OPERATING SYSTEMS

OPERATING SYSTEMS

A Design-Oriented Approach

Charles Crowley
University of New Mexico

IRWIN

Chicago • Bogotá • Boston • Buenos Aires • Caracas
London • Madrid • Mexico City • Sydney • Toronto

Irwin Book Team

Publisher: _Tom Casson_
Senior sponsoring editor: _Elizabeth A. Jones_
Senior developmental editor: _Kelley Butcher_
Project supervisor: _Lynne Basler_
Senior Production supervisor: _Laurie Sander_
Director, Prepress Purchasing: _Kimberly Meriwether David_
Compositor: _Interactive Composition Corporation_
Typeface: _10/12 Times Roman_
Printer: _Times Mirror Higher Education Group, Inc., Print Group_

Times Mirror
Higher Education Group

Library of Congress Cataloging-in-Publication Data

Crowley, Charles (Charles Patrick)
    Operating systems : a design-oriented approach / Charles Crowley.
      p. cm.
    Includes bibliographical references and index.
    ISBN 0-256-15151-2
    1. Operating systems (Computers)   I. Title.
QA76.76.063C77   1997
005.4'3—dc20   96–43708

To Mom, Pat, Cathy, Ella, and Kendra

PREFACE

In this book I have tried to approach the traditional, junior or senior level operating systems course in a new way. There are several areas where I have done things differently:

- *Describe the external operating system interface:* I start with a description of the system call interface to an operating system.
- *Use of code:* I have tried to steer a middle course between a concepts approach and a case study approach.
- *Development of concepts:* I have tried to show how the operating system concepts developed into their present form.
- *Design orientation:* I have tried to show how ideas from the design of operating systems relate to the design of other types of programs.

EXTERNAL OPERATING SYSTEM INTERFACE

Many students come to an operating system class without a clear understanding of what an operating system really does. These students should understand how operating system services are used before learning how these services are implemented. To deal with this, the book begins with a simplified, UNIX-like set of system calls. The book includes a discussion of these calls, example programs using these calls, and a simple shell program to integrate the examples.

CONCEPTS OR CASE STUDIES

There have always been two approaches to the operating systems class. The first approach is the *concept* or *theory* approach which concentrates on the basic conceptual issues in the design of operating systems. These courses discuss each of the basic problems in operating systems design and the range of common solutions to those problems. The books are mostly text and diagrams with very little code. The second approach is the *case study* method which concentrates on an example operating system that is simple but complete. The books contain a lot of code and spend a lot of pages explaining the code in detail.

There are advantages and disadvantages to both approaches. Some people feel the ideal situation is to take both classes but this is rarely possible in an already crowded computer science curriculum so one is required to make a choice.

USE OF CODE

I have tried to find a middle course between the two approaches. This book is basically a concepts oriented book with more code than is usual. I have found that seeing actual code allows the students to understand the concepts more deeply, feel more comfortable about the material, and ask questions they wouldn't have thought to ask in a purely concepts oriented course. The code does not comprise a complete operating system however and it as simple as possible in order to reduce the amount of pages devoted to explaining it.

DEVELOPMENT OF CONCEPTS

I have tried to show how these ideas developed. Many of the concepts in operating systems have developed over many years and the current solutions were developed slowly, in several stages. Each new solution had a problem that the next solution tried to fix. I think it helps the student to understand this development and see that these ideas were not brilliant flashes of insight that came out of nowhere but ideas that were improved by many people over many years. The development was a series of good ideas where each improvement made sense in the context in which it was developed. Seeing this development helps to understand why the solutions have their present form. In addition, it is useful to know the design constraints that caused solutions to develop into their present form because technological advances often change these constraints and old solutions that used to be inferior suddenly become practical again. Finally these developments give students examples of the design process through a series of potential but flawed solutions to a problem to a final solution that is acceptable.

DESIGN ORIENTATION

Finally there is a concentration on design. In some ways designing an operating system is a pretty specialized activity having to do mainly with resource management. But many basic design ideas run through all designs and they show up in operating systems as much as anywhere else. Throughout the book I note places where we are presented with typical design problems. I abstract the operating systems related problems and solutions from the book into the general design problems and solutions and present them in a way that they can be applied to design problems in other areas of computer science.

Clearly it is not possible to cover all design topics and issues. I am striving for two things. First, I want to give the student an awareness of design issues, where they come up, which techniques to apply, how they can be generalized, etc. I do not present an organized survey of design techniques but a series of useful ones that come up in the context of operating systems. I hope to make the student aware of design and to enable the student to start doing their own generalizing about design. Second, I present a collection of useful design techniques that the students can use in their design toolkit.

Very few computer professionals will participate in the design of an operating system during the course of their careers. While it is important that students of computer science have a good foundation in the basic concepts in specialized areas such as operating systems, it is not necessary that every computer science student understand all the details. However, there is a thread running through all areas of software engineering: the concept of design. There are many issued which are tackled during the design of an operating system which can be generalized and applied to other areas of computer science. In this book, I attempt to focus on these design issues and their implications for other areas.

I have oriented this book to provide a solid preparation for the larger design projects the student will encounter in later software engineering courses and as preparation for their career as a software professional designing, implementing and maintaining a wide variety of systems. This orientation also enables the operating systems course follows modern developments in the field of computer science. The interrelations between the separate areas of computer science are becoming more important. For example, in the area of high speed parallel machines, it is clear that it is necessary to think of the hardware, the operating system, and the programming language as a single system to get maximum performance. Optimization in any part of the system will have consequences for the other parts of the system.

The design techniques are noted in side bars as they come up and longer explanations of each design topic are placed in separate chapters from the operating system material. The instructor can structure a course with varying degrees of concentration on design aspects. The goal is that the design sections are independent of the main flow of the text and independent from each other. This will allow the instructor to pick and choose those design sections he or she finds to be useful.

USING THIS BOOK IN A COURSE

There is more material in this book than can be comfortably covered in a one-semester course. A number of the sections of the book have been marked with an asterisk. This indicates that they can be skipped with no loss of continuity in the presentation. In addition, all of the design chapters and design sidebars can be skipped with no loss of continuity. If you skip all the design chapters you can probably just cover the book in a semester. I expect that most instructors will choose to skip some of the design sections and some of the optional sections and teach a course that is about 90 percent operating systems and 10 percent design issues. Alternatively, the design issues could be covered in a separate one-unit course, strictly on design, that is taken along with the operating systems course.

ACKNOWLEDGMENTS

I want to thank my colleague Barney Maccabe who started out as my co-author on the book but had too many other commitments to work on the book. Our discussions lead to the conception of the book and the design orientation. I have talked with Barney on many aspects of operating systems and computer science and those discussions shaped many of my ideas.

I also want to thank John Brayer who used drafts of the book in several of his operating systems courses and put up with many typos, badly written sections, and unfinished sections. His comments helped in the development of the book.

I also want to thank my other colleagues in the Computer Science Department at the University of New Mexico. Continuing "in-the-hall" discussions with them have helped me formulate and improve my ideas.

Many students in CS 481 have used drafts of the books and have provided many useful comments and suggestions. I want to particularly thank Dave Rosenbaum who provided extensive comments on the entire draft, found numerous errors and typos and taught me some things about writing good English as well.

My treatment of the design chapters was greatly influenced by the design patterns developments in recent years and particularly the fine book by Gamma et el. (1995). I used their presentation format in the design chapters.

I want to thank all the people who reviewed this book while it was being developed. I corrected many problems and got many ideas for the presentation from their careful reviews and comments. The design chapters especially profited from their comments.

- Mustaque Ahamad, Georgia Institute of Technology
- Jim Alves-Foss, University of Idaho
- Anish Arora, The Ohio State University
- Brent Auernheimer, California State University - Fresno
- Anthony Q. Baxter, University of Kentucky
- Mahesh Dodani, University of Iowa
- H. George Friedman, Jr., University of Illinois - Urbana
- Tim Gottleber
- Stephen J. Hartley, Drexel University
- Giorgio P. Ingargiola, Temple University
- Stephen J. Krebsbach, South Dakota State University
- Donald S. Miller, Arizona State University
- Matt W. Mutka, Michigan State University
- Richard Newman-Wolfe, University of Florida
- Steve Reichenbach, University of Nebraska - Lincoln
- Bernhard Weinberg, Michigan State University

Finally my wife, Ella Sitkin, put up with many bad moods and excuses that I was "too busy" during the years this book was developed. As if that wasn't enough, she also edited several chapters.

CONTENTS

18

Design Techniques IV   745

19

Resource Management   770

OPERATING SYSTEMS

1

Introduction

Operating systems run on computer hardware and serve as platforms for other software to run on. In this chapter, we present an overview of an operating system. We focus on four questions:

- Where does an operating system fit in a computing system?
- What does an operating system do?
- How is an operating system structured?
- Do we need an operating system?

We look at an operating system from two viewpoints: as a resource manager and as a virtual machine manager. We also look at how the operating system stands between the hardware and the user software.

1.1   WHERE DOES AN OPERATING SYSTEM FIT IN?

operating system

An *operating system* is the layer of a computer system between the hardware and the user programs (user software). (See Figure 1.1.) An operating system does what all software does: it implements some desired functionality by building on the functionality available in lower levels. Software transforms one interface into another interface. For example, a BASIC interpreter transforms a computer into a BASIC machine, a statistical package transforms a computer into a statistics machine, a computer game program transforms a computer into a game machine, etc.

An operating system is built directly on the hardware interface and provides an interface between the hardware and the user programs. The first thing we will do in this book is look at exactly what kind of interface the operating system implements. Then, in the rest of the book, we will look at how the operating systems interface is implemented.

A computer system, as it comes "out of the box," is not easy to use—it requires an operating system and application software to run on it. An application software package, as it comes "out of the box" (or "out of the shrinkwrap"), will not run directly on the computer hardware—it requires an operating system to run it.[1] An operating system is the layer of software that nearly every application software package expects to be present. The operating system is the first program run on a computer when the computer boots up. There can be only one operating system running on a computer.[2]

> The operating system is the layer between the hardware and the software.

1.1.1   SYSTEM LEVELS

Figure 1.1 illustrates the layered structure of the hardware, the software, and the operating system. The *hardware interface* consists of things like program counter, registers, interrupts, disks, terminals, etc. The hardware interface consists of everything you need to know about the hardware in order to write programs that will execute on the hardware. In Chapter 2, we describe the hardware interface for the example hardware used in this book. The *operating system interface* is described in Chapter 3.

hardware interface

operating system interface

---

[1]This is not true in all cases. There are some special programs that are intended to be run on the bare hardware. One example would be a program that fixes disk problems. These are special cases, however, and are not common.

[2]Technically this is not always true since it is possible to have a "virtual" operating system that runs other operating systems. The correct statement is that only one operating system is in direct control of the hardware at any one time.

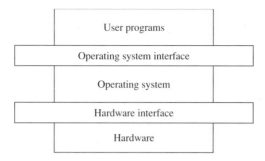

Figure 1.1   Levels in a computer system

An operating system shares characteristics with both hardware and software. An operating system is software, that is, it is a program that is compiled, linked, and run on a computer. However, it is like hardware in that only one copy of the operating system runs on a computer and it extends the capabilities of the hardware. The services of the operating system are invoked with a special "trap" or "system call" instruction that is used just like any other hardware instruction.

DESIGN TECHNIQUE: TWO-LEVEL IMPLEMENTATION

An operating system is a lower level of software that user programs run on. Together they form a two-level structure where the operating system implements functionality used by the user program. This idea is called a *two-level implementation* and it is seen in many places in computer science. We will see several more examples later in the book.

A programming language is another example. It is the lower level used to implement programs. Special-purpose languages are an even better example. The special-purpose language provides low-level primitives for solving certain kinds of problems, and the user writes programs in that language. Some examples are the 4GL languages for producing reports from database information, and spreadsheet macro languages.

In a two-level implementation, you use the "*divide and conquer*" strategy by dividing the problem into two parts and solving each part separately. A two-level implementation is a special case of a modular implementation, but the two-level case occurs so often that it is useful to discuss it as a separate design technique from modular implementation. It is common for the lower level to implement a language that the upper level is written in.

Two-level implementations are especially useful when the lower level can be reused by more than one upper level. This is the case with an operating system and most languages. A good lower level can be reused many times.

Two-level implementations are used in operating systems to separate mechanism from policy. A **mechanism** is a set of basic facilities that can be used in many different ways. For example, a programming language is a mechanism for writing programs. A **policy** is the use of a mechanism for a particular purpose—for example, a program to solve a specific equation. An example from operating systems is the protection of files. UNIX provides a protection mechanism that determines whether other people can read, write, or execute your files. You decide on the policy, that is, which files are readable, writable, or executable. The distinction between mechanism and policy is a basic concept in operating systems and will reappear in many places in this book.

You can learn more about two-level implementations in Section 4.4.

1.2   WHAT DOES AN OPERATING SYSTEM DO?

The functions of an operating system can be viewed in two ways:

*   As a resource manager.

*   As an implementor of virtual computers.

By *virtual computer* we mean an implementation of the functionality of a computer in software. In this section we will introduce both viewpoints.

> An operating system is a resource manager and a virtual computer manager.

1.2.1   HARDWARE RESOURCES

hardware resource

The operating system manages the hardware resources of the computer system. The main *hardware resources* in a computer system are:

*   *Processor*—the processor is the part of the computer system capable of executing instructions.

*   *Memory*—the memory contains all instructions and data used by a processor.

*   *Input/output (I/O) controllers*—processors that know how to transfer data between memory and devices.

*   *Disk devices*—disks provide long-term storage for data.

*   *Other devices*—hardware components that accept data from or generate data for I/O controllers. Examples are terminals, networks, tape drives, etc.

Figure 1.2 shows the resources in a computer system.

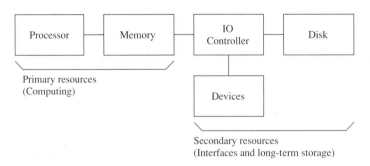

Figure 1.2   The hardware resources in a computer system

1.2.2   RESOURCE MANAGEMENT

Resource management is: resource management

- *Transforming*—creating a new resource from an existing resource. The created resource will act as a substitute for the existing resource but will be easier to use.
- *Multiplexing*—creating the illusion of several resources from one resource.
- *Scheduling*—deciding which programs should get each resource and when they should get it.

To give a more concrete meaning for transformation and multiplexing, we consider the construction of multiple virtual printers—one for each virtual computer.

Transformation   Hardware resources have moderately complex interfaces. The hardware interface to a printer might consist of a data register, a control register, and a status register. To send a character to the printer, you need to poll (repeatedly read) the status register until it indicates that the printer is ready to accept the next character. Once the printer is ready, the data value needs to be written to the data register and a "send" command written to the control register. None of this is particularly difficult, but it is tedious and error prone: you need know the addresses of the data, control, and status registers and you need to know the structure of the bits in the control and status registers.

Operating systems *transform* physical resources into virtual resources to avoid   transformation
the difficulties associated with using hardware resources. A *virtual resource* provides   virtual resource
the essential functionality of the hardware resource, but is easier to use because the details of the hardware interface are hidden. For example, an operating system might provide a virtual printer that is capable of printing a character. To use this virtual resource, an application only needs to specify the character to be printed. The virtual printer provides the essential functionality of the hardware printer, while the operating system handles the details that make the hardware interface difficult to use (register addresses, register formats, and wait until the printer is ready for each character).

> Operating systems transform physical resources into virtual resources that provide functionality which is similar to the physical resources, but have a simpler interface.

Multiplexing   When there are more virtual computers than physical resources, the operating system needs to make sure that the virtual computers can share the physical resources. The sharing of physical resources is called *multiplexing*. Continuing with   multiplexing
our printer example, suppose your system only has one printer. If you run two or more applications, the operating system needs to make it appear as if each virtual computer has its own printer. That is, the operating system needs to make sure that the characters printed by one virtual computer are not mixed with the characters printed by another virtual computer.

To create the illusion of multiple printers, the operating system can implement a virtual printer using a disk file. In this solution, each virtual computer has its own "printer file." Every time the application prints a character, the operating system simply appends the character to the end of the printer file which belongs to the virtual computer being used for that application. When the application finishes, the operating system queues the application's printer file. The software that drives the physical printer only prints files.

spooling

Historically this solution was called *spooling*, and the application's "printer file" is called a *spool file*. *SPOOL* is an acronym for *Simultaneous Peripheral Operations On Line*. Simultaneous refers to the fact that two or more virtual computers can issue printer operations at the same time. On line refers to the fact that the hardware printer is connected to the same computer as the virtual printers are running on. The alternative to on-line printing is to write the print file to a tape and print the tape on a different computer. See Section 5.16.1 for a more detailed explanation of off-line printing.

time-division multiplexing

time-sharing

Our printer example illustrates a simple form of *time-division multiplexing*. In time-division multiplexing, the resource is used for different virtual computers at different times. In many contexts, time-division multiplexing is called *time-sharing*.

This form of time-division multiplexing is relatively simple because the printer does not begin printing the output for a virtual computer until the application is finished. Moreover, the printer finishes printing all of the output for one virtual computer before it starts to print the output for another virtual computer. Other instances of time-division multiplexing may involve switching between virtual resources while they are still being used by applications. Time-division multiplexing is appropriate when the resource cannot be divided into smaller versions of itself.

space-division multiplexing

space-sharing

In *space-division multiplexing*, a resource is divided into smaller versions of itself and each virtual computer is given a part of the resource. Space-division multiplexing is used in multiplexing primary and secondary storage (memory and disks). Although not commonly used, the term *space-sharing* is a synonym for space-division multiplexing.

Multiplexing (sharing) of a single physical resource involves dividing the resource based on time or space.

An operating system multiplexes, transforms, and allocates hardware resources.

1.2.3   VIRTUAL COMPUTERS

An operating system creates software copies of the processor (the capability to execute instructions) and the memory (the capability to store information). It also transforms the disk devices into a file system and the other input-output devices into more abstract (less detailed) and easily used devices. Thus an operating system:

- Creates multiple *processes* (simulated processors) out of the single processor and allocates them to programs. It accomplishes this by time-multiplexing the processor.

  process

- Creates multiple *address spaces* (memory for a process to run in) out of the memory and allocates them to processes. It accomplishes this by space-multiplexing the processor.[3]

  address space

- Implements a *file system* and input/output (I/O) system so that processes can easily use and share the disks. It accomplishes this by space-multiplexing the disks and time-multiplexing the I/O channels.

  file system

The operating system creates what we will call *virtual computers* from the physical computer. The first thing we need to look at is how a virtual computer differs from the physical computer.

virtual computer

The most significant difference is that there are many virtual computers while there is only one physical computer. The operating system creates the illusion of many virtual computers by transforming the single, physical computer. Figure 1.3 shows the structure.

Each virtual computer is similar to the physical computer in many ways but it is easier to use than the physical computer.

A computer has four basic parts: processor, primary memory, I/O, and secondary memory. Let us look at each of these in turn and see how our virtual computer differs from the physical computer.

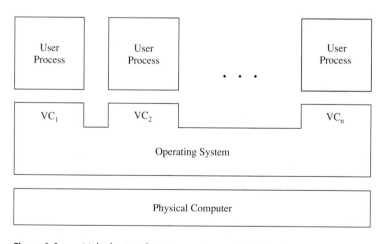

Figure 1.3   Multiple virtual computers in an operating system

---

| [3]Virtual memory systems time-multiplex memory.

> Computing requires a processor and some memory.

1.3   A VIRTUAL COMPUTER

A virtual computer is a computer implemented in software using the hardware resources of the physical computer. It has the same four basic components (processor, memory, I/O, and disk) as the physical computer. Each virtual resource will be a transformed and multiplexed version of the physical resource. Figures 1.4, 1.5, 1.6, and 1.7 show the multiplexing of the four virtualized resources. Note that all of the multiplexing is done in the same way: the physical resource is broken up into discrete pieces and these pieces are put together to create the virtual resources. In some cases the pieces are spatial (space-multiplexing) and in some cases they are pieces of time (time-multiplexing).

In the next few sections we will describe the ways in which these resources are transformed into virtual resources.

> Operating systems create virtual computers that can solve the same problems as a real computer, but that are easier to use.

1.3.1   VIRTUAL PROCESSOR

The virtual processor has nearly the same interface to the user as the physical processor, that is, it has nearly the same set of instructions. One reason for this is that it is implemented by using the physical processor directly. The operating system will rapidly switch the services of the physical processor between the virtual computers to implement the virtual processors.

The operating system removes some of the physical processor instructions and adds some other operations. The instructions it removes are the ones that control the physical resources of the computer (processor, memory, I/O). These are the instructions that affect access to memory, provide direct access to the devices, and change the protection state of the processor. In return for the instructions, the operating system adds instructions that allow the virtual processor to request virtual resources from the operating system. These instructions are called *system calls*. System calls allow a programmer to:

system call

- Create new virtual computers;
- Communicate with other virtual computers;
- Allocate memory as needed;
- Do I/O; and
- Access a sophisticated file system.

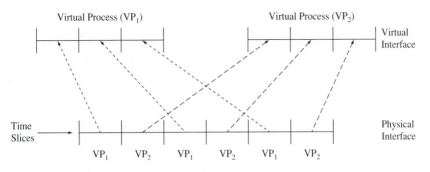

Figure 1.4   Multiplexing the processor by time-slicing

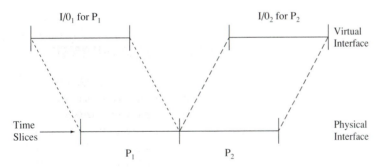

Figure 1.5   Multiplexing the physical memory by dividing it into pieces

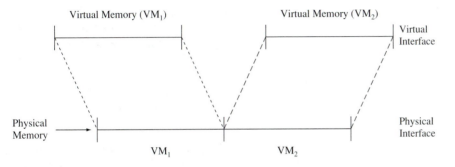

Figure 1.6   Multiplexing the I/O processor by sequential use

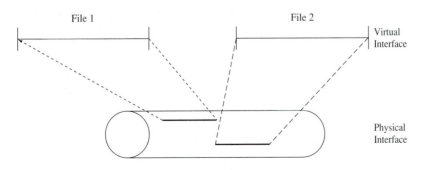
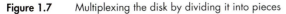

Figure 1.7   Multiplexing the disk by dividing it into pieces

Modern processors provide system call instructions precisely because operating systems need them to provide users with safe access to operating system services.

We can summarize the relationship in the equation (where P is a processor):

$$P_{\text{virtual}} = P_{\text{physical}} - \{\text{Dangerous instructions}\} + \{\text{Useful replacements}\}$$

The virtual processor does not change the instruction set of the physical processor very much since the main goal of the operating system is to create virtual copies of the processor. Creating an improved virtual instruction set is a complex job and is done by compilers and interpreters.

Modern processors make removing the resource control instructions easy by providing two processor modes: system and user. In user mode, the instructions that control the physical resources of the computer are not allowed. Processors have processor modes precisely because operating systems need them to provide a safe virtual processor. The operating system is managing the hardware resources of the computer and it must keep control of them. It allows the virtual computer to *use* these resources but not to *control* them.

1.3.2   VIRTUAL PRIMARY MEMORY

The memory of the virtual computer is very similar to the hardware memory, that is, it is a long sequence of cells with sequential, numerical names. The operating system will divide up the physical memory into parts and give a part to each virtual computer. The operating system usually creates, with help from the hardware, the illusion that the memory seen by each virtual computer is named with numerical names starting at 0. The operating system may also create the illusion that the virtual computer has more memory than the physical computer has physical memory. This is called virtual memory.

The programming language concept of an array is taken directly from this model of memory, so you are already familiar with the software emulation of physical memory, although you may not have realized it.

1.3.3   VIRTUAL SECONDARY MEMORY

Secondary storage provides long-term storage for data. This is done physically on disk blocks and virtually in disk files. The virtual computer sees a file system consisting of hierarchically named files that can be of any size and can be read and written in any size units. A considerable amount of operating system code is required to create this illusion.

1.3.4   VIRTUAL I/O

The I/O operations of the virtual computer are completely different than the I/O operations of the physical computer. The physical computer has devices with complex control and status registers. For example, the disks are basically large sequences of physical blocks with no structure. They can only be read or written in large blocks (of, say, 1024 bytes). Figure 1.8 summarizes the situation.

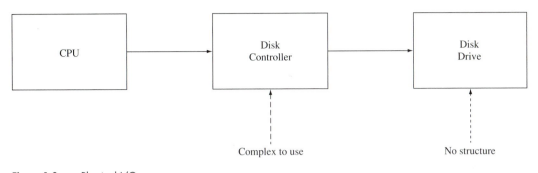

Figure 1.8 Physical I/O

By comparison, the virtual I/O provided by the virtual computer is simple and easy to use. We will see examples in Chapter 3.

You share a resource by dividing it up into pieces and distributing the pieces. These could be pieces of time or space.

1.4 DO WE NEED AN OPERATING SYSTEM?

It is not essential to have an operating system to use a computer. Some special-purpose computers do not have an operating system. For example, almost all microwave ovens have a small computer chip inside to control the oven, but few of the computer chips in microwave ovens have operating systems. Controlling a microwave oven is a very specialized task and it is the only task the computer chip is responsible for, so a full operating system would be wasteful and unnecessary. However, many of the tasks that are traditionally done in an operating system (managing devices, scheduling, pseudo-parallelism, etc.) would have to be done by the code in the microwave oven, so if you were designing such code you would want to be familiar with the techniques used in operating systems.

There are many examples of specialized computers that do not use an operating system but, in each one, the duties of the operating system are taken over by application code.

A general-purpose computer system must be able to run a wide range of programs. For such a system, an operating system is the most natural way to go. Otherwise each application would have to program its own operating system services. An operating system is useful because it contains a library of reusable services. The operating system implements many necessary features that are used by nearly every program. It is a good investment to implement them once, in the operating system, rather than in each application program.

METRIC PREFIXES

In all parts of computer science, and in the study of operating systems in particular, we often have to deal with very small numbers and very large numbers. The time of a memory access or instruction execution is getting shorter all the time and the size of disks and memories is getting larger. In this section we will show the metric prefixes that we will be using throughout the book.

First we will look at the small numbers.

Power of 10	Decimal Fraction	Prefix	Abbre-viation
10^{-1}	0.1	deci	ds
10^{-2}	0.01	centi	cs
10^{-3}	0.001	milli	ms
10^{-6}	0.000001	micro	μs
10^{-9}	0.000000001	nano	ns
10^{-12}	0.000000000001	pico	ps
10^{-15}	0.000000000000001	fempto	fs
10^{-18}	0.000000000000000001	atto	as

In this book, we will only discuss small time intervals so the abbreviations are for fractions of a second. In the study of computer hardware we might be interested in nanometers and the like.

Note that the low powers of 10 have irregular names but, starting with 10^{-6}, they all end with "o".

This is because the first few prefixes have been in common use for some time but the higher ones were established by standards committees and so are regular.

The abbreviations all work out well except for the fact that millisecond and microsecond begin with the same letter and both would be candidates for being abbreviated as ms. Millisecond gets that honor and we use the greek letter mu (μ) in the abbreviation for microseconds (μs).

Here are the large numbers.

Power of 10	Number	Prefix	Abbre-viation
10^1	10	deka	Dbyte
10^2	100	hecto	Hbyte
10^3	1,000	kilo	Kbyte
10^6	1,000,000	mega	Mbyte
10^9	1,000,000,000	giga	Gbyte
10^{12}	1,000,000,000,000	tera	Tbyte
10^{15}	1,000,000,000,000,000	peta	Pbyte
10^{18}	1,000,000,000,000,000,000	exa	Ebyte

Again, they are regular starting with 10^6. We will only use these large numbers to discuss numbers of bytes, so that is how we are showing the abbreviations.

1.5   SUMMARY

An operating system is the layer of software that runs directly on the hardware and provides support for other software running on the hardware. An operating system is implemented on the hardware interface and implements a virtual computer interface. The operating system interface is similar in basic functionality to the hardware interface but is easier to use. In addition, many virtual computers can run on a single physical computer. A user program runs as a process in a virtual computer.

We can share a resource by dividing up the times it can be used (time-division multiplexing) or or we can divide up the resource itself (space-division multiplexing).

A hardware computer system has five types of hardware resources: processor(s), memory, I/O controllers, disk devices, and other input/output devices. A virtual computer provides software versions of each of these resources. A virtual processor can run programs and uses essentially the same instruction set as the hardware processor. Some hardware instructions (the ones that control the hardware itself) are not available on the virtual processor. The virtual processor has additional instructions, called system calls, which provide access to the services of the operating system. The virtual memory is used to store the user program and data. The operating system provides a separate virtual memory area for each virtual computer. Virtual input/output devices provide (indirect) access to the hardware devices. The disk devices are virtualized as a file system.

The function of an operating system can be viewed in two different ways. The operating system is a resource manager that manages (allocates and frees), multiplexes (provides multiple copies of), and transforms (makes easier to use) the hardware resources. The operating system is also a virtual computer manager that provides virtual computers for processes to run in.

An important reason for using an operating system is that it represents reusable software.

1.5.1   TERMINOLOGY

After reading this chapter, you should be familiar with the following terms:

- address space
- file system
- hardware interface
- hardware resource
- mechanism
- multiplexing
- operating system
- operating systems interface
- policy
- process
- resource management
- space-division multiplexing
- space sharing
- spooling
- system call
- time-division multiplexing
- time sharing
- transformation
- virtual computer
- virtual resource

1.5.2   REVIEW QUESTIONS

The following questions are answered in the text of this chapter:

1. What are the activities of resource management? What are the five main hardware resources in a computer system?
2. What are the advantages of virtualizing a hardware resource?
3. What do we mean by the transformation of a resource?
4. What are the four resources of a virtual computer?
5. Give a brief definition for the term *multiplexing*.
6. What is the advantage of multiplexing a resource?
7. What hardware instructions are removed from the virtual processor? Why are they removed? How are they removed? What are they replaced with?
8. Explain the difference between sharing a resource and multiplexing a resource.
9. What is a reason for not using an operating system on a computer system?
10. What do we call a millionth of a second? What do we call a billion bytes?

1.5.3   FURTHER READING

There are many good books on operating systems where you can get different viewpoints than you will find in this book. These include Silberschatz and Galvin (1994), Tanenbaum (1992), Stallings (1992), Finkel (1988), Bic and Shaw (1988), and Lister and Eager (1995).

1.6   PROBLEMS

 1. A process implements a virtual computer. Consider the idea of running another operating system on the virtual computer, that is, running an operating system as a program on another operating system. There are two ways we could do this. Discuss each one in terms of practicality and efficiency.

   a. You load the operating system code directly into the virtual computer (with no other additional software) and run it.

   b. You first load an emulator into the virtual computer. The emulator creates a virtual version of some computer. Then you load the operating system to run on this emulator.

2. In this chapter we looked at level models. In software engineering we divide a system into modules. Compare the level model with the module model for dividing up systems.

3. A window system manages three hardware resources: the display, the mouse, and the keyboard. Discuss a window system as an operating system. What are the virtual resources? What things are multiplexed and how (space or time or both)? Are the resources transformed for easier use?

4. Imagine a program to control a microwave oven. What operating systems–like functions would it need? Resource management (what resources)? Transformation of resources? Multiplexing of resources?

2

The Hardware Interface

In this chapter we consider the hardware interface. Our goal is to introduce a simple computing system that we will use in the remainder of this text. We will use a simplified, generic RISC processor with some CISC elements. We call it the Composite RISC Architecture 1 (CRA–1). We will not describe the entire architecture, but only the parts that we will use in later chapters. We will only see a small part of the instruction set, for example.

Figure 2.1 presents an overview of the CRA–1. This system provides a *CPU* (also known as a *processor*) for executing programs, a *memory* for storing instructions and data during the execution of a program, and a *disk system* (disk controller and disk) for permanent storage of programs and data. These components are interconnected using a *system bus*.

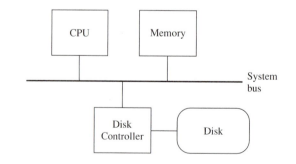

Figure 2.1   CRA–1 organization

2.1   THE CPU

2.1.1   GENERAL-PURPOSE REGISTERS

The CPU provides 32 *general-purpose registers,* each 32 bits long. In assembly language, these registers are referenced using the names *r0* through *r31*. As is common with RISC machines, *r0* always holds the value 0. The other registers are for general use, but a few have conventional uses in most programs:

cpu processor

general purpose register

- *r1*—return values from procedures.
- *r8*—first parameter to a function call (or system call).
- *r9*—second parameter to a function call (or system call).
- *r10*—third parameter to a function call (or system call).
- *r11*—fourth parameter to a function call (or system call).
- *r29*—the frame pointer.
- *r30*—the stack pointer.
- *r31*—the return address from a procedure call.

Procedure calls send their arguments in registers *r8*, *r9*, *r10*, and *r11*, and return values in *r1*.

Two registers are used to support programming language stacks. The stack register is used by the stack instructions. The stack can be used for procedure arguments beyond the four provided for in the registers. The frame pointer is used by the programming language to address items in stack frames.

2.1.2   CONTROL REGISTERS

The *control registers* hold values that control the execution of the processor. The control registers are all 32 bits long.

control register

- *ia*—The *instruction address register* contains the address of the next instruction.
- *psw*—The *program status word* has two significant bits. Bit 0 (the low-order bit) is 1 if the processor is in user mode, and 0 if the processor is in system mode. Bit 1 is 1 if interrupts are enabled, and 0 if interrupts are masked.
- *base*—The memory *base register* is added to all addresses when the system is in user mode.

base register

- *bound*—The memory *bound register* is the address limit. In user mode, all addresses must be less than the *bound* register; otherwise a program error interrupt (with *ip* of 2) will occur. The comparison is done before the *base* register is added.

bound register

- *iia*—The *interrupt instruction address register* stores the value of the *ia* register before an interrupt. When an interrupt occurs, the *ia* register is saved in the *iia* register before the *ia* register is loaded with the address of the interrupt handler.

- *ipsw*—The *interrupt program status word* stores the value of the *psw* register before an interrupt. When an interrupt occurs, the *psw* register is saved in the *ipsw* register before it is loaded with 0.

- *ip*—The *interrupt parameter register* contains data about the last interrupt (if any is necessary).

- *iva*—The *interrupt vector address register* is the location in memory where the interrupt vector table is located.

- *timer*—The *interval timer register* is decremented once every microsecond unless it is already zero. When it is decremented from 1 to 0, a timer interrupt is generated. Storing a zero in this register clears any pending (but masked) timer interrupts.

2.1.3   PROCESSOR MODES

system mode

user mode

The processor can either be in *system mode* (if *psw* bit 0 is 0) or in *user mode* (if *psw* bit 0 is 1). In system mode, all instructions are legal and all addresses are physical addresses (see Section 2.2). In user mode, the instructions that modify the control registers are not legal and will cause a program error interrupt (with *ip* of 1). In user mode, all addresses must be less than *bound* and will have *base* added to them before memory is accessed.

Interrupts can occur only if *psw* bit 1 is 1.

2.1.4   INSTRUCTION SET

We will only specify a few instructions because that is all we will need for the purposes of this book. The instructions we will use are shown in Table 2.1.

In a load/store architecture, there are two main instructions that access memory, one to load a register from memory and another to store a register into memory. We will assume that the load and store instructions can load into and store from a control

Table 2.1   Some CRA–1 instructions

Operation	Instruction	Format
Load register	load	*address, rN*
Store register	store	*rN, address*
Load registers	loadAll	*address*
Store registers	storeAll	*address*
Move register	move	*rM, rN*
System call	syscall	
Return from interrupt	rti	

register as well as a general register.[1] For convenience we have an instruction that will store all the general registers to 32 words of memory and another instruction that will load all the general registers from 32 words of memory.[2] There is also an instruction to move one register to another. This instruction will work with general registers and control registers.[3]

The system call instruction is executed by a user process in order to request a system service. This instruction causes an interrupt which puts the processor into system mode and transfers to the system call interrupt handler in the operating system. The arguments to the system call (including the system call number) are assumed to be in the user's registers at the time of the system call.

Finally there is an instruction to return from an interrupt. We will discuss it in more detail in Section 2.3.

2.1.5   MACHINE INSTRUCTIONS IN C++ CODE

We will need to write short sequences of machine instructions at a few places in the book. Many C++ compilers allow the insertion of assembly language in an *asm block*. For example, the following code sets the timer to a new value.

asm block NOT available in most C & C++ compilers

```
SetTimer (int timerValue) { asm {move timerValue, timer} }
```

We will assume that we can put passed arguments in the assembly language code (as we did with timerValue in the above example) and the compiler will do the addressing correctly.

2.2   MEMORY AND ADDRESSING

The smallest addressable unit will be an 8-bit byte and addresses will be 32 bits long. When the processor is in system mode, all addresses are *physical addresses*, which means that the address generated by the instruction is sent directly to the memory by placing it on the system bus as a memory address. Physical addresses are also called *absolute addresses*.

physical address

When the processor is in user mode, all addresses are *logical addresses*. When an instruction generates a logical address, the processor will first check to be sure that the logical address is less than the *bound* register. If it is not, then a program error interrupt (with *ip* of 2) is generated. Otherwise, the *base* register is added to the logical address to generate a physical address. This physical address is then placed on the system bus as a memory address.

logical address

---

[1]In an actual machine, this might be a different instruction or you might have to load into a general register and then move into a control register.

[2]Register *r0* will always have a value of 0 no matter what is loaded into it.

[3]In an actual instruction set, the instructions to move to and from control registers will probably be different than those to move between general registers. We will assume here that the assembler will work out these details.

The upshot of all this is that, in user mode, a program is restricted to a portion of the physical addresses. It cannot access any physical address less than the value of the *base* register (since it is added to every address) and it cannot access any physical address greater than (or equal to) the sum of the *base* and *bound* register (since this limit is checked for each logical address). This is a simple form of memory protection.

physical address space

The *physical address space* consists of all the physical addresses that a program can generate. It is all the addresses between 0 and 0xFFFFFFFF. The physical address space is divided up into the memory address space and the I/O address space.

memory address space

The *memory address space* is the part of the physical address space where we can place memory. In the CRA–1, the memory address space is from 0 to 0xEFFFFFFF. Only a part of the memory address space will have actual memory responding to those addresses. We will normally be assuming our CRA–1 has 16 megabytes (16M) of actual memory at addresses 0 to 0xFFFFFF. The *I/O address space* is the part of the physical address space reserved for I/O devices and consists of the physical addresses 0xF0000000 to 0xFFFFFFFF.

I/O address space

logical address space

A *logical address space* is the range of addresses that a program running in user mode can use. This starts with 0 and goes up to the value of the *bound* register. Each logical address is mapped into a physical address when the *base* register is added to it.

2.3   INTERRUPTS

interrupt

An *interrupt* is an immediate transfer of control caused by an event in the system. There are several events that can cause an interrupt in the CRA–1.

1. *System call*—A system call instruction was executed.
2. *Timer*—The interval timer counted down to zero.
3. *Disk*—The disk device finished a transfer.
4. *Program error*—The program made an error. The *ip* register indicates exactly what happened.

   - $ip = 0$—an undefined instruction.
   - $ip = 1$—an illegal instruction in user mode. This is a move to control register instruction (which is not allowed in user mode).
   - $ip = 2$—a logical address greater than or equal to the *bound* register.

When an interrupt occurs, the CRA–1 does the following:

1. The *psw* register is saved in the *ipsw* register.
2. The *psw* register is set to 0.
3. The parameter of the interrupt (if it is a program error interrupt) is put in the *ip* register.
4. The *ia* register is saved in the *iia* register.
5. The interrupt number (system call = 0, timer = 1, disk = 2, program = 3) is multiplied by 4 and added to the contents of the *iva* register to get the interrupt vector slot. The address in that slot is loaded in the *ia* register.

First the processor saves the *psw* register in the *ipsw* register, and resets *psw* to put the processor in system mode with interrupts disabled (by storing a 0 in the *psw*). Then it stores the interrupt argument (if there is one) in the *ip* register. The processor then saves the *ia* register in the *iia* register, gets the address of the interrupt handler by looking in the appropriate slot in the *interrupt vector area* (pointed to by the *iva*   interrupt vector area register), and loads the address into the *ia* register. This completes the handling of the interrupt by the hardware, and normal instruction execution resumes. The address of the next instruction is taken from the *ia* register, which has just been set to the beginning of the interrupt handler for this interrupt.

The return from interrupt (*rti*) instruction reverses the effect of an interrupt. The *rti* instruction moves the contents of the *iia* register to the *ia* register, moves the contents of the *ipsw* register to the *psw* register, and then begins normal instruction execution. This will restart the program that was running when the interrupt occurred at the point it was interrupted. If no registers have been changed (or if they were saved and then restored just before the *rti*), then the process will continue on as if nothing had happened.

The *iva* register points to an area in memory which contains the addresses of the interrupt handlers. There is a slot in the interrupt vector area for each interrupt. The offset in the interrupt vector area depends on the interrupt number. A table of the slots is shown in Table 2.2.

Some interrupts can only occur when bit 1 of the *psw* register is 1. If it is 0, the interrupts are *masked*, meaning that the fact that they occurred is recorded but   masked the interrupt is not actually processed until interrupts are unmasked by setting bit 1 of the *psw* register to 1. Only the timer and disk interrupts are masked; the program error and system call interrupts can occur even if bit 1 of the *psw* register is 0.

If interrupts are enabled and both the timer and disk interrupts are pending, then the timer interrupt is taken first.

2.4   I/O DEVICES

The CRA–1 uses *memory-mapped I/O*, meaning that communication between the   memory-mapped I/O I/O devices and the processor is done through physical memory locations in the I/O address space. Each I/O device will occupy some locations in the I/O address

Table 2.2	Layout of the interrupt vector area

Offset	**Interrupt**
0–3	System call
4–7	Timer
8–11	Disk
12–15	Program error

space. That is, it will respond when those addresses are placed on the bus. The processor can write those locations to send commands and information to the I/O device, and read those locations to get information and status from the I/O device. Memory-mapped I/O makes it easy to write device drivers in a high-level language as long as the high-level language can load and store from arbitrary addresses.

2.4.1 DISK CONTROLLER

The CRA–1 has one disk controller and it controls one fixed disk. Disk commands are initiated by storing them in the disk controller control register (see Figure 2.2). Disk blocks (also called sectors) contain 4096 data bytes. There are only two commands: load disk block from the disk into memory, and store disk block from memory to the disk. The disk block is specified by the disk block number, which is 20 bits long. This allows for about a million blocks on the disk, and a total disk size of 4 gigabytes.

The address to load into or store from in memory is specified by the disk memory address register, which should be loaded before the disk control register is loaded with a command.

When a disk transfer command is initiated, the disk controller goes into a busy state and remains busy until the transfer is completed. When the transfer completes, the disk controller can optionally cause a disk interrupt to inform the CPU that the disk is no longer busy. The disk_status_reg can be read to determine if the disk is busy.

```
const int BlockSize = 4096;

enum disk_command {LoadBlock=0, StoreBlock=1};

struct disk_control_reg {        1 bit for command
  unsigned int command : 1;
  unsigned int interrupt_enabled : 1;    1 bit for interrupt-enabled
  unsigned int disk_block : 20;     20 bits for disk-block
  unsigned int padding : 10;      10 leftover bits - need to make
};                                            up 32 bits

volatile disk_control_reg *Disk_control=
  (disk_control_reg *)0xF0000000;
void **Disk_memory_addr = (void **)0xF0000004;  - move pointer 4 bytes
void *Disk                                             over

enum disk_status {DiskIdle=0, DiskBusy=1};
struct disk_status_reg {
  unsigned int busy : 1;     1 bit if it's busy
  unsigned int padding : 31;   - leftover not needed
};

disk_status_reg *Disk_status = (disk_status_reg *)0xF0000008;
```

Figure 2.2   Declarations for the disk controller

2.5   SUMMARY

The CRA–1 hypothetical computer system has 32 general-purpose registers. Some have special purposes: always zero (*r0*), passing arguments (*r8, r9, r10,* and *r11*), stack (*r29, r30*), and procedure calls (*r1* and *r31*). It has nine control registers intended for use by the operating system. It has user and system processor modes. It is byte-addressed and uses 32-bit words and addresses. It has four types of interrupts: system call, timer, disk, and program error. And it has a disk and disk controller.

2.5.1   TERMINOLOGY

After reading this chapter, you should be familiar with the following terms:

- asm block
- base register
- bound register
- control register
- CPU
- general-purpose register
- I/O address space
- interrupt
- interrupt vector area
- logical address
- logical address space
- masked
- memory address space
- memory-mapped I/O
- physical address
- physical address space
- processor
- system mode
- user mode

2.5.2   REVIEW QUESTIONS

The following questions are answered in the text of this chapter:

1. What is the difference between a control register and a general-purpose register?
2. How do the base and bound registers control access to memory in user mode?

3. What happens when an interrupt occurs?

4. What happens when an *rti* is executed?

5. How do you specify machine instructions in C++?

6. What is memory-mapped I/O?

2.5.3   FURTHER READING

There are many books on computer organization and architecture that discuss in more detail the topics in the chapter. Some examples are Hamacher et al. (1990), Herzog (1996), Maccabe (1993), and Tanenbaum (1990).

The hardware reference manuals for some current RISC machines are also helpful. The major ones are the HP Precision (Hewlett Packard 1994) (`http://www.hp.com/nsa/acd.html`), the IBM RIOS (May et al. 1994) (`http://www.austin.ibm.com/tech`), and the SPARC (SPARC International 1992) (`httpp://www.prenhall.com/~rich/013/825000/82500-0.html`).

2.6   PROBLEMS

1. Why is there more physical address space than physical memory?

2. What is the alternative to memory-mapped I/O?

3. Why can't you mask off the system call and program error interrupts?

4. Show the code to read disk block 100 into address 0x2000.

5. Give the computation that shows that the disk controller can access a disk of up to 4 Gbytes.

6. Why is *r0* always 0? How is this useful?

7. What if a procedure has more than four arguments? What would you do?

8. Why aren't the base and bound registers used in system mode? What if they were used in system mode? Would this work? What other changes to the hardware would be necessary?

9. Why can't you change the control registers in user mode?

10. Most older processors required the interrupt vector area to be in the first part of the physical address space. Give a reason why it is better to have an *iva* register to determine the location of the interrupt vector area.

11. The interval timer only counts down to zero. Suppose we wanted to keep the time of day. How could we use the interval timer to keep the time of day?

12. Some processors save the *ia* register and the *psw* register on a stack when an interrupt occurs. What are the advantages and disadvantages of this?

13. Change the definitions of the disk controller to allow for up to four disks on a single disk controller. Then change the status register to allow it to return error codes when an operation fails.

chapter
3

The Operating System Interface

Before we look at how an operating system is implemented, we need to look at what functions will be implemented. So, in this chapter we will look at the interface the operating system provides to user programs. This interface is accessed with special machine instructions called traps or system calls. First we will look at exactly what system calls are and then we will look at the kinds of system calls that are provided by a typical operating system. We will see how files are used, how processes are created and destroyed, how processes communicate, and how shells provide interactive access to operating system functions.

3.1   WHAT ARE SYSTEM CALLS?

only work in C or assembly

Almost all modern processors provide instructions that can be used as system calls. A system call instruction is an instruction that does not execute a specific function in hardware but instead generates an interrupt that causes the operating system to gain control of the processor. The operating system then determines what kind of system call it is and performs the appropriate service for the system caller. In our hardware the syscall instruction is used for system calls.

   Figure 3.1 illustrates the flow of control during a system call. A system call goes through the following steps:

1. The program executes the system call instruction.

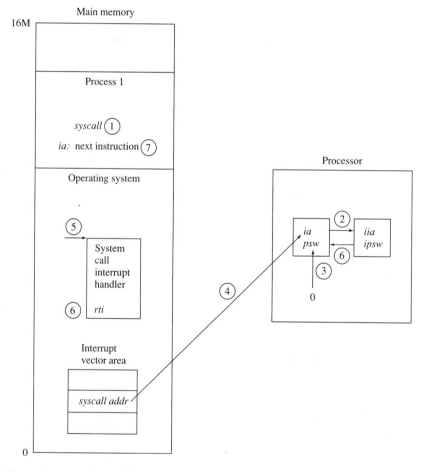

Figure 3.1   System call flow of control

2. The hardware saves the current *ia* and *psw* registers in the *iia* and *ipsw* registers.

3. The hardware loads a value of 0 into the *psw* register, which puts the machine in system mode with interrupts disabled.

4. The hardware loads the *ia* register from the system call interrupt vector location. This completes the execution of the system call instruction by the hardware.

5. Instruction execution continues at the beginning of the system call interrupt handler (whose address was in the system call interrupt vector location).

6. The system call handler completes and executes a return from interrupt (*rti*) instruction. This restores the *ia* and *psw* from the *iia* and *ipsw*.

7. The process that executed the system call instruction continues at the instruction after the system call.

The system call appears to be a single instruction to the caller but is implemented by many instructions in the operating system. It is similar to a procedure call instruction except that:

- The address of the procedure is not given; instead, an integer system call number is given.
- The processor mode changes from user mode to system mode.

The system caller must provide an integer argument, which is the system call number. This is usually used by the operating system as an index into a system table that determines what code is actually branched to. Since a system call is a switch to the operating system, the processor mode is changed to system mode.[1]

The system calls are the instruction set of the operating system virtual processor.

3.1.1 HOW TO MAKE A SYSTEM CALL

A system call is made using the system call machine language instruction. Few compilers will allow you to make system calls directly, so they must be made from an assembly language program. In C++ you use a library of assembly language routines that make system calls for you. The library is accessed through C++ procedure calls.

Since our hypothetical C++ compiler allows in-line assembly language, we can show how to make system calls directly from C++. The following code shows how such a system call library routine would look.

---

[1] Actually this is not necessarily so. It is possible to execute a system call while in system mode. In this case, the processor mode does not change. However, it is unusual to execute a system call in system mode.

MAKING A READ SYSTEM CALL

```
void open( char * file_name ) {
   asm {
      load    ReadSystemCallNumber,r8
      move    file_name,r9
      syscall
   }
}
```

The arguments are passed in registers. The return value of the system call will be passed back in register 1, which is also the register used for the return value for C++ procedures. Thus the value returned by the system call is passed back to the C++ caller.

3.1.2   WHAT IS A SYSTEM CALL INTERFACE?

The operating system provides a set of operations which are called system calls. These extend the native hardware instructions. All services that the operating system provides can be requested through system calls. From the point of view of a user, the entire functionality of the operating system is defined by the system calls. A *system call interface* is the description of the set of system calls implemented by the operating system.

system call interface

3.2   AN EXAMPLE SYSTEM CALL INTERFACE

For the purposes of this chapter we will define a simple system call interface to be used as an example. This interface is quite similar to a subset of the UNIX system call interface. Many of these calls will run unchanged on a UNIX system. We will generally *not* mention instances where the UNIX interface provides additional functions beyond what we define in this interface. You can see a complete list of the UNIX system calls by executing the UNIX command `man 2 intro` (on BSD-derived systems) or `man -s 2 intro` (on SVR4-derived systems)

3.2.1   SYSTEM CALL OVERVIEW

We will start with a brief overview of all the system calls and then describe each of them in some detail.

File and I/O System Calls:

   Open—get ready to read or write a file.

   Creat—create a new file and open it.

Read—read bytes from an open file.

Write—write bytes to an open file.

Lseek—change the location in the file of the next read or write.

Close—indicate that you are done reading or writing a file.

Unlink—remove a file name from a directory.

Stat—get information about a file.

Process Management System Calls:

CreateProcess—create a new process.

Exit—terminate the process making the system call.

Wait—wait for another process to Exit.

Fork—create a duplicate of the process making the system call.

Execv—run a new program in the process making the system call.

Interprocess Communication System Calls:

CreateMessageQueue—create a queue to hold messages.

SendMessage—send a message to a message queue.

ReceiveMessage—receive a message from a message queue.

DestroyMessageQueue—destroy a message queue.

3.2.2 HIERARCHICAL FILE NAMING SYSTEMS

Before we look at the file-related system calls, let us look briefly at how files are named. All operating systems need a way to name files. Most operating systems use what are called hierarchical file names, where file names are structured as a tree with the internal nodes being file directories. In this section we will briefly present the idea of hierarchical file names. We will discuss this topic again in Chapter 16.

A basic concept in a hierarchical file naming system is a directory. A *directory* is a collection of names, each referring to a file or another directory. If a name leads to another directory, then we can use that directory as a collection of names, each referring to a file or another directory. This creates a tree structure where leaf nodes are files and interior nodes are directories. There is a special directory that is the root of the tree and it is called the root directory. Figure 3.2 gives an example of a *hierarchical file naming system.*

Each directory is a collection of names, and all the names in a directory are unique. A directory forms a name space, and a directory also includes the mapping from each name to the file or directory it refers to. So, given a name and a directory, you can find the file or directory the name refers to. This is called a *name lookup.*

Files in a hierarchical file system are named with structured, multipart file names. A file name represents the path from the root directory to the file being named. A special character is used to separate the names in the path. In the example file hierarchy in Figure 3.2, the name of the directory `ch1` is `/users/faculty/crowley/book/ch1`.

directory

hierarchical file naming system

name lookup

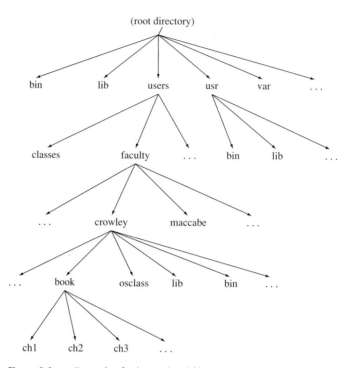

Figure 3.2   Example of a hierarchical file system

Since we see only one `ch1` in the directory tree, you know which file we mean when we say `ch1`, but if we were to refer to directory `bin` we could mean any of three directories (`/bin`, `/usr/bin`, or `/users/faculty/crowley/bin`). We will call the path names with separators (like `/usr/bin`) *full path names*. Each part in the full path name (like `usr` and `bin`) will be called a *component name*. Each component name is looked up in a directory.

Almost all modern operating systems use hierarchical file names because they have many advantages over the most common alternatives, which are a flat name space or a two-level name space. If the root directory could contain only file names and not directory names, you would have a *flat name space*. A *two-level name space* is a hierarchy that is limited to only two levels, so only the root directory can contain other directories.

full path names
component name

flat name space
two-level name space

Most operating systems provide hierarchical file names because they are easy to understand and powerful to use.

3.2.3 FILE AND I/O SYSTEM CALLS

The following table summarizes the system calls for file operations. We assume a hierarchical file system like the one used in UNIX and most other operating systems.

Call	Parameters	Returns	Notes
open	name,flags	fid	Create open file connected to a file
creat	name,mode	fid	Create file and connect to open file
read	fid,buffer,count	count	Read bytes from open file
write	fid,buffer,count	count	Write bytes to open file
lseek	fid,offset,mode	offset	Move position of next read or write
close	fid	code	Disconnect open file from file
unlink	name	code	Delete the named file

In order to use a file, you first need to ask for it by name. This is called *opening* the file. Opening a file creates an operating system object called an *open file*. The open file is logically connected to the file you named in the open system call. What this means inside the operating system is that the open file data structure has a pointer to the data structure that represents the file you opened.

open file

An open file has a *file location* associated with it. It is the offset in the file where the next read or write will start.

file location

After you open a file, you can read or write the open file. When you are done using the open file, you close it.

Here is a complete specification of the file-related system calls:

- `int open ( char * pathName, int openFlags );` —The named file is opened and an integer, the *open file identifier,* is returned. The file location is initialized to 0. The flags argument can be one of:

open file identifier

  0—open for reading.

  1—open for writing.

  2—open for reading and writing.

If an error occurs in trying to open the file, a negative integer is returned. The possible error codes are:

  −1—the file path name was invalid.

  −2—the `openFlags` argument is out of range (not 0, 1, or 2).

  −3—the file is not readable and you opened for reading.

  −4—the file is not writable and you opened for writing.

- int creat (char * pathName, int fileMode);[2]—The named file is created as an empty file and opened for writing, and an integer, the open file identifier, is returned. The file location is initialized to 0. The fileMode argument is the file protection mode and is not used in this operating system because we have not defined file protection modes. If some error occurs in trying to create the file, then creat will return a negative integer to indicate the error. The possible error codes are:

  −1—the file path name was invalid.

  −2—the fileMode argument is invalid.

- int read(int openFileID, char * bufferAddress, int count);—The operating system tries to read count bytes from the open file designated by openFileID. The bytes are read from the file starting at the offset provided by the file location. If fewer than count bytes are left before the end of the file, all the remaining bytes will be read. This is not considered to be an error. The openFileID must be one returned by an open call (with openFlags of 0 or 2). The bytes read are placed into the array of bytes starting at bufferAddress. The file location is increased by the number of bytes read. The return value is the number of bytes that were actually read. This might be less than count if the file location is very near the end of the file. A return value of 0 indicates that the end of the file has been reached (the file location is equal to the size of the file) and no more bytes can be read. A negative return value indicates that some error occurred in the read. The possible error codes are:

  −1—the openFileID is invalid (does not represent an open file).

  −2—the bufferAddress is an invalid address.

  −3—the count is invalid.

  −4—reading is not allowed on this open file.

  −5—I/O error.

- int write(int openFileID, char * bufferAddress, int count);— The operating system tries to write count bytes to the open file designated by openFileID. The bytes are written to the file starting at the offset provided by the file location. The openFileID must be one returned by a successful open call (with openFlags equal to 1 or 2) or a creat call. The bytes are taken from the array of bytes starting at bufferAddress. The file location is increased by the number of bytes written. The return value is the number of bytes that were actually written.[3] A negative return value indicates that some error occurred in the write. The possible error codes are:

  −1—the openFileID is invalid (does not represent an open file).

---

[2]The final "e" is left off create just because UNIX does it that way. We are following the UNIX spelling so that the examples will run under UNIX. We are not sure why the "e" was left off in the name of the UNIX system call—possibly to keep all the basic system call names to five characters or less.

[3]For all practical purposes this will be count. The only way the bytes could not be written is if the write encountered the end of the medium or the disk it was writing on filled up before it could write all the bytes.

−2—the bufferAddress is an invalid address.

−3—the count is invalid.

−4—writing is not allowed on this open file.

−5—I/O error.

- int lseek(int openFileID, int offset, int moveMode);[4]—The file location associated with the open file is changed to a new value. The new value is computed by adding the offset to the base. The base is selected according to the moveMode as described below. The legal values for moveMode are:

0—use 0 as a base (move from the beginning of the file).

1—use the current file location as a base (for relative moves).

2—use the current file size as a base (move from the end of the file). Positive values of offset will cause the next write to be beyond the current end of the file. A 0 value will cause the next write to extend the file.

The returned value is the new file location. An lseek call with an offset of 0 and a moveMode of 1 will not change the file position but will return the current file position. This is how you query the current file position. A negative return value indicates that an error occurred in the seek. The possible error codes are:

−1—invalid file location (negative).

−2—invalid openFileID (not an open file).

−3—the moveMode is invalid (not 0, 1, or 2).

- int close(int openFileID);—The file is closed. The openFileID must have been obtained from either open or creat. A return value of 0 means the close succeeded. A return value of -1 means that the openFileID did not refer to an open file.
- int unlink(char * pathName);—The file is deleted.[5] A return value of 0 means the unlink succeeded. A return value of -1 means that the pathName could not be found.

The open file identifiers returned by open and creat are local to the process making the call. That is, open file identifier 3 in one process is not related to open file identifier 3 in another process.

One thing to note is that the read system call specifies which file to read, how much to read, and where to put the read characters, but it does not indicate which characters in the file to read (where in the file to read). The location in the file is not passed with the calls but is kept with the open file information as part of the file state.

---

[4]The "l" in lseek is again for compatibility with UNIX. When UNIX was a 16-bit system, there was a seek system call that was more complex than this one. Later it was changed to use 32-bit (long) integers and so added the new system call lseek (long seek).

[5]This is called unlink in UNIX because of how directories are implemented. Directories in UNIX contain only the file name and a pointer to the file descriptor. The unlink system call in UNIX only removes a file name from a directory and decrements the link count in the file descriptor. The last unlink of a file reduces the link count to 0 and the file itself is deleted as a side effect. We will use the UNIX name, but in this operating system this instruction deletes the file itself.

The file location starts at 0 and is moved whenever bytes are read from (or written to) the file. Thus the file is read (or written) sequentially by default. If the file was opened for update (openFlags = 2), then reads and writes can be intermixed and they both affect the file position.

The lseek system call is used to achieve random access into the file since it changes the file location that will be used for the next read or write.

Figure 3.3 shows a flow chart for using a file.

3.2.4   OPEN FILES

file

It is important to understand the difference between a file and an open file. A *file* is a passive container of data, a named sequence of bytes. The principal operation on an existing file is the open system call, which returns an open file. The creat system call creates an empty file and then opens it for writing. An *open file* is a dynamic object that can provide bytes from the file or accept bytes to be stored in the file (or both). The operations on an open file are the read, write, lseek, and close system calls. An open file is generally associated with a file and allows access to the file. Later we will generalize the notion of an open file and see how an open file can be associated with other things than a file, such as input or output devices.

In Figure 3.4 we show how the open system call creates the open file and connects it to the file being opened. The read system call gets data from the file,

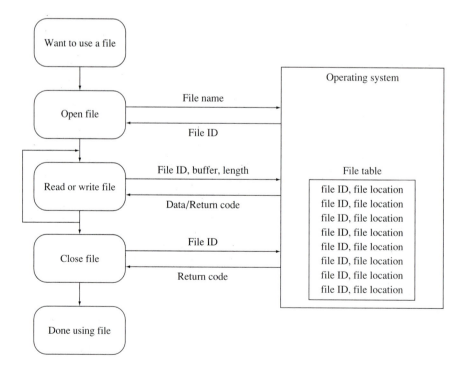

Figure 3.3   Steps in using a file

through the open file, and copies it into the I/O buffer, in the process making the
read system call.

> Files are passive containers of data. Open files are active sources and sinks for data.

Figure 3.5 shows the relationship between process objects (see Section 3.6), open
file objects, and file objects. These three objects (processes, open files, and files) are
different types of objects with different operations, but they are logically connected to
each other because processes have open files and open files are connected to files.

> Operating systems implement objects for users. The system calls create and operate on operating
> system objects.

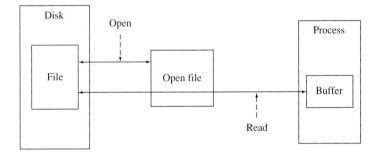

Figure 3.4   Files and open files

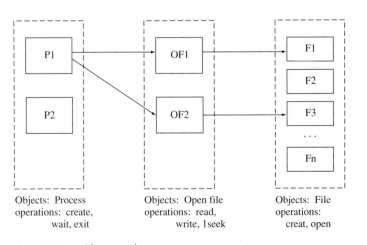

Objects: Process	Objects: Open file	Objects: File
operations: create,	operations: read,	operations:
wait, exit	write, lseek	creat, open

Figure 3.5   Objects and operations in an operating system

3.2.5   EXAMPLES OF FILE I/O

These system calls make it very easy to work with files. Here is the code to do a file copy.

FILE COPY

```
enum { Reading=0, Writing=1, ReadAndWrite=2,ReadWriteFile=0644 };
// This procedure takes as arguments two file path names.
// The first file is copied to the second file.
void FileCopy( char * fromFile, char * toFile ) {
    // open the source file for reading
    int fromFD = open( fromFile, Reading );
    if( fromFD < 0 ) {
        cerr << "Error opening " << fromFile << endl;
        return;
    }
    // create the destination file with protection mode read and write
    int toFD = creat( toFile, ReadWriteFile );
    if( toFD < 0 ) {
        cerr << "Error opening " << toFile << endl;
        close( fromFD );
        return;
    }
    // This loop reads one character at a time from the
    // source file and writes it to the destination file.
    while( 1 ) {
        char ch;
        int n = read( fromFD, &ch, 1 );
        // if 0 characters were read we are at the end of file
        if( n <= 0 )
            break;
        // throw away the value returned by write
        n = write( toFD, &ch, 1 );
        if( n < 0 ) {
            cerr << "Error writing " << toFile << endl;
            return;
        }
    }
    // close the two files and return
    close( fromFD );
    close( toFD );
}
```

We read and write one character at a time so the "array" of characters in the buffer is only a single character. We have to pass the address of the character because the system call expects the address of the first character of the buffer. The

variable ch is being used as an array of one character. We could have declared it as
char ch[1].

> Basic I/O is simple: open, read/write/seek repeatedly, then close.

The Reverse program will copy a file and reverse it while copying. It demonstrates the use of lseek.

REVERSE

```
enum { Reading=0, Writing=1, ReadAndWrite=2 };
enum { SeekFromBeginning=0, SeekFromCurrent=1, SeekFromEnd=2 };
// This procedure reverses the bytes in a file and writes the
// reversed version in a new file.
void Reverse( char * fromFile, char * revFile ) {
    // open the source file
    int fromFD = open( fromFile, Reading );
    if( fromFD < 0 ) {
        cerr << "Error opening " << fromFile << endl;
        return;
    }
    // move the internal file pointer so the next character read will
    // be the last character of the file
    int ret=lseek( fromFD, -1, SeekFromEnd );
    if( ret < 0 ) {
        cerr << "Error seeking on " << fromFile << endl;
        close( fromFD );
        return;
    }
    int revFD = creat( revFile, 0 );
    if( revFD < 0 ) {
        cerr << "Error creating " << revFile << endl;
        close( fromFD );
        return;
    }
    // Loop while reading from the end of the source file to
    // the beginning. The loop is exited in the middle.
    while( 1 ) {
        char ch;
        int n = read( fromFD, &ch, 1 );
        if( n < 0 ) {
            cerr << "Error reading " << fromFile << endl;
            return;
        }
        n = write( revFD, &ch, 1 );
        if( n < 0 ) {
```

```
            cerr << "Error writing " << revFile << endl;
            return;
        }
        // exit the loop if lseek returns an error.
        // The expected error is that the computed offset will
        // be negative.
        if( lseek(fromFD, -2, SeekFromCurrent) < 0 )
            break;
    }
    close( fromFD );
    close( revFD );
}
```

We start at the end of the file by setting the file position to one less than the end-of-file file position. (Remember that the system calls read and write the *next* byte at the file position.) Each time we read a character we move the file position back two, one for the byte we just read (which moved the file position up one) and one more so that we back up one byte.

Figure 3.6 shows the process of reading a byte from the source file, writing it to the destination file, and backing up the file pointer by two bytes.

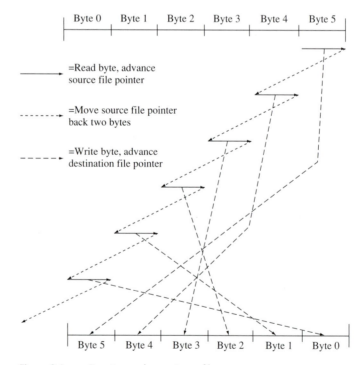

Figure 3.6   Copying and reversing a file

DESIGN TECHNIQUE: INTERFACE DESIGN

The reverse program requires an `lseek` in every iteration of the loop. For this particular program, it would be better to change the interfaces to `read` and `write` to include, as an explicit parameter to the call, the file offset at which to read or write. For example, the call might look like this: `read(fromFD, offset, &ch, 1)`. This would save one system call for each iteration of the loop and also express our intentions more clearly.

When we design an operating system (or any program, for that matter) we design two things: the interface and the implementation (for an operating system, the interface consists of the system calls and their arguments). When designing an interface it is useful to consider several design alternatives. As in any interface design, we have to consider who will be using the interface and how they will be using it. The original interface (with an implied file offset and a separate `lseek` to set it) is optimized for sequential reading and writing. For sequential file access, no `lseek` calls are required. The new interface proposed here (with explicit offsets in each read and write) is optimized for random access to the file. Experience tells us that sequential access is much

more common, and so we are led to accept the original design.

But can't we support both interfaces? We could have two sets of `read` and `write` system calls. One set would be the original set and one set would have explicit file offsets. We can do this, but this approach has other costs: more for users to learn, more decisions for users, possible confusions and mistakes by mixing up the two kinds of calls, longer manuals, and more code to implement the two sets of calls. It is better for the designers to make the decision.

You should follow this pattern in all interface designs.

- Determine who will use the interface and how they will use it.
- Think of several possible interfaces.
- Evaluate each alternative based on user and usage information.

This analysis is inexpensive, gives you a chance to examine your assumptions, and leads to improved interfaces.

See Section 4.5 for a longer discussion of interface design issues.

3.3   INFORMATION AND META-INFORMATION

Let us look at files in a more general way. Information is generally not a pure, complete, self-describing entity. Usually we want to record information about the information, that is, *meta-information*. A good example is a file. The file contains   meta-information
information itself, but the operating system also keeps meta-information about the file:

- Who owns the file.
- Who can use the file and how.
- When the file was created.
- When the file was last modified.
- When the file was last read.
- How long the file is.

There is a system call that will return to you all the meta-information about a file:

- int stat(int fileName, StatStruct * statInfo);[6] — The filename is looked up in the file system and the meta-information about the file is returned in the structure statInfo, which must be a pointer to a StatStruct. A return code of 0 means the stat succeeded and the information was written into statInfo. A return code of -1 means the file could not be found and no status information was returned.

*[handwritten annotation above "int": char *]*

We will expand on the contents of StatStruct in Chapter 16.

The ls command in UNIX (DIR in MS/DOS) can be used to display any of the information that the stat call returns. The ls command has many command line options since stat returns so much information. The command man stat will return a description of the meta-information kept in a UNIX file descriptor.

Most of the meta-information about a file is set by the operating system as a side effect of other operations. For example, when you modify a file the date of last modification is set. There is one type of meta-information that the owner of the file can set directly, and that is the protection status of the file, that is, who can use the file and how. There is usually a system call to do this. In UNIX, the system call is chmod (change mode).

> Information is data. Meta-information is information about the data.

3.4 NAMING OPERATING SYSTEM OBJECTS

In Section 3.2.2, we discussed how the file system uses hierarchical names for naming files and directories. We want to generalize that idea a little bit so we can use the file naming system for other kinds of operating system objects.

In a file system, the names map into either files or directories. A file is an object that you then do some operation on (usually open), while a directory is another name map that you use for the next step of the file name lookup.

So far, we have used the file system to name files and directories. In practice, the names in a file system really map into file object descriptors on disk, and these file object descriptors point to the file objects themselves (see Figure 3.7). We can easily extend this file naming system to name other kinds of operating system objects as well. When a user or program needs to refer to an object, it needs a name for that object. So it is convenient to use the file name naming system to name all the objects that need names. In Figure 3.7, we have shown the file naming system naming a number of different kinds of objects, some of which we haven't yet discussed (processes and queues).

| [6]The name stat is a shortening of "status."

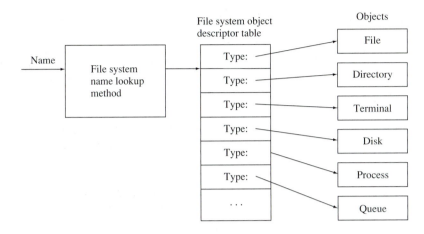

Figure 3.7   File system names mapping to objects

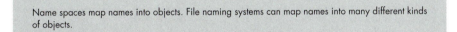

Name spaces map names into objects. File naming systems can map names into many different kinds of objects.

3.5   DEVICES AS FILES

We have seen how the operating system provides two related concepts for dealing with files. A *file* is a collection of information on disk, and an *open file* is an object (returned by an open or a creat) that you can read data from or write data to. So we can think of an open file as a source of bytes or a sink for bytes.

But objects other than files can also provide data and accept data. For example, the keyboard on a terminal or workstation is a source of bytes (keystrokes), and a terminal screen or a window on a workstation can accept bytes (characters) and display them on the screen. In fact, all I/O devices either receive data or send data or both. Given this similarity between devices and open files, it is useful to try to unify the concepts of file and device in an operating system. Let's see how that is done.

Every file has a name in the hierarchical file naming system. Since devices need names also, we will give them names in the file name hierarchy too. We will add special entries in the file system for the devices. In UNIX, there is a specially named directory, /dev, where most devices names are kept.[7] For example, a terminal attached to the computer might have the name /dev/tty13.[8] If we open

---

[7]This is just a convention in UNIX, not a requirement. Device files can legally occur in any directory but, in practice, it is rare to have a device file that is not in /dev or a subdirectory of /dev.

[8]Terminals are often called "ttys" for historical reasons. The first terminals were called teletypes, and that was abbreviated as tty.

the "file" name /dev/tty13, we get an open file object back. When we read from that open file, we are really reading from the keyboard of the terminal. When we write to that open file, we are really writing to the screen of the terminal.

For example, suppose we are sitting in front of a terminal whose name in the file system is /dev/tty17. The command

copy fileToList /dev/tty17

will list the file fileToList on the terminal /dev/tty17 and the command

copy /dev/tty17 fileToRewrite

will take input from terminal /dev/tty17 and write it into the file fileToRewrite. A program does not need to know whether it is reading from (or writing to) a file or a device. This is called *device independence*.

We can do the same thing with all devices: tape drives, floppy disks, terminals, communication lines, etc. We can even do it with windows on a workstation screen. Windows are sometimes called *pseudodevices* since they act like devices (terminals in particular) but are not real, physical devices.

device independence

> Unifying devices and files makes programs device independent.

3.5.1   UNIFICATION OF THE FILE AND DEVICE CONCEPTS

The file system has two distinct parts to its services. The first part is the file naming system, which maps hierarchical names into objects (files). There is no particular reason that a name has to refer to a file since it just maps to some object. Most operating systems take advantage of that fact and use the file naming system to provide names that users can use to refer to a number of different objects. In particular, you can use the file naming system to give names to I/O devices. Later we will see the file naming system used to name other machines, processes, interprocess communication mailboxes, etc. This technique does not unify devices and files but merely uses the same system to name them.

The second part of the file system provides access to (that is, reading and writing of) files, and treats a file as a source or a sink for data. We have seen in this section how the file concept can be generalized to include devices. By unifying the concepts of file and device, we make things easier for users. A program does not need to know whether it is writing to a device or a file, so programs are simpler.

3.6   THE PROCESS CONCEPT

We previously discussed how the operating system creates a number of virtual computers. When we execute a program on one of these virtual computers, we call the executing program a *process*. The principal goal of an operating system is to implement virtual computers and the processes that run on them. A virtual computer is created

process

for each process, thereby giving the process the illusion of running on its own physical computer. The virtual computer extends the hardware instruction set with a set of system calls that request operating system services. The virtual computer is the execution environment created by the operating system, and the process is the program execution that occurs in that environment.

Many users are not aware of the process concept because they just run a program in a single process on the computer. Normally other programs create processes for you. For example, a shell (a command interpreter in UNIX) creates your first process "for free," that is, it is automatically created for you and starts up running the program you requested. Many users use multiple processes in their work, even though they may not realize it. A shell pipeline is implemented by creating a process for each program in the pipeline. If you compile a program in the background and edit in the foreground, you are using multiple processes.

3.6.1 PROCESSES AND PROGRAMS

It is important to understand the distinction between a program and a process. A *program* is a static object that can exist in a file. It contains the instructions (the algorithm). A *process* is a dynamic object that is a program in execution. A program is a sequence of instructions. A process is a sequence of instruction executions. A program exists at a single place in space and continues to exist as time goes forward. A process exists in a limited span of time. Let's look at an example of the difference. Consider the following C program:

program

```
main() {
    int i, prod = 1;
    for( i = 0; i < 100; ++i )
        prod = prod * i;
}
```

The program contains one multiplication (`prod = prod * i`), but the process will execute 100 multiplications, one each time through the loop.

	Program	**Process**
Exists in	Space	Time
Is	Static	Dynamic
Consists of	Instructions	Instruction executions

A program is a static object. A process is a dynamic activity.

3.6.2 PROCESS MANAGEMENT SYSTEM CALLS

We will present the process management system calls in several versions so that we can introduce one process-related concept at a time. Only the last of these versions (in Section 3.8) is compatible with the UNIX system calls.

Process Creation Without Arguments   The operating system will allow a process to create new processes, to terminate itself, and to wait for a process it created to complete. There are just three system calls dealing with processes:

- int SimpleCreateProcess(char * programName);—A new process is created and the program programName is run in that process. The return value is the process identifier of the new process.
- void SimpleExit(void);—The process making the system call is terminated.
- void SimpleWait(int pid);—The calling process will wait until the process specified by the process identifier pid terminates.

The operating system creates the very first process when it initializes. That process then starts all other processes in the system using SimpleCreateProcess system calls. Each process makes a SimpleExit system call when it is finished. This terminates the process and releases any resources it was holding.

The operating system assigns to each process a unique number, which is used to identify the process. This is called the process identifier or PID. A process can wait for any other process to exit (as long as it knows the process identifier of the process it wants to wait for).

> Processes are created, are waited for by their parent process, and exit when they are done.

Suppose you wanted to run two programs at the same time. One program is named compiler, the other is named editor. The following code creates a process for each program to run in and runs the processes at the same time. The procedure CreateProcess1 must be called by a running process.

SIMPLE CREATE PROCESS

```
// This procedure creates two processes and waits for them
// to complete.
void CreateProcess1( void ) {
    // Create the two processes.
    int pid1 = SimpleCreateProcess( "compiler" );
    if( pid1 < 0 ) {
        cerr << "Could not create process \"compiler\"" << endl;
        return;
    }
```

```
int pid2 = SimpleCreateProcess( "editor" );
if( pid2 < 0 ) {
    cerr << "Could not create process \"editor\"" << endl;
    return;
}
// Wait until they are both completed.
SimpleWait( pid1 );
SimpleWait( pid2 );
// "compiler" and "editor" end by making SimpleExit system calls
SimpleExit();
}
```

Figure 3.8 shows the process hierarchy this creates.

Process Creation with Arguments   Our `SimpleCreateProcess` is easy to use but does not allow us to pass any information to the process we create. Most programs require some arguments to tell them what to do. Let's extend the `Simple CreateProcess` system call to allow us to send arguments to processes we create. Different programs require different numbers of arguments, so we need a method that allows a variable number of arguments. We will use the method used in UNIX systems, that is, the arguments will be packaged as an array of strings.

In addition to passing information to a process, we want a process to return information to us when it exits. The information returned is status information about whether the child process was successful. Therefore, we allow an exiting process to send an integer return code to the process that waits for it.

The following table summarizes the process-related system calls and their arguments:

Call	Arguments	Returns	Notes
CreateProcess	Program file,args	Pid	Create the process
Exit	Return code	Does not return	Destroy the process
Wait	Pid	Return code	Wait for pid to Exit

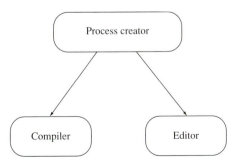

Figure 3.8   Creating two processes

The new system calls are specified as follows:

- int CreateProcess(char * programName, int argc, char *argv [ ]);—A new process is created and the program programName is run in that process. If the process creation is successful, the return value is the process identifier of the new process. The arguments are in the argument vector argv which is an array of strings, that is, an array of pointers to characters. argc gives the argument count, that is, the number of pointers to strings in argv. The return code is -1 if the process could not be created because process table space was not available. The return code is -2 if the programName could not be read for execution.

- void Exit(int returnCode);—This system call causes a process to exit. The return code is returned to the parent process when it executes the Wait system call.

- int Wait(int pid);—This system call will cause the calling process to wait until the process specified by pid exits. The return value is the return code provided by the process when it exited. Normally a return code of 0 means the process was successful.

Let's look at an example:

CREATE TWO PROCESSES

```
// This procedure creates two processes and waits for them
// to complete.
void CreateProcess2( void ) {
    // Create the argument list for the first process as an
    // array of strings created at compile time.
    static char * argb[3] = {"compiler", "fileToCompile", (char *) 0 };
    // Create the first process.
    int pid1 = CreateProcess( "compiler", 3, argb );
    if( pid1 < 0 ) {
        cerr << "Could not create process \"compiler\"" << endl;
        return;
    }
    // Create the argument list for the second process
    // at run time by assignments to the array components.
    char * argv[3];
    argv[0] = "editor";
    argv[1] = "fileToEdit";
    argv[2] = (char *) 0;
    // Create the second process.
    int pid2 = CreateProcess( "editor", 3, argv );
    if( pid2 < 0 ) {
        cerr << "Could not create process \"compiler\"" << endl;
        return;
    }
```

```
// Wait for both processes to complete.
(void) Wait( pid1 );
(void) Wait( pid2 );
Exit( 0 );
}
```

In this example we created one argument list at compile time in a static variable. The second argument list we created at run time by filling in the array values. It is more flexible to create argument lists at run time since then they can depend on information only available at run time. We ignore the return values of the processes. Figure 3.9 shows the process hierarchy this creates.

How Arguments Are Passed   For compiler we constructed the argument vector when we declared argb using array initialization. We added a 0 pointer to mark the end of the array. This is not strictly necessary because we give an argument count, but it is a UNIX convention so we might as well follow it. For editor we constructed the argument list in the code.

Notice that the first argument is the name of the program itself. This is another UNIX convention that is widely followed, so we will follow it here. Generally, programs know what name they are called by so this information is superfluous, but some programs do make use of this information. For example, the vi full-screen text editor and the ex line editor are really the same program. The program looks at the name it was called with and goes to either full-screen mode or line mode, depending on whether that name is vi or ex. The same is true of compress, uncompress, and zcat, which are all the same program. The function performed is determined by the name by which the program is called.

The operating system will take these arguments and make them available to the new process by copying them from the memory of the creating process to the (newly allocated) memory of the created process (see Figure 3.10).

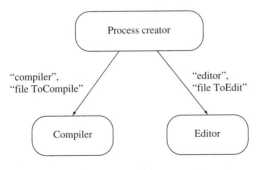

Figure 3.9   Creating two processes with arguments

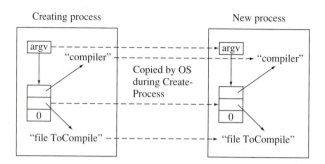

Figure 3.10   Passing arguments by copying between processes

The following code example shows how the process can get access to these arguments. It is a program that simply prints out its arguments.

PRINT ARGUMENTS

```
// This program writes out its arguments.
#include <iostream.h>
void main( int argc, char * argv[ ] ) {
    int i;
    for( i = 0; i < argc; ++i ) {
        cout << argv[i] << " ";
    }
    cout << "\n";
}
```

A main program has two arguments, the argument count and the argument vector. The operating system takes the argument vectors from the calling process and copies them to the new process. It builds these arguments on the process's stack before the process begins execution. The operating system takes care of the copying from the memory of the creating process to the memory of the created process since they do not share any memory.

3.6.3   PROCESS HIERARCHY

parent process

child process

process hierarchy

When one process creates another process, we say the creator is the *parent process* and the created process is the *child process*. This parent/child relationship can be shown as a tree structure of the processes in the system (see Figure 3.11), and this tree structure is called the *process hierarchy*.

Generally a parent is in control of a child process. The parent can stop the child temporarily, cause it to be terminated, send it messages, look inside its memory, etc.

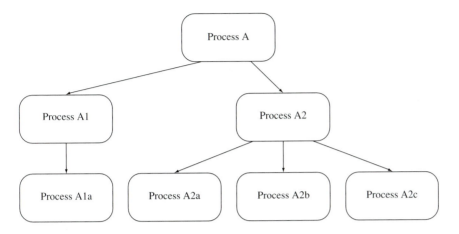

Figure 3.11   An example of process hierarchy

The operating system usually accumulates accounting information for the children in the parent. Sometimes resource control is handled through the hierarchy, that is, a parent allocates resources to the children who then allocate them to their children, etc. Usually only a parent can wait for a child process to complete. In some systems, if a parent process terminates, then the children are automatically terminated also. Other systems can "reparent" the orphan children by moving them somewhere else in the process hierarchy (UNIX does this).

Processes are organized in hierarchies. Parent processes have control over their child processes.

3.7   COMMUNICATION BETWEEN PROCESSES

Using the process system calls, we can send arguments to a new process and get a return code when that process completes. Sometimes, we will also want processes to communicate with each other while they are running. We call this *interprocess communication* or *IPC*.

interprocess communication
IPC

We will add a message system and provide system calls to send and receive messages between processes. We will allow a process to send a message even though the receiver is not yet ready to receive it. We will do this by *buffering* the messages, that is, we will save the message until the receiver asks for it. We buffer the message in a *message queue,* which holds messages that have been sent but not yet received. Message queues will be a type of object supported by the operating system. A process can create a message queue, and then any processes can send messages to it or receive messages from it.

buffering

message queue

Messages will be addressed to message queues. The alternative design would be to address a message directly to another process. In that case, we would have a message queue associated with each process. The process's message queue would hold messages that had been sent to it but that it had not received yet. We will see that addressing messages to message queues rather than specific processes has a number of advantages.

Each message will contain eight words. This is rather a small message size; therefore it will be difficult to send large quantities of data between processes. But for now we will use this small, fixed message size since we want to concentrate on the message passing and not the problems of message buffering.

Figure 3.12 shows several processes and message queues and how they are connected. Notice that a process can send to several message queues and receive from several message queues. Similarly, a message queue can be sent to by several processes and be received from by several processes.

> Processes implement separate activities, but processes often need to communicate with each other.

3.7.1 COMMUNICATION-RELATED SYSTEM CALLS

We need system calls to create message queues and to send and receive messages. The following table summarizes the communication-related system calls:

Call	Parameters	Returns	Notes
CreateMessageQueue	None	qid	Create a message queue
SendMessage	qid, msg	return code	Send a message
ReceiveMessage	qid, msg	return code	Receive a message
DestroyMessageQueue	qid	return code	Destroy a message queue

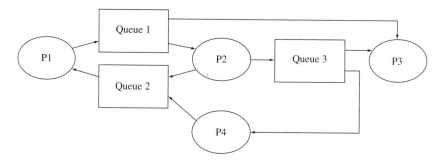

Figure 3.12   Complex message-passing paths between processes

The new system calls are described below.

- int CreateMessageQueue(void);—A new message queue is created and an identifier for the new message queue is returned to the caller. The message queue identifier is used in the send and receive message system calls. All message queue identifiers are global to the system; therefore all message queues can be accessed by all processes. The message queue will continue to exist until it is destroyed with a call to DestroyMessageQueue. A valid message queue identifier will always be a positive integer. The return value is -1 if there was a problem that prevented the queue from being created (such as no available memory).

- int SendMessage(int msg_q_id, int * message_buffer);—The message in message_buffer is sent to the message queue with identifier msg_q_id. The message_buffer is an array of 8 integers. The information in the message is not examined by the operating system but is simply transferred to the message queue and later to the receiver. The return value is 0 if the message is sent successfully. The return value is -1 if msg_q_id is not a valid message queue identifier, and -2 if message_buffer is an invalid address.

- void ReceiveMessage(int msg_q_id, int * message_buffer);—The oldest message in the message queue whose identifier is msg_q_id will be copied into message_buffer, an array of 8 integers. If there are no waiting messages, then the system call will not return until a message is sent to that message queue. The return value is 0 if a message is received successfully. The return value is -1 if msg_q_id is not a valid message queue identifier, and -2 if message_buffer is an invalid address.

- int DestroyMessageQueue(int msg_q_id);—The message queue with identifier msg_q_id will be destroyed. Any unreceived messages will be discarded. The identifier msg_q_id will no longer be valid for message sending and receiving. A return value is 0 if the message queue was destroyed. The return value is -1 if msg_q_id is not a valid message queue identifier.

3.7.2   EXAMPLE OF INTERPROCESS COMMUNICATION

Messages provide a basic communication capability between two processes. As an example, we will look at a program that will read a file and send the file to another process. The other process will count the number of characters in the file and return the count to the first process. This is not exactly a realistic example, but it does show the use of messages.

The following is the code for the file sender program:

MESSAGE: FILE SENDER

```
// A convenience procedure to make packaging and sending messages easier.
// Only for message of three or fewer words.
void SendMsgTo( int msg_q_id, int msg0=0, int msg1=0, int msg2=0 ) {
```

```
    int msg[8];
    msg[0] = msg0; msg[1] = msg1; msg[2] = msg2;
    (void)SendMessage( msg_q_id, msg );
}
// This process sends the bytes in a file (one at a time)
// to another process.
enum { Reading=0, Writing=1, ReadAndWrite=2 };
enum { FileToOpen=1, SendQueue=2, ReceiveQueue=3 };
void main( int argc, char * argv[ ] ) {
    //The first argument is the file to send. Open for reading.
    int fromFD = open( argv[FileToOpen], Reading );
    if( fromFD < 0 ) {
      cerr << "Could not open file " << argv[FileToOpen] << endl;
      exit( 1 );
    }
    // The second argument is the message queue to which bytes will be sent.
    int to_q = atoi(argv[SendQueue]);
    // atoi = ASCII to integer (in C++ library)
    // Loop once for each byte in the file.
    while( 1 ) {
      char ch;
      // Read the next byte.
      int n = read( fromFD, &ch, 1 );
      //If there are no bytes left then exit the loop.
      if( n <= 0 )
        break;
      // Send each byte in a message to the message queue.
      SendMsgTo( to_q, ch );
    }
    close( fromFD );
    // Signal the end of file to the process receiving the bytes.
    SendMsgTo( to_q, 0 );
    int msg[8];
    int from_q = atoi(argv[ReceiveQueue]);
    ReceiveMessage( from_q, msg );
    // Receive the message containing the byte count and print it out.
    cout << msg[0] << " characters\n";
    exit( 0 );
}
```

We are sending the characters one per message. Obviously we could pack 32 characters per message (assuming a 32-bit word, eight bits per character, and eight-word messages), but that would complicate the code without revealing anything more about message passing in operating systems.

Here is the code for the receiver.

MESSAGE: FILE RECEIVER

```
//This process receives bytes one at a time and counts them up.
enum{ SendQueue=1, ReceiveQueue=2 };
```

```
void main( int argc, char * argv[ ] ) {
    //start the count at zero.
    int count = 0;
    int msg[8];
    int from_q = atoi(argv[SendQueue]);
    while( 1 ) {
      ReceiveMessage( from_q, msg );
      if( msg[0] == 0 )
        break;
      //Any message with nonzero content is a character to count.
      ++count;
    }
    //Send the count back to the sender.
    int to_q = atoi(argv[ReceiveQueue]);
    (void) SendMsgTo( to_q, count );
    exit( 0 );
}
```

Finally, here is the code for the process that starts these two processes. Assume that the file sender has been compiled and linked, and the executable is in file **File-Sender**. Similarly, the executable for the file receiver is in **FileReceiver**.

MESSAGE: START FILE SENDER AND FILE RECEIVER

```
//Convenience procedure for creating a process with up to 3 arguments
int CreateProcessWithArgs(char * prog_name, char * arg1=0,
                    char * arg2=0, char * arg3=0) {
    char *args[5];
    //Create the argument array and create the process.
    args[0] = prog_name; args[1] = arg1;
    args[2] = arg2; args[3] = arg3; args[4] = 0;
    int argc = 4;
    if( arg3 == 0) --argc;
    if( arg2 == 0) --argc;
    if( arg1 == 0) --argc;
    return CreateProcess( prog_name, argc, args );
}
//Convert integers to strings
char * itoa( int n ) {
    char * result = new char[8];
    sprintf( result, "%d", n);
    return result;
}
//This process creates two message queues and then the two
//processes. No error code checking is done.
void main( int argc, char * argv[ ] ) {
    //Create the message queues the processes will use.
    int q1 = CreateMessageQueue();
    int q2 = CreateMessageQueue();
    //Create the two processes, sending each the identifier
    //for the message queues it will use.
```

```
int pid1 = CreateProcessWithArgs( "FileSend", "FileToSend",
                    itoa(q1), itoa(q2) );
int pid2 = CreateProcessWithArgs( "FileReceive",
                    itoa(q1), itoa(q2) );
//Wait for the two processes to complete.
int ret1 = wait( pid1 );
int ret2 = wait( pid2 );
//We do not use the return code ret1 and ret2 in this example.
//Destroy the message queues.
DestroyMessageQueue( q1 );
DestroyMessageQueue( q2 );
Exit( 0 );
}
```

The process must create the message queues first so that it can send the message queue identifiers to each process it creates. Having a common parent is an easy way to set up communication between two processes.

Figure 3.13 shows the creation and message-sending relationships between the three processes.

Message passing is a simple form of interprocess communication that is widely used in distributed operating systems. In centralized systems, more-optimized forms of interprocess communication are often used. In either case, a layer of software is placed above message passing to make interprocess communication simpler for users to use.

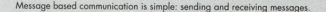

Message based communication is simple: sending and receiving messages.

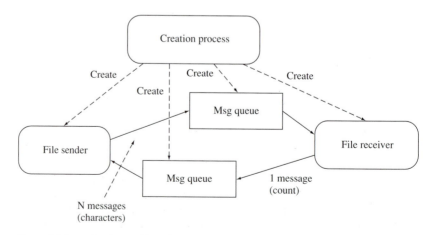

Figure 3.13   Sending a file with messages

3.8   UNIX-STYLE PROCESS CREATION

UNIX uses a very different method of process creation. In UNIX, two system calls are necessary to create a new process running a different program, one to do the actual creation of a new process and the other to run a specific program in the new process. In Section 3.9 we will discuss why UNIX does this. For now we will present the UNIX process system calls and show how they are used.

The following table summarizes the UNIX process-related system calls:

Call	Parameters	Returns	Notes
fork	None	pid or 0	Duplicate process
execv	programFile,args	None	Execute program in process
exit	return code	Does not return	Destroy process
wait	return code address	pid	Wait for process to exit

Here is their specification:

- int fork(void);—A new process is created that is an exact copy of the process making the system call. The return value to the parent is the process identifier of the new process. The return value to the child is 0.   fork

- int execv(char * programName, char *argv[ ]);—The program programName is run in the calling process. The program in the calling process is overwritten and will no longer exist. The arguments are in the argument vector argv, which is an array of strings, that is, an array of pointers to characters.   execv

- void exit(int returnCode);—This system call causes a process to exit. The return code is returned to whoever waits for the process.

- int wait(int * returnCode);—This system call will cause the calling process to wait until *any* process created by (that is, forked by) the calling process exits. The return value is the process identifier of the process that exited. The return code of that process is stored in returnCode.

The fork system call is somewhat unusual. A copy of the calling process is made and runs as a new process. The copy is of the memory of the calling process at the time of the fork system call, not the program the calling process was started from. The new process does not start at the beginning but at the exact point of the fork system call. Right after the fork there are two processes with identical memory images. Each one is about to return from a fork system call. The only difference between the two processes is the return value the operating system will give to the two returning forks. The fork of the parent returns the process identifier of the newly created process (the child process). The fork of the child returns a 0. Note that the fork system call returns twice, once to the parent process and once to the child process.

The UNIX wait system call is slightly different from the one we have seen before. The UNIX wait system call waits for *any* process to exit. You cannot control which one is waited for. The system call returns the first one it finds. As a consequence, the system call has to return the pid of the process that exited.

Sometimes it is more convenient to wait for any exited process and sometimes you want to wait for a specific process to exit. You can get the best of both worlds with a wait system call that waits for a specific process unless you pass in a special, unused pid (such as 0 or -1), which means to wait for any process to exit.

Figure 3.14 gives an example of a UNIX fork.

Let's redo the process creation example on page 46 with the UNIX process system calls.

UNIX: CREATE PROCESS

```
void CreateProcess3( void ) {
    int pid1, pid2;
    static char * argv[3] = { "compiler", "fileToCompile", 0 };
    //The fork will create a process that is a copy of this one.
    pid1 = fork();
    if( pid1 == 0 ) {
        //Child process code begins here.
        //Child return pid1 == 0
        execv( "compiler", argv ); //Child executes the compiler
        //Child process code ends here.
        //execv does not return so control in the child
        //never returns here.
    }
    //Parent skips the "if" body and executes here because pid1!= 0
    argv[0] = "editor";
    argv[1] = "fileToEdit";
    argv[2] = 0;
    //Assign and test the return value from fork differently.
    if( (pid2 = fork()) == 0 ){
        execv( "editor", argv );
    }
    int reta, retb;
    int pida = wait( &reta );
    int pidb = wait( &retb );
}
```

In the fork method of process creation, the open files are inherited by the child process. This is an advantage that we will discuss in the next section.

In UNIX, pure process creation is logically separated from executing a new program in an existing process.

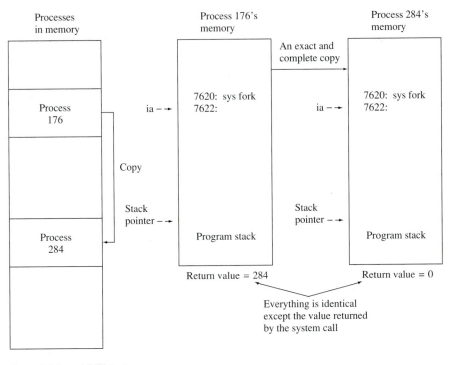

Figure 3.14   UNIX fork

3.9   STANDARD INPUT AND STANDARD OUTPUT

We have noted that programs can read from and write to open files, and that open files are named with integers that are returned by open and creat. We called these integers open file identifiers. In UNIX the open file identifiers 0 and 1 are treated specially. Open file identifier 0 is called *standard input* and open file identifier 1 is called *standard output*.

standard input
standard output

Many programs read data, transform it, and write it out again. By convention, in UNIX, these programs read their input from standard input (file identifier 0) and write their output to standard output (file identifier 1). When the shell starts a program, standard input and standard output are normally the user's terminal, but they can be changed by a method called *redirection*. If we start a shell process as follows:

redirection

```
someprog <infile >/dev/tty23
```

then the program will run with standard input reading from the open file infile and standard output writing to the device named /dev/tty23. A program whose main function is to read a sequence of bytes from its standard input, transform the stream in some way, and then write it to standard output is called a *filter*.

filter

Figure 3.15 shows how input and output can be redirected.

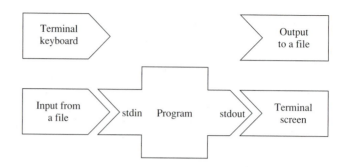

Figure 3.15   Standard input and output redirection

How does the shell do this? The UNIX `fork` system call makes a duplicate of the running process, and part of that duplication is that all the open files of the parent process (that called the `fork`) are copied (duplicated in UNIX jargon). When an `exec` is executed, the program running in the process is changed but all open files are preserved. So if the parent shell has its standard input reading from the user's terminal and its standard output writing to the user's terminal, then so will the child process. By default, the child inherits the standard input and output of the parent.

In UNIX, an open file is an object that exists independently of the process that created it. The process holds a pointer to the open file. When the process `forks`, the pointer is copied; thus, the child process can also use the open file.

If we want to redirect standard input from the user's terminal to a file, we can close standard input and open it again as file `infile`. UNIX has a system call that will open a file and give it a specific open file identifier. With this system call you can guarantee that the open file identifier will be 0. The open file already in 0 will be automatically closed.

We redirect standard input and output after the `fork` (so the `fork`ing process's standard input and output are not affected) and before the `exec` (so the new standard input and output will already be in effect when the new program begins execution). By separating process creation from execution of a new program in a process, we can create a process, set up its open files (standard input and output in particular), and then execute the program. This is the main advantage of the UNIX method of creating processes.

To achieve this effect with the `CreateProcess` form of process creation, we would need to modify the `CreateProcess` system call. For example, we might have a form of the call:

- `int CreateProcessWithStdio( char * programName, int stdin, int stdout );`—A new process is created and the program `programName` is run in that process. Open file `stdin` will be duplicated and made the standard input of the new process. Similarly, the open file `stdout` will be duplicated and made the standard output of the new process. The return value is the process identifier (pid) of the new process.

This still is not as flexible as the UNIX `fork/exec` method because it does not allow us to share other open files, only standard input and standard output.

Another approach would be to redefine `CreateProcess` as:

- `int CreateProcessAndDuplicateOpenFiles(char * programName
  );`—A new process is created and the program `programName` is run in that
  process. All of the open files in the parent process will be duplicated and be open
  files in the child process. The return value is the process identifier of the new
  process.

So to set the standard input and output for the child process, the parent process will
change its standard input and output to the desired open files, create the child
process, and then change the standard input and output back to their original values.
This is less convenient than the UNIX `fork/exec` method since it requires the parent to change its own standard input and output before the create and change it back
afterwards. It also requires the parent to share all of its open files instead of allowing
it to selectively close files after the `fork` and before the `exec`.

3.10   COMMUNICATING WITH PIPES

We have seen how devices can be named using the file system hierarchical naming
system and how these devices are used in the same way as files. We can use the
same idea to allow interprocess communication through a technique called *named
pipes* (also called a *fifo*). A *pipe* is an object that can act like a file, that is, it can be
written to and read from. We can write bytes to the pipe. When we read from a pipe,
we get the same bytes that were written and in the same order as they were written.
A pipe is useful when we want to write from one process and read from another.
This allows us to use pipes as a method of communication between processes, an alternative to messages.

> fifo
> pipe

Note how different this method is from messages. With messages, there is a
fixed message size which both sender and receiver must adhere to. With a pipe, a
process writes to the other process as if it were writing to a file. There are no
fixed-size blocks. For example, the process writing the pipe can write in units of
100 bytes and the process reading the pipe can read in units of 20 bytes. (See
Figure 3.16.)

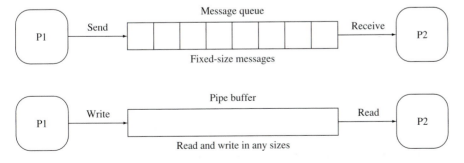

Figure 3.16   Messages and pipes

In addition, we use the familiar file access interface instead of having to learn a new interface involving sending and receiving rather than writing and reading.

It is possible for a pipe to have several writers and several readers, although in that case it is hard to keep sorted out what belongs to whom.

The example we used in Section 3.7.2 to show the use of the message system calls has three processes. A sender process read a file and sent it, one character at a time, to a receiver process. The receiver process counted the characters and sent back a count when the end of file was reached. There was also a main process that created the sender and the receiver. Let's redo our message example with named pipes. First, the file sender will look like this:

PIPE: FILE SENDER

```
enum { Reading=0, Writing=1, ReadAndWrite=2};
void main( int argc, char * argv[ ] ){
    //The first argument is the file to open.
    int fromFD = open( argv[1], Reading );
    //The second argument is the pipe to write it on.
    int to_pipe = open( argv[2], Writing );
    while( 1 ) {
        char ch;
        int n = read( fromFD, &ch, 1 );
        if( n ==0 )
            break;
        write( to_pipe, &ch, 1 );
    }
    close( fromFD );
    //Closing the pipe will cause the receiver to get an
    //end of file after it reads all the characters currently
    //in the pipe.
    close( to_pipe );
    //The third argument is the pipe from which to read the count.
    int from_pipe = open( argv[3], Reading );
    int n;
    //We are assuming the int n is four bytes long,
    //so we read four bytes.
    read( from_pipe, &n, 4 );
    close( from_pipe );
    cout << n << " characters\n";
    exit( 0 );
}
```

Here is the code for the receiver.

PIPE: FILE RECEIVER

```
enum { Reading=0, Writing=1, ReadAndWrite=2 };
void main( int argc, char * argv[ ] ) {
    int count = 0;
    //The first argument is the pipe to read from.
    int from_pipe = open( argv[1], Reading );
    while( 1 ) {
        char ch;
        int n = read( from_pipe, &ch, 1 );
        if( n == 0 )
            break;
        ++count;
    }
    close( from_pipe );
    //send the count back to the sender.
    //The first argument is the pipe to write to.
    int to_pipe = open( argv[2], Writing );
    write( to_pipe, &count, 4 );
    close( to_pipe );
    exit( 0 );
}
```

In the message version, the file receiver receives a message containing a zero, which indicates the end of file. In the pipe version, it gets an actual end of file (a read count of 0) from the read on the pipe.

Finally here is the code for the process that starts these two processes:

PIPE: START FILE SENDER AND FILE RECEIVER

```
void main( int argc, char * argv[ ] ) {
    int pid1 = CreateProcessWithArgs( "FileSend", "FileToSend",
                        "PipeToReceiver", "PipeToSender" );
    int pid2 = CreateProcessWithArgs( "FileReceive",
                        "PipeToReceiver", "PipeToSender" );
    int ret1 = wait( pid1 );
    int ret2 = wait( pid2 );
    exit( 0 );
}
```

It is possible to connect several processes together with pipes. Figure 3.17 shows a pipeline created by connecting the standard output of one process to the standard input of another process. The two processes communicate through a pipe.

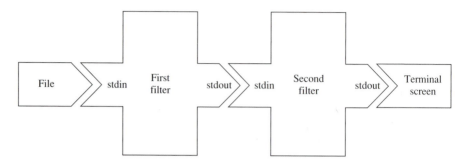

Figure 3.17   A pipeline of two processes with redirection at both ends

Pipes connect program tools together to make larger tools.

3.10.1   Naming of Pipes and Message Queues

One difference between named pipes and message queues (as we specified them) is how they are named. Named pipes are named by the file system naming system and they are implemented by an entry in the file system indicating that they are a named pipe. There is a system call to create a named pipe in the file system. Thus they have some kind of existence even when no process is using them. Any two processes can communicate if they both know the name of the pipe. They just both open the pipe and use it as an open file.

Message queues have no name and no existence before they are created by a process. When they are created they are given an internal (operating system defined) name for use by processes wanting to pass messages. This name can be passed to other processes, but passing the name requires some form of communication. That limits the processes that can receive the name to descendants of the process that created the message queue. So two processes need a common ancestor in order to communicate.[9] This is much less convenient than the named pipe approach.

There is nothing inherent in message queues that requires them to be named as we have specified in this chapter. We could also allow message queues to have a place in the file system and use the file naming system. Instead of creating a message queue, we could "attach" to a message queue and get an internal name to use in message sends and receives. When we were done, we could unattach the queue,

---

[9]It is possible to emulate the named pipe communication in the following way. A process could create a message queue and write its name to a file. Then another process could read the name from the file and the two processes could communicate. This would work, with message queue names as we defined them, but a better solution would be to get the operating system to help you find the name.

DESIGN TECHNIQUE : CONNECTION IN PROTOCOLS

Sometimes an operating system service requires a sequence of interactions—for example, reading a sequence of blocks from a file or exchanging a sequence of message with another process. Usually there is some initial cost in setting up the service. For example, to read a file it is necessary to look up its name in a sequence of directories. This may require a number of disk reads. In this case we use a *connection* protocol where there are separate operations to connect to (open) the file and disconnect from (close) the file.

Connection protocols are more efficient because the setup is only performed once for each connection. But there are other tradeoffs. Connections sometimes tie up resources unnecessarily and are less efficient if there is only one transaction. Connections require reliable communication partners and assume that future use can be accurately predicted.

The distinction between connection and connectionless protocols is especially important in networks of computers. Some network connection protocols use connections and some do not. Which is best depends on many factors about the network and the communication. Loose connections like the Internet are better served with connectionless protocols. For example, World Wide Web protocols are connectionless.

See Section 4.6 for more discussion of connection and connectionless protocols.

---

which would be like destroying the message queue. The first *attach* operation would create the message queue as an operating system data structure, and subsequent attaches would return an internal identifier to that data structure.

Similarly, we could have named pipes with an internal name only. A process would create a pipe by calling `CreatePipe` and get an internal identifier back, which could then be opened to get an open file. The original UNIX pipes were like this, except they combined the creating of the pipe with the opening of the pipe. Thus pipe creation returned two open file identifiers, one to write the pipe and one to read it. These open files were passed to `forked` processes in the same way as any other open files. This method of naming pipes also required processes to have a common ancestor in order to communicate with pipes. It was this limitation that led to the concept of named pipes in UNIX.

> Object names can be global or local to a process and its descendants.

3.11 SUMMARY OF SYSTEM CALL INTERFACES

We have looked at a number of system calls and some alternative ways to specify some of the system calls. The system calls fall into a few categories:

- *File and I/O*—open, creat, read, write, lseek, close, unlink, stat. These gave us the ability to create and destroy files and to read and write them.

- *Processes*—CreateProcess, Wait, Exit. These gave us the ability to create and terminate processes and to wait for a child process.
- *Interprocess Communication*—CreateMessageQueue, SendMessage, Receive Message, DestroyMessageQueue. These gave us the ability to create and destroy message queues and to send and receive messages using message queues.

This set represents the core functionality needed in an operating system. A real operating system will have many more system calls, but most of them will be used in specific situations to satisfy certain requirements. As an operating system evolves, its system call interface may expand to meet new needs. The biggest omission in our system call interface is the lack of facilities to deal with directories—create and destroy directories, and to create and destroy directory entries. The other missing system calls are minor but necessary functions like: getting your own process ID, getting your parent's process ID, handling networks, using shared memory, etc.

Our system call interface is based on the UNIX system call interface, and many of the calls are the same. Most UNIX systems have over a hundred system calls. We could list them here, but many of them require knowledge about operating systems that we have not covered yet.

3.12   OPERATING SYSTEM EXAMPLES

Throughout the book we will provide examples from existing operating systems. First we will discuss a topic in general terms without mentioning specific operating systems. Then we will have a section where we describe how a service is defined and implemented in several existing operating systems. In this section we will introduce several of the operating systems that will serve as running examples throughout the book.

3.12.1   UNIX

The UNIX operating system will be one of our most frequently cited examples. UNIX has a special place in the history of operating systems. The first implementations of UNIX was developed at Bell Telephone Laboratories in the early 1970s by Dennis Ritchie and Ken Thompson. It was first used inside Bell Labs, but soon it was licensed (at a very low cost) to universities for educational and research purposes. UNIX was the first widely used operating system to be written almost entirely in a high-level language (the C language). This made it feasible to port UNIX to various computer architectures. During the 1970s, UNIX proliferated at universities and was ported to several different architectures. It became the most common operating system used in university computer science departments. UNIX was widely used in computer science by students for classwork and projects and by faculty for operating systems research. This was fostered by the fact that the source code for UNIX was available for modification.

This led to many changes, improvements, and variations in UNIX. The most well-known variation was developed at the University of California at Berkeley, which distributed the Berkeley Software Distribution (BSD) version of UNIX. The BSD versions of UNIX provided many technical improvements in UNIX, including virtual memory, a faster file system, TCP/IP support, sockets, and more.

AT&T (the owner of Bell Labs) also developed a version of UNIX called System V (the "V" is the roman numeral 5) UNIX. The latest version is release 4 and is usually known as SVR4.

Many commercial workstation vendors have developed their own versions of UNIX (for example, SUN Solaris, HP UNIX, Digital UNIX, SGI IRIX, and IBM AIX). These are either derived from the BSD version or the System V version. Recently there has been some standardization on SVR4, but there are still many minor variations between UNIX systems from different vendors.

UNIX has been the basis for operating systems research for a number of years, and most of the technical developments in operating systems originated in UNIX systems. In addition, the UNIX system call interface and implementation has been widely influential, and most other operating systems developed in the last 20 years have borrowed to some degree from the UNIX interface and implementation. As a result, this book will draw heavily on UNIX and its variants.

The system call interface discussed in this chapter is nearly identical to a subset of the UNIX system call interface. Actual UNIX systems, of course, have many more system calls.

3.12.2 MACH

In the mid 1980s, researchers at Carnegie-Mellon University began working on a new operating system based on the idea of a *microkernel*, that is, a small operating system (the *kernel*) that provides only the basic services. The rest of the usual operating system functionality was provided by processes running outside the kernel. Mach provides processes that emulate the UNIX environment, so UNIX programs can be run on it. A consortium of computer vendors has developed an operating system called OSF/1, which uses Mach as its basis.

microkernel

The ideas developed in Mach have also been highly influential, and almost all operating systems developed since Mach have borrowed some ideas from Mach. As we go though the book, we will look at the basic ideas in Mach more closely.

3.12.3 MS/DOS

When IBM came out with their personal computer in the early 1980s, they also arranged for Microsoft to provide the MS/DOS operating system. MS/DOS was developed for very small personal computers and did not have many of the features expected of operating systems for larger computers. But the PC and its clones became much more successful than most people had imagined, and MS/DOS has grown to be the most widely used operating system in the world. As the power and capabilities of the PC increased, features were added to MS/DOS to deal with the new hardware. Although MS/DOS is quite primitive by modern operating system standards, it is an open system (due to the fact that there is no protection at all) and so it could be adapted and modified by add-on programs. MS/DOS has gone through six major versions over the years since the first PC was introduced.

The MS/DOS system call interface is modeled after UNIX and has a similar set of system calls. One major difference is that it does not have the UNIX `fork` or `exec` system calls, but has a system call more like the `CreateProcess` described earlier in this chapter.

One add-on to MS/DOS is the Microsoft Windows windowing environment. Windows adds significant functionality to MS/DOS and could be considered an operating system on its own.

3.12.4   WINDOWS NT

The deficiencies in MS/DOS became apparent as it was moved to more and more powerful hardware. MS/DOS started out as an operating system for a small personal computer with a small memory, no hard disk, no protection, no memory management, and no network. A small and simple operating system was appropriate for this hardware. But as personal computers became more powerful, they got to the point where they needed and could support a full-featured operating system. Many facilities were added on to MS/DOS, including networking and a windowing system, but it had basic problems that could not be easily fixed.

As a consequence, Microsoft decided it needed a modern operating system for personal computers and decided to develop Windows NT (for New Technology). Design for Windows NT was started in late 1988 and the first version was released in 1993. The designers of Windows NT took advantage of many of the new ideas that had been developed in operating systems up to that point, including ideas from UNIX and Mach. We will describe many of the design features of Windows NT in the course of this book.

3.12.5   OS/2

OS/2 is IBM's operating system for personal computers. It was developed to remedy the known deficiencies in MS/DOS. OS/2 version 1.0 was released in 1987 and was a simple extension of MS/DOS to more capable hardware. OS/2 version 2.0 was released about 1990 and was a substantial revision and extension of OS/2. With version 2.0, OS/2 became a modern full-featured 32-bit operating system.

3.12.6   MACINTOSH OS

The other significant operating system for personal computers is the Macintosh OS (MacOS) for Apple Macintosh computers. The Macintosh provided a significant challenge to the domination of the IBM PC and PC clones in the personal computer market. The Macintosh provided a full-fledged graphical interface and was significantly easier to use than PCs. Although the Macintosh never captured much more than 10 percent of the personal computer market, it influenced the PC market and caused the growth of MS Windows as an add-on to MS/DOS.

MacOS was a more complete operating system than MS/DOS. It did not have all the features of operating systems like UNIX but it provided substantial functionality to support the graphical user interface. It also had a sophisticated file system and support for networks and virtual memory fairly early on.

*3.13   THE USER INTERFACE TO AN OPERATING SYSTEM

3.13.1   WHY YOU NEED A SHELL

All operating system services are available through system calls. But in order to issue a system call you have to be running a process. How does the first process get started? As we said before, the operating system constructs the first process. This initial process then starts all the other processes.

But suppose you want to communicate *interactively* with the operating system. If we wrote an interactive program that communicated with the user through a terminal and with the operating system through the system calls, we could make all the operating system services available interactively to a user sitting at a terminal. This is exactly what a *shell* is: a user interface to the operating system built on the programming (system call) interface. Figure 3.18 shows two viewpoints of a shell.

shell

As another example of using system calls, we will write a simple shell.

3.13.2   THE SPECIFICATION OF THE SHELL

The shell executes commands of the form:

`commandName [argument1...]`

The shell executes (via `fork` and `exec`) the program `CommandName` and passes the argument on the command line to it (via the `argv` array of strings). Then the shell waits for the command to exit.

3.13.3   IMPLEMENTING THE SHELL

In this section we will describe a C++ program that implements the shell interface using the system call interface. Below is the code to implement a simple shell using the system call interface. First, here are the declarations, definitions, and global data.

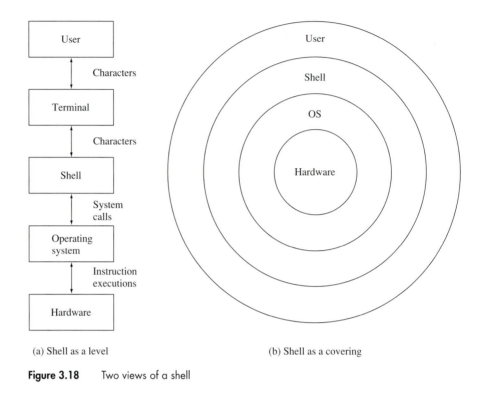

(a) Shell as a level   (b) Shell as a covering

Figure 3.18   Two views of a shell

SHELL GLOBALS

```
#include <iostream.h>

//some constants
constant int ARGSIZE = 50;   //maximum size of any one argument
constant int NARGS = 20;     //maximum number of arguments

//token types returned by getWord()
constant int STRING = 1;
constant int INREDIR = 2;
constant int OUTREDIR = 3;
constant int NEWLINE = 4;

//define the argv structure
char *argv[NARGS]; //space for argv vector
char args[NARGS][ARGSIZE]; //space for arguments.
```

We set limits on the number and length of the argument to shell commands. A real shell would handle this more dynamically and allocate space as needed. We are going to parse the command line with a parsing procedure. The constant definitions give the types of the tokens found by the parser.

We will assume we have a scanner that reads the input, handles quoting, detects the special symbols, and deals with tokens that are too long. We will assume the scanner has a procedure **getWord** that returns the token type and copies the token itself into the string it is passed.

Here is the code for the shell.

SHELL MAIN PROGRAM

```
//This program is a very simple shell.
void main( int argcount, char *arguments[ ] ) {
    int wasInRedir, wasOutRedir;
    char inRedir[ARGSIZE], outRedir[ARGSIZE];

    //each iteration of this loop will parse one command
    while( 1 ) {
        //display the prompt
        cout << "@";
        //So far we have not seen any redirections
        wasInRedir = 0;
        wasOutRedir = 0;
        //Set up some other variables.
        int argc = 0;
        int done = 0;
        char word[ARGSIZE];
        //Read one line from the user.
        while( !done ) {
            //getWord is the scanner, it gets one word from the line.
            int argType = getWord(word);
            //getWord also returns the type of the word it read.
            switch( argType ) {
            case INREDIR:
                //We saw an input redirection character (a <).
                //Record seeing it and read the input file name
                //(which is the next word on the line).
                wasInRedir = 1;
                (void)getWord(inRedir);
                break;
            case OUTREDIR:
                //We saw an output redirection character (a >).
                //Record seeing it and read the output file name
                //(which is the next word on the line).
                wasOutRedir = 1;
                (void)getWord(outRedir);
                break;
            case STRING:
                //everything else is a string to put into the
                //list of arguments.
                strcpy(args[argc], word);
                argv[argc] = &args[argc][0];
                ++argc;
                break;
```

```
                            case NEWLINE:
                                //When we see the newline the command has ended.
                                //(We do not allow commands to span lines.)
                                done = 1;
                                break;
                    }
            }
            //terminate the argument list
            argv[argc] = NULL;
            //The logout command is not executed, instead it exits the shell.
            if( strcmp(args[0], "logout") == 0 )
                break;
            //Fork a child process and set up stdin and stdout.
            if( fork() == 0 ) {
                //handle input redirection (if any)
                if( wasInRedir ) {
                    close(0);//close standard input
                    open(inRedir, 0;)//reopen it as the redirect file
                }
                //handle output redirection (if any)
                if( wasOutRedir ) {
                    close(1);//close standard output
                    enum { UserWrite=0755 };
                    creat(outRedir, UserWrite);
                    //reopen it as the redirect file
                }
                //Look for the command name in two places:
                //(1) the current directory
                //(2) the /bin directory.
                char cmd[60];
                strcpy(cmd, "./"); strcat(cmd, args[0]);
                execv(cmd, &argv[0]);
                strcpy(cmd, "/bin/"); strcat(cmd, args[0]);
                execv(cmd, &argv[0]);
                //The execv only returns if the exec failed.
                cout << "Child: could not exec \"" << args[0] << "\"\n";
                exit(1);
            }
            //wait for the child to finish
            int status;
            (void) wait(&status);
        }
finish;
    cout << "Shell exiting. \n";
}
```

Basically the shell collects words, puts them in an argument array, and forks off a process to execute the command. The shell must handle input and output redirection.

Real shells (for example, sh, csh, ksh, bash, etc.) are much more complicated than this one (they comprise tens of thousands of lines of code), but conceptually they are the same as this shell. Their extra complexity is in providing a sophisticated user interface: history, quoting, programming facilities, etc.

DESIGN TECHNIQUE: INTERACTIVE AND PROGRAMMING INTERFACES

System calls allow a running process to use operating system services. A shell allows a user to use operating system services interactively. Many programs have only an interactive interface. For example, a drawing program allows you to create drawings by direct interaction, but you cannot create drawings from another program. This makes it tedious to create a complex but regular drawing (for example, a drawing consisting of 100 squares in a ten-by-ten array where each square is 10 percent smaller than the one above it and the one to the left of it).

Most programs could benefit from having both kinds of interfaces. Some operating systems now have *scripting architectures* that define a standard protocol for programming interfaces to applications, encourage all applications to provide a programming interface (often called a scripting interface), and provide a system-wide scripting language (and language support) that allows programmers to write programs that interact with other programs.

For more discussion of interactive and programming interfaces, see Section 4.7.

A shell is an interactive interface to an operating system. System calls are the programming interface to an operating system.

3.14   SUMMARY

The interface an operating system presents to user programs is called the system call interface. A system call is a hardware instruction that transfers control to the operating system, which then performs some service for the user. The system call interface has three main parts: the file and I/O system calls, the process management system calls, and the interprocess communication (IPC) system calls.

An operating system provides a naming system for files, devices, message queues, and other objects. This is usually a hierarchical naming system based on a tree of directories. Each directory maps names into objects. Some of the objects named in a directory are other directories and this forms the tree structure.

Files are passive containers of data on a disk. A file must be opened (a system call) before it can be used. Opening a file returns an open file. The open file can be read and written (via system calls), either sequentially or randomly. The file location keeps track of the offset at which the next read or write will take place. An open file is closed when access to it is no longer needed. Many operating systems name hardware devices in the same way as files and allow access to devices using the same interface as to files: open, read, write, close.

Operating systems keep meta-information about each file: who owns it, when it was created, who can access it, how long it is, etc. There is a system call to read the meta-information and several system calls to write it.

A process is the execution of a program. All user computation in an operating system is done through processes. The three basic system calls for processes are:

create a new process, exit the current process, and wait for another process to exit. Process creation allows the transfer of arguments to the new process. A created process is the child process of the creator, which is the parent process. This creates a process hierarchy where a parent has some control over its children.

Operating systems provide methods for processes in execution to communicate with one another. This is called interprocess communication or IPC. One basic method of interprocess communication is the transfer of messages between processes. Messages are like letters, and they are often addressed to message queues, which are like mail boxes. A process can send messages to and receive messages from message queues.

Another method of IPC (different from message passing) is to use a pipe. A pipe is a mechanism that allows IPC to look like reading and writing an open file. Instead of writing to a file, you write to another process. Each process has a standard input and a standard output.

UNIX uses a different method of process creation which separates the creation of a new process (a fork) from the execution of a new program in an existing process (an exec).

The system call interface allows a running process to request operating system services by making system calls. A shell is an interactive user interface to an operating system that allows a user to enter commands as character strings or through a graphical user interface. The shell converts them to system calls to the operating system. System call results and other information from the operating system are presented to the user through an interactive interface.

3.14.1   TERMINOLOGY

After reading this chapter, you should be familiar with the following terms:

- buffering
- child process
- component name
- device independence
- directory
- execv
- fifo
- file
- file location
- filter
- flat name space
- fork
- full path name
- hierarchical file naming system

- interprocess communication (IPC)
- message queue
- meta-information
- microkernel
- name lookup
- open file
- open file identifier
- parent process
- pipe
- process
- process hierarchy
- program
- redirection
- shell
- standard input
- standard output
- system call interface
- two-level name space

3.14.2   REVIEW QUESTIONS

The following questions are answered in the text of this chapter:

1. What is a system call interrupt handler?
2. Go through the flow of control during a system call.
3. What is a directory?
4. Why does a read advance the file location?
5. Why do files need to be opened?
6. What are the file modes that you can open a file in?
7. What does it mean when a `read` system call returns a 0?
8. How do you find out the current value of the file location?
9. What is the purpose of the `lseek` system call? Why is it necessary?
10. What does it mean to name a device with the file naming system?
11. What does it mean for a program to be device independent?
12. Explain the difference between a program and a process.
13. Explain the interactions between the `CreateProcess`, `Wait`, and `Exit` system calls.
14. Explain how arguments are passed to child processes.

15. In C++ argument passing there is a variable argc. What is argc used for and why can it not be 0?

16. What process is at the root of the process hierarchy tree?

17. What is message buffering? Why is it useful?

18. Explain how file identifiers are local to a process.

19. Explain how queue identifiers are global to all processes.

20. Explain the difference between the CreateProcess and the fork system calls.

21. Explain the difference between the CreateProcess and the execv system calls.

22. Explain what standard input and standard output are.

23. Explain how pipes allow you to use variable-sized messages.

3.14.3 FURTHER READING

There are many books about UNIX. An excellent book on UNIX internals is Vahalia (1996). Other books on UNIX internals are Bach (1986) and Leffler et al. (1989). Goodheart and Cox (1992) describe System V Release 4. Deitel and Kogan (1994) describe OS/2 2.0. The Open Software Foundation (1993) has a book about OSF/1 which is based on Mach. Baron et al. (1990) is one of many places to find information about Mach. Custer (1993) is the main reference on Windows NT.

3.15 PROBLEMS

1. Suppose a computer did not have a special system call instruction but it did have a typical interrupt system. How could you simulate a system call instruction on such a computer?

2. Should terminating a process also terminate all of its children? Give an example where this is a good idea and another example where it is a bad idea.

3. Should the open files of a process be closed automatically when a process exits?

4. Why do most programs require arguments? Give an example of a program that never requires any arguments.

5. Give some of the differences between opening a file and opening a device.

6. Why does the creat system call also open the file? What if it didn't? Can we do it ourselves and get the same effect?

7. The "Reverse" program on page 37 does not work for files of length 0. Why not?

8. Suppose we wanted to implement a linked data structure in a disk file rather than in memory. Explain how you would use the read, write and lseek system calls to do this. Compare this with implementing linked structures in an array using array indices as pointers.

9. Design a form of the open system call that subsumes the functions of the creat system call.

should be courier font

10. Write a program using the file system calls (open, creat, read, write, lseek, close, unlink) that determines the length of a file without using a loop in the code.

11. Modify the file copy program to read and write in blocks of 1024 bytes instead of just one byte at a time. Do *not* assume that the file will have a length that is a multiple of 1024.

12. Modify the file copy program to check for all possible errors that can occur and return an error code of 0 if there is no error and a different negative value for each type of error that you can detect.

13. Modify the reverse program to reverse the file in place, that is, reverse the file without using any other files and using a fixed amount of memory (that does not depend on the size of the file being reversed). *Hint:* You need to open the file for reading and writing. *Hint:* Exchange the bytes, in pairs, outside-in to the middle.

14. The form of `read` we defined first in this chapter specified the file descriptor, the buffer address, and the number of bytes to read. The file position was kept up to date by the system and not directly specified in the `read` system call. The `lseek` system call was used to change the file position.

Suppose we want to remove the buffer address from the `read` system call. We add a new system call `SetIOBufferAddress` with one argument that sets the buffer address for subsequent `read` (and `write`) system calls. This must be called before any `reads` or `writes` (else they will return an error code). `SetIOBufferAddress` can be called more than once and the last one is the one that is used. Rewrite the file copy program to use this form of `read`, `write`, and `SetIOBufferAddress`.

Examine the tradeoffs between this kind of I/O interface and the original interface we defined. In which cases is this better and in which cases it is worse?

15. Consider the previous problem. Suppose we copy a file with the file copy program on page 36 and that a system call takes 300 microseconds plus 20 microseconds per argument. Now consider the same program but changed as described by using the `SetIOBufferAddress` system call (once outside the loop). What is the shortest file where the `SetIOBuffer Address` version will take less time in system calls?

Compute the same answer assuming that we read and write the file 1024 bytes at a time.

16. In the chapter, we discussed standard input and standard output. UNIX also defines open file identifier 2 as *standard error*. Why would they do this? *Hint:* Think about errors in pipelines.

17. Suppose you wanted to write a program that could take input from one of two possible sources and count the length of the input. The two input are either:

- A pipe or a file.
- A message queue or a file.

Discuss which of the programs would be easier to write. Relate this to device independence as mentioned in Section 3.5.

18. What are the advantages of named pipes (with names in the file system) over pipes with internal names? Are there any disadvantages?

19. Suppose we want to eliminate all the arguments from the `read` system call. We define a new system call: `int CreateIOState( int fileDescriptor, char * bufferAddress, int count )`. This sets all the I/O parameters for a particular I/O state, and returns a system identifier for that I/O state. You can create as many I/O states as you want. You can create an I/O state once and use it on as many system calls as you want. The restriction is that each call will have exactly the same parameters, but fortunately this is the usual case (see the examples in this chapter). Each `read` and `write` system call has only one parameter: the I/O state identifier that was returned by `CreateIOState`. Rewrite the file copy program using this form of I/O system calls.

Examine the tradeoffs between this kind of I/O interface and the original interface we defined. In which cases is this better and in which cases is it worse?

20. Make the file copy program into an executable program and run it. Compare it against the system copy (`cp`) program for speed, size, and robustness.

21. Consider the message-sending process in Section 3.7.2. What will happen if the file being sent contains a byte with value 0?

22. Consider the message-creation process in Section 3.7.2. There is a potential bug in the program related to the fact that message queue ids are 32-bit integers. Explain the bug.

23. Consider the message creation process in Section 3.7.2. This program contains a "storage leak" in `itoa`. Explain what this is.

24. Suppose we wanted to use message passing to replace `argc/argv`. Explain how this could be done using named message queues. *Hint:* Use the process identifier to create a standard name for an argument-passing message queue.

25. Should a message queue be destroyed automatically when the process that created it exits? Give a reason for doing this and a reason against doing it.

26. Modify the file sender and receiver processes to send as many characters at a time as possible given the message format we defined. *Hint:* You will have to include a count field.

27. Consider the following suggestion: Since we can send messages to running programs, we do not really need to pass arguments to processes when they are created (in `CreateProcess` or `exec`). Instead we could just send them messages containing the arguments. Would this scheme work? Is there anything that we can do with passing argument to created processes that we cannot do with this scheme? How is one better than the other?

28. Suppose we wanted to change the message system so that you sent messages directly to another process rather than to a message queue. The message queue concept will not be visible to the programmer. Redesign the message queue system calls in Section 3.7.1 for this message system and describe your calls as we described our calls in that section. Then redo the message-passing example in Section 3.7.2 to use your new message-passing system calls.

29. Suppose we wanted to add a command separator in our simple shell in Section 3.13. When it reads a semicolon (;) it will end the command and execute it before executing the rest of the command line. Modify the shell to do this.

30. Modify the shell in Section 3.13 to allow a "&" at the end of a command. If a command ends with a "&" it will not wait for the command to finish but will return immediately with another prompt.

31. About 10 lines from the end of the shell code is a line exit(1). It looks like this line exits the shell if you type in a command that it cannot find in the current directory or in the /bin directory. Why is this not so?

32. Modify the shell in Section 3.13 to handle pipes. Assume the scanner will return a token of type PIPE. *Assume:* A system call pipe(fids) that takes an array of two integers as an argument. When it returns, it will have set up a pipe where fids[1] is an open file identifier of the writing end of the pipe and fids[0] is an open file identifier of the reading end of the pipe. *Hint:* Handle each part of the pipeline in a separate iteration of the main loop. Use variables to remember the pipes that are outstanding.

33. Does it make sense to run a shell in another shell?

4

Design Techniques I

The study of operating systems leads naturally to the study of the design principles used in operating systems, and this leads to the study of the application of these design principles in other contexts. Every few chapters, we will include a chapter that summarizes the design principles we have seen in the previous chapters and generalizes these principles to see how they apply in other design situations. Our hope is that your design skills will improve as you learn about operating systems.

This chapter is the first of these design chapters. In this chapter we will discuss design in general and then a number of specific design techniques that you will find useful in solving many design problems. You have already seen side bars on most of these design techniques.

4.1   OPERATING SYSTEMS AND DESIGN

Most people who take an operating systems class intend to be computer science, software engineering, or computer engineering professionals. An operating systems course is one of many that you will take towards that goal. But what do you need to know to be a computer professional? First, you must have a general knowledge of the core areas in computer science: programming, software engineering, data structures, algorithm design, computer organization and architecture, compilers, operating systems, etc. Second, you need to become a competent designer.

Design is a key activity common to all engineers as well as many other professionals such as architects, graphic designers, industrial designers, etc. The basic design problem is to plan an artifact (a man-made object) that meets certain goals and satisfies certain constraints.

4.1.1   THE DESIGN PROCESS

Good design follows a *design process,* which guides the designer through the necessary steps in the design. Learning good design involves both learning the design process and learning how to execute each of the design steps. All design follows roughly the same process, but we will present it here in the specific context of software engineering—the steps in the process of creating a software product.

design process

- *System Analysis and Requirements Analysis*—Gather the information necessary for the design process and determine the specific needs that this software product must fulfill.

- *System Specification*—Specify the external interface of the software product to be built, what it will look like (the syntax) and how it will work (the semantics), that is, what its interface will be and what functionality it will provide.

- *Architectural Design*—Decide on the major modules of the software product, what each will do, and how they will interact.

- *Module Design*—Design each module, its specific interface, and how its functionality will be implemented. This includes decisions on algorithms and data structures.

The courses you take in a computer science degree program all support learning about this design process (either directly or indirectly). In a software engineering course, you concentrate on the design process itself and its management. Most of the other courses are aimed at giving you the skills to accomplish one or more steps in the design process.

Figure 4.1 shows the design process and the related skills required to complete the design process.

We will concentrate on three design steps: system specification, architectural design, and module design. Figure 4.2 shows the relationships between them and how they relate to the system requirements. The requirements are determined by the role the system must

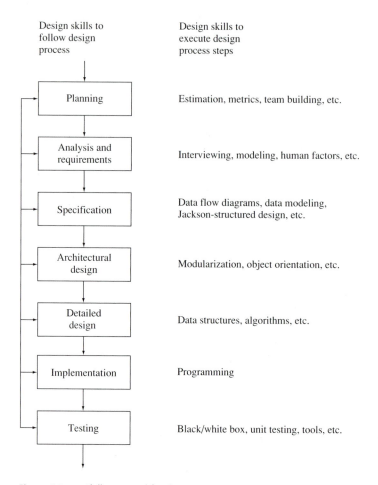

Design skills to
follow design
process

Design skills to
execute design
process steps

Planning — Estimation, metrics, team building, etc.

Analysis and requirements — Interviewing, modeling, human factors, etc.

Specification — Data flow diagrams, data modeling, Jackson-structured design, etc.

Architectural design — Modularization, object orientation, etc.

Detailed design — Data structures, algorithms, etc.

Implementation — Programming

Testing — Black/white box, unit testing, tools, etc.

Figure 4.1   Skills required for design

play in its environment. This role could be filled by a number of different systems, and the system specifications define one particular system that meets the requirements. The architectural design determines the general structure of the system that will implement the system specification. The architectural design divides the system into modules, and module design determines how these modules are specified and implemented.

The design process is actually recursive since module design really consists of defining the interface of the module (the system specification), then deciding how to organize the module (architectural design), and then implementing the parts (module design).

4.1.2   RELATIONSHIP TO SOFTWARE ENGINEERING

In this book we are only dealing with the design aspects of software development, and not the much larger area of software engineering. We have included system

System

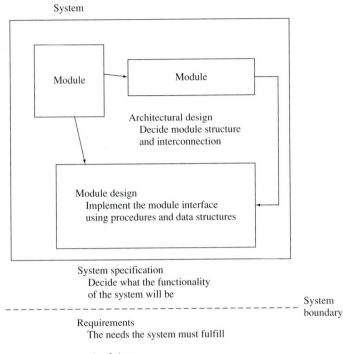

Architectural design
Decide module structure
and interconnection

Module design
Implement the module interface
using procedures and data structures

System specification
Decide what the functionality
of the system will be

System
boundary

Requirements
The needs the system must fulfill

Figure 4.2   Levels of designs

analysis and requirements analysis in the previous section for completeness only. We will not cover either of these topics in this book.

We left out a number of other topics that would concern a software engineer, such as implementation, testing, delivery, planning, estimating, project management, etc. These topics are all important but are not ones that are within the scope of this book.

4.1.3 A DESIGN EXAMPLE

Suppose you are presented with a situation in a program where you have to look up a string in a set of strings. This is a typical design situation where you have a general problem and there are a variety of methods you could use to solve the problem. Which solution you choose depends on the details of the design situation. If all the strings are known before the program begins and there are a large number of them, you would probably use binary search. If it was a small number, say only 50 or 100 strings, you might consider a perfect hashing function. If strings are continually added to the list, then you might consider a hash table or a binary tree. You might decide on a balanced binary tree if you suspect the strings will not be randomly distributed. If strings will be deleted frequently, that will affect your decision. In some simple cases, you might decide to use an unordered list and linear search.

Your education has prepared (or will prepare) you to meet this design situation and decide on a good solution to the problem that meets the design goals and satisfies the design constraints. In these design chapters, we would like to expand the number of design situations which you are prepared for.

4.1.4 LEARNING DESIGN THROUGH OPERATING SYSTEMS

In this book you will learn about the design of operating systems. We will present the major parts of an operating system. Operating systems are so well studied that there are only a few different architectural designs that are used. We will look at each of these and go over their strengths and weaknesses. For each major component of an operating system, we will talk about the typical goals and constraints in designing this component. We will talk about the design situations that come up, the range of known solutions, and the strengths and weaknesses of each solution.

The design situations that come up in operating systems are often specific not only to operating systems but represent design situations that come up in a wide range of computer systems. By learning these problems and their standard solutions, you will be adding to your set of tools and techniques that can be used in other design situations in software development.

In fact it is these general design techniques that will prove the most useful in your career as a software engineer. Unfortunately there are very few opportunities for people to actually design an operating system, but almost all of you will design other programs that require similar design skills. The design skills you learn in this book will serve you in those situations as well, and make you a more accomplished designer.

In a sense, this book is two parallel books, an operating systems book and a design techniques book. Both books will enhance your skill as a computer science professional. Knowing how operating systems are designed is useful for anyone using operating systems. It will help you understand the system you are using and use it more effectively. The design techniques you learn here are potentially useful in every design project you undertake.

4.2 DESIGN PROBLEMS

During the design of programs, you repeatedly come across situations where you need to achieve a certain goal in a certain situation subject to certain constraints. This is what we call a *design problem*. Let's take, as an example, one of the most studied design problems in computer science and the one we introduced in the previous section.

design problem

You need to write a map module where you save data indexed by a character string. Here are the two procedures in the interface:

- void Enter(Map * m, char * key, struct data d)—The data structure d is stored in the map m. A later Lookup with key key will return structure d.

- `struct data Lookup( Map * m, char * key )`—The data structure previously entered with key `key` will be returned.

This is the associative lookup problem that comes up all over in computer science. One example is the symbol table in a compiler.

The design problem here is to decide which data structure to use to implement the map. We haven't given enough information yet to answer this question because a design problem needs more constraints than the basic functionality required. First, we need to expand the requirements to include the performance required. How fast does it need to be? Second, we have to specify the constraints of the problem. How much memory can we use? What languages and libraries can we use? How much development and testing time can we use? Third, we need to know more about how the procedures will be called. How often will each procedure be called? Will we enter a key and look it up only once or thousands of times? Will we redefine the structure associated with a key? Will all the `Enters` occur before any `Lookups`?

You probably know the types of algorithms that might be suitable to solve this design problem: unordered linear array with sequential search, ordered linear array with binary search, linked list, binary search tree, balanced binary search tree (several kinds), B-tree, skip list, dynamic hash table, perfect hash table, etc. Each of these solutions has some good points and some bad points. When confronted with this design problem, you need to look at the situation, the requirements, and the constraints, and decide which of these solutions best fits the problem at hand.

4.2.1 DESIGN SKILLS

The above example is typical of the design situations you will encounter during the detailed design of a system.

- The design problem is a fairly general one that you are likely to encounter many times in your career.
- There are several (even many) possible solutions to the problem.
- Each potential solution has advantages and disadvantages.
- Each potential solution is only appropriate in some situations.

The design skills you need to solve a design problem are:

- Learning how to frame the problem in a general way so that it fits a pattern and you can see it as a general design problem.
- Knowing the range of potential solutions to the general design problem.
- Knowing how to evaluate each potential solution in the particular environment of your specific design problem and pick the best one for the situation.

The design problem example we used, a map, is unusual in that almost all computer science students are trained to solve this problem when they take a data structures class. Most of the design problems you encounter will be far less studied than the map data structure problem. That is the reason for the design chapters.

4.2.2 DESIGN SPACE

One way to look at design is as a search through the *design space* of the problem. Designing the system will require many (hundreds or thousands) of design decisions. Most of the decisions can have several right answers. As a result there are a huge number of different possible designs. We can think of a multidimensional space where each design decision is one dimension, so there are hundreds or thousands of dimensions. Figure 4.3 shows the idea, but with only three dimensions of design decisions.

The design space is not continuous because most design decisions have to be decided in one of a few different ways. So the design space consists of a huge number of points in *n*-dimensional space, where each point represents a possible design. Each design can be evaluated according to how well it meets the requirements of the system. Some designs will be better than others.

The task of design is to search through this design space and find the design that evaluates the highest, that is, that best meets the requirements. But this is a difficult task for several reasons. First, two points close to each other might evaluate very differently because one bad decision can degrade the whole system. So you cannot start from a solution and improve it a little at a time and gradually move to a good solution. Second, it is very hard to evaluate designs unless you build them. Third, the design space is so huge that you cannot hope to cover any more than a tiny fraction of it.

Design skill consists of being able to move around the design space and find good points. This includes skills in evaluating designs and good intuition as to what parts of the design space to search. Even constructing the design space is an important design skill. You need to know what the design dimensions are, and what are the possible choices in each dimension.

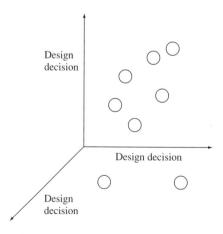

Figure 4.3   The design space of a design
problem (three dimensions)

4.2.3 DESIGN LEVELS

The goal of design is to create a pattern for a software system from a set of requirements. A software system consists of a set of modules, each module is a set of procedures, and each procedure is a sequence of statements. Design problems can occur at
any of these levels:

- How should we divide a system into modules, what should each module do, and
  how should modules communicate?
- What is the set of procedures each module defines, which are exported
  (hence what is the external interface), and how should the procedures
  communicate?
- What data structures should the module maintain?
- What algorithms and data structures should a procedure use?

At the higher levels, the problems are more structural: how the parts of the solutions should be organized. At the lower level, the problems are more algorithmic and
data structure issues. We will be looking at design issues at all levels, but we will
concentrate more on the lower levels.

Figure 4.4 shows the design decisions that must be made in designing a system.

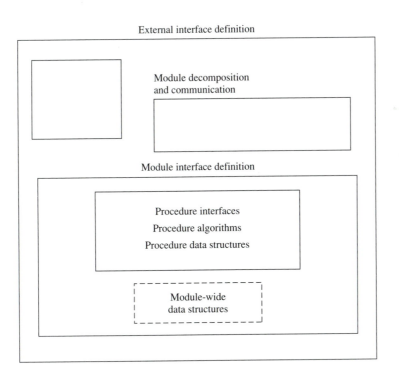

Figure 4.4   Design levels

4.3   DESIGN TECHNIQUES

Now that we have looked at design in general, it is time to explore some specific design techniques. In the next few sections we will discuss some useful design techniques. In Chapters 1, 2, and 3 you have seen each of these techniques applied in the context of an operating system. Now it is time to concentrate on the techniques themselves and see what other situations they apply to.

We will present the design techniques using a standard format that includes the following sections:

- **Overview:** This is a short section that summarizes the purpose of the technique.
- **Motivation:** This section gives an example of the use of the technique.
- **Operating System Examples:** This section gives examples of the use of the technique in operating systems. Some of the examples refer to sections of the book that have not been covered yet.
- **Computer Science Examples:** This section gives examples of the use of the design technique in other areas of computer science (and sometimes outside of computer science).
- **Applicability:** This section explains when the technique is appropriate to use.
- **Consequences:** This section describes the good and bad effects of using the technique.
- **Implementation Issues and Variations:** This section presents issues that come up when you use this technique and also gives examples of variant ways of using the technique.
- **Related Design Techniques:** This section mentions other design techniques that are similar to or are used with this design technique.

Sometimes one or more of these sections is omitted if it is not appropriate.

This organization is borrowed from the format used in the book on design patterns by Gamma et al. (1995).

4.4   TWO-LEVEL IMPLEMENTATION

4.4.1   OVERVIEW

Implement a system on two levels where the upper level is implemented by using the interface implemented by the lower level. The lower level implements a language that the upper level uses to solve the original problem.

4.4.2   MOTIVATION

The first thing we noted about an operating system was that it was a layer of software between user programs and the computer hardware (see Section 1.1). The operating system defined a system call interface that the user programs used to obtain services from the operating system. This two-level structure is the first general design principle we want to talk about.

A key principle in software design is *modularity*. The first step in the design process is deciding how to decompose the system into the modules. If the interactions between the modules are simple, then we can design each module independently of the others. Thus we can break the system down into smaller and smaller pieces until we get to ones we can easily implement.

modularity

You do not need a lot of modules to get the advantages of modularity. What we have done in an operating system is a special case of the modularity principle that we are calling *two-level implementation*. Here there are just two modules, and there is a sense that the upper module is running "on" the lower module, that is, the lower level defines an interface that is really a language to solve problems in. Instead of solving the problem directly, we write a lower-level module that implements a language which is designed to make it easier to implement the problem we have. Then the upper level solves the problem using this language.

two-level implementation

Figure 4.5 shows two levels and the interface between them.

4.4.3   OPERATING SYSTEM EXAMPLES

Operating System   This technique is used when we provide an operating system to run programs on a computer. The operating system is the lower level and the user program is the upper level.

Memory Management   The operating system (the lower level) allocates large chunks of memory to processes, and the per-process memory allocator (the upper level) allocates small chunks of memory to the program that is running. (See Chapter 10.)

Virtual and Real Terminals   The upper level uses a virtual terminal and the lower level implements the virtual terminal interface on a specific, real terminal. (See Chapter 14.)

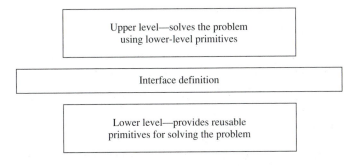

Figure 4.5   Two-level implementation

Device Drivers   The upper level implements a common device driver interface for the rest of the operating system. The lower level performs input/output requests on a specific device. (See Chapter 15.)

I/O and File Systems   The I/O system is the lower level and the file system is the upper level. (See Chapter 16.)

4.4.4   COMPUTER SCIENCE EXAMPLES

File and Database Systems   The file system is the lower level and provides a base on which to build a database management system, which is the upper level.

Language Translators   The lower level implements a programming language (either by interpretation, compilation, or a mixture of the two). The upper level is a program written in the language implemented.

Subroutine or Class Libraries   A subroutine or class library is the lower level and the program that uses it is the upper level.

Scripting Languages   Many applications are programmable in a language called a *macro language* or a *scripting language*. In this case the application is the lower level and the program in the scripting language is upper level. The next example is a specific case of this.

There is a movement now to implement interapplication scripting languages. These allow you to combine the capabilities of several programs together in a single script. In a certain sense, that is what an operating system command language is.

Little Languages   The implementation of the little language is the lower level and the program written in the little language is the upper level. We will discuss little languages further in the Implementation Issues section (Section 4.4.7).

4.4.5   APPLICABILITY

Use a two-level design when:

- You can find a natural intermediate-level interface. The interface can be a language or a set of functions.
- You want to implement a mechanism and experiment with different policies that use that mechanism.
- You want to provide user programmability.
- You want to separate the parts likely to change (in the upper level) from the parts less likely to change (in the lower level).

The most important test of the applicability of a two-level implementation is: does the system divide naturally into two levels, that is, can you define an intermediate interface and describe clearly the functions at each level? If such a division can be found, then a two-level implementation technique can be applied. If no natural division can be found, then it is better to try other techniques.

4.4.6 CONSEQUENCES

- The problem is divided into two parts.
- It is easy to change the solution by rewriting only the upper half. This is useful when the details of the solution change but its general nature stays the same.
- You can reuse the lower half to solve other related problems.
- Communication between the two halves is less efficient than communication within a single module.
- It may be hard to define the language the lower half implements. The problem may not be one that easily divides up this way.

We could dispense with the operating system and write each program to run on the bare hardware, implementing the operating system functionality directly in the program. There are three reasons why it is useful to implement a two-level structure in a program.

- *Modularity*—It is easier to write two programs than one program that is twice as large.
- *High-level programmability*—It is easier to write a program in a higher-level language than a lower-level language.
- *Reusability*—It is even easier to not write a program at all and instead use an existing program.

The benefits of *modularity* are widely known and will not be repeated here, other than to say that modularity is one technique that does live up to its hype.

We will discuss *high-level programmability* in the Implementation Issues section (Section 4.4.7).

By *reusability* we mean that we use the lower level of the implementation more than once, that is, with different upper levels. Not all two-level structures are reusable, but when they are you get an additional benefit. An operating system is a reusable lower level and is, in fact, reused with many thousands of user programs. You can't get better return on investment than that!

4.4.7 IMPLEMENTATION ISSUES AND VARIATIONS

Languages and Interfaces   The two levels in a two-level implementation must communicate with each other. We can divide two-level implementation into two categories according to how they communicate. The first category we will call *programming interfaces*, where the upper level is a program that calls the lower level with procedure calls (or things that are similar to procedure calls). The communication might be an actual procedure call, a remote procedure call (which is a network version of a procedure call), a message, or writing to a pipe or socket.

programming interface

language interface

The second category we will call *language interfaces* where the upper level might be a user or a program that sends the lower level a program to execute. The program is in the form of text. The form is useful if the upper level is not a program. Programming features (such as variables, control structures, etc.) can be provided by the lower level. The only interfaces in the second category are little languages or scripting languages.

Actually, this distinction is only useful in certain ways. An interface is a collection of functions that can be invoked. Whether you make a program call or encode a program call in a text string is not really that important.

Little Languages   Two-level structures are used in a software design technique that is called *little languages* (see Bentley (1988), Chapter 9, and Aho and Kernighan (1988)). The idea of a little language is that it provides interactive access to a collection of functions related to a task. One example is a language for studying sorting techniques. The language is interpreted from a command line and includes primitives for creating test data sets, displaying data sets, applying various sort algorithms to the data sets, timing algorithms, etc. One can write up functions for the basic sorting techniques and use the language to experiment with them.

little language

Printf Example   The `printf` format strings in C are an example of a little language for describing formatted output. This idea has been borrowed a number of times. For example, suppose you want to let users of a mail program print mail messages. The problem is that the program does not know the exact UNIX command to give to get something to print. Such commands vary from system to system and often depend on the device you are printing to. You can solve this problem by letting the user specify the print command template to the mail program. But the user specifying a print command template does not know what file is to be printed. So the file name is given in the template as a special string %f. When the mail program goes to generate a print command it takes the template, substitutes the real file name for the %f, and executes the command. For example, the print command template might be:

```
format %f | lpr
```
or
```
enscript -2rG %f
```

Title Line Example   As another example, suppose that a text editor wants the user to be able to specify what information goes in the title line of the text window. We define the following replacement strings:

- %n—name of the file being edited.
- %N—full path name of the file being edited.
- %l—line number the cursor is on.
- %c—character number the cursor is on.
- %e—* if the file has been changed, empty otherwise.

The user specifies title lines like:

- File: %n at char %c"
- "%e%N : line %l"

This technique allows users to easily customize the title line without having to modify the program code.

Using two levels can greatly increase your power of expression. The reason is reusability. The little language captures the reusable functions. Using those building blocks, you can create a variety of useful structures easily.

> To solve a problem, first design and implement a little language to solve it in, and then solve the problem in that language.

Internal and External Little Languages   There are two distinct cases when you might use a little language. The first is when the little language is a user-level language that is used by people using the program rather than the programmer writing the program. This allows users to use the program in a number of ways. The little language gives them the basic tools to use to build up the system they want. This is a good idea when you are not sure exactly how people might use the facilities you provide, or you feel that new and unexpected uses may arise. It allows easy experimentation with different policies using the same set of basic mechanisms.

The other place you use a little language is internally in a system where you need to experiment with policies. The considerations are similar here. If you are not sure of the system specifications and you need to be able to change system policies after delivery, then you should think about a little language.

The little language in this case can be more complicated and based on internal system concepts because only people familiar with the internals of the system will be using it. It can require a lot of sophistication to use and can be very powerful.

Avoiding Design Decisions   It may not be a good idea to use a little language if you do have a good idea how the facilities will be used. You should not use a little language to avoid making design decisions. You should give the user some choices where they are in the best position to make the choice. But if you, the designer, are in the best position to make the choice, you should make it and not pass the decision on to the user. In this case, you should provide higher-level mechanisms that do exactly what the user needs, and not make the users build the system for themselves.

There is a compromise decision, and that is to provide the little language but also provide prewritten programs in the little language to handle the expected standard uses. This way, beginners can use the high-level facilities provided, and experienced users can write their own custom facilities. This solution is good when you have a wide range of users and you need to provide solutions for them all. But do not think that you avoid all the problems with this middle solution. Having the little language affects things and makes the system more complicated. If it is not needed, then do not use a little language.

Separation of Policy from Mechanism   Choosing the right level for the little language is an important decision. It is an example of what we often call in operating systems a *policy versus mechanism* decision. We want the little language to provide all the necessary mechanism to do whatever the user (of the little language) wants to do. But we do not want to build our idea of how things should be (the policy) into the little language. For example, in the above text editor title language we allow the user to arrange the title line in many different orders and allow whatever information the user wants to see to be displayed. However, we are requiring that the symbol for a changed file be an asterisk (*). This is really a policy decision and should be left to the user. An alternative, more policy-free version would be:

policy versus mechanism

- %e/text—If the file has been changed then text is displayed, otherwise the empty string. The delimiter can be changed to any character that does not appear in text.

    Thus %e/*/ would simulate the original %e. This would allow a title string like:

- "%N : line %1 %e/ (Modified)/"

This facility allows any string to be used but does not allow a bitmap, so there is still some policy enforced. Another way to make the facility more policy-free would be to allow a specification like %e/modified-msg/unmodified-msg/, which allows a string for the unmodified case also.

> Develop general mechanisms that allow you to experiment with different policies.

Isolate What Changes   Another way to look at the policy versus mechanism dichotomy is based on how likely decisions are to change. Mechanisms are low-level building blocks that are closely related to the problem area itself. Policies are higher-level constructions built out of mechanisms. Policies are more closely related to the solution of the problem. Because policies are more complicated, there are more possibilities and they are more likely to change. Mechanisms are simple and are less likely to change. Builders have been using 2×4 boards unchanged for a long time, but the buildings they build with them have changed a lot.

Policies require testing and experimentation. We want to design the system so that we can experiment with policies without having to rewrite everything.

Defining Requirements   The hardest part of a software system is defining the requirements, that is, deciding what the system should do. It is said that more systems are not successful because of incorrect requirements than because of bad implementation. What this says is that it is common to not know exactly how a system should function. Often the only course is to build something, try it out, and see what is wrong with it. The separation of policy and mechanism is one way to experiment quickly. Instead of solving the problem directly, you develop a set of mechanisms that solve problems of that general class, and then use those mechanisms to experiment with solutions to the problem at hand. You are rarely solving just one problem; rather you are solving a class of related problems. As time goes on and requirements change, the problem changes but the general class of the problem remains the same.

Object-Oriented Design   Object-oriented design and implementation is also based on separation of policy and mechanism. The objects are general mechanisms for the class of problem you are solving. The exact requirements of the problem may change, but the types of objects you are working with are less likely to change.

Other Examples   The separation of policy and mechanism is such a good idea that it is seen in many contexts both inside and outside of computer science. Here are some examples:

- In the U.S. federal government, the Congress makes the laws (the policy) and the Executive branch enforces the laws (the mechanism). The laws are the policy and the police enforce them. The police do not formulate the laws.

- In a company, the managers set the salaries of the employees, but the payroll department is in charge of actually paying the employees. The payroll department can pay according to any policy the management decides upon.

- At a private party, the hosts decide who to send invitations to (the policy), and the people at the door check for invitations before they let anyone in (the mechanism).

- A programmer decides what the code should do, but the compiler actually converts it to machine language.

- In the C library, there is a sorting routine, `qsort`, which can sort according to any sorting order (the mechanism). A comparison function is passed to `qsort` and determines the policy of what is less than what.

- A procedure can perform a class of functions (the mechanism). The parameters sent to the procedure decide exactly what it will do.

User-Level Programming   A little language can bring some of the power of programmability to the user level. This can be at the simple level of programming the format of a message information line, or at the more complicated level of full programming languages or *scripting languages* like the shell programming languages. The little language idea is so useful that there are many examples in commercial and noncommercial products.

    The Motif X toolkit defines a little language called UIL (user interface language), which describes the look of a graphical user interface. It is used to specify all the widgets in the interface and their attributes. The Tcl language (Ousterhout (1994) and Welch (1995)) is a more advanced version of a little language. Tcl (tool command language) is intended as a generic macro or scripting language for software tools. Tcl

scripting languages

provides the language framework of variables and control structures. Tcl is customized into a little language by adding commands (implemented in C) that control the program. For example, a text editor would add commands to tcl that give access to all the text editing capability of the editor. The expanded tcl then becomes a little language for text editing.

Reusability of Two-Level Implementation   The use of two-level implementation involves doing a job in two steps:

1. Create the lower level, and
2. Use it to get the job done.

What are the advantages of doing the job in two steps? First we have the usual one: divide and conquer. It is easier to implement in two independent steps than to try to do it all at once. Second, reusability is an important factor. You can implement the lower level once and use it for several different jobs. The first operating systems were programs that virtualized the I/O (input/output) on computers. This made I/O operations significantly easier for everyone to use. The personal computer (PC) revolution recapitulated this development in that the early PC operating systems were based on I/O virtualization. This included the BIOS (basic input/output system) for CP/M, the BIOS for MS/DOS, and the "toolbox" for Macintoshes (which virtualized graphical I/O).

Two-level implementation is most useful when many programs will use the lower level, but it is even useful in a single project. A project of any size always seems to have changes during its development and use. Thus it is not really a single program but a series of related programs—perfect for reusing a lower level. Prototyping is becoming an accepted practice in developing software. Use of a lower level allows you to prototype new versions faster. Thus a program can go through several "versions" before it is even released.

Size of Two-Level Implementations   Our first example of a two-level implementation was an operating system where the entire implementation was a two-level structure. We have also seen examples of smaller two-level implementations where the two-level implementation was only a small part of the design. The way you print a status line is a small part of the design of a mail reader, but we used a two-level implementation to solve that problem. The two-level structure can be used at all levels.

Multiple-Level Structures   All software transforms a computer into something else, usually something very different from the underlying computer. Through software, the computer can become a word processing machine, a database machine, a spreadsheet machine, a game playing machine, etc. Each time we transform a computer to perform a new function, we call it a software level.

A level structure is made up of interfaces and implementations. Each level is defined by an interface. An *interface* is a specification of the capabilities of a level. An interface is a contract between the implementor of the interface and the clients of the

interface

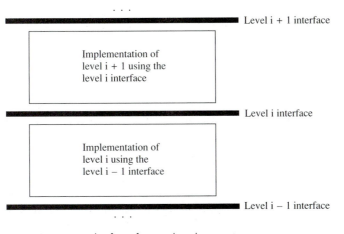

Figure 4.6   Levels of interface and implementation

interface. Thus we always draw interfaces with a thin line. An interface does not *exist* in the software but rather is *implemented* by the software.

Figure 4.6 shows a level structure. Each level has an interface which is used by the next level up. Each interface is supported by the *implementation* below the interface. Each implementation uses the interface below it. Eventually we get down to a hardware interface where we stop worrying about the implementation and just buy it from the hardware vendor. Going up we eventually get to an interface that is the solution to the problem we are interested in.

implementation

Level structures simplify software.

4.4.8   RELATED DESIGN TECHNIQUES

Two-level implementation is an example of *modularity* with only two modules. Often the lower level implements the *mechanism* and the upper level implements the *policy.*

4.5   INTERFACE DESIGN

interface design

4.5.1   OVERVIEW

Often there is a range of possibilities in the design of an interface. The best approach is to think of the various possibilities and look at their tradeoffs.

4.5.2 MOTIVATION

In this section we will consider the design of the interface using the file system calls as an example. We will look at possible variations of the calls we introduced in Section 3.2.3.

When you design a module in a system you have two related design problems:

- Design the interface the module will export to the rest of the system. This is a set of procedure call prototypes.

- Design the implementation of the interface. This is a set of data structures and procedure bodies.

The programming interface to the virtual machine is an important decision in the design of an operating system. There are several issues that must be weighed:

- Ease of use,

- Flexibility, and

- Efficiency of use (number of calls required).

Explicit Offsets   Suppose we decide to add an explicit file offset to read and write rather than have them be implicit. We will add them as the second argument. We will no longer need the lseek system call since all reads and writes will specify a file location.

With this interface the copy procedure is about the same:

FILE COPY (WITH EXPLICIT OFFSETS)

```
void FileCopy( char * fromFile, char * toFile) {
    int fromFD = open( fromFile, 0 );
    int toFD = creat( toFile, 0 );
    int offset = 0; // CHANGED <————————
    int n;
    char ch;
    while( 1 ) {
        n = read( fromFD, offset, &ch, 1 ); // CHANGED <—
        if( n == 0 )
            break;
        (void) write( toFD, offset++, &ch, 1 ); // CHANGED <-
    }
    close( fromFD );
    close( toFD );
}
```

But the reverse procedure has one less system call in each iteration of the loop. We will need to know the total size of a file so we can start at the end. We will add a system call fileSize to ask that.

REVERSE (WITH EXPLICIT OFFSETS)

```
void Reverse( char * fromFile, char * revFile ) {
    int fromFD = open( fromFile, 0 );
    int fromPosition = fileSize( fromFD);//NEW <——
    int revFD = creat( revFile, 0 );
    int newPosition = 0; // NEW
    int n;
    char ch;
    while( fromPosition >= 0 ) {
        n = read( fromFD, --fromPosition, &ch, 1 ); // CHANGED <-
        (void) write( revFD, toPosition++, &ch, 1 ); // CHANGED <-
    }                         new
    close( fromFD );
    close( revFD );
}
```

The tradeoffs between this version of the system call interface and the old one are:

- This version requires an extra argument on every read and write, so each call takes a little more time.
- This version requires the user to keep track of the file location
- This version does not require lseek calls.

This version is better for random access, and the original version is better for sequential access. This argues for the first interface unless you are in a design situation where random access is more common than sequential access. Since almost all file access is sequential, the first interface is better.

Figure 4.7 shows the two styles of file interface.

Two Kinds of Calls   Another way to decide this issue is to have both kinds of reads and writes. There would be a seqRead, which was like the first version and a ranRead, which was like the second version. The user can decide which one to use depending on the situation.

But what are the costs of making this "nondecision"? First, it adds two more system calls, and there are a number of costs associated with this:

- There are more system calls for the users to learn.
- A user has to decide in each case which one to use.
- Beginning users will be confused about the difference between the two forms of read and write.
- The manuals will be longer to describe the extra calls.
- The system code will be longer to implement the two calls.

Complicating an interface unnecessarily is a bad idea. It is probably better here to just make a decision and stick with it. Keeping both forms seems like an easy way out, but it has many disadvantages.

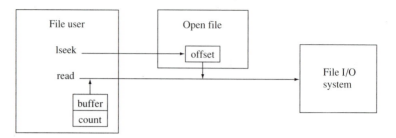

(a) File I/O with implicit offsets

(b) File I/O with explicit offsets

Figure 4.7   Two models for file I/O system calls

A motto we might bring up here is due to Alan Kay:

Simple things should be simple and complicated things should be possible.

The UNIX solution to make sequential reading simple and random reading possible is a good one, given the preponderance of sequential reading of files.

> It is not usually a good idea to avoid making a hard design decision by offering both alternatives.

Interface Models   There is another aspect of this issue that we might bring up. Often software abstractions are based on hardware. For files, there are two possible hardware models we could use: disks and tapes. The first version with sequential reads and writes is based on the tape model. A physical tape is always at some position, and reading and writing is only possible at that one position. So read and write commands to a tape do not have a position argument. The second version of the read and write system calls is based on the disk model. In a physical disk, each command specifies the disk block desired.

Disks are more versatile and generally better than tapes in all respects except cost per byte stored. But the tape model is simpler and is a better model for a file.

> Use analogies to generate ideas, *not* to evaluate them.

> Design and compare several interfaces. Compare them by solving typical problems.

4.5.3 APPLICABILITY

You should look at interface variations whenever you design an interface.

4.5.4 CONSEQUENCES

- Finds good alternatives.
- Takes time and effort.

Design is the balancing of tradeoffs. This technique is just reminding you to spend some time at the beginning and think about alternatives. It usually does not cost much at the beginning to at least think about different possible interfaces to a set of functions.

Some of the the other design techniques (such as little languages) allow you to defer the final specification of interfaces to later in the design cycle. This usually means you can try more alternatives and find the one that is best suited to the situation.

Some people say that if you cannot think of at least two feasible design alternatives you should look carefully at your problem specification and see if it is really a solution specification instead of a problem specification. It is easy to have a solution in mind and write down a specification of that solution instead of the real problem you are trying to solve.

4.5.5 RELATED DESIGN TECHNIQUES

Little languages allow experimentation with interfaces.

4.6 CONNECTION IN PROTOCOLS

4.6.1 OVERVIEW

Increase the efficiency of a series of communications with a server by establishing a connection with the server. Connecting and disconnecting is sometimes called opening and closing.

4.6.2 MOTIVATION

Messages are a communication system that is based on the *postal system model,* that is, they are like regular mail. Each individual message is sent from one place to another and messages are not grouped in any way. We could also call this the *telegram model* and this is the basis of the term *datagram,* which is used in networking to describe a message that is sent in isolation from other messages.

We could also model a communication system based on the *telephone system model,* that is, where you set up a persistent *connection,* send a number of messages along the connection, and then break the connection when you are done. This is the

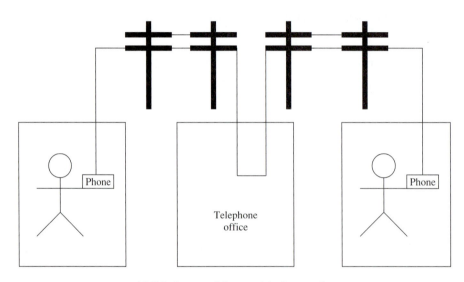

(a) Telephone model — persistent connection

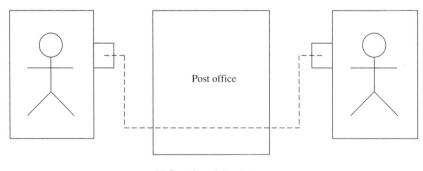

(b) Postal model — letters

Figure 4.8   Message sending models

model we used for the file system. First, you had to open a file that set up a connection to the file. Then you read or wrote the file any number of times. When you were finished with the file, you would close the file, which would break the connection to the file. Figure 4.8 shows the two models.

Any time you have multiple transactions with the same partner you have to decide whether a connection or connectionless strategy will be followed. For higher speed transactions we are most familiar with using connection strategies: telephones, talking to someone in their office, connecting to a computer, using ftp to get remote files. Transactions with longer turnaround time are more often connectionless: writing letters, e-mail.

4.6.3 OPERATING SYSTEM EXAMPLES

File I/O   File I/O almost always uses a connection protocol. Before you can access the file you must connect to the file by *opening* the file. When you are finished using the file you disconnect from the file by *closing* the file.

Message Passing   Messages are a connectionless protocol. Each message stands on its own and is not connected to other messages.

Pipes   A pipe is a connection protocol for communication between processes. It borrows the file open and close protocol.

Interacting with an Operating System   A user interacting with an operating system uses a connection protocol. You must sign on and authenticate yourself to the operating system before you can execute any commands.

Network and Distributed Operating Systems   In a network operating system, you must sign on to each machine you use. In a distributed operating system, you sign on only once and can then use any of the machines that are running the distributed system. This is an important difference between network and distributed operating systems.

4.6.4 COMPUTER SCIENCE EXAMPLES

World Wide Web Connections   World wide web connections use a connectionless protocol. Each communication with the web site is separate from the other. You are never "connected" to a Web page.

FTP   The Internet file transfer protocol (FTP) is a connection protocol. You must sign into a system (often as an "anonymous" user) before you can make FTP transfers.

Electronic Mail   E-mail is a connectionless protocol. Each e-mail message stands on its own.

4.6.5   APPLICABILITY

Use a connection protocol when:

*   You know for sure that you will communicate with the server several times.
*   The server is reliable and unlikely to fail during the connection.
*   There is significant setup cost for the communication.

Use a connectionless protocol when:

*   You are not sure how long the communication will be.
*   The server is likely to fail and the failure will invalidate the connection.

4.6.6   CONSEQUENCES

*   In a connection protocol, you only incur the setup cost once, at the beginning of the connection. In a connectionless protocol, the setup cost occurs for each interaction.
*   Connectionless protocols are more fault tolerant since they do not depend on state in the server that can be lost if the server fails.
*   Connectionless protocols do not tie up resources while they are not being used. Thus connectionless protocols are best when you are not sure of the future interactions you might make.

The telling factor is the ratio of the time for a transaction to the time between transactions. The World Wide Web protocol uses connectionless protocols to avoid tying up systems with connections. As communication lines and computers get faster, we can expect more use of connectionless protocols to avoid the overhead and fault sensitivity of connection protocols.

With a connection, you are reserving resources with the expectation that you will be using them again very soon. This is a bet that pays off if you do use the resources again fairly soon, but otherwise you tie up the resources doing nothing. Given the difficulty in predicting the future, connectionless protocols are better except in cases where you know a lot about the expected communication activity or in cases where the cost of keeping a connection is low. For example, we usually open files before we use them even if we use them sporadically after that. The cost of keeping a file open is a slot in a few system tables, a very low cost, and the cost of looking up a file name can be fairly high, so it is useful to remember that information.

4.6.7   IMPLEMENTATION ISSUES AND VARIATIONS

Connectionless File Access   Reading a file using the system calls we have seen so far is done in three stages:

1. *Open the file.* The operating system looks up the name of the file in the directory hierarchy and finds the file on disk. A token is returned to the user to represent the open file.

2. *Read the file.* All read calls pass the open file token so the operating system knows which file we are reading.

3. *Close the file.* Clean up operating system data structures.

We can express these steps in a more general way:

1. *Connect to the file.* Establish a connection between the process and the file. Return a token that represents that connection.

2. *Communicate with the file over the connection.* All read and write calls pass the connection token.

3. *Close the connection.* Return the token and break the connection.

It is possible to use files without opening them first if we have a different set of system calls from those we saw in Section 3.2.3:

- ```
  int read( char * fileName, int offsetIntoFile, char * bufferAd-
  dress, int bytes ToRead );
  ```

- ```
  int write( char * fileName, int offsetIntoFile, char * bufferAd-
  dress, int bytesToWrite );
  ```

In this form of read and write, each call stands by itself and does not require an open file. We specify everything necessary to do the operation in the system call. This form of read and write is called connectionless because no persistent connection is established to the file and each file operation stands on its own.

What are the tradeoffs in doing things this way? Some of the advantages of connectionless I/O are:

- It is simpler for the user since there are fewer types of system calls and they do not depend on each other.

- Fewer system calls are made while the program is running.

- Each call stands on its own. If the file server is on a remote computer and that computer goes down while you are reading a file, you will not be as much affected as you would be in a connection protocol.

Some of the disadvantages are:

- The name-to-file lookup must be done with every call.

- The sequential form of read (and write) where the file offset is kept by the connection is no longer possible.

We are reminded of an old Bob Newhart comedy routine where he is calling up a department store to report a man hanging from a ledge of their building. As he is transferred from one person to another, he has to repeat his whole story over and over again. The joke is that he is experiencing a connectionless protocol which requires the setup to be done each time he talks to a person. You may have had similar experiences calling offices.

Connections in Interprocess Communication   The first form of interprocess communication (IPC) we used was messages. Messages are a connectionless protocol for IPC because each message is individually addressed and independent of the others. Messages are received one at a time and as complete messages, not part of a message.

> There are two general models of communication: connection and connectionless. Neither is always better than the other. Consider both types before you decide.

The second form of IPC we looked at used named pipes and was modeled after the file system calls. This was a connection protocol because you had to open the connection before you communicated on it and you closed it when you were finished. In this form of IPC, the messages are not discrete units but are considered as a stream of bytes. A receiver can read part of a message or bytes from several messages at one time. Figure 4.9 illustrates this distinction.

4.6.8   RELATED DESIGN TECHNIQUES

A connectionless protocol is an example of *late binding.* A connection protocol is more *static* and a connectionless protocol is more *dynamic.*

(a) Connectionless protocol—messages—no connection

(b) Connection protocol—fifos—continuous connection

Figure 4.9   Connection and connectionless IPCs

4.7   INTERACTIVE AND PROGRAMMING INTERFACES

4.7.1   OVERVIEW

Make a program more versatile by providing a user interface *and* a programming interface so other programs can control it directly. The communication may be by procedure calls, messages, or other forms of communication.

4.7.2   MOTIVATION

Once you go to the trouble of implementing a set of functions, it is useful to have them available as widely as possible. If you only have an interactive interface, then other programs cannot gain access to the functionality and you cannot combine the power of two different programs.

For example, suppose you have a drawing program that you like to use. If you could control it from your favorite programming language, then you could combine the nifty graphics from the drawing program with the clever programs you write.

Your programs gain in power when they can be combined with other programs—your own programs and other people's programs.

In Section 3.13, we saw that a shell was an interactive interface to the operating system that was also accessible from programs through system calls. Most programs have interactive interfaces, that is, they get input and perform actions based on the input. Take a drawing program as an example. We can, using a mouse and keyboard, create all sorts of interesting figures with a drawing program. But what if we wanted to create a drawing that consisted of 100 little boxes in a 5 by 20 array? Or suppose we wanted to create a sequence of 100 lines of length 1, 2, 3, up to 100. It would be very tedious to create these drawings using the interactive interface to the drawing program.

It would be much nicer if the drawing program had a programming interface, that is, if we could run a program and send drawing commands to the drawing program. Then the tasks mentioned above would be very simple program loops.

Figure 4.10 shows a drawing program with an interactive and programming interface.

We can think of a drawing program as a collection of drawing functions with a graphical user interface. We can execute the functions through the interface or through a program. Sometimes it is easier to use a program interactively and sometimes it is easier to run a program from another program.

Most programs would benefit from having both kinds of interface. Database systems usually have both kinds of interface, but many other types of programs do not. It would be useful to have programming interfaces to spreadsheets,[1] word processors, communications programs, drawing programs, etc.

---

[1] A macro language is a partial solution, but it would be even nicer to control a spreadsheet from another program.

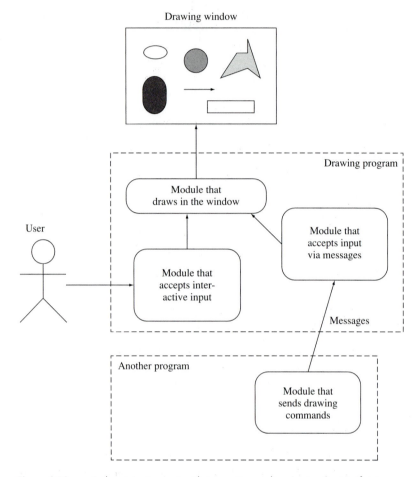

Figure 4.10   A drawing program with interactive and programming interfaces

> It is useful to have an interactive interface and a programming interface to all programs.

4.7.3 OPERATING SYSTEM EXAMPLES

Operating System Shells   The system call interface is the programming interface to an operating system. The command interpreter (often called the shell) is the interactive interface to an operating system.

System-Level Scripting   Some operating systems support system-level scripting. Programs provide programming interfaces to their functions that can be accessed from a scripting language supported by the operating system. Scripts can combine functionality from a number of different programs.

4.7.4 COMPUTER SCIENCE EXAMPLES

Tool Command Language   Tcl (tool command language) is intended to be a general macro language for tools. Each tool embeds a Tcl interpreter and defines Tcl commands to expose all of the tool's functionality. The tool can still be used interactively, but it can also be used by another program by sending it Tcl commands to execute.

Socket Listening Programs   Any program can create a socket and listen on the socket for messages from other programs. It can interpret these messages as commands and execute them.

4.7.5 APPLICABILITY

Provide both an interactive and a programming interface if:

*   You want the program to be able to be controlled from other programs.
*   You have a solution to the security problem involved.

    It is not always safe to execute any command that is sent to you. You have to be sure this is a command from a process that you trust.

4.7.6 CONSEQUENCES

*   Users can use the program interactively.
*   Programmers can control the system from a program and achieve useful effects like demonstrations and scripting.
*   It makes the program reusable by other programs through the programming interface.
*   It makes it easy to combine programs into larger systems without changing any of the component programs.
*   It allows a system-wide scripting language that can control many applications.
*   It is a little more trouble.
*   Security holes may arise in the programming interface.

4.7.7 IMPLEMENTATION ISSUES AND VARIATIONS

Embeddable Systems   The current fashion is to develop languages that are *embeddable*. This means that they are implemented as a procedure library that can be   *embeddable*
included in any program. The prototype program that includes them is a language

processor that reads programs and runs them through the language processor. Perl and Tcl are both implemented this way.

Communication   There are several ways the communication of commands can be handled. It must be some form of interprocess communication. Some possibilities are:

- In an X window system, you can send X events to other processes.
- Using Tcl/Tk, you can use the send command.
- You can use sockets in most systems.
- You can use remote procedure calls.

4.7.8   RELATED DESIGN TECHNIQUES

Little languages can be used as an intermediate form to provide both an interactive and programming interface.

---

decomposition patterns

4.8   DECOMPOSITION PATTERNS

4.8.1   OVERVIEW

There are several different strategies for decomposing a system. We can decompose it into:

- A strict hierarchy of procedures.
- A DAG of procedures.
- A sequence of levels where each level is a module.
- A collection of modules that export and import interfaces from other modules.

The first two patterns do not have a module structure and so are not used except in small systems, or in the lower levels of a design where the modules are so small they are a single procedure.

A directed graph of modules, each of which may export and/or import interfaces, is the most general model and is widely used today and taught in software engineering classes.

4.8.2   MOTIVATION

Implicit in the design step of architectural design is that it is "a good thing" to divide a system up into modules, and then recursively divide those modules in submodules, and so on. This process stops when a module is small enough to be implemented in a single procedure. Decomposition into modules is an application of the general principle of *divide and conquer*. It is easier to solve two small problems than one problem twice as large. The reason for this is that the number of interactions between the parts of a problem goes up with the square of the size of the problem.

So once we have convinced ourselves of the importance of decomposing a system into modules, we must confront the problem of how to do that. The modules must be chosen carefully or they will interact too much and we will lose the advantage of modules (low growth in the number of interactions). A lot of the work in design has been to come up with strategies for decomposing a system into modules. In this section we will look at four patterns of decomposition that have been used over the years. Figure 4.11 shows the four patterns of decomposition that we will be talking about.

When early software designers thought about decomposition, they looked to existing complex systems for guidance. Natural systems, such as the human body, are very complex, but they seem to be organized into a rough hierarchy: body, organs, tissues, and cells. Complex artificial systems, such as governments, are also divided up into a

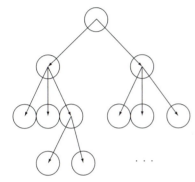

(a) Strict hierarchy

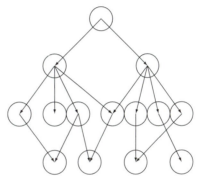

(b) Directed acyclic graph

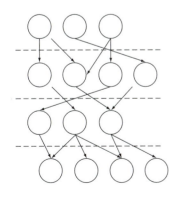

(c) Level structure

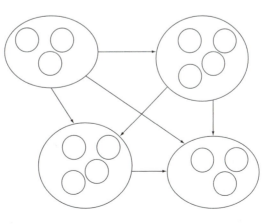

(d) Graph structure

Figure 4.11   Four patterns of decomposition

hierarchy: country, state, county, city, and neighborhood. So many early designers tried to organize their systems into hierarchies of procedures. This process was called step-wise refinement or step-wise decomposition, and it worked very well in some systems. Each node of the hierarchy is a procedure, and so the procedures form a tree where an edge from one procedure to another means that one procedure calls another.

A strict hierarchy (that is, a tree) means that a node cannot have two parents. That means that no procedure could be called by two other procedures. This was clearly too restrictive since a system usually depended on a number of low-level utility procedures that did common tasks for other procedures. So these designers generalized the structure a little to allow a node to have two parents, but still no cycles were allowed. This is called a *directed acyclic graph* or *DAG*.

directed acyclic graph

Gradually designers came to think of their systems as being structured in levels rather than individual procedures. It was still a DAG of procedure, but the procedures were logically grouped into levels and each level was a module. Each level called procedures at the level below and was called by procedures at the level above. A procedure could not call two or three levels down, only one level. The level model provided a method of modularization and so provided two levels of organization, the procedure and the module.

One problem with the level structure for modules was that often a procedure needed to call another procedure two or more levels down. One solution was to provide, at each level, procedures which simply called a procedure at the next level down. These procedures effectively transferred a procedure up one level. This kept the purity of the organization but, once designers realized that some procedures had to be transferred through several levels, they decided that maybe this organization was too artificial and did not reflect the natural organization of the system.

It was then that designers moved on to the newest pattern, a directed graph. The system was divided into modules, each of which *exported,* that is, implemented, an interface with a certain functionality. A module that needed some functionality could import the interface exported by the module that provided it. This pattern of exports and inputs formed a directed graph. This pattern of decomposition is the one most-commonly-used technique today, although the level structure model is also widely used. The directed graph pattern is the basis of the *client-server model* that we will look at later in the book.

4.8.3 OPERATING SYSTEM EXAMPLES

Levels   Operating systems are often implemented in levels.

Interfaces   Some new operating systems are object oriented and basically export a number of useful interfaces.

4.8.4 COMPUTER SCIENCE EXAMPLES

Top-Down Design   Top-down design creates a hierarchy.

Functional Decomposition   Functional decomposition creates a hierarchy.

Modular Decomposition   Modular decomposition creates a collection of modules that import and export interfaces.

4.8.5 APPLICABILITY

You should consider these decomposition structures whenever you are deciding on how to modularize a system.

4.8.6 CONSEQUENCES

* Strict hierarchy is well behaved but too restrictive for most designs. It supports only top-down design.
* A DAG is an improvement on a strict hierarchy and improves the ability to do some bottom-up design.
* Levels are an improvement on DAGs and provide a structuring method so you can better organize your system.
* An interface (directed graph) structure is the most flexible but also provides the least structure.

Most systems will have some level structure and some directed graph structure.

4.8.7 IMPLEMENTATION ISSUES AND VARIATIONS

Level Model versus Server Model   The overall purpose of an operating system is to implement the process abstraction, that is, to create a level above the hardware where several programs can run simultaneously. We will call this the *level model* because the operating system creates a virtual machine level that hides the hardware level. Another approach is the *server model* (or client-server model) where each server provides a service in the form of an exported interface or set of service calls. A server is implemented using other servers or levels, but it does not hide them.

    In programming languages, we can design an entirely new language or we can add a subroutine library to an existing language. Lisp is a particularly good language for adding on "server" subsystems that provide new functionality while the original Lisp functionality is still available.

    The level model is more centralized. It takes an interface and creates a new interface to replace it. The server model is decentralized. It provides services and a client gets services from several servers to create a computing environment. Figure 4.12 shows the two models.

    We can make an analogy with software engineering. The most widely used model in software engineering is the *module model*. In this model, a system is made up of a number of modules. Each module has an interface which provides a collection of related services. Some modules depend on the services of other modules.

level model

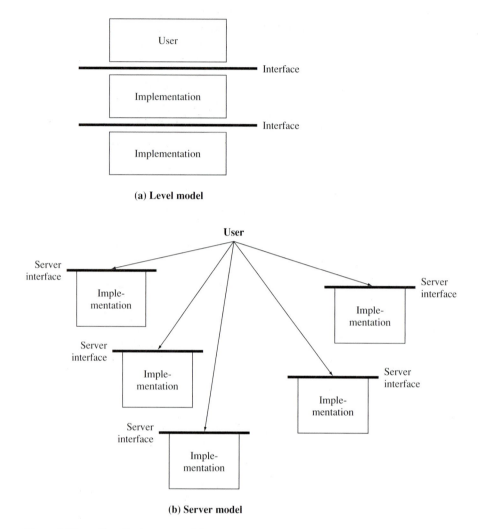

(a) Level model

(b) Server model

Figure 4.12   The client server model

Each module is essentially a server, and some modules are clients of other modules. The modules do not form a strict linear hierarchy, but rather a graph with no dependency cycles.

4.8.8   RELATED DESIGN TECHNIQUES

Decomposing a system into parts is an example of the *divide and conquer* technique.

4.9   SUMMARY

Design is the planning of artifacts that meet goals and satisfy constraints. There is a design process that is similar in all design fields. A good designer knows the steps of the design process and has the skills to carry out each step. In this chapter, we looked at several design techniques that are useful at various points in the software design process.

Two-level implementations are used to modularize a system into an upper level which is implemented in terms of a lower level. Little languages are a good example. We should look at interface design alternatives whenever we have to design an interface. We should decide about protocol connection whenever a client and server interact. All programs with useful functionality should consider having a programming and interactive interface. All systems can be decomposed into one of a few general decomposition patterns.

4.9.1   TERMINOLOGY

After reading this chapter, you should be familiar with the following terms:

- connection protocol
- connectionless protocol
- decomposition pattern
- design problem
- design process
- design skill
- design space
- directed acyclic graph (DAG)
- embeddable system
- implementation
- interface
- interface design
- language interface
- level structure
- little language
- policy versus mechanism
- programming interface
- scripting language
- two-level implementation

4.9.2 REVIEW QUESTIONS

The following questions are answered in the text of this chapter:

1. What are the steps in the software design process?
2. What is a design problem?
3. Relate two-level implementation to software modules.
4. Why is a little language useful?
5. What is a connection protocol? Give some examples.
6. What is a connectionless protocol? Give some examples.
7. Why should interactive programs also have programming interfaces?
8. How does one program communicate with another?
9. What are the benefits of a directed graph structure for module communication?

4.10   PROBLEMS

1. In the chapter, we discussed the design process for a software system. Describe the design process for an interactive, virtual community for sports fans or for mystery fans on the Internet.

2. Suppose you are designing an e-mail reader program. List five important design decisions you will have to make and list several possible choices for each design decision.

3. Suppose you need to prepare graphs of a large number of experimental results using a basic graphics system (lines, circles, rectangles, text, etc.). Describe a two-level implementation for this.

4. Suppose you have to control a TV and VCR from a C++ program. Define a little language for controlling a TV and VCR.

5. Design a little language for developing voice mail systems.

6. Suppose you have a very large database about movies. Define a little language for accessing and presenting information from the database.

7. Suppose that we have implemented Prolog in Lisp and we are running it on a Lisp interpreter on a typical computer system. Draw a diagram showing all the levels of hardware and software in such a system.

8. Consider two variations in I/O system calls in the book. The first set is the same as we discussed in the book.

   a. **IOSetA**—openA, readA, writeA, lseekA, closeA—You open the file and then read, write, and lseek, and then close the file. The file offset is not given in the readAs and writeAs but is kept by the system and can be changed with the lseekA.

b. **IOSetB—readB, writeB**—Each `readB` and `writeB` contains the name of the file and the file offset (as well as the buffer address and the number of bytes to transfer). There are no open files because you give the file name in each call. There is no seek because you give the file offset in each call.

Suppose our operating system implemented IOSetB but we wanted to write a program that used IOSetA. Can we write a set of library routines (openA, readA, writeA, lseekA, closeA) that will implement the semantics of IOSetA in terms of the I/O system calls in IOSetB? (That is, the library routines contain only calls in IOSetB.) You should ignore error code reporting when deciding whether IOSetA can be implemented with IOSetB, but in your discussion of how it can be done, discuss error codes and how you would handle them (if they cannot be handled correctly).

If it can't be done, explain why not, and if it can be done, sketch out how you would implement each routine in IOSetA.

Now answer the same question for the other direction, about implementing IOSetB in terms of IOSetA.

9. Design a connection protocol for using a random number generator package.

10. Suppose that all text editors and graphics programs had a programmable interface. Describe how you would design a debugger that allowed the user to use his or her favorite text editor and graphics program in the debugger (the text editor to display source code being debugged and the graphics program to visualize data structures in the program being debugged). Describe the advantages and disadvantages of having a core set of functions that were implemented in every text editor and graphics program. Describe a core set of text editor functions that a debugger would use.

11. Mail reader programs (e.g., `mail`, `elm`, `mush`) generate lists of pending mail messages with one line of description for each mail message. There is a lot of information about a mail message (length of the message, who it is from, who it is to, when it was sent, when it arrived, the subject, the contents of the message, the first few words of the contents, etc.) and not all of it can fit in a one-line description. But different users might want different things to be on the line and in different orders. Describe a way that the user can specify the format of the one-line descriptions to fit his or her tastes. *Hint:* Use a little language.

12. Is two-way radio a connectionless (postal model) or connection (telephone model) method of communication? Or is it some of both? Explain your reasoning.

13. In a very fast network, it is possible to log into a system, execute some commands, and log out again within a few hundredths of a second. How could you use this to implement something that appears to be a connection model but really uses a connectionless model underneath?

5

Implementing Processes

Now that we have seen the system call interface of an operating system and the hardware it will be implemented on, it is time to look at how the system call interface would be implemented. We start that explanation in this chapter and continue it for the rest of the book. The most fundamental object implemented by an operating system is the process. The process concept is at the center of operating systems, and we spend the next few chapters examining it and its implications.

We look at process implementation through a simple operating system that implements processes and interprocess communication. The operating system is simplified, but it provides the same basic services that a real operating system does. Seeing code gives you a deeper understanding of the issues in process implementation than textual description of an implementation would. We have tried to give enough detail so that you can see how it is done without creating confusion with excessive detail. The simple operating system also shows the internal structure of an operating system and how the parts fit together.

In Chapter 3 we introduced the idea of a process, a program executing in a virtual computer which is implemented by the operating system. In this chapter we will show how an operating system implements processes. The basic idea is the one we mentioned in Chapter 3, switching the real processor rapidly between all the virtual machines. Each process will be represented as a data structure that we will call a process descriptor. Each process will get to run on the real hardware for a short period of time, and then the next process will run for a short period of time, and so on. That is, we will interleave the execution of all the processes (see Figure 5.1) to give the illusion that all processes are actually running in parallel. We call this activity *time sharing*.

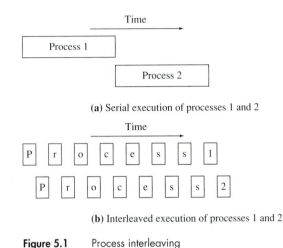

(a) Serial execution of processes 1 and 2

time sharing

(b) Interleaved execution of processes 1 and 2

Figure 5.1   Process interleaving

5.1   THE SYSTEM CALL INTERFACE

In this chapter we will examine the code for a simple operating system that will demonstrate the basic ideas in implementing processes. We will start with a description of the system call interface to be implemented by the simple operating system.

This interface is different than the one described in Chapter 3. In that chapter we were trying to present a fairly realistic system call interface. In this chapter we use a simplified system call interface because we are trying to show the basic ideas of process implementation.

All system calls in this simple operating system return a nonnegative integer if they complete successfully. Some system calls return a positive number that is the result of the system call. If there is nothing useful to return, a zero is returned. Negative return values signify an error in the system call. First, the process-related system calls:

- `int CreateProcess( int blockNumber, int numberOfBlocks );`—This system call creates a new process and returns the process ID. The process code and data image are on disk in `numberOfBlocks` consecutive disk blocks, starting with disk block `blockNumber`. A return code of −1 means that the process was not created because there were no free process descriptor slots in the process table.

- `void ExitProcess( int exitCode );`—The calling process is terminated and its resources returned to the operating system. This call always succeeds (and does not return).

This interprocess-communication-related system calls are:

- `int CreateMessageQueue( void );`—A new message queue is created and its identifier is returned. A return code of −1 means that the message queue table was full and the message queue was not created.

- int SendMessage(int msg_q_id, int * msg);—The integer pointer msg points to an array of eight integers, which is the message. msg_q_id is the identifier of the message queue the message is to be sent to. Usually the first word in the message is the type of the message, but this interpretation is the business of the message senders and receivers.

  A return code of −1 means that the msg_q_id was not a valid message queue identifier. A return code of −2 means that there were no available message buffers. In both of these cases, the message was not sent.

- int ReceiveMessage(int msg_q_id, int * msg);—This system call returns the oldest message in the message queue with identifier msg_q_id. If there are no messages in the queue, then the system caller is blocked until a message is sent to the queue. The msg argument is the address of an eight-word array (allocated by the caller of ReceiveMessage) where the message will be placed.

  A return code of −1 means that the msg_q_id was not a valid message queue identifier and no message was received.

The simple operating system does not have a file system, so it will not have file system calls like the ones we described in Chapter 3. Instead, we will provide basic disk access with system calls to read and write disk blocks. In Chapter 15 we will see that these system calls are the same functions that are implemented by a *disk driver*. The disk-I/O-related system calls are:

- int ReadDiskBlock(int blockNumber, char * buffer);—Disk block blockNumber is read into buffer. This system call always succeeds and returns zero.

- int WriteDiskBlock(int blockNumber, char * buffer);—Disk block blockNumber is written from buffer. This system call always succeeds and returns zero.

In terms of user-visible objects defined by the simple operating system, and the system calls as operations of those objects, we have this table:

- Process object
  - -CreateProcess
  - -ExitProcess
- Message queue object
  - -CreateMessageQueue
  - -SendMessage
  - -ReceiveMessage
- Disk object
  - -ReadDiskBlock
  - -WriteDiskBlock

Figure 5.2 shows the system calls and system objects and how they relate.

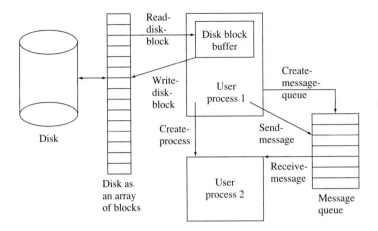

Figure 5.2   Operating system objects and operations

We have simplified this interface from the one given in Chapter 3. In particular, we have not defined a `Wait` system call or a `DestroyMessageQueue` system call. These system calls would be easy to add, but they have been left out to reduce the size of the code.

5.2   IMPLEMENTATION OF A SIMPLE OPERATING SYSTEM

We are going to present the code for a simple operating system. This will comprise about 300 lines of actual C++ code and about 600 lines with comments. It is difficult to understand this much code in any case, even more difficult when it is systems code, and still more difficult if you are learning fundamental operating system concepts at the same time. We feel it is important that you understand this code in some detail, and to help you do this we will explain the code from several different points of view. We are sure that you will find it necessary to reread these sections several times before you understand the simple operating system. This is quite normal and the only way to understand a complicated program. Each time through, you will understand a little more. So do not despair if it seems hard the first time through, or even the fourth time through!

5.2.1   GUIDE TO THE CODE

Here is a guide to the sections and subsections that follow.

- The *Architecture* section (5.2.2) describes the overall structure of the system. It should be read first.

- The *System Constants* section (5.2.3) describes the constants that are used in the code. Look this over briefly the first time, and go back and refer to it when you encounter the constants in the code.

- The *Global Data* section (5.2.4) describes the data types and data structure that comprise the main operating system tables. Look this over briefly the first time through, and go back to the definitions as you encounter the use of the data structures in the code.

- The *Process Creation* section (5.3.1) describes how processes are created. This is a good place to start looking through the code.

- The *Process States* section (5.3.2) describes the various states a process can be in and why it moves from state to state.

- The *Process Dispatching* section (5.3.3) describes how processes get run. This is the last thing the operating system does after it is entered with an interrupt, but it is good to read and understand this code early.

- The *System Stack* section (5.3.4) describes the unusual way the system stack is used. This section should help you understand dispatching better.

- The *Timer Interrupts* section (5.3.5) is the first example of an interrupt handler. An interrupt is an entry into the operating system, and is the next system event after a process is dispatched (assuming the process uses up its entire time slice).

- The *System Initialization* section (5.4) describes how the operating system starts up. Read this section quickly, and go back to it as you see the data structures that it sets up used in the system.

- The *Switching between Processes* section (5.5.1) is another view of the mechanics of switching processes.

- The *Flow of Control* section (5.5.2) is still another view of process switching and how the *ia* and stack change as it happens.

- The *System Call Interrupt Handler* section (5.6) shows how system calls are handled. This is the core of the functionality of the operating system. Try to understand it one case at a time, and expect to go over it several times. The cases interact with one another.

- The *Disk Driver Subsystem* section (5.8) shows the code to read and write disk blocks. Read this section after you have a good understanding of the previous sections.

- The *Implementation of Waiting* section (5.9) deals with some important but subtle points about how you wait for events in the simple operating system. Read this after you have a good understanding of the previous sections.

- The *Flow of Control through the Operating System* section (5.10) shows how control moves through the operating system for each system call. This is a good section to look at in your early readings of this chapter because it gives an overall view of the working of the system.

5.2.2   THE ARCHITECTURE

The first thing to understand is the overall structure of the code, what is called the *architecture* of the system. Figure 5.3 shows the components of the simple operating system. In Figure 5.3, the gray rectangles are data and the rounded rectangles are code modules. Dotted lines show data access, solid lines show transfer of control, and dashed lines show transition of control from system calls and returns.

    The operating system itself has two major subsystems. The *process management subsystem* creates the process abstraction. It maintains the process tables and message queues, handles system calls, and dispatches processes to run on the processor. The *disk driver subsystem* creates the disk abstraction for the user processes. It communicates with the disk hardware and handles disk interrupts. It includes a device driver that accepts disk operation requests and schedules them onto the disk.

architecture

process management subsystem

disk driver subsystem

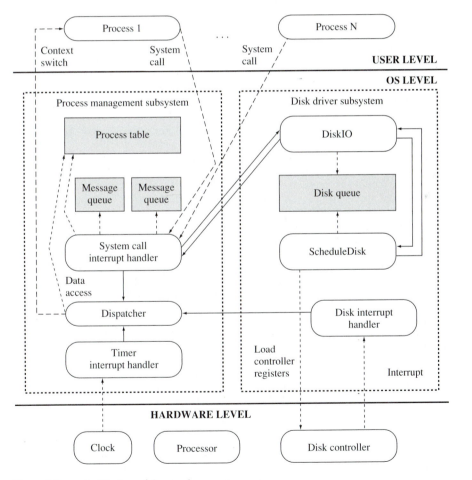

Figure 5.3   Architecture of the simple operating system

In the following sections we will look at the code that implements each part of the simple operating system. The simple operating system will implement all the system calls described in the previous section.

5.2.3   SYSTEM CONSTANTS

First we define some constants needed by the operating system and the system callers.

SYSTEM CONSTANTS

```
// Boolean values
enum { False=0, True=1 };

// hardware constants (determined by the hardware)
const int DiskBlockSize = 4096;
const int NumberOfRegisters = 32;

// system constants (we can change these constants to tune the operat-
ing system)
const int SystemStackSize = 4096; // bytes
const int ProcessSize = 512*1024; // bytes
const int TimeQuantum = 100000; // 100000 microseconds = 100 milli-
// seconds
const int MessageSize = 8; // 8 words = 32 bytes
const int InitialProcessDiskBlock = 4341; // disk block number
const int EndOfFreeList = -1;

// system limits (we can change these)
const int NumberOfProcesses = 20;
const int NumberOfMessageQueues = 20;
// This is the number of message buffers for ALL the message queues.
const int NumberOfMessageBuffers = 100;

// event handler offsets (determined by the hardware)
const int SystemCallHandler = 0;
const int TimerHandler = 4;
const int DiskHandler = 8;
const int ProgramErrorHandler = 12;

// system call numbers (arbitrary numbers, as long as they are all dif-
// ferent)
const int CreateProcessSystemCall = 1;
const int ExitProcessSystemCall = 2;
const int CreateMessageQueueSystemCall = 3;
const int SendMessageSystemCall = 4;
const int ReceiveMessageSystemCall = 5;
const int DiskReadSystemCall = 6;
const int DiskWriteSystemCall = 7;
```

There is a maximum number of processes and message buffers, but these maximums can be set to any number and the system recompiled. Hence there is no theoretical limit on either. That is, there is nothing fundamental in how the code is structured that limits how large these numbers can be. We are assuming here that the code for the initial process is in disk block 4341. This disk block number was chosen arbitrarily. We have to read the initial process from somewhere. We give numbers to all the system calls.

5.2.4 GLOBAL DATA

This code defines the global data used by the operating system. This is data that records the state of the system. It is described after the code.

GLOBAL DATA

```
// A save area allocates space to save all the hardware registers.
// We use it to record the hardware state of a process.
struct SaveArea {
    int ia, psw, base, bound, reg[NumberOfRegisters];
};

// A process is always in a state. These are the possible states.
enum ProcessState {Ready, Running, Blocked};
typedef int Pid;

// The process descriptor is the data structure that records the
// state of a process. It includes the register state and the
// process state.
struct ProcessDescriptor {
    int slotAllocated; // Boolean: is the slot free or used?
    int timeLeft; // time left from the last time slice in milliseconds
    ProcessState state; // ready, running or blocked
    SaveArea sa; // register save area
};
//
// OPERATING SYSTEM GLOBAL DATA

//
// ********** Processes
//
// The current process is the one that is currently running.
// It is possible for this to be 0 indicating that no process is running.
int current_process;
// This reserves space for the stack used when you are running in the
// system (as opposed to a user process).
int SystemStack[SystemStackSize];

ProcessDescriptor pd[NumberOfProcesses]; // pd[0] is the system

//
// ********** Messages
```

```
// A pool of message buffers
typedef int MessageBuffer[MessageSize];
MessageBuffer message_buffer[NumberOfMessageBuffers];
int free_message_buffer; // points (into array) to head of free list

// The message queues
// Keep track of which queues are allocated
int message_queue_allocated[NumberOfMessageQueues];
// Each logical message queue is implemented with two
// C++ queues, one (message_queue) to hold the messages
// and another (wait_queue) to hold WaitQueueItems which
// record processes that are waiting for messages on the queue.
Queue <MessageBuffer *> * message_queue[NumberOfMessageQueues];
// Note that "message_queue" is an array of pointers to Queues
// and each Queue holds pointers to message buffers.

// This structure is what we put in the wait_queue following.
struct WaitQueueItem {
    Pid pid;
    // This is the address of the buffer in pid's process of the
    // buffer to read the message from or write the message to.
    // Thus this is not a system mode (unmapped) address
    char * buffer;
}
Queue <WaitQueueItem *> * wait_queue[NumberOfMessageQueues];
// Note that "wait_queue" is an array of pointers to Queues
// and each Queue holds pointers to WaitQueueItems.

//
// ********** Interrupt vector area
//
// These are the addresses of the four procedures that
// will act as interrupt handlers.
char * SystemCallVector = &SystemCallInterruptHandler;
char * TimerVector = &TimerInterruptHandler;
char * DiskVector = &DiskInterruptHandler;
char * ProgramErrorVector = &ProgramErrorInterruptHandler;

//
// ********** Disk queue—of disk requests waiting to be serviced.
//
int process_using_disk;
// The structure type for a disk request.
struct DiskRequest {
    int command;
    int disk_block;
    char * buffer;
    int pid;
};
Queue <DiskRequest *> disk_queue;
// The items on this Queue are pointers to DiskRequests

//
// Procedures for allocating and freeing message buffers.
```

[handwritten margin note: Queue <int>]
[handwritten annotation near "pointers to": the index of a]

```
//
int GetMessageBuffer( void ) {
    // get the head of the free list
    int msg_no = free_msg_buffer;
    if( msg_no != EndOfFreeList ) {
        // follow the link to the next buffer
        free_msg_buffer = message_buffer[msg_no][0];
    }
    return msg_no;
}

void FreeMessageBuffer( int msg_no ) {
    message_buffer[msg_no][0] = free_msg_buffer;
    free_msg_buffer = msg_no;
}
```

The first part defines the necessary types. The register save area has space for all the processor registers that need to be saved when we change processes. A process is always in a process state: ready, running, or blocked. We will discuss this more in Section 5.3.2. The process descriptor contains a process state, a register save area, and the amount of time left to run in the last time slice the process received.

If a process is currently running then its process number is recorded in cur-rent_process. If no process is currently running (all are blocked), then cur-rent_process will be 0. The operating system itself is written in C++, and C++ programs expect to have a stack to hold procedure call frames. So we reserve space for the system stack. We define a process descriptor table (the array pd of Process-Descriptor). This contains the process descriptor for each process in the system.

The next few definitions support the implementation of message queues. We are assuming a template queue data type (Queue) is already defined. We define a pool of message buffers to hold messages that have been sent but not yet received. We define an array that tells us which message buffers are allocated. Next, we define an array of message queues to use when they are created. The items are pointers to Queue be-cause we will allocate them as the user processes create the message queues. We also need to provide for a queue of processes waiting for a message from a message queue, so we have a parallel stack of wait queues. At least one of these two queues will be empty, since either there are messages waiting to be received, processes waiting for a message to arrive, or neither of these. Each item in a wait queue contains a process identifier and a pointer to a message buffer (in the process) to use.

To summarize message queues: The process sees a logical concept of a message queue, which is an object implemented by the operating system that the process can send messages to and receive messages from. We use two internal Queue data structures to im-plement a single, logical message queue. We need one queue to hold messages that have been sent but not yet received, and we need the second queue to hold processes that want to receive a message from the queue. We use the abstract data type Queue to implement these internal queues. The two paired queues (one for messages and one for processes) exist in two arrays of Queues. The paired queues have the same index in each array.

The disk queue holds disk requests that are waiting to be serviced.

We define two utility procedures (`GetMessageBuffer` and `FreeMessage-Buffer`) to allocate and free messages.

> Operating system objects are represented in the operating system by data structures and implemented with procedures that operate on those data structures.

5.3   IMPLEMENTATION OF PROCESSES

5.3.1   PROCESS CREATION

The internal operating system procedure that creates processes (`Create-ProcessSysProc`) is shown below. The operating system creates the first process when it starts up by calling `CreateProcessSysProc` directly. All other processes are created when a `CreateProcess` system call is executed. The code below is followed by an explanation.

PROCESS CREATION

```
// This is the internal OS procedure for creating a process.
// It will be called when a CreateProcess system call is made.
// It is also called once during system initialization to
// create the initial (first) process.

int CreateProcessSysProc( int first_block, int n_blocks ) {
    // The code to run in the process is in a sequential file
    // on disk (meaning that it is in consecutive blocks on the disk)
    // first_block is the disk block address of the first block of
    // the code file and n_blocks is the number of following blocks
    // it takes up.
    int pid;
    // Look for a free slot in the process table.
    for( pid = 1; pid < NumberOfProcesses; ++pid ) {
        if( !pd[pid].slotAllocated )
            break;
    }
    if( pid >= NumberOfProcesses ) {
        // We did not find a free slot, the create process fails.
        return -1; // ERROR
    }
    pd[pid].slotAllocated = True; // Mark the slot as allocated.
    // Initialize the fields of the process descriptor.
    pd[pid].state = Ready; // processes start out ready
    // In this simple OS memory is divided into 20 equally sized
```

```
// blocks and each process gets one.
pd[pid].sa.base = pid * ProcessSize;
pd[pid].sa.bound = ProcessSize;
pd[pid].sa.psw = 3; // user mode, interrupts enabled
pd[pid].sa.ia = 0; // begin execution at address 0
// We leave the registers uninitialized
// since we have no idea what they should be.
// They will be initialized by the process itself and saved
// and restored when the process is interrupted and dispatched.

// Read in the image of the process.
// First get the address of the beginning of the area of physical
// memory that is assigned to this process.
char * addr = (char *)(pd[pid].sa.base);
for( i = 0; i < n_blocks; ++i ) {
    // Read one block.
    IssueDiskRead( first_block + i, addr, 0/*no interrupt*/ );
    while( DiskBusy() )
        ; // busy wait for the disk I/O to complete
    // Move to the address of the next block to read in.
    addr +=DiskBlockSize;
}
return pid;
}
```

[handwritten margin note: partial fix for bug – if disk driver has disk busy here then we should wait for it. But the disk interrupt will still be lost.]

We call this procedure `CreateProcessSysProc` to make it clear this is the internal operating systems procedure and not the create process system call. The `CreateProcessSysProc` procedure first finds an empty slot in the process table for this new process. Failure to find a free slot will cause the system call to return a failure return code. Then it initializes process descriptor and reads the program code in from the disk. Note that we do not turn on the disk interrupt when we start the disk I/O. Only the *psw* and *ia* registers are initialized in a new process. Instead we wait for the disk block read to complete. We do it this way to make the procedure simpler. If we wanted to go on to the next process while waiting for the disk read to complete, we would have to save the current state of the create process system call and continue it later when the disk block is read. See Sections 5.9.2 and 5.9.3 for a discussion on how to go about suspending a system call.

We are not concerning ourselves with memory management in this simple operating system. We will assign each process 50K bytes. Since there are 20 process and 1M bytes of main memory, we put processes every 50K bytes. There is no process 0, and so the first 50K bytes are reserved for the operating system. Memory management is important, but we can afford to ignore it for now and concentrate on other issues. In Chapter 10 we will examine memory management in detail.

Process creation consists of setting up the fields of the process descriptor.

5.3.2   PROCESS STATES

process states

A process can be in one of several possible *process states*. The process states that are possible vary from operating system to operating system, but here are three that occur in all systems.

running

- *Running*—A process in the running state is currently being executed by a real processor.

ready

- *Ready*—A process in the ready state is ready to be run by a processor, but there are currently no free processors to run it.

blocked

- *Blocked*—A process in the blocked state is waiting for some event (for example, waiting for a disk block read to complete), and cannot be run even if there is a free processor to run it.

Figure 5.4 shows the state diagram for a our simple operating system. Processes move from state to state as events occur. The events in Figure 5.4 are:

- *Create process*—A new process enters the system. The operating system creates it in response to a `CreateProcess` system call.
- *Dispatch process*—When the processor becomes free, it picks a ready process and starts it running. This is called *dispatching* a process.
- *Block for I/O or message*—When a process makes a read or write system call, it must wait for completion of the transfer before it can be resumed. It is said to be blocked while it is waiting for the transfer. All process blocks are caused by making a system call. A process can block waiting for a message to arrive in a (currently) empty message queue.
- *I/O done*—When an I/O operation completes, the process that was waiting for it can be made ready.
- *Message sent*—When a message is sent to a queue that a process is waiting to receive from, the process that was waiting for it can be made ready.

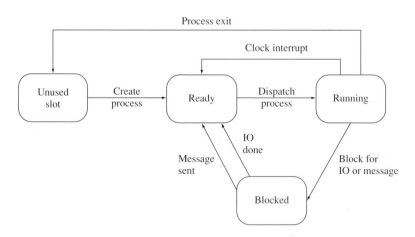

Figure 5.4   Process states

DESIGN TECHNIQUE: STATE MACHINES

The process state graph in Figure 5.4 is an example of a *state machine*. A state machine is a graphical and mathematical notation for describing systems that move from state to state depending on the current state and events that occur. When an event occurs, the state machine may perform some action (or produce some output) and then move to a new state. Systems like this are called *reactive systems* because they react to events. State machines are a useful formal model for reactive systems. An additional advantage to the state machine model is that it can be mechanically converted into a program. See Section 9.2 for more discussion of state machines.

• *Process exit*—A process leaves the system when it executes an `ExitProcess` system call.

5.3.3 PROCESS DISPATCHING

The *dispatcher* finds a ready process and starts it running. If no process is ready to run it waits for an interrupt.

dispatcher

The `Dispatcher` code is shown below. It looks through the processes (the `pd` array) and "dispatches" the next process it finds that is not blocked. By *dispatch* of a process, we mean loading its process state, which causes it to begin executing at the point where the process state was last saved.

THE DISPATCHER

```
void Dispatcher( void ) {
    // Pick a process to run.
    current_process = SelectProcessToRun();
    // and run it.
    RunProcess( current_process );
    // This procedure call will not return.
}

int SelectProcessToRun( void ) {

    // next_proc is a static variable so that we will remember
    // the last process we selected and start searching from there.
    // We start with a high value that will be wrapped to 1 the
    // first time the dispatcher is called.

    static int next_proc = NumberOfProcesses;

    // If the process was interrupted by a disk interrupt or made a
    // system call that did not block, then we let it use the rest
    // of the time slice that was alloted to it.

    if( current_process > 0 && pd[current_process].slotAllocated
      && pd[current_process].state == Ready
      && pd[current_process].timeLeft > 0 )
        return current_process;
        { pd [current-process]. state = Running;
          return current process;
        }
```

```
        // We start from the current value of next_proc and wrap around when
        // we get to the end.
        // i counts the number of iterations so we can easily tell when
        // we have looked through the entire array.

        for( int i = 1; i < NumberOfProcesses; ++i ){
            // If we have gotten to the end of the process table then wrap
            // around to the beginning.
            if( ++next_proc >= NumberOfProcesses )
                // Slot 0 and pid 0 are reserved for the OS,
                // so start with slot 1
                next_proc = 1;

            // next_proc is the process we are looking at.
            if( pd[next_proc].slotAllocated && pd[next_proc].state == Ready ){
                // If the process is ready then pick it to run.
                pd[next_proc].timeLeft = TimeQuantum;
                pd[next_proc].state = Running;
                return next_proc;
            }
        }
        //If we drop through the loop then no process is ready to run.
        return -1;
}

void RunProcess( int pid ) {
    // Was a process picked to run?
    if( pid >= 0 ) {
        // Dispatch the process
        SaveArea * savearea = &(pd[pid].sa);
        int quantum = pd[pid].timeLeft;
        asm {
          // ia and psw will be taken from iia and ipsw by
          // the rti instruction
          load   savearea+0,iia
          load   savearea+4,ipsw
          // restore base and bound registers from saved values
          load   savearea+8,base
          load   savearea+12,bound
          // restore all the saved general registers
          loadall savearea+16
          // set the interval timer
          load   quantum,timer
          // return from interrupt restarts the process
          rti
          // rti does not return, since it sets the ia register
        }
    } else {
        // If there is no process to run then they must all be waiting
        // for an interrupt. Loop the processor and wait for interrupts.

        waitLoop: goto waitLoop;
        // control never drops through the tight loop
    }
}
```

The dispatcher has two jobs: figure out which process to run (Select-ProcessToRun) and then run it (RunProcess).

The SelectProcessToRun procedure checks to see if the process that made the system call (or was interrupted by a disk interrupt) is still ready and has time left in its most recent time slice. This will be the case for disk interrupts and for system calls that do not block the calling process. Otherwise Select-ProcessToRun looks through the array of process descriptors and picks the first one it finds that is ready.

The order it looks at processes determines the priority of the processes. A simple method would be to always start at the beginning of the array. This gives priority to processes that are near the beginning of the array. In order to avoid this bias, we do not start looking for a ready process at the beginning of the array but rather from the point where we found the last ready process to run. We do this by saving the position in the array in a static variable, which will retain its value from call to call. This will give equal priority to all processes. The pointer next_proc will continually cycle through the array. Since we do not start at the beginning of the array, we have to find a way to determine when we have looked through the entire array. This would happen when no process is ready to run. This will happen quite frequently. What we do is to keep another counter of how many process slots we have looked at, and exit the loop when we have looked at them all without finding a ready process. When we find a process to run, we set its time allocation to TimeQuantum and return.

The RunProcess procedure does the actual starting of the chosen process. If no process is ready to run, then the system loops until an interrupt occurs. Otherwise it starts the process by loading its registers and using the rti instruction to start up the new process. Since this will be a user process, its *psw* will be 3, and so the process will run in user mode with interrupts enabled. Section 5.3.5 shows where this register information is saved.

The Dispatcher is called from various points in the operating system, but it never returns from a call. The operating system is entered in only one way, through an interrupt. In this operating system, it is either a system call interrupt, a timer interrupt, a disk interrupt, or a program error interrupt. In more complex operating systems, there could be dozens of devices that could cause interrupts. Each interrupt causes the operating system to be entered and causes it to take various actions. In the course of interrupt processing, several levels of procedure calls are made, and the final one is always to the process dispatcher.

In *preemptive scheduling,* we will not allow a process to run for as long as it likes, but allocate a block of time to it. This block of time is called a *time slice* or *quantum*. We will set the interval timer to interrupt at the end of the time slice and then start a process running. If the process executes a system call before the end of the time slice, we disable the timer interrupt and schedule another process. If the system call does not block the process, then it will get to run for the rest of its time slice after the system call completes. If the timer interrupt occurs while the process is still running, we change the running process to the ready state and dispatch another process. Thus a process in an infinite loop will keep getting time slices, but it will be unable to use *all* the processor time.

preemptive scheduling
time slice
quantum

> Process dispatching consists of deciding which process to run and resuming its execution.

5.3.4   THE SYSTEM STACK

system stack

As the dispatcher is about to run a user process, the *system stack* contains a record of all the procedure calls that have been made by the system and not yet returned from. In a normal program, all called procedures are returned from, and this stack is used to do those returns. An operating system, however, is different. After the operating system does its work, it wants to start a user process. Any important state information has been recorded in operating system data tables. There is nothing on the stack that needs to be saved, and so there is no need to save the stack or to return to the calling procedures. When the operating system is called again, it will start at the interrupt handler again, and it will be a new transaction. For this reason, the current contents of the operating system's stack can be ignored, so we reset the stack pointer to the top of the stack. When the operating system is entered again, it will just write over any old stack information.

So we see that a system call is not like a procedure call and does not return in the same sense. The operating system is playing tricks by changing the basic machine registers. The operating system creates the process environment for the users, but does not run as a process itself.

> Operating systems use stacks in unusual ways that are not expected by the compiler.

5.3.5   TIMER INTERRUPTS

timer interrupt handler

The *timer interrupt handler* is shown next. It is called when a timer interrupt occurs. A timer interrupt indicates that the time slice has run out, so the current process has used up its allocation of time for now. It saves the state of the current process and calls the dispatcher. The dispatcher will then pick a process to run. It will pick the current process again when all the other processes have been given a time slice.

TIMER INTERRUPT HANDLER

```
// This procedure is called when a timer interrupt occurs.
void TimerInterruptHandler( void ) {
    if( current_process > 0 ) { // was there a running process?
```

```
    // Save the processor state of the system caller.
    // Dispatch will later use this to restart the process.
    SaveArea * savearea = &(pd[current_process].sa);
    asm {
        // processes ia and psw are saved in iia and ipsw
        store  iia,savearea+0
        store  ipsw,savearea+4
        // save the base and bound registers
        store  base,savearea+8
        store  bound,savearea+12
        // save all the general registers
        storeall savearea+16
        // set up the system stack
        load  SystemStack+SystemStackSize,r30
    }
    pd[current_process].timeLeft = 0;
    pd[current_process].state = Ready;
}
// else the processor was idle waiting for an interrupt
// and so there is no current process to save the state of

// Pick another process to run (it could be the same one)
Dispatcher();
}
```

This is a typical interrupt handler. The first thing it does is save the *context* (the state) of the current process. Saving a process context is called a *half context-switch*. The other half of the context switch is the restoring of the context of the next process to run.

context

half context-switch

The saving of the context of one process and the restoring of the context of another process switches the current process and so is called a (full) *context switch*.

context switch

Once we have saved the context of the interrupted process, we are ready to handle the interrupt. The timer interrupt, however, does not have any processing to do since it just times out one process and lets the next one run. So we immediately call the dispatcher. The dispatcher will decide which process to run, and do the second half context-switch that starts the next process.

5.4   SYSTEM INITIALIZATION

The system initialization code is shown next. First, we set up the interrupt vectors. Next, we initialize the process table by setting slotAllocated to False. The index into the process table is also the process ID. We reserve process 0 for the operating system, and we will see later how this will be used. We create one process initially to get things going, and it will create any other processes we need. Next, we put all the message buffers on the free list (actually a stack). Finally, we go to the dispatcher to start a process running.

SYSTEM INITIALIZATION

```
// This is the main program for the operating system. It is executed
// only once, when the operating system is initialized.

int main( void ) {
    // Set up the system's stack
    asm{load SystemStack+SystemStackSize,r30 }

    // Set up the interrupt vectors area
    asm{ load &SystemCallVector,iva }

    // set up the process descriptors
    // Process 0 is reserved for the system, never dispatch it.
    pd[0].slotAllocated = True;
    pd[0].state = Blocked;
    // The other process slots start out free.
    for( i = 1; i < NumberOfProcesses; ++i )
        pd[i].slotAllocated = False;
    // Process 1 is the initialization process.
    (void) CreateProcessSysProc( InitialProcessDiskBlock, 1 );

    // set up the pool of free message buffers
    for( i = 0; i < (NumberOfMessageBuffers-1); ++i )
        // link each one to the next one
        message_buffer[i][0] = i+1;
    // The last message buffer in the free chain has a marker so
    // you can tell you are at the end of the list.
    message_buffer[NumberOfMessageBuffers-1][0] = EndOfFreeList;
    free_message_buffer = 0;

    // All the message queues start out unallocated.
    for( i = 0; i < NumberOfMessageQueues; ++i )
        message_queue_allocated[i] = False;

    // Let's go!
    process_using_disk = 0; initialize this to 0 => no process.
    current_process = -1;
    Dispatcher();
}
```

5.4.1 THE INITIAL PROCESS

Initial process

It limits our flexibility to build into the operating system which processes to create initially. Instead, we assume that there is an *initial process* that is located at a fixed location on disk (at disk block number **InitialProcessDiskBlock**). The operating system starts this as the first process. The initial process then creates any other necessary processes. Part of the operating system initialization has been moved out of the operating system and into the initial process. The initial process is logically part of the operating system, even though it operates as a user process. This makes it easier to change that part of the initialization.

The code for the initial process is next.

THE INITIAL PROCESS

```
void main( ) {
    // start the two processes
    (void)CreateProcess( UserProcessA, UserProcessASize );
    (void)CreateProcess( UserProcessB, UserProcessBSize );
    // There is nothing else for this process to do.
    // We haven't implemented a Wait system call, so just exit.
    ExitProcess( 0 );
}
```

The initial process makes system calls to start two user processes and then exits. We can make the operating system do different things by changing the initialization process. The call to **CreateProcess** here is a system call, not a direct call to the operating system procedure named **CreateProcessSysProc**. The user-level, C++ library **CreateProcess** procedure will make a **CreateProcess** system call, which will transfer to the operating system's **CreateProcessSysProc** procedure.

The initial process is an ordinary process that is compiled and linked separately from the operating system and runs as a normal user process. Contrast this with the **CreateProcessSysProc** in the operating system code. The operating system initialization code is part of the operating system, and the **CreateProcessSysProc** is a procedure call.

Figure 5.5 shows how the initial process is created specially by the operating system and is the common ancestor of all other processes.

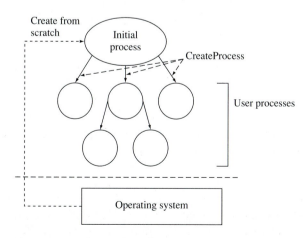

Figure 5.5   The initial process creates other processes

The operating system creates the first process internally. All other processes are created by this first process and its descendants.

5.5   PROCESS SWITCHING

5.5.1   SWITCHING BETWEEN PROCESSES

The instruction address determines which instruction is executed next, so the instruction address determines which process is executing on the computer. The other registers determine what data the program operates on: the *base* register determines what part of physical memory the instructions and data come from, the *bound* register determines how much of the physical memory can be accessed, and the general registers contain working data for the program. All together, these registers provide a context for the process to operate in—what instructions it executes and what data it operates on. In this section, we will see how to use these registers to achieve process switching.

In implementing processes, it is necessary to run a process for a short time and then switch the processor to another process. Some care must be taken when you do this because a running process has a memory area that it is using, and it keeps values in processor registers that it needs in its computation. If you switch the processor to another process, it is necessary to save the values in the registers since the next process will want its own values in the registers. We do this by saving all the registers when a process loses the processor, and restoring them all again when it is resumed. This activity is called context switching, and it is the thing that makes process switching work.

Figure 5.6 shows the way register values are moved around in a context switch caused by an interrupt. The numbers in the rest of this paragraph correspond to the numbers in Figure 5.6. (1) When an interrupt occurs, the *ia* and *psw* are moved to control registers *iia* and *ipsw* by the hardware interrupt mechanism. This hardware mechanism also sets the *ia* register to the address of the interrupt handler, which starts the interrupt handler running. (2) The first thing the interrupt handler does is to save the *iia* and *ipsw* registers in the save area for the process that was interrupted. (3) Then the interrupt handler saves all the other registers in the save area. (4) Now that the state of the interrupt process has been saved, the interrupt is handled by the operating system. (5) When the operating system has done what it needs to do, it calls the dispatcher. The dispatcher then loads the processor state (that is, the hardware registers) of the next process to run. (6) Then it moves the saved *iia* and *ipsw* registers to *iia* and *ipsw*. (7) This starts the process with a return from interrupt instruction.

Operating system code does not run as a process, but rather it implements processes so user code can run as a process.

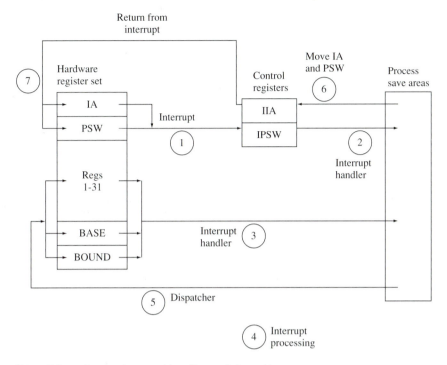

Figure 5.6   First level interrupt handling and dispatching

5.5.2 FLOW OF CONTROL

In a normal program, we are used to a very orderly flow of control. The *ia* does jump around for loops and conditionals, but the major breaks are when a procedure is called. This moves the *ia* to another procedure where it computes for a while and then returns to where it was called from. Figure 5.7 shows the flow of control within a single process. The figure also shows the stack which records which procedures have been called but not returned from yet. This orderly model is handled by the compiler, which manages the stack and transfers of control.

When several processes are running in an operating system, however, the situation is much more complex. The *ia* will, in fact, jump all over the place as interrupts occur and processes are switched. Each process and the operating system will have its own stack, and the processor will frequently change the stack it is using. Figure 5.8 shows how the flow of control (that is, the *ia*) moves when we switch between two processes. Let's go through the flow of control as Process 1 makes a system call, Process 2 is started, Process 2 gets interrupted, and we return to Process 1.

1. Process 1 is running. It is using the process stack.
2. Process 1 executes the `syscall` instruction. We switch to system mode and the system stack, which starts out completely empty each time we enter the operating system.

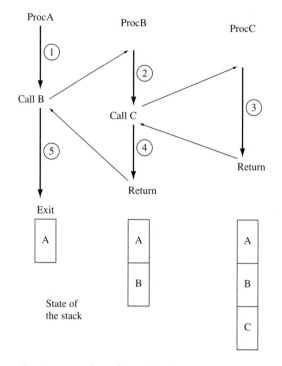

Figure 5.7   Flow of control within process

3. The operating system figures out the kind of system call, and calls Procedure A to handle it. The system stack has one stack frame on it, for the enter OS code.

4. We are in Procedure A. The system stack has two stack frames on it. When the work is completed, we call the dispatcher (with a normal procedure call).

5. We are running in the dispatcher. The system stack has three stack frames (EnterOS, ProcA, and Dispatcher). It chooses Process 2 to restart.

6. The *rti* instruction switches to user mode and jumps to Process 2. The system stack pointer was reinitialized, so the system stack is empty again. We are running on the stack for Process 2.

7. We are running inside Process 2 using its stack. Eventually, the I/O will complete, and an I/O interrupt will occur.

8. The I/O interrupt switches the computer to system mode and enters the operating system.

9. The operating system code figures out who responds to I/O interrupts. We are now using the system stack, and it has one stack frame on it.

10. Now we are in Procedure B, which is handling the I/O interrupt. This handling will make Process 1 ready again.

11. We call the dispatcher (with a normal procedure call).

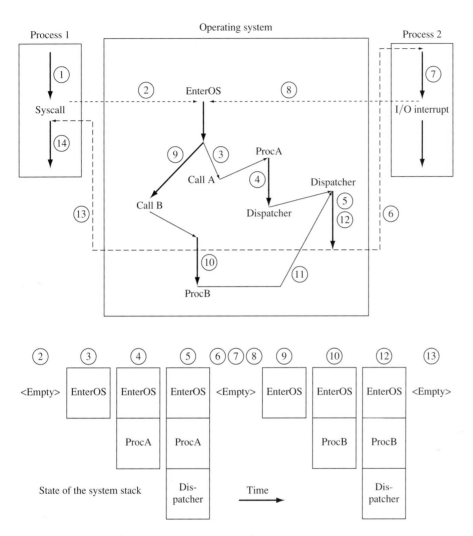

Figure 5.8   Flow of control during process switching

12. The dispatcher is running. The system stack has three stack frames on it. The dispatcher decides to restart Process 1.

13. The dispatcher reinitializes the system stack (making it empty) and switches to Process 1 with an *rti* instruction.

14. We are finally back in Process 1 after the system call. We are using the stack for Process 1.

You can see that control moves all around between the operating system and the processes. Control changes within a process or the operating system are all procedure calls. Interrupts switch control from a user process to the operating system.

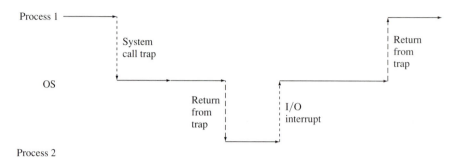

Figure 5.9   Flow of control during process switching (another view)

The return from interrupt instruction switches control from the operating system to a user process. All this rapid switching occurs behind the scenes, however. Each process sees a nice orderly flow of control, with procedure calls and returns as we saw in Figure 5.7. A process cannot tell when it is interrupted, except that the virtual computer seems to run more slowly.

The operating system is written in a high-level language. The compiler assumes that it is running as a normal process with a normal stack. Since the operating system is different, we have to trick the compiler into doing what we want. We do this by reinitializing (and hence throwing away) the system stack whenever we dispatch a process. The procedure call to the dispatcher inside the system will never be returned from, but the compiler sets up a stack frame assuming that it will.

Figure 5.9 shows this in another way. Process 1 is running until a system call switches to the operating system. Then it handles the system call by starting the I/O, and restarts Process 2. Process 2 runs until the I/O interrupt occurs, which switches back to the operating system and then back to Process 1.

5.6   SYSTEM CALL INTERRUPT HANDLING

system call interrupt handler

We have already seen the timer interrupt handler. In this section, we will look at the *system call interrupt handler* The disk interrupt handler will be discussed when we cover the disk management subsystem.

The system call interrupt handler contains most of the functionality of the operating system and takes some time to understand. Figure 5.10 shows a flow chart of the system call interrupt handler. Study this first to get an idea of the overall flow of control through the system call interrupt handler.

Once you have a feel for that, you can go on to look at the actual code for the interrupt handler. You might find it useful to go back to the flow chart while you are reading the code. We hope these two views, at two different levels of detail, will help you understand this complex procedure.

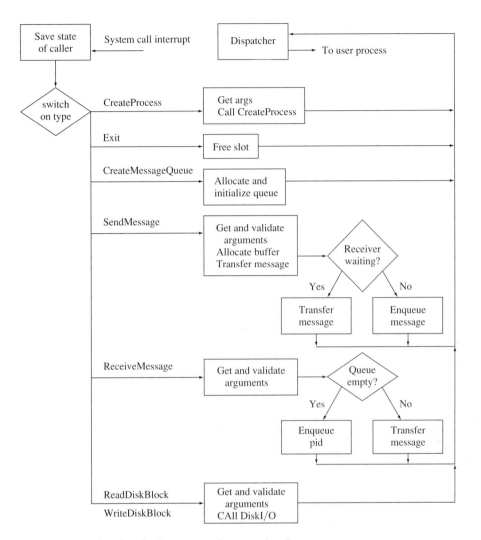

Figure 5.10 Flowchart for the system call interrupt handler.

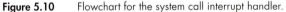

SYSTEM CALL INTERRUPT HANDLER

```
// This procedure is called when a process makes a system call.
void SystemCallInterruptHandler( void ) {

    // Save the processor state of the system caller.
    // Dispatch will later use this to restart the process.
    SaveArea * savearea = &(pd[current_process].sa);
    int saveTimer;
    asm {
```

```
        // stop the interval timer and clear any pending timer interrupt
        store  timer,saveTimer
        load   #0,timer
        // process's ia and psw are saved in iia and ipsw
        store  iia,savearea+0
        store  ipsw,savearea+4
        // save the base and bound registers
        store  base,savearea+8
        store  bound,savearea+12
        // save all the general registers
        storeall savearea+16
        // set up the stack
        load   SystemStack+SystemStackSize,r30
    }
    pd[current_process].timeLeft = saveTimer;
    pd[current_process].state = Ready;

    // fetch the system call number and switch it on
    int system_call_number; asm {store r8,system_call_number}
    switch( system_call_number ) {

    case CreateProcessSystemCall:
        // get the system call arguments from the registers
        int block_number; asm {store r9,block_number}
        int number_of_blocks; asm {store r10,number_of_blocks}

        // put the return code in R1
        pd[current_process].sa.reg[1]
            = CreateProcessSysProc( block_number, number_of_blocks);
        break;

    case ExitProcessSystemCall:
        char * return_code; asm { store r9,return_code }
        // we don't save the return code in this OS so
        // just free up the pd slot
        pd[current_process].slotAllocated = False;
        break;

    case CreateMessageQueueSystemCall:
        // find a free message queue
        int i;
        for( i = 0; i < NumberOfMessageQueues; ++i ) {
            if( !message_queue_allocated[i] ) {
                break;
            }
        }
        if( i >= NumberOfMessageQueues ) {
            // signal the error, message queue overflow
            // return a value that is invalid
            pd[current_process].sa.reg[1] = -1;
            break;
        }
        // Create the two Queues and return the index to the
        // message queue.
        message_queue_allocated[i] = True;
        message_queue[i] = new Queue<MessageBuffer *>;
                                          <int>
```

```
        wait_queue[i] = new Queue<WaitQueueItem *>;
        pd[current_process].sa.reg[1] = i;
        break;

case SendMessageSystemCall:
        // get the arguments
        int * user_msg; asm {store r9,user_msg}
        int to_q; asm {store r10,to_q}

        // check for an invalid queue identifier
        if( !message_queue_allocated[to_q] ) {
            pd[current_process].sa.reg[1] = -1;
            break;
        }
        int msg_no = GetMessageBuffer();
        // make sure we have not run out of message buffers
        if( msg_no == EndOfFreeList ) {
            pd[current_process].sa.reg[1] = -2;
            break;
        }
        // copy the message vector from the system caller's memory
        // into the system's message buffer
        CopyToSystemSpace( current_process, user_msg,
                           message_buffer[msg_no], MessageSize );
        if( !wait_queue[to_q].Empty() ) {
            // some process is waiting for a message, deliver it immediately
            WaitQueueItem item = wait_queue.Remove();    wait_queue[to_q].Remove();
            TransferMessage( msg_no, item.buffer );
            pd[item.pid].state = Ready;
        } else {
            // otherwise put it on the queue
            message_queue[to_q].Insert( msg_no );
        }
        pd[current_process].sa.reg[1] = 0;
        break;

case ReceiveMessageSystemCall:
        int * user_msg; asm {store r9,user_msg}
        int from_q; asm { store r10,from_q }

        // check for an invalid queue identifier
        if( !message_queue_allocated[from_q] ) {
            pd[current_process].sa.reg[1] = -1;
            break;
        }
        if( message_queue[from_q].Empty() ) {
            pd[current_process].state = Blocked;
            WaitQueueItem *item = new WaitQueueItem;
            item->pid = current_process;
            item->buffer = user_msg;
            wait_queue[from_q].Insert( item );
        } else {
            int msg_no = message_queue[from_q].Remove();
            TransferMessage( msg_no, user_msg );
        }
```

```
            pd[current_process].sa.reg[1] = 0;
            break;

    case DiskReadSystemCall:
    case DiskWriteSystemCall:
            char * buffer; asm { store r9,buffer }
            buffer += pd[current_process].sa.base;
            //convert to physical address
            int disk_block; asm { store r10,disk_block }

            DiskIO (system_call_number, disk_block, buffer);
            pd[current_process].sa.reg[1] = 0;
            break;
    }
    Dispatcher();
}
// A convenience procedure to do the two parts of receiving a message.
// Both SendMessage and ReceiveMessage might call this procedure.
static TransferMessage( int msg_no, int * user_msg ) {
    CopyFromSystemSpace( current_process, user_msg,
                         message_buffers[msg_no]), MessageSize );
    FreeMessageBuffer( msg_no );
}
```

The SystemCallInterruptHandler is called when a process executes a SystemCall instruction because we initialized that interrupt vector with the address of SystemCallInterruptHandler. Before executing this instruction, the system call procedure (called by the process making the system call) put the arguments to the system call in the argument passing registers ($r8$, $r9$, $r10$, and $r11$).

First, the handler saves the process state of the system caller so it can be restored later by the Dispatcher.

The handler gets the system call number from $r8$ and uses it to switch to the appropriate code. The CreateProcessSystemCall gets the arguments and lets the CreateProcessSysProc procedure do the work. The ExitProcessSystemCall simply frees the process slot. The CreateMessageQueueSystemCall allocates a message queue slot, initializes the two queues, and returns the index of the message queue in the arrays of message queues. We use two internal queues to represent a single message queue. One queue is a queue of messages that have been sent to the message queue but not yet received by a process. The other queue is a queue of processes that are waiting for a message from the message queue. At any one time, at most one of the queues can have something in it because there cannot both be messages waiting to be received and processes waiting for messages to be sent.

The SendMessageSystemCall copies the message from the caller's memory area to the operating system's memory area, sets the sender process ID field, and places it on the message queue. If a process is waiting to receive the message, then the receiving process is made ready and the message is transferred. The ReceiveMessageSystemCall checks to see if any messages are waiting to be received. If not, it blocks the receiver until one arrives. If so, it copies the message into the receiver's memory area. For a DiskReadSystemCall system call, we then fetch the two arguments we will need. Then DiskReadSystemCall and DiskWriteSystemCall call DiskIO to do the work.

> System call interrupt handlers are big case statements.

5.6.1 COPYING MESSAGES BETWEEN ADDRESS SPACES

Process addresses are relocated (by the hardware) by adding in the process's memory base register, but operating system addresses are not relocated because the operating system runs in system mode. So we have to adjust for this in order to copy data from a process address to an operating system address. CopyToSystemSpace and CopyFromSystemSpace do that.

If memory management is more complicated than simple relocation, then this operation will be more complicated. We separate it out into a procedure because it uses specific information about memory management. When we have a memory management module in the operating system, this function will be part of that module.

TRANSFER BETWEEN USER AND SYSTEM MEMORY

```
void CopyToSystemSpace( int pid, char * from, char * to, int len) {
  // We are in system mode so addresses are not related by the base
  // the 'from' address is relative to process 'pid's base so we
  // relocate it ourselves                                    relocated
  from += pd[pid].sa.base;
  // now that both addresses are system mode addresses
  // we can simply move the data
  while( len-- > 0)
    *to++ = *from++;
}

void CopyFromSystemSpace( int pid, char * to, char * from, int len ) {
  // We are in system mode so addresses are not related by the base
  // the 'to' address is relative to process 'pid's base so we
  // relocate it ourselves
  to += pd[pid].sa.base;
  // now that both addresses are system mode addresses
  // we can simply move the data
  while( len-- > 0 )
    *to++ = *from++;
}
```

See Figure 5.11 for a diagram of this copying.

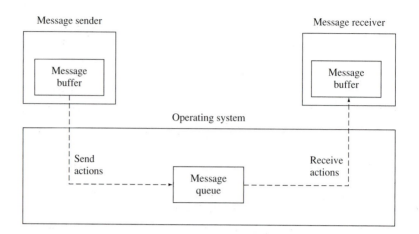

Figure 5.11   Actions required to send and receive a message

5.7   PROGRAM ERROR INTERRUPTS

When a program error occurs, we will forcibly exit the program just as if it had executed the exit system call.

In a real operating system there would be more processing to exit the process, and an error return code would be generated.

PROGRAM ERROR INTERRUPT HANDLER

```
// This procedure is called when a process makes a program error.
void ProgramErrorInterruptHandler( void ){

    asm {
        // stop the interval timer and clear any pending timer interrupt
        load  #0,timer
        // no need to save the processor state
        //
        // set up the stack
        load  SystemStack+SystemStackSize,r30
    }
    pd[current_process].slotAllocated = False;
    Dispatcher();
}
```

5.8   DISK DRIVER SUBSYSTEM

disk driver subsystem

The second major subsystem of the simple operating system is the *disk driver subsystem*. **DiskReadSystemCall** and **DiskWriteSystemCall** call **DiskIO** to put the request on the disk queue.

DISK I/O

```
// The procedure is called from the system call interrupt handler.
void DiskIO( int command, int disk_block, char * buffer ) {
    // Create a new disk request and fill in the fields.
    DiskRequest * req = new DiskRequest;
    req->command = command;
    req->disk_block = disk_block;
    req->buffer = buffer;
    req->pid = current_process;
    // Then insert it on the queue.
    disk_queue.Insert( req );
    pd[current_process].state = Blocked;
    // Wake up the disk scheduler if it is idle.
    ScheduleDisk();
}
```

DiskIO simply saves the relevant information in a DiskRequest structure and places it on the disk queue. Then DiskIO calls ScheduleDisk to see if the request can be handled immediately.

The ScheduleDisk code is shown below. It returns immediately if the disk is busy or if there are no disk requests to service. Otherwise, it remembers the process that it is doing the I/O for, and starts the disk transfer. Finally, ScheduleDisk returns to SystemCallInterruptHandler, which calls Dispatcher to start up a process that is not blocked.

DISK SCHEDULING

```
void ScheduleDisk ( void ) {
    // If the disk is already busy we cannot schedule it.
    if( DiskBusy() )
        return;
    // Get the first disk request from the disk request queue.
    DiskRequest * req = disk_queue.Remove();
    // Simply return if there is no disk request to service.
    if( req == 0 )
        return;
    // remember which process is waiting for the disk operation
    process_using_disk = req->pid;
    // issue the read or write, with disk interrupt enabled
    if( req->command == DiskReadSystemCall )
        IssueDiskRead( req->disk_block, req->buffer, 1 );
    else
        IssueDiskWrite( req->disk_block, req->buffer, 1 );
}
```

When the disk interrupt is detected by the hardware, it goes to the vector location, finds the address of DiskInterruptHandler, and jumps to it. Disk-InterruptHandler first saves the state of the process that was interrupted. Note that it is possible that no process was executing when the disk interrupt occurred. If all processes are waiting on the completion of a system call, the Dispatcher will call the WaitForInterrupt instruction that will cause the processor to halt and wait for an interrupt. In this case, current_process will be 0 and there will be no process state to save, and so the SaveProcessorState instruction will be skipped.

Then it marks the process that was waiting for the disk I/O as ready (not Blocked), and calls Dispatcher to start some other process.

DISK INTERRUPT HANDLER

```
void DiskInterruptHandler( void ) {

    if( current_process > 0 ) { // was there a running process?
        // Save the processor state of the system caller.
        // Dispatch will later use this to restart the process.
        SaveArea * savearea = &(pd[current_process].sa);
        int saveTimer;
        asm {
            // stop the interval timer and clear timer interrupts
            store   timer,saveTimer
            load    #0,timer
            // process's ia and psw are saved in iia and ipsw
            store   iia,savearea+0
            store   ipsw,savearea+4
            // save the base and bound registers
            store   base,savearea+8
            store   bound,savearea+12
            // save all the general registers
            storeall savearea+16
            // set up the stack
            load    SystemStack+SystemStackSize,r30
        }
        pd[current_process].timeLeft = saveTimer;
        pd[current_process].state = Ready;
    }

    // The process waiting for the disk is now ready to run
    pd[process_using_disk].state = Ready;
    process_using_disk = 0;

    // Wake up the disk driver
    ScheduleDisk();

    // now run a process
    Dispatcher();
}
```

Interrupts (including system call interrupts) are the only entry to an operating system.

5.8.1   COMMUNICATING WITH THE DISK CONTROLLER

There are two basic procedures left to define, `DiskBusy` and `IssueDiskRead`. These are the procedures that know the exact format of the disk controller registers. We will show how they are implemented in this section.

The following code shows the implementation of the disk interface.

DISK INTERFACE IMPLEMENTATION

```
int DiskBusy( void ) {
    // pick up the appropriate bit in the disk status register.
    disk_status stat = *Disk_status;
    // and return it.
    return stat.busy;
}

void IssueDiskRead( int block_number, char * buffer,
            int enable_disk_interrupt ) {
    // block_number is the disk block address
    // buffer is the address of to read into
    // Sometimes we want the disk controller to interrupt
    // after the transfer is completed and some times we
    // want to busy wait for the transfer to complete.
    // The enable_disk_interrupt flag determines whether
    // the interrupt is turned on (it is controlled by a
    // bit in the disk control register).
    disk_control_reg control_reg;

    // assemble the necessary control word
    control_reg.command          = 1;
    control_reg.disk_block       = block_number;
    control_reg.interrupt_enabled = enable_disk_interrupt;

    // store the control words in the disk control register
    *Disk_memory_addr = buffer;
    *Disk_control_reg = control_reg;
}
```

If a different disk were used with different control registers, the disk interface would remain the same even though the implementation details might vary. If the system had two different kinds of disks, they could be accessed using an identical interface. The operating system hides the complexity of device I/O from the user and provides a simpler, easier to use, and more general disk interface.

Abstract disk interfaces are useful and easy to implement and use.

5.9   IMPLEMENTATION OF WAITING

5.9.1   WAITING FOR MESSAGES

There is an interesting problem here that we solved in the code but didn't mention in the commentary, and that is the problem of suspending a system call and completing it later, after another event has occurred. We will discuss the problem first in the context of the send and receive message system calls.

The "natural" order for a message transfer is for the message to be sent before it is received. If a message is sent by SendMessage and the receiver is not waiting for it, the message is put on the message queue. Later, when the ReceiveMessage system call is made on this message queue, the message is transferred to the receiver's message buffer. The SendMessage system call moves the message from the sender's address space into a message buffer in the system's address space, and puts that message buffer on the message queue. The ReceiveMessage system call takes the message buffer off the message queue, and moves the message to the receiver's message buffer in the receiver's address space. (See Figure 5.11.)

But suppose the ReceiveMessage system call occurs before the SendMessage system call.[1] Now we have a problem because the message cannot be received because it hasn't been sent yet. The ReceiveMessage system call cannot be completed immediately because it must wait for the matching SendMessage to occur. The receiving process must be suspended, of course, and this is done by setting its state to blocked. The receiving process will not be selected by the dispatcher, and its memory and registers (its "state") will be preserved. When the matching send message occurs, the SendMessage system call code does double duty. It does the send message work of moving the message into a message queue, but it also does the receive message work if there is a ReceiveMessage system call waiting to be completed. Luckily, we have not signed a contract with the SendMessage code giving a restrictive job description, so we can press it into duty doing receive message work.

See Figure 5.12 for a pictorial view of the two possible timings of the send and the receive. Note the asymmetry of SendMessage and ReceiveMessage. Send

---

[1] This can easily happen if the receiving process starts first.

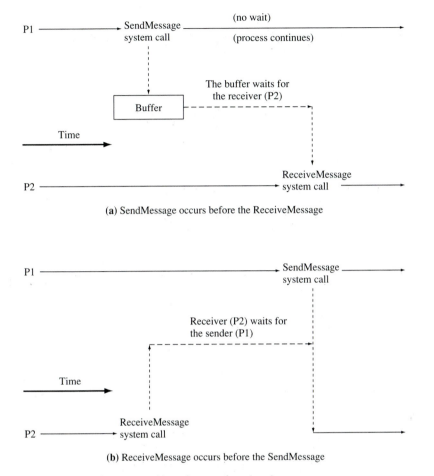

Figure 5.12   The two possible orderings of send and receive message

Message never waits because the message buffer does the waiting for it. The buffer is a proxy waiter for the process making the SendMessage system call. ReceiveMessage does wait unless a message is available.

5.9.2 WAITING INSIDE A SYSTEM CALL

Suspending the process making the receive system call is not enough. The receive system call itself must also be suspended. Remember that once you make a system call, you are no longer executing in the calling process but instead you are executing in the operating system. The operating system "activity" of handling the ReceiveMessage system call cannot complete and must be suspended. But that activity itself also has a state, so we must remember the address in the receiver's address space to put message. This operating system activity of executing the ReceiveMessage system call is not completed, even though we finish the ReceiveMessageSystemCall case of the *switch* in the system call interrupt handler and go on to dispatch another process. Like the "show," the operating system must go on. It cannot complete the ReceiveMessage system call, but it must dispatch other processes or the SendMessage will never occur. The operating system must record that the system call has been made and set things up so it will be completed later.

When the corresponding SendMessage system call is finally executed, it will complete the ReceiveMessage by transferring the message into the receiver's address space. The operating system activity of executing the ReceiveMessage system call was suspended and resumed later, just like a process. In fact, what we have done is implement a facility to block and resume operating system code. For processes, the operating system does this implementation, but there is no suboperating system below this operating system to do this for us. The operating system must handle its own blocking and resuming.

It seems like we have made little progress, since the operating system must solve for itself the same problem that it was supposed to solve for processes. But we *have* made some progress. We have reduced the problem to a simpler case. To suspend a process, we needed to save a lot of information, but to suspend an operating system activity, we only need to save a few words of data. We remembered the fact that the ReceiveMessage system call was not completed in the process state by making the state Blocked, and we put the receiver's process identifier and the system call argument (the receiver's buffer address) in the wait_queue corresponding to the message_queue the message was sent to. We have handled the activity blocking "by hand," that is, by allocating storage and using process states to handle the problem. Our solution to the suspending and receiving problem is not general as is the operating system's solution for processes, but it is specific to this case, a special-purpose solution.

Let us review what we are saying here. The process making the receive system call has a state which includes its memory area and its registers. The operating system will save the registers and ensure that the memory is not modified, and it will suspend the process by marking in its pd that the process is blocked, preventing it from being dispatched. The activity of handling the receive system call, however, is not part of the process making the receive system call; it is an activity of the operating system. (We have chosen another word here, "activity," instead of "process," to make the difference clear.) The operating system activity must also be suspended (and later resumed) because it cannot be completed immediately. The state of this operating system activity (handling the receive system call) is very small (the process's pid and I/O buffer address), and that state is saved in the wait queue. The fact that the ReceiveMessage system call is suspended and must be resumed (and completed) later is recorded by putting the wait structure (including the process ID) on the wait queue that corresponds to the message queue that is being waited on. When the matching send is made, the receive system call activity will be completed.

5.9.3 SUSPENDING SYSTEM CALLS

In general, when we suspend a system call we have to do two things: we have to save the system call arguments that we will need later, and we have to record the fact that the system call needs completion.

When a read disk block system call is made, it cannot be completed because it has to wait for the disk operation to complete. In this case, we save the necessary information in the disk request queue.

To summarize, when the operating system needs to suspend an activity (the processing of a system call), it does the following:

- Finds a place to save the state of the system call for later use, and
- Makes sure the system call will be resumed later by keying it to the event that will allow the system call to be completed.

In the disk scheduler:

- We saved the process ID in the disk request queue.
- The disk interrupt was the event we were waiting for, and we had it complete the system call.

In the receive message system call:

- We saved the receiver's pid and address in the wait queue.
- The SendMessage event finds the wait queue entry and completes the system all.

In Chapter 8 we will see a more general way to handle the problem of suspending system calls.

5.10 FLOW OF CONTROL THROUGH THE OPERATING SYSTEM

Let us look at the flow of control in the system calls as they move through the operating system. This should give you some perspective on the operating system. Figure 5.13 shows the sequence of events of a disk read (or write) system call.

1. System call—disk read (enter SystemCallInterruptHandler).
2. Call Disk IO (operating system procedure).
3. Put request in disk queue.
4. Wake up ScheduleDisk.
5. Get request from disk queue.
6. Start disk controller.
7. Return from ScheduleDisk.
8. Return from Disk IO.
9. Call Dispatcher.
10. Context switch to another process.

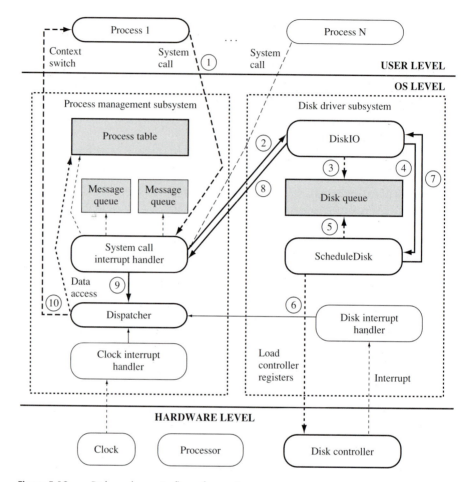

Figure 5.13   Disk read or write flow of control

Figure 5.14 shows the sequence of events of a create process or exit process system call.

1. System call—create process (enter `SystemCallInterruptHandler`).
2. Allocate and initialize process table slot.
3. Call `Dispatcher`.
4. Context switch to another process.

Figure 5.15 shows the sequence of events of a create message queue system call.

1. System call—create message queue (enter `SystemCallInterruptHandler`).
2. Allocate and initialize message queue.
3. Call `Dispatcher`.
4. Context switch to another process.

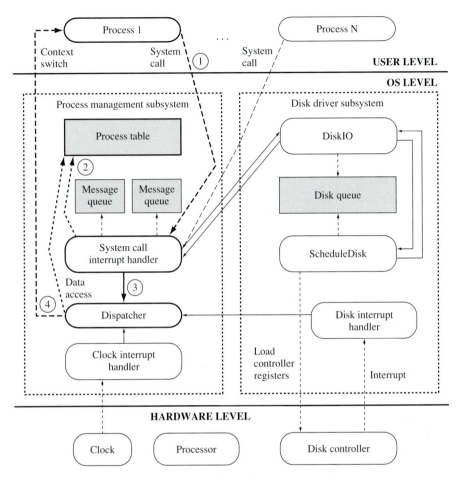

Figure 5.14   Create or exit process flow of control

Figure 5.16 shows the sequence of events of a send (or receive) message system call.

1. System call—send (or receive) message queue (enter `SystemCallInter-ruptHandler`).

2. Allocate message buffer and transfer data into it (for a send) or check if there is a message in the queue (for a receive).

3. For send: if a process is waiting, then transfer the message and unblock the waiting process, or else queue the message. For receive: if message is waiting, then transfer it in, or else block receiver.

4. Call `Dispatcher`.

5. Context switch to another process.

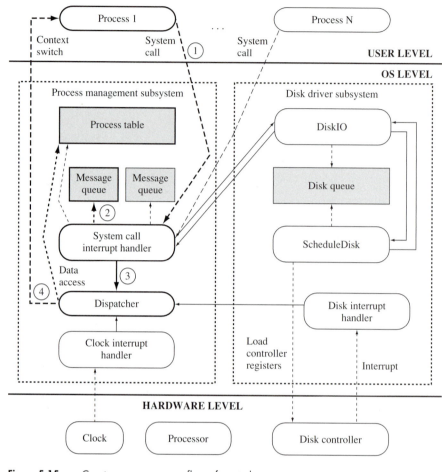

Figure 5.15   Create message queue flow of control

5.11   SIGNALING IN AN OPERATING SYSTEM

The DiskIO and ScheduleDisk procedures communicate principally through the disk queue, but how does ScheduleDisk know when DiskIO has put something in the queue? This is a "signaling problem," and there are various ways to solve it. In this operating system, we simply have DiskIO call ScheduleDisk. But this call has no arguments and does not pass any data. The call signals the fact that data has been put into the disk queue. The purpose of the procedure call is to "wake up" the disk scheduler (if necessary). In Chapter 8, we will see better ways of doing this signaling—ways that do not require a direct transfer of control between the procedures.

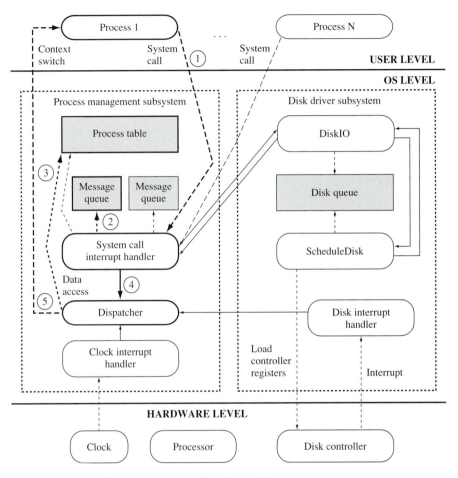

Figure 5.16   Send or receive message flow of control

5.12   INTERRUPTS IN THE OPERATING SYSTEM

We have defined our hardware so that all events are disabled when we enter system mode. The operating system does not enable them while it is in system mode. The context switch back to user mode in the dispatcher will reenable interrupts. This makes it easier to write the operating system code, since we do not have to worry about an interrupt when it is not ready for it. But it is a long time to keep interrupts disabled.

    This is not a realistic restriction for an operating system, since it is generally not a good idea to inhibit interrupts for too long. Some devices (like disks) will just wait, so inhibiting their interrupts only reduces their actual speed of operation, but other devices (like communication lines) cannot be ignored for very long or else data will be lost.

It is not hard to improve this situation by reenabling interrupts while still in system mode, but it requires some careful planning to make this work. For now, let us just look at an example of what could go wrong if we did not have this restriction.

Suppose a process makes a system call, and control enters `SystemCallInterruptHandler`. The procedure saves the register state of `current_process`, and then a disk interrupt occurs. The first action the disk interrupt handler will take is to save the register state into the very same save area (since the value of `current_process` will not have changed yet). The old state will have been lost. This is called a reentrancy failure, since the second time we enter (when we *re*enter) the operating system we write over a common data area. The problem is that the operating system needs a few instructions to save the state of the interrupted process before it can tolerate another interrupt.

5.13　OPERATING SYSTEMS AS EVENT AND TABLE MANAGERS

One useful view of an operating system is as a system that responds to events. Events generally change the process state of one or more processes. Some of the events are generated by the processes themselves (via system calls), and some of the events are generated externally (device interrupts). As such, operating systems are not active but rather are passive entities. They do not do things on their own, but instead respond to events. These are sometimes called *reactive systems*. This type of system can be described by a state machine.

reactive system

What does an operating system do in response to an event? Normally it looks things up in one or more tables, and probably makes some changes in the tables. By *tables* we mean arrays and linked lists of structures. The state of an operating system is the state of its tables.

Here is a table of the events this operating system reacts to and the data structures that are read or changed in responding to each event.

Interrupt	Data Updated	Processing Done
Timer	pd	Switch processes
Disk	pd	Unblock process and start next I/O

System Call	Data Updated	Processing Done
CreateProcess	pd	Initialize process table slot
Exit	pd	Free process table slot
CreateMessageQueue	pd, message_queue	Initialize message queue
SendMessage	pd, message_queue, message_buffer	Queue or transfer message
Receive Message	pd, message_queue, message_buffer	Block process or transfer message
ReadDiskBlock	pd, disk_queue	Queue disk request
WriteDiskBlock	pd, disk_queue	Queue disk request

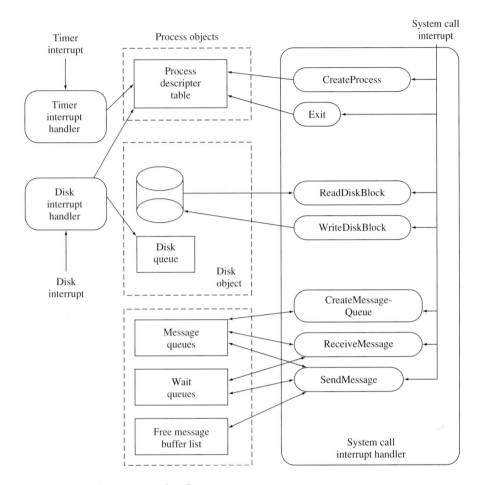

Figure 5.17   Interrupt event handling

Figure 5.17 shows the operating system events and tables and how they interact.

An operating system is a collection of procedures that access and update tables in response to events.

Operating systems are reactive systems—they react to interrupts.

5.14   PROCESS IMPLEMENTATION

In this chapter we have seen the basic ideas of the implementation of processes in an operating system. This implementation rests on a few simple ideas:

- The execution of the operating system code is not a process but implements processes.
- Each process is represented by a data structure called the process descriptor or PD. The process descriptor is kept in the operating system's memory.
- Each process runs on the actual hardware with some provisos:
  - The hardware processor is shared between all processes and is rapidly switched between them.
  - The memory area of each process is restricted using memory mapping hardware.
  - A process is prevented from using certain machine instructions since it runs in user mode.
- A process communicates with the operating system through system calls.
- A process can be interrupted at any time by an interrupt from a device.
- When an interrupt occurs (system call or device interrupt), the operating system gets control, handles the interrupt, and then gives control back to some process.

5.14.1   THE PROCESS TABLE AND PROCESS DESCRIPTORS

process table

process descriptor

The *process table* is the central data structure used to implement processes. It contains an entry, called a *process descriptor* (PD), for each process in the system. The descriptor contains all the information that the operating system needs to know about the process. The PDs in the simple operating system were small and simple, but the PDs in real operating systems contain many other fields. Over the next few chapters, we will continue to add necessary fields to the PD as the operating system requires more information in order to perform more services.

The following list gives some of the fields you might find in a PD:

- Process ID
- Process name
- Memory allocated to the process
- Open files
- Process state
- User name
- User protection privileges
- Register save area

- CPU time used so far
- Pending software interrupts
- Parent process
- User ID.

The process table might be implemented as an array or a linked list, but logically it is a *set* of PDs.

Another process management data structure is the *ready list*. This is a list of the processes that are currently ready to use the processor and so are candidates for dispatching. This might be implemented as a separate list, as a list threading through the PDs, or implicitly in the state field of each PD. The dispatcher needs to pick a process from the ready list each time the operating system is called and completes its work.

ready list

> Process descriptors contain everything the operating system needs to know about a process.

5.15   EXAMPLES OF PROCESS IMPLEMENTATION

All operating systems use a structure similar to what we have described in this chapter. Processes are described by a process descriptor and dispatched by a dispatcher. System calls and interrupts cause control to be transferred to the operating system, which saves the state and handles the event.

Most newer operating systems implement threads as well as processes. In addition, most operating systems allow the processes (or threads) to run in kernel mode. In the next chapter we will see what threads are, how they are implemented, and how they can run in kernel mode.

Most UNIX systems divide up the process descriptor into two parts. One part is always kept in main memory, and the other part is saved on the disk to save space in main memory when the process is idle.

The disk subsystem we described is really a disk driver (see Chapter 15), and a complete operating system would provide a file system (see Chapter 16).

There are several books that give the code of complete operating systems. See Section 5.17.3 for references.

*5.16   MONOPROGRAMMING

In Chapters 3 and 5, we introduced the concept of multiprogramming, that is, running several processes at the same time. Why should we go to all this trouble? Why try to run several processes at the same time? Just run one program at a time. That

monoprogramming

process runs to completion, and then another program is run. This is called *monoprogramming*. Early mainframe operating systems and personal computer operating systems (MS/DOS and the Macintosh OS) worked this way—they ran only one program at a time. There are two reasons for handling the problem this way. One is that if you only have a small amount of memory, it is not worth the trouble to share it since two programs won't fit into the memory anyway. This was the case in early mainframe and PC systems. The other reason to only allow monoprogramming is that it is easier for the operating system to implement.

throughput

Monoprogramming is simple to implement, but it is not really an acceptable solution. What are the reasons for wanting to run more than one program at a time? For noninteractive systems, the only reason was efficiency—specifically *throughput,* getting the most processes run in a given amount of time. If there was only one program in memory, then there was only one program to run. If that program was waiting for I/O, then the memory space and processor time were being wasted since the program was not using them but no other program could use them.

5.16.1   BATCH SYSTEMS

Early computers were slow by today's standards, but the I/O devices were even slower. This was in the days when the input was from cards and the output was to a printer. Reading cards was very slow. The typical fast card readers could read 1000 cards a minute, but that still is only 17 cards a second or one card every 59 milliseconds. Even with the slow computers of the day, this was still thousands of instruction times wasted waiting for each card to be read in. And the printers were not any faster than the card readers.

People soon realized that almost all of a computer's time was spent waiting for I/O operations to complete, and that they had to deal with this problem in order to increase the efficiency of computer use.

batch operating system

The first solution to this problem was to speed up the I/O. But how could they do that since printers and card readers were as fast as they could be with the technology available? The answer was the "batch" operating system. A *batch operating system* would use two computers: a small, slow, cheap computer to read cards onto tape and print lines from tape; and a larger, fast, expensive computer that would read from the tape and write print lines to the tape. (See Figure 5.18.) Reading and writing tape was much faster than reading cards and printing lines. Several jobs would be read onto a tape and the tape carried over to the fast machine. The output of a batch of jobs was written on a tape and the tape was carried back over to the slow computer to be printed. After it was printed you could get your output. The jobs on a single tape were called a *batch*. If you got in at the end of a batch, you would get better turnaround time because you would not have to wait for the batch to fill up. It was like crossing a river on a big ferry that only ran when it was filled with cars.

While batch systems do not exist any more, the word "batch" that came out of these systems is still used in computing to mean noninteractive computation, that is,

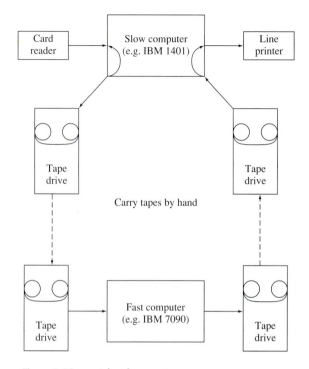

Figure 5.18   A batch operating system

a system where you present your input to the system and then, sometime later, you get your output. Compiling is a batch process in this sense. Word processors like T$_E$X that format a whole document at a time without user input are called batch-style formatters.

5.16.2 MULTIPROGRAMMING AND I/O OVERLAP

Tape I/O was slow compared to the speed of the processor, and the industry had to move on to operating systems that kept more than one program in memory at the same time, that is, *multiprogramming*. This meant that while one program was wait- multiprogramming ing for an I/O operation to complete, another program could be computing, and both the processor and the I/O devices could be kept running at close to maximum speed. The parts of a computer system were expensive, and it was important that they be efficiently used.

A major task of an early operating system was to keep the system in "balance," that is, to keep the processor busy all the time and to keep all the devices running at maximum speed. The way to do this was to keep as many jobs in memory as possible, since then there were more potential users of the processor and I/O devices. The speed of these early systems was determined by how many jobs they could pack into the memory.

Figure 5.19 shows the three stages of I/O overlap: Monoprogramming, with no overlap between computing and I/O; monoprogramming with no overlap but faster I/O; and multiprogramming with overlap between I/O and processing. Figure 5.20 shows how the compute and I/O time were related in these three types of systems.

The table below shows the efficiency of the three methods of reducing the cost of I/O. The third line overlaps input, processing, and output so the efficiency is 100 per cent even though each of these three activities takes as long as it does in line two.

Method	Read Card	Process	Print Line	Process/Total	Efficiency
Slow I/O	60 ms	10 ms	60 ms	10/130	8 %
Fast I/O	10 ms	10 ms	10 ms	10/30	33 %
Overlapped I/O	10 ms	10 ms	10 ms	30/30	100 %

Note that, in multiprogramming systems, individual processes do not run any faster, but more processes are run in a given period of time.

5.16.3   PERSONAL COMPUTER SYSTEMS

Consider the early personal computers (PCs and Macintoshes). They were relatively cheap and there was only one user, so it did not matter whether the I/O devices were used efficiently. A monoprogramming operating system would seem sufficient for them, but this did not turn out to be the case. This is because there is a second reason why you want to run more than one program at a time, and that is because the humans who use computers like to do more than one thing at a time. A person sitting at a computer might be writing a document with a word processor, get a telephone call, and have to look something up in a database. Or the user might have to do a calculation. An irony of early personal computers was the picture of a calculator sitting next to a personal computer. A person working in a word processor does not want to save the file, exit the word processing program, start up the calculator program, do the calculation, write down the answer on a block of paper, exit the calculator program, start up the word processing program, and go back to the place they were working—all just to do a calculation. The same applies to looking up a phone number, making a note on a to-do list, or scheduling an appointment.

People want multiprogramming not for efficiency of computer use but to save their own time. They do not need two programs to be running at the same time, but

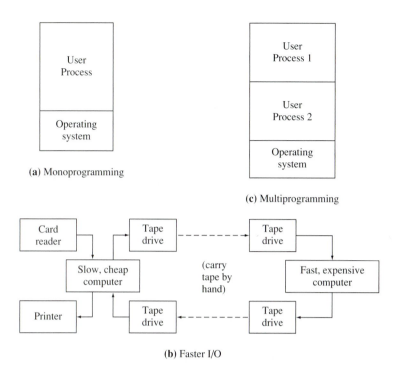

(a) Monoprogramming

(c) Multiprogramming

(b) Faster I/O

Figure 5.19   Monoprogramming, faster I/O, and multiprogramming

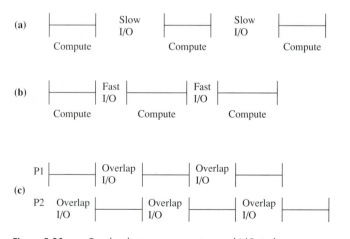

Figure 5.20   Overlap between computing and I/O in these systems

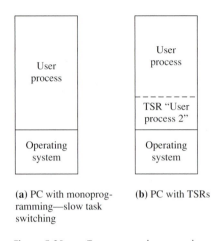

(a) PC with monoprogramming—slow task switching   **(b)** PC with TSRs

Figure 5.21   Terminate and stay resident programs (TSRs) In PCs

they need to be able to switch between programs as they are interrupted without having to save their entire work context and later reestablish it.

Early on in the PC world, people realized this limitation of monoprogramming and tried to find a solution for it. It turned out that a partial solution was available. The crucial thing to realize is that, even in a monoprogramming system, there are really two programs running, the application program and the operating system. The solution is to find a way to add things to the operating system. This was done in PCs with a trick called a TSR (*terminate and stay resident*) program (see Figure 5.21). This was a program that you would run and, when it finished, the operating system would not reclaim the memory it used (that is, it would stay "resident" in memory) so it would, in some sense, become part of the operating system. The TSR would attach itself to the keyboard interrupt (that is, it would arrange to be called whenever a key was pressed) and reactivate when it saw certain special key combinations (such as both shift keys held down at the same time). This TSR program could then start running again while the application program was running, and we would essentially have multiprogramming. The details are not important here, but the scheme did work.[2] The Macintosh operating system had a similar hook, which was something they called a *desk accessory*. These techniques were used until the operating systems started providing a limited form of multiprogramming (Macintoshes using MultiFinder and PCs using DeskView or Windows).

---

[2]One problem that TSRs had to face was that the MS/DOS operating system was not reentrant. If they tried to make an MS/DOS system call while the main application was also making one, then the system might crash. Fortunately, there was a (undocumented) flag you could test to detect and avoid this.

5.17   SUMMARY

The main subject of this chapter is a sample implementation of an operating system that has many of the components of a real operating system but is as simple as possible.

We began by defining the system call interface that the simple operating system will implement. This was a subset of the system call interface we defined in Chapter 3. It included `CreateProcess`, `ExitProcess`, `CreateMessageQueue`, `SendMessage`, `ReceiveMessage`, `ReadDiskBlock`, and `WriteDiskBlock`.

The simple operating system contains two subsystems: process management and the disk driver. The process management subsystem is larger and implements processes, dispatching, system call interrupt handling, and messages. The disk driver supports reading and writing of disk blocks.

An operating system maintains a number of tables and data structures. Each system object (a process, a message, a message queue, a disk, a disk request) has an associated data structure, and these are kept in tables or queues. An operating system responds to events (timer interrupts, disk interrupts, program exception, system calls) by consulting and modifying these data structures.

A process is executed by loading its context (the hardware registers it uses). Since this context includes the *base* and *bound* registers, the context defines not only the registers but the area of memory used by the process. The operating system switches processes by switching process contexts.

Each process has its own stack, and the operating system itself has a stack. When the system is in user mode, it is using the stack of some process. When the system is in system mode, it is using the system stack.

System calls are handled by a large case statement, with one case for each system call.

The disk driver subsystem contains two parts. The upper part receives disk requests from system calls and puts them on a queue of disk requests. The lower part of the disk driver subsystem takes disk requests from the disk queue and executes them on the disk.

Messages are buffered so they can be sent before they are received. This allows the sending process to do other things instead of having to wait for the receiver. A process making a receive message system call may have to wait until the message is sent. Doing this requires the simple operating system to be able to suspend a system call because we have to suspend the receive message system call and let other processes run.

There are two reasons we want to have several processes in memory at the same time: efficiency of resource use, and responsiveness to user demands.

5.17.1   Terminology

After reading this chapter, you should be familiar with the following terms:

- architecture
- batch operating system

- blocked (process state)
- context
- (full) context switch
- disk driver subsystem
- dispatch
- dispatcher
- half-context switch
- initial process
- monoprogramming
- multiprogramming
- preemptive scheduling
- process descriptor
- process management subsystem
- process state
- process table
- quantum
- reactive system
- ready (process state)
- ready list
- running (process state)
- system call interrupt handler
- system stack
- throughput
- time sharing
- time slice
- timer interrupt handler

5.17.2   REVIEW QUESTIONS

The following questions are answered in the text of this chapter:

1. What are the three objects the simple operating system implements, and what operations are allowed on them?

2. What are the two main subsystems of the simple operating system, and what are their functions?

3. Why are two Queue data structures required for each message queue?

4. What is the `TimeQuantum` constant used for?

5. Why does the process descriptor have a `TimeLeft` field? What is it used for?

6. Why is the initial psw set to 3 in `CreateProcessSysProc`?

7. What are the two reasons a process can be blocked?

8. Explain what process dispatching is.

9. If a process makes a system call that does not block (for example a `SendMessage` system call), it will be dispatched again after the system call. Where is the code that ensures this will happen?

10. What is the purpose of the `next_proc` variable in the procedure `SelectProcessToRun`, and why is it declared static?

11. Why does the operating system need a stack?

12. What does it mean when the timer interrupts? State this is terms of what is going on in the simple operating system.

13. What is the initial process?

14. What makes it hard to copy messages from a user process to the operating system message buffers?

15. Why is it necessary for `DiskIO` to call `ScheduleDisk`?

16. Which system calls might not be able to be completed immediately when they are first called?

17. Why is it hard to delay the completion of a system call?

18. Why do we call the operating system an event and table manager?

19. What are the advantages of multiprogramming over monoprogramming?

5.17.3 FURTHER READING

Horning and Randell (1976) look at the concept of a process independent of any particular operating system.

Comer's book on XINU (Comer 1984) gives a complete implementation of a simple operating system. Tanenbaum (1987) also gives a complete implementation of a simple operating system called MINIX. The NACHOS operating system is another complete operating system available for educational use. It can be obtained from `http://http.cs.berkeley.edu/~tea/nachos/`.

John Lions of The University of New South Wales in Australia published the complete code and a useful commentary on an early version of UNIX (Level Six). These books were published by the University of New South Wales and later by Bell Laboratories, but are no longer available.

5.18 PROBLEMS

1. In implementing process timing, we had to check how much time was left on the timer when a process was interrupted. Why would a process have time left if it was interrupted?

2. The process table contains all the information the operating system keeps about each process. The process table is normally kept in the operating system's own memory and is not accessible by user processes. Why don't the user processes need access to the process table?

Could we put the process table information for each process in the address space of each process? What problems would that cause?

3. Section 5.12 gives an example of the problems that can occur if you allow interrupts while the operating system is running. Give a different example of a problem that can occur if the operating system could be interrupted.

4. In the process dispatcher code, there is a procedure named SelectProcessToRun. It will return the current value of current_process immediately if three conditions hold. Explain how it might come about that each one of the three conditions might fail to hold, that is, how could it happen that:

$\leq$

a. current_process $\neq$ 0

b. pd[current_process].state != Ready

c. pd[current_process].timeLeft == 0

d. pd[current_process].slotAllocated == False

Suppose that one or more of these conditions is false, and we start going through pd to find a process to run. Is it possible that SelectProcessToRun still might return the current value of current_process? Explain how it can happen or why it can't happen.

5. Suppose we wanted to change the message size used in the simple operating system from 8 words to 1024 words. What changes in the code would be required? What would be the effect of this change on users of the operating system? Give some good and some bad effects.

6. When we load a process from disk, we do not turn on the disk interrupt and wait for the disk I/O. Explain why it would be hard to use the disk interrupts for this loading. *Hint:* How would you wait for it?

7. Modify the simple operating system to have two types of blocked states: BlockedOnDIskIO and BlockedOnReceive. Make sure the state always reflects the correct reason the process is blocked.

8. The time quantum for this operating system was set at 100 milliseconds. Modern operating systems often use a quantum of 10 milliseconds. What do you think is the lowest reasonable value of the time quantum? *Hint:* Consider the overhead of context switching.

9. In Section 5.2.3 on system constants, the event handler offsets are set to 0, 4, 8, and 12. What is the hardware basis of these numbers?

10. In the message systems we have seen so far, message receivers must wait for message senders, but message senders do not ever wait for message receivers. Explain why that is. Why don't message senders ever have to wait?

11. The program loader in the simple operating system is very primitive. It assumes that the initial program counter is at word 0 of the program, and that the disk block contains an exact image of how the program should appear in memory. In this problem, we will describe a more complex program format and ask you to modify the program loader to handle this new format.

The program is assumed to reside in consecutive disk blocks starting with the disk block number passed to `CreateProcessSysProc`. The first block contains three words of header information and the first 4084 bytes of the program image itself (assuming disk blocks of 4096 bytes each). The format is:

- Word 0 (bytes 0–3): A special bit pattern to mark this as an executable program. This pattern will always be `0x80808080`. Do not load the program unless this bit pattern is present (since that would indicate that this is not really an executable program).

- Word 1 (bytes 4–7): The number of bytes in the executable program. The first 4084 will be in this block and the rest will be in following disk blocks.

- Word 2 (bytes 8–11): The initial program counter to set when the program is started.

Rewrite `CreateProcessSysProc` to handle this format for executable programs.

12. The simple operating system does not have a `Wait` system call that allows a process to wait for a child process. Specify and implement a `Wait` system call. Model it after the `Wait` system call in Chapter 3. Be sure to keep the return code from the `Exit` and pass it on to the `Wait`. Be sure to handle both cases: (1) where the `Exit` occurs before the `Wait`, and (2) where the `Wait` occurs before the `Exit`. You will have to add several fields to the process descriptor to store the information you will have to keep. You will have to add a new process state. You will have to modify `Exit` and write `Wait`.

13. System calls are much more expensive than procedure calls. In this question, we will estimate how much more expensive. Use the machine we defined in Chapter 2 and assume that all instructions take the same amount of time.

First estimate the cost of a procedure call that passes one argument but does not do any actual processing. Just count the time to set up the stack, make the call, and then return.

Then estimate the cost of a system call that passes in one argument. There will be no actual system call processing. Include the time to set up the stack, make the system call, do the first-level interrupt handling (saving the registers), and dispatch another process. Look at the C++ code and make estimates of how many instructions they would require.

14. Suppose we wanted to add a system call that would block the process for a number of microseconds (the number is an argument to the system call). To do this, we have to multiplex the clock. Implement this system call in the simple operating system. Use the hardware interval timer. To make this problem simpler, assume that the simple operating system will *not* be using the timer for process time slices. Assume it uses some other timer to do that. *Hint:* A virtual timer will be an entry in a list kept in time order. The time interrupts when the first entry in the list expires.

15. Consider the following C program for execution on a UNIX system.

```
/* #define NOSYSCALL */
#ifdef NOSYSCALL
int getpid() { return 55; }
#endif
int main( int argc, char * argv[] ) {
    int i, a, limit = atoi(argv[1]);
    for( i = 0; i < limit; ++ i ) a = getpid();
}
```

The system call `getpid` performs almost no processing. It looks up your pid and returns it. All the time it takes is system call overhead that is present in every system call. Likewise, the procedure call `getpid` does nothing but return a value. All the time it takes is procedure call overhead that is present in every procedure call.

Run this program for a million or two iterations and see how long it takes. Then uncomment out the `#define` and run it for 30 or 40 million iterations and see how long it takes. What do you conclude about the relative speed of a system call and a procedure call?

16. Suppose we wanted to change the disk I/O system call so that it did not wait for the disk transfer to complete but returned immediately. Describe the changes to the simple operating system required to implement this change.

One problem with this change is there is no sure way for the process to know when the disk transfer is completed. Describe a method of solving this problem. This will be a new system call (or calls) or a change to an existing one (or ones). Just describe the new or changed system call(s). You do not have to say how to implement it.

17. Suppose we wanted to record how long each process executes. Add code to the operating system to do this. You will need to use the microsecond interval timer register for doing the timing. Add a field to the process descriptor to record the time used. Try not to count the time in the operating system against any process.

18. Implement the following change to the simple OS. When a process makes a system call, the time it has remaining is recorded. The next time it executes, it gets that time plus 100 more milliseconds. But no process can get more than 300 milliseconds.

19. Suppose we decided to keep track of which process creates a message queue, and to destroy the message queue automatically when the process that created it exits. What problem would this solve? What problem would this cause?

20. In `CreateProcessSysProc` (in Section 5.3.1), we read in the code for the process from the disk and busy wait for each disk block to be read (this is near the end of `CreateProcessSysProc`). Now consider the discussion in Section 5.8 about waiting for events inside of a system call. We can use the same techniques that we used in the read disk block system call and the receive message system call to eliminate this busy waiting. Sketch out how that would be done. What exactly do we have to do and when do we do it?

21. Add a new system call `DestroyMessageQueue`. This will allow the message queue to be used over again. Specify the call and show how to implement it. Make sure it returns any message buffers in the queue to the free buffer pool. Keep track of the message queues that are still active, and change `CreateMessageQueue` so that it will reuse message queues that have been destroyed.

Then change Exit so that, when a process exits, any message queues it has created will be destroyed automatically.

22. Consider the code for `Receive Message` in the simple operating system. Suppose we want to change the system call so that there is one more parameter called `Wait-ForMessage`. If this new parameter is 1, then the system call works just like it does now, but if the parameter is 0 and there is no message waiting in the message queue, the system call returns immediately with an error code indicating no message is waiting. This allows a process to find out if a message is waiting without being blocked until a message arrives.

Modify the code in the system call interrupt handler to implement this new version of `ReceiveMessage`.

23. Processes "call" the operating system with system call interrupt instructions. Why can't processes make ordinary procedure calls to call the operating system? Why do we need a separate facility that is much more expensive than procedure calls?

24. Consider the two varieties of process creation we looked at:

   a. Create-process—where the process-related system calls are `CreateProcess1`, `Wait1`, and `Exit1`. The `CreateProcess1` call specifies the program to run in the new process.

   b. Fork-exec—where the process-related system calls are `Fork2`, `Exec2`, `Wait2`, and `Exit2`. The `Fork2` call creates a duplicate of the calling process. The `Exec2` call specifies a program to run in the calling process.

Suppose our operating system implemented the fork-exec style of process creation. Could we implement a library of routines (`CreateProcess1`, `Wait1`, and `Exit1`) that implemented the create-process style of process creating, using the fork-exec style system calls?

How about the other direction? Can we implement the fork-exec system calls using the create-process system calls?

In both cases describe how each of the implementations would be done (if they are possible).

25. Right now, the `SendMessage` system call assumes a free message buffer is available for the message. Suppose we want to modify it to check to see if a free message buffer is available and, if not, wait until one is available. The send message system caller will be blocked until a free message buffer becomes available. Modify the system call interrupt handler to implement this new version of `SendMessage`.

26. Suppose we added three more disks to the system. What changes to the disk I/O system will this cause?

27. Consider the procedure CopyToSystemSpace on page 131. Where is the other place in the operating system that we copy data from the process's address space into the operating system's address space?

28. Compare the three different concepts: procedure call, system call, and context switch. How are they different and how are they the same?

29. Pick an operating system that you have access to and find out the command that lists out the processes in the system. (This is the ps command in UNIX.) Read the documentation for the command, and from it figure out the fields that are in the process descriptors of this operating system.

30. Does it make sense for the operating system to make a system call? Why or why not?

31. Describe some noncomputer situations where batch processing is done. Think about things like offices, stores, amusement parks, parking, dealing with the government, processing forms, etc.

6

Parallel Systems

In Chapter 5, we implemented a simple operating system that allowed user processes to operate in pseudo-parallel. By **pseudo-parallel** we mean that the processes run in an interleaved fashion with the appearance of running in parallel, although they do not literally run at the same time since there is only a single processor in the computer system. A user process can get interrupted at any time, that is, between any two instructions, and cannot predict when another process might get control of the processor.

Some computer systems have more than one processor. In fact, this is becoming quite common. In these systems, we can have **true parallelism** where we have two processes executing simultaneously. Figure 6.1 shows the differences between pseudo-parallelism and true parallelism. Both pseudo-parallelism and true parallelism can cause problems for processes that do not take care in how they handle their communication with other processes. In fact, the problems that come up are the same in both types of systems, although the very lowest-level solutions are a little harder in a true parallel system.

True parallelism is also called **physical parallelism.** We use the term "physical" because there is more than one physical processor running in parallel. Another name for pseudo-parallelism is **logical parallelism.** We use the term "logical" because it is not true or physical parallelism, but it shares many of the logical characteristics and problems with physical parallelism.

In this chapter, we will introduce the topic of parallel systems. First, we will look at a two-processor version of our example hardware, and show how to extend our simple operating system to run on this new hardware. In the course of this, we will see the problems of parallelism that come up and see one way to solve them. Then we will examine the idea of threads, see how to implement threads for user processes, and then see how to implement threads inside the operating system. In the next chapter, we will examine common patterns of communication between systems running in parallel.

In our simple operating system, we avoided problems of logical parallelism inside the operating system itself by not allowing interrupts while executing operating system code. This made the system simpler and allowed us to concentrate on other issues. But now we want to examine the problems of parallelism. Rather than allow

pseudo-parallel
true parallelism
physical parallelism
logical parallelism

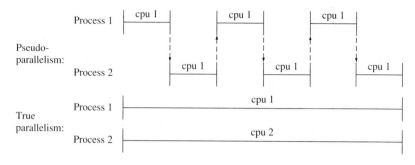

Figure 6.1   Pseudo-parallelism and true parallelism

interrupts in operating system code to allow logical parallelism (we will do this later, in Section 6.8), we will add a second processor and allow true parallelism.

The same sort of problems appear in logical parallelism and physical parallelism.

6.1   PARALLEL HARDWARE

By two processors, we mean two CPUs as described in Chapter 2 and shown in Figure 6.2. In particular, each processor will have its own set of registers. The two processors share the memory, and each has access to all locations in the memory. A disk interrupt will go to either processor, but only to one of them. A system call or program error interrupt will go to the processor that executed the system call

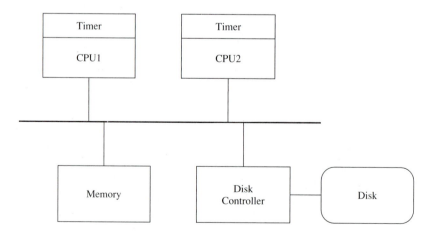

Figure 6.2   A two-processor system

instruction or the instruction that caused the program error. There will be two interval timers, one for each processor. Each timer will belong to a processor, and its interrupts will go to that processor.

6.2 AN OPERATING SYSTEM FOR A TWO-PROCESSOR SYSTEM

How can we extend our simple operating system to run on a two-processor system? There seem to be two possibilities. We can have a separate operating system for each processor, or we can share the operating system between the two processors.

6.2.1 USING TWO SEPARATE OPERATING SYSTEMS

The two processors share a common memory. We could divide this memory into two parts and allocate one part to each processor. Each processor would have its own operating system in its part of memory. (See Figure 6.3.) Each processor and operating system would operate independently. Each would have its own set of processors and its own process table.

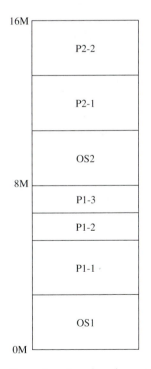

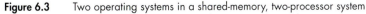

Figure 6.3   Two operating systems in a shared-memory, two-processor system

This organization will work, but there are several reasons why we do not want to do this.

- Two operating systems must reside in memory, taking twice the space a shared operating system would take.

- Processes in the two systems would not be able to communicate easily.

- We assume that the operating system controls the hardware, but then which processor controls the memory and disk (of which there is only one)?

- We have a single machine with two processors, so we should have a single operating system.

The two-operating-system solution is not a good one.

6.2.2 SHARING THE OPERATING SYSTEM

The second solution is to have both processors share a single copy of the operating system. As you might expect, we will have to make some changes to the operating system to make this work, but the changes are not too difficult. In this chapter, we will show what changes are necessary and why.

First, we will examine in more detail what exactly we mean by sharing the operating system. Then we will look at what problems the sharing might cause. Finally, we will look at the solution to these problems.

Figure 6.4 shows one view of the configuration. There will be only one copy of the operating system code. Both processors share this code, and they might even be executing in the operating system code at exactly the same time. But there is no problem with this, since the code is read-only. Each processor can be fetching instructions from the code at the same time, and they will not interfere with each other.

Each processor has its own set of registers. Each processor will have its own system stack. They cannot share a system stack since they both write into the stack and they would write over each other's data. All local variables in a procedure go onto the stack, so while a processor is running in the operating system, the local variables in the procedures it uses will be on its own system stack. So even if both processors are executing the same procedure, they will have their own copies of the local variables.

But what about the global variables in the operating system? We can make separate copies of some of the global variables and allow each processor to have its own copy. We can see these separate data areas in Figure 6.4. Some global data, however, require that we maintain only one copy of the data, and so it must be shared between the processors. This is the area where we will have to be more careful.

Let's look at our simple operating system and see what data are global.[1] The global data are:

---

[1] Our operating system does not have any static data, but if it did we would treat it just like the global data.

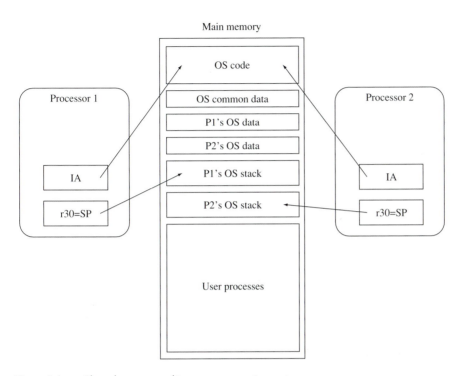

Figure 6.4   Shared memory multiprocessor operating system

1. The stack—`SystemStack`.
2. The current process—`current_process`.
3. The process using the disk—`process_using_disk`.
4. The disk queue—`disk_queue`.
5. The process table—`pd`.
6. The message queue data—`message_buffer, free_message_buffer, valid_message_queues, message_queue,` and `wait_queue`.

In converting from a single processor to a multiprocessor system, we have two options with global data. The easiest course is to have two copies of the data, one for each processor. This means that the two processors do not have to share the data, and so there are no sharing problems. We have seen that the system stack is duplicated, and each processor has its own private stack. Some data cannot be duplicated, however, and for these we have to deal with the problems of sharing.

We will duplicate the current process variable (`p1_current_process` and `p2_current_process`), since each processor will have its own current process that it is running.

The process table, the disk queue, and the message queues must be shared between the processors, and some precautions must be taken to make this sharing work.

First we will look at the kinds of problems that can occur, and then we will present a solution to these problems.

> Some global data in a multiprocessor operating system can be duplicated for each processor, but some must be shared between the processors.

6.3   RACE CONDITIONS WITH A SHARED PROCESS TABLE

A problem can occur if both processors try to examine and modify the process table (pd) at the same time. Consider the following sequence of events:

1. The process running on processor 1 makes a system call and is blocked, and so processor 1 starts looking for another process to run.
2. The process running on processor 2 makes a system call and is blocked, and so processor 2 starts looking for another process to run.
3. Processor 1 finds that pd[10].state == Ready, but at exactly the same time . . .
4. Processor 2 finds that pd[10].state == Ready.
5. Processor 1 sets pd[10].state = Running.
6. Processor 2 sets pd[10].state = Running.
7. Processor 1 starts running the process in pd[10].
8. Processor 2 starts running the process in pd[10].

(See Figure 6.5.) We do not want both processors to be running the same process at the same time. It is wasteful, and because of the unpredictable rates at which the two processors execute instructions, the process will not run correctly.

race condition
   This situation is called a race condition. A *race condition* is a situation where two processes are interacting in some way, and the relative speed at which the processes run will affect the output they produce.

   The problem is that there is a delay between the time a processor finds out that the process is Ready and the time it sets the state to Running. During this delay, the other processor can examine the state of the same process. The solution to the problem is to make the reading of the old value of the process state and the writing of the new value into a single action by one processor that does not allow the other processor to read the process state until the first processor has read and changed it.

> A race condition is a situation where the relative timing of the events in two separate processes could affect their output.

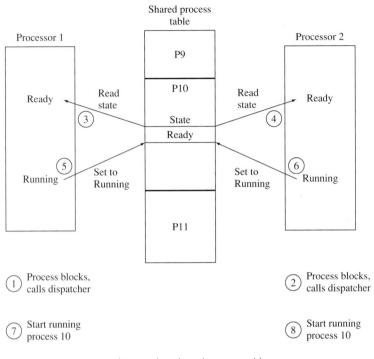

Figure 6.5   Race condition with a shared process table

6.4   ATOMIC ACTIONS

Memory hardware ensures that a single read or write of a memory cell cannot overlap with another read or write. If one processor tries to read a memory cell at the same time another processor tries to write it, the reading processor will get either the old value or the new value. It will not get a word that is a combination of the old and new values. The hardware ensures that a write (or a read) is an *atomic action,* that is, two writes (or a read and a write) cannot overlap each other. If two writes are requested at exactly the same time, the memory arbitrarily picks one of them to go first, and the resulting value in the memory location will contain either one value or the other, and *not* a combination of the two.

atomic action

As we said, the problem is that reading the process's `state` variable and writing a new value in it is not an atomic operation, that is, two read-then-write operations can be interleaved, and this is what causes the problem.

One solution is to appeal to the memory-accessing hardware to define an atomic read-then-write operation. This is, in fact, how most machines solve this problem. The hardware defines an operation that reads the current contents of a memory cell and writes a new value there as an atomic operation. One form of this operation is called *ExchangeWord*, and it exchanges the contents of a memory cell and a hardware register as an atomic operation. Consider the following situation:

1. Memory cell 200000 contains a 0.
2. Processor 1 sets its R1 to 1.
3. Processor 2 sets its R2 to 2.
4. Processor 1 executes ExchangeWord(R1,200000) at exactly the same time as . . .
5. Processor 2 executes ExchangeWord(R2,200000).

After this happens, either:

1. $R1 = 0$, $R2 = 1$, and memory(200000) = 2, or
2. $R1 = 2$, $R2 = 0$, and memory(200000) = 1.

It is not possible that the two operations overlapped, so we get either:

1. $R1 = 0$, $R2 = 0$, and memory(200000) = 2, or
2. $R1 = 0$, $R2 = 0$, and memory(200000) = 1.

The four events of interest are:

1. P1 read.
2. P1 write.
3. P2 read.
4. P2 write.

We know that ExchangeWord has to read the cell before it can write it or the value would be lost, so we have: $time(P1read) < time(P1write)$, and $time(P2read) < time(P2write)$. The ExchangeWord instruction ensures that: $time(P1write) < time(P2read)$, or $time(P2write) < time(P1read)$. So only two of the six possible orderings of these events are possible. Figure 6.6 shows this graphically.

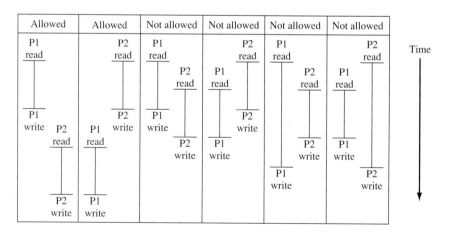

Figure 6.6   ExchangeWord is an atomic operation and cannot be overlapped with another ExchangeWord

This instruction allows us to solve the problems of sharing the process table and the message queues. Now we can proceed and show the modified operating system.

An atomic action is one where no intermediate state (between the beginning of the atomic action and the end) can be seen by any other process.

6.4.1   HARDWARE IMPLEMENTATION OF ATOMIC ACTIONS

To implement the `ExchangeWord` instruction, the hardware has to read and then write a memory cell without any possibility of the other processor accessing the cell between the read and the write. If you look back at Figure 6.2, you can see that the only way either processor can access a memory cell is by communicating with the memory module over the system bus. In order to use the system bus you must become a *bus master*. There is a hardware unit that grants bus mastership to the processors and controllers that request it. Normally, you are bus master for one bus cycle, which is long enough to read or write a memory cell.

The `ExchangeWord` instruction is implemented by allowing a processor to remain bus master for two consecutive bus cycles. This is long enough to read a cell and then write it. Since no other processor can gain access to the bus, it cannot access the cell during this time.

The Intel 80486, Pentium, and i860 processors have an interesting variant of this idea. They have an instruction that holds the bus for 30 bus cycles. You then have 30 cycles to do whatever uninterruptable things you need to do. You can release the bus early, but if you do nothing the bus is always released after 30 bus cycles. This is usually enough time to get an atomic action done. An instruction like this gives the programmer more flexibility and allows the construction of custom atomic actions that exactly fit the current needs of the programmer.

6.5   A MULTIPROCESSOR OPERATING SYSTEM

In this section, we will discuss a multiprocessor version of our simple operating system. We will show only the parts that need to be changed because of the presence of two processors instead of just one. First, here are the global data definitions.

PROCESS DESCRIPTORS

```
//... Most of what we had before plus:
//
//OPERATING SYSTEM ***PER PROCESSOR*** GLOBAL DATA
//
//Each processor is running a process (its "current" process)
int p1_current_process;
```

```
    int p2_current_process;

    // Each processor has its own system stack
    int p1_SystemStack[SystemStackSize];
    int p2_SystemStack[SystemStackSize];

    //
    // OPERATING SYSTEM ***SHARED*** GLOBAL DATA
    //
    ProcessDescriptor pd[NumberOfProcesses]; //pd[0] is the system

    // the message buffers
    typedef int MessageBuffer[MessageSize];
    MessageBuffer message_buffer[NumberOfMessageBuffers];
    int free_message_buffer;

    // the message queues
    int message_queue_allocated[NumberOfMessageQueues];
    Queue<MessageBuffer *> * message_queue[NumberOfMessageQueues];
    Queue<WaitQueueItem *> * wait_queue[NumberOfMessageQueues];

    // the disk queue
    int process_using_disk;
    Queue<DiskRequest *> disk_queue;
```

The system initialization must be done by a single processor. We will assume that processor 1 starts running alone and does the initialization of its own data and the shared data (the process table, the disk queue, and the message queues). Then, at the end of the initialization, processor 1 starts processor 2, and processor 2 initializes its own stack and **p2_current_process**. After that they are both running and will call the Dispatcher to choose a process to run.

SYSTEM INITIALIZATION

```
int main( void ) {//Processor 1 system initialization
                //assumes processor 2 is not running yet
    // Set up the system's stack
    asm { load p1_SystemStack+SystemStackSize,r30 }
    // set up the interrupt vectors
    //. . . as before
    // set up the pds
    //. . . as before
    // process 1 is the initialization process
    //. . . as before
    // set up the pool of free message buffers
    //. . . as before
    process_using_disk = 0;
    p1_current_process = 0;
    //start processor 2
    Dispatcher();
}
```

```
int main( void ) { // Processor 2 system initialization
    // Set up the system's stack
    asm{ load p2_SystemStack+SystemStackSize,r30 }
    p2_current_process = 0;
    Dispatcher();
}
```

6.5.1 THE CURRENT PROCESS VARIABLE

Each processor will have to use its own current_process variable (p1_current_process and p2_current_process). This variable occurs throughout the code, and we will not show all the places where it occurs even though each one has to be changed. Each time current_process is accessed, the processor has to check which processor it is and use the correct one. We might decide to make it an array of length two, and have the processor number in a register that is used to index into the array.

6.5.2 DISPATCHING WITH A SHARED PROCESS TABLE

We have seen the problems that can occur if both processors try to pick a process to run at the same time. We will deal with this problem by only allowing one processor at a time to access the process table. If a processor wants to use the process table while it is in use, then it will have to wait.

We use the ExchangeWord instruction to implement this waiting. First we define procedures to call to gain exclusive use of the process table.

PROTECTING ACCESS TO THE PROCESS TABLE

```
// A global variable to restricts access to the process table
int ProcessTableFreeFlag = 1;

void StartUsingProcessTable( void ) {
    int flag;
    while( 1 ) {
        asm{
            move r0,r1
            exchangeword r1,ProcessTableFreeFlag
            store r1,flag
        }
        // Busy wait until you get a 1 from the shared flag.
        if( flag == 1 )
            break;
    }
}
void FinishUsingProcessTable( void ) {
    ProcessTableFreeFlag = 1;
}
```

The flag ProcessTableFreeFlag starts out at 1, and a call to StartUsing-ProcessTable sets it to 0. Subsequent calls to StartUsingProcessTable will stay in the while loop until the first processor executes FinishUsingProcessTable and sets ProcessTableFreeFlag back to 1.

Note that even if two processors call StartUsingProcessTable at the same time, the ExchangeWord instruction will ensure that only one of them will see a 1. Thus one processor will drop out of the loop and start accessing the process table, but the other processor will continue looping until ProcessTableFreeFlag is set back to 1.

The following code shows how the dispatcher is changed to adapt the system to two processors. The procedures Dispatcher and RunProcess are unchanged.

PROCESS DISPATCHING AND SCHEDULING

```
int SelectProcessToRun( void ) {
    static int next_proc = NumberOfProcesses;
    int i, return_value = -1;
    // Get exclusive access to the (shared) process table.
    StartUsingProcessTable();  // <——————— NEW CODE
    // Figure out which current_process to use.
    int current_process;
    if( ProcessorExecutingThisCode() == 1 )
        current_process = p1_current_process;
    else
        current_process = p2_current_process;
    if( current_process > 0
     && pd[current_process].state == Ready
     && pd[current_process].timeLeft > 0 ) {     pd[next_proc].state =Running!
      return_value = current_process;
    } else {
      for( i = 1; i < NumberOfProcesses; ++i ) {
          if( ++next_proc >= NumberOfProcesses )
              // Slot 0 and pid 0 are reserved for the OS.
              next_proc = 1;
          if( pd[next_proc].slotAllocated
   should be     && pd[next_proc].state == Ready ) {
   indented          pd[next_proc].state = Running;
                     pd[next_proc].timeLeft = TimeQuantum;
                     return_value = next_proc;
                     break;
              }
          }
    }
    // Release exclusive access to the process table.
    FinishUsingProcessTable(); // <——————— NEW CODE
    return return_value;
}
```

The only change is the call to `StartUsingProcessTable` before you begin the search loop and the call to `FinishUsingProcessTable` after the search loop is completed and the state of the selected process is changed. This ensures that only one processor at a time will be searching for a process to run. If they both want to do this at the same time one of the processors will have to wait inside `SelectProcessToRun` until the other processor has chosen a process to run and set its process state to Running.

6.5.3   BUSY WAITING

In the code given above we were trying to prevent two different processors from using the process table at the same time. The way we did this was to require each processor to enter a waiting loop (inside of `StartUsingProcessTable`) before it used the process table. The loop was structured so that the processor executed the *ExchangeWord* instruction over and over again until it found a 1 in the `ProcessTableFreeFlag` variable. This means that the processor is executing in this loop while it is waiting to use the process table. We call this *busy waiting* because the processor is busy executing instructions while it is waiting. We can contrast this with a processor that is idle while it is waiting for an interrupt.

busy waiting

You might wonder if the processor could find something more useful to do while it is waiting for permission to use the process table. There are several problems in trying to find other work for the processor. First it is not clear what other work it could do. It is waiting for the process table in order to find a process to run. This implies it does not have anything else to do anyway. But suppose we had some background process that was always ready to run and which the processor can switch to while it is waiting. Even if the processor found something useful to do, the time it has to wait is fairly small. The other processor will only execute a few hundred instructions in searching the process table. If you consider the time it takes to switch in another process to run and then switch it out again when the process table becomes free there is very little time left for any actual computing. A final problem is how the processor can be informed when the other processor has finished and the process table is available for use. The processor will have to periodically check to see if there is a 1 in `ProcessTableFreeFlag`. This checking has to be included in the background process.

Given these problems it is just as efficient to busy wait than to try to find something else for the processor to do.

The variable `ProcessTableFreeFlag` and the code that uses it is called a *spin lock*. It is a lock because it protects a shared variable. It is a spin lock because busy waiting is roughly analogous to spinning. You can think of the *ExchangeWord* instruction spinning variables between the register and the lock variable.

spin lock

6.5.4   HANDLING THE QUEUES

What we have just seen is a general technique that can be used to protect access to any shared variables and that constitutes a general solution to those problems in a multiprocessor system. The one drawback is that a processor may have to busy wait for the other processor and hence waste processor time.

We can use the same solution to protect access to the disk queue and the message queues. In this case, we will not show the exact code, but will show graphically how the solution works for the message queues.

In Figure 6.7, the "Key" is the permission to access the message queues gained by getting the "1" flag using the `ExchangeWord` instruction. Once you have the key, you can enter the room and access the message queues. If the other CPU comes along, then it will have to wait until you replace the key by putting the "1" back in the flag variable.

6.5.5   GROUPING OF SHARED VARIABLES

We have considered all the message queues together as a single area of shared memory, and allowed only one processor to access the area at a time. But we could be more permissive than this without causing any problems. It is okay if two processors access two *different* message queues at the same time. We only have a problem if two processors try to access the same message queue simultaneously. So instead of having a message queue flag for all the message queues, we could have a separate one for each message queue. (See Figure 6.8.) This technique would forbid simultaneous access only when absolutely necessary, and so will allow more parallelism.

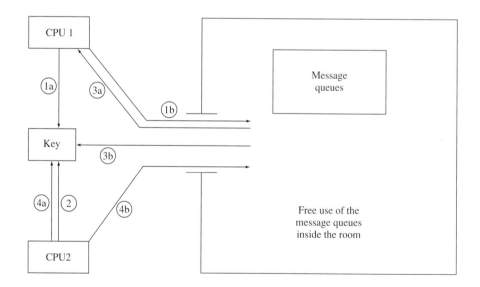

1. CPU1 (a) gets key and (b) enters the room.
2. CPU2 fails to get the key but keeps on trying.
3. CPU1 (a) leaves the room and (b) returns the key.
4. CPU2 (a) succeeds in getting the key and (b) enters the room.

Figure 6.7   Message queues protected by mutual exclusion

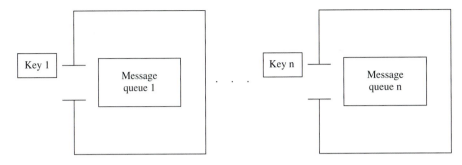

Figure 6.8   Individual message queues protected by mutual exclusion

6.5.6   A GENERAL SOLUTION

The way we have handled the flags means that we need a separate pair of procedures for each shared memory area we want to protect. This would be a problem if we decided to make each message queue a separate shared memory area.

If we pass in the shared memory flag into the procedures, we can reuse the same procedures for all shared memory areas.

PROTECTING ACCESS TO ANY SHARED MEMORY

```
void StartUsingSharedMemory( int * shared_memory_flag ) {
    int flag;
    while( 1 ) {
        // check first to see if we have a chance
        while( *ProcessTableFreeFlag == 0 )
                    shared_memory_flag
            ;
        asm{
            move r0,r1
            exchangeword r1,*ProcessTableFreeFlag
            store r1,flag        shared_memory_flag
        }
        // Busy wait until you get a 1 from the shared flag.
        if( flag == 1 )
            break;
    }
}
void FinishUsingSharedMemory( int * shared_memory_flag ) {
    *shared_memory_flag = 1;
}
```

All that is necessary is to have an integer that is the shared memory flag for each area of shared memory. All such flags are initialized to 1.

We added two extra lines to avoid tying up the memory bus so much. Before we use the **ExchangeWord** instruction, we first check for a 1 in the flag. This avoids writing the flag repeatedly even when it contains a 0.

Let's see how we would use this general solution on the message queues. The modified code for the send message system call in the system call trap handler is show below.

SEND MESSAGE FOR TWO PROCESSORS

```
// Add this to the system global data
int message_queue_flag[NumberOfMessageQueues]
   = {1,1,1, . . . ,1}; // NEW CODE
// . . .
// This is the new version of the send message case
case SendMessageSystemCall:
   // get the arguments
   int * user_msg; asm { store r9,user_msg }
   int to_q; asm { store r10,to_q }

   // check for an invalid queue identifier
   if( !message_queue_allocated[to_q] ) {
       pd[current_process].sa.reg[1] = -1;
       break;
   }
   int msg_no = GetMessageBuffer();
   // make sure we have not run out of message buffers
   if( msg_no == EndOfFreeList ) {
       pd[current_process].sa.reg[1] = -2;
       break;
   }
   // copy the message vector from the system caller's memory
   // into the system's message buffer
   CopyToSystemSpace( current_process, user_msg,
                      message_buffer[msg_no], MessageSize );
   StartUsingSharedMemory( &message_queue_flag[to_q] ); // NEW CODE
   if( !wait_queue[to_q].Empty() ) {
       // some process is waiting for a message, deliver it immediately
       WaitQueueItem item = wait_queue.Remove();
       TransferMessage( msg_no, item.buffer );
       pd[item.pid].state = Ready;
   } else {
       // otherwise put it on the queue
       message_queue[to_q].Insert( msg_no );
   }
   FinishUsingSharedMemory( &message_queue_flag[to_q] ); // NEW CODE
   pd[current_process].sa.reg[1] = 0;
   break;
```

We have added another array of flags, one for each message queue. The SendMessageSystemCall case only requires two additional lines of code. We surround the code that accesses the message queue with a StartUsingSharedMemory and a FinishUsingSharedMemory. This ensures that only one processor at a time will try to use a message queue. Since we have a separate flag for each message queue, it is still possible for each processor to be simultaneously using a different message queue.

When we noted that the message queues would have to be shared, we included the message buffers that go on the queues as well. Since they are shared, they will have to be protected. In the above we have the line

int msg_no = GetMessageBuffer( );

If both processors try to execute this at the same time, the links in the free buffer list could be set incorrectly. To deal with this problem, we need to protect these operations with a shared memory flag. Here are the modified versions of the message buffer procedures.

MESSAGE BUFFER MANAGEMENT

```
int message_buffer_flag = 1; // NEW CODE
int GetMessageBuffer( void ) {
    // get the head of the free list
    StartUsingSharedMemory( &message_buffer_flag ); // NEW CODE
    int msg_no = free_msg_buffer;
    if( msg_no != EndOfFreeList ) {
        // follow the link to the next buffer
        free_msg_buffer = message_buffer[msg_no][0];
    }
    FinishUsingSharedMemory( &message_buffer_flag ); // NEW CODE
    return msg_no;
}
void FreeMessageBuffer( int msg_no ) {
    StartUsingSharedMemory( &message_buffer_flag ); // NEW CODE
    message_buffer[msg_no][0] = free_msg_buffer;
    free_msg_buffer = msg_no;
    FinishUsingSharedMemory( &message_buffer_flag ); // NEW CODE
}
```

One final change is required for message queues. We need to change the create message queue case so that only one processor at a time can create a new message queue. This will require another shared memory flag.

A similar change must be made to protect access to the disk queue.

In general, we define a shared memory flag for each shared variable (or array), and make a call to StartUsingSharedMemory before we start using the shared variable and a call to FinishUsingSharedMemory after we finish using the shared variable.

With two processors, each will sometimes have to busy wait until the other finishes some activity.

busy waiting

Busy waiting is using the processor to continuously check whether another activity has completed.

6.5.7 USING TWO PROCESS TABLES

Another solution to sharing a single process table would be to have two separate process tables, one for each processor. We could give each processor half the processes. The problem with this solution is what to do if one processor's process list had no ready processes, and so that processor was idle, while the other processor was busy and still had other ready processes in its process table. There would be work to do, but one processor would be idle anyway. See Figure 6.9.

This is analogous to a situation in a grocery store where there are two checkers with individual lines. The customers have to schedule themselves by line hopping. If one line is empty, people from the other line will move into it. Unfortunately, processes do not do this, since they are not impatient and autonomous agents like grocery store customers. It is better to have a single line that all processors draw from. The race condition problem does not come up in the grocery store scenario because of physical constraints, that is, a customer can only go to one checker or the other—you cannot make a copy of him and his groceries and check them both out at the same time.

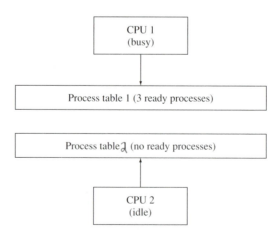

Figure 6.9   Problem with two process lists

6.6   EXAMPLES OF MULTIPROCESSOR OPERATING SYSTEMS

Multiprocessors are already becoming common in workstations and will soon be common in personal computers. As a result, almost all newer versions of operating systems provide for the possibility of multiple processors.

Most modern versions of UNIX will run on multiprocessors. This includes System V Release 4 from AT&T, Solaris from SUN, HP UNIX from HP, Digital UNIX from Digital, AIX from IBM, and IRIX from SGI.

Any operating system can be converted to work on multiprocessors by protecting all the shared data structures from simultaneous use by two or more processors. *Spin locks* are used to protect these variables. The actual details take some time to work out, but the basic ideas are fairly simple.

spin lock

Newer operating systems like Windows NT and Mach were designed from the beginning to work on multiprocessors.

6.7   THREADS

6.7.1   THE THREAD CONCEPT

Almost all operating systems implement processes. A process is an abstraction of a stand-alone computer. Processes do not share memory but communicate with messages which are based on the way computers on a network communicate with one another. But we have just seen a computer with two processors sharing the same memory, which we used to implement processes in pretty much the same way as we implemented them on a single-processor machine.

Having done this, we could look at our two-processor system and imagine what a software abstraction of a two (or more) processor shared memory computer would be like. Two processes can run at the same time (in pseudo-parallel or in true parallel on a two-processor machine), but they do not share memory. Suppose we provided software entities that could run at the same time but also shared memory. Such entities exist in many newer operating systems, and they are called *threads*.[2] A thread has some of the characteristics of a process, but it is possible to have several threads sharing the same memory space.

thread

Figure 6.10 shows two processes, one with two threads and one with three threads. The lines represent a thread of execution moving through the code in the memory of the process. We can think of time passing as we move along a thread (a line in the diagram). The relative times of the various threads are not important; they are intended to show paths through the code.

---

[2]We sometimes talk about the sequence of instructions executed by a process as its *thread of control*. The idea is that control moves (threads) around the code. It is this phrase that the term "thread" is taken from.

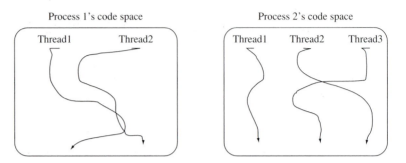

Figure 6.10 Threads executing inside two processes

The threads can execute anywhere in the code space of the process. They might execute the exact same code at the same time (or at different times), but even when they do execute the same code, it is not the same execution, just the same instructions—that is, they are fetching and executing the same instructions, but in different contexts (with different registers and stack).

To make this idea clear, let us extend our operating system to implement threads. The operating system will still provide processes and it will still be possible to create new processes, but we will also be able to create new threads. A process will have an associated address space, and a thread will have an associated process in whose address space it runs. When a process is created, an initial thread will also be created in it. This thread can then create new threads in the same process. These threads can exit at any time, and the process will exit when the last thread in the process exits. Each thread will have its own stack and its own set of registers.

6.7.2 THREAD SYSTEM CALLS

Let's look at the system calls that will allow the programmer to use threads:

- int CreateThread(char * startAddress, char * stackBegin);—A new thread is created which starts executing at address startAddress and has a stack at stackBegin. The return value is the thread identifier of the new thread.

- void ExitThread(int returnCode);—This system call causes the thread making the call to exit. If this is the last thread to exit in a process, then it ends the process as well as the thread, and the return code is returned to the parent process when it executes the Wait system call. Otherwise returnCode is passed to the thread that calls WaitThread on it.

- int WaitThread(int tid);—This system call will cause the thread making the system call to wait until the thread specified by tid exits. The value returned is the return code from the ExitThread call.

The creator of the new thread is responsible for allocating stack space for it to use. The creator also determines where it will start execution. We have defined Exit-

`Thread` to exit the thread and to exit the process only if it is the last thread to exit. We have defined a new call `WaitThread` to wait for a thread to exit. There will still be the `Wait` system call to wait for a process to exit. A process exits when its last thread exits. The `Wait` system call is executed by a thread in one process to wait for (the last thread in) another process to exit.

Notice that these calls are nearly the same as the process calls we saw before. The one difference is that, when you create a process, you give it a program to run. The operating system finds memory for it, and the new program allocates its own state from that memory. In a thread, you have to allocate the stack space and tell the `CreateThread` call where it is. No new program is loaded, but you pass an address in the current program at which to start executing.

6.7.3 ADVANTAGES OF THREADS

We motivated threads by using the analogy with a two-processor computer, but what good are threads in programming? Threads provide parallel (or pseudo-parallel) processing, like processes, but they have one important advantage over processes: they are much more efficient. Threads are cheaper to create and destroy because they do not require allocation and deallocation of a new address space or other process resources (such as duplicating open files). So you can use multiple threads much more freely and create a thread to do a small task (like a few thousand instructions).

It can be faster to switch between threads than processes if the dispatcher tries to dispatch a thread in the same process that was just running. It will be faster since the memory mapping does not have to be set up and the memory and address translation caches do not have to be invalidated.[3]

Threads are also more efficient because they share memory. They do not have to use system calls (which are slow because they require context switches) to communicate; they can communicate through memory. So threads are especially good for parallel activities that are tightly coupled and use the same data structures.

Another name used for a thread is *lightweight process* to emphasize the fact that a thread is like a process but is more efficient and uses fewer resources (hence, is "lighter").

lightweight process

> Threads are lightweight (low overhead) processes that can share an address space.

6.7.4 USES OF THREADS

When an operating system implements both processes and threads, the programmer can choose to have parallelism at two levels, the process level or the thread level. Processes provide an upper level of parallelism for parallel activities that do

---

| [3]We will see the costs of memory management and address translation in Chapter 10.

not interact heavily and do not need to share very much data. The process level of parallelism is ideal for separate activities, such as when one user is editing a file and another user is running a statistical package. Threads provide the possibility for parallel activities inside a single process. This level is best for parallel activities that interact heavily with each other and share a lot of data. In this section, we will look at some examples where threads are a more natural unit of parallelism than processes.

Threads to Partition Process Activities   Let's look at some typical uses of threads. Suppose we have a spreadsheet program that is displaying a large spreadsheet. We might have one thread that manages the recalculation of the spreadsheet, another that manages the updating of the screen, and another that gets input from the user and executes the commands. If you make a change to a cell that causes a long recalculation, the recalculate thread will start running. It will communicate closely with the screen update thread. When a cell is recalculated, it will inform the screen update thread to redisplay the cell. At the same time, the user can type in another command and the command thread will read it in and act on it, at the same time as the recalculation and screen update is going on. If it turns out that the next command required another recalculation, the command thread can stop the recalculate thread and have it start over. This way the user does not have to wait for the old recalculation that is no longer relevant. Figure 6.11 shows the threads that might be in a spreadsheet program.

There are several advantages to such an organization. First, the program is more responsive to the user. It will always accept input from the user, and screen update goes on in parallel with other activities. Second, it is often easier to program the system with this type of organization. Separate activities are in separate threads, and you do not have to worry about interleaving them or deciding what to do next. Each activity has one goal and one sequence of events. The scheduler handles the interleaving. Third, it

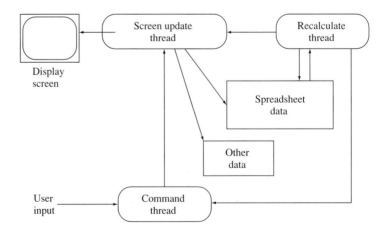

Figure 6.11   Threads in a spreadsheet program

is efficient to wait for things with threads. A thread is only a part of a program, and if it is blocked, say waiting for a disk transfer, the rest of the threads are still active. For example, suppose reading the mouse and reading the keyboard are separate system calls, and they both block if there is no input to read. You can have two threads, one waiting for events from the mouse and another waiting for events from the keyboard.[4]

Of course, threads have the same problems of parallelism that processes do, but the same solutions can be used to handle these problems. In fact, since threads share memory, very efficient synchronizing primitives are possible for use by threads.

Threads to Wait for You   Suppose your operating system uses *blocking I/O*, meaning that, when you try to read a disk block, the read system call does not return until the block has been read into memory. Suppose you do not want to wait for the read, but have some other computation to do while the block is being read. You can have one thread wait for the I/O to complete, and another thread do the other computation.

Threads to Replicate Activities   Another natural use of threads is in a server process. A *server process* is one that receives requests from many other processes. It acts on the requests and does what is requested. For example, a disk block server will accept requests to read and write disk blocks. A server will often have several requests pending at the same time, and it does not want to serve only one request at a time. One solution is to assign a separate thread to each request. If a thread blocks (on disk I/O), then only that one thread is blocked and there will still be other threads to serve new requests. Figure 6.12 shows a disk block server that uses a thread for each request.

server process

Of course, threads are not the only way to solve this problem, but they are a clean and simple solution. If we did not have threads, the server would have to keep a table of pending requests that have been started but not yet completed. When a request requires a disk operation, the request is put on the pending request table and a message is sent to the disk driver to start the transfer. When the transfer completes the disk driver will send a completion message to the disk block server. When a disk completion message comes in, it is matched with the request that caused it, and that request is continued. In effect, the server would be implementing a specialized version of threads. It is simpler to implement threads once in the operating system, and let all servers use them.

*6.7.5   THREAD IMPLEMENTATION

In the previous sections, we have talked about threads in general. In this section, we will look at what it takes to implement threads in our simple operating system.

Threads exist inside of processes, so we will still have processes in the operating system. However, some of the functions of processes will be taken over by threads. In fact, the main changes will be to redistribute these functions. We will still have a process table and a process descriptor, but the process descriptor will have less information in it. Memory is allocated to a process, so the process descriptor will

---

[4]Most graphic user interface systems already combine events from the various devices into a single event stream, and so this example is not realistic for those systems.

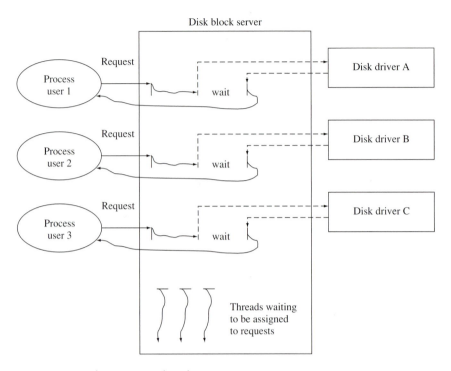

Figure 6.12   Disk server using threads

record the base and bound values for the memory area allocated to the process. Each process will have one or more associated threads, so the process descriptor will contain the head of the list of threads associated with this process.

We will also have a thread table containing thread descriptors. The thread descriptor contains a register save area because the threads will be dispatched and interrupted and will need to save their processor state. The thread descriptor also contains the pid of the process it belongs to, pointers so it can be put on a list of threads, and a thread state (which is equivalent to the process state in our simple operating system).

The dispatcher will look in the thread table for a thread that is not blocked and dispatch it. Here are the new or changed data declarations.

PROCESS AND THREAD DESCRIPTORS

```
enum ThreadState { Ready, Running, Blocked };
struct ThreadDescriptor {
    int slotAllocated;
    int timeLeft;
    // Pointers so the thread can be put on a linked list of threads.
    int nextThread, prevThread;
    int pid; // The process this thread runs in.
```

```
   ThreadState state; // Each thread has its own state.
   SaveArea sa; // Each thread has its own register save area.
};
struct ProcessDescriptor {
   int slotAllocated;
   int threads; // A circular list of threads.
   // The process is allocated an area of memory. The base and bound
   // are saved here and used to initialize the base and bound registers
   // for any threads associated with this process.
   void * base, * bound;
};
// OPERATING SYSTEM GLOBAL DATA
// This is the thread currently running.
int current_thread;
// We need a process table and a thread table.
ProcessDescriptor pd[NumberOfProcesses]; // pd[0] is the system
ThreadDescriptor td[NumberOfThreads];
int thread_using_disk;
```

Now threads, instead of processes, have a state and a save area. A process keeps track of its memory and its threads. We do not use **ProcessState** anymore because processes no longer have a state; only threads have a state because only threads are active.

We extend system initialization to initialize the new thread table.

SYSTEM INITIALIZATION

```
int main( void ) {
   // Other initialization is the same . . .
   // The thread slots start out free.
   for( i = 1; i < NumberOfThreads; ++i )
      td[i].slotAllocated = False;
   // Other initialization is the same . . .
}
```

Now we look at the process and thread creation code.

PROCESS AND THREAD CREATION

```
// This procedure creates a new process.
int CreateProcess( int first_block, int n_blocks ) {
   // Look for a free slot in the process table.
   int pid;
   for( pid = 1; pid < NumberOfProcesses; ++pid ) {
      if( !(pd[pid].slotAllocated) )
           break;
   }
   if( pid >= NumberOfProcesses ) {
```

```
            return −1; // ERROR
    }
    // Initialize the fields of the process descriptor.
    pd[pid].slotAllocated = True;
    pd[pid].base = pid * ProcessSize;
    pd[pid].bound = ProcessSize;

    // Read in the image of the process.
    // Use busy waiting to avoid having to split the loop
    // over a series of interrupts.
    char * addr = (char *)(pd[pid].sa.base);
    for( i = 0; i < n_blocks; ++i ) {
        IssueDiskRead( first_block + i, addr, 0/*no interrupt*/ );
        while( DiskBusy() )
            ;        // Busy wait for the disk I/O to complete.
        addr += DiskBlockSize;
    }

    // Create the initial thread in the process and link it up.
        // Assume that the stack for the initial process is at the
        // end of the memory for the process.
    int tid = CreateThread( pid, 0, ProcessSize );
    pd[pid].threads = tid;
    td[tid].nextThread = td[tid].prevThread = tid;
    return pid;
}
// This procedure creates a new thread.
int CreateThread( int pid, char * startAddress, char *stackBegin ) {
    // startAddress is the address in the process address space to
    // begin execution (it is the initial IA).
    // stackBegin is the initial value of r30.
    //
    // Look for a free slot in the thread table.
    int tid;
    for( tid = 1; tid < NumberOfThreads; ++tid ) {
        if( !(td[tid].slotAllocated) )
            break;
    }
    if( tid >= NumberOfThreads ) {
        return −1;// ERROR
    }
    td[tid].slotAllocated = True;
    // Initialize the fields of the thread descriptor.
    td[tid].pid = pid;
    td[tid].state = Ready;
    td[tid].sa.base = pd[pid].base;
    td[tid].sa.bound = pd[pid].bound;
    td[tid].sa.psw = 3;
    td[tid].sa.ia = startAddress;
    td[tid].sa.r30 = stackBegin;
    // We leave the registers uninitialized
    // since we have no idea what they should be.
    // The process itself will initialize these registers.
    return tid;
}
```

(handwritten annotation:) if (tid == −1) return −1;

In process creation, we allocate the process slot and the memory for the process, read in the program, and create the first thread to execute in the process. We create the initial thread for the process because all processes must have at least one thread. We link the threads together on a doubly linked circular list.

For thread creation, we allocate a slot in the thread table and initialize the save area. Now we look at the changes in the Dispatcher.

THE DISPATCHER

```
void Dispatcher( void ) {
    current_thread = SelectThreadToRun();
    RunThread( current_thread );
}

int SelectThreadToRun( void ) {
    static int next_thread = NumberOfThreads;
    if( current_thread > 0
        && pd[current_thread].state == Ready
        && pd[current_thread].timeLeft > 0 )
        return current_thread;
    for( int i = 0; i < NumberOfThreads; ++i ) {
        if( ++next_thread >= NumberOfThreads )
            next_thread = 0;
        if( td[next_thread].slotAllocated
            && td[next_thread].state == Ready ) {
            td[next_thread].state = Running;
            return next_thread;
        }
    }
    return -1; // No thread is ready to run
}

void RunThread( int tid ) {
    //... same except it uses tid instead of pid
}
```

[handwritten annotations: td (over pd); && td[current_thread].slotAllocated; { td[current_thread].state = Running; }; pd ? td ?]

The Dispatcher now runs threads instead of processes, but otherwise it is essentially unchanged from process dispatching.

Now we look at the system call interrupt handler.

SYSTEM CALL INTERRUPT HANDLER

```
void SystemCallInterruptHandler( void ) {

    //...
    //New or changed cases:
```

```
// The Exit system call is eliminated. You exit a process by
// exiting from all its threads.

case CreateProcessSystemCall:
    int block_number; asm { store r9,block_number }
    int number_of_blocks; asm { store r10,number_of_blocks }
    td[current_thread].sa.reg[1]
              = CreateProcess( block_number, number_of_blocks);
    break;

case CreateThreadSystemCall:
    int start_addr; asm { store r9,start_addr }
    int stack_begin; asm { store r10,stack_begin }

    int pid = td[current_thread].pid;
    int new_thread = CreateThread( pid, start_addr, stack_begin );
    td[current_thread].sa.reg[1] = new_thread;
    // Insert the thread into the double linked circular thread list.
    int next_thread = td[current_thread].nextThread;
    td[new_thread].nextThread = next_thread;
    td[new_thread].prevThread = current_thread;
    td[current_thread].nextThread = new_thread;
    td[next_thread].prevThread = new_thread;
    break;


case ExitThreadSystemCall:
    td[current_thread].slotAllocated = False;
    int next_thread = td[current_thread].nextThread;
    int pid = td[current_thread].pid;
    // Is this the last thread in the process?
    if( next_thread == current_thread ) {
        // if so exit from the process, by freeing its slot
        pd[pid].slotAllocated = False;
        // We have no other exit process processing. In a real
        // OS we might free memory, close unclosed files, etc.
    } else {
        //Unlink it from the list and make sure pd[pid]
        //is not pointing to the deleted thread.
        int prev_thread = td[current_thread].prevThread;
        td[next_thread].prevThread = prev_thread;
        td[prev_thread].nextThread = next_thread;
        pd[pid].threads = next_thread;
    }
    break;
}
Dispatcher();
}
```

CreateProcessSystemCall is about the same as before. CreateThread SystemCall calls the CreateThread procedure to do the main work, and then makes sure all the list pointers are updated correctly. ExitThread unlinks the thread from the process's thread list and checks to see if this is the last thread in the process. If so, then the process is exited.

6.7.6   SPLITTING THE PROCESS CONCEPT

Our first definition of a process was an entity that had its own address space and would be allocated processor time when it needed it. We also saw how processes could open files and use them over a period of time. The process had two main purposes. First, it was an entity that could request and hold resources (for example, memory, open files). Second, it was an entity that could be scheduled by the dispatcher and be executed by the processor.

By introducing threads, we split up the process concept into two parts. A thread becomes the entity that is scheduled by the dispatcher and receives processor time to execute. The (new) process is the entity that can request and hold resources. Splitting the concept allows more flexibility. Now we can have several threads in a single process and get the benefits of multiprocessing inside a process.

If concepts can be used independently, then it is useful to split them up.

6.7.7   LIGHTWEIGHT PROCESSES AND USER THREADS

The threads we have described are usually called *lightweight processes* because they are a cheaper version of processes. They are implemented by the operating system and so require a change to the operating system.

We could also implement threads at the user level without any assistance at all from the operating system. All we have to do is implement a little scheduler in a process that will switch between threads. Thread switching within a process does not require any change in the memory mapping; it is basically just a change in the registers and a jump instruction. A user process does not need to be in system mode to do this. This technique is called *user threads*.   user threads

User threads are much more efficient than lightweight processes because they do not require a switch to the operating system to change threads. But they are not recognized by the operating system and so you cannot use them as flexibly as kernel threads. For example, you can use lightweight processes to wait for messages on several different message queues. A lightweight process blocking will not prevent the other lightweight processes in the process from continuing to execute. But if a user thread blocks, the entire process blocks (because the operating system does not know anything about the other threads).

There is another related concept, and that is to implement threads inside the operating system. This is sometimes called *kernel threads*. Kernel threads are discussed in the next section (Section 6.8).

> User threads are more efficient and kernel threads are more flexible.

6.7.8   EXAMPLES OF THREADS

Most modern operating systems (Mach, Solaris, OS/2, Windows NT, and almost all recent versions of UNIX) implement lightweight processes. The main exception is System V Release 4, which does not implement threads.

Another exception is Plan 9, which instead implements a very flexible form of the `fork` system call where you can specify exactly which parts of the parent process you want duplicated in the child and which parts you want to be shared between the parent and the child. They feel that this, along with a fast fork implementation, provides all the benefits of threads and more.

In addition, most operating systems provide user thread packages that implement user threads. These two forms of threads can be combined in a system where you have one or more user threads executing on each lightweight process. Figure 6.13 shows an example of this. The operating system implements lightweight processes (LWPs) and allocates one or more of these to each process. In this example, Process 1 has one LWP and Processes 2 and 3 each have two LWPs. Each process can use the user threads package to implement user threads. The user threads package knows about LWPs, can allocate LWPs, and assigns one or more user threads to each LWP. The LWPs are more expensive than user threads. If only one user thread is assigned to an LWP, then it is essentially an LWP, but if two or more user threads are assigned to an LWP, then we get the advantages of user threads (faster dispatching).

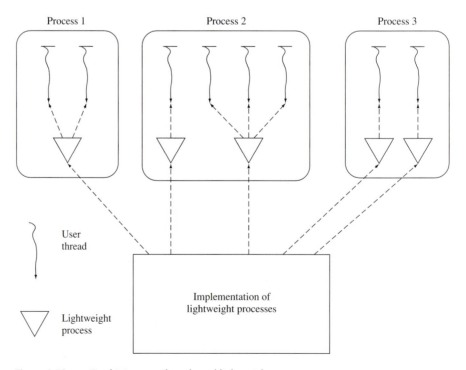

Figure 6.13   Combining user threads and lightweight processes

---

DESIGN TECHNIQUE: SEPARATION OF CONCEPTS

We started with the concept of a process: an object that holds resources (e.g., memory, open files) and can be scheduled for execution. We found it useful to separate the process concept into two concepts: a new concept of process which can own resources, and a thread which can be scheduled for execution. This allowed us to use multiple threads inside a single process and to achieve effects that were not possible before.

This technique can be used in many places. If we separate two concepts, we allow the possibility of using them separately or combining them in different ways while still allowing us to use them together as we did before. The important factor is whether the concepts are used separately often enough to justify the implementation cost of separating them.

To read more about separations of concepts, see Section 9.4.

DESIGN TECHNIQUE: REENTRANT PROGRAMS

Threads are multiple executions in the same address space, and so allow the possibility of the same code being used simultaneously by two threads. This creates a new class of problems that did not occur with processes. If the code depends on global or static variables, the two threads will interfere with each other.

Now that threads are becoming more common, we are finding out that a lot of code is not **thread-safe**, that is, it no longer works correctly if two or more threads are executing it simultaneously. We call a program **reentrant** if it is thread-safe.

The techniques for making programs reentrant are well known but they take more work and require planning. The idea is to allocate a block of storage for each execution that holds the global and static data. This block of storage is the *state* of an execution of the code. It takes more effort to write programs this way, but the work produces general benefits.

To read more about reentrant code, see Section 9.6.

Some very recent operating systems do not implement LWPs at all, and depend on user threads and a technique called *scheduler activations* to give user threads the desirable features of LWPs. The idea is that whenever a user thread makes a system call that would block, the operating system calls another user thread in the process, called the scheduler thread. The scheduler thread then blocks the thread that made the system call and schedules a different thread. When the thread making the system call should be unblocked, the operating system makes another call to the scheduler thread. This allows most thread scheduling to be done efficiently in user libraries, but removes the problem of user threads making blocking system calls.

---

*6.8 KERNEL-MODE PROCESSES

In Chapter 5, there were two places where the operating system had to wait for some event before it could complete a system call. If there was no message in the message queue when a process executed the receive message system call, the operating system could not complete the system call and had to wait for a message to be sent to the queue. In the disk read (or write) system call, the operating system had to wait for the disk transfer to complete before it could complete the system call. In each case, we dealt with the problem by saving the essential state of the system call and blocking the process. We saved the message receiver's pid and buffer address in the message queue, and we saved the pid of the process requesting disk I/O in the disk queue. Later, when the event we were waiting for occurred (a message send or a disk I/O interrupt), we found the information we had saved and completed the processing of the system call.

This method worked because we did not have much state to save (only a word or two) and we did not have much more to do in processing the system call after the wait. We had to have the send message code finish the receive message system call for the receiver of the message. This approach to the problem is ad hoc and complex. A more general way to solve this problem is to allow processes to run in system mode, inside the operating system. This will also allow us to enable interrupts while we are in the operating system.

When the operating system is entered (always via an interrupt), we will give the process a new stack in the address space of the operating system and save the process registers in a save area on that stack. We will allocate this stack in the process descriptor for the process. Essentially we will be making a thread out of the process. This thread or *kernel-mode process* will be scheduled through the same process slot. The process's registers will be saved on the system stack.

kernel-mode process

The *kernel* is the part of an operating system that implements the most basic functions of the system. The kernel always runs in system mode and is the core of the operating system. When we use the term *kernel* in kernel-mode process we indicate that this is a process that is running in system mode.

kernel

Since the process has a new stack, we could consider it a new process. Actually it is a new thread, since all kernel-mode processes run in the same address space (the address space of the operating system). Another word for operating system is kernel, and so kernel-mode processes are also called *kernel threads*.

kernel threads

The advantage of doing this is that we will use the same process save and restore mechanism for process switching, and so we can save the state of a system call on the stack. We can wait for events in the operating system by having the process wait.

The techniques we used in Chapter 5 were essentially implementing an ad hoc version of threads in the operating system. We might as well implement operating system threads directly and get all the benefits of a complete thread implementation.

First we will look at the implementation, and then we will discuss some of its advantages and disadvantages.

6.8.1 DATA STRUCTURES FOR KERNEL-MODE PROCESSES

The code below shows the data structure changes required.

CHANGES FOR KERNEL-MODE PROCESSES

```
struct ProcessDescriptor {
    int slotAllocated;
    int timeLeft; //time left from the last time slice
```

```
    ProcessState state;
    // SaveArea sa; <- ELIMINATED
    int inSystem; //initialize to 0 in CreateProcess <- NEW
    int * lastsa; //The most recent save area on the stack <- NEW
    char sstack[SystemStackSize]; //system mode stack <- NEW
};
// We don't need a common system stack any more
// int SystemStack[SystemStackSize]; <- ELIMINATED

// CHANGED: this is now a queue of ints.
Queue<int> * wait_queue[NumberOfMessageQueues];
```

We have added three new fields to the process descriptor. inSystem is a count of how many times we have entered system mode. CreateProcess will initialize this field to 0. lastsa is a pointer to the most recent save area we have used. sstack is a stack to use while we are in system mode. We have eliminated the old save area because we will save the processor state in our system stack instead.

Each time we enter the system, a save area will be allocated on the stack and linked to the previous save area on the stack (if there is one). The lastsa variable will record the location of this save area. Then we will save the registers in the save area.

6.8.2   PROCESS CREATION WITH KERNEL-MODE PROCESSES

In the simple operating system, when we created a process we had to read in the code and data from the process. We did this because it was too complicated to wait for each disk block and still remember where you were in the iteration. Now we can wait easily, and so we can do other things while a new process's code and data are being read from the disk. In fact, we can call DiskIO and have it do the I/O for us.

PROCESS CREATION

```
int CreateProcessSysProc( int first_block, int n_blocks ) {
    //. . . the beginning part is the same as it was before except
    pd[pid].inSystem = 0;

    //Read in the image of the process.
    char * addr = (char *)(pd[pid].sa.base);   ← this uses "sa" which we eliminated. To fix it must
    for( i = 0; i < n_blocks; ++i ) {               allocate & set up a save area when we create process.
        DiskIO( DiskReadSystemCall, first_block + i, addr );
        addr += DiskBlockSize;
    }
    return pid;
}
```

6.8.3   INTERRUPT HANDLERS FOR KERNEL-MODE PROCESSES

Here are the changes for the system call interrupt handler.

SYSTEM CALL INTERRUPT HANDLER FOR KERNEL-MODE PROCESSES

```
void SystemCallInterruptHandler( void ) {
    // *** BEGIN NEW CODE ***
    //     All this initial interrupt handling is new.
    char **savearea;
    int saveTimer;
    if( pd[current_process].inSystem == 0 ) {
        //This is the first entry into system mode
        savearea = &(pd[current_process].sstack + SystemStackSize
            -sizeof(SaveArea)-4);
    } else {
        //we were already in system mode so the system stack
        //already has some things on it.
        asm { store r30,savearea }
        //allocate space on the stack for the save area
        savearea -= sizeof(SaveArea)+4;
    }
    asm {
        //stop the interval timer
        store  timer,saveTimer
        load   #0,timer
        //process's ia and psw are saved in iia and ipsw
        store  iia,savearea+4
        store  ipsw,savearea+8
        //save the base and bound registers
        store  base,savearea+12
        store  bound,savearea+16
        //save all the general registers
        storeall savearea+20
        //set up the system stack
        load   savearea,r30
    }
    pd[current_process].timeLeft = saveTimer;
    pd[current_process].state = Ready;
    *savearea = pd[current_process].lastsa; //link to previous save area
    pd[current_process].lastsa = savearea;
    ++(pd[current_process].inSystem);

    //enable interrupts now that the state has been saved
    asm { load #2,psw }
    // *** END NEW CODE *** for interrupt handling code

    // fetch the system call number and switch based on it
    int system_call_number; asm { store r8,system_call_number }
    switch( system_call_number ) {

    case CreateProcessSystemCall:
```

```
        //. . . the same

case ExitProcessSystemCall:
        //. . . the same

case CreateMessageQueueSystemCall:
        //. . . the same

case SendMessageSystemCall:
        // get the arguments
        int * user_msg; asm { store r9,user_msg }
        int to_q; asm { store r10,to_q }

        // check for an invalid queue identifier
        if( !message_queue_allocated[to_q] ) {
            pd[current_process].sa.reg[1] = -1;
            break;
        }
        int msg_no = GetMessageBuffer();
        // make sure we have not run out of message buffers
        if( msg_no == EndOfFreeList ) {
            pd[current_process].sa.reg[1] = -2;
            break;
        }
        // copy the message vector from the system caller's memory
        // into the system's message buffer
        CopyToSystemSpace( current_process, user_msg,
                           message_buffer[msg_no], MessageSize );
        if( !wait_queue[to_q].Empty() ) {
            // some process is waiting for a message, unblock it
            int pid = wait_queue.Remove();
            pd[pid].state = Ready;
        }
        // put it on the queue
        message_queue[to_q].Insert( msg_no );
        pd[current_process].sa.reg[1] = 0;
        break;

case ReceiveMessageSystemCall:
        int * user_msg; asm { store r9,user_msg }
        int from_q; asm { store r10,from_q }

        // check for an invalid queue identifier
        if( !message_queue_allocated[from_q] ) {
            pd[current_process].sa.reg[1] = -1;
            break;
        }
        if( message_queue[from_q].Empty() ) {
            pd[current_process].state = Blocked;
            wait_queue[from_q].Insert( pid );     current_process
            SwitchProcess();
        }
        int msg_no = message_queue[from_q].Remove();
        TransferMessage( msg_no, user_msg );
```

```
        pd[current_process].sa.reg[1] = 0;
        break;

    case DiskReadSystemCall:
    case DiskWriteSystemCall:
        //. . . the same
    }
    Dispatcher();
}
}
```

The first action we take is to allocate a save area for the registers of the system caller. If this is the first entry into the system (the usual case), then we allocate space at the top of the system stack area for this process. Otherwise, we allocate the next free space in the system stack. We allocate enough space for the register save area and one more word for a linked list of all the save areas. The process descriptor field **lastsa** records where the most recent save area on the stack is located. The first word of each save area on the stack points to the previous save area. The register saving code is about the same, except that the offsets are four bytes larger to allow for the save area link pointer. We set up the system mode stack just below the register save area. Next we link up the save areas, remember the most recent one, and increment our count of entries into the system. Finally, we enable interrupts. We can do this safely since we have saved the state, and an interrupt now will allocate new space on the system stack and not disturb our save area.[5]

The send message code is a little simpler because it does not have to deliver messages to message receivers. It just unblocks the first waiting message receiver and puts the message in the queue. The next time the receiver process runs, it will receive the message, as we see in the receive message code explained next.

The receive message code is also simpler. If there is no message waiting, then the process puts itself on the message waiting queue, blocks itself, and calls SwitchProcess, which will save the state of the process (just as if it had made a system call) and call the dispatcher. Later, when the message is sent, the send message code will unblock it. When the dispatcher finally runs it again, Switch-Process will return, and the receiving process will remove the message from the queue.

6.8.4 SWITCHING PROCESSES FOR KERNEL-MODE PROCESSES

Now let's look at SwitchProcess to see how it does this.

---

[5]The code shown here to save the register state will not really work. The problem is that the C code at the beginning that determines the correct save area to use will change a few of the registers before we get a chance to save them in the save area. The solution is to do the whole thing in assembly language, and be very careful to save registers before you use them. This can be done, but we did not want to complicate the code by showing so much assembly language.

SWITCH PROCESSES

```
void SwitchProcess( int pid ) {
    // Called when a system mode process wants to wait for something
    int * savearea; asm { store r30,savearea }
    savearea -= sizeof(SaveArea)+4;
    asm {
        // save the registers
        // arrange to return from the procedure call when we return
        store   r31,savearea+4
        store   psw,savearea+8
        store   base,savearea+12
        store   bound,savearea+16
        storeall savearea+20
    }
    pd[current_process].state = Blocked;
    Dispatcher();
}
```

This procedure is called from a kernel-mode process when it wants to wait for something. The register state is saved, and the saved *ia* register is set up to return from the procedure when the state is restored. Then the dispatcher is called and runs another process.

The other interrupt handlers (the disk interrupt handler and the timer interrupt handler) both will be changed in the same way that the system call interrupt handler was changed. They will save the register state on the system stack, keep the save areas linked, and remember how many times the system has been entered. We will not show the code for these interrupt handlers.

6.8.5   How the System Stack Is Used

In order to understand how system mode processes work, let's go through an example to see how the stack frames work.

Suppose a process makes a system call to read a disk block. When it enters the system call interrupt handler, a save area will be set up on the system stack to save the state of the process at the time of the system call. Then it will call DiskIO, and DiskIO will call SwitchProcess. SwitchProcess will then set up another save area and link it to the first one. Figure 6.14 shows the stack frame at this point.

The process is now blocked. SwitchProcess will now call the Dispatcher, which will pick another process to run.

When the disk transfer completes, this process will be put in the Ready state. When the Dispatcher picks it to run, it will reload the state from the second save area and start the process running again. The *ia* in that save area is the return address from the call to SwitchProcess, and so the process will start up in DiskIO, just

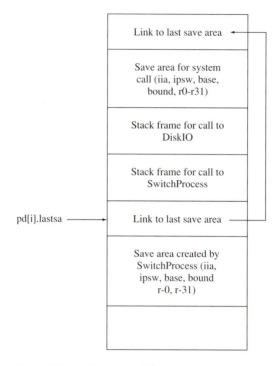

Figure 6.14   System stack for a kernel-mode process

having returned from `SwitchProcess`. It will immediately return from `DiskIO` to the system call interrupt handler, which will drop out of the case statement and call the dispatcher again. The dispatcher will then detect that this process is still ready and dispatch it again, this time using the first save area. This dispatch will return to the process that made the system call.

6.8.6   WAITING WITH KERNEL-MODE PROCESSES

A kernel-mode process can call `SwitchProcess` from anywhere to wait for an event. The `DiskIO` will call it to wait for the disk transfer to complete.

DISK I/O

```
// The procedure is called from the system call interrupt handler.
void DiskIO( int command, int disk_block, char * buffer ) {
    // Create a new disk request and fill in the fields.
    DiskRequest * req = new DiskRequest;
    req->command = command;
    req->disk_block = disk_block;
    req->buffer = buffer;
    req->pid = current_process;
    // Then insert it on the queue.
```

```
    disk_queue.Insert( (void *)req );
    pd[current_process].state = Blocked;
    // Wake up the disk scheduler if it is idle.
    ScheduleDisk();
    SwitchProcess(); //NEW CODE
}
```

The only thing different here is the call to **SwitchProcess**. This call will not
return until the process is unblocked.

SwitchProcess does not arrange for the process doing disk I/O to be unblocked;
that is taken care of by the request it puts in the disk queue. In the next chapter, we will
cover an operating system object called a *semaphore* which kernel-mode processes
could use to wait in the operating system and get unblocked at the right time.

6.8.7 DISPATCHING WITH KERNEL-MODE PROCESSES

Now we look at the other side of things and see how the dispatcher will use these
save areas to dispatch the process after it is unblocked.

THE DISPATCHER FOR KERNEL-MODE PROCESSES

```
void RunProcess( int pid ) {
  if( pid >= 0 ) {
    // Disable interrupts while we modify the save area.
    asm { move #0,psw }
    int * savearea = pd[pid].lastsa;
    pd[pid].lastsa = *savearea;
    --(pd[pid].inSystem);
    int quantum = pd[pid].timeLeft;
    asm {
        // ia and psw will be taken from iia and ipsw by rti
        load  savearea+4,iia
        load  savearea+8,ipsw
        // restore base and bound registers from saved values
        load  savearea+12,base
        load  savearea+16,bound
        // restore all the saved general registers
        loadall savearea+20
        // set the interval timer
        load  quantum,timer
        // return from interrupt restarts the process
        rti
        // rti does not return, since it sets the ia register
    }
  } else {
    waitLoop: goto waitLoop;
  }
}
```

The dispatcher uses the most recent save area to restore the processor registers from. It goes down the save area chain, and makes the next save area the most recent one. Then it loads the process state from the save area and starts it running.

We have to do all this with interrupts disabled because we cannot allow an interrupt while the save area chain and system stack are being changed. We do not have to reenable interrupts because that will be done by the rti.

6.8.8   KERNEL-MODE-ONLY PROCESSES

Once we allow processes to run in the operating system, we have the possibility of a process that runs only in the operating system, that is, a process that never runs in user mode. The purpose of such kernel-mode-only processes is to handle periodic activities that are not a direct result of a system call.

An example is the lower half of the disk driver. Its job is to take disk requests from the disk queue and start the disk transfer necessary to satisfy the disk request.

DISK SCHEDULING

```
void ScheduleDisk( void ) {
    StartUsingProcessTable();
    if( pd[scheduleDiskPid].state == Blocked )
        pd[scheduleDiskPid].state = Ready;
    FinishUsingProcessTable();
}
void RealScheduleDisk( void ) {
    while( 1 ){ // NEW CODE
        // If the disk is already busy, wait for it.
        if( DiskBusy() )
            SwitchProcess(); // NEW CODE
        // Get the first disk request from the disk request queue.
        DiskRequest * req = disk_queue.Remove();
        // Wait, if there is no disk request to service.
        if( req == 0 )
            SwitchProcess(); // NEW CODE
        // remember which process is waiting for the disk operation
        process_using_disk = req->pid;
        // issue the read or write, with disk interrupt enabled
        if( req->command == DiskReadSystemCall )
            IssueDiskRead( req->disk_block, req->buffer, 1 );
        else
            IssueDiskWrite( req->disk_block, req->buffer, 1 );
    }
}
```

The old `ScheduleDisk` was called from `DiskIO` and from the disk interrupt handler. To avoid changing the code in those two procedures, we redefine a new `ScheduleDisk` that just unblocks `RealScheduleDisk`, which is an infinite loop. Whenever `RealScheduleDisk` is unblocked, it looks for a free disk and a disk request. If it finds them, then it starts a disk request. Then it blocks itself by calling `SwitchProcess`.

Somewhere in the initialization of the operating system, this `RealScheduleDisk` process must be created. We will not show this code as it is a bit complicated. We have to set up the kernel-mode stack and a save area that will start the process executing in the `RealScheduleDisk` procedure.

6.8.9 TRADE-OFFS OF KERNEL-MODE PROCESSES

We gain several advantages by using kernel-mode processes. Waiting in the operating system is now handled in a simple and general way. All state is preserved (on the system stack), and processes can wait anywhere in the system and be restarted later. We showed how this was done with the receive message and disk I/O system calls.

In addition, we are now allowing interrupts in the operating system with no additional work. The interrupts save the state on the system stack, and so do not interfere with previous saved states.

In later additions to our simple operating system(to add virtual memory and a file system), we will have much more complicated sorts of waiting to do, and kernal-mode processes will handle it easily.

There is one important disadvantage of kernel-mode processes, and that is that every process needs a kernel-mode stack in addition to a user mode stack. Each stack takes at least 4 Kbytes, and so all these kernel stacks take up quite a bit of space.

UNIX and systems modeled after UNIX have used kernel-mode processes from the beginning because it is such an easy way to organize the system. Some modern versions of UNIX are starting to get away from this model because of the large memory overhead for kernel stacks. They have only one kernel stack, and use the techniques we discussed in Sections 5.9.2 and 5.9.3 to deal with the problem of suspending system calls.

6.8.10 EXAMPLES OF KERNEL-MODE PROCESSES

The original UNIX implementation was one of the first operating systems to use kernel-mode processes. Almost all UNIX implementations since then have followed along and used kernel-mode processes. Windows NT and OS/2 also use kernel-mode processes. Some newer UNIX implementations are trying to get away from using kernel-mode processes because of the memory space consumed by the required kernel stack for every process or thread.

6.9   IMPLEMENTATION OF MUTUAL EXCLUSION

In Chapter 5, we looked at messages as methods of interprocess communication and synchronization. Implementing messages involves two issues. The first issue is the algorithms necessary to implement the semantics of message passing. We have already seen messages implemented in the simple operating system. The implementation is quite simple, just involving queuing messages and transferring them to the right place at the right time.

The second issue is to implement the mutual exclusion necessary for these algorithms to work correctly. In this chapter, we examined some of the problems that can occur when two processors try to share data. The message queues were shared data, and so we had to ensure serial access to them. In the simple operating system, we assumed that no interrupt would occur when we were in system mode. This meant that the message operations did not have to worry about interference from another process. In this chapter, we used the `ExchangeWord` instruction to implement locks on shared variables.

So we have already seen two solutions to the mutual exclusion problem in implementing messages, disabling interrupts, and special hardware instructions. We will briefly review them, and then look at another solution that does not require any hardware assistance.

6.9.1   FIRST SOLUTION: DISABLING INTERRUPTS

The problems occur when two processes are changing a shared data structure. With a single processor machine, there is only one process active at a time, and another process starts only when an interrupt occurs. If we prevent interrupts from occurring, then no other process can run, and we do not have to worry about interference.

This solution works well on single processor machines, and has been the solution of choice in operating system for many years. It is cheap and easy and does the job.

Unfortunately, disabling interrupts does not extend easily to a multiple processor system. We could consider an instruction that disables interrupts on one machine and halts all the other machines. This would be rather hard to implement and would reduce the productivity for multiprocessors. Also, it would not scale up well to hundreds or thousands of processors.

So the solution of disabling interrupts only works well on uniprocessors.

6.9.2   SECOND SOLUTION: USING EXCHANGEWORD

This solution uses a special instruction that allows one processor to read and modify a word in memory without any other processor getting access to the word between the read and the write. The example of this kind of instruction we looked at was `ExchangeWord`.

This solution requires help from the hardware. In particular, the hardware mechanisms that control access to memory must support this kind of memory access. Given that hardware help, this solution is simple and straightforward and works well on multiple processors.

There are several variations of this same instruction that do about the same thing. Another class of instructions is the "test and set" instructions. They read a word from memory, test it (for zero and sign), and write another word into the same memory location, all in one uninterruptable action.

6.9.3   THIRD SOLUTION: SOFTWARE SOLUTIONS

It is easy to appeal to the hardware designers to provide atomic read-then-write operations, and this is an efficient way of handling the problem. But it is interesting to note that one does not need special hardware instructions to solve this problem. There are purely software solutions to the problem as well.

When we say "purely software," we mean no special instructions that hold the bus. We will still be relying on the fact that the memory hardware will provide atomic reads and writes, that is, two simultaneous writes will happen in one order or the other, and will never result in a word that is a combination of the two values written.

It is not obvious how this can be done, and it took some very clever people to work it out. The first solution was discovered around 1965 and showed that it could be done. This solution (due to Dekker) was somewhat complicated and hard to understand. In 1981, Peterson came up with a simpler solution and we will present his solution here.

First let's give a clear statement of the problem to be solved. Two processes are structured as follows:

IMPLEMENTING MUTUAL EXCLUSION

```
void Process1( void ) {
  while( 1 ) {
    DoSomeStuff();
    EnterCriticalSection( 0 );
    DoCriticalSectionStuff();
    LeaveCriticalSection( 0 );
  }
}
void Process2( void ) {
```

```
while( 1 ) {
  DoSomeStuff();
  EnterCriticalSection( 1 );
  DoCriticalSectionStuff();
  LeaveCriticalSection( 1 );
}
}
```

Each process has some other things to do that do not require the use of shared variables. A process will call EnterCriticalSection before accessing the shared variables, perform the operations of the shared variables, and then call LeaveCriticalSection when it is done. Note that the two processes execute exactly the same code to enter and leave their critical section (except for the argument, which is the process number).

The ground rules are:

1. When a process wants to enter its critical section, it will be allowed to do so within a finite time, that is, it will not have to wait forever inside EnterCriticalSection.
2. It is not possible for both processes to be in their critical section at the same time.
3. Processes will only spend a finite time in their critical section, and will not fail inside their critical section (and hence fail to execute the LeaveCriticalSection).
4. A process may spend any amount of time outside its critical section without entering its critical section. Therefore a process that wants to enter its critical section cannot be made to wait for the other process to enter its critical section.

A solution is an implementation of EnterCriticalSection and LeaveCriticalSection that adheres to the rules stated above. Here is Peterson's solution:

IMPLEMENTING MUTUAL EXCLUSION

```
enum { False = 0, True = 1 };

// This is global data available to both processes
int interested[2] = {False, False};
int turn = 0;

void EnterCriticalSection( int this_process ) {
    int other_process = 1 - this_process;
    interested[this_process] = True;
    turn = this_process;
    while( turn == this_process && interested[other_process] ) {
        // do nothing, just wait for this loop to exit
    }
}
void LeaveCriticalSection( int this_process ) {
    interested[this_process] = False;
}
```

First suppose that one process wants to enter but the other is not interested in entering the critical section. It is clear that the process will proceed immediately, since it will find interested[other_process_number] false and the loop will exit immediately.

Now suppose that process 0 gets to point IsInterested, and so interested[0] is true. After this has happened, process 1 cannot possibly exit from the while loop without help from process 0. The reason is that since interested[0] is true, it can only exit the while loop if turn != this_process_number and process 1 will set them equal before it enters the loop.

Eventually both process 0 and process 1 make the assignment turn = this_process_number and enter the loop. If process 0 gets to the loop test before process 1 executes interested[this_process_number] = True, then process 0 will drop out of the loop and enter its critical section. Otherwise it depends on which process executes turn = this_process_number *last*. The one that executes it last will allow the other process to drop out of the loop and enter its critical section.

Look carefully at the code and be sure you understand how and why it works.

6.9.4 WHEN TO USE EACH SOLUTION

All three of these solutions have their advantages, and each is useful in certain situations. Let's look at the strengths and weaknesses of each implementation.

Disabling interrupts:
- Is very fast.
- Does not involve busy waiting.
- Only works with one processor.
- Is the best solution for a single processor.

Using ExchangeWord:
- Requires busy waiting.
- Requires hardware assistance.
- Works with multiple processors.
- Is the best solution for multiprocessors which share memory.

Peterson's solution:
- Requires busy waiting.
- Does not need hardware assistance.
- Works with multiple processors.
- Is the best solution for distributed systems with no central control.

6.9.5 EXAMPLES OF IMPLEMENTING MUTUAL EXCLUSION

What we talked about in this section was the lowest-level implementation of mutual exclusion. This is the mutual exclusion used inside the operating system. This low-level mutual exclusion can then be used to implement message passing or other similar primitives that implement mutual exclusion for processes.

Traditionally, operating systems have run on a single processor and have implemented mutual exclusion by disabling interrupts. This is a simple and fast solution and works well in a single processor. Almost all single-processor operating system do this. Multiprocessors all use some form of hardware solution like `ExchangeWord`.

*6.10   VARIETIES OF COMPUTER MODELS

We have looked at a system with shared memory and two processors. Let us examine other ways we can add processors to a computer system.

We will start out with a basic computer model which consists of three components:

$$Computer = Processor + Memory + Input/Output$$

What different ways can we have two copies of these things? Suppose we had two input/output devices:

$$Computer = Processor + Memory + 2 * Input/Output$$

Well, this is nothing special. Lots of computers have multiple disks, tapes, CD-ROM drives, terminals, etc. We already meant for the *Input/Output* to include multiple devices anyway.

What about having two memories?

$$Computer = Processor + 2 * Memory + Input/Output$$

It is not clear exactly what this might mean. How are two memories different than one large memory? Some older computers had two speeds of memory: some fast memory and some larger, slower memory. This was called *Large Core Storage* on IBM machines and *Extended Core Storage* on CDC machines.

We are especially interested in configurations with more than one processor so more than one user program can be executing at the same time. There are three ways we can look at this. The first is to replicate the processor only.

$$Computer = 2 * Processor + Memory + Input/Output$$

shared-memory
multiprocessors

We call this a *multiprocessor*. The processors share the memory, and these are often called *shared-memory multiprocessors* to emphasize that fact. It is easy for the processors in such a system to communicate because they share a memory and they can communicate using the memory. This is the simplest kind of system with multiple processors, and it is the kind of system we assumed in the operating system in Section 6.5.

We could also replicate the processor and memory as a unit.

$$Computer = 2 * \{Processor + Memory\} + Input/Output$$

multicomputer

This is called a *multicomputer*. The equation does not show it, but there is usually some form of communication between the processor units. This is generally in the form of a wire of some sort, either a bus or a point-to-point connection.

A wire connection is fundamentally different than a memory connection because signals on a wire are transient, the bits are put on the wire one at a time, and each bit replaces the previous one. A wire is like a one-bit shared memory that is constantly changing. A memory retains its value until it is written over again. Messages model a wire connection between processors.

Finally, we could replicate all three.

$$Computer = 2 * \{Processor + Memory + Input/Output\}$$

This is not significantly different for our purpose than the previous configuration, and this is also called a multicomputer.

6.10.1 MULTIPROGRAMMING

The term *multiprogramming* refers to a situation where two or more programs are in memory at the same time, sharing the processor and appearing to be running in parallel. This rapid interleaving of processes is sometimes called logical parallelism. We might loosely say the processes are running in parallel or simultaneously or concurrently, but none of these words is really correct since they all imply running literally at the same time. Multiprogramming assumes a single processor that is being shared. *multiprogramming*

> Multiprogramming switches one processor among several programs kept in a common memory at the same time.

6.10.2 MULTIPROCESSING

The term *multiprocessing* refers to a situation where there is more than one processor in the system. In such a system, it is possible for two processes to run in parallel, something that can only be simulated by a multiprogramming system. *multiprocessing*

Some multiprocessing systems have several processors that share a common memory. These are not that different from a single processor system, and it is possible to take a single processor operating system and modify it to work in such a situation.

On the other hand, some multiprocessing systems have completely separate processors that each have their own memories. This is sometimes called a multicomputer system. The separate computers communicate through communication lines, rather than shared memory. Such a system requires a significantly different kind of operating system. We will look at these kinds of operating systems later in the book.

Figure 6.15 shows three varieties of computer system.

> Multiprocessing switches two or more processors among several programs kept in a common memory at the same time.

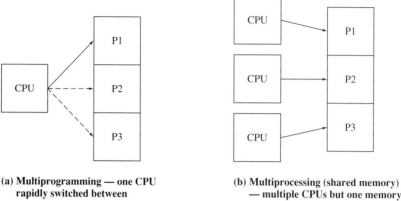

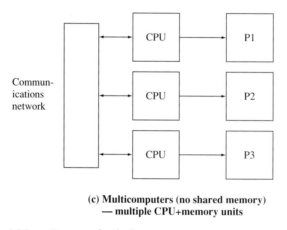

(a) **Multiprogramming — one CPU rapidly switched between processes**

(b) **Multiprocessing (shared memory) — multiple CPUs but one memory**

(c) **Multicomputers (no shared memory) — multiple CPU+memory units**

Figure 6.15   Varieties of multiple processors

DESIGN TECHNIQUE: USING MODELS FOR INSPIRATION

A model is a structure of objects and the relations between them that can be mapped into another system. An example would be using a mathematical equation to model the trajectory of a rocket. One use of models is to understand the system we map the model into. We understand the mathematical equation and transfer that understanding to understand better how a rocket will move. Another use of models is to give us ideas about how to structure the system we map it into. We structure the system so that we can easily map the objects and relations of the model into the system.

The hardware models in this section can give us ideas for software architectures that are structured in similar ways. What we are doing is reusing good ideas. A structure that works in the model may also work well in the system. For example, we used a single processor memory system as a model for processes. The shared memory multiple processor is a model for threads.

It is important to remember, however, that we use the model to generate ideas not to prove them correct or effective. The idea (the new structure) must prove itself useful in the system it is transferred to.

For more discussion of models, see Section 9.7.

> Multicomputing has two or more processor-memory combinations, with one or more processes in each separate memory.

6.11   SUMMARY

Many current computer systems have multiple processors, and in the near future it seems that most computer systems will have multiple processors. This requires the programs running on these systems to share the code and data of the operating system. Sharing the code caused no problem, since the code is read-only. Each processor has its own system stack, so we did not need to share the local variables of the procedures in the operating system. The only variables they had to share were the global variables relating to messages and processes.

Race conditions can occur when two parallel processes are modifying the same variables. The solution is to prevent the two processors from modifying the same variables at the same time. This can be done in a general way with a solution based on a hardware instruction that read and wrote a word in memory in a single, uninterruptable action.

Many systems implement a form of lightweight process called a thread. Several threads can be executing in the same process and can communicate through the (shared) address space of the process. This allowed a simple solution to the problem of how to structure a server process. The implementation of threads consisted mainly of dividing up the two concepts of a process that owns an area of memory and a thread which can be dispatched by the dispatcher. Threads can be implemented in the operating system (kernel threads or lightweight processes) or by the user (user threads). Kernel threads are more flexible, but user threads are more efficient.

Many operating systems implement system calls by allowing the process to run inside the operating system code. After a system call, the process gets a system stack (in the operating system's address space) and runs as a kernel-mode process. This makes waiting inside the operating system easier, since only the process waits, not the whole operating system. It also allows us to allow interrupts while in system mode. The implementation of kernel-mode processes is accomplished by giving each process a kernel-mode stack and saving process state on that stack.

There are three low-level solutions to the mutual exclusion problem. The first solution is to disable interrupts. This solution only works on a single processor system. The second solution is to use a hardware instruction that implements mutual exclusion in the hardware. This is the solution used in multiprocessor systems. The third solution is based on an algorithm by Peterson which implements mutual exclusion in software. This solution is best in systems with no central control.

6.11.1   TERMINOLOGY

After reading this chapter, you should be familiar with the following terms:

- atomic action

- busy waiting
- kernel
- kernel-mode process
- kernel threads
- lightweight process
- logical parallelism
- multicomputer
- multiprocessing
- multiprogramming
- physical parallelism
- pseudo-parallelism
- race condition
- reentrant
- server process
- shared memory multiprocessor
- spin lock
- thread
- thread-safe
- true parallelism
- user threads

6.11.2   Review Questions

The following questions are answered in the text of this chapter:

1. What is the difference between logical and physical parallelism?
2. What are the disadvantages of using two operating systems in a multiprocessor system?
3. What data must be shared in a multiprocessor operating system?
4. What is it about the `ExchangeWord` instruction that makes it the solution to our race condition problem?
5. Why does each processor have its own `current_process` variable?
6. What is busy waiting? What is the alternative?
7. What are the advantages of threads?
8. What are some examples of programs that can use threads?
9. Explain the difference between a process and a thread.
10. Compare user threads and lightweight processes. What advantages do they share and what are their advantages and disadvantages?

11. What are the advantages of kernel-mode processes?

12. Explain why kernel-mode processes are really the same thing as threads in the operating system.

13. State the three ways to implement basic mutual exclusion in an operating system.

14. Compare a multiprocessor with a multicomputer.

15. Why does each process require a kernel stack if we want to use kernel-mode processes?

6.11.3 FURTHER READING

Dijkstra did a lot of early work on software mutual exclusion. Dekker's algorithm is presented in Dijkstra (1968) and (1965) and is the first published solution to the problem. Lamport (1974) developed the bakery algorithm, which is simpler and works naturally for any number of processes. Peterson (1981) developed an even simpler solution.

For discussions of threads, see: Anderson, Lazowska, and Levy (1989); Draves, et al. (1991); Kogan and Rawson (1988); Tevanian, et al. (1987), Massalin and Pu (1989); and Marsh, et al. (1991). Birrell (1989) gives guidelines for programming with threads.

6.13 PROBLEMS

1. In the multiprocessor operating system, we used spin locks (using the **Exchange-Word** instruction) instead of blocking interrupts. Explain why we had to do this.

2. We defined the clock in Chapter 2 so that setting the clock to 0 also cancels any pending clock interrupts. Suppose that the clock did not do this. Explain how a race condition could occur between the clock interrupt and the system call interrupt.

3. Suppose we tried to protect access to the process state directly with the **Exchange-Word** instruction. Consider the following code that does that.

```
int SelectProcessToRun( void ) {
    int i;
    for( i = 0; i < NumberOfProcesses; ++i ) {
        if( pd[i].state == Ready ) {
            R14 = Running;
            ExchangeWord( R14, pd[i].state );
            if( R14 == Ready )
                // We grabbed the "Ready" so this is the one to run
                return i;
```

```
                //else another processor grabbed this one so keep looking
            }
        }
        return -1;
    }
```

This is more direct, but it has a subtle problem. It will ensure that only one processor will run a process, but it may inadvertently change the state of a ~~running~~ process. *being run by the other processor* Explain what can go wrong here. *Hint:* Consider a situation where one processor is much faster than the other—so fast that it can grab the process, start it, and run it for a while before the other processor can execute even a few instructions.

4. In Section 6.3, we showed a race condition with the process table. Show another race condition with the message buffer pool that will also cause an error to occur.

5. In Section 6.3, we showed a race condition with the process table. Show another race condition with the message queues that will also cause an error to occur.

6. Why is static data treated the same as global data when you are converting an operating system to run on a multiprocessor?

7. How do you decide what data to duplicate for each processor and what data to share between processors when converting an operating system to a multiprocessor operating system?

8. In our parallel hardware, why does each CPU need its own timer?

9. We noted in Section 6.5.5 that we could have one flag to protect all the message queues, or a separate flag for each message queue, and that this would allow more parallelism. Consider the possibility of having a separate flag for each slot in the process table. Would this be a good idea or not? Explain your answer.

10. Suppose we decided to have just one mutual exclusion flag for the entire operating system. It will guard access to the process table, the messages queues, the message buffers, and the disk queue. Will this work? If not, describe what can go wrong. If it does work, indicate whether you think it is a good idea and what problems it might cause even though it does protect the variables.

11. We showed in this chapter how we can easily extend our simple operating system to work with two processors. Does this solution extend also to three processes with only minor changes in the code? That is, will our spin lock idea work for three processors? How about 10,000 processors? What other problems might crop up with 10,000 processors? Would this be a feasible system?

12. In Section 6.5.2, we showed how to implement mutual exclusion in the use of the process table using the ExchangeWord instruction. Suppose we have a different instruction, TestAndSet:

    • int TestAndSet(int wordToTest, int valueToSetItTo);—This instruction reads the current value of wordToTest, sets wordToTest to valueToSetItTo, and returns a 1 if the current value of wordToTest was non-zero and a 0 if the current value of wordToTest was zero.

Recode StartUsingProcessTable using TestAndSet instead of ExchangeWord while still keeping it safe for two processes(like the ExchangeWord version is).

13. We proposed using two ready lists in a two-processor system (one for each processor) to avoid having to solve the problem of sharing the ready list between the two processors. We pointed out that one problem with this solution is that it might happen than one ready list is empty while there are still processes in the other ready list. Thus one processor will be idle while there is work to do. Suppose we try to solve this problem by moving processes from the nonempty ready list to the empty ready list. Why is this not a real solution to the problem?

14. Add code to the system call interrupt handler to implement the WaitThread system call.

15. Change the implementation of threads to use a single-linked thread list.

16. In the implementation of the CreateThread system call, we copy the base and bound values from the process descriptor to the thread descriptor. Why is this necessary? Why isn't the copy in the process descriptor sufficient?

17. In order to implement user threads, we need to be able to set a timer and get a user-level interrupt when the timer goes to 0. Why do we need user-level timer interrupts like this?

Design a system call to request a timer interrupt. Explain what the parameters to the system call would be.

Describe how the operating system would implement this system call. Just give the outline of the implementation describing the problems that you would have to deal with and how you would deal with them.

18. One potential problem with threads is that all threads get an equal chance to be run, and so a process can get more processor time by creating more threads. Suppose we wanted to treat the processes more equally and give equal time to each process no matter how many threads it had. Describe a method for doing this.

19. Look at the implementation of SendMessage and ReceiveMessage in the implementation of kernel-mode processes. Describe what has changed from the original implementation (in Section 5.6), and explain why the changes were made.

20. Dekker's solution to software mutual exclusion goes like this:

IMPLEMENTING MUTUAL EXCLUSION (DEKKER)

```
// This is global data available to both processes
int interested[2] = {False, False};
int turn = 0;

void EnterCriticalSection( int this_process ) {
    int other_process = 1 - this_process;
    interested[this_process] = True;
    while( interested[other_process] ) {
        if( turn == other_process ) {
            interested[this_process] = False;
```

```
            while( turn == other_process )
                /* do nothing*/ ;
            interested[this_process] = True;
        }
    }
}
void LeaveCriticalSection( int this_process ) {
    int other_process = 1 - this_process;
    turn = other_process;
    interested[this_process] = False;
}
```

Compare this with Peterson's solution and describe the simplifications he made. What are the insights he had that simplified the solution? Explain why they are correct.

21. Consider Peterson's solution to the mutual exclusion problem given on page 194. Suppose we make a small change to the problem and change the line:

$$turn = this\_process\_number;$$

to:

$$turn = other\_process\_number;$$

This change will cause the program to no longer be correct. Describe what can go wrong if this change is made. That is, describe a sequence of events that leads to a situation where either:

- Both processes can be in their critical section at the same time, or

- A process wants to enter its critical section, but it cannot and loops infinitely waiting to enter.

22. Suppose we wanted to extend Peterson's algorithm to three processes. Say we call them A, B, and C. One way to do this is to use the algorithm twice, once between A and B and once between C and the winner of A and B. Describe in more detail how this would work, and give an argument that it actually does work.

23. Consider Peterson's solution to the mutual exclusion problem given on page 194. Suppose we wanted to extend this to three processes instead of two. We do this by changing the code to this new version:

```
enum{ True = 1, False = 0 };
int interested[3]; // changed from [2]
void EnterCriticalSection( int this_process_number ) {
    int other1, other2;
    switch( this_process_number ) {
        case 0: other1 = 1; other2 = 2; break;
        case 1: other1 = 0; other2 = 2; break;
        case 2: other1 = 0; other2 = 1; break;
```

```
        }
    interested[this_process_number] = True;
    turn = this_process_number;
    while( turn == this_process_number
        && (interested[other1] || interested[other2] ) {
            // do nothing in the loop, just wait for an exit
    }
}
void LeaveCriticalSection( int this_process_number ) {
    interested[this_process_number] = False;
}
```

The big change is in the waiting loop. The second part of the wait condition used to test whether the other process was interested. Now it tests whether *either* of the other processes are interested.

This generalization to three processes is not correct. Describe what can go wrong, that is, describe a sequence of events that leads to a situation where either:

•   Two processes are in their critical section at the same time, or

•   A process wants to enter its critical section, but it cannot and loops infinitely waiting to enter.

7

Interprocess Communication Patterns

The concept of a process is based on the idea of a program executing on a virtual processor that is independent of all other virtual processors. Since the processes may be executing on the same physical computer, they will compete for processor time (and other hardware resources) and slow each other down, but other than that they operate independently. This is the model that best describes situations when you compile and edit at the same time, or when you have two windows running programs at the same time. But sometimes we want to elaborate on this model and allow processes to communicate with each other. Processes communicate with each other for many reasons and in many different ways, but certain patterns of communication occur over and over again. These patterns model the relationships between processes as they cooperate and compete. In this chapter, we will examine these recurring patterns of interprocess communication.

7.1   USING INTERPROCESS COMMUNICATION

Why are we spending so much time on patterns of communication between user processes? When we talk about memory management in Chapter 10, we will not spend much time explaining to you why you need memory and what you should use it for. In Chapter 16, when we talk about file systems, we will not spend much time telling you why you should use files and explaining techniques for file use. We do not do this because you already know these things. You already know that you need memory to solve problems in software, memory for code, memory for large arrays, memory for other dynamic structures. You know that files are useful and you know how to use them.

The situation with interprocess communication is different, however. It is not common for typical computer users to use more than one process except in carefully controlled situations like shell pipelines or in situations where no interprocess communication is required. Typical programmers do not normally write code where processes have to communicate. As a consequence, we think it is important to spend time here talking, not just about how to implement interprocess communication in an operating system, but about how to use the interprocess communication system calls that an operating system provides. It is important to understand the use of these calls in order to appreciate the reasons they are implemented the way they are. In addition, this style of programming is becoming more and more common for programmers who are not systems programmers. It is now common to have to deal with processes, threads, networks, pipes, sockets, messages, shared memory, semaphores, etc.

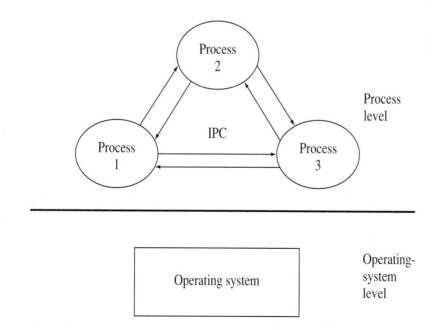

Figure 7.1   Interprocess communication (IPC) at the process level

In this chapter, we will discuss the problems one encounters when programming multiple processes and interprocess communication. For each problem, we will discuss the typical solutions and the common idioms and styles of this type of programming.

We will present these problems at the process level (see Figure 7.1) but, as we saw in Chapter 6, the problems of communication between concurrent activities are the same at the process level and the operating system level.

7.2   PATTERNS OF INTERPROCESS COMMUNICATION

In the previous chapters, we have seen two styles of communication between processes. The first one we saw was the use of messages for communication. This was a simple method, similar to sending letters or e-mail. We also looked at named pipes, which make communication between processes look like reading and writing files. A third method of communication is possible between threads (which share memory), and that is to communicate through the reading and writing of common memory. These three approaches to interprocess communication differ considerably in their details, but in principle they are the same—one process sends information and events to another process. In this chapter, we will use all three methods in our examples.

7.2.1   COMPETING AND COOPERATING

There are two main reasons why we have implemented processes in our operating systems. The first is to allow processes to proceed separately (in parallel) and share the resources of the computer system. In this case, each process has its own task to do, but it needs to interact with other processes in order to share the resources. For example, suppose that two processes would like to print a file on the printer. They have to communicate in order to decide which process will get to use it first, and the second process must wait until the first process is done using the printer. We call this
process competition. Another reason we have implemented processes is so that we can have two processes work together on a single task. For example, we might want to search for something in a large number of files. You can have two (or more) processes working on different files at the same time. UNIX pipelines are another example of using two or more processes to do a single task. The idea in pipelines is that each process is a specialist and does one job well. A more complicated job is done by
process cooperation
combining several specialist processes together. This is called *process cooperation.*

As processes compete for resources and cooperate on tasks, they must communicate with one another. We have called this interprocess communication or IPC. For the examples in the first part of this chapter, we will use messages as our IPC method. The processes will communicate with messages, but the more interesting question is what will they say to each other? It turns out that there are a few standard patterns of interprocess communication that cover almost all the ways that processes interact.

process competition

We will present a survey of these standard IPC patterns. Once we understand these, we will be able to understand most IPC problems and solutions.

In Chapter 6, we looked at the problem with competition for data structures in a multiprocessor operating system. In the following sections, we will look at similar problems at the user process level.

There is just one basic IPC pattern for interprocess competition, and that is the mutual exclusion pattern. We will start by motivating the problem at the user level, and then show the mutual exclusion IPC pattern. In the following sections, we will look at a number of different patterns of process cooperation and a complex variant of the mutual exclusion problem—the database access and update IPC pattern.

> Processes interact by competing for resources and cooperating in accomplishing a task.

7.3   PROBLEMS WHEN PROCESSES COMPETE

Suppose we have a network with several computers on it, where all user files are kept in a file server. Two users are trying to edit the same file at the same time (see Figure 7.2). For example, suppose everyone in the operating systems class is asked to add their names and e-mail addresses to a common class file, and two students try to do it at the same time.

The way almost all text editors work is that they read into memory a copy of the file to be edited when the edit program is started. While the version in memory is being edited, the version on disk is not changed. When the edited file is finally saved, the disk version is changed.[1] Suppose we assume that each read or write of the (entire) disk file is a single event that cannot take place simultaneously with other reads

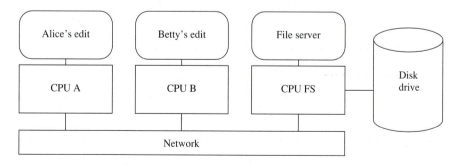

Figure 7.2   Two simultaneous edits using a common file server

---

[1]What is maintained in memory is often not an actual copy of the file being edited, but rather data structures that represent a copy of the file. This is an implementation issue, and the semantics are the same: The editor maintains its version of the file, and the version on disk is unchanged.

and writes. Then there are two significant events in each of the two editing sessions: edit classList (read the file) and write classList. These four events can take place in six different orders:

Order 1			Order 2			Order 3		
edit-a			edit-a			edit-a		
write-a					edit-b			edit-b
	edit-b		write-a					write-b
	write-b				write-b	write-a		

Order 4			Order 5			Order 6		
	edit-b				edit-b			edit-b
	write-b		edit-a			edit-a		
edit-a					write-b	write-a		
write-a			write-a					write-b

Note that we are assuming that the operating system will not allow a read and a write to occur simultaneously, but will always order them one way or the other.

Of these six orders, only 1 and 4 will result in a correct file. Orders 3 and 5 will lose Betty's edits and orders 2 and 6 will lose Alice's edits. Alice and Betty are in competition for access to the file. In order for things to work correctly, they have to edit the file one at a time, that is, each one has to exclude the other when she is editing the file.[2] This is a specific example of a general class of problems that can occur whenever two processes share data. The general problem is called the *mutual exclusion problem*. A sequence of actions that must be done one at a time is called a *critical section*.

mutual exclusion

critical section

This is the identical situation we had when looking into the problem of implementing our operating system on a two-processor system in Chapter 6. The problem here is the same as the problem there: the read-then-write is not an atomic operation, and so the reads and writes can be interleaved and we might get incorrect results. The solution there was to make the read-then-write into a single, uninterruptable operation using the new ExchangeWord instruction.

The same solution will work here: make the read-edit-write into an uninterruptable operation. But that solution is harder to implement here. We cannot just appeal to the hardware designers because it is not sensible to make reading a file, editing it, and writing it out an uninterruptable machine operation. Instead, we have to come up with a software solution, that is, the ability to create an uninterruptable operation out of any sequence of instructions. Section 7.6 shows how to do this.

---

[2]Some text editors will detect, before writing a file, that it has been changed since it was read into the editor buffer and will produce a message and ask the user what she wants to do. This prevents the old edits from being overwritten, but it does not solve the basic problem.

Permission to use the file is a resource that can only be given to one process at a time. It is what we call a *logical resource,* meaning that it is not a piece of hardware of which there is only one copy, but it is a logical object defined by the operating system. A resource that can only be used by one process at a time and which can be returned and used by another process is called a *serially reusable resource*. Memory and disk space are also reusable resources. We say "serially reusable" since it can be used by only one process at a time (serially), but once a process is finished with it, another process can use it (reusable).

logical resource

serially reusable resource

7.4 RACE CONDITIONS AND ATOMIC ACTIONS

In Section 7.3, we looked at the problem that can occur when two processes try to edit the same file at the same time. The problem was that when the second editor's write occurs, the changes made by the first edit are overwritten and lost. Stated more generally, the problem is that the relative timing of the two writes makes a difference in the outcome. Normally, when two processes are running at the same time, the results come out the same no matter which one finishes first. When the order of process completion does make a difference the problem is called a *race condition,* because it is a race between the two processes to see who finished first.[3] A race condition can only occur when there is some sort of communication between the two processes. In this case, the communication is in the form of shared memory, that is, the shared file.

race condition

A race condition can only occur when the two processes are running in parallel. If they run sequentially, in either order, then no problem occurs and both edits are preserved. This observation leads to the solution to the problem: do not allow the two processes to run in parallel. But how can we do this? The whole idea of processes is that the operating system creates a virtual processor for each process, and they can all run in parallel. This model works most of the time, since most of the time processes are not communicating or using shared memory. What we need is an additional mechanism that prevents some processes from running in parallel when two or more of them are using shared memory.

Figure 7.3 shows a very simple race condition involving the incrementing of a shared variable. In order to increment the shared variable, a process must:

1. Read the shared variable into a register.
2. Increment the value in the register.
3. Store the new value into the shared variable.

The problem occurs if one process reads the shared variable, then a second process reads it before the first process can write it out again (see Figure 7.4). They will both increment the same value, and one increment will be lost.

| [3]Actually it is a reverse race, since the process that finished last has its edits prevail and can be said to win.

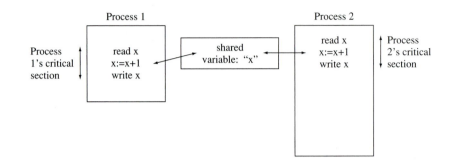

Figure 7.3   Race condition on a shared variable

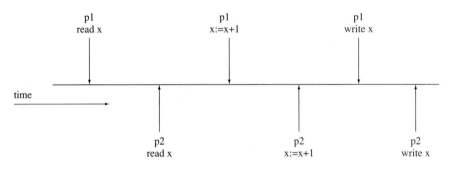

Figure 7.4   Race condition timing chart

The solution to the problem is not to allow any other process to access the variable while one process is using it. Figure 7.5 shows the exclusion areas.

atomic action

In most machines, a single machine instruction is an *atomic action,* that is, once the instruction has begun execution, the entire instruction executes before any interrupts are handled.[4] If you have a single processor that is time shared between a number of processes, a timer interrupt can occur and the running process can change between any two instructions, but not within a single instruction. We need to generalize this idea to allow a sequence of instructions to be atomic.

The section of the process's program that uses the shared memory will be called the critical section of the process. Each process sharing some memory has a corresponding critical section where it uses the shared memory. What we require to solve the race condition problem is to ensure that only one process at a time will be executing in its critical section. Another way to say this is to make an execution of the critical section an atomic action with respect to the other process's executions of their critical sections, that is, they execute their critical sections in sequence and not in parallel.

---

[4]There are, of course, some machines where this is not true. Some processors have a few lengthy instructions that can be interrupted in the middle and later restarted. An example of such an instruction is one that moves a large block of memory. The VAX architecture has several instructions that are interruptible.

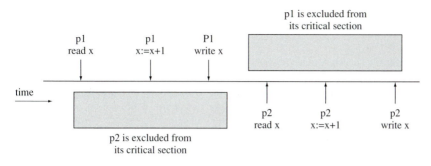

Figure 7.5   Critical section to prevent a race condition

We do not exclude processes from running in parallel in the general case: we only exclude them from running in parallel when both of them are in their critical section. A process that is not in a critical section is free to execute at any time the dispatcher will let it. But a process trying to execute in its critical section must wait for, and cannot run in parallel with, another process that is in its critical section. So we take away the privilege of running in parallel in a few selected instances where it can cause problems.

Figure 7.5 shows how to avoid race conditions by excluding a process from executing in its critical section while another process is executing in its critical section.

But how can we prevent two processes from running in their critical sections at the same time? Let's review how we solved the problem in our simple operating system. When we extended the simple operating system to handle multiple processors, we had a mutual exclusion problem with accessing and changing the fields of the process descriptor. The critical section was the reading and writing of the state field in the process descriptor. We solved the problem by making the reading of the current value of a memory cell and the writing of a new value an atomic action. We did this by assuming the memory-passing hardware would do it for us.

This memory hardware atomic action is enough to deal with that mutual exclusion problem, but it cannot be used to solve our problem with the simultaneous editing of a single file by two text editors. To solve this problem, we need an operating system mechanism that can implement atomic actions. We will see that message passing can be used to solve these problems. We have previously seen that we can implement messages using ExchangeWord.

Let us summarize the terms and the issues: each communicating process has a sequence of instructions that modify shared data, and this sequence of instructions is called a *critical section*. If two processes are executing in their (respective) critical sections at the same time, then they will interfere with each other, and the result of their executions will depend on the order in which they do things and the relative speed of execution of each process. This situation is called a *race condition* and should be avoided. The way to avoid race conditions is to only allow one process at a time to be executing in its critical section. That is, any process executing in its critical section must exclude all the other processes from executing in their critical

DESIGN TECHNIQUE: WIN BIG, THEN GIVE SOME BACK

Multiprogramming provides many benefits. One process can run while another does input or output. The processor can be shared between processes and each can think it has the entire hardware processor to itself. But multiprogramming can cause problems when the processes share data. If we forbid processes that share data from running in parallel while they are using the shared data, we will lose a little of the benefits of multiprogramming, but it solves the mutual exclusion problem that multiprogramming creates. We give a little back to solve a problem the optimization (multiprogramming) created, but we still come out way ahead.

This technique can be used in many places where an optimization loses some important property or creates a problem. But giving a little back, we can solve the problem the optimization caused, and this can make the optimization acceptable. The same idea occurs outside of computer science. For example, when a college increases tuition, it usually increases scholarship assistance to help those students who cannot afford the extra tuition.

You can read more about this design technique in Section 9.3.

sections at the same time. How to achieve this is called the *mutual exclusion problem*. The mutual exclusion problem can be solved by making the execution of the entire critical section a single action on the shared data that cannot occur at the same time as a similar action by any other process. That single action is called an *atomic action*.

7.5   NEW MESSAGE-PASSING SYSTEM CALLS

In Section 3.10.1, we discussed various ways in which we could name message queues. In this chapter, it will be convenient to have message queues named in the file system. This avoids having to specify a parent process that starts them both up and passes them the message queue identifiers. Here are the new system calls to attach to a message queue. The `SendMessage` and `ReceiveMessage` system calls are unchanged.

- `int AttachMessageQueue( char * msg_q_name );`—The message queue named `msg_q_name` is looked up in the file naming system. If the name does not exist, it is created as a "message queue file." The attach count for the message queue is increased by one. An identifier to the message queue is returned. All processes that attach to the message queue of the same name will be given the same message queue identifier, and it will refer to the same queue. The message queue identifier will be an integer that has meaning to the operating system, but is just an arbitrary number of the system caller. The message queue identifier is used in the send and receive message system calls. A valid message queue identifier will always be a positive integer. The return value is -1 if there was a problem that prevented it from being created (such as no available memory).

- `int DetachMessageQueue( int msg_q_id );`—The attach count for the message queue is decreased by one. If this is the last process to detach from the message queue, then the name of the message queue file is deleted from the file system. The return value is -1 if the identifier is not a valid message queue identifier.

When a process exits, any message queues still attached will be detached. This is the same thing that we did for open files. Since the operating system knows the process is exiting, and it knows what files it has open and what message queues it has attached, it can easily close the files and detach the message queues if the user fails to do so. It is better to do this than to require the user to remember to do so. It is common to forget things like this, and programs that fail unexpectedly will not have a chance to do so.

> Do not require the user to clean things up if the operating system has sufficient information to do so for the user.

7.6   IPC PATTERN: MUTUAL EXCLUSION

Now we will show the solution to the mutual exclusion problem using messages. It turns out that the basic message transfer system solves the problem for us, and so the solution at the user process level is straightforward.

Consider two processes, A and B, that both need to make some changes to a file named F. If they both try to change the file at the same time, they will interfere with each other and the file will not come out right. What we need is for these two processes to share access to the file so that, at any one time, only one of them is trying to change the file. The solution involves using a message queue to guard access to file F.

TWO-PROCESS MUTUAL EXCLUSION

```
// Convenience procedure to receive an empty message
void WaitForEmptyMsg( int msg_queue ) {
    int msg[MsgSize];
    ReceiveMessage( msg_queue, msg );
}
// Both processes (process A and process B) have the same code.
void main( int argc, char * argv[ ] ) { // Process A or B
        // The name "/usr/queue/FMutex" in the file system does not name
        // a file but rather a message queue.
    int mutex_queue = AttachMessageQueue( "/usr/queue/FMutex" );
        // Only one of the two processes should "seed" the message
        // queue with an initial message. We postulate a function to
        // tell the process whether it is process A or process B.
    if( IAmProcessA() ) // start with exactly one message in the queue
        SendMsgTo( mutex_queue );
        // Each process loops forever, alternately doing things outside of
        // its critical section and then using file F.
```

```
while( 1 ) {
        // In this part of the loop it is not interested
        // in using file F.
    DoOtherThings( );
        //
        // This is the code to enter the critical section.
    WaitForEmptyMsg( mutex_queue );
        //
    UseFileF( );
        //
        // Exit the critical section.
        // Replace the message in the queue.
    SendMsgTo( mutex_queue );
    }

}
```

Figure 7.6 shows the pattern of messages. The message queue starts out with one message in it.

None of the messages have any information in them; it is just the existence of the messages that is important. We define a convenience procedure, **WaitForEmpty Msg,** which is used whenever we do not care about the contents of the message.

It is necessary to "seed" the queue with exactly one message. One process (and only one) must be chosen to do this. In this case we have chosen process A. Another solution is to have a special startup process whose whole job is to initialize the queues.

Processes A and B look for the message (that is, try to receive it) in the queue when they want to write into the file F. Once one process receives the message, then the queue is empty and the other process cannot receive a message from it until the first process finishes using the file F and sends another message to the queue. The message in that queue acts like a kind of ticket. The holder of the ticket can write into the file F.

In some cases, a process will receive the same message it sent. It is unusual to read from the same message queue that you send to, but in this case the messages are like tickets, and so you can replace the ticket and then pick it up again later. Even though each message in the queue is actually a new message, replacing the

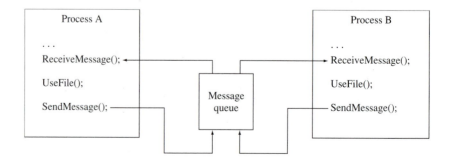

Figure 7.6   Mutual exclusions message pattern

old one, it is useful to think of it as always the same message. When you receive the message, you just hold it for a while (while you are using file F), and then you put it back again later (when you are finished using file F).

7.6.1 N Process Mutual Exclusion

The solution as shown above will work for any number of processes. Only one process at a time will be able to use file F. The only difference is that there might be several processes waiting for a message from the message queue.

7.6.2 Voluntary Cooperation in Mutual Exclusion

If we look at the solution to the mutual exclusion problem given in the previous section, we can see that we are depending on each process to voluntarily "do the right thing" and not try to access file F without first trying to receive the message from the queue. In many cases, this is an acceptable solution. Often, processes sharing a resource all want it to be shared properly, so they will go through the proper protocols. There would be no advantage to not using the mutual exclusion pattern, because then your edits to file F might be lost.

But there are situations when you cannot depend on the processes to act according to the mutual exclusion rules, either because they could gain from cheating or because the processes are not guaranteed to be debugged. What can we do in those situations to ensure that the processes go through the proper procedures before file access?

One solution to this problem is to combine the mutual exclusion control and the data modification into a single procedure. Then the process doing the modification

---

DESIGN TECHNIQUE: REDUCING A PROBLEM TO A SPECIAL CASE

As we see from this section, messages can be used to solve the mutual exclusion problem. But in Chapter 6 we found that we had to solve a mutual exclusion problem in order to implement messages. We call this a recursive design problem. While trying to solve a problem with a certain method, we run into another instance of the same problem we are trying to solve. It is common to find that you have to solve a special case of a problem while trying to solve the general case of the problem. Usually, the special case of the problem can be solved with a method that would not work for the general case of the problem.

We cannot use busy waiting to solve the general mutual exclusion problem because it is too wasteful of processor time for the potentially long waits possible in general mutual exclusion. But we can use busy waiting to protect message queues because the waiting intervals are very short.

Consider a totally different example. Programs should provide help so that the users do not need to remember how to use every feature of the program. But it is not unreasonable to expect users to remember how to use the help system itself. By knowing that special case, they can get help on any other problem they encounter.

You can read more about reducing a problem to a special case in Section 9.5.

cannot avoid going through the mutual exclusion. There is a mechanism called *monitors* that does this. We can also implement this with messages by having a process that you call to do the modifications for you.

7.7   IPC PATTERN: SIGNALING

Suppose you have a special process that informs you when interesting events occur. It will put up a window on your screen if it thinks you are working on your terminal (based on keystrokes and mouse activity), send you mail, or even beep your beeper! This works so well that you would like all events to be signaled through this process.

Now suppose you send a file to be printed, and you tell the printer control process (sometimes called the *printer daemon*) to send a message to your informer process when the printing is completed. This is an interprocess signaling pattern, and the solution is extremely easy: The printer daemon sends a message to your informer process. Here is the code:

SIGNALING AN INFORMER PROCESS

```
void main() { //Printer Daemon
    while( 1 ) {
        PrintJob();
        SendMsgTo( informer_queue[i], PrintingDone );
    }
}
void main() { // Informer Process
    int msg[MsgSize];
    while( 1 ) {
        //wait for a message to display
        ReceiveMessage( my_queue, msg );
        //inform the person the printing is done.
    }
}
```

signaling

The general *signaling* pattern is shown next.

SIGNALING

```
void main() { //Signal Sender
    int signal_queue = AttachMessageQueue( "/usr/queue/receiver" );
    // Do what you need to do, then signal completion
    SendMsgTo( signal_queue );
}
void main() { //Signal Receiver
    int signal_queue = AttachMessageQueue( "/usr/queue/receiver" );
    int msg[MsgSize];
```

```
    // wait for the sender process to send the signal
    ReceiveMessage( signal_queue, msg );
    // Do something in response to the signal
}
```

The signal sender is doing some task, and the signal receiver wants to know when the task is completed. The task completion event is signaled by sending a message to the signal queue (here /usr/queue/receiver). The signal receiver might have other activities to carry out first, but will eventually have to wait for the signal message. When the message comes, it knows the task is completed and it can go on to do whatever it needs to do after that event (the completion of the task) has happened.

In one-way signaling, the signal sender process never waits for the signal receiver process; it just sends the message and goes on to other things. The signal receiver process, however, might have to wait for the signal. Figure 7.7 shows process signaling.

7.8   IPC PATTERN: RENDEZVOUS

Sometimes it is necessary for two processes to synchronize and do something at exactly the same time. For example, suppose we have a computer game for two people on two different computers. A process on each computer runs the game for one person. When the game begins, we want both players to start at the same time. The code to handle this is straightforward. Note the symmetry of the solution.

TWO-PROCESS RENDEZVOUS

```
void main( int argc, char *argv[ ] ) { // Game Player A
    int b_queue = AttachMessageQueue( "/usr/queue/gpb" );
    SendMsgTo( b_queue, ReadyToStart );
    int a_queue = AttachMessageQueue( "/usr/queue/gpa" );
    WaitForEmptyMsg( a_queue );
}
void main( int argc, char *argv[ ] ) { //Game Player B
    int a_queue = AttachMessageQueue( "/usr/queue/gpa" );
    SendMsgTo( a_queue, ReadyToStart );
    int b_queue = AttachMessageQueue( "/usr/queue/gpb" );
    WaitForEmptyMsg( b_queue );
}
```

A *rendezvous* is really just two one-way signals, one in each direction. Signaling is not symmetric, since the signal sender never waits for the signal receiver, but the signal receiver might have to wait for the signal sender. In a rendezvous,

rendezvous

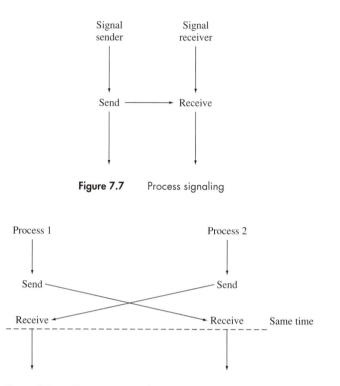

Figure 7.7   Process signaling

Figure 7.8   Two-process rendezvous

each process is signaling the other and so the situation is symmetric. The process that gets to the rendezvous point first will have to wait for the other process.

We send the message "ReadyToStart" mainly as a comment to the reader. The receiver does not look at the message contents. We do not worry about the message contents because we assume that no other processes will be sending messages to these particular queues. The message queue you read the message from implies what event has occurred.

Figure 7.8 shows two-process rendezvous.

Another example of the rendezvous pattern would be where two processes each administer half of a database. Suppose they wanted to write out a checkpoint of the entire database so they could reconstruct it later if the processes fail. They should both save their part of the database at the same time so a consistent version is saved. They would rendezvous and then save their part of the database before they made any further changes to it. This would ensure a consistent version of the database.

7.8.1   MANY-PROCESS RENDEZVOUS

If we want to start three or more players at the same time, we can generalize this by using a separate process as the game coordinator. Every player sends a message to the game coordinator when he or she is ready to go, and when all the messages are in, the game coordinator starts all the processes. The code is shown below.

MANY-PROCESS RENDEZVOUS

```
#define NumberOfPlayers 3
void main ( int argc, char *argv[ ]) { //Game Coordinator
    int msg[MsgSize];
    int player[NumberOfPlayers];
    int coordinator_queue = AttachMessageQueue( "/usr/queue/coordq" );
    // wait unitl all the players are ready to start
    for( i = 0; i < NumberOfPlayers; ++i) {
        ReceiveMessage( coordinator_queue, msg );
        player[i] = msg[1];
    }
    // now let them all start
    for(i = 0;i < NumberOfPlayers; ++i ) {
        SendMsgTo( player[i], Begin Playing );
    }
}
void main( int argc, char *argv[]) {// Game Player i
    int coordinator_queue = AttachMessageQueue( "/usr/queue/coordq" );
    char qname[32];
    sprintf( qname, "/usr/queue/%s", argv[1]);
    int my_queue = AttachMessageQueue( qname );
    SendMsgTo( coordinator_queue, ReadyToStart, my_queue );
    WaitForEmptyMsg( my_queue );
}
```

Each player process sends a message containing its message queue identifier to the coordinator process. When the coordinator has received all the messages, it sends go signals to all the player processes. Note how we are passing a message queue identifier from one process to another. The message queue identifiers are operating-system-wide identifiers and have the same meaning in all processes.

Actually, the first player will receive the go signal before the others, but we are assuming here that the messages are all sent rapidly and this will not be noticed. In fact, message sending on computers is very fast, and all the messages will go out and be received within a small fraction of a second (assuming a relatively unloaded, local area network).[5]

Figure 7.9 shows three-process rendezvous. The generalization to N processes is obvious. This solution assumes that no process will fail, which is unrealistic in a distributed system. One problem with a coordinator process is that the whole system depends on that one process.

7.9　IPC PATTERN: PRODUCER-CONSUMER

In order to see the Adobe fonts known to the X server, we might run the pipeline:

　　xlsfonts | grep adobe

---

[5]We cannot really assume this in general, but we will accept it for the purpose of this example. Dealing with unpredictable network delays is a difficult problem.

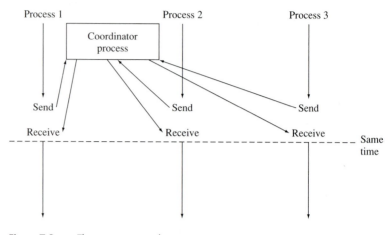

Figure 7.9   Three-process rendezvous

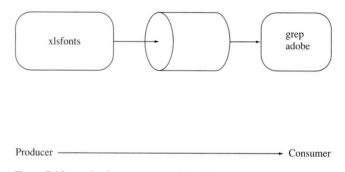

Figure 7.10   Producer-consumer IPC pattern

We use a pipeline to piece together tools. The first tool, xlsfonts, generates the font list. The second tool, grep adobe, filters out the ones we are not interested in.

These two tools are independent processes, but they need to communicate with each other to work in a pipeline. These processes are communicating in what we call a *producer-consumer* pattern. xlsfonts produces lines of text which are consumed by grep adobe. Figure 7.10 shows this graphically.

The producer-consumer relationship is the most basic pattern of cooperative inter-process communication. The producer-consumer pattern occurs when one process, the producer, is producing something that a second process, the consumer, needs. The idea is that, to complete a task, the producer must first work on it, and then the consumer must finish the work. In fact, almost all forms of process cooperation can be considered to be variations on the producer-consumer pattern. This seems reasonable when you think about it. Why would two processes be working together? It must be that each one is doing part of a task. Unless they can work on the task at the same time, one process has to start the work and the other process has to complete it. The major exception is when the task can be separated into disjointed parts that can be worked on in parallel by separate processes.

producer-consumer

The pipeline we described above (xlsfonts | grep adobe) can be implemented using messages as follows.

IMPLEMENTING A PIPELINE

```
void main() { // xlsfonts (the producer)
    int grep_queue = AttachMessageQueue( "/usr/queue/grep" );
    while( 1 ) {
        // find the next font name
        SendMsgTo( grep_queue, fontName );
  }
}
void main() { // grep (the consumer)
    int msg[MsgSize];
    int grep_queue = AttachMessageQueue( "/usr/queue/grep" );
    while( 1 ) {
      ReceiveMessage( grep_queue, msg );
      if( end_of_font_names )
            break;
      if( font_name_matched_pattern ) {
            // print font name
      }
    }
}
```

We have skipped over some details, such as what happens if the font name is too long to be sent in a single message and how the end of the font name is encoded. But these are simple to fix once the basic IPC pattern is established.

7.9.1 THE BASIC PRODUCER-CONSUMER PATTERN

In order to look at some variations, we will now show the pattern in a more abstract form.

THE PRODUCER-CONSUMER IPC PATTERN

```
void main( ) {// The Producer
    int consumer_queue = AttachMessageQueue( "/usr/queue/consumer_q" );
    while( 1 ) {
        // Produce a message
        SendMsgTo( consumer_queue, msg );
    }
}
void main() { //The Consumer
    int msg[MsgSize];
    int consumer_queue = AttachMessageQueue( "/usr/queue/consumer_q" );
    while( 1 ) {
        ReceiveMessage( consumer_queue, msg );
```

```
        // consume the message
    }
}
```

Notice that this pattern is just the one-way signaling pattern, but in a loop this time. In signaling, we only looked at a single interaction. Here, the producer can signal a number of messages before the consumer starts consuming them. The messages are queued by the operating system until the consumer can receive them. We say the operating system is *buffering* the messages. This allows the producer to get ahead of the consumer.

What is the use of buffering? Buffering is useful when the producer is *bursty*, that is, when it produces buffers at an uneven rate. If the consumer consumes buffers at a steady rate, then this avoids forcing the producer to wait for the consumer. For example, a program might compute for a while, then produce many lines of output. The printer prints output at a steady rate. Buffering allows the program to produce lots of lines quickly, and then go off and compute while the printer is printing.

Similarly, the consumer might be bursty. In this case, the steady producer can build up a queue of things, and then the consumer can consume them very quickly once it starts up.

7.9.2   LIMITING THE NUMBER OF BUFFERS USED

But there is a limit to the usefulness of buffering. If the producer produces megabytes of information for a slow consumer, it will fill up all the buffers in the operating system. It is useful to limit buffering to a reasonable level.

Suppose we decide to limit the number of buffered messages to 20. Here is how we would change the producer-consumer pattern (also see Figure 7.11).

THE PRODUCER-CONSUMER PATTERN WITH LIMITED BUFFERING

```
#define BufferLimit 20
void main() {// The Producer
    int buffer_queue = AttachMessageQueue( "/usr/queue/buffer_q" );
    int producer_queue = AttachMessageQueue( "/usr/queue/producer_q" );
    int msg[MsgSize];
    while( 1 ) {
        // wait, if the buffer limit has been reached
        WaitForEmptyMsg( producer_queue );
        // Produce a message
        SendMsgTo( buffer_queue, msg );
    }
}
void main() { // The Consumer
    int buffer_queue = AttachMessageQueue( "/usr/queue/buffer_q" );
    int producer_queue = AttachMessageQueue( "/usr/queue/producer_q" );
    int msg[MsgSize], i;
    // start with BufferLimit empty buffers
```

buffering

bursty

```
for( i = 0; i < BufferLimit; ++i )
    SendMsgTo( producer_queue );
while( 1 ) {
  ReceiveMessage( buffer_queue, msg );
  // consume the message
  // tell the producer another buffer is now available
  SendMsgTo( producer_queue, EmptyBuffer );
}
}
```

The producer waits for a message from the consumer before it sends a full buffer. The consumer initializes the interaction by sending 20 messages to the producer, one for each free buffer. The consumer also sends a message for each buffer it receives. The messages from the consumer to the producer have no useful content; it is their existence that is important.

What we have now is really two producer-consumer relationships. The consumer consumes full buffers and produces empty buffers, while the producer consumes empty buffers and produces full buffers.

Notice that BufferLimit buffers are used at all times. Some are empty buffers in the producer-queue and some are full buffers in the buffer_queue, but the total number of buffers in the two queues is always BufferLimit.

If we set the buffer limit to 1, then we have a pattern very similar to the rendezvous except that we do it over and over again. The two processes rendezvous to exchange the buffer.

7.9.3 MULTIPLE PRODUCERS AND CONSUMERS

The code for the basic producer-consumer pattern will work even if there are multiple producers and multiple consumers (see Figure 7.12). In this model, we would assume that all the consumers are equivalent, and it does not matter which one handles the buffer. An example of this would be a printing system. Any process that wanted to print a file would send a message to the printer queue and any number of printers could take a message from the print queue.

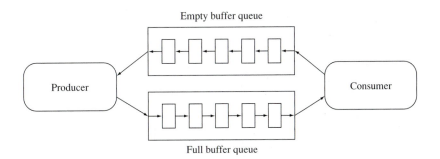

Figure 7.11   Producer-consumer IPC pattern with limited buffers

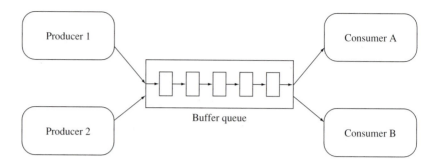

Figure 7.12   Multiple producers and consumers

We can also have longer sequences of producers and consumers. In this case, the middle processes take part in two producer-consumer relationships, one as a consumer and one as a producer. UNIX pipelines are a good example of this.

We could also have more complex networks of producers and consumers. See Figure 7.13 for an example. In this figure, we have four processes, four queues, and four producer-consumer relationships. The process in the top right is a consumer of items produced by Producer 1, and a producer of two types of products which it places in Queue 2 and Queue 3. The process in the lower right consumes from two queues.

7.10   IPC PATTERN: CLIENT-SERVER

Sometimes you have a resource that is best managed centrally, or a service that must be done centrally. Some examples are:

- *File servers* are central storage facilities that store files for several users on the network.

- *Name servers* translate names into network addresses.

- *Authentication servers* issue unforgeable credentials that a process is who it says it is.[6]

- *Print servers* accept print requests from any user in the network.

In these cases, it is usual to have one process that "owns" the resource or service and is in charge of managing it. This process accepts requests from other processes to use the resource or service. The process that owns the resource and does this management is called a *server process* because it services requests for use of the resource. Other processes, called *client processes,* send service requests to the server.

Client processes need to know the name of the queue to send service requests to, so this name must be publicly available. The server process, on the other hand, does not solicit business, it just waits for requests to come in. As a consequence, it does not need to know the name of any other message queue (except maybe that of another server that it uses). So the client knows the name of the server's queue, but the server

server process
client processes

| [6]In Chapter 19 we will see how this can be done.

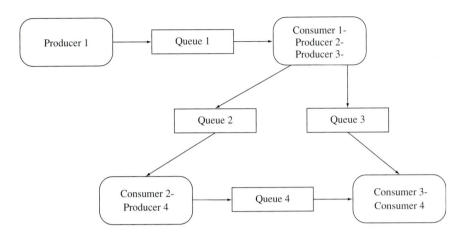

Figure 7.13   Complex networks of producers and consumers

does not know the name of the client's queue. However, a service request that requires a response will include the name of a message queue to reply to.

The pattern of communication between clients and servers is the *client-server*   client-server
IPC pattern. Let's start with a trivial example of a "squaring server," that is, a server
that will square a number for you–maybe not the most useful service you could think
of, but it will serve as an example.

A "SQUARING" SERVER

```
void main() { //Squaring Client
    int msg[MsgSize];
    int my_queue = AttachMessageQueue( "client_queue" );
    int server_queue = AttachMessageQueue( "/usr/queue/squarer" );
    SendMsgTo( server_queue, 23, my_queue ); // square 23
    ReceiveMsg( my_queue, msg );   get response or verification
    // msg[0] will contain 23*23
}
void main() { Squaring Server
    int server_queue = AttachMessageQueue( "/usr/queue/squarer" );
    int msg[MsgSize];
    while( 1 ) { //Main server loop
        ReceiveMessage( server_queue, msg );
        SendMsgTo( msg[1], msg[0]*msg[0] );
    }
}
```

The client creates a message queue for the response. It sends the server a message containing the number to square and the message queue identifier of the queue to respond to. This is necessary because the server does not know where to send replies. Any number of clients can use this server.

Most servers offer more than one type of service. The service request message contains a code indicating the type of service desired. The server handles messages with a case statement switched on the service code. Here is an example of a server (called **server17**) which has several services. One of these services has code 43.

CLIENT SERVER

```
enum { Service43=43 };
void main() { // Client
    int msg[MsgSize];
    int my_queue = AttachMessageQueue( "client_queue" );
    int server_queue = AttachMessageQueue( "/usr/queue/server17" );
    // do other stuff not requiring the server
    SendMsgTo( server_queue, Service43, my_queue, otherData );
    ReceiveMsg( my_queue, msg );// get response or verification
}
void main() { // Server
    int server_queue = AttachMessageQueue( "/usr/queue/server17" );
    int msg[MsgSize];
    while( 1 ) { // Main server loop
        ReceiveMessage( server_queue, msg );
        switch( msg[0] ) { // switch on the service requested

        case Service43:
            // get parameters and serve request
            // send response
            SendMsgTo( msg[1], responseData );
            break;
        //
        //... other cases are structured similarly
        }
    }
}
```

The most common server in a networked computer system is a file server. It provides a range of file services (most importantly read and write). Figure 7.14 shows this pattern in the case of a file server. Any client can send a file request to the message queue used by the file server. The file server does not actually read and write the file blocks itself: instead, it uses the services of a disk block server. A *disk block server* is a process that will read and write disk blocks for you. The disk block server uses the file server's message queue to send back responses to disk block requests. It is common for one server to use another, and hence to be both a client and a server at the same time.

A file server may not be able to completely service a request when it gets it. It may, for example, have to request some blocks from the disk block server. To handle situations like this, the file server has to make a record of pending requests

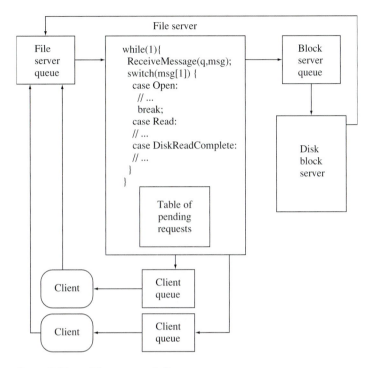

Figure 7.14   File server and clients

that it has started but not completed. This is the "Table of pending requests" in the figure.

The file server uses a case statement to decide which type of message it has received. Some cases are for the file requests and some are for replies from the disk block server. These replies might mean that the file server can complete a pending request.

You may have noticed the similarity between this IPC pattern and the producer-consumer IPC pattern (the variant with multiple producers). The client-server pattern is really a variant of the producer-consumer pattern. The emphasis is a little different here in several ways. First, the client is not always sending data to the server to be processed in another step; instead, it sends requests for service. Second, the pattern is more asymmetric than we think of with producer-consumer. In the producer-consumer IPC pattern, the two processes are equal and know about each other. In the client-server pattern, the server does not know about the client and serves anyone who asks. Third, the relationship between the client and the server is temporary. A client sends a request, the service is rendered, and a reply is sent. After that, the relationship is terminated until the client has another request. We will see later that sometimes a longer sequence of messages takes place between the server and the client, but the transient nature of the connection is still there. In the producer-consumer pattern, we think of the two processes as having a longer-term relationship.

*7.11 IPC PATTERN: MULTIPLE SERVERS AND CLIENTS

Sometimes we want to have several servers that provide the same service. Clients do not care which server they get as long as the service is performed. Suppose we have a large system with several printers, and we have a process controlling each printer. When a process wants to print something, it might not care which printer it uses, so it can send the request to any of the printer control processes. Rather than having to know the names of the queues used by all the printer control processes, we would like to have a system where you contact a printing coordinator who matches you up with an available printer control process. This is the general pattern of communication that we are presenting in this section.

We will generalize the pattern to have several servers, all of which are equivalent, and clients arrive and must be matched up with a server. It is possible that all the servers are busy, in which case the client must wait for a server to become available.

The code for this IPC pattern is as follows.

MULTIPLE SERVERS AND CLIENTS IPC PATTERN

```
// This is the code for a client process.
// Clients are continually entering and leaving the system.
void main( int argc, char *argv[ ] ) {
    int msg[MsgSize];
    // Get the message queue identifier of the message queue used
    // to send message to the (unique) coordinator process.
    int coordinator_queue = AttachMessageQueue( "/usr/queue/coord" );
    char qname[32];
    // Figure out the name of my message queue and get its identifier.
    sprintf( qname, "/usr/queue/%s", GetPid() );
    int my_queue = AttachMessageQueue( qname );

    // Tell the coordinator I need to be assigned a server.
    SendMsgTo (coordinator_queue, INeedService, my_queue );
    Receive Message( my_queue, msg );
    // Communicate with server whose pid is in msg[1].
    // Then leave the system.
}
// This is the code for a server process.
// There are a fixed number of server processes in the system.
void main( int argc, char *argv[] ) {
    int msg[MsgSize];
    // Get the message queue identifier of the message queue used
    // to send message to the (unique) coordinator process.
    int coordinator_queue = AttachMessageQueue( "/usr/queue/coord" );
    char qname[32];
    // Figure out the name of my message queue and get its identifier.
    sprintf( qname, "/usr/queue/%s", GetPid() );
    int my_queue = AttachMessageQueue( qname );

    // Servers do not ever leave the system but continue to
    // serve clients as they are assigned to them.
```

```
    while ( 1 ) {
        // Tell the coordinator I am free.
        SendMsgTo( coordinator_queue, ImFree, my_queue );
        // Wait for an assignment to a client process.
        Receive Message( my_queue, msg );
        // Serve the client whose pid is in msg[1].
    }
}
// This is the code for the coordinator process.
// There is exactly one coordinator process in the system.
void main() {
    int msg[MsgSize];
    int coordinator_queue = AttachMessageQueue( "/usr/queue/coord" );

    // Wait for requests by clients and servers and match them up.
    while( 1 ) {
        // Wait for a request.
        ReceiveMessage( coordinator_queue, msg );
        // See what kind of a request it is.
        switch( msg[0] ) {
        case INeedService:
            // This is a request from a client to be assigned a server.
            if( ServerQueue.Empty() ) {
                // If no servers are available then put the request
                // on the client queue for later assignment when a
                // server becomes free.
                ClientQueue.Insert( msg[1] );
            } else {
                // If there are free servers then assign one to the
                // client.
                queue = ServerQueue.Remove();
                // Inform both the server and the client of the as-
                // assignment.
                SendMsgTo( msg[1], YourServerIs, queue );
                SendMsgTo( queue, YourClientIs, msg[1] );
            }
          break
        case ImFree:
            // This is a request from a server, to be assigned a client.
            if( ClientQueue.Empty() ) {
                // If no clients are waiting for a server then put the
                // server on the server queue for later assignment.
                ServerQueue.Insert( msg[1] );
            } else {
                // If there are clients waiting for a server then
                // assign this server to one of them.
                queue = ClientQueue.Remove();
                // Inform both the server and the client of the as
                // assignment.
                SendMsgTo( msg[1], YourClientIs, queue );
                SendMsgTo( queue, YourServerIs, msg[1] );
            }
        }
    }
}
```

We are assuming a system call GetPid that will return the process identifier of the calling process. This is an easy way to get a unique number for creating a name for the message queue to receive replies on. This message queue is attached by the client, and the message queue identifier is sent to the server. The server can send messages to the queue, even though it has not attached the queue, because the message queue identifiers are global identifiers.

Figure 7.15 shows the pattern of multiple servers and clients.

Clients arrive, get served, and leave the system. They announce their presence to the coordinator and get a message back when a server is assigned to them. Servers operate in a continuous loop, serving clients. They tell the coordinator they are free and wait for a client assignment. After a client and server have been matched up, the coordinator does not communicate with them further. They handle the service themselves.

The coordinator handles all requests. Each arriving client tells the coordinator it needs service. If there is a free server, the client is matched to it immediately. If all the servers are busy, then the client is put on a wait queue. When a server becomes free, it is matched to the next waiting client. If there are no waiting clients, then the server is put on a queue to wait for the next client.

7.12   IPC PATTERN: DATABASE ACCESS AND UPDATE

Suppose we have a graphics display system that displays the current state of some dynamically changing data. For example, the graphical display might show the state

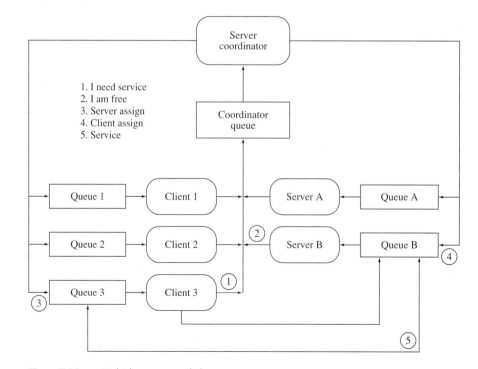

Figure 7.15   Multiple servers and clients

of the queues in an operating system. If the data model being displayed is a linked structure, then it cannot be read at the same time it is being written because changing the data structure causes it to temporarily enter invalid states where the links are not consistent. To avoid problems, we prevent reading while updates are taking place, and we prevent updates while reading is taking place.

This is modeled directly by the *database access and update* IPC pattern. In this system, there is a common database and several readers and several writers. The readers can share access to the database with each other, but not with a writer. This pattern is often called the *readers-writers problem*.

database access and update

readers-writers problem

Figure 7.16 shows the readers-writers problem as it is programmed below. We have three readers accessing the database. New readers can enter immediately. New writers must wait for all the readers to leave. If a writer is writing, then other readers and writers must wait (see Figure 7.17).

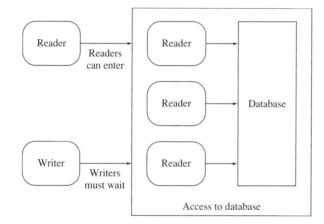

Figure 7.16   The readers-writers problem with readers reading

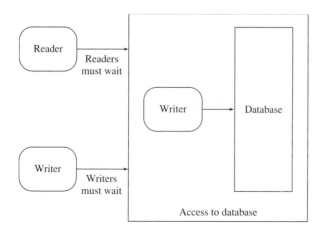

Figure 7.17   The readers-writers problem with a writer writing

Here is the code for the readers-writers pattern.

DATABASE ACCESS AND UPDATE

```
// This is a reader process. There are several readers in the system.
void main( int argc, char * argv[]) {
    // Get the identifier of the coordinator's message queue.
    int coordinator_queue = AttachMessageQueue( "/usr/queue/coord" );
    char qname[32];
    // Figure out the name of my input queue and gets its identifier.
    sprintf(qname, "/usr/queue/%s", GetPid() );
    int my_queue = AttachMessageQueue( qname );
    // Readers do other things for a while, read, and then repeat.
    while( 1 ) {
        DoOtherThings();
        // Request permission to read the database.
        SendMsgTo(coordinator_queue, RequestToStartReading, my_queue);
        // Wait for permission to begin reading.
        WaitForEmptyMsg( my_queue );
        ReadTheDatabase();
        SendMsgTo( coordinator_queue, EndRead );
    }
}
// This is a writer process. There are several writers in the system.
void main( int argc, char * argv[]) {// A writer
    // Get the identifier of the coordinator's message queue.
    int coordinator_queue = AttachMessageQueue ( "/usr/queue/coord" );
    char qname[32];
    sprintf( qname, "/usr/queue/%s", GetPid() );
    // Figure out the name of my input queue and gets its identifier.
    int my_queue = AttachMessageQueue( qname );
    while( 1 ) {
        DoOtherThings();
        // Request permission to write the database.
        SendMsgTo(coordinator_queue,RequestToStartWriting,
            my_queue);
        // Wait for permission to begin writing.
        WaitForEmptyMsg( my_queue );
        WriteTheDatabase();
        SendMsgTo( coordinator_queue, EndWrite );
    }
}
// This is the database coordinator process.
// There is only one database coordinator process in the system.
// The database coordinator does the scheduling of access to
// the database.
void main() { //The Database Coordinator
    // Get the identifier of my message queue.
    int coordinator_queue = AttachMessageQueue("/usr/queue/coord");
    // Define the necessary queues and counter variables.
    int NReaders = 0;
    Queue ReaderQueue;
    int NWriters = 0;
    Queue WriterQueue;
```

```
    int msg[MsgSize];

// This loop handles one scheduling request each iteration.
while( 1 ) {
    // Wait for a scheduling request.
    ReceiveMessage( coordinator_queue, msg );
    // See what kind of a request it is.
    switch( msg[0] ) {
    case RequestToStartReading:
        // Request from a reader to start reading.
        if( NWriters==0 && WriterQueue.Empty() ) {
            // If there is not a writer writing and
            // no writer is waiting to write,
            // then allow the reader to start reading.
            //
            // Keep a count of the number of readers
            // in the database.
            ++NReaders;
            // Tell the reader it can begin reading the database.
            SendMsgTo( msg[1], OkayToStartReading );
        } else {
            // Otherwise the reader must wait, so put it
            // on the queue of waiting readers.
            ReaderQueue.Insert( msg[1] );
        }
        break;
    case EndRead:
        // A reader has finished reading.
        // Keep a count of the number of readers in the database.
        --NReaders;
        if( NReaders == 0 && !WriterQueue.Empty() ) {
            // If this is the last reader and there are
            // writings waiting in the writer queue,
            // then let the first writer proceed.
            //
            // Keep a count of the number of writers
            // in the database.
            ++NWriters;
            // Get the writer that has waited the longest.
            // (WriterQueue is a first-in, first-out queue.)
            queue = WriterQueue.Remove();
            // Tell the writer it can begin writing the database.
            SendMsgTo( queue, OkayToStartWriting );
        }
        break;
    case RequestToStartWriting:
        // A request by a writer to begin writing.
        if( NReaders == 0 && NWriters == 0 ) {
            // If there are no readers or writers in the
            // database, then let this writer proceed.
            ++NWriters;//Keep a writer count.
            // Tell the writer to proceed.
            SendMsgTo( msg[1], OkayToStartWriting );
        } else {
            // Otherwise, we have to make the writer wait.
```

```
                    WritersQueue.Insert( msg[1] );
                }
            break;
        case EndWrite:
            // A writer is leaving the database.
            --NWriters;  //Keep a count of the writers.
        if( !ReaderQueue.Empty() ) {
            // If there are readers waiting,
            // then let them all in to read the database.
            while( !ReaderQueue.Empty() ) {
                // Get the next reader and tell it to proceed.
                queue = ReaderQueue.Remove();
                SendMsgTo( queue, OkayToStartReading );
            }
        } else if( !WriterQueue.Empty() ) {
            // If there are no readers waiting but there is
            // a writer waiting, then let it proceed.
            queue = WriterQueue.Remove();
            SendMsgTo( queue, OkayToStartWriting );
        }
        // If there are not readers or writers waiting then
        // the database is idle for a while.
        break;
    }
}
```

Indent more

Both readers and writers treat this as a mutual exclusion pattern. Before they start, they send a request message to the coordinator, they wait for a "go" signal from the coordinator, and, after they finish, they send a completion message to the coordinator. What makes this pattern different from the basic mutual exclusion pattern is the two types of processes and the use of a coordinator process. This pattern is more complicated because the database coordinator process is doing complex scheduling of processes. The coordinator will allow any number of readers to access the database simultaneously. Concurrent reading is not a problem. But the coordinator will ensure that if a writer has access to the database, then no other writer or any reader can have simultaneous access.

This solves the problem in terms of preserving the integrity of the data, that is, it is not possible for two writers, or a reader and a writer, to have simultaneous access. But there is also a scheduling problem here that is more interesting than it was in the basic mutual exclusion pattern.

7.12.1 SCHEDULING

The original solution to the mutual exclusion problem did not use a coordinator process, but used a message queue instead. There are two reasons why we did not use that solution here. The first is the additional problem specification that multiple readers could share access to the database. If we had used a simple queue, it would have required the readers to access the database one at a time. Second, a queue implies that processes get access to the database on a first-come, first-served basis. By using a queue, we are accepting the first-come, first-served scheduling implicit in queuing. This method of scheduling is fair, but sometimes we want to use more complex scheduling methods.

Suppose that a writer finishes, and there are both readers and writers waiting (see Figure 7.18). You could allow either one to go and still maintain the correctness of the solution. The decision now is not one of correctness, but one of priority and scheduling. In the code above, we allow the readers to go first, figuring that a writer just had control of the database so now it is the readers' turn.

A similar scheduling problem comes up when a reader arrives when other readers are reading and a writer is waiting. We can decide to allow the reader to start reading, since there are other readers who already have access to the database(see Figure 7.16). But the danger is that a continuous stream of readers will prevent a writer from ever gaining access to the database. To avoid this problem in the code above, a reader that arrives when a writer is waiting is required to wait, and when the last reader leaves, the writer is allowed access (see Figure 7.19).

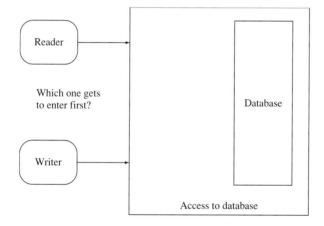

Figure 7.18   Do readers or writers have priority?

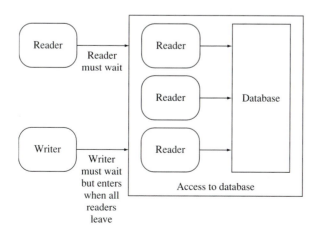

Figure 7.19   Must incoming readers wait for a waiting writer?

These two decisions ensure that no process will wait forever, but we might have made other decisions depending on the exact situation and who we want to give priority to.

7.12.2 PRIORITY

priority

We can think of this in terms of priority. By *priority* we mean which process gets to go first when more than one is ready. We can give priority to readers or writers, or we can treat them equally. Anytime you are scheduling a resource, you are deciding about priority between processes.

7.12.3 SCHEDULING QUEUES

private scheduling queues

In this solution, each reader and writer had a queue that it used to receive "go" signals from the coordinator process. These are called *private scheduling queues,* and they are necessary to implement a custom scheduling method. The coordinator must have a way to let any process go next. Each process has a private scheduling queue, and it is the only process that will ever wait for that queue. So sending a message to that queue guaranteed that that process will get released.

Releasing a process using a private scheduling queue is an example of the signaling IPC pattern.

7.13   REVIEW OF INTERPROCESS COMMUNICATION PATTERNS

We have gone through a number of different patterns of interprocess communication, and now it is time to summarize the patterns that we have seen.

7.13.1 MUTUAL EXCLUSION

- *Name:* Mutual exclusion.
- *Variant of:* None.
- *Classes of processes:* 1.
- *Number of resources:* 1 (the critical section).
- *Problem:* To make sure that only one process uses the resource at a time, and all processes get to use the resource eventually.
- *Example:* Changing your password requires exclusive write access to the password file.
- *When to use:* When two or more processes are sharing a resource that can only be used by one process at a time.

This is the basic pattern to use when two or more processes are sharing a serially reusable resource (that is, one that can only be used by one process at a time). It requires one message queue for each resource that is to be protected. You can set up mutual exclusion between any number of processes.

7.13.2   Signaling

- *Name:* Signaling.
- *Variant of:* None.
- *Classes of processes:* 2 (sender and receiver).
- *Number of resources:* 1 (the "go" signal).
- *Problem:* To make sure that the receiver waits for the signal from the sender but the sender is never held up by the receiver.
- *Example:* Waiting for a document to finish printing.
- *When to use:* When one process needs to wait for an event to occur in another process.

Signaling is used when one process needs to wait for an event in another process. A signal goes in one direction only, and only one of the two processes ever has to wait. Signaling is always between exactly two processes.

7.13.3   Rendezvous

- *Name:* Rendezvous.
- *Variant of:* Signaling (it is two-way signaling).
- *Classes of processes:* 1.
- *Classes of resources:* 1 (the "go" signal).
- *Problem:* To make sure that each process waits for all the others to arrive at a common point.
- *Example:* Several processes starting a game at the same time.
- *When to use:* When two or more processes want to synchronize in time and do an activity together, or start an activity at the same time.

A rendezvous is basically a two-way signaling pattern. Each process gets to a point in its execution and waits for the other process to get to a corresponding point in its execution. When they are both at the common point, they both proceed.

Rendezvous is used when you want two processes to start an activity at the same time, like the start of a race. A rendezvous can be between any number of processes.

7.13.4   Producer-Consumer

- *Name:* Producer-consumer.
- *Variant of:* Signaling (it is repeated signaling plus data transfer).

- *Classes of processes:* 2 (producers and consumers).
- *Classes of resources:* 1 (resources are produced).
- *Problem:* To make sure that the consumers and producers wait for each other when necessary.
- *Example:* One process produces lines for another process in a shell pipeline.
- *Other issues:* Buffering of resources is involved. This is built on signaling.
- *When to use:* When you have two processes working together on a task where one process does the first part of the work and the other process does the second part of the work.
- *Notes:* There are many variations of the producer-consumer pattern. You might have several producers or consumers or both. You might have more than two stages, and so the middle processes are both consumers and producers.

The producer-consumer pattern is one of the most common. It is used when two processes are working on a task of processing a number of items in sequence, and when one process does the first step in the processing and the other process does the second step of the processing.

There are many possible variations of the producer-consumer pattern. You can have any number of producers and consumers. It is also possible to have producers producing different kinds of products and consumers requiring some combination of products of various kinds.

7.13.5 CLIENT-SERVER

- *Name:* Client-server.
- *Variant of:* Producer-consumer (requests are produced by clients and consumed by the server) and mutual exclusion.
- *Classes of processes:* 2 (clients and servers).
- *Number of resources:* 1 or more (the resource the server manages).
- *Problem:* Multiple clients request services of the server and the server handles the requests.
- *Example:* A file server.
- *When to use:* When you have a process that manages a resource that other processes need to use.

This is also a variation of the mutual exclusion pattern where we have more control of process priority.

7.13.6 MULTIPLE SERVERS AND CLIENTS

- *Name:* Multiple servers and clients.

- *Variant of:* Client-server and mutual exclusion (a server can only be accessed by one client at a time).

- *Classes of processes:* 2 (servers and clients).

- *Number of resources:* Not applicable.

- *Problem:* To match up servers with clients.

- *Example:* Managing multiple printers.

- *When to use:* When you have clients and servers and you need to dynamically match them up.

When you have several servers, you use this pattern to match up servers and clients.

7.13.7   Database Access and Update

- *Name:* Database access and update.

- *Variant of:* Mutual exclusion (with explicit scheduling).

- *Classes of processes:* 2 (readers and writers).

- *Number of resources:* 1 (the database).

- *Problem:* To make sure that no writer changes the database at the same time as any other process and that all processes eventually gain access to the database.

- *Examples:* A password database, an airline reservation system.

- *Other issues:* Multiple readers can use the database simultaneously. This is a generalization of the simple mutual exclusion problem.

- *When to use:* When you have a shared database with both readers and writers, and when the writers need exclusive access to the database.

It is common to have a shared database that is read and written. If writing the database puts it, temporarily, in an inconsistent state that you do not want other processes to see, then you use this pattern.

7.14   A PHYSICAL ANALOGY

People are like processes in that they can each work on a task independently of other people, and in that they often cooperate on tasks or compete for resources. For example, suppose one person is addressing envelopes containing wedding invitations, and the other person is putting on the return address, sealing, and stamping them. The (human) "addresser" produces the addressed envelopes one at a time, and can never get ahead of the stamper/sealer since the addressed envelopes will not exist yet. The coordination happens naturally.

DESIGN TECHNIQUE: REUSABLE PATTERNS

OVERVIEW

A *pattern* is a design, a program structure, or an approach to a problem. When we identify a pattern, we have the chance of reusing it in a later design.

MOTIVATION

A pattern is a reusable design. It is a way to organize a program and to solve a particular task. Good designs are harder to come up with than good code, and you get more benefit out of reusing a design than reusing code. In object-oriented terminology, a reusable design is called a *framework*.

There has been a lot of attention recently given to patterns in computer science. In fact, these design chapters are all about reusable patterns. All the design principles we are looking at are reusable patterns in design.

A lot of the work in solving a problem is planning the solution rather than actually carrying it out, that is, the design of the solution. In a program, a design is a module structure, a data structure, an algorithm, etc. If we have a collection of designs that have worked well in the past, we can use them over and over again. This saves work in new designs. It also increases the reliability of the designs since they are used many times and there are many chances to find problems.

OPERATING SYSTEM EXAMPLE

IPC Patterns   In Chapter 7, we presented a number of IPC patterns that are commonly used. We gave code for each pattern, but our intent was not that you would reuse the code in your programs. What we expected you to reuse was the *design,* the organization of the communication—who sent messages, to whom, and when.

COMPUTER SCIENCE EXAMPLE

Design patterns   Design patterns are patterns of objects in an object-oriented design. Gamma et al. (1995) is an excellent introduction to design patterns.

APPLICABILITY

Patterns should be used wherever they are appropriate, that is, wherever they meet the goals and constraints of the design problem.

CONSEQUENCES

- Patterns save work because designs are reused.
- Patterns improve quality because designs are tested many times.
- Sometimes a pattern does not fit the situation well but is used anyway.

pattern

framework

Similarly, if a guest is signing the guest book at a wedding[7] and another guest comes up and wants to sign it, there is no chance that the second guest will accidentally try to sign on the same line. The second guest will see the first guest is there, and will wait until he is done. The fact that there is only one physical guest book means the competition for it is handled naturally.

In a computer system, we need additional mechanisms to handle these problems since a text editor cannot tell, when it reads a file, that another text editor is already editing that file, and a program reading data from another program cannot tell whether a section of memory contains new data or not.

---

[7]We will continue with our wedding theme.

7.15   FAILURE OF PROCESSES

In all of these patterns, we assume that no process will fail. One form of failure is when a process will suddenly stop and not execute any further instructions. In an even worse form of failure, a process will suddenly start executing random instructions. If a process fails while another process is waiting for a message from it, then that process will wait forever and the system will probably come to a halt.

This assumption of no failure is not really a very practical one, since processors and processes do fail for a variety of reasons. This is especially true in distributed systems. We can take steps to deal with the problem of the failure of processes. Doing this successfully takes a lot of care and effort, but we can give you the outline of the solution.

The idea is to have two processes together represent the server process. The first process is the one that responds to service requests, and the second one is a shadow process that keeps track of the requests the server has received and not yet finished processing. The shadow process periodically sends a message to the server asking it if it is still alive. Obviously, the server will not respond if it has failed, so we have a timeout period in which we expect a response from the server. If the shadow process does not get a response within the timeout period, then it assumes the server has failed; it starts another one and replays the requests that have not been completed.

Below is the outline of a shadow process. In this code, we are assuming there is a timer server which will accept messages that give a return message type and a time interval. The time server will send that message back to you after the time interval has expired.

The server has a few additions to it. First it recognizes AreYouAlive messages and responds to them, saying it is alive. It also forwards all requests and replies to the shadow process. Figure 7.20 shows the system.

CLIENT SERVER WITH FAILURE DETECTION

```
void main() {// Client
    // ...same as before
}
void main() {// Server
    int msg[MsgSize];
    int server_queue = AttachMessageQueue( "/usr/queue/server17" );
    // get the identifier for the message queue of the shadow process.
    int shadow_queue = AttachMessageQueue( "/usr/queue/shadow17" );
    while( 1 ) {// Main server loop
        ReceiveMessage( server_queue, msg );
        // Forward a copy of all requests to the shadow process.
        SendMsgTo( shadow_queue, msg );
        switch( msg[0] ) {//switch on the service requested

        case AreYouAlive:
            // Respond to "are you alive" messages.
```

```
                    SendMsgTo( shadow_queue, YesImAlive );
                    break;

              case Service43:
                    // Get parameters, serve request and send response.
                    SendMsgTo( msg[1], responseData );
                    // Inform the shadow process that I have handled
                    // this request so it does not have to keep a record
                    // of it any longer.
                    SendMsgTo( shadow_queue, msg[1] );
                    break;
              //
              // other cases are structured similarly
              }
        }
}
void main() { // Server's shadow process
     int msg[MsgSize];
     int server_queue = AttachMessageQueue( "/usr/queue/server17" );
     int shadow_queue = AttachMessageQueue( "/usr/queue/shadow17" );
     int timer_queue = AttachMessageQueue( "/usr/queue/timer" );
     int timeout_pending = 0;

     // Start the timer for the first watch interval.
     SendMsgTo( timer_queue, shadow_queue, CheckServer, WatchInterval );
     while( 1 ) { // Main server loop
         ReceiveMessage( shadow_queue, msg );
         switch( msg[0] ) {// switch on the service requested

         case CheckServer:
              // If the watch interval has expired then see if the
              // server is still alive.
              SendMsgTo( server_queue, AreYouAlive );
              // Wait a certain amount of time (TimoutInterval) for a
              // response.
              SendMsgTo( timer_queue, TimeoutServer, TimoutInterval );
              timeout_pending = 1;
              break;

         case YesImAlive:
              // The server is still alive.
              // Record the fact that it did answer.
              timeout_pending = 0;
              break;

         case TimeoutServer:
              // The response time is expired. Has the server responded?
              if( timeout_pending ) {
                  // The server did not respond to the AreYouAlive mes-
                  // sage in the allotted time. We assume that the server
                  // had died so we start another server and forward to
                  // it all the requests in the pending request table.
              }
              // Start another watch interval time out.
              SendMsgTo( timer_queue, CheckServer, WatchInterval );
```

```
        break;

    default:
        // Otherwise it is message about a request.
        if( RequestFromClient() ) {
            // A new request has arrived at the server.
            // Record the request in the pending request table.
        } else if( ReplyByServer() ) {
            // A request has been serviced so we no longer have
            // to keep a record of it for retry in case the
            // server fails.
            // Remove the request from the pending request table.
        break;
    }
}
}
```

The shadow process arranges to periodically check the server process. So, every **WatchInterval** time units the shadow process gets **CheckServer** message from the timer server. It then sends an **AreYouAlive** to the server and sets another timer interval for the time it will wait before it assumes the server has failed and will not respond (**TimoutInterval**). If it gets the response from the servers it sets a flag indicating that fact. When the timeout comes, it checks to see if a response was received. If not, it takes steps to recover. It recovers by starting a new server process and sending it all the requests that the previous, failed server process received but did not finish servicing. The shadow process knows which ones they are because the server process forwards all requests and replies to the shadow process. The shadow process keeps a table of requests that have not been responded to.

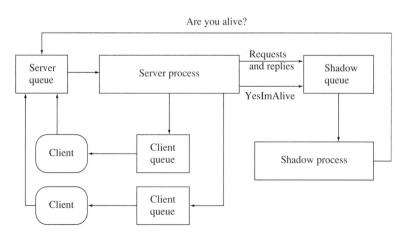

Figure 7.20   Fault-tolerant server system

7.15.1   RECOVERY FROM FAILURE

If you look at this organization, you will realize that there are a lot of holes in it, and that it does not protect completely against failure or always recover smoothly. Let's look at some of the problems with this outline solution.

If the shadow process fails, then the server process has no backup, and if the server process subsequently fails, the service will not recover (at least not automatically). We can easily fix that by reversing the procedure. The server process also uses timeouts to make sure the shadow process has not failed, so they check on each other. Even with this modification, we can still have an overall failure if the server process and the shadow process both fail at about the same time (although this is unlikely).

The shadow waits for `TimoutInterval` to decide whether the server is still alive. It is possible that the server is very busy and it will not respond in the required time period, even though it is alive. This problem can be ameliorated by having a special queue for `AreYouAlive` messages that the server always checks before it checks its request queue. This requires a nonblocking receive (see Section 8.13.2), and the problem could still happen (although it is far less likely). The shadow needs a foolproof way of detecting whether the server process is still alive, but there is really no way to do this since there are no bounds on network delays.

The recovery mechanism is also flawed. We assume that the new server process will read from the same queue as the previous, failed server process so no requests are lost that way. But if the server process fails after receiving a request and before it can be forwarded to the shadow process, then the request will be lost. Clients can have timeouts themselves and resend requests that timeout, so this is not too bad of a problem. In fact, we could have assumed this mechanism for all client requests and not have the server process remember any requests. When a server fails, then a number of requests will be timed out and will have to be resent.

There is another problem with serving requests more than once. When the server receives a request, it starts serving it. Suppose it finishes serving the request, but then fails before it can reply to the client process (and the shadow process). The request will be reissued and done over again. In some cases, this is fine, for example, writing a disk block. In some cases, this wastes resources, for example, printing a long document. In some cases, this will lead to incorrect behavior, for example, subtracting a check from a bank balance.

These problems are solvable, but the solutions are too complex to present here.

7.16   SUMMARY

There are standard ways in which logically and physically parallel processes communicate with one another. This communication usually follows one of several patterns of communication that are common in parallel systems. These patterns fell into two groups, sharing and cooperating.

Race conditions can occur when parallel processes share storage that can be written by one or both of them. The problem comes when they both try to access the shared storage at the same time. The solution to the problem is to only allow one process at a time to access the shared storage. Doing this is called mutual exclusion. It makes the execution a critical section and atomic action.

The most common pattern in sharing is the mutual exclusion pattern. In this pattern, two processes ensure that a process will eventually gain exclusive access to shared storage. The mutual exclusion pattern is easily realized using message-passing mechanisms.

Sharing occurs because processes are running on the same system (maybe a single computer, maybe a networked environment) and need to share the resources of the system. Cooperation occurs when two or more processes cooperate to achieve a common goal. This form of interaction is voluntary (processes would rather not compete with each other) and comes in many varieties. There are five common patterns of cooperation: signaling, rendezvous, producer-consumer, client-server, and database access/update.

The most basic pattern is where one process needed to know that a second process had reached a specified point before the first process could proceed. The signaling pattern appears as a subpattern in all the other patterns of cooperation.

The rendezvous pattern is two signaling patterns linked together. It occurs when two or more processes have to all start from a specified point at the same time.

The producer-consumer pattern is the most common one in process cooperation. It occurs when one process has to process items that are then passed to a second process for further processing. The two processes are each doing one part of a task. It involves signaling, since the first process needs to inform the second process that an item is ready for it. There are many variations on the producer-consumer pattern which vary the number of producers, the number of consumers, the number of types of items produced, and the number of buffers to hold the items.

The client-server pattern occurs when one process (the server) is providing a service required by several other processes (the clients). This pattern is common in computer networks where most network resources are managed by servers. This pattern has an important variation where there are multiple servers and clients and they need to be matched up.

The database access/update pattern (also known as the readers-writers problem) is really the mutual exclusion problem with some scheduling thrown in. The database can be accessed by one or more readers or by one writer at a time. An important aspect of the pattern is the scheduling of waiting processes. This pattern introduces the idea of the scheduling of shared resources.

Reusable patterns are the basis of many of these design principles in this book. They are also a way to classify programming techniques and have been used effectively in object-oriented design.

It is not uncommon in distributed systems for a process to fail, and so a careful implementation of any of these patterns of communication should allow for the failure of a process. A common technique for dealing with failure is to have one process keep watch over another process, and restart it when it fails.

7.16.1 TERMINOLOGY

After reading this chapter, you should be familiar with the following terms:

- atomic action
- buffering
- bursty
- client process
- client-server
- critical section
- database access and update
- framework
- logical resource
- mutual exclusion
- pattern
- priority
- private scheduling queue
- process competition
- process cooperation
- producer-consumer
- race condition
- readers-writers problem
- rendezvous
- serially reusable resource
- server process
- signaling

7.16.2 REVIEW QUESTIONS

The following questions are answered in the text of this chapter:

1. Relate the terms race condition, atomic action, critical section, and mutual exclusion.
2. Why is mutual exclusion the most important IPC pattern for competition for resources?
3. What is the basic idea of the mutual exclusion IPC pattern?
4. What is the basic idea of the signaling IPC pattern?
5. What is the basic idea of the rendezvous IPC pattern?
6. Explain how a rendezvous pattern consists of two signaling patterns.

7. What is the basic idea of the producer-consumer IPC pattern?

8. Explain how a shell pipeline uses the producer-consumer IPC pattern.

9. What is the basic idea of the client-server IPC pattern?

10. What is the basic idea of the multiple servers and clients IPC pattern?

11. What is the basic idea of the database access and update IPC pattern?

12. Why does process failure cause problems with our IPC patterns?

13. What can be done about the possibility of process failure?

7.16.3   FURTHER READING

Ben-Ari (1982) is a complete and entertaining treatment of the issues of concurrency. A later book [BA90] expands the treatment to distributed systems.

Andrews and Schneider (1983) survey many issues in concurrent processes.

Many books and articles on design patterns are starting to come out. A book on the First Annual Conference on Pattern Languages of Programs (1995) has a wide range of interesting articles. Gamma et al. (1995) is a catalog of design patterns and is very instructive reading.

7.17   PROBLEMS

1. Modify the code for the database access and update IPC pattern so that each reader or writer has an externally assigned priority. Allow them to go in order of priority so that no reader or writer will be delayed by a reader or writer with a lower priority(unless the lower priority reader or writer was already using the database when the higher-priority reader or writer entered the system).

2. Modify the code for the database access and update IPC pattern so that readers have the strongest possible priority.

3. Explain how the database access and update IPC pattern is really a complicated variation of the mutual exclusion IPC pattern.

4. In the client-server pattern, the client creates a message queue called client_queue. What exactly will go wrong if two clients in the same directory try to use the client-server pattern? How can this problem be corrected?

5. Explain how every IPC pattern includes the signaling pattern.

6. Modify the code for the many-process rendezvous pattern so that the coordinator is one of the players.

7. Consider the two-process mutual exclusion program in Section 7.6. Suppose we made a mistake, and both process A and process B put an initial message into the message queue (instead of just process A doing it). What would go wrong with the solution if we did this?

8. In the definition of `AttachMessageQueue`, we said that the first attach will create the file name and the last detach will remove it. An alternative specification would require that the name already exist in the file naming system as a special "message queue" file. Give the advantages and disadvantages of this method compared to the one described in the book.

9. Explain the relationship between signaling, rendezvous, and the producer-consumer patterns.

10. Suppose we had a producer-consumer situation where there was one consumer and three producers. To consume, the consumer needed the product from any two of the three producers. Program a solution to this problem along the lines of the solution given in Section 7.9.

11. Suppose we had a producer-consumer situation where there was one consumer and three producers. To consume, the consumer needed the product from any one of the first two producers and the product of the third producer. Program a solution to this problem along the lines of the solution given in Section 7.9.

12. Consider the case of two students editing a common file, as described in Section 7.3. Suppose that three (instead of two) students were trying to edit the same file at around the same time. How many possible orderings of the six edit and write events are there, and how many of them lead to a correct file at the end? By "correct" file, we mean one where the edits of all three students are contained in the file.

13. Consider a hamburger shop with the following features:

- A line of customers waiting to place their orders.
- Several clerks who take orders from people in line, get the food, and give it to the customer.
- One cook making hamburgers.
- One cook making french fries.
- A drive-up line where cars first come to a speaker and give their order to one of the clerks (the same clerks who handle the inside line of customers), and then move up to the drive-up window and get their order.

Give all the IPC (Inter-People Communication) relationships between people in this system. Include instances of cooperation and competition.

14. In Section 7.9.2, we talked about a limit on the message number of buffers a process can use. Explain what can go wrong if a process uses too many message buffers. What steps could an operating system take to prevent this from happening?

15. For each of the IPC patterns we discussed, consider what would go wrong if one of the participating processes failed. For each pattern, describe what would happen if a process failed. For several of them, the consequences are different depending on which process fails and where in its execution it fails. Try to describe all the cases.

16. For each of the IPC patterns we discussed, consider what would go wrong if one of the messages in the communication was lost. For each pattern, describe what would happen if a message was lost. For several of them, the consequences are different depending on which message gets lost. Try to describe all the cases.

17. Suppose we wanted to improve the failure tolerance of the client-server code in Section 7.15. Modify the code so that the server process also checks up on the shadow process, and starts a new one if the shadow process fails.

18. Consider the following IPC patterns:

- Mutual exclusion.
- Signaling.
- Rendezvous.
- Producer-consumer.
- Client-server.
- Multiple servers and clients.
- Database access and update.

For each of the following situations, decide which of the above IPC patterns models the situation most closely. In some situations, more than one pattern will be appropriate. In those cases, list all that you think apply, but also indicate which pattern you think is the most central to the issues of the problem.

- The upper and lower half of a disk driver.
- Processes in a UNIX pipeline.
- Updating and accessing (at logon) the password file.
- Two processes communicating by sending messages to and receiving messages from a mailbox.
- Processes sending messages to a print request queue, which is serviced by two printer-driver processes.
- A disk driver and the disk controller.
- Two people communicating by e-mail.
- Two people communicating by telephone.
- A program that lets you know when e-mail has arrived.
- Two people meeting at the top of the Empire State Building at noon on Christmas Eve.
- An airline reservation system where there are many travel agents trying to book flights.
- Several media transfer programs that will transfer data between a WORM (write-once, read-many) drive, a CD-ROM drive, a floppy disk drive, and two different sizes of cartridge tape drives.

19. In Chapter 6 we saw the problems that race conditions can cause in the kernel. The solution was to make modifications to shared data into atomic actions using the ExchangeWord instruction. In this chapter we looked at problems with race conditions between user processes and our solution was to build atomic actions using messages. Why were different solutions needed in the two cases?

20. Besides mutual exclusion, what other IPC patterns are needed in the implementation of an operating system? Which IPC patterns are definitely not needed in an operating systems?

21. Explain why we say that data access and update is an type of mutual exclusion problem. How is scheduling handled in the mutual exclusions IPC pattern?

22. Explain where signaling is used in the data access and update IPC pattern.

chapter
8

Processes

In this chapter, we will look at a range of topics relating to processes: process scheduling, deadlock, starvation, process synchronization, and interprocess communication.

8.1   EVERYDAY SCHEDULING

Before we talk about processor scheduling, we will motivate the ideas by talking about how people schedule things in noncomputer situations.

8.1.1   FIRST-COME, FIRST-SERVED SCHEDULING

first-come, first-served scheduling

Suppose you go to the supermarket, pick out the food you want, and go to the check-out line. You go to the end of the line and wait until everyone in front of you has been checked out, and then you get checked out. This is called *first-come, first-served scheduling* (FCFS), and most people consider it a fair scheduling algorithm. In fact, just about everyone considers "cutting in line" to be cheating because it goes against the essential fairness of FCFS. FCFS lines are used in supermarkets, post offices, banks, and airports—in fact, virtually everywhere lines are used. FCFS is also called *first-in, first-out*, or FIFO.

first-in, first-out

> First-come, first-served scheduling treats everyone equally.

Figure 8.1 shows first-come, first-served scheduling. We assume that customers arrive by some unknown mechanism. They enter the system, choose a line, wait in the line, are served, and then leave the system.

People normally wait in a line in the order they arrive. Sometimes, it is inconvenient to have people wait in an actual line. Instead of this, some stores (bakeries come to mind) have a machine that dispenses numbers. When you arrive, you take the next number, and the people are served in the order of their numbers. This effectively prevents cutting in line and allows people to walk around and even leave for a while and still maintain their position in line. The numbers form a "virtual line."[1] Restaurants that take your name and put it on a list are doing the same thing.

8.1.2   SHORTEST-JOB-FIRST SCHEDULING

But sometimes at the supermarket you will have a full basket of food and someone will get in line behind you who has only one or two things to buy. They might ask you if they can go first, or you might spontaneously allow them to go first. Why would you do this if FCFS is already considered to be fair? If FCFS is fair, then letting someone else go first would be unfair.

The reason you do let a person with only a few things go first is that people understand the advantage of letting small checkouts go first. For example, suppose the person with one item takes one minute to be checked out, and your groceries take 10

---

[1] And you probably thought that virtualization was something that only happened in operating systems.

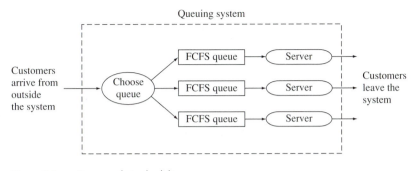

Figure 8.1   Supermarket scheduling

minutes. If you go first, then you wait zero minutes and they wait 10 minutes, and the average waiting time for both of you is 5 minutes. If they go first, then they wait zero minutes, and you wait one minute and the average waiting time for both of you is 30 seconds. You, in fact, are worse off, but only by a small amount with respect to the overall time to check out, and the other person is much better off.

So we have two possible standards of fairness:

1. Treat everyone the same (so everyone will have the same expected waiting time).

2. Have the lowest average waiting time (over all customers).

The first standard is easy to agree on and treats all individuals the same. The second standard considers the good of the group over the good of the individual, and some individuals will have their waiting time increased (over what it would have been using FCFS) in order to decrease the overall average waiting time.

But some people might not be as public-spirited as you, and only consider their own waiting time, not allowing short orders ahead of them. So supermarkets usually have a special line just for short orders (10 items or less, or something like that). This means that people with a few items always have a quick line to go to, and do not have to depend on public-spirited people to let them go first. This also seems fair, since most people intuitively realize that the overall waiting time is reduced by these methods, and they figure that sometimes they will be the ones with just a few items to check out. This also means that we are modifying our definition of "fair" to include some idea that your waiting time should be proportional to the amount of time you will take to check out. We call this method *shortest-job-first scheduling* (SJF).   shortest-job-first scheduling

We will often use the term *job* to refer to the things that are getting scheduled. Processes (or people) come into the system with a specific job to do. This job will take a certain amount of time. Usually the time a job will take is not known in advance, but, of course, it is always known by the time the job finishes.

Shortest-job-first scheduling favors short jobs and minimizes the average wait time over all processes.

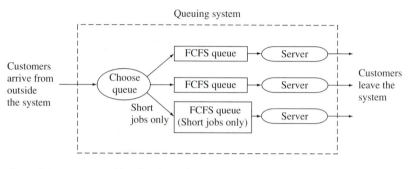

Figure 8.2   A special line for short jobs

Figure 8.2 shows first-come, first-served scheduling with a special line for short jobs. Only short jobs are allowed in the short job line.

8.1.3   HIGHEST-RESPONSE-RATIO-NEXT SCHEDULING

Let's look at another situation. You have a long article to copy and there is only one copy machine. If someone else has only one page to copy, you will generally let them go first. If another person comes in with only one or two pages to copy, you will also let them go ahead of you. If people with a few pages keep coming in and going first, you soon get to feel that this SJF stuff is not really fair because you are having to wait a long time. In fact, the main problem with SJF is that, in a busy system, long jobs can wait a very long time.

The SJF scheduling strategy needs to be modified in a busy system to avoid discriminating too much against long jobs. One strategy that is more moderate is called *highest-response-ratio-next scheduling*. By *response ratio* we mean the sum of your waiting time and the time your job takes, divided by the time your job takes.

highest-response-ratio-next scheduling

$$ResponseRatio = \frac{Wait\ Time + Job\ Time}{Job\ Time}$$

The job with the highest response ratio is chosen to go next. Long jobs are discriminated against for a while because their long job time keeps their expected response ratio low, but as their waiting time increases, their response ratio starts to go up and eventually they get to go ahead of short jobs.

True "highest-response-ratio-next" could only be used in an operating system because of the complex calculations necessary to implement it, but having special lines for short jobs is one way of approximating it in noncomputer situations.

> Highest-response-ratio-next scheduling is a compromise between first-come, first-served and shortest-job-first because it discriminates less against long jobs.

8.1.4   PRIORITY SCHEDULING

Now suppose you are scheduling your time at work. Most of us use some elements of SJF and do the short things first. This serves to get them out of the way. But the basic work scheduling strategy used by most people is a *priority scheduling*. Some things   priority scheduling are considered more important, and you do those first. If you need to prepare for a presentation for an important customer, that will take priority over a weekly report.

     The priority scheduling algorithm requires you to assign a priority to each task. You do the task with the highest priority first. The algorithm is simple. The hard part is deciding the priority of each task.

> Priority scheduling is best when processes have different levels of importance.

8.1.5   DEADLINE SCHEDULING

Scheduling of work also sometimes uses a *deadline scheduling* system. That is, you   deadline scheduling do the job that will be late if you do not start doing it right away. In deadline scheduling, you look at all the jobs and their deadlines, and figure out when you have to start a job to complete it by its deadline. You do this by starting the job whose deadline is closest (Stankovic et al. 1995).

8.1.6   ROUND-ROBIN SCHEDULING

Now suppose a group of you are playing a video game. A video game usually has natural stopping points, and although you might want to continue playing, you can, at a stopping point, allow someone else to play a game and then later play another game yourself. We say that *preemption* is possible, that is, you can stop using the game and then go back to it later without any loss of time. Compare this with checking out groceries. If you are halfway checked out, it is not easy to stop checking you out, start checking someone else out, and then, when they are done, start checking your groceries out again. Most cash registers will not handle this, for one thing. Checking out groceries is not really preemptable, but playing a video game and using a processor are.

     When several people want to use a video game, most people would use a sharing system. One person gets to play for 10 minutes, then the next person for 10 minutes, and so on. When everyone has played once, you start over. In computer systems, this is called *round-robin (RR) scheduling*. Most people consider round-   round-robin scheduling robin to be a fair method of sharing something that can be preempted.

> Round-robin scheduling is a good way to schedule processes that can be preempted.

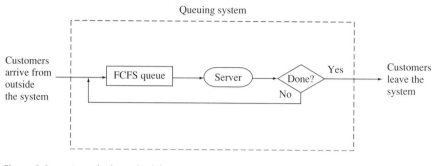

Figure 8.3   Round-robin scheduling

Figure 8.3 shows round-robin scheduling.

8.1.7   SUMMARY

From everyday life situations, we see the major scheduling methods that are used:

- First-come, first-served
- Shortest-job-first
- Highest-response-ratio-next
- Priority
- Deadline
- Round-robin.

These six scheduling methods are the basic ones used in computer systems as well. Since preemption of the processor is quite cheap, we generally prefer round-robin, or variants of it, in computer systems.

8.2   PREEMPTIVE SCHEDULING METHODS

In this section, we will look at several methods of preemptive scheduling of the processor. We will assume a system where processes enter the processor scheduling system and remain there (sometimes executing and sometimes waiting to execute) until they have finished execution. By "finished execution," we do *not* mean that the process terminates; rather, we mean that the process becomes blocked waiting for an event (waiting for a message or an I/O operation to complete). At that point, the process can no longer use the processor, and so it is considered to be finished. (See Figure 8.4.)

A process will enter and leave the processor scheduling system many times during its entire execution, maybe hundreds of thousands of times. Still, each one is a separate transaction as far as the processor scheduling system is concerned. The processor scheduling algorithm might look at the history of the process, that is, what

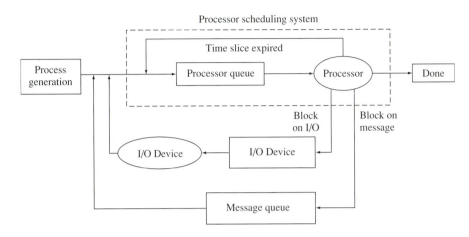

Figure 8.4   The flow of processes in an operating system

happened on previous trips through the processor scheduling system. For example, the scheduler might want to estimate how much processor time the process will consume on this trip through the scheduling system. One rough estimate would be the same amount of time it used last trip. A better estimate might be a weighted average of the last 10 trips.

8.2.1   SCHEDULING OVERVIEW

Figure 8.4 is a diagram of the flow of processes through the system. Processes flow in several circles. A process that is ready to run waits in the processor queue until it is scheduled to run. Its execution can end in several ways. It may block on a system call requesting an I/O transfer or a message receive, it may use all of its time slice, or it may finish. Unless it actually finishes, it enters another queue and is scheduled again.

Usually, we will look at one scheduler at a time. For example, in this section we will look at processor scheduling. From the point of view of the process scheduler, a process runs for up to, say, 50 milliseconds, and then it is finished. By "finished" we mean that it leaves the processor scheduling system. We can see by the diagram that it leaves the processor scheduling system to enter another scheduling system, and it will soon be back in the processor scheduling system. But when it comes back it will be considered a "new" process.

8.2.2   ROUND-ROBIN SCHEDULING

Round-robin scheduling in a computer is the same as we described in Section 8.1.6, and Figure 8.3 is still valid. There is one queue, and processes entering the processor scheduling system are placed at the end of that queue. When the processor is

quantum

time slice

free, it picks the first process in the queue (the process that has been waiting in the queue the longest) and runs it for a fixed length of time. This length of time is called the *quantum* or *time slice*. If the process is blocked by a system call, then it leaves the system for another queue, and it is considered to have finished. If the quantum runs out, the processor is preempted from the process, and the process is placed at the end of the queue. Note that newly entering processes and processes that are preempted are treated the same.

Round-robin scheduling is easy to implement. It is just a matter of maintaining a queue of processes. The hard part is deciding what the length of the time slice should be. Each quantum requires saving the process state and executing the interrupt handling code in the operating system. Longer time slices are more efficient because they cause fewer clock interrupts (with their associated overhead). On the other hand, if the time slice is too long, then it will take a long time for each process to get its turn, and interactive response will be poor.

The usual solution is to pick a compromise value. For example, we might pick 20 milliseconds. This is time enough to do a substantial amount of computation, and if there are 50 or fewer processes in the ready queue, each process will get a turn at least every second.

The adaptive solution would be to determine what you want your interactive response time to be, and continually change the length of the time slice to provide that response time. For example, say we want an interactive response time of 100 milliseconds. Before we start a process running, we see how many processes are in the ready queue, say 5. Then we divide that number into 100 milliseconds to get the time slice, 20 milliseconds (100 milliseconds/5) in our example.

Let's develop a simple model to help us understand about time slices. Suppose we include the time spent in context switching (the cost of preemption) in the time slice, and measure the length of the time slice in terms of multiples of this context switching time. For example, if the context switching time was 200 microseconds, then a time slice of 10 milliseconds would be 50 context switching times. If the time slice is one context switching time, then the overhead for context switching is 100 percent. If the time slice is 100 context switching times, then the overhead for context switching is 1 percent. In between, it will follow the curve $1/N$, where N is the number of content switching times in the time slice. Figure 8.5 shows this curve, which we might nickname the "diminishing returns" curve because it shows how increasing the size of the time slice rapidly decreases the percent overhead at the beginning, but later it changes quite slowly.

What insights can we get from this? Well, clearly it is bad to have a very small time slice, and the minimum you might consider is at least five times the context switching time. But after that, the decrease in overhead is small, and your decisions about the size of the time slice should be based on other factors.

One simple strategy would be to determine the response time you want, say 250 milliseconds, and then use a time slice that ensures this. A time slice of 250/*NumberOfProcesses* will ensure a 250-milliseconds response time. You should also put a lower limit on the time slice of 10 times the cost of a context switch.

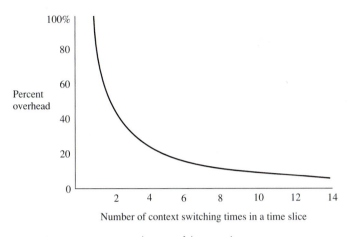

Figure 8.5   Determining the size of the time slice

8.2.3   HEAVILY LOADED SYSTEMS

What happens when a round-robin system is heavily loaded? Suppose our minimum time slice is 10 milliseconds (.01 seconds). If we have 500 jobs in the ready queue, then each one will get a time slice every 5 seconds (500 ∗ .01). This is a very slow response time, and users on such a system would rapidly get disgusted and do something else until the load goes down (or move to another machine).

We would like to find ways to make the system degrade more gracefully. In particular, we would like interactive response for short jobs to remain good even if long jobs take a very long time. Round-robin does not do this, but there are scheduling methods that do.

8.2.4   TWO QUEUES

One goal of a time-sharing system is to maintain good interactive response, that is, a user making a new request should get a response quickly if the request does not require much processor time. For example, a person editing text expects nearly instant response when a key is typed. The way to achieve good interactive response is to not allow long jobs to slow down the short jobs. One way to do this is to have two queues, one for newly ready processes and one for processes that have already used up a time slice. The first queue has a short time slice (say 10 milliseconds) and has priority over the second queue. The second queue has a longer time slice (say 100 milliseconds). The dispatcher will always run a process in the first queue (if there are any). If there are no processes in the first queue, a process from the second queue is run. A process that uses up its entire time slice is put in the second queue.

two-queue scheduling

Figure 8.6 show a *two-queue scheduling* system. Two-queue scheduling solves the problem of the degradation of interactive response when the system is heavily loaded. Jobs that finish within one short time slice will get very good response in almost all cases.

8.2.5 MULTIPLE QUEUES

The two-queue method divides processes into two classes: those that have not yet received and used up one (short) time slice, and those that have. We give the former processes priority in the name of fast interactive response times. The idea is to give better response to very short jobs. But suppose we want to give better response to medium jobs than long jobs? We might decide we want more than two classes of processes, and generalize this idea with three or more queues, each with a longer time slice. A process that completes its time slice moves on to the next-higher queue.

multiple-queue scheduling

We call this *multiple-queue scheduling*.

Figure 8.7 show a three-queue scheduling system. We will explain the details of this figure in the next section.

8.3 POLICY VERSUS MECHANISM IN SCHEDULING

Process scheduling is a perfect example of where it is very easy to separate policy and mechanism. First, let us define a general scheduling mechanism. We use a multiple queue system with three queues. For each queue, there is a scheduling parameter, which is the quantum length of that queue. We call these $q1$, $q2$, and $q3$. Also, for

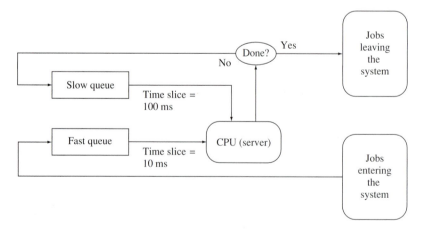

Figure 8.6   Two-queue scheduling

all but the last queue, we have a scheduling parameter, which is the number of times a process can go through this queue. We call these $n1$ and $n2$.

At any point in time, we choose a job from $q1$ if there are any jobs in $q1$, else from $q2$ unless it is empty, else from $q3$. The job is given the time quantum appropriate for the queue it came from. When it completes, it may go to the end of the queue it came from (if it has gone through this queue less than $n1$ or $n2$ times) or to the end of the next queue up.

Figure 8.7 shows the parameterized scheduler (the mechanism) and the scheduling module (the policy). This mechanism can become any of a number of scheduling policies, depending on the parameters we use. If $n1$ and $q1$ are infinite, we have FCFS. If $n1$ is infinite and $q1$ is finite, we have round robin. If $q1$ and $q2$ are finite and $n2$ is infinite, then we have a two-queue system. The scheduler can set scheduling policy by changing these five scheduling parameters. For example, suppose the system is heavily loaded and response time is going up. We can reduce $q1$ and $n1$ to get jobs through the first queue more quickly and improve response time. If we are spending too much time switching between jobs, we can increase one or more of $q1$, $q2$, and $q3$, and maybe decrease $n1$ or $n2$. If we need additional scheduling flexibility, we can parameterize the algorithm on the number of queues, instead of setting it to three.

This is an ideal example of the policy/mechanism split, since we can define a general scheduling mechanism and control it by setting a few parameters. The dispatcher mechanism is in the kernel and is fixed. We can have a scheduling process that wakes up every minute and examines how the system is performing. It can then choose to make adjustments in the scheduling parameters, if that is necessary to improve system performance. This makes it easy to try out new schedulers, since they are in a process rather than the kernel.

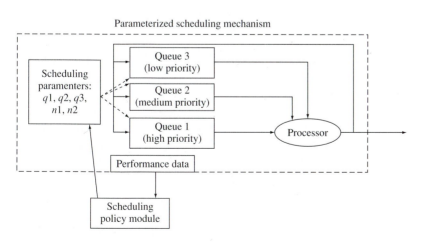

Figure 8.7   Three-queue scheduling

8.4   A SCHEDULING EXAMPLE

Let's see how the choice of scheduling algorithms affects the execution of a set of jobs. Consider the following jobs:

Job	Time	Arrival	Priority
1	10	0	3
2	2	0	2
3	5	0	1
4	3	0	4

All the jobs arrive at time 0 (but in the order 1, 2, 3, then 4) and have an execution time and a priority. The priority is only used for priority scheduling, and is ignored in the other scheduling methods. Figure 8.8 shows the order of the four jobs and the time each job completes.

Shortest-job-first does the best job in minimizing the average time to completion, and first-come, first-served is the worst. The performance of round-robin in this example depends on the time slice. We are not counting process switching overhead, but the completion time of the individual jobs depends on how big the time slice is. The first round-robin figure shows a time slice of 2. The limiting case of round-robin is called *processor sharing*, and it assumes an infinitely short time slice so that the active processes all share the processor equally and progress exactly the same amount in any time period. Thus, during the first eight minutes, each process gets two minutes of time, and, at the end of that period, job 2 completes.

It may be surprising to you that round-robin does so poorly in average time to completion. Round-robin is not intended to give short average completion time, but to give fair response to all jobs. A principle advantage of round-robin is that you do not have to know ahead of time how long a job will run. Round-robin "samples" the jobs by giving them time slices. Short jobs finish in fewer time slices and so get out faster, but not at the extreme of ignoring long jobs; they also get a share of the time.

This is an advantage because you rarely know exactly how long a job will run. Shortest-job-first is very efficient, but it is not practical unless you know in advance how long a job will run, and this is rarely the case in a computer system.

We can estimate a job's expected completion time by keeping a running average of how long it took on previous trips through the ready queue.

8.5   SCHEDULING IN REAL OPERATING SYSTEMS

There is a remarkable uniformity in the scheduling algorithms in modern operating systems. Almost all of them use a priority scheduling system with from 32 to a few hundred levels of priority. They are preemptive, so the highest-priority process is al-

Margin notes (handwritten):

$T_s = 2$

FCFS — Time Average = $\dfrac{10+12+17+20}{4}$ = 14.75

SJF — $T_A = \dfrac{2+5+10+20}{4}$ = 9.25

RR — $T_A =$ No Order $\dfrac{4+13+17+20}{4}$ = 13.5

| 1 | 2 | 3 | 4 | 1 | 3 | 4 | 1 | 3 | 1 | 1 |

RR - SJF $T_A = \dfrac{2+9+15+22}{4}$ = 12

| 2 | 4 | 3 | 1 | 4 | 3 | 1 | 3 | 1 | 1 |

Priority $T_A = \dfrac{5+7+17+20}{4}$ = 12.25

processor sharing

ways running. If there are several processes at a priority-level, they are run round-robin. The upper levels are reserved for real-time processes, which stay at a specific priority. Interactive jobs go in the lower levels, and move up and down in priority according to how much processor time they use and how much I/O they do.

8.5.1 SCHEDULING IN UNIX SVR4

System V, Release 4 UNIX is considered the standard UNIX. It uses a priority scheduler with 160 priority levels. Processes at levels 0–59 are in the time-sharing class. Interactive processes run in this class. Processes at levels 60–99 are for system priorities. Processes that are running in kernel mode run in this class. Processes at levels 100–159 are in the real-time class. The process with the highest priority is always running. Processes with the same priority are scheduled round-robin.

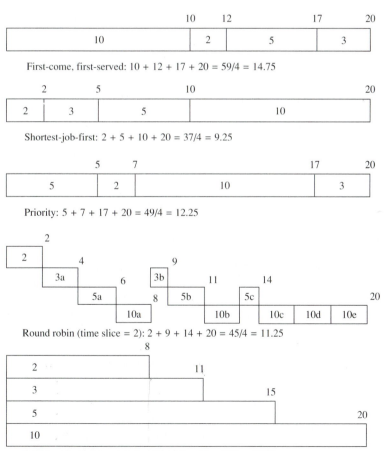

First-come, first-served: 10 + 12 + 17 + 20 = 59/4 = 14.75

Shortest-job-first: 2 + 5 + 10 + 20 = 37/4 = 9.25

Priority: 5 + 7 + 17 + 20 = 49/4 = 12.25

Round robin (time slice = 2): 2 + 9 + 14 + 20 = 45/4 = 11.25

Round robin (continuous): 8 + 11 + 15 + 20 = 54/4 = 13.50

Figure 8.8   Scheduling example

The priorities of the processes in the time-sharing class vary dynamically. The priority of a time-sharing process goes down if it uses up its time quantum. Its priority goes up if it waits for an event (usually an I/O completion) or has to wait a long time for its time quantum.

The time quanta range from 100 milliseconds for priority 0 to 10 milliseconds for priority 59.

8.5.2   SCHEDULING IN SOLARIS

The Solaris scheduler is very similar to the SVR4 scheduler. It adds another class of processes and 10 more priority levels: levels 160–169 are for interrupt handling. The time quanta are shorter, ranging from 4 to 20 milliseconds.

Solaris uses priority inheritance to avoid the problem of priority inversion. When a process waits on a lock, the process holding the lock will inherit its priority (if it is higher than its own priority).

8.5.3   SCHEDULING IN OS/2 2.0

OS/2 is IBM's main PC operating system. It uses a priority thread scheduler with 128 levels in four classes. The time-critical class is at levels 96–127. These are real-time threads. The server class is at levels 64–95 and is for server threads that are essentially part of the operating system. The regular class is at level 32–63 and is for normal time-sharing threads. The idle class is for daemon threads doing background tasks.

The time slice is from 32 to 248 milliseconds and is set on system initialization.

Threads in the foreground (interactive) have their priority increased. Threads just completing an I/O operation have their priority increased. Threads that have waited a while to get a time slice have their priority increased.

8.5.4   SCHEDULING IN WINDOWS NT 3.51

Windows NT is Microsoft's high-end operating system. It uses a priority thread scheduler with 32 levels in two classes. Real-time threads have fixed priorities in the range 16–31. Time-sharing threads have variable priorities in the range 1–15. Threads get their priority increased for doing disk I/O, increased more for doing keyboard or mouse I/O, and decreased when they use up their time quantum. This keeps interactive threads at the higher variable priorities, I/O bound jobs in the middle priorities, and compute bound jobs at the lowest priorities.

8.5.5   SCHEDULING IN OTHER OPERATING SYSTEMS

Mach has 128 priority levels. It also has what is called *hand-off scheduling*. When a process sends a message and the receiver is waiting to receive it, then the receiver is scheduled immediately, without going through any scheduling queues. This helps to speed up message passing.

8.6   DEADLOCK

In the last few sections, we have been concerned with how best to allocate resources so that they are efficiently and fairly used. There is another important goal in scheduling resources, and that is to avoid deadlock and starvation.

Deadlock is a situation where two or more processes are each waiting for a resource that another process in the group holds. These processes will wait forever, since none of them can make any progress and release its resources unless it obtains certain resources, and those resources are held by other processes that cannot make any progress because they are waiting for resources.

deadlock

Let's take a simple example. There are two programs which each need to use the CD-ROM drive and the DAT drive. Suppose things happen in this order:

1. Process A requests the CD-ROM drive from the resource manager.
2. Process A is granted exclusive use of the CD-ROM drive.
3. Process B requests the DAT drive from the resource manager.
4. Process B is granted exclusive use of the DAT drive.
5. Process A requests the DAT drive from the resource manager.
6. Process B requests the CD-ROM drive from the resource manager.

Figure 8.9 shows the situation. At this point, Process A is holding the CD-ROM drive and will not release it until it gets use of the DAT drive. Process B is holding the DAT drive and will not release it until it gets use of the CD-ROM drive. The two processes are deadlocked.

Processes can deadlock on consumable, software resources as well as hardware resources. Suppose Process A and Process B are structured as follows:

Process A	Process B
`receive( B, msg );`	`receive( A, msg );`
`send( B, msg );`	`send( A, msg );`

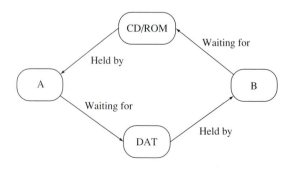

Figure 8.9   Two-process deadlock

If they are started, they will immediately deadlock since they are each waiting for a message from the other one.

A deadlock might involve more than two processes. We can easily construct a similar situation with four processes, each waiting for a message from another process in the group.

Process A	Process B
receive(D, msg);	receive(A, msg);
send(B, msg);	send(C, msg);

Process C	Process D
receive(B, msg);	receive(C, msg);
send(D, msg);	send(A, msg);

In each of these situations, you might say that processes just should not do that, and you would be right. But sometimes mistakes happen, and processes do do this sort of thing. Sometimes errors occur in the system—for example, messages sometimes get lost in transit. Suppose Processes A and B were structured like this:

Process A	Process B
while(1) {	while(1) {
send(B, msg);	receive(A, msg);
receive(B, msg);	send(A, msg);
}	}

If no messages are lost, then this communication works well, but suppose we have the following scenario:

1. B waits for a message from A.

2. A sends a message to B.

3. The message from A to B is lost in transit.

4. A waits for a return message from B.

The processes will deadlock.

Let's take an example from an airline reservation system. Suppose agent A is booking a flight from Los Angeles to New York with a stopover in Chicago, and agent B is booking a similar flight. Each agent needs to book two flights that connect to one another. When booking a flight, you gain exclusive access to the flight record so that it is not possible to book the same seat twice. Agent A locks a Los Angeles to

Chicago flight and makes a reservation, and agent B locks a Chicago to New York flight and makes a reservation. Then each tries to lock the flight the other has locked. Here is the algorithm used by each agent:

Agent A	**Agent B**
Lock(laToChi);	Lock(chiToNy);
see if space is available	*see if space is available*
Lock(chiToNy);	Lock(laToChi);
see if space is available	*see if space is available*
Unlock(chiToNy);	Unlock(laToChi);
Unlock(laToChi);	Unlock(chiToNy);

Again we get a deadlock.

8.7   WHY DEADLOCK IS A PROBLEM

In each of the situations we have described, it is not difficult to see how to handle the deadlock problem. In fact, in centralized systems it is generally easy to deal with the deadlock problem. The important thing is to realize that deadlock is possible and to take steps to prevent it or recover from it. We will see in a later section how to do this.

Of course, in complicated situations, deadlock may be hard to detect or prevent. For example, suppose we have a database with millions of records, each of which can be individually locked. Each record is a resource. A transaction might need to lock dozens of records in order to complete, and hundreds of transactions might be executing at the same time. In such a complex situation, deadlock could easily occur.

8.8   CONDITIONS FOR DEADLOCK TO OCCUR

There are certain conditions that must be true for a deadlock to occur. First, let us rephrase exactly what deadlock is. Deadlock is a situation in which a process is waiting for another process, which is waiting for another process, etc., until finally a process in the chain is waiting for the original process—that is, there is a cycle of processes where each one is waiting for the next one. If processes are deadlocked, it is logically impossible for any of them to proceed since they are waiting for each other.

The four necessary conditions for deadlock are:

1. Resources are not preemptable.

2. Resources are not shared.

3. A process can hold one resource and request another.

4. Circular wait is possible.

Deadlock involves waiting for a resource, so if you can simply preempt the resource, then you don't have to wait for it and no deadlock can occur. Similarly, if you can share the resource, then you do not have to wait for another process to finish using it. Deadlock requires that a process be holding a resource while waiting for another resource. Finally, deadlock requires the waiting process to be in a cycle.

8.9   HOW TO DEAL WITH DEADLOCK

There are three strategies for dealing with deadlock:

1. *Prevention*—Place restrictions on resource requests so that deadlock cannot occur.
2. *Avoidance*—Plan ahead so that you never get into a situation where deadlock is inevitable.
3. *Recovery*—Detect when deadlock has occurred and recover from it.

deadlock prevention

8.9.1   DEADLOCK PREVENTION

Deadlock requires the four conditions enumerated above. If we can prevent any one of these conditions from occurring, we can prevent deadlock.

Allowing Preemption   If we can preempt resources, then deadlock is not possible. All resources can be preempted, but often the cost is too high to be practical.

Avoiding Mutual Exclusion   Sometimes we can virtualize a resource so that there seem to be an unlimited number of them. A good example of this is printer spooling. If a program prints by writing directly to the printer, it has to wait for exclusive use of the printer. With printer spooling, you "print" to a disk file and send a message to the print spooler process to print it when its turn comes up. The print spooler is the only process that ever accesses the hardware printer, and it always has exclusive access to it. Since we can "print" to disk files, we have an unlimited number of virtual printers.

As attractive as this solution is, it cannot be used in all cases where deadlock can occur. It is useful when you want to share a hardware device and you do not need "real-time" access to it.

Avoiding Hold and Wait   If a process acquires all of the resources it needs at one time, then it will never be in a situation where it is holding a resource and waiting for another resource. This will prevent deadlock.

This solution works and is used in some situations, but it can lead to inefficient use of resources. Suppose you have a long process that uses a tape drive for the first 10 minutes and then a CD drive for a few seconds. If you have to acquire them both at the same time, then you will be holding the CD drive for 10 minutes without using it.

This solution also assumes that you know all the resources you will need before you start, and sometimes this is not true. For example, a database transaction might not know what records it needs until it starts looking at some records. One record will lead to another. In such a situation, you cannot predict at the beginning which records you will need to lock.

Avoiding Circular Wait   We can give each resource a unique, positive integer, and only acquire resources in ascending, numerical order. This will prevent any circular wait.

This method is actually pretty good and is often used. However, it can also lead to inefficient use of resources since, again, you might have to acquire a resource way before you intend to use it because of the way resources are ordered.

8.9.2   DEADLOCK AVOIDANCE

It turns out that there are algorithms you can use to avoid deadlock. Whenever you are about to make an allocation, you can run the algorithm and see if making that allocation would lead to a deadlock. This seems like the ideal method, but it has several important drawbacks. The first is that the algorithms are not that fast, and there is a lot of overhead in running them before every resource allocation. An operating system might be allocating resources hundreds of times a second. Second, the algorithms assume that processes know their maximum resource needs, but this is often not the case. Third, they assume they know what resources are available in the system. Hardware can go down and resources can become unavailable. This can lead to deadlocks that could not be predicted.

8.9.3   DEADLOCK RECOVERY

Deadlock recovery involves two steps. The first is deadlock detection. This is essentially finding a cycle in a graph of resource requests. This is not too hard, but not that fast either. Fortunately, we do not have to detect deadlock after each resource allocation. Instead, we can check periodically for deadlock, say every few seconds.

Once we have discovered a deadlock, we have to figure out how to break it. This involves preempting a resource, which might mean canceling a process and starting it over.

Deadlock detection and recovery is the optimistic solution to the problem. We assume deadlock is unlikely, but detect it and recover from it when it occurs rather than spending resources trying to prevent it or avoid it.

The VMS operating system uses a simple but effective method of deadlock detection. Whenever a resource request fails and must wait, VMS starts a timer of 10 seconds. If the timer goes off and the request is still waiting, then it runs its deadlock detection algorithm. That is, it does not run the deadlock detection algorithm until it has some reason to suspect that a deadlock might exist.

8.10   A SEQUENCE OF APPROACHES TO THE DEADLOCK PROBLEM

In this section, we will review the solutions in the previous sections and discuss a progression of ways to deal with the deadlock problem. Each solution is more liberal than the previous one in how it grants resources.

1. *Never grant resource requests*—In this "solution," we never grant any resource requests. No deadlock can occur, but processes will make no progress since they will have no resources. This is not a practical solution, but an extreme case for comparison only.

2. *Serialization*—In this solution, we require processes to run one at a time. Deadlock cannot occur, since you have to have at least two processes requesting resources in order to have a deadlock. This solution works and might be used in some extreme cases, but it is a very severe (and slow) solution.

3. *One-shot allocation*—In this solution, we require a process to request all the resources it will require at one time. This solution works and is practical in some cases, but it requires processes to always assume the worst-possible case and can lead to inefficient use of resources.

4. *Hierarchical*—In this solution, resources are arranged in a hierarchy or sequence, and you have to request resources in a specified order. This is a reasonably good solution and is often used, but it can also lead to inefficient use of resources. Again, it requires worst-case planning since you have to acquire a resource in order or not at all. If you are not sure whether you will need it, you have to acquire it to make sure.

5. *Advance claim*—In this solution, the processes have to declare in advance how much of each resource they will need. The system uses a deadlock avoidance algorithm. This is the most liberal method that guarantees to avoid deadlock, but it is not really practical in real-world situations.

6. *Always allocate*—In this solution, you always allocate the resources that are requested (if you have them). You detect and recover from deadlock if it occurs. This is the most liberal policy, but it does not prevent deadlock.

As you can see, there is no ideal solution to the deadlock problem. Each approach has some defects.

8.11   TWO-PHASE LOCKING

There is a method used in databases that avoids deadlock and combines some of the previous techniques. Databases allow you to *lock* a record. This gives you exclusive access to the record until you unlock it. This allows you to make changes in the record without worrying about interference from other processes. It is assumed that

all processes accessing the database will lock a record before changing it. Called *two-*
phase locking, the idea is that a database transaction goes through two phases, a locking phase and a changing phase. In the locking phase, it goes through and decides
what changes it needs to make and what record locks it needs to acquire. It does not
make any changes to the database in this phase. If it fails to acquire a lock in this
phase, then it releases all the locks it holds and starts over. Deadlock cannot occur in
this stage because it never waits for a lock while it is holding a lock.

After a transaction has locked all the records, it goes into the second phase
where it makes all the changes. Then it releases all the locks. Deadlock is not possible in this stage because it does not try to lock any more locks. They are all acquired
in the first stage.

This algorithm does avoid deadlock, but it is vulnerable to starvation. We will
look into the starvation problem in the next section.

8.12   STARVATION

Starvation is a situation in which a process is prevented from proceeding because
some other process always has the resources it needs. It is different from deadlock
because it is possible for the process to get the resources it needs; it just doesn't happen to because of bad luck in the timing of resource requests.

In the simplest starvation situation, you have a random queue, that is, a queue
where the next process is chosen at random from all the processes waiting in the
queue. If, by chance, one process is continually passed over, it will never get out of
the queue and will be "starved" for resources.

You might say this is unrealistic, and a random queue is not fair and never happens. In fact, things like random queues are not that uncommon. If you are trying to
call a popular phone number (like a radio station), you have to call over and over
again if the line is busy. If you are unlucky, you will never get through since you will
never happen to call exactly as another caller hangs up. Phone callers trying to get
through to a busy number are essentially in a random queue. The same thing is true
of popular *ftp* sites that reject *ftp* connections over a certain set limit.

The solution is to use an FCFS queue, and that is what companies who have multiple phone lines that are answered by a machine do. They always answer your call,
and then you are put in an FCFS line to talk to someone.

But the FCFS solution only works if you are waiting for a single resource. Suppose your system avoids deadlock by requiring you to acquire all the resources you
need in a single request, and you need a DAT drive and a CD-ROM drive so you ask
for the two of them together. When you make the request, let's say the CD-ROM
drive is free but the DAT drive isn't, so you have to wait. A little later, another
process acquires the CD-ROM drive, and then the DAT drive becomes free. You still
cannot be allocated the resources since the CD-ROM drive is no longer free, so you
still must wait. A little later, the DAT drive is acquired by another process, and then
the CD-ROM drive becomes free again. This could go on for a long time, and there
might never be a time when they are both free at the same time.

One solution is for the system to reserve whatever it can for you when you make the request, and then wait for the other resources to becomes available. But then you are in a hold and wait situation, and deadlock again becomes possible.

So you can see that, although deadlock and starvation have similar effects, they conflict in that solutions to the deadlock problem can make starvation more likely, and solutions to the starvation problem can make deadlock more likely.

We will see the standard solution to the starvation problem in Section 15.2.3 on disk head scheduling, and that is *aging*. A process that is waiting for a resource ages as it waits, and as it ages, its priority increases. When its priority gets very high, then other processes are prevented from going ahead of it.

For example, in the DAT and CD/ROM example, we would wait for a while (say five minutes) for both to be free. After that, we would acquire them one at a time. We might acquire them in a system-determined order in order to avoid deadlock.

8.13   MESSAGE-PASSING VARIATIONS

8.13.1   USING PIDs AS MESSAGE ADDRESSES

In the message-passing systems we have discussed up to now, we have always sent messages to message queues. We could consider simplifying the system by sending messages directly to processes instead of message queues. We already have a way of naming processes, namely process identifiers, so they would be used as addresses. Each process would have an associated message queue to buffer messages sent to that process. The operating system would still have to support message queues as an internal object inside the operating system, but user processes would not need to know anything about them.

Figure 8.10 shows how this would work. Each process would have an associated message queue, and messages sent to that process would be put onto that queue. This is similar to the concept of a port described later (see Section 8.21.2), except that it is not possible for another process to take over receiving messages from the port if the first process receiving from it fails.

Sending messages directly to processes would simplify the system by removing one kind of object (message queues), but there are important disadvantages. Such a system is less flexible than the message queue system. The level of indirection provided by the message queues means that several processes can receive from the same queue. It means that a process can receive from several different queues.

8.13.2   MESSAGE PASSING WITH NONBLOCKING RECEIVES

It is not possible to wait on more than one message queue at a time because the first ReceiveMessage system call will block the calling process until a message arrives at that queue. One way around this problem is to simulate this facility with extra processes. You start by creating a process to wait on each queue you are interested in. That process will forward any messages to a common queue. Then you just wait on

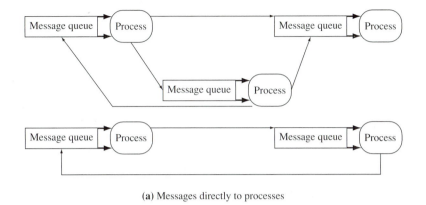

(a) Messages directly to processes

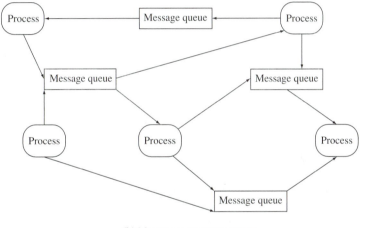

(b) Message-to-message queues

Figure 8.10   Addressing messages to processes or message queues

the common queue, and messages from all other queues will be forwarded to that one queue. The defect of this solution is that it requires the overhead of extra processes whose only purpose is to wait for messages.

Another solution to the problem is possible if we add a nonblocking version of ReceiveMessage, called ReceiveMessageNoWait, which will check the queue for messages and return a message if there is one waiting, but return with a failure code if there is not a message waiting. This is called a *nonblocking receive*. Using non-   nonblocking receive
blocking receives, it is possible to wait on several queues by repeatedly trying to receive from each one in turn using ReceiveMessageNoWait. Usually the process will try each queue and, if they are both empty, go to sleep for a while (say 100ms to 1 second) and try again when it wakes up. The problem with this solution is that it involves busy waiting, since the process makes an unbounded number of ReceiveMessageNoWait calls.

DESIGN TECHNIQUE: INDIRECTION

Sending messages directly to a process is simpler, but it is not as flexible as sending messages to a message queue. Message queues allow the possibility of several processes receiving from the same message queue, and allow the possibility of changing the process reading from the message queue. This allows recovery if the process receiving from a message queue fails unexpectedly.

This is an example of the idea of indirection—going through an intermediate object to gain access to another object. Indirection provides a single point at which to monitor and modify accesses to the final object, and this allows us to easily provide additional services on each access or on selected accesses. In the message queue place, we can provide the facility of directing the message to a different process if one fails.

Objects only allow access to private variables through functions that get and set the variable. This allows the object to monitor the use of the variable. Thus, it could maintain a graphical display of the current value of the variable. The object could also avoid storing the value, and instead recalculate it each time it is read. Or the value could be calculated in a lazy fashion, on the first access to it.

Indirection allows us to delay the creation of an object until it is first used. This technique can be used to delay the creation of windows in a graphical user interface until they are needed. This will speed up the initialization of the application.

Indirection is discussed at greater length in Section 9.1.

DESIGN TECHNIQUE: ADDING A NEW FACILITY TO A SYSTEM

We looked at three solutions to the problem of waiting for two queues at the same time. We can generalize these three solutions as follows:

1. Using an existing facility to build a solution to the problem (such as using a separate process to wait on each queue).

2. Adding a new, low-level facility that can be used to build a solution to the problem (such as changing the ReceiveMessage system call so that it will return with an error code if there are no messages in the queue to be received).

3. Adding a new, high-level facility that solves the problem directly (such as a new form of the ReceiveMessage system call that will wait on two queues at the same time).

The same three types of solutions are possible in many other situations. For example, suppose you want to provide system calls that allow a process to read a directory of file names. The problem here is that a directory is of unknown length. It may contain two names or two hundred names. Here are the three solutions to this problem:

1. Allocate enough memory to hold all the names and return the allocated memory, that is, use the existing memory allocation facility that can handle objects of variable size.

2. Provide two new system calls: one that will return the first name in a file directory, and one that will return the next name in a file directory. This solution adds a low-level facility.

3. Provide a system call that will iterate over all the names in a file directory and call a function provided by the process on each file name. This provides a high-level, direct solution to the problem.

For more discussion of this design technique, see Section 9.8.

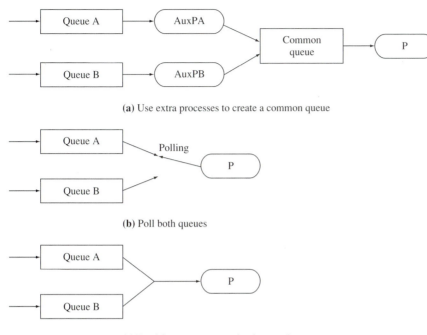

(a) Use extra processes to create a common queue

(b) Poll both queues

(c) Read from two queues simultaneously.

Figure 8.11   Three ways to read from two queues simultaneously

A third solution would be to add a new primitive operation which allows you to specify a list of message queues to wait on. The primitive operation would return when there was a message on any of the queues.

Figure 8.11 shows the three methods of solving this problem.

8.13.3   MESSAGE PASSING WITH BLOCKING SENDS

We can go the opposite direction on waiting and remove the need for message buffers. Suppose the `SendMessage` call waits until there is a process ready to receive the message. Then the message is transferred directly from the sender to the receiver, with no intermediate copying or buffering. This removes the burden of managing buffers from the operating system. This is called a *blocking send.*   blocking send

We can go a step further and require the sender to wait for a reply. This is based on the *client-server model* of communication (see Section 7.10 and Chapter 20). We send a message to a server, it receives the message, and it sends a reply. We need to expand our set of system calls as follows:

*   void SendMessage(int toMsgQueue, MessageBuffer msg);
*   void ReceiveMessage(int fromMsgQueue, MessageBuffer msg);
*   void SendReply(int toMsgQueue, MessageBuffer msg);

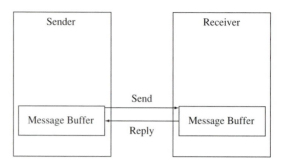

Figure 8.12   Send-receive-reply message passing model

The `SendMessage` call sends the message and then blocks the calling process until a reply is received. The return message is placed in the same message buffer that the sent message was in. The receiver gets the message with `ReceiveMessage` and replies to it with `SendReply`.

Figure 8.12 shows the data movement for the send-receive-reply model of message passing. This is the sequence of events:

1. Sender calls `SendMessage`. Sender is blocked.
2. Receiver calls `ReceiveMessage`.
3. Message is transferred from the sender's buffer directly to the receiver's buffer.
4. Receiver does the processing required to handle the message.
5. Receiver calls `SendReply`. Message reply is transferred from the receiver's buffer directly to the sender's buffer.
6. Sender is unblocked.

Events 1 and 2 on the above list can occur in either order, but the rest of the events will occur in the order listed. The receiver is blocked until the `SendMessage`, but the sender is blocked until the `SendReply`.

8.13.4   REMOTE PROCEDURE CALLS

The version of message sending that waits for a reply is much more structured than our previous versions. In fact, it looks almost like a procedure call between two processes because the sending process is blocked until a reply is received from the receiver. This observation has led to the idea of structuring message passing so that it doesn't look to the user like message passing at all. Instead it looks like procedure calling. This concept is known as *remote procedure call* or *RPC*.

remote procedure call
(RPC)

The Basic RPC Mechanism   First we will explain in general terms how a remote procedure call is implemented. Then we will discuss some details that complicate the implementation.

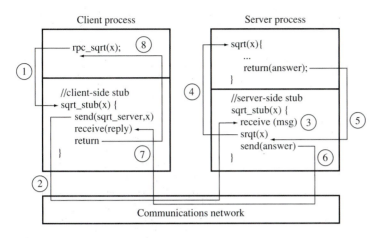

Figure 8.13   Remote procedure call

Figure 8.13 shows the sequence of events in a remote procedure call. The numbered items in the following list match with the numbers in Figure 8.13.

1. The client makes a remote procedure call.
2. The client-side stub turns it into a message on the network.
3. The server-side stub receives the message.
4. The server-side stub calls the real procedure on the server.
5. The real procedure performs the requested work and returns to the server-side stub.
6. The server-side stub sends the result back in a message.
7. The client-side stub receives the result message.
8. The client-side stub returns to the remote procedure caller.

The client-side stub acts as a proxy for the real *sqrt* procedure. It accepts calls for the procedure and arranges for them to be forwarded to the server. It works with its partner, the server-side stub, which is in the same address space as the *sqrt* procedure. The server-side stub receives the message, calls the *sqrt* procedure, and returns the result (in a message) to the client-side stub. Finally, the client-side stub returns the result to the original RPC call. The two stubs (client-side and server-side) work together to "transfer" the procedure call from the client's address space to the server's address space.

The next code segment shows the RPC and the client-side stub procedure in more detail.

IMPLEMENTING REMOTE PROCEDURE CALLS

```
// The remote procedure call (RPC)
retValue = RemoteService( arg1, arg2, arg3 );
```

```
// Client-side "stub" procedure
int RemoteService( int arg1, int arg2, int arg3 ) {
    MessageBuffer msg;
    msg[0] = RemoteServiceCode;
    msg[1] = arg1;
    msg[2] = arg2;
    msg[3] = arg3;
    SendMessage( RemoteServer, msg );
    ReceiveMessage( RemoteServer, msg );
    return msg[1];
}
```

Advantages of Remote Procedure Calls   There are several advantages to the remote procedure call form of message passing. First, procedure calling is well-understood by programmers. It is more familiar than message passing, which is more oriented towards the hardware configuration of multicomputers. Second, message fields are unnamed, untyped data, but procedure arguments are named and typed. Thus the RPC interface serves to define the arguments and return values of the remote service more explicitly, and the argument types are checked by the procedure calling mechanism. This serves to standardize the service and make it more generally useful.

Implementation Issues with Remote Procedure Calls   There are some difficult issues to consider when implementing a remote procedure call. The first issue is how the arguments are sent. The arguments will be sent in a message to another address space. This means that it is not reasonable to send a local address, since it will not have any meaning in the address space of the server. So we cannot pass an argument by reference. Instead, we must pass complete copies of all arguments. The same is true of return values. If you want the remote procedure call to update an array, you have to pass the entire array in the message, and return the entire (updated) array in the reply.

The second issue in remote procedure calls is where to send the message. The client-side stub must know the network address of the server process. This can be a problem because processes sometimes run on different machines at different times.

The third issue in remote procedure calls is the problem of errors. It is possible for a message to get lost in the network. It is also possible for the machine the server process is running on to fail, and so there will be no server process to send the message to. What should the client-side stub do in these cases? First, it has to detect that an error has occurred. Sometimes it is hard to tell the difference between a machine being down and it being very slow. Once it discovers an error, it has do something about it. Presumably, it will return from the procedure with an error.

The general problem is that we are representing something as a procedure call when it really is not a procedure call, but rather something quite a bit more complex. This is an advantage when it works, but sometimes we cannot prevent the underlying complexity of the service from showing through.

RPC Libraries There is a lot of code involved in implementing an RPC mechanism, but once you have implemented one, the next one is a lot easier since most of the code is independent of the particular remote procedure called. Because of this, operating systems often provide libraries of functions that assist you in implementing RPCs.

There are two parts to implementing an RPC. The first part is implementing the server-side stub and process that does the real procedure you are providing. The second part is implementing the client-side stub that can be included in any client process that wants to make use of the RPC. This is generally provided as an include file and a library that includes the client-side stub. The RPC support in an operating system will provide assistance in developing both these parts.

8.14 SYNCHRONIZATION

8.14.1 DEFINITION OF SYNCHRONIZATION

In common English usage, synchronization means to make things happen at the same time. Synchronization has a technical meaning in computer science that is related to this meaning but somewhat different. The most basic type of *synchronization* of processes is what we called signaling in Section 7.7. In the signaling IPC pattern, when one process reaches its signal point, it waits for the other process to reach its signal point. This was implemented by a message receive at the signal receiver's signal point and a message send at the signal sender's message point.

synchronization

In broader terms, process synchronization is when one process waits for notification of an event that will occur in another process. The other IPC patterns were more complicated versions of signaling, and were all synchronization patterns. In the rendezvous pattern, two processes were each signaling the other. (The two processes synchronize so they are both at specific points in their codes.) In the producer-consumer pattern, the producer is repeatedly signaling the consumer. (The producer and consumer keep synchronized so that the producer does not get too far ahead of the consumer.) In the client-server pattern, a single consumer (the server) can be signaled by a number of producers (the clients). (The client and server synchronize so they can communicate.)

The mutual exclusion pattern is also a version of signaling, but it has some important differences. In the mutual exclusion pattern, a process must wait for another process to leave its critical section. The event it waits for is the end of another process's critical section. But it only needs to wait for this event if the other process is in its critical section. So, even though mutual exclusion can be construed as a variation of signaling, it is better thought of as a second basic type of synchronization.

In signaling, one process waits for another process to do something (signal an event), and in mutual exclusion, one process waits for another process to not be doing something (not be in its critical section). Signaling is the most basic form of process cooperation, and mutual exclusion is the most basic form of process competition.

To complete our review of IPC patterns, database access and update is a form of mutual exclusions, with scheduling considerations thrown in.

8.14.2   REVIEW OF SYNCHRONIZATION

So far, we have talked about a number of aspects and instances of synchronization. This is an important issue, and so in this section we would like to review what we have done and try to place it all in a framework that you can understand as a whole.

Figure 8.14 shows, in table format, where in the book you can find discussions of each of several topics in synchronization. The following paragraphs expand on the information in this table.

First, in Chapter 5, we developed the process concept. Processes are logically parallel, that is, they seem to be running at the same time. Processes running in parallel are not a problem, since the processes cannot communicate with each other. But, we wanted processes to communicate and cooperate, so we added a message-passing facility to the operating system to allow and promote this communication.

In Chapter 7, we discussed at length the issues of competition and cooperation between processes. The patterns in Chapter 7 are a catalog of different forms of process synchronization.

Synchronization Issue	Operating System Level	User Process Level
mutual exclusion problem	protecting OS data (Ch. 6)	file update (Ch. 7) increment counter (Ch. 7) mutual exclusion IPC pattern (Ch. 7)
mutual exclusion solutions	disable interrupts (Ch. 5) spin locks (Ch. 6) Peterson's algorithm (Ch. 6)	IPC patterns (Ch. 7) messages (Ch. 7) semaphores (Ch. 8) monitors (Ch. 8)
signaling problem	Delaying completion of a system call (Ch. 5)	signaling IPC pattern (Ch. 7)
signaling solutions	kernel-mode processes (Ch. 6) semaphores in OS (Ch. 8)	IPC patterns (Ch. 7) messages (Ch. 7) semaphores (Ch. 8) monitors (Ch. 8) RPC (Ch. 8)
interprocess communication	shared memory (Ch. 5)	shared memory (threads) (Ch. 8) shared memory (virtual memory) (Ch. 11) messages (Ch. 5) RPC (Ch. 8)
threads and processes	processes (Ch. 5) light-weight processes (Ch. 6) kernel threads (Ch. 6)	user threads (Ch. 6)

Figure 8.14   Discussions of synchronization in this book

The patterns we developed in Chapter 7 assumed that the operating system provided message-passing primitives. In Section 6.9, we noted that implementing message-passing primitives required mutual exclusion in the operating system. This creates two levels of implementation of mutual exclusion. The operating system can implement message passing using mutual exclusion, and the user process can implement mutual exclusion using message passing.

In Chapter 5, we implemented mutual exclusion in the operating system by disabling interrupts when we were running operating system code. This prevented logical parallelism and solved the mutual exclusion problem. But the second aspect of the synchronization problem was still present. This is the problem of signaling, that is, of allowing a process to wait until another process signals an event. In Sections 5.9.2 and 5.9.3, we noted the problem of system calls (like `SendMessage`) that could not be completed immediately.

In Chapter 6, we had to deal with the mutual exclusion problem inside the operating system because we moved the simple operating system to a two-processor system that added physical parallelism. Our original solution of disabling interrupts would not work in this situation, and so we introduced a hardware instruction (*ExchangeWord*) which could be used to implement mutual exclusion using busy waiting. We noted that this was a general solution to the problem for any number of processors. The busy waiting solution works because the waiting time is short because critical sections are short.

Signaling can also be done at the operating system level with busy waiting, but this is not a good solution at the user level because the waiting times are too long and too much processor time would be wasted doing busy waiting. Instead, we used message passing to implement signaling at the user level. Kernel-mode processes allow us to use semaphores for signaling at the operating system level (see Section 8.18).

Levels of Synchronization   We have discussed mutual exclusion at two levels: the user level and the operating system level. Each level had the same basic problem: race conditions caused by logical or physical parallelism. Each level has the same solution: critical sections need to be made into logically atomic actions. This solution was implemented with a mechanism to provide mutual exclusion. At the operating systems level, we either inhibited interrupts or used spin locks. At the user level, we used message passing to implement mutual exclusion.

Inhibiting interrupts and spin locks are the standard solutions to the mutual exclusion problem at the operating systems levels, and are used in every operating system. But there are other common mechanisms to implement mutual exclusion at the user level, and we will look at some of them in the next few sections. The two main mechanisms we will look at are semaphores and monitors. Semaphores are an operating-system-level solution, like message passing, and monitors are a programming-language-level solution. We will also look at synchronization in Ada 95, which has the most advanced synchronization facilities of the commonly used languages.

The other part of the synchronization problem is the signaling problem. We have seen how it can be solved with messages, but the same mechanisms that provide mutual exclusion also solve the signaling problem. As we look at these other methods, we will see how they solve both of these basic synchronization problems.

The IPC patterns in Chapter 7 are above the synchronization primitive level. These same patterns will occur with messages, semaphores, and monitors. As we introduce semaphores and monitors, we will show how some of these patterns are implemented using those primitives.

8.15 SEPARATING DATA TRANSFER AND SYNCHRONIZATION

If you look at the IPC patterns in Chapter 7, you will see that there are two aspects to the communication: processes waiting for each other, and processes transferring data. In a message system, waiting and data transfer are combined into a single concept, the message. One process will signal another process that an event has occurred by sending it a message, and the other process waits for the event by waiting for the message. Many of the messages contained no information, since they were only signaling that a particular event had taken place.

Messages combine these two aspects of IPC, but it is also possible to define IPC system calls where these two aspects are separated. For example, in a shared memory system, we can transfer data between processes through the shared memory. The main problem then becomes one of synchronization—one process waiting for another.

In Section 6.7, we introduced the concept of threads that existed in a shared memory space. We did not discuss how threads would synchronize with each other. Messages would be a possibility, but it seems unnecessary for threads to synchronize with messages since they can easily communicate information through their common memory.

Early operating systems were built on computer systems with one processor and shared memory, and operating system designers were concerned mainly with solving the synchronization problem. The early operating system designers developed a number of synchronization primitives that assumed shared memory, and solved the synchronization problem of logically parallel processes. These solutions are also useful for threads, which also share memory. The most widely known and widely used of these synchronization primitives is called a semaphore, and we will discuss it in the next section.

8.16 SEMAPHORES

In Section 7.2.1, we saw that there were two basic reasons why processes needed to communicate: to compete for shared resources, and to cooperate on a task. To share resources, they have to solve the mutual exclusion problem, and to cooperate on a task, they have to solve the signaling problem. There is a primitive called a *semaphore* that solves both these problems quite neatly.

semaphore

Semaphores have to be named in some way, just like message queues and pipes. Just for a change, we will use a different naming scheme than we have before. The semaphore name will be an integer identifier. The semaphore identifiers are global to all processes, that is, if two different processes use the same semaphore identifier, then they will get the same semaphore. These global semaphore identifiers can be any integer, and are chosen by the user processes. They are similar to names in the file naming system in that they are global, but they are different from names in the file naming system in that they are integers and they do not have an existence in the file naming system.

8.16.1   SPECIFICATION OF SEMAPHORE OPERATIONS

Semaphores are created by an `AttachSemaphore` operation, which takes as a parameter the global identifier the semaphore will have. Subsequent `AttachSemaphore` operations with the same global identifier will not create a new semaphore, but instead attach to the exiting one. The `AttachSemaphore` operation will return a local identifier for this instance of the semaphore. This identifier is similar to an open file identifier. When a process has completed using a semaphore, it will call a `DetachSemaphore` operation. If a process exits, the system will automatically call `DetachSemaphore` for all semaphores it still has attached. This way, the system can keep track of which processes are using a semaphore, and it can delete semaphores that are no longer in use.

A semaphore is an object with two operations: `Wait` and `Signal`. Here is the definition of the system calls to attach and detach a semaphore and perform the `Wait` and `Signal` operations on the semaphore.

- `int AttachSemaphore( int sema_gid );` —The operating system attaches, the semaphore with global identifier `sema_gid` is looked up, and a local identifier to the semaphore is returned. All processes that attach to the semaphore of the same global identifier will be operating on the same semaphore. The local identifier will be an integer that has meaning to the operating system but is just an arbitrary number of the system caller. The local identifier is used in the `Wait` and `Signal` system calls. The local identifier is only valid for the process that called `AttachSemaphore`, and should not be passed to any other process. The first time a process attaches a semaphore, it is created by the operating system. Semaphores are created in a "busy" state. A valid semaphore identifier will always be a positive integer. The return value is −1 if there was a problem that prevented it from being created.

- `int Wait( int sema_id );` —If the semaphore is not busy, then the state is changed to busy and the system call returns. If the semaphore is busy, then the system call is blocked and the calling process is put on the semaphore's wait queue.

- `int Signal( int sema_id );` —If the wait queue of the semaphore with identifier `sema_id` is empty, then the state of the semaphore is changed to not busy.

If the wait queue is not empty, then some process is removed from the wait queue for this semaphore and unblocked.

• int DetachSemaphore(int sema_lid); —This announces to the system that the calling process is no longer using this semaphore.

8.16.2 IMPLEMENTATION OF SEMAPHORES

Let's look at the pseudo-code for these operations to make sure we understand exactly what they do.

IMPLEMENTATION OF WAIT AND SIGNAL (BINARY SEMAPHORE)

```
void Wait( int sema_id ) {
    Semaphore * sema = GetSemaphoreFromId( sema_id );
    Lock( sema->lock ); // a busy waiting spin lock
        if( !sema->busy ) {
            sema->busy = True;
        } else {
            sema->queue->Insert( current_process );
            Block( current_process );
        }
    Unlock( sema->lock );
}
void Signal( int sema_id ) {
    Semaphore * sema = GetSemaphoreFromId( sema_id );
    Lock( sema->lock ); // a busy waiting spin lock
        if( sema->queue->Empty() ) {
            sema->busy = False;
        } else {
            process = sema->queue->Remove();
            Unblock( process );
        }
    Unlock( sema->lock );
}
```

The operating system has some way (GetSemaphoreFromId) of finding the semaphore data structure from the semaphore identifier. The semaphore operations themselves must be atomic, that is, no other process can execute an operation on this semaphore at the same time. We ensure this with a spin lock (sema—>lock). A process that calls Wait on a busy semaphore is blocked. This ensures it will not run again until unblocked by a Signal operation. When a process is unblocked, it is eligible for execution. We are not specifying any particular scheduling here, that is, it is not necessarily the very next process to run.

The Wait and Signal operations are atomic and are not allowed to overlap with a wait or signal by another process. This means the check of the semaphore state and the subsequent setting of the state are atomic.

The semaphore we have just defined is called in *binary semaphore*. It is also called a *mutex* to emphasize its use in providing mutual exclusion. There is also a slightly more general version called a counting semaphore, which we will discuss later.

binary semaphore

mutex

8.16.3   AN ANALOGY

We can make an analogy between a semaphore and a key which normally hangs on a hook—say a key to the bathroom at a gas station. When a process calls Wait, it is like looking for the key on the hook. If the key is on the hook, then it is removed and the Wait caller continues. If not, then the Wait caller waits around the hook until the key is placed back on the hook. A Signal caller replaces the key on the hook.

Semaphores were originally proposed by Dijkstra in Dijkstra (1968) and Dijkstra (1971). In those papers, he used the operation names P and V for Wait and signal. These names are the first letters of the Dutch words for these operations. You sometimes still see these operations named P and V.

8.16.4   MUTUAL EXCLUSION WITH SEMAPHORES

We can easily adapt all the IPC patterns in Chapter 7 to use semaphores if we assume that they can communicate information using shared memory. Let's start by looking at the mutual exclusion IPC pattern. Here is how it would be with semaphores:

TWO PROCESS MUTUAL EXCLUSION WITH SEMAPHORES

```
// This is the code for process A or B
void main( int argc, char * argv[ ] ) {
    // The semaphore is named a unique global identifier.
    int mutex_sema = AttachSemaphore( FMutexID );
    if( ThisIsProcessA() )
        Signal( mutex_sema ); // Initialize the semaphore to not busy
    while( 1 ) {
        DoOtherThings();
        // The critical section
        Wait( mutex_sema );
            UseFileF();
        Signal( mutex_sema );
    }
    DetachSemaphore( mutex_sema );
}
```

Note that it is virtually identical to the message solution, with `Signal` replacing `SendMsgTo` and `Wait` replacing `WaitForEmptyMsg`.

8.16.5   RENDEZVOUS WITH SEMAPHORES

Now let us look at the two-way synchronization (that is, rendezvous) IPC pattern.

TWO PROCESS RENDEZVOUS WITH SEMAPHORES

```
// Game player A
void main( int argc, char *argv[ ] ) {
    int a_sema = AttachSemaphore( GPAID );
    int b_sema = AttachSemaphore( GPBID );
    // Tell B that A is ready to go.
    Signal( b_sema );
    // Wait until B is ready to go.
    Wait( a_sema );

    DetachSemaphore( a_sema );
    DetachSemaphore( b_sema );
}
// Game player B
void main( int argc, char *argv[ ] ) {
    int b_sema = AttachSemaphore( GPBID );
    int a_sema = AttachSemaphore( GPAID );

    // Tell A that B is ready to go.
    Signal( a_sema );
    // Wait until A is ready to go.
    Wait( b_sema );

    DetachSemaphore( a_sema );
    DetachSemaphore( b_sema );
}
```

Again, the solutions are nearly the same.

8.16.6   PRODUCER-CONSUMER (ONE BUFFER) WITH SEMAPHORES

Finally, we will look at the producer-consumer IPC pattern with a single buffer.

THE PRODUCER CONSUMER IPC PATTERN WITH SEMAPHORES (1 BUFFER)

```
Buffer buffer;// global buffer

void main() {// The Producer
```

```
    int empty_buffer = AttachSemaphore( EmptyBufferID );
    int full_buffer = AttachSemaphore( FullBufferID );

    while( 1 ) {
        Wait( empty_buffer );
        FillBuffer( buffer );
        Signal( full_buffer );
    }

    DetachSemaphore( empty_buffer );
    DetachSemaphore( full-buffer );
}
void main() {// The Consumer
    int empty_buffer = AttachSemaphore( EmptyBufferID );
    int full_buffer = AttachSemaphore( FullBufferID );
    Signal( empty_buffer); // buffer is not full initially

    while( 1 ) {
        Wait( full_buffer );
        ConsumeBuffer( buffer );
        Signal( empty_buffer );
    }

    DetachSemaphore( empty_buffer );
    DetachSemaphore( full_buffer );
}
```

In order to extend this solution to *N* buffers, we need to look at counting semaphores.

8.16.7   COUNTING SEMAPHORES

A binary semaphore is either busy or not, because it is intended for mutual exclusion where only one process at a time can be in its critical section. There are some situations where you want to limit the number of processes in some state, but the limit is greater than one. For example, you might only allow three processes to be printing because you have three printers.

One way to handle this situation is to use a counting semaphore. A *counting semaphore* is similar to a binary semaphore, except it maintains an integer count instead of just a busy flag. Here is the pseudo-code for a counting semaphore.

counting semphaore

IMPLEMENTATION OF WAIT AND SIGNAL (COUNTING SEMAPHORE)

```
void Wait( int sema_id ) {
    Semaphore * sema = GetSemaphoreFromId( sema_id );
    Lock( sema->lock );
        if( sema->count > 0 ) {
            --sema->count;
        } else {
```

```
                    sema->queue->Insert( current_process );
                    Block( current_process );
            }
        Unlock( sema->lock );
}
void Signal( int sema_id ) {
    Semaphore * sema = GetSemaphoreFromId( sema_id );
    Lock( sema->lock );
        if( sema->queue->Empty() ) {
            ++sema->count;
        } else {
            process = sema->queue->Remove();
            Unblock( process );
        }
    Unlock( sema->lock );
}
```

If the count never gets above one, then it is equivalent to a binary semaphore.

8.16.8   PRODUCER-CONSUMER (N BUFFERS) WITH SEMAPHORES

We have to be concerned with the buffers now, since semaphores only handle synchronization and not data transfer. This means we are always in the bounded buffer situation. We can no longer depend on the operating system to manage buffers for us. As a result, this looks like the producer-consumer with limited buffers solution.

Suppose we wanted to increase the number of buffers. Let us assume we have a queue data structure that will hold the buffers. We have to enforce mutual exclusion on manipulation of the buffer queue. Here is the code to do that.

THE PRODUCER CONSUMER IPC PATTERN WITH SEMAPHORES (N BUFFERS)

```
enum { MaxBuffers = 20 };
Queue<Buffer>buffer_queue; // Queue of buffers

void main() {// The Producer
    int use_buffer_queue = AttachSemaphore( UseBufferQueueID );
    int empty_buffer = AttachSemaphore( EmptyBufferID );
    int full_buffer = AttachSemaphore( FullBufferID );
    Buffer buffer;

    while( 1 ) {
        // Fill the local buffer
        FillBuffer( buffer );
        // Wait for a slot in the buffer queue
        Wait( empty_buffer );
        // Ensure mutual exclusion using the buffer queue
```

```
        Wait( use_buffer_queue );
        // Insert the full buffer into the buffer queue
        buffer_queue.Insert( buffer );
        Signal( use_buffer_queue );
        // Notify the consumer that a buffer is ready
        Signal( full_buffer );
    }

    DetachSemaphore( use_buffer_queue );
    DetachSemaphore( empty_buffer );
    DetachSemaphore( full_buffer );
}
void main() { // The Consumer
    int use_buffer_queue = AttachSemaphore( UseBufferQueueID );
    int empty_buffer = AttachSemaphore( EmptyBufferID );
    int full_buffer = AttachSemaphore( FullBufferID );
    Buffer buffer;
    Signal( use_buffer_queue ); // Buffer queue is initially free

    // Initially there is space for MaxBuffers buffers
    for( int i = 0; i < MaxBuffers; ++i )
        Signal( empty_buffer );
    while( 1 ) {
        // Wait until a full buffer is available
        Wait( full_buffer );
        // Ensure mutual exclusion using the buffer queue
        Wait( use_buffer_queue );
        // Get a full buffer from the buffer queue
        buffer = buffer_queue.Remove();
        Signal( use_buffer_queue );
        // There is space for one more buffer in the buffer queue
        Signal( empty_buffer );
        ConsumeBuffer( buffer );
    }

    DetachSemaphore( use_buffer_queue );
    DetachSemaphore( empty_buffer );
    DetachSemaphore( full_buffer );
}
```

Both the producer and consumer have a local buffer for holding one bufferful of data. They share a buffer queue between them, and they use a semaphore to ensure mutual exclusion on the buffer queue. The full_buffer semaphore tells the consumer when to look in the buffer queue. The empty_buffer semaphore tells the producer when to try to place another buffer in the buffer queue.

So we can see that semaphores are used for synchronization in about the same ways as messages are. Messages have the advantage that they transfer information, but the disadvantage that they are more complicated and less efficient to implement.

Threads commonly use semaphores for synchronization.

8.16.9 SEMAPHORES AND MESSAGES

Using semaphores is logically the same as sending and receiving empty messages. In fact, we can convert a semaphore program to a message passing program as follows. For each semaphore, have a message queue. Translate `Signal` to `SendMessage` and `Wait` to `ReceiveMessage`.

But in message systems, we have overhead in allocating message buffers and keeping them on queues. Since in a semaphore all "messages" are empty, we can just keep a count of them. So semaphores can be implemented very efficiently and require no memory allocation.

Messages are more appropriate for IPC between processes that do not share memory. They are especially appropriate for IPC over a network. Semaphores are more appropriate for processes that share memory and communicate through the shared memory. This shared memory does not have to be main memory; it could be a shared file system.

*8.17   IMPLEMENTING SEMAPHORES

Semaphores provide a general mechanism for waiting in a shared memory environment, and so are ideal for use in the operating system itself whenever we need to wait for an event. In this section, we will look at an implementation of semaphores in our simple operating system.

8.17.1 SYSTEM CONSTANTS

We need a few additional constants relating to semaphores.

SYSTEM CONSTANTS

```
// system limits (we can change these)
const int NumberOfSemaphores = 50;

// system call numbers (arbitrary numbers, as long as they are all
// different)
const int AttachSemaphoreSystemCall = 8;
const int DetachSemaphoreSystemCall = 9;
const int SignalSemaphoreSystemCall = 10;
const int WaitSemaphoreSystemCall = 11;

// semaphore data structures
struct Semaphore {
    int allocated;
    int count;
    int use_count;
    int id;
```

```
    Queue<Pid> queue;
};
Semaphore sema[NumberOfSemaphores];
```

We need to initialize the semaphore array.

SYSTEM INITIALIZATION

```
int main( void ) {
    //...all what we had before, plus

    //initialize all semaphores to "not allocated"
    for( i = 0; i < NumberOfSemaphores; ++i )
        sema.allocated[i] = False;
}
```

In the system call interrupt handler, we need to define the new semaphore-related system calls. We also change the send and receive message system calls to use semaphores to wait for messages.

SYSTEM CALL INTERRUPT HANDLER

```
// New cases

case AttachSemaphoreSystemCall:
    int sema_id; asm { store r9,sema_id }
    pd[current_process].sa.reg[1] = AttachSemaphore( sema_id );
    break;

case DetachSemaphoreSystemCall:
    int sid; asm { store r9,sid }
    pd[current_process].sa.reg[1] = DetachSemaphore( sid );
    break;

case SignalSemaphoreSystemCall:
    int sid; asm { store r9,sid }
    pd[current_process].sa.reg[1] = SignalSemaphore( sid );
    break;

case WaitSemaphoreSystemCall:
    int sid; asm { store r9,sid }
    pd[current_process].sa.reg[1] = WaitSemaphore( sid );
    break;

case SendMessageSystemCall:
    // get the arguments
```

```
    int * user_msg; asm { store r9,user_msg}
    int to_q; asm { store r10,to_q }

    // check for an invalid queue identifier
    if( !message_queue_allocated[to_q] ) {
        pd[current_process].sa.reg[1] = -1;
        break;
    }
    int msg_no = GetMessageBuffer();
    // make sure we have not run out of message buffers
    if( msg_no == EndOfFreeList ) {
        pd[current_process].sa.reg[1] = -2;
        break;
    }
    // copy the message vector from the system caller's memory
    // into the system's message buffer
    CopyToSystemSpace( current_process, user_msg,
        message_buffer[msg_no], MessageSize );
    // put it on the queue
    message_queue[to_q].Insert( msg_no );
    // notify any waiters that it is there
    SignalSemaphore( message_semaphore[to_q] ); // NEW CODE
    pd[current_process].sa.reg[1] = 0;
    break;

case ReceiveMessageSystemCall:
    int * user_msg; asm { store r9,user_msg }
    int from_q; asm { store r10,from_q }

    // check for an invalid queue identifier
    if(!message_queue_allocated[from_q]) {
        pd[current_process].sa.reg[1] = -1;
        break;
    }
    WaitSemaphore( message_semaphore[from_q]); // NEW CODE
    int msg_no = message_queue[from_q].Remove();
    TransferMessage( msg_no, user_msg );
    pd[current_process].sa.reg[1] = 0;
    break;
//
// Semaphore implementation procedures
//
int AttachSemaphore( int sema_id ) {
    int i;
    int free_slot = -1;
    // Look for an allocated semaphore with this id.
    // Also look for a free slot in case we don't find one with this id.
    for( i = 0; i <NumberOfSemaphores; ++i ) {
        if ( sema[i].allocated ) {
            if( sema[i].id == sema_id)
                break;
        } else {
            free_slot = i;
        }
    }
    // Did we go through the entire array without finding
```

```
        //one with the correct id?
        if( i>= NumberOfSemaphores ) {
            // Did we find a free slot?
            if( free_slot  == -1 )
                //No free slots for new semaphores, return an error code.
                return -1;
            // Allocate a semaphore with this id
            i = free_slot;
            sema[i].allocated = True;
            sema[i].count = 0;
            sema [i].use_count = 0;
            sema[i].id = sema_id;
            sema[i].queue = new Queue<Pid>;
        }
        ++sema[i].use_count;
        return i;
}
int DetachSemaphore( int sid ) {
        if( !sema[sid].allocated ) {
            pd[current_process].sa.reg[1] = -1;
            break;
        }
        if( --sema[sid].use_count == 0 ) {
            sema[sid].allocated = False;
            delete sema[sid].queue;
        }
        return 0;
}
int SignalSemaphore( int sid ) {
        if( !sema[sid].allocated ) {
            pd[current_process].sa.reg[1] = -1;
            break;
        }
        if( sema[sid].queue->Empty() )
            ++sema[sid].count;
        else {
            int pid = sema[sid].queue->Remove();
            pd[pid].state = Ready;
        }
        return 0;
}
int WaitSemaphore( int sid ) {
        if( !sema[sid].allocated ) {
            pd[current_process].sa.reg[1] = -1;
            break;
        }
        if( sema[sid].count > 0 )
            --sema[sid].count;
        else {
            sema[sid].queue->Insert(current_process);
            pd[current_process].state = Blocked;
        }
        return 0;
}
```

We add four new cases for the four semaphore operations. Each one is implemented in a procedure. We have changed the send message system call to signal the message_semaphore for the message queue to which the message was sent. The receive message system call waits on the semaphore for the message queue from which it is trying to receive a message. It will get through the semaphore immediately if there are messages in the queue, and it will wait for a message if none are available. This shows how cleanly semaphores solve this kind of problem.

AttachSemaphore searches for a semaphore with the same id as was passed in. If none is found, then it finds a free semaphore data structure and allocates it.

DetachSemaphore decrements the semaphore use count, and deletes the semaphore when the count reaches zero. This happens when the number of detaches is equal to the number of attaches.

SignalSemaphore increments the semaphore count if there are no waiters, and releases the first waiter if there are waiters on the semaphore.

WaitSemaphore decrements the semaphore count if it is greater than zero. If the count is zero, then the wait semaphore system caller is blocked and placed in the semaphore waiter queue for later release by SignalSemaphore.

8.18   USING SEMAPHORES IN THE SIMPLE OPERATING SYSTEM

Now that we have semaphores, we can use them for synchronization. Since we are using kernel-mode processes, we could actually make system calls while executing in the operating system, but it is more efficient to call the operating system procedure that implements the system call directly.

First we have to create the semaphores we will need.

SYSTEM INITIALIZATION

```
processTableSemaphore = AttachSemaphore( ProcessTableID );
disk_queue = AttachSemaphore( DiskQueueID);
disk_free = AttachSemaphore( DiskFreeID );
```

We can use semaphores to wait for exclusive access to the process table. This replaces StartUsingProcessTable and FinishUsingProcessTable.

PROCESS DISPATCHING AND SCHEDULING

```
int SelectProcessToRun( void ) {
    static int next_proc = NumberOfProcesses;
    int i, return_value = -1;
```

```
    // Get exclusive access to the (shared) process table.
    WaitSemaphore(processTableSemaphore); // NEW CODE

    // ... use process table as before
    SignalSemaphore(processTableSemaphore); // NEW CODE
    return return_value;
}
```

We can also use semaphores with the disk queue. We signal the semaphore when a request is added to the disk queue, and we wait on the semaphore before we try to take something out of the disk queue.

Each process will have a private semaphore for waiting on. Disk requests will use the private semaphore to wait for the completion of the disk request. We no longer need to save the process ID; instead, we use the private semaphore to wait on and pass the semaphore identifier with the disk request. When the semaphore gets signaled, the kernel-mode process continues (after the semaphore wait).

DISK I/O

```
// The procedure is called from the system call interrupt handler.
void DiskIO (int command, int disk_block, char * buffer){
    // Create a new disk request and fill in the fields.
    DiskRequest * req = new DiskRequest;
    req->command = command;
    req->disk_block = disk_block;
    req->buffer = buffer;
    req->semaphore = pd[current_process].semaphore;
    //Then insert it on the queue.
    disk_queue.Insert ( req );
    // Wake up the disk scheduler if it is idle.
    SignalSemaphore ( disk_queue );
    WaitSemaphore ( pd[current_process].semaphore );
}
```

The ScheduleDisk procedure will use semaphores to wait for the disk to be free and for a request to be placed in the disk queue. It will record the semaphore to signal on disk transfer completion in the global variable disk_completion_semaphore.

DISK SCHEDULING

```
void RealScheduleDisk( void ){
    while( 1 ) { // NEW CODE
        WaitSemaphore( disk_free ); //NEW CODE
```

```
        WaitSemaphore( disk_queue );  // NEW CODE

        // Get the first disk request from the disk request queue.
        DiskRequest * req = disk_queue.RemoveFirst();

        // remember which process is waiting for the disk operation
        disk_completion_semaphore = req->semaphore;

        // issue the read or write, with disk interrupt enabled
        if( req->command == DiskReadSystemCall )
            IssueDiskRead( req->disk_block, req->buffer, 1 );
        else
            IssueDiskWrite( req->disk_block, req->buffer, 1 );
    }
}
```

The disk interrupt handler will signal two semaphores. One semaphore signal is to release the kernel-mode process that is waiting for the transfer to complete. The second semaphore signal is to notify the disk driver that the disk is now free. The semaphore is being used instead of checking with the hardware disk controller (via DiskBusy).

DISK INTERRUPT HANDLER

```
void DiskInterruptHandler( void ){

    if( current_process > 0 ) { // was there a running process?
        // Save the processor state of the system caller.
        // ... as before
    }

    // Notify the waiting process that the disk transfer is complete
    SignalSemaphore( disk_completion_semaphore );

    // Notify any waiters that the disk is free
    SignalSemaphore( disk_free );

    // now run a process
    Dispatcher();
}
```

8.19   PROGRAMMING-LANGUAGE-BASED SYNCHRONIZATION PRIMITIVES

Both message passing and semaphores are operating-system-based synchronization primitives. By this we mean that they are implemented with system calls and do not have any effect on the language being used. There is another class of synchronization primitives that are implemented as primitives in the programming language. They are not accessed directly with system calls, but with basic language constructs.

We will look at two examples of language-based synchronization primitives: monitors, and the synchronization primitives in Ada 95.

8.19.1 MONITORS

A monitor is a construct that could be added to any programming language, but that can most naturally be added to languages that already have a concept of a module or an abstract data type.

A *monitor* is a module with the following components:

- *variables*—The monitor can contain any kind of data variables.

- *condition variables*—The monitor can also contain a special kind of variable, called a condition variable, which is used for signaling inside the monitor.

- *procedures*—The monitor can contain procedures which can be called from outside the monitor.

The variables in the monitor are protected data that can only be used by procedures inside the monitor. This means a monitor can be used to hide data and control access to it, just like any abstract data type or module mechanism. The condition variables are used for signaling. We will discuss them later.

The procedures can be called from outside the monitor, but the monitor ensures that only one procedure at a time can be called. If Process A calls a procedure in a monitor, it sets a lock on the monitor that will prevent any other process from entering the monitor. If another Process B calls the same or another procedure in the same monitor, then Process B must wait until Process A returns from the procedure, leaves the monitor, and releases the lock on the monitor. The call by Process B is held up, and Process B is blocked until the monitor lock is free. In other words, the procedures in a monitor are all mutually exclusive. Thus the monitor provides mutual exclusion.

Let's look at a simple example. A basic mutual exclusion problem is the atomic counter update problem. Several processes each are incrementing a single counter, and they must do it atomically to avoid losing a count. This is easy to do with a monitor.

COUNTER MONITOR

```
monitor Counter {
private:
    int count = 0;
public:
    void Increment( void ) {
        count = count + 1;
    }
    int GetCount( void ) {
        return count;
```

```
        }
    }

int main() {// one process
    while( 1 ) {
        // ... Do things other than incrementing the counter
        Counter.Increment();
        // ... continue on
        int n = Counter.GetCount();
    }
}

int main() { // another process
    while( 1 ) {
        // ... Do things other than incrementing the counter
        Counter.Increment();
        // ... continue on
    }
}
```

If two processes call **Increment** at the same time, one will get to go first and the other will wait.

Mutual exclusion is built into the definition of the monitor. Signaling is provided by a facility called condition variables. A *condition variable* is a special kind of variable than can be defined only inside a monitor. There are two operations on a condition variable: **wait** and **signal**. If a process calls **wait** on a condition variable, it will be blocked until some other process calls **signal** on the same condition variable. If a process calls **signal** on a condition variable, it will unblock *all* the other processes that are waiting on the same condition variable.

condition variable

Condition variables are not the same as semaphores. In particular, they have no memory. If **signal** is called on a condition variable 10 times and then a process calls **wait** on the variable, the process will still be blocked. A **wait** waits for the *next* call to **signal**. Past calls to **signal** are not considered.

Another feature of **wait** is that a process that calls **wait** on a condition variable gives up the lock on the monitor, and so other processes can now call the procedures in the monitor. If any other process is blocked on a monitor call, then it is allowed to enter the monitor.

Let's see how condition variable can be used for signaling.

SIGNALING MONITOR

```
monitor Signal {

private:
    int IsSignaled = 0;
    condition SendSignal;
```

```
public:
    void SendSignal( void ) {
        IsSignaled = 1;      != free
        signal( SendSignal );
    }

    void WaitForSignal( void ) {
        If( !IsSignaled )  = 1 then wait
            Wait( SendSignal );
    }
}

int main() { //the Signal Sender
    // ... Do things up to the signal point
    Signal.SendSignal();
    // ... continue on
}

int main() { // the Signal Receiver
    // ... Do things up to the signal point
    Signal.WaitForSignal();
    // ... continue on when the signal is received
}
```

Note that the **signal** operation is not sufficient to implement general signaling because it has no memory. We need a regular variable (not a condition variable) to remember that the signal has been sent. The signal receiver uses condition variables to wait for the signal if it has not yet arrived when **WaitForSignal** is called.

Let's look at a more complex example that uses condition variables. We will use the producer-consumer problem as an example. Here is the monitor for the producer-consumer problem.

PRODUCER-CONSUMER MONITOR

```
monitor BoundedBufferType {

private:
    BufferItem * buffer;
    int NumberOfBuffers;
    int next_in, next_out;
    int current_size;
    condition NotEmpty, NotFull;

public:
    BoundedBufferType( int size ){
        buffers = new BufferItem[size];
        NumberOfBuffers = size;
        next_in = 0; next_out = 0; current_size = 0;
    }
```

```
        void Put( BufferItem item ) {
            if( current_size == NumberofBuffers )
                wait( NotFull );
            buffer[next_in] = item;
            next_in = (next_in+1) % NumberOfBuffers;
            if( ++current_size == 1 )
                signal( NotEmpty );
        }

        BufferItem Get( void ) {
            if( current_size == 0 )
                wait( NotEmpty );
            BufferItem item = buffer[next_out];
            next_out = (next_out+1) % NumberOfBuffers;
            if( --current_size == NumberofBuffers-1 )
                signal( NotFull );
            return item;
        }
}

BoundedBufferType BoundedBuffer;

int main() {// the Producer
    while( 1 ) {
        BufferItem item = ProduceItem();
        BoundedBuffer.Put( item );
    }
}

int main() {// the Consumer
    while( 1 ) {
        BufferItem item = BoundedBuffer.Get();
        ConsumeItem( item );
    }
}
```

Monitors are not a feature of C++, but we have speculated on how they would be added to the language. The monitor definition would be a variant of a class definition. The private variables are for the private use of the monitor procedures. A constructor for the monitor initializes the data. In this case, it allocates the buffer pool and initializes several variables. The two public procedures of the Bounded-BufferType monitor class are BufferPut and BufferGet. We have assumed a type called BufferItem, which is the type of object the buffers hold.

The BufferPut procedure begins by testing if all the buffer slots are full. If so, then it waits on the condition variable NotFull. Then it moves the item into the next free buffer. The buffer pool is used circularly, so we increment the buffer pointers using modular arithmetic. If this item was the first item placed in an empty buffer, we signal the condition variable NotEmpty, just in case some other process is waiting for a buffer. If no process is waiting, then the signal has no effect.

The BufferGet procedure begins by testing if all the buffer slots are empty. If so, then it must wait for a buffer to be inserted. It does this by calling **wait** on the condition variable NotEmpty. We saw how BufferPut will signal this condition when the buffer becomes nonempty. Then it removes the next item from the buffer. If the buffers were previously all full, then we signal NotFull. This will release any process that called BufferPut and found all the buffers full. Finally, we return the item we removed from the buffer.

The definition of BoundedBufferType was like a class definition, that is, it only describes monitors of this type but does not create one. We make a definition to create a monitor of this type.

The producer and consumer are processes that run in parallel. The producer calls BufferPut and the consumer calls BufferGet.

As a final example, we will show how to implement a semaphore using a monitor.

COUNTING SEMAPHORE MONITOR

```
monitor Semaphore {

private:
    int count = 0;
    condition NotBusy;

public:
    void Signal( void ) {
        if( ++count > 0 )
            signal( NotBusy );
    }

    void Wait( void ) {
        while( count <= 0 )
            wait( NotBusy );
        --count;
    }
}

int main() { //one process
        while( 1 ) {
        // do other stuff
        // enter critical section
        Semaphore.Wait();
            // do critical section
        Semaphore.Signal();
    }
}

int main() { // another process
    while( 1 ) {
        // do other stuff
        // enter critical section
```

```
            Semaphore.Wait();
                // do critical section
            Semaphore.Signal();
        }
    }
}
```

When the semaphore count goes above 0, the Signal procedure will signal Not-Busy. This will unblock all the processes waiting in NotBusy. Because of this, we need the while loop in Wait. After the Wait call is unblocked by a signal to Not-Busy, the process must check to make sure that Count is still greater than 0 before it tries to decrement it. If two or more processes are releases, the first one allowed to enter the monitor will find Count equal to 1 and decrement it to 0. The other processes that enter after that process will find Count equal to zero again, and will wait on NotBusy again (because of the while loop).

Monitors can be used to implement all of the IPC patterns in Chapter 7.

8.19.2   Synchronization Primitives in Ada 95

Ada 95 has two mechanisms for synchronization: rendezvous and protected variables.

Rendezvous   Ada 95 also has a powerful mechanism called a rendezvous that combines synchronization, mutual exclusion, and interprocess communication.

Ada uses the term *task* for what we have been calling a thread. That is, all tasks share the same address space. A rendezvous is similar to a remote procedure call. One task calls an entry in another task, and when the call is accepted, the two tasks *rendezvous*. During the rendezvous, the calling task is blocked.

rendezvous

First, let's see how a rendezvous can be used to implement simple mutual exclusion. We will use the example of a counter that will be incremented by two or more processes.

MUTUAL EXCLUSION WITH RENDEZVOUS IN ADA 95

```
-- declare the interface to the task
task Counter is
    entry GetCount( count : out integer );
    entry Increment;
private
    count : integer;
end Counter;

-- define the implementation of the protected variable
task body Counter is
    loop
        select
            accept GetCount( count_out : out integer ) do
```

```
                count_out := count;
            end;
        or
            accept Increment do
                count := count + 1;
            end;
        end select;
    end loop;
end Counter;

-- using the counter
task body OneProcess is begin
    loop
        -- do other things than incrementing the counter
        Counter.Increment;
        -- do other things
        Counter.GetCount( n );
    end loop;
end OneProcess;
task body AnotherProcess is begin
    loop
        -- do other things than incrementing the counter
        Counter.Increment;
        -- do other things
    end loop;
end AnotherProcess;
```

We define a separate task to manage the counter. The task defines two entries: GetCount and Increment. The only job of the Counter task is to make rendezvous with other tasks, so its code is an infinite loop. The body of the loop is a select/accept statement, which indicates that it will accept a rendezvous with either type of call. It accepts one rendezvous per loop iteration. GetCount returns the current count, and Increment increases the count by one. The Counter task can only accept one rendezvous at a time, so only one call to Increment at a time is possible. This provides the necessary mutual exclusion.

The mutual exclusion task would accept Increment calls repeatedly (so it used a loop) and would accept GetCounter calls at any time (so it used a select). Signaling is simpler, since we only have to accept two rendezvous(no loop) and in a specific order (no select). Here is how we would implement signaling with a rendezvous.

SIGNALING WITH RENDEZVOUS IN ADA 95

```
task Signal is
    entry SendSignal;
    entry WaitForSignal;
end Counter;

task body Signal is
```

```
        accept SendSignal do
            null;
        end;
        accept WaitForSignal do
            null;
        end;
end Signal;

-- using the signal
task body SignalSender is begin
    -- get to point where event occurs
    Signal.SendSignal;
    -- go on to other things
end SignalSender;
task body SignalReceiver is begin
    --- get to the point where you need to wait for the event
    Signal.WaitForSignal;
    -- respond to event
end SignalReceiver;
```

Again, we must use a task to represent the signal. This task first accepts SendSignal, and then WaitForSignal. If WaitForSignal is called first, the calling task will be blocked until the Signal task gets to the accept WaitForSignal.

In order to implement a bounded buffer, we have to use **guarded entries**, that is, entries that will only be accepted if a specified condition is true.

PRODUCER-CONSUMER IN ADA

```
-- declare the interface to the buffer
task BoundedBuffer is
    entry Put( x : in Item );
    entry Get( x : out Item );
end BoundedBuffer;

-- define the implementation of the buffer
task body BoundedBuffer is
    NumberOfBuffers : constant integer := 20;
    buffers : array(1 .. NumberOfBuffers) of Item;
    current_size : integer range 0 .. NumberOfBuffers := 0;
    next_in, next_out : integer range 1 .. NumberOfBuffers := 1;
begin
    loop
        select
            when current_size < NumberOfBuffers =>
                accept Put( x : in item ) do
                    buffers( next_in ) := x;
                end;
                next_in := (next_in mod NumberOfBuffers) + 1;
                current_size := current_size + 1;
```

```
         or when current_size > 0 =>
             accept Get( x : out Item do
                 x := buffers(next_out);
             end;
             next_out := (next_out mod NumberOfBuffers) + 1;
             current_size := current_size - 1;
         or
             terminate;
      end select;
   end loop;
end BoundedBuffer;

-- using the buffer: producer and consumer
task body Producer is begin
   loop
      item := ProduceItem;
      BounderBuffer.Put( item );
   end loop;
end Producer;
task body Consumer is begin
   loop
      BounderBuffer.Get( item );
      ConsumeItem( item );
   end loop;
end Consumer;
```

As a final rendezvous example, we will show how to implement a counting semaphore with Ada tasks and rendezvous.

COUNTING SEMAPHORE WITH RENDEZVOUS IN ADA 95

```
-- declare the interface to the semaphore
task type CountingSemaphore( StartCount : Integer := 1 ) is
   entry Wait;
   entry Signal;
   entry Count( count_out : out integer );
private
   CurrentCount : Integer := StartCount;
end CountingSemaphore;

-- define the implementation of the semaphore
task body CountingSemaphore is begin
   loop
      select
         when CurrentCount > 0 =>
            accept Wait do
               CurrentCount := CurrentCount - 1;
            end;
      or
         accept Signal do
```

```
                CurrentCount := CurrentCount + 1;
            end;
        or
            accept Count( count_out : out integer ) do
                count_out := CurrentCount;
            end;
        end select;
    end loop;
end CountingSemaphore;
```

The semaphore is implemented with a task that accepts rendezvous. It will accept **Signal** and **Count** whenever it is at the **select**, but it will only accept a **Wait** if the semaphore count is positive.

These examples do not really show rendezvous in its best light. They are too simple for the powerful rendezvous mechanism. In each case, we had to introduce a new task just to handle some simple synchronization problem like signaling or a semaphore. As we suggested, a rendezvous is like a remote procedure call. A rendezvous works best when it is embedded in a task that would occur naturally in the program anyway. A rendezvous allows two tasks to synchronize and transfer information in both directions. For these simple examples, the simpler Ada mechanism, the protected variable, is more appropriate.

protected variable   **Protected Variables**   Ada 95 is the new version of the Ada 83 language. The rendezvous is powerful, but also expensive to implement. The designers of Ada 95 felt Ada needed a second synchronization mechanism which was simpler and cheaper to implement, so they added protected variables. Protected variables are similar to monitors. A rendezvous can only be made with another task, so any protected object must be a task, which is an active entity with fairly high implementation overhead. A protected variable is just a special kind of data structure, and it has lower implementation overhead.

Lets look at the implementation of a counter with atomic updates using protected variables. Here is the Ada 95 code.

MUTUAL EXCLUSION WITH PROTECTED VARIABLES IN ADA 95

```
-- declare the interface to the protected variable
protected Counter is
    function GetCount return integer;
    procedure Increment;
private
    count :integer;
end Counter;

-- define the implementation of the protected variable
protected body Counter is
    function GetCount return integer is begin
        return count
```

```
        end GetCount;
        procedure Increment is begin
            count := count + 1;
        end Increment;
end Counter;

-- using the counter
task body OneProcess is begin
    loop
        -- do other things than incrementing the counter
        Counter.Increment;
        -- do other things
        n := Counter.GetCount;
    end loop;
end OneProcess;
task body AnotherProcess is begin
    loop
        -- do other things than incrementing the counter
        Counter.Increment;
        -- do other things
    end loop;
end AnotherProcess;
```

Ada divides up an object declaration and its implementation (called the *body* in Ada). The declaration of Counter declares the procedures and the data item count. The body defines the procedures. The procedures of a protected variable are like those of a monitor: only one can be executing at the same time. So protected variable provides mutual exclusion.

Our second example will be to implement signaling with protected variables.

SIGNALING WITH PROTECTED VARIABLES IN ADA 95

```
protected Signal is
    procedure SendSignal;
    entry WaitForSignal;
private
    IsSignaled : boolean := False;
end Signal;
protected body Signal is
    procedure SendSignal is begin
        IsSignaled := True;
    end SendSignal;
    entry WaitForSignal when IsSignaled is begin
        null;
    end WaitForSignal;
end Signal;

-- using the signal
task body SignalSender is begin
    -- get to point where event occurs
```

```
    Signal.SendSignal;
    -- go on to other things
end SignalSender;
task body SignalReceiver is begin
    --- get to the point where you need to wait for the event
    Signal.WaitForSignal;
    -- respond to event
end SignalReceiver;
```

The WaitForSignal is called an *entry*. An entry is similar to a procedure, but it can have a *guard* condition associated with it. When a process calls the entry, the guard is evaluated. If the guard is true, then the call is made. If the guard is false, then the process is blocked and will wait for the guard to become true before the call can begin. This is exactly what we need for the signal. The guard when IsSignaled will delay the WaitForSignal call until the signal arrives.

The next section of code shows the producer-consumer problem implemented with protected variables.

PRODUCER-CONSUMER WITH PROTECTED VARIABLES IN ADA 95

```
-- declare the interface to the buffer
protected type BoundedBuffer is
    entry Put( x : in Item );
    entry Get( x : out Item );
private
    buffers : ItemArray(1..NumberOfBuffers);
    next_in, next_out : integer range 1..NumberOfBuffers := 1;
    current_size : integer range 0..NumberOfBuffers := 0;
end BoundedBuffer;

-- define the implementation of the buffer
protected body BoundedBuffer is
    entry Put( x : in Item ) when current_size < NumberOfBuffers is begin
        buffers(next_in) := x;
        next_in := (next_in mod NumberOfBuffers) + 1;
        current_size := current_size + 1;
    end Put;
    entry Get( x : out Item ) when current_size > 0 is begin
        x := buffers(next_out);
        next_out := (next_out mod NumberOfBuffers) + 1;
        current_size := current_size − 1;
    end Get;
end BoundedBuffer;

-- using the buffer: producer and consumer
task body Producer is begin
    loop
        item := ProduceItem;
        BounderBuffer.Put( item );
    end loop;
```

```
end Producer;
task body Consumer is begin
    loop
        BounderBuffer.Get( item );
        ConsumeItem( item );
    end loop;
end Consumer;
```

Both Get and Put have guards, so must be entries. Put is only allowed when the buffer is not full, and Get is only allowed when the buffer is not empty.

As a final example, we will show how to implement a counting semaphore with a protected variable.

COUNTING SEMAPHORE WITH PROTECTED VARIABLES IN ADA 95

```
-- declare the interface to the semaphore
protected type CountingSemaphore( StartCount : Integer := 1 ) is
    entry Wait;
    procedure Signal;
    function Count return Integer;
private
    CurrentCount : Integer := StartCount;
end CountingSemaphore;

-- define the implementation of the semaphore
protected body CountingSemaphore is
    entry Wait when CurrentCount > 0 is begin
        CurrentCount := CurrentCount - 1;
    end Wait;
    procedure Signal is begin
        CurrentCount := CurrentCount + 1;
    end Signal;
    function Count return Integer is begin
        return CurrentCount;
    end Count;
end CountingSemaphore;
```

8.20   MESSAGE-PASSING DESIGN ISSUES

8.20.1   COPYING MESSAGES

In our simple operating system, we buffered messages for the processes, that is, when a message was sent, it was copied into a message buffer in the operating system. When the message was received, it was copied from the system buffer into the user's address space. (See Figure 8.15).

This was done even if the receiver was already waiting for the message when it was sent. If the message is sent before the receiver is ready for it, then either the operating system must buffer the message, or the sender must wait for the receiver to become ready to receive the message. The message was always copied twice.

We can improve on this situation if we require the sender to wait for the receiver. Then the message can be copied just once, directly from the sender's buffer into the receiver's buffer. This halves the copying time, which tends to be a large portion of the message-passing overhead.

In a network, the situation can be even worse since there are two operating systems to deal with. Figure 8.16 shows the situation.

The message is copied four times. We can do several things to reduce this cost. The first thing is to delay the send until the message can be put directly onto the network from the sender's buffer. This saves the first copy, and operating system A does not have to worry about message buffers. This delay is fairly small un-

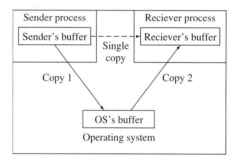

Figure 8.15   Copying messages

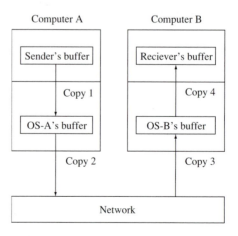

Figure 8.16   Copying messages over a network

less the network is very busy, and, in that case, any sort of message passing will be slow.

The second way we can try to avoid copies is to not send the message unless the receiving process is ready to receive it. This avoids one copy and message buffering at the receiving end.

If we combine both of these optimizations, we have only the necessary copy through the network hardware. But a sender will be delayed until the receiver is ready and the network is available for transmission of the message.

8.20.2 LONGER MESSAGES

The messages that we have defined are very small; only eight words of data can be transferred in a message. Clearly, a longer message size is desirable, say 1024 to 8192 bytes of data per message.

Making the messages longer means that processes will require fewer messages to send large quantities of data to one another, but also it means that more space will be taken up with message buffers and time with copying of messages. The longer the messages are, the more incentive there is to reduce copying and buffering.

It is also possible to have variable-sized messages where the sender indicates how long the message is. This leads to efficiency in one area: messages will always be exactly as long as they need to be. But variable-sized messages mean extra work in a number of areas. All message buffers will now have to be variable in size, and so will have to be allocated each time they are used. A receiver might not provide a buffer that is large enough, so the receive system call must have a way of indicating that the message was truncated and determining how long the message actually is so the receiver can provide a large enough buffer.

When we study paging systems in Chapter 11, we will see ways to transfer messages without memory-to-memory copying.

8.21 IPC IN MACH

The Mach operating system has an interesting IPC structure that has been influential in operating system design since it was introduced. In this section, we will discuss the concepts in Mach IPC.

8.21.1 TASKS AND THREADS

A Mach *task* is what we have called a process. It is the object that holds resources, principally an address space. A Mach *thread* is just like the threads we have discussed. A process contains one or more threads, all sharing the same address space.

task

task

8.21.2   PORTS AND MESSAGES

port

A Mach *port* is a variation of what we have called a message queue. Only one task can receive messages from a port, but any number of tasks can send messages to a port. A task can create ports and pass them to other tasks, allowing those tasks to send messages to the port. A port can be passed by inheritance to a child, or it can be sent in a message (sent through another port).

A *message* is sent to a port and will be received by the task that is receiving from that port. The message can contain three types of data:

- *Data*—Any number of bytes can be sent in the message. A copy of this data is transferred from the sender to the receiver.
- *Out-of-line data*—Some part of the address space of the sender can be sent to the receiver. The data is transferred using an optimization called copy-on-write (see Section 12.13.3) that allows the transfer of large amounts of data efficiently (with no copies).
- *Ports*—Ports can be passed from one task to another in a message.

8.21.3   OBJECTS

Mach is an object-oriented operating system. The Mach kernel implements a number of objects, and each object has one or more methods that can be called to perform operations on the object. A Mach port represents an object. You perform operations on the object by sending messages to the port that represents the object. These messages are sent in the context of a remote procedure call, and so it looks to the task as if it is calling methods of the object. If you have a port, that means you have the ability to call any method of the object.

8.22   IPC AND SYNCHRONIZATION EXAMPLES

8.22.1   SIGNALS

signal

It is useful for one process to be able to notify another process that an event has occurred. In UNIX, this is done with a signal. A *signal* is an event notification that is sent to a process by another process.

Signals in UNIX are used for many different purposes. UNIX defines 30 or so specific events that can be signaled. Some signals are sent to a process when they get an interrupt: illegal instruction, addressing error, arithmetic error. Some signals are external events: interrupt (usually the user typed control-C on the keyboard), kill (one process tries to destroy another process), alarm (a timer set by the process has expired), child (status of child process has changed), socket (an urgent condition on a socket), IO (I/O possible on an open file), window (window size changed). Some signals are for other errors: syscall (bad argument to a system call). Two are general signals that can mean anything: user1 and user2.

The thing all signals have in common is that there is some event that the process needs to know about. A signal is really a software version of a hardware interrupt. When the event occurs, the current activity of the process is stopped and control is passed to a signal handler. This is basically like a procedure call that is forced on the process between any two machine instructions.

A process can tell the system which procedure to call when a signal arrives. This procedure is called the signal handler.

8.22.2   SVR4 UNIX

Like all UNIX systems, SVR4 implements signals to allow one process to signal an asynchronous event to another process, and pipes to allow processes to send data to each other. SVR4 also implements semaphores with the usual operations. One interesting feature of SVR4 semaphores is that they allow arrays of semaphores and indivisible operations on arrays of semaphores. This allows you to wait on several semaphores at the same time.

SVR4 also implements message queues and message sending. Messages can be of any length.

SRV4 also implements shared memory. This allows two processes to set up part of their address space as shared between the two processes. This is a fast way to transfer large quantities of information. Shared memory is discussed at some length in Section 12.12.

8.22.3   WINDOWS NT

Windows NT has a pair of facilities, called *alerts* and *asynchronous procedure calls,* which work together to achieve an effect similar to signals.

The main IPC method in Windows NT is message passing. The message-passing facility is structured as a mechanism, based on RPC, called LPC (local procedure call). LPC is optimized for communication between processes on a single machine. Windows NT has *port* objects (like Mach), which are message queues. Messages up to 256 bytes can be sent over a port. To pass a data area larger than 256 bytes, you can pass a section of memory to the receiving process through a port. The memory is passed efficiently using memory mapping (see Chapter 11).

Windows NT also supports regular remote procedure calls and named pipes for communication over networks. It uses busy-wait spin locks for multiprocessor synchronization.

Windows NT has a range of synchronization primitives. A thread can wait on an I/O object for an I/O completion. Or it can wait on another thread or process until the thread or process exits. In addition, they have mutexes (binary semaphores), general semaphores, and general events (that are signaled by another thread).

8.22.4   OS/2

OS/2 has the usual set of synchronization and IPC facilities. It has shared memory, binary semaphores, general semaphores, message queues, signals, and pipes.

8.22.5   SOLARIS

Solaris has several primitives for thread synchronization. It has binary semaphores (which they call *mutexes*) and general semaphores. Both of these have an operation which will lock a mutex or semaphore if it is available, but return with an error code if it is already locked. This allows a thread to check a mutex or semaphore without the chance of getting blocked. There is a special reader/writer lock to solve the readers/writers problem. It has a read lock operation and a write lock operation. There are also nonblocking versions of these locks. Finally, Solaris has condition variables that can be used in conjunction with mutexes to wait for arbitrary conditions.

8.23   SUMMARY

Most everyday scheduling is nonpreemptive. The common methods are first-come, first-served, shortest-job-first, priority, and deadline scheduling. Round-robin scheduling is a preemptive scheduling method that is used occasionally in everyday life, and also used extensively in processor scheduling in computers.

Processor scheduling is almost always preemptive. The main processor scheduling methods are round-robin, multiple queues, deadline, and priority. Scheduling is a good example of a place where it is useful to separate mechanism from policy. Most real operating systems use a priority scheduling system in which most processes move up and down in priority.

Deadlock occurs in a cycle of processes when each holds a resource that another process in the cycle needs and waits for a resource that another process in the cycle holds. You can deal with deadlock in three ways. In deadlock prevention, the operating system policies make deadlock impossible. In deadlock avoidance, the operating system uses an avoidance algorithm each time a resource is allocated to make sure deadlock never occurs. In deadlock recovery, the operating system detects when a deadlock has occurred and recovers from it by preempting resources from a process. Two-phase locking is a method used in databases to prevent deadlock. Starvation occurs when a process is prevented from getting the resources it needs for a long time.

There are several variations of message passing. *Ports* are message queues with only one receiver. It is also possible to associate a message queue directly with a process and address messages by process identifier. A nonblocking message receive allows you to check for messages without the possibility of blocking your process. A blocking send eliminates the need for message buffering by waiting until a receiver is ready to receive the message. A remote procedure call (RPC) is a way to put a procedure call interface on a message-passing system. The advantage is that programmers are familiar with using procedure calls.

Synchronization is the means by which one process informs another process that an event has occurred. The two basic synchronization operations are signaling and mutual exclusion.

Semaphores provide a means of process synchronization without any data transfer. Semaphores are simpler and more efficient than messages, and are most useful for threads which can use shared memory for data communication. Semaphores can be used for all the IPC patterns in Chapter 7.

Semaphores can be easily added to our simple operating system, and they can be used to implement waiting in the simple operating system.

A monitor is another example of a synchronization primitive. It is a programming language construct that can solve the same synchronization problems as a semaphore (or messages), but with more structure.

The Ada 95 language provides two synchronization primitives: a rendezvous that is similar to an RPC, and a protected variable that is similar to a monitor.

It is possible to reduce the amount of data copying by changing to a blocking send.

8.23.1   TERMINOLOGY

After reading this chapter, you should be familiar with the following terms:

- binary semaphore
- blocking send
- condition variable
- counting semaphore
- deadline scheduling
- deadlock
- deadlock prevention
- first-come, first-served scheduling (FCFS)
- first-in, first-out scheduling (FIFO)
- highest-response-ratio-next scheduling (HRN)
- monitor
- multiple-queue scheduling
- mutex
- nonblocking receive
- port
- priority scheduling

- processor sharing

- protected variable

- quantum

- remote procedure call (RPC)

- rendezvous

- round-robin scheduling (RR)

- semaphore

- shortest-job-first scheduling (SJF)

- signal

- starvation

- synchronization

- task

- time slice

- two-phase locking

- two-queue scheduling

8.23.2 REVIEW QUESTIONS

The following questions are answered in the text of this chapter:

1. Why is first-come, first-served scheduling fair?

2. What is the main advantage of shortest-job-first scheduling?

3. What is the advantage of highest-response-ratio-next scheduling over shortest-job-first scheduling?

4. What is a response ratio?

5. Why is preemptive scheduling better?

6. What happens to processes that leave the processor scheduling system? When, if ever, do they come back?

7. What is a quantum in round-robin scheduling?

8. Explain why round-robin is also called time slicing.

9. Why is the context switch time important in choosing a time quantum in round-robin scheduling?

10. How does round-robin do if the system is heavily loaded? What would do better?

11. What is the advantage of a multiple queue scheduling system?

12. Describe a typical scheduling system in a real operating system.

13. What is the difference between a port and a message queue?

14. When are nonblocking receives useful?

15. What is the advantage of a blocking send?

16. What are the advantages of remote procedure calls over regular message passing?

17. Give an analogy between messages and semaphores.

18. Why are semaphores more efficient than message passing?

19. Why is it a good idea to reduce message copying?

8.23.3   FURTHER READING

Ben-Ari (1982) is a complete and entertaining treatment of the issues of concurrency. A later book (Ben-Ari 1990) expands the treatment to distributed systems. Andrews and Schneider (1983) survey many issues in concurrent processes.

Coffman and Kleinrock (1968), Lampson (1968) and Bunt (1976) discuss scheduling techniques. Ruschitzka and Fabry (1977) discuss a unified view of scheduling.

Dijkstra (1968) was the first to discuss the deadlock problem. Deadlock avoidance in OS/360 using resource ordering is discussed by Havender (1968). Deadlocks were surveyed by Coffman et al. (1971), Isloor and Marsland (1980), and Holt (1972). Holt also discussed starvation. Howard (1973) presents a mixed solution to the deadlock problem. The operating systems text by Bic and Shaw (1988) has a good treatment of deadlock.

Semaphores were first described by Dijkstra (1968, 1971). Hoare (1974) discusses monitors.

For discussions of RPCs, see Birrell and Nelson (1984) and Shrivastava and Panzieri (1982).

8.24   PROBLEMS

1. Explain how a preemptive priority scheduling system would work.

2. Of the following scheduling methods, which only make sense as preemptive scheduling policies, which only make sense as nonpreemptive scheduling policies, and which could be either?

    a. First-come, first-served.

    b. Round-robin.

    c. Priority.

    d. Multiple queues.

    e. Shortest job first.

3. If you want to separate scheduling policy and mechanism, you have to parameterize the scheduling algorithm to set the policy. What are the parameters (if any) of each of the following scheduling algorithms?

a. First-come, first-served.

b. Round-robin.

c. Priority.

d. Multiple queues.

e. Shortest job first.

4. Suppose we run each of the following scheduling algorithms in a system that is very heavily overloaded. Describe how each of these algorithms acts in the face of overloading. Discuss how this overloading affects the average waiting time of short jobs, medium jobs, and long jobs (if they are affected differently). That is, discuss how the average waiting time changes (for short, medium, and long jobs) when going from a lightly loaded system to a heavily loaded system. Be sure to discuss the overhead of extra context switches caused by the scheduling algorithm (if any).

a. First-come, first-served.

b. Highest response ratio next.

c. Round-robin.

d. Multiple queues.

e. Priority.

f. Shortest job first.

5. In preemptive scheduling the operating system may stop a process at an arbitrary point in its code and run another process in its place. This will occur when the new process has a higher priority than the one that was running.

A nonpreemptive scheduler will only switch processes when the running process voluntarily gives up control to the operating system. It does this when it needs some system service such as I/O where it cannot use the CPU any more until the I/O is completed.

Give a noncomputer example of preemptive and nonpreemptive scheduling. Consider any system where people (or things) use some kind of resources and compete for them.

6. Repeat the calculations in Section 8.4, but with the following jobs:

Job	Time	Arrival	Priority
1	8	0	3
2	4	0	2
3	6	0	1
4	1	0	4

7. Consider two jobs, A and B, in a deadline scheduling system. The deadline for A is before the deadline for B. Explain why we should run A before B, that is, show that if running A, then B, fails to meet some deadline, then running B before A will also fail to meet some deadline.

8. Consider a variant of round-robin called *selfish round-robin*. In selfish round-robin, there is a maximum number of processes that can be in the round-robin queue. After that maximum is reached, newly entering processes are placed in a holding queue. Processes in the holding queue do not get any time slices. When a process in the round-robin queue completes and leaves the system, the oldest process in the holding queue is allowed to enter the round-robin queue.

   How do you think selfish round-robin will do in a heavily loaded situation? Compare it to the two-queue system and ordinary round-robin.

   Relate selfish round-robin to the two-queue scheduling system. How are they the same and how are they different?

9. Consider a variation of round-robin that we will call *priority round-robin*. In priority round-robin, each process has a priority in the range of 1 to 10 (higher numbers are better). When a process is given a time slice, the length of the quantum is some basic constant (say 50 ms) times the priority of the job. Compare this system with an ordinary priority system, in which the highest-priority job is always executing.

10. Consider a variation of round-robin we will call *progressive round-robin*. In progressive round-robin, each process has its own quantum. This starts out at 50 ms, and increases by 50 ms each time it goes through the round-robin queue. So long jobs keep getting longer and longer time slices. Give the advantages and disadvantages of this variant over ordinary round-robin.

11. In the two-queue system, we did not say what happens when a job from the slow queue is running and a new job arrives at the short queue. We could either wait until the time slice is finished, or we could preempt the job from the slow queue and place it back at the front of the slow queue (with a reduced time slice, depending on how much it has used so far). Which alternative do you think would be better, and why?

12. Show a deadlock using semaphores. Give the program for each process.

13. We mentioned in the chapter that one method of preventing a circular wait is to number each resource and require processes to acquire resources in ascending numerical order. Explain why this method prevents circular waits.

14. Two-phase locking can lead to starvation. Explain how this can happen. Explain why deadlock is not possible.

15. Some systems have a message receive system call that allows you to specify the process you want to receive a message from. Such system calls usually have a special process identifier that means you want to receive from any process. What is the advantage of this type of message receive? Are there any disadvantages to this form of the receive system call?

16. We have talked about message systems with blocking and nonblocking receives and blocking and nonblocking sends. Consider three sets of message system calls:

    a. **MessageSet1**—nonblocking sends and blocking receives.

    b. **MessageSet2**—nonblocking sends and nonblocking receives.

    c. **MessageSet3**—blocking sends and blocking receives.

Suppose we wanted to write libraries that simulated one set of system calls with another set. Consider each of the six possible simulations, and explain what problems there would be (if any) with the simulation. If there are no problems with the simulations, state that.

    a. Simulate MessageSet1 using MessageSet2 calls.

    b. Simulate MessageSet1 using MessageSet3 calls.

    c. Simulate MessageSet2 using MessageSet1 calls.

    d. Simulate MessageSet2 using MessageSet2 calls.

    e. Simulate MessageSet3 using MessageSet1 calls.

    f. Simulate MessageSet3 using MessageSet2 calls.

17. Suppose we try to develop an algorithm similar to two-phase locking but that will prevent starvation. We will describe the algorithm, and you have to decide whether it really solves the starvation problem or not. We will describe the algorithm two times, first very generally, and then in more detail.

    The idea of the algorithm is to use aging to prevent starvation. (Aging is the standard way to prevent starvation.) When a process fails to lock a record, it must release all its locks and start over (just like in two-phase locking). But it also increases its age by one, and marks all the records that is has already locked and the one it failed to lock. It marks these records with its own (unique) pid (process identifier) and its age (after the incrementing). Then it starts over.

    In addition, whenever any process tries to lock a record, it can only do so if no process with a higher age has marked the record.

    Now let's try to state this more precisely. All records start out with no marks. When a process starts a transaction, it will have no records locked at all, and its age will be zero. It starts trying to lock records. It can lock a record if (a) the record is unlocked, and (b) the age of the locking process is not less than the age in any of the list of marks associated with the lock.

    If the process fails to lock a record (for either reason (a) or (b)), it then does the following:

- Increases its age by one.

- Creates a mark that includes its pid and its (new) age.

- Adds a copy of this mark to the record that it failed to lock and to all the records it currently has locked. But if it has already marked a record, it leaves the mark but increases the age on the mark to its new age.

- Unlocks all the records it has locked.

- Starts over from the beginning trying to lock records.

At all times, each record will have a list of marks associated with it. Often the list will be empty. If not, the list consists of pairs (pid, age), and no pid appears twice on the list.

When a process completes a transaction, it does the following:

- Removes its mark from all the records it has locked.

- Unlocks all these records.

- Sets its age back to zero.

Does this algorithm prevent starvation? Does this algorithm prevent deadlock? Of course, you must explain.

18. Consider the following variation of two-phase locking. Each time a process fails to get a lock and has to release all its locks and start over, it increases its age by 1. As soon as a process reaches age 10, then all other processes that are in phase 1 have to release all their locks and wait (they do not start trying to get locks again). Then this process starts trying to get locks, but when it cannot get a lock it just waits for it. When this process completes phase 1 and enters phase 2, then all the other processes in phase 1 can start trying to get locks again.

Does this algorithm prevent deadlock? Does it prevent starvation? Explain your reasoning for each answer.

19. Suppose we add another feature to the algorithm in the previous question. Once a process reaches age 25, then all other processes that are trying to get resources release all their resources and wait until the process that reached age 25 gets its resources and completes. Any new process trying to get resources must also wait.

Does the algorithm with this change prevent starvation? Does the algorithm with this change prevent deadlock? Of course, you must explain your reasoning.

20. Message deadlock is when there is a cycle of processes, each waiting for a message from the previous process in the cycle. This is nearly identical to resource deadlock. This can happen in a distributed system. Suppose we have a distributed system with 100 computers, each of which is running a kernel. Each kernel runs only one process at a time. The processes are numbered with the computer number (0 . . . 99). You can send a message to any kernel, and ask the kernel if its process is waiting to receive a message and, if so, what process it is waiting for a message from.

Describe an algorithm that can detect message deadlock on this system. Suppose the deadlock detection algorithm runs on computer 0. The algorithm can be described in pseudo-code or whatever means you think is clear. Assume common mathematical algorithms, like cycle finding in a graph, are available to you (that is, you do not need to specify them).

21. *Message deadlock* can occur when we have a cycle of processes, each waiting for the next one to send a message. For example, suppose that only process PA sends to message queue QA, and only process PB sends to message queue QB. If PA is waiting for a message from QB and PB is waiting for a message from QA, then they are deadlocked.

{ nearly identical to #20

Suppose you had a table which told you, for each process, which message queues it can send to and which message queue (if any) it is currently waiting for. Describe an algorithm that uses this information and can detect a message deadlock between the processes.

Suppose, in the above example, that another process, PC, can send to message queue QA. In that case, the processes may not be deadlocked because it is possible that PC will send a message and break the cycle. Make sure your algorithm detects this and does not report a deadlock in cases like this.

22. Consider the statement, "Any synchronization problem that can be solved with semaphores can be solved with messages, and vice versa." Is this statement true or false? Explain the reasoning you used to come up with your answer.

23. Semaphores assume some shared memory, but the method of sharing can be indirect (as noted in Section 5.4). Suppose we had two different computers on a network, and a message system between them. The message system sends messages addressed with specific process identifiers (pids), *not* to mailboxes. There can be several processes on each computer, but processes do not share any memory, even processes on the same computer. Do not assume a common file system, either. These processes can communicate *only* via messages.

Describe a way to implement a semaphore on such a system. That is, describe the messages that will correspond to the semaphore operations send and receive, which processes the messages are from and to, what extra processes you will need (if any) and what they will do, and where the semaphore data structures are kept.

24. Suppose we had a message system where messages were addressed to specific processes rather than to message queues (as described in Section 8.13.1). This would prevent the mutual exclusion pattern, as described in Section 7.6, from working, since it depends on the message queue. Recode this solution to provide mutual exclusion for three processes, using messages sent directly to processes.

25. Suppose we had a message system where messages were addresses to specific processes rather than to message queues (as described in Section 8.13.1). For most of the IPC patterns described in Chapter 7, we could easily make changes to use message addresses directly to processes rather than to message queues. Look over the seven patterns, and indicate which ones would require substantial changes and which ones could be easily changed.

26. Rewrite the database access and update IPC pattern using semaphores and shared memory instead of messages.

27. Some simple operating systems use nonpreemptive scheduling. Give an example of a problem that can occur when the operating system uses nonpreemptive scheduling.

28. In some ways, starvation and deadlock seem like opposite problems. Sometimes, solutions to the deadlock problem cause more starvation and solutions to the starvation problem can cause deadlock. Give an example of each of these. Give a reason why you think deadlock and starvation are related in this way.

29. Show how to implement counting semaphores at the user level using binary semaphores. Give the code for the implementation.

30. Give the code to implement the database access and update problem using semaphores. Use the version whose code is given in chapter 7. This version gives equal priority to readers and writers.

Same as #26

31. Give the code to implement the rendezvous IPC pattern using semaphores.

32. Give the code to implement the database access and update problem using Ada. Use the version whose code is given in chapter 7. This version gives equal priority to readers and writers. You can use either the Ada rendezvous or protected variables.

chapter
9

Design Techniques II

9.1 INDIRECTION

9.1.1 OVERVIEW

Instead of accessing an object directly, access it indirectly though a third object. This allows more control over access to the object. In particular, it allows you to gain control each time the object is accessed.

The term *indirection* comes from its use in talking about addresses and pointers. An indirect reference is one where a pointer points to another pointer, rather than directly to an object. Figure 9.1 shows indirection in C++.

9.1.2 MOTIVATION

Suppose you are writing a document and defining a number of new terms in the text. You would like to format a word in a special font at the point you define it. Suppose you decide to put words that are being defined in italics. So you mark each one with the italics formatting attribute.

After you do this, you decide that you really want them to be in bold so they really stand out. To make this change, you have to go through the text and change every defined word from italics to bold. You cannot just change all the italicized words to bold because you also used italics to emphasize words, so you have to look carefully at each italicized word and change some of them to bold.

You can avoid this work by changing to indirect formats (see Figure 9.2). The formatting system allows you to mark any word with a user-defined formatting code. Say you use the code "definition" for all words that are being defined. Then you tell the formatter to format all "definition" words in italics. When you decide to change to bold, you tell the formatter to format all "definition" words in bold. The emphasized words have format code

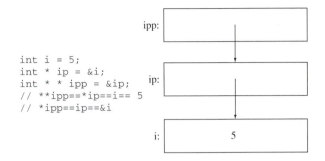

```
int i = 5;
int * ip = &i;
int * * ipp = &ip;
// **ipp==*ip==i== 5
// *ipp==ip==&i
```

Figure 9.1   Indirection in C + +

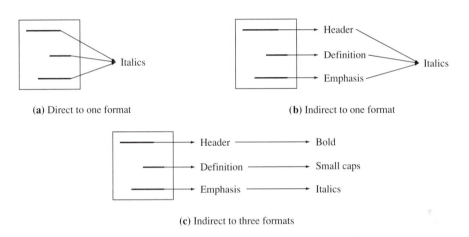

(a) Direct to one format

(b) Indirect to one format

(c) Indirect to three formats

Figure 9.2   Indirect formatting

"emphasis," and so they remain in italics. We added a level of indirection to achieve this flexibility. Instead of giving the format directly, we give the name of the format.

We can look at this in a different way, and see that the change to indirect formats is really allowing us to not lose information when we assign format codes to the text. When we format a defined word as italic, we are recording two decisions. First we are marking this as a defined word, and second we are deciding to format defined words in italics. By using indirect formats, we record each decision separately, and so we can change them independently.

9.1.3   OPERATING SYSTEM EXAMPLES

Message Queues   In Section 8.13.1, we discussed the idea of sending messages directly to processes instead of to message queues. We noted that sending to message queues was more flexible.

Initial process   The idea of indirection is too powerful and useful to restrict its use to pointers. In Section 5.4.1, we used the idea of having an initial process that starts all the other processes. In using an initial process in an operating system, the indirection is in creating a process. Instead of creating a process we want directly, we create a process that will, in turn, create the process we actually want. Process creation is our "pointer."

The operating system starts one initial process when it starts up. The initial process then starts up all the processes needed. This initial process can be changed and represents a level of indirection in process creation. The flexibility it provides is to allow the specific processes created to vary without changing the operating system.

RPC Implementation   A remote procedure call is implemented by calling a local (stub) procedure, which makes the call over the network using whatever means of network communication is available. The procedure is called indirectly. The advantage we gain is the ability to use any available method of communication.

Shared Memory   (See Chapter 11.) It is possible to implement shared memory on machines that do not share hardware memory. This is done through the memory management system. When the "shared" memory is used it traps to the operating system, which accesses the memory (possibly communicating with another machine that holds the actual memory) and simulates the effect of local, shared memory. We gain control on each access and simulate the shared memory.

Dynamic Loading   (See Chapter 10.) A simple way to implement dynamic loading is to make all the calls to procedures in the dynamically loaded module into indirect calls which always fail. The first time they are called they trap to the operating system, which does the dynamic loading. Then it fixes up the indirect calls to actually call the desired procedure (which is now loaded). By gaining control on each access we can detect the first access.

Character Generator Memory   (See Chapter 14.) The character generator memory is an example of indirection to save space. Instead of sending down a bitmap of 114 bits to describe a character we send a character of 8 bits and look it up in the character generator memory. This is the same thing as passing a pointer to an object instead of the object itself to avoid moving a large object.

9.1.4   COMPUTER SCIENCE EXAMPLES

Two Level Implementations   Some two level implementations are mainly to allow indirection and increased flexibility. The virtual terminal interface is an example of this. (See Chapter 14.)

Private Data in an Object   In object-oriented systems it is common for a variable to be private to an object. If a procedure outside the object wants to read or write the variable it must do it indirectly through functions provided by the object. A function that reads a variable is called an *accessor* function and a procedure that sets a variable is called a *settor* procedure. The advantage of going through a procedure is that you get control at the time the variable is accessed. This allows you to do things like monitor changes or delay generating the value of the variable until it is asked for.

A variant of this technique is to only allow access to a resource through an accessor function. This gives you control right before (and after) a resource is used. This can be used to implement a protection policy, mutual exclusion, and other similar ideas.

Indirection in Memory Management   Suppose we have a large block of memory and we are dynamically allocating blocks of memory. If we use direct pointers we cannot move the blocks or else dangling pointers will result (see Figure 9.3). If we use indirect pointers we can move the blocks with no problems (see Figure 9.4).

These indirect pointers are often called *handles*. The rules of using handles require that you always do the double indirection and never dereference the handle once to get the direct pointer. This will defeat the goal of being able to change the direct pointer without having to notify the users of the blocks.   handle

Sorting Large Objects   Sorting requires the repeated movement of the objects sorted. If the objects are large these moves can get expensive. A simple solution is to create an array of pointers to the objects. Then sort the pointers (which are small). The objects are sorted as long as you access them indirectly. See Figure 9.5.

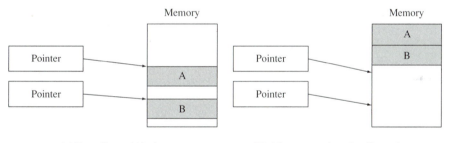

(a) Two allocated blocks   (b) After compaction, dangling pointers

Figure 9.3   Dangling pointers after compaction

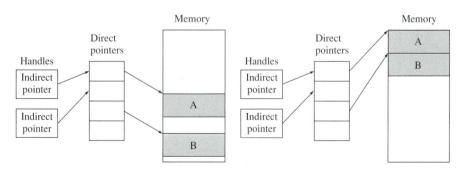

(a) Two allocated blocks with indirect pointers   (b) After compaction, pointers still valid

Figure 9.4   Indirection using memory handles

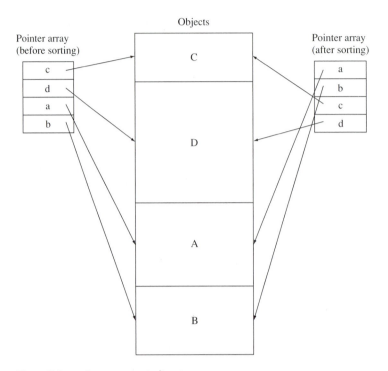

Figure 9.5   Sorting using indirection

Passing by Reference   Many programming languages pass arguments by value, that is, they pass a copy of the argument to the called procedure. If the object is large then the copy will be expensive. If the procedure does not change the passed object, it will be cheaper to pass a pointer to the object rather than the object itself. This use of indirection saves a large copy.

Defined Constants   You may recognize this technique as the same one you use when you define named constants in a program. Instead of using constants directly in the code, you use the name of the constant and then define the constant in one place. The compiler follows the indirect link for you.

   The preprocessor facility of including a file within another file is another example of indirection.

Formatting with Styles   This example is explained in the Motivation section.

9.1.5   DISCUSSION

It is useful to look at the concept of indirection more generally to help us better understand it. We frequently have to access an object, and we do it with a name or an address. For example, in a program you access a variable by giving its name. When the compiler translates the program to machine language, the variable is referenced with an address.

If we add a level of indirection, we just do this twice, that is, we refer to an indirect object (with a name or address), and that object then refers to the actual object we are interested in.

The following table shows the indirect object and the method of referring for the examples we looked at above.

Source Object	Reference	Indirect Object	Reference	Desired Object
Process	Send	Message queue	Receive	Process
OS	Create by hand	Initial process	Create	Processes
Client process	RPC call	RPC Client Stub	Server RPC	Server process
Process	Memory reference	Indirect pointer	Memory reference	Data object
Statement	Name	Symbolic constant	Table lookup	Value
Characters	Name	Abstract style	Style sheet	Concrete format

All the examples use indirection, but there are differences between them. An important difference is which entities are active and which are passive. In the message sending example, the two processes are active and the message queue in the middle is passive. In the initial process example, the OS and the initial process are active. In the RPC example, all three entities are active. In the indirect pointer example, the process is the only active entity, and the other two are passive data. In the symbolic constant example, none of the entities is really active, and all the activity is in the compiler that is translating the statement. Similarly, in the formatting style example, the entities are all passive, and the formatting system is doing the style sheet lookups.

9.1.6 APPLICABILITY

Use indirection whenever you want to have control of the access to an object. This is useful for a number of reasons. It can allow you to:

- Move the object pointed to.
- Create the object only when it is first referenced.
- Allow only certain kinds of access to an object.
- Dynamically change the object referred to.
- Simulate access to an object that is in another address space.
- Do reference counting on the object.

Indirection is probably the most powerful design technique in a software designer's repertoire. There are many examples of the use of indirection in design, and we will see some more in later design chapters.

It is usually possible to add a level of indirection to any reference, and doing so will usually make the design more flexible and powerful.

9.1.7 Consequences

- You get control each time the data are accessed.
- You can trade time or space when you get control.
- It adds an extra step to the processing.

Adding a level of indirection almost always increases flexibility at a small cost in time and space.

9.2 USING STATE MACHINES

9.2.1 Overview

Use a graphical notation to show system states and state transitions.

In Section 5.3.2, we used a state machine to describe the states of a process. Operating systems are reactive systems that respond to events. *State machines* are generally a good way to describe such systems.

state machine

9.2.2 Operating System Example

Process States   Processes move from state to state, and a state diagram is the best way to explain process states.

9.2.3 Computer Science Example

String Recognition   State machines are theoretically equivalent to regular expressions. As a result, they are ideally suited to recognizing regular expressions, that is, strings in certain formats. Figure 9.6 shows a state machine for recognizing quoted strings.

9.2.4 Applicability

Use state machines whenever you have a system that has discrete state and whose behavior changes depending on the state it is in.

In fact, any time a state machine *can* be used in describing the operation of a system, it probably *should* be used. The reason for this is the state machine is a precise

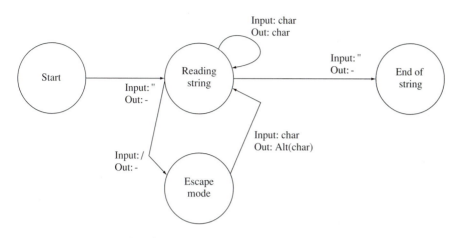

Figure 9.6   State machine for recognizing quoted strings

yet intuitive way of describing a system that responds to input events. It is pictorial, yet formal, and often state machines can be translated into code almost mechanically.

As with all powerful tools, there is a temptation to use state machines beyond the scope where they are effective. You should not try to do that. What we are saying is that, for systems within their scope, they are a very powerful and easy-to-use method.

State machines are a formal graphical technique for describing systems that react to events, produce outputs, and maintain a state that remembers the important parts of the history of previous events. They are useful in describing any system like that.

9.2.5 CONSEQUENCES

- State machines are easy to visualize.
- State machines are easy to create.
- State machines can be automatically translated to code.

9.2.6 IMPLEMENTATION ISSUES AND VARIATIONS

Implementation of State Machines   State machines can be used as a conceptual tool to understand a system that is state oriented. This is how we use state machines in operating systems.

It is possible to implement state machines by a fairly mechanical translation in a programming language. Sometimes they are implemented with a matrix. The rows are states and the columns are inputs. Each entry tells what to do and what state to go to next. This is an easy and efficient implementation of a state machine.

If the state processing is too complex to encode in a matrix cell, we can implement state machines with a case statement. This is not as easy or efficient, but it is more general.

9.3 WIN BIG, THEN GIVE SOME BACK

9.3.1 OVERVIEW

Sometimes you use a technique to save a lot of time or space, but it causes you to lose a desirable feature. You can often use some (but not all) of your gains to regain the feature.

9.3.2 MOTIVATION

Video frames compress very well since two sequential frames are nearly identical. To compress video, put out the first frame as a complete frame, describing all the bits in the frame. For the second frame, put out a small record that records the differences between the first frame and the second frame. For every subsequent frame, just put out the differences between it and the previous frame.

This method will allow a huge compression factor, but it will also create a problem. Now you always have to start at the beginning of the stored video, because all frames except the first are relative to the one before them. This means you cannot start playing in the middle.

We can solve this problem by giving back some of our compression. Suppose we put a full frame every 10 frames, and the next 9 are just the differences from the previous frame. Then we can start in the middle by backing up to the next full frame (which must be within 10 frames) and starting from there. Figure 9.7 shows the two compression methods.

How much do we lose by this? Suppose the average compression of a difference frame over a full frame is 99 percent; for example, if a full frame takes 2 Mbytes, then a difference record takes (on the average) 20 Kbytes. For a long sequence, the average cost per frame of full compression will approach 1 percent of a frame, or 20 Kbytes. For the other method, 10 frames will take 2 Mbytes plus 9 times 20 Kbytes, or 2.18 Mbytes or 218 Kbytes per frame. So the new method is only 89 percent

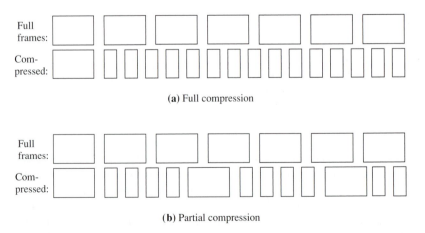

(a) Full compression

(b) Partial compression

Figure 9.7   Video compression

compression instead of 99 percent, but it is still very good. But we gain the advantage of being able to start in the middle of the tape. If we decide to put full frames every 100 frames, then our compression will be 98 percent.

9.3.3 OPERATING SYSTEM EXAMPLES

Multiprogramming and Multiprocessing   We gained two big advantages by going to pseudo-parallelism in the form of multiple processes. Processes allow more efficient utilization of resources, and they allow a user to do several things at the same time. By going to a two-processor system, we gained processing speed for the overall system.

But in both these cases, we also ran into problems with the synchronization of parallel processes. The solution to the problem is *not* to allow processes to run in parallel if they might interfere with each other. We give back some of the gains we achieved by allowing parallelism in order to solve the problems it created. We still have a large improvement because we gained a lot and gave back only a little.

Shortest-Response-Ratio-Next Scheduling   Shortest-job-first scheduling minimizes the average waiting time, but it discriminates severely against long jobs. In a heavily loaded system, a long job can wait forever. The shortest-response-ratio-next scheduling algorithm prevents this from happening by running long jobs that have waited a long time. This still gives a low average wait time, but prevents some jobs from never being run.

We will see this same idea in the aging and batching algorithms described in Chapter 15.

9.3.4 COMPUTER SCIENCE EXAMPLES

Video Compression   We can compress video frames, but we lose the ability to start the video from any point. By adding uncompressed frames periodically, we can regain that ability.

9.3.5 APPLICABILITY

Sometimes a technique will be very successful and we will realize a large gain in time or space efficiency. These are situations where you might think about "reinvesting" some of these gains to get back some features that you lost using the new technique. You still have some of your gains, and you have no loss of features.

9.3.6 CONSEQUENCES

• You get the same features.
• You save time or space.

This is a technique that allows you to "save" an optimization that didn't quite work. If the problem was that you lost some essential feature, you may be able to use the optimization anyway by expending some additional resources to regain the lost feature. If the additional resources are less than what you gained by the optimization, then you come out ahead.

9.4   SEPARATION OF CONCEPTS

9.4.1   OVERVIEW

Take a concept and divide it into two parts, each of which can be used individually.

Some concepts combine two (or more) smaller concepts into a single concept. This is a good idea if the component concepts are always used together because we can generally handle them more efficiently as a unit. But sometimes the component concepts are useful on their own, and we can find places where one is useful without the other. In these cases, it is better to separate the concepts and allow each one to be used on its own. This allows new uses that you would not think of if the concepts were bundled. It follows a building block approach, where we provide the primitives to create solutions rather than providing complete solutions.

9.4.2   MOTIVATION

In Chapter 6, we introduced the idea of threads. We took our original concept of a process and broke it up into two separate concepts. The original process concept was something that could own resources (like memory space, address mapping, open files, attached message queues), and it could be given processor time by the dispatcher. With threads, we separate those two concepts so that the new process only owns resources and the thread is the dispatchable unit. A process must have at least one thread, and so you must create both a process and a thread in it in order to run a program.

It was useful to separate these concepts because then we could get effects that were not possible otherwise. In particular, we could have several threads in the same process that shared the same address space.

Similarly, if you never run more than one thread in a process, then it is not worth the effort to split the two concepts. But if you often run multiple threads and gain efficiency from having parallel threads in the same address space, then it is useful to separate the concepts.

9.4.3   OPERATING SYSTEM EXAMPLES

Processes and Threads   If we separate resource ownership (process) from the ability to be scheduled for processor time (thread), we can have several threads per process.

Create Process and Fork   In Section 3.8, we saw that in UNIX the concept of process creation was divided into two separate concepts. The fork created a new process, but it was running the same code as the parent process. The exec runs a new program in the same process. This separation allows effects that are not possible with a unified concept of creating a process. We noted in Section 3.9 that this allowed the easy manipulation of standard input and standard output. It also makes some other things simple, like process login where the serial line watching process execs the login process (which gets and checks the password) and then execs a shell.

This separation comes at a high cost, however. The fork must duplicate the parent process by copying all its memory. This effort is generally wasted, since 99 percent of the time the process will immediately execute an exec and the entire just-copied memory space is discarded. In the original UNIX system, this did not matter much since processes were small and always in memory, but when UNIX moved to machines that allowed larger address spaces, they had to devise a variant of fork called vfork (virtual fork), which did not copy the actual memory but borrowed the parent's address space temporarily. The use of "copy-on-write" pages (see Chapter 12) can also be used to make fork more efficient.

Messages and Semaphores   We saw another example of separating concepts in Section 8.15, where we noted that messages combine the concepts of synchronization and data transfer, and semaphores and shared memory separate them.

9.4.4   COMPUTER SCIENCE EXAMPLES

Stack Operations   Let's look at an example in the area of module specification. Suppose we are implementing a stack module. There are two possible sets of stack operations:

- *pop*—pop the stack and return the top item.
- *push*—push an item on the stack.

In this interface, the concepts of getting the value of the top item on the stack and removing the top item on the stack are combined. We can separate those concepts with this interface:

- *top*—return the top item on the stack.
- *pop*—remove the top item on the stack (no return value).
- *push*—push an item on the stack.

The first interface is best if we always pop off values. The second interface is best if we frequently look at the top of the stack without popping it.

Actually, in this case we have another option, and that is to have both the top operation and the *old* pop operation. When we only want to pop the stack, we can ignore the return value. The reason this is an acceptable option is that returning a value from an operation is a very cheap thing to do and only involves one extra machine instruction.

In other cases, having it both ways would not be so cheap, and we would have to make the choice. For example, we can always use empty messages to simulate semaphores, but then we do not get any of the implementation simplicity and efficiency of semaphores.

9.4.5 APPLICABILITY

Separate two concepts when you think they each might be useful on their own.

9.4.6 CONSEQUENCES

- Separation of concepts gives you more flexibility.
- With separated concepts, you can choose what you want more precisely.
- Separate concepts can be less efficient.

There are good and bad things about separating a concept into two concepts. The separated concepts give you more flexibility and can be more efficient if used separately. But separating the concepts always has some cost, and using them together will be a little more expensive than using the combined concept. If the concepts are only used separately once in a while, the extra cost may not be worth it for these few cases.

For example, we could get the effect of threads with two processes and shared memory. It is possible that this solution is more efficient than separating the concepts of process and thread.

> Separate concepts if you think you will use them separately in ways that were not previously possible.

9.4.7 IMPLEMENTATION ISSUES AND VARIATIONS

Process Creation   We noted that UNIX separates the concept of process creation (fork) from the concept of running a program in a process (exec). The advantage is that the fork also copies the open files, and this allows easy communication between the parent and child process.

Many current UNIX systems allow you to specify which open files are to be copied on a fork and which are not. A few of them generalize this even further. A process has many attributes:

- Code space
- Data space
- Stack space
- Threads
- Open files
- IPC structures.

When you create a new process, there are many possible variations on what you might want to copy in the child. You might want to copy the code, but not the data and stack. You might want only one thread copied. One possibility is to allow the user to decide, with each fork, which things will be copied from the parent process and which things will not.

9.4.8 RELATED DESIGN TECHNIQUES

In Section 18.5, we will discuss unifying concepts that are similar, and the main example will be unifying devices and files. In that case, we will talk about combining two very similar concepts into a single unified concept. In this section, we have been talking about separating a concept into two parts. The two parts are not similar concepts but the two components of the single concept. For example, data transfer and synchronization are not similar concepts, but they are combined into the message concept.

9.5 REDUCING A PROBLEM TO A SPECIAL CASE

9.5.1 OVERVIEW

We have a general problem for which simple solutions are not adequate. We solve the problem with a method that, to implement, requires us to solve a special case of the general problem. But then the simple solutions are adequate for the special case.

9.5.2 MOTIVATION

Sometimes we try to solve a problem and run into a recursive instance of the same problem. We call this a *recursive design problem.* This happened in the implementation of messages on a multiprocessor in Chapter 6. Messages can be used to implement mutual exclusion (see Section 7.6), but to implement messages we have to solve the mutual exclusion problem with respect to access to the message queue data structures. But now we have a special case of the mutual exclusion problem. The general case involves any two processes, and the time a process may be in a critical section has no limit (it could be seconds, minutes, even hours). In the case of access to the message queue data structures, the critical section is only a few machine instruction executions long. We can use a busy waiting solution in this case because the time in the critical section is so short.

recursive design problem

9.5.3 OPERATING SYSTEM EXAMPLES

Mutual Exclusion   We need a special case of mutual exclusion to implement general mutual exclusion. General mutual exclusion was used for critical sections of any length. The special case in the implementation of mutual exclusion had critical sections of only a few machine instruction executions. For that special case, simple solutions like spin locks or disabling interrupts were adequate.

Process Blocking   In Section 5.9.1, we discussed how the operating system needs to suspend itself in the course of suspending a process during a system call. This special case of suspending was handled with a special case solution.

Name Servers   A problem in networks is knowing the addresses of servers. Often we know the name of the server we want but not its address. If we can get the address of the name server, then it can translate server names to network addresses.

Unique Global Names   In Section 18.3, we will see how to reduce the problem of assigning unique names in a distributed system to the problem of assigning unique names at each level of the system. Since each level is managed centrally, the unique name problem is easily solved.

9.5.4   Computer Science Examples

Help Systems   Requiring people to remember how to execute all the commands in a system is too much of a memory load. But we can require that they remember how to execute one command, the help command, and this gives them assistance on all other commands. This is an instance of the same principle—reducing a problem to a special case, and then using a simple method for solving the general case.

Text Editor Data Structures   A text editor must keep a long sequence of text and make frequent insertions and deletions to the sequence. A simple array of characters would require too much moving around of characters, since a sequence of text may have tens or hundreds of thousands of characters. If you deleted the first character of a 50,000 character file, you would have to move 49,999 characters down one position in the array. But suppose we decide to keep each line of text together and have a sequence of pointers to the lines. If we edit within a line, we put the edited line in a new area and change the line pointer to it. The vi text editor uses this data structure.

On the other hand, keeping the characters in a linked list, one node per character, would be terribly inefficient in space, even though insertion and deletion would be easy. But we could keep line pointers in a linked list because there are many fewer lines than characters.[1]

9.5.5   Applicability

It is common in a design problem to think of simple solutions that are not quite adequate for some reason. They might be too slow or take too much space. In developing more complex solutions, we sometimes encounter another instance of the same design problem we are trying to solve. But usually this recursive design problem is different—in most cases, simpler than the original one. This means

---

[1] There are better data structures for text editors than these. The most popular is the "gap" method, which keeps the characters in a large array with a gap in the middle, at the insertion point.

that the simple solutions that would not work in the general case might work in the simplified case.

9.5.6 CONSEQUENCES

This technique is of general use. Often a problem has no good solution, but it can be reduced to a special case, and a solution that did not work in the general case does work in the special case.

9.5.7 IMPLEMENTATION ISSUES AND VARIATIONS

Changing Design Problems   We noted in Section 4.2 that a design problem included a lot of information about the problem beyond the simple statement of the problem— information like how often the problem occurs, how big the data structures will be, etc. When we encounter a recursive design problem, the general statement of the problem is the same but this related information is different. These differences allow a different set of solutions.

9.6 REENTRANT PROGRAMS

9.6.1 OVERVIEW

Write a program with no static or local data so two threads can use it at the same time. This is called a *reentrant program*.

reentrant program

9.6.2 MOTIVATION

Suppose you are writing a program where you display a file browser which shows the names of all the files in a directory. If you are only planning a single browser, you might be tempted to use global variables to keep the state information for the browser. The code below shows this method. We have simplified the browser state to include only two variables.

BROWSER USING GLOBALS

```
WindowID wBrowser;
char *wCurrentDirectory;
void redrawWindow( void ) {
    char ** list = GetFileList( wCurrentDirectory );
    UpdateListBox( wBrowser, list );
}
```

This code sample includes two things, the code (the redrawWindow procedure) and the state data for the browser (wBrowser and wCurrentDirectory). They are mixed together in the code, but they are fundamentally different sorts of things.

This method works, but suppose later you discover that you would really like to have more than one browser. You will have to make several changes to the program to allow for this. You might have to make arrays out of all your state variables.

A better solution is to collect all the browser state information into a record, and allocate it dynamically. The code below shows this solution.

BROWSER USING STATE STRUCTURE

```
typedef struct browserStruct {
    WindowID browserID;
    char *currentDirectory
} Browser;
void redrawWindow( Browser * browser ) {
    char ** list = GetFileList( browser->currentDirectory );
    UpdateListBox( browser->browserID, list );
}
```

The only differences are that each reference to a global variable requires an indirection. If that is too slow, you can read the value into a local variable in the procedure and use it instead. The code that initialized the overall program will dynamically allocate the storage for a browser. That storage will represent the browser, rather than the two global variables we used before.

Clearly, it is very easy to add another browser window. You just allocate another instance of the structure and pass it in to the functions that access the browser window. This solves two potential problems. It makes it easy to have multiple copies of the browser window, and it makes the code reentrant since it eliminates the global variables.

9.6.3 OPERATING SYSTEM EXAMPLES

Threads   Sometimes it happens that the same copy of a program is executed by two different threads or processors at the same time. These two threads are not executing the same exact instructions simultaneously, but just in the same code. This can also happen in an operating system when it gets an interrupt. It was executing somewhere in the operating system, and the interrupt causes it to start executing in another part of the operating system. This can also happen within a user process if threads (processes sharing the same memory space) are provided.

Shared Data in a Multiprocessing Operating System   The problem with reentrancy is the shared data, and it is exactly the same problem of parallelism that we dealt with in Chapters 6 and 7. But we usually look at the problem in a different light when we talk about reentrancy. We talk about reentrancy when the two executions don't really have anything to do with one another, other than sharing the code. So they have no need to share storage or worry about mutual exclusion. Instead, reentrant programs ensure that no two executions will share any storage, and so they will not interfere with each other.

MPOS   For example, when we moved our simple operating system to a multi-processor, we gave each processor its own stack and its own copy of the *current_ process* variable. To make a program reentrant, we have to be careful not to have any common storage. The trick that makes that work is the hardware registers. We assume that each process has its own set of hardware registers, and so there cannot be any interference in register use. When we need storage beyond what will fit in the registers, we make sure that it is not global or static storage, but storage that is allocated dynamically and accessed through a register pointer.

MS/DOS   Another example is the MS/DOS operating system. Many early MS/DOS programs had to do all sorts of tricks to get around the fact that MS/DOS was not reentrant. Since the early PCs had no protection and interrupts could occur at any time, you could easily have an interrupt while executing in MS/DOS, and then the interrupt handling code would make a system call and reenter MS/DOS.

9.6.4   Computer Science Example

Object-Oriented Programming Languages   This technique is part of the philosophy behind object-oriented programming languages. An object in C++, for example, is really just a record with procedures attached to it. The idea of an object is that it is a collection of data. Each time you create an object, you are dynamically allocating an instance of a structure.

9.6.5   Applicability

These days, threads are common, and it is a good idea for all programs to be written reentrantly. Otherwise, you will run into problems later with threads.

Reentrancy is fairly easy to achieve if you plan for it, but, when one is writing a program, it is often easier to simply use global storage than to always allocate storage. Thus, a lot of programs are not reentrant just because the programmers were not careful about this.

9.6.6   Consequences

- With reentrant programs, it is easy to make multiple copies of the object.
- You can use the reentrant program in a multithreaded environment.
- Reentrant programs require extra indirection steps because all data is accessed through pointers.

> Reentrant programming makes multiple copies easier.

9.6.7   IMPLEMENTATION ISSUES AND VARIATIONS

Reentrant Programs Are Not Processes   Reentrancy is a property of a program, not a process. That is, it can be determined by inspecting the code and checking if there is any global or static data.

Why do we use global or static variables? To save state from one call of a procedure to the next. The local variables are not saved from one call to another. The purpose of a global or static variable is to save state information, but the state is associated with the process, not the program. The solution is to pass in the state data that is needed. The procedure itself is stateless.

9.6.8   RELATED DESIGN TECHNIQUES

As we observed above, object-oriented programming strongly supports writing reentrant code.

9.7   USING MODELS FOR INSPIRATION

9.7.1   OVERVIEW

model

Use the analogy between a *model* and a system to give you ideas about how the system should be specified or implemented.

9.7.2   MOTIVATION

The process model is basic to an operating system and is based on the idea of a standalone computer. We wanted to have one computer, but have it act as if it were several separate computers. But we quickly learned that it is useful if processes communicate with one another. The kind of interprocess communication used in early operating systems was based on the shared memory model. But separate computers can communicate by hooking them up with wires and sending messages along the wires. The physical model inspired the message-based model of interprocess communication. Besides separate computers connected with wires, we also have multiprocessors that share memory. From this physical model, we get the logical model of threads— processes that share memory.

We also discussed the idea that file I/O can be based on the disk model or the tape model.

In each of these cases, we have a physical system as the inspiration of a logical model, but this is really just a coincidence. The important fact is that one model was used as inspiration for the design of another kind of model. Also, in each case, we did not slavishly follow the analogy between models in every detail, but instead used the source model to help us generate ideas for how the target model might be designed.

In Section 6.10, we started with the simple model *Computer = Processor + Memory + I/O,* and used it to explore the various ways in which the components of a computer might be replicated. This is another example of using a simple model for inspiration.

9.7.3   OPERATING SYSTEM EXAMPLES

Hardware Models   Computer hardware is a rich source of models for computer software.

File I/O   File I/O can be based on either of the two devices a file might be implemented on: disks or tapes.

9.7.4   COMPUTER SCIENCE EXAMPLES

Blackboards   Programs to assist people working in a group sometimes use the shared blackboard (these days, a whiteboard) model for communication.

Graphs   Hypertext is based on the graph model.

Markets   People have used the idea of a free market to control the allocation of computing resources in a network of workstations.

9.7.5   APPLICABILITY

This is a powerful technique for generating useful ideas, and we see it frequently in computer science. The more ideas you have early on, the better off you are. It is fairly cheap to investigate ideas to see how useful they are.

9.7.6   CONSEQUENCES

- Models can be a rich source of ideas.
- Models can lead to bad ideas.

9.8   ADDING A NEW FACILITY TO A SYSTEM

9.8.1   OVERVIEW

When you want to add a new facility to a system, you have three choices: build on existing mechanisms, add a new low-level mechanism and build the facility with that, or add a new high-level mechanism that provides exactly the facility you need.

9.8.2 MOTIVATION

In Section 8.13.2, we discussed the problem of waiting for a message from two queues at the same time. We looked at three solutions to the problem.

- Use two helper processes. Each helper process waits on one message queue and forwards messages to a common queue. Then the main process waits on the common queue.

- Use a nonblocking receive. Use the nonblocking receive to check for messages in one queue and then the other. This is a busy waiting solution.

- Use a special-purpose receive. The operating system provides a form of receive that waits for two queues at the same time.

Each of these solutions has good and bad features. The process solution builds on existing facilities and does not require any new system calls or operating system services. But it is fairly inefficient since processes are expensive to create and destroy.

The nonblocking receive solution requires a new system call (or a change in the semantics of an existing system call). The solution also requires busy waiting. Note that the nonblocking receive does not solve the problem directly, but it provides the key building block you need to construct the solution yourself.

The two queue receive also requires a new system call. But the operating system can take over the busy waiting and allow the process to sleep while waiting. The operating system can recheck the queues when they change, and so the waiting will not really be busy. This solution is the only one that solves the problem directly.

The process and nonblocking receive solutions generalize easily to N queues. The two queue receive can be generalized to pass in an array of semaphores to wait on. In fact, System V UNIX has such a primitive for semaphores.

9.8.3 OPERATING SYSTEM EXAMPLES

Receiving from Two Queues   This was discussed in the Motivation section.

Implementing Mutual Exclusion   We encountered a partial application of this design principle when we discussed the implementation of mutual exclusion in an operating system. The first method we used was to disable interrupts during a critical section. This is an example of building the solution using an existing facility. In a multiprocessor, disabling interrupts does not work, and so we tried the solution of adding a low-level hardware facility, `ExchangeWordWithRegister`, to handle the problem. This was an example of adding a new, low-level facility that we can use to build up our solutions.

We did not discuss the third possibility in terms of implementing mutual exclusion. That would be to add system calls to solve specific mutual exclusion problems, that is, to protect specific sets of variables. A mechanism called *monitors* (see Brinch Hansen 1970) has been suggested that is along these lines.

Implementing Threads   Threads are a useful facility that can be added to an operating system. We can implement threads at the user level. This is an example of using an existing facility. We can implement a dispatcher at the user level and implement threads with no help at all from the operating system.

The other alternative is to implement threads at the operating system level. This is essentially the high-level facility solution because threads are exactly what we need.

What would a low-level primitive solution to this problem be? The problem with user threads is that they might block the entire process. A solution to that would be for the operating system not to block a process, but to call a *scheduler thread* when it would have blocked and call it again when it would have released the block. This allows the scheduler in the process to block the thread, run other threads, and unblock the thread when the operating system operation is completed. These solutions and variants have been proposed by Draves et al. (1991), Massalin and Pu (1989), and Marsh et al. (1991).

9.8.4   COMPUTER SCIENCE EXAMPLES

Iterating Over a Data Structure   Suppose you want a system call (or system calls) that will give you a list of the files in a directory. The problem is that the list is of variable length. There might be only one file in the directory or there might be 500 files. We can use the three approaches we just mentioned.

First, we can use the existing facility that allocates variable-sized chunks of memory. The operating system can figure out how much memory it will take to hold the entire list, allocate the memory from the memory allocator, put the list in the memory, and pass the memory back to the caller.

Or we could provide a pair of system calls: GetFirstFileInDirectory and GetNextFileInDirectory. The user then creates a loop in the program that uses these system calls to retrieve the directory one name at a time.

Finally, we could have a system call that will go through the directory for you and do something with each entry.

We see the same tradeoffs. Using an existing facility tends to be inefficient. Here the problem is that we might generate all the names but we might be looking for a particular one. Providing low-level functions and implementing the facility yourself is more work but more flexible. Having the system do one special thing is easy but not flexible.

9.8.5   APPLICABILITY

This principle provides guidance when you are implementing a new facility. You will have to do it one of these three ways. What the principle says is that you should look at all three ways and see which one is the best in your situation.

This principle is a guide to give you ideas on implementation. It does not say that all three methods are reasonable in every situation, just that they are possible. Examine the three approaches and pick the best one.

These three solutions represent three general approaches to providing a new facility for users within the context of an existing system.

- Use an existing facility. Sometimes there is a facility that already exists that you can build a solution on.

- Provide a basic function to build on. The operating system can provide some basic functionality that provides the "hook" you need. You build the solution yourself from this.

- Special-purpose solution. The operating system provides a new facility that is a specific solution to your problem.

The first solution does not require any changes, but sometimes the existing facility is not quite right and the solution is too slow or too expensive.

The second solution provides a general facility that can be used to solve this problem, and maybe other problems as well. But since it is general, it may be inefficient.

The third solution is usually the most efficient because the operating system can do exactly what is necessary and no more. But it is not general since it solves only this problem. If a similar problem comes up, another new solution will be required.

You will usually be able find these three types when implementing a new facility. Each one is useful in certain contexts and bad in others.

9.8.6 CONSEQUENCES

- *Features of using existing facilities:*

    -No changes to the system are required.

    -There are no new concepts to learn.

    -Their use can be inefficient if the existing facilities are not appropriate for the problem.

- *Features of using low-level mechanisms:*

    -They are easier to implement than high-level mechanisms.

    -They can be used for other purposes, encouraging exploration of new solutions.

    -They are flexible.

    -They are harder to use, because you must build the solutions yourself.

- *Features of using high-level mechanisms:*

    -They can be very efficient.

    -They are easier to use, because the solution is ready-made for you.

    -They are not as flexible as low-level mechanisms because they can only be used for this particular problem.

    -They can be made more secure because you know exactly what the user is doing and do not have to provide for general cases.

9.8.7   RELATED DESIGN TECHNIQUES

The difference between adding a high-level primitive that solves the problem directly and a low-level primitive that can be used to solve the problem is related to the idea of separation of concepts. The low-level primitive is better when it can be used in other ways to solve other problems. If it cannot be used in any other ways, you might as well package it up in a high-level solution and save the user some work.

9.9   SUMMARY

Indirection is adding an intermediate step to access an object. This allows you to get control on each access, and modify or control access to the object.

State machines are easy to create and easy to understand. They are an excellent method of representation for any system which depends on states.

Sometimes an optimization saves a lot of time or space, but it loses some essential functionality. In these cases, you can sometimes use some extra time or space (often redundant data structures) to regain the functionality without losing all the gains made by the optimization.

Sometimes it is useful to separate a concept into two smaller concepts. The advantage comes when you can use the smaller concepts by themselves.

When you are looking for a solution to a design problem, it is common to come up with simple solutions that work but do not meet the constraints of the problem. Later, you come up with a more complex solution that reduces the problem to a special case of the original problem. Often the simple solutions you first came up with will work for the special case because the constraints on it are different.

A reentrant program can be executed simultaneously by two threads because it does not use any global or static data.

A model is a system that is similar or analogous to the system you are working on. Models are useful for thinking up new ideas and approaches to problems.

When you have to add a new function to a system, there are three general approaches. The first approach is to use some existing facility in a new way. This approach does not require any new primitives in the system. The second approach is to provide a new low-level primitive that allows the user to program the new facility. This approach allows for the use of the primitive in different ways. The third approach is to add a high-level facility that does exactly what is wanted. This approach solves the problem with the least effort by the user.

9.9.1   TERMINOLOGY

After reading this chapter, you should be familiar with the following terms:

- handle
- indirection
- model

- recursive design problem
- reentrant program
- separation of concepts
- state machines

9.9.2   REVIEW QUESTIONS

The following questions are answered in the text of this chapter:

1. Why is indirection useful?
2. How can indirection help in memory management?
3. What are the three entities and two links involved in indirection?
4. What do we mean by reducing a problem to a special case?
5. What prevents a program from being reentrant?
6. Why do we run into reentrancy problems when threads are introduced into a system?
7. Why are models better for inspiring ideas than for proving that an idea will work?
8. How are the disk and tape models relevant to I/O?
9. What are the three general strategies for adding a new facility to a system?

9.10   PROBLEMS

1. Explain how indirect formats (section 9.1.2) are an example of separation of concepts.

2. Can our method of video compression be used if you need to be able to play the video backwards? Explain how it would be done or why it cannot be done.

3. Explain how a state machine could be used in a formatting program.

4. Explain how passing procedure arguments by reference is an example of indirection. What do you do if the procedure is not supposed to change the argument?

5. If a procedure contains a single instruction, then calling the procedure takes more space than executing the single instruction. How many instructions does a procedure have to have before calling the procedure takes less space than doing it inline? Use the machine language and stack frame defined in Chapter 2.

6. In C++, the class definition has a public part, which defines the data and procedures that anyone can access, and a private part that defines the data and procedures that only the member procedures can access. Some languages divide these two parts up into an interface part that only includes the public specification, and an implementation part that defines the private data and procedures and the rest of the implementation. But this separation creates a problem for the compiler if it only has access to the public part and needs to reserve space for the object on its stack frame. What is the problem and how can indirection solve the problem?

7. Explain how #include statements in C++ are a form of indirection.

8. Suppose you have a process with a large number of threads (say 10) working on a problem that requires a large table. There are five different tables that can be used, and one thread will change the current table from time to time. You cannot change the table in place by copying, because such a large copy is slow and is not an atomic operation anyway. The thread could send a message to all the other threads telling them the location of the new table. Think of another solution to this problem that does not require the threads to communicate.

9. A photo CD is a CD that contains digitized images of photographs taken with an ordinary camera. When the photographs are developed, they are digitized and put on the CD. A CD holds about 500 megabytes of data and can hold about 100 photographs. Each photograph is stored in several different ways: two icon sizes and five picture sizes of different resolutions. Give some reasons why they didn't just store one high-resolution image on the CD. Then give some design alternatives to this method of storing, and indicate in which situations your new designs would be better.

10. A Postscript image consists of a Postscript program which you execute to generate the image. Sometimes it takes a lot of processing to generate the image, and, in all cases, it requires a Postscript processor, which is a complex piece of software. Many word processing programs will allow you to insert a Postscript image created by some other program in a document, but, since the word processor does not contain a Postscript processor, the on-screen version of the document has an empty space where the Postscript image should be. Design a way to represent Postscript images that solves this problem.

11. A file system contains files of many different types: text files, object files, compressed files, Postscript files, WordPerfect files, tiff files, etc. Suppose you are designing a file browser that allows you to move around the file system and pick a file. Often, the file name alone is not sufficient information for you to decide if this is the file you want, and you really need to see the first part of the file in order to decide. We want to design the file browser so it can do this for all the file formats in the file system. Give two different designs that will allow this to be done. *Note:* Your designs are not restricted to how the browser works. You may require other programs in the system to do things to help the browser.

12. Explain how hashing is an example of reducing a problem to a special case.

13. Explain how a hierarchical naming system is an example of reducing a problem to a special case.

14. Consider a random number generator as follows:

```
int random( int n ) {
   static int seed = 1;
   seed = 3645651*seed + 237457;
   return seed % n; // seed mod n
}
```

Why is this procedure not reentrant? Modify it so it is reentrant. You will have to change the parameters you send to random.

15. Why is a dynamic memory allocator important in writing reentrant programs?

16. We defined I/O system calls modeled after disks and tapes. Suppose we wanted to model our I/O system calls after the concept of a deck of index cards with information written on each one. How would such a set of system calls look?

17. We discussed using disks and tapes as models for I/O. In the old days, people used decks of punched computer cards to hold programs and data, and they used card readers and card punches to read and write the decks. Define an I/O model based on card decks, card readers, and card punches.

18. Computer file systems are based on the disk model in that they allow files to be modified. Now we have WORM devices that can only be written one time and never modified after that. Suppose we wanted to model our file system on the WORM model rather than the disk model. What changes would we make to the ways we use files? *Note:* Several existing file systems (e.g., VMS) are already based on this model to some extent.

chapter
10

Memory Management

So far, we have talked about processes, the active part of a computation. But a computation also requires memory. In this chapter, we will look at the basic ideas in memory management. In Chapter 11, we will look at virtual memory. In Chapter 12, we will look at page replacement algorithms and some other issues related to memory management.

Main memory is generally the most critical resource in a computer system in terms of the speed at which programs run, and it is important to manage it as efficiently as possible. The operating system is responsible for allocating memory to processes. In this chapter, we will look at the problems of memory management and a range of possible solutions.

10.1   LEVELS OF MEMORY MANAGEMENT

Figure 10.1 shows the two levels of memory management that go on in a running system. The memory manager is the subsystem of an operating system in charge of allocating large blocks of memory to processes. Each process gets, from the operating system, a block of memory to use, but the process itself handles the internal management of that memory.

Each process has a memory allocator for that process. In C++ (and Ada and Pascal), this is the `new` memory allocator, and in C it is the `malloc` memory allocator. These memory allocators do not call the operating system each time they get a memory request. Instead, they allocate space from a large block of free memory that is allocated, all at once, to the process by the operating system. When the per-process memory allocator runs out of memory to allocate, it will ask for another large chunk of memory from the operating system.

In this chapter, we will look at both levels of memory management. We will look at the per-process memory management first. Once we understand memory management inside a single process, we will consider the additional issues that come up in operating system memory management.

10.2   LINKING AND LOADING A PROCESS

In order to understand how memory management inside a process works, we first have to understand how the memory in a process is set up initially, when the process is started. This initialization sets up the memory pool that is allocated from by the per-process memory manager.

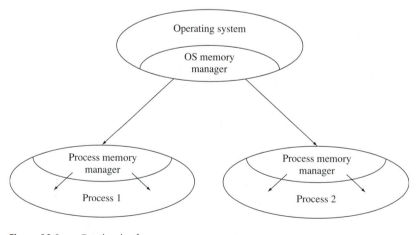

Figure 10.1   Two levels of memory management

A program must go through two major steps before it can be loaded into memory for execution. First, the source code is converted into a load module (which is stored on disk). Second, when a process is started, the load module is loaded from disk into memory.

10.2.1 CREATING A LOAD MODULE

The process of creating a load module from a source program is shown in Figure 10.2. First, the source code file is compiled by the compiler. The compiler produces an *object* module. Let's look at the contents of an object module, and then we will go back to discussing Figure 10.2 and see how object modules are linked together into a load module.

object module

Object modules   Figure 10.3 shows one possible structure of an object module. There are many object module formats. They differ in details, but all contain the same basic information. An object module contains a header which records the size of each of the sections that follow (as well as other information about the object module), a machine code section which contains the executable instructions compiled by the compiler, an initialized data section which contains all data used by

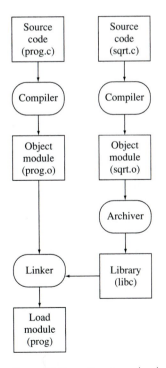

Figure 10.2   Creating a load module

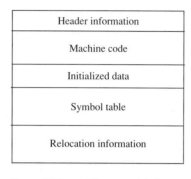

Figure 10.3   Object module format

```
#include <iostream.h>
#include <math.h>
float arr[100];
int size = 100;
void main( int argc, char * argv[ ] ) {
    int i;
    float sum = 0;
    for( i = 0; i < size; ++i ) {
        cin >> arr[i]; //or " >> "(cin, arr[i]);
        arr[i] = sqrt(arr[i]);
        sum += arr[i];
    }
    cout << sum; //or " << "(cout, sum);
}
```

Figure 10.4   Sample C++ program

the program that requires initialization, and the symbol table section which contains all the external symbols used in the program. Some of the external symbols are defined in this object module and will be referred to by other object modules, and some of these symbols are used in this object module and defined in another object module. The relocation information is used by the linker to combine several object modules into a load module.

Let us use a specific example to help understand this process. Consider the program in Figure 10.4.

The object module for this will look something like the one shown in Figure 10.5. The comments fields are not, of course, a part of the object module, but are there in the diagram for explanation. All numbers are written in decimal.

header section   The *header section* contains the sizes necessary to parse the rest of the object module and create the program in memory when it eventually gets loaded.

Offset	Contents	Comment
		Header Section
0	94	Number of bytes of machine code
4	4	Number of bytes of initialized data
8	400	Number of bytes of uninitialized data
12	72	Number of bytes of symbol table
16	?	Number of bytes of relocation information
		Machine Code Section
20	XXXX	Code for top of for loop
50	XXXX	Code arr[i] << cin statement
66	XXXX	Code for arr[i] = sqrt(arr[i]) statement
86	XXXX	Code for sum += arr[i] statement
98	XXXX	Code for bottom of for loop
102	XXXX	Code for cout << sum statement
		Initialized Data Section
114	100	Location of size
		Symbol Table Section
118	?	"size" = 0 (in data section)
130	?	"arr" = 4 (in data section)
142	?	"main" = 0 (in code section)
154	?	" >> " = external, used at 42
166	?	"sqrt" = external, used at 62
178	?	" << " = external, used at 90
		Relocation Information Section
190	?	Relocation information

Figure 10.5   Object module for the sample C++ program

The *machine code section* (also called the *text section*) contains the generated machine code. We have put Xs in for the machine code, and put the source code in the comments. We have roughly estimated how many bytes of code will be required for each statement. Different values would only affect the offsets of later items in the object module. *(machine code section)*

The only item in the *initialized data section* is the constant 100 (named size). Note that the variable sum is initialized, but it is a stack variable and does not appear in this section. The initialized data section only contains global and static, initialized data. *(initialized data section)*

The *uninitialized data section* also contains only global and static data. In this case, that includes only the array arr, which is 400 bytes long. Note that the uninitialized data section is not represented explicitly in the object module; only its size is recorded. The initial value of uninitialized data is undefined, so there is *(uninitialized data section)* no need to record it. The space will be allocated when the program is loaded into memory.

symbol table

external symbol

undefined external symbol

defined external symbol

The *symbol table* contains two classes of external symbols: undefined symbols and defined symbols. *External symbols* are the symbols in the symbol table. They are distinguished from local symbols that are only used in a single object module. *Undefined external symbols* are used in this program but defined in another object module. For each of these symbols, we record the symbol name and the places it is used. When the program is linked, these locations will be filled in with the correct value. *Defined external symbols* are defined in this object module, and may be used as undefined symbols in other object modules.[1] For each of these symbols, we record the symbol name and the value of the symbol. We have assumed that each symbol table entry takes 12 bytes. Note that the symbol offsets used are not the offsets in the object module (shown in the left-hand column), but offsets into the section (machine code or data) that the symbol is in. So, `size`, which is at offset 114 in the object module, is at offset 0 in the data section. The same is true for the offsets given for the undefined external symbols. For example, `sqrt` is used in code at offset 82 in the object module, but at offset 62 in the load module (since the code section starts at offset 20 in the object module).

linker

load module

library

Creating a Load Module   Now, getting back to Figure 10.2, the job of the *linker* is to combine one or more object modules and zero or more libraries into a *load module,* which is a program ready to be executed.

A *library* is an archive of object modules that are collected into a single file in a special format. There is a library manager (called an "archiver" in Figure 10.2) which manages libraries. The linker knows the library format, and can fetch object modules from the library.

The linker has several jobs:

- Combine the object modules into a load module.

- Relocate the object modules as they are being combined.

- Link the object modules together as they are being combined.

- Search libraries for external references not defined in the object modules.

Here is the process the linker goes through to create a load module.

1. Initialize by creating an empty load module and empty global symbol table.

2. Read the next object module or library name from the command line.

3. If it is an object module, then:
   a. Insert the object module (code and data) in the next available space in the load module. Remember the address (in the load module) where it was loaded.
   b. Relocate the object module to its new load address. Also relocate all the symbols in the object module's symbol table.

---

[1] With certain compiler options, the symbol table will contain local (internal) symbols also. These are not necessary for linking, but are used by symbolic debuggers.

   c. Merge the object module's symbol table into the global symbol table. Steps *d* and *e* describe this process in more detail.

   d. For each undefined external reference in the object module's symbol table:

      (1) If the reference is already defined in the global symbol table, then write its value into the object module you just loaded.

      (2) If the reference is not yet defined in the global symbol table, then make a note to fix up the links when the symbol is defined (during the loading of a later object module).

   e. For each symbol definition in the object module's symbol table, fix up all previous references to this symbol noted in the global symbol table (these are references in object modules loaded earlier).

4. If it is a library, then:

   a. Find each undefined external reference in the global symbol table.

   b. See if the symbol is defined in any of the object modules in the library.

   c. If it is, then load the object module from the library as described in Step 3 for an object module listed on the command line.

5. Go back to Step 2.

The linker takes one or more object modules and combines them into a load module. In doing this, it has to relocate each object module (except the first one) and link all the object modules together. We will discuss the relocation and linking steps in the next few sections.

Load Module Sections   The linking algorithm we described above is inaccurate in one detail. We implied that the object modules are placed sequentially in the load module as they are loaded. Actually, the three sections of each object module (the code, initialized data, and uninitialized data) are separated, and the sections of each type are loaded together in the load module. That is, all the code sections are loaded sequentially together in the first part of the load module, all the initialized data sections are loaded next, and finally all the uninitialized data sections are placed together. The result is that the load module has these same three sections: code, initialized data, and uninitialized data.

This makes the relocation a little more complicated, since each section has its own load address. It also makes management of the memory in the load module more complicated, since you have three sections, each of which is growing.

Relocation of Object Modules   The relocation section records the places where symbols need to be relocated by the linker. When an object module is being compiled, the compiler must assume some specific address where it will be loaded because certain places in the program require absolute addresses (that is, addresses that are not relative to a machine register but are a constant value). The compiler usually assumes that the object module will be loaded at address 0, but it records (in the relocation information) all the places that assume a load address of 0.

When the linker combines several object modules, only one of them can actually be loaded at address 0. The rest have to be relocated to higher addresses. When the linker does this, it goes into the object module and modifies all the absolute addresses to account for the new starting address. If the assumed load address is 0, this comes down to adding the real load address to these locations. Otherwise, we add in the difference between the actual load address and the assumed load address.

The linker creates a load module that it assumes will be loaded at address 0. We can think of each object module as an address space starting from 0 and going up to the size of the object module. The linker combines these address spaces into a single address space. In doing so, it must change some of the addresses in the object modules—the ones that assumed that the object module started at address 0.

Figure 10.6 shows two object modules being combined into a load module. The first object module is 110 bytes long, and so has an address space of 0 to 109. It is loaded first into the load module, and so it keeps its addresses, 0 to 109. The second object module is 150 bytes long, and so has an address space of 0 to 149. At address 136, there is a data cell named **x**, and at address 80, there is a reference to that address, and so the value 136 is used. When this object module is loaded into the load module, it is placed after the first object module, and so it occupies ad-

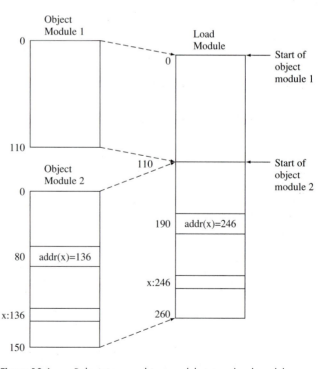

Figure 10.6   Relocating an object module into a load module

dresses 110 to 259 in the address space of the load module. The data cell named **x** is now at address 246, and so the reference to it (now at address 190) must be changed from 136 to 246.[2]

The compiler (or assembler) that creates an object module makes a record of each place where the address in the object module assumes a loading address of 0. When the object module is loaded into a load module, the linker goes to all these places and changes the value based on the real load address, which is now known. The process is straightforward and depends on the the appropriate tables being created in the object module.

Figure 10.6 only shows one value being relocated, but, in general, there will be a number of locations requiring relocation. The amount of relocation necessary depends on the hardware architecture. Modern architectures do not require much relocation, but still some absolute addresses must be used.

The location we are discussing here is called *static relocation*. Static relocation is done once, by the linker, as the load module is created. When the load module is executed on our hardware, each address will have the contents of the *base* register added to it before it is sent to the memory. This is called *dynamic relocation* because it happens each time the address is used during the execution of the program.

static relocation

dynamic relocation

The load module the linker creates (described in the next section) will be dynamically relocated when it is executed using a base register, but the object modules must be statically relocated because they all share the same base register. If we had a separate base register for each object module, then no static relocation by the linker would be necessary. This is the case in a segmented system (see Section 12.11).

Linking of Object Modules   A linker combines several object modules into a single load module. The reason you want to combine the object modules is that they refer to each other. One object module may call procedures in another object module, or use data defined in another object module. Each object module may define some external symbols (procedures or data) that will be referenced by other object modules. When the compiler compiles a program into an object module, it builds a symbol table in the object module that contains the undefined external references that are used in the object module and the external symbols that are defined in the object module. The compiler compiles a zero for the external references to allocate space for the reference. Later, the linker will write in the correct value.

Another function of the linker is to link up these undefined external references with the external symbols to which they refer, and this process is called *linking*. As the linker loads and relocates the object modules, it also creates a global symbol table for the entire load module. All the external symbols are kept in this table, which is just the combination of the symbol tables of all the individual object modules. When an external reference is encountered, the linker looks it up in this global table. If it is found, then the linker writes the correct value into the space for

linking

---

[2]Again, this diagram is misleading because, in reality, the code sections of the object modules will be loaded together, as will the two data sections.

the reference in the load module. If the symbol is not found, the linker makes a note to link the reference later, when the external symbol is defined in a later object module. Figure 10.7 shows this process.

When the linker is instructed to load a library, it does not load all the modules in the library. Instead, it looks through its global symbol table and finds all the undefined external references. It then goes through the library and loads any object modules that define one or more of these external references.

Differences between Linking and Relocation   It is important to remember that the linker is doing two distinct and separate tasks when it creates a load module out of object modules. We will review them here to be sure that you understand the differences. The first task is relocation. Relocation is the combining of the address spaces of all the object modules into the single address space of the load module. Relocation involves modifying each code and data location that assumes the object module starts at address 0. Relocation consists of adding the actual starting address of the object module in the load module to each of these locations.

Linking is the modification of addresses where one object module refers to a location in another object module (such as when code in one object module calls a procedure in another object module). When such an external address is required, the compiler has no idea what the correct value is, and so just writes in a zero and records the location of the address in the object module symbol table. When the linker puts

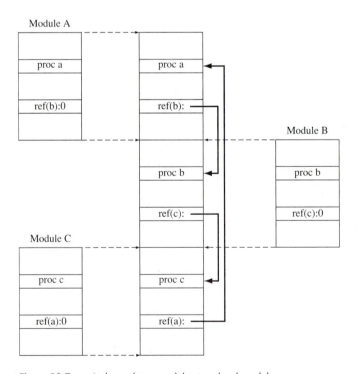

Figure 10.7   Linking object modules in a load module

all the object modules together, it knows all the external addresses, and it can correctly set these external addresses.

Load Modules   The format of a load module is similar to that of an object module. A load module, like an object module, will have a code section, an initialized data section, an uninitialized data section (not actually stored in object or load modules but its size is recorded), a symbol table section, and a relocation section. The relocation information is not necessary since most systems use dynamic relocation, and so programs are loaded at (logical) address 0. Since that is what the linker assumes, no further relocation is necessary. The symbol information is no longer necessary, but is kept with the load modules for use by symbolic debuggers.[3]

10.2.2   LOADING A LOAD MODULE

When a program is executed, the operating system allocates memory to the process (we'll see later in this chapter how it does this) and then loads the load module into the memory allocated to the process. Figure 10.8 shows how this loading is done. The executable code and initialized data are copied into the process' memory from the load module. In addition, two more areas of memory are allocated. One is for the uninitialized data. This area is allocated but does not need to be initialized. Some operating systems will initialize this area to all zeros (UNIX does this).[4] The second area is for the stack. Programming languages usually use a run time stack for keeping information about each procedure call (called activation records or procedure contexts). The stack starts out empty, and so there is no need to store it in the load module.

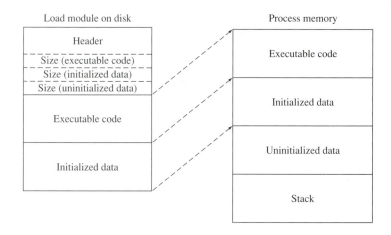

Figure 10.8   Loading a program into a process

[3]UNIX has a command called `strip` which removes the symbol table information from load modules. You can use this to save disk space if you are sure you will not want to symbolically debug the program.

[4]This belies the name "uninitialized data" so we can think of this as data that is not initialized to a specific value by the compiler. In a computer system, no memory is really "uninitialized" since the bits there must have some value at all times. By "uninitialized" we generally mean that it does not have an easily predictable value.

Before the loader does any of this, it computes how much memory the process will require and requests that much memory from the operating system. The memory required is the sum of the sizes of the executable code, the initialized data, the uninitialized data, and the stack. The first three of these sizes are obtained from the load module. The loader reads the load module header first, then allocates the memory, and then completes the loading.

How big is the stack? The loader has a default initial size for the stack (and most loaders have a command line option to change this default size). It starts the stack out at this size. When the stack fills up, more space will be allocated to it. This process will continue until the stack reaches some predefined maximum size. We will defer a discussion of exactly how this happens until we talk about memory mapping.

> Object modules have been compiled, but not linked, and cannot be executed. Load modules have been compiled, linked, and are ready to be executed.

10.2.3   ALLOCATING MEMORY IN A RUNNING PROCESS

Most programming languages allow you to allocate memory while the program is running. We saw in Section 10.1 that this is done with a call to the memory allocator, which is called `malloc` in C and `new` in C++, Pascal, and Ada. Where does this memory come from? To see this, we have to revise our diagram of a loaded process from that given in Figure 10.8. Figure 10.9 shows the loaded module, with a new memory area between the uninitialized data and the stack called "free space."

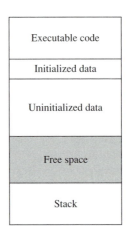

Figure 10.9   Memory areas of a running process

This free space is the memory that the per-process memory allocator allocates. In Sections 10.4 to 10.10 we will talk about how it does this allocation, and that will complete our discussion of the first level of memory management. After that, we will talk about memory management by the operating system. But before we go on to these topics, we will discuss some other methods used in program loading.

10.3   VARIATIONS IN PROGRAM LOADING

We discussed the creation and loading of load modules in Section 10.2. Figure 10.10 shows the process of linking and loading again.

These days, some programs are very large. There are two problems with large load modules. The first is that they take a lot of space on the disk, and the second is that they take a long time to load. Operating systems often use techniques to alleviate each of these problems.

10.3.1   LOAD TIME DYNAMIC LINKING

The large executable problem is especially apparent these days with window systems. It takes a lot of code to run the window interface, and most of this code is in the window libraries provided with the window systems. For example, a minimum X windows program is about 500K bytes long. About 450K of this is window libraries. If you have 11 such programs, you have 10 times 450K, or 4.5M bytes, of duplicated information. This can start filling up your disk pretty quickly.

One solution is to use a technique called *load time dynamic linking*. When the linker is linking from a library that has been designated as a load time dynamic link library, it does not insert the library object modules into the load module. Instead, it

load time dynamic linking

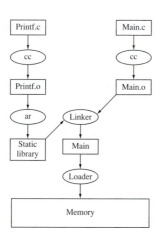

Figure 10.10   Normal linking and loading

inserts information about where to find the library, which of the library modules to load, and where to load them in the program's address space. When the program is actually loaded, the run time loader notices these load time dynamic link library references, goes to these libraries, and completes the library loading process at that time. Figure 10.11 shows this process.

Loading with load time dynamic link libraries takes a little longer, since the loader has more work to do, but it saves a lot of disk space that would have been wasted with duplicate copies of library modules.

Load time dynamic linking will only work if the libraries are in exactly the same place in the file system when the program is loaded as they were when the program was linked. System files like libraries seldom move, and so this is generally the case, but occasionally there is a system reorganization that moves things around and, after this happens, it is possible that some load modules that use load time dynamic link libraries will fail to load correctly.

Another problem is new versions of libraries. Most linkers record the version of the load time dynamic link library they looked at and, when object modules are finally loaded, if the version has changed, a warning message will be generated. Usually, the load will continue, and the resulting program will run correctly. But if it does not, then the version change is one place to look for a reason for the failure.

If you move an executable program from one machine to another, the libraries may be in different locations even though it is the same operating system on the same type of hardware. System managers have flexibility in how they lay out the system files in the file system, and often there are variations between installations.

10.3.2   RUN TIME DYNAMIC LINKING

What about the second problem? A big program might take a long time to load, since there is so much information to read into memory from disk. Most X windows executables are millions of bytes long. Even with load time dynamic link libraries, there is still the problem of moving from disk into memory.

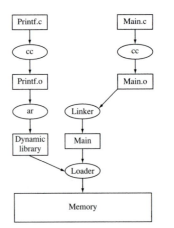

Figure 10.11   Load time dynamic linking

Many newer (and a few older) operating systems provide a service to deal with this problem, and it is called *run time dynamic linking,* or simply, *dynamic linking.* Dynamic linking is the idea of load time dynamic linking taken one step further. With load time dynamic linking, you defer the linking of library modules until just before a program is about to begin execution. With dynamic linking, you defer the loading to the last possible moment, that is, until the module is actually needed for the execution of the program. Figure 10.12 shows this process.

run time dynamic linking

Here is how you can do this. You add code to the program to check if a module has been loaded. This can be done efficiently by accessing the module indirectly through a pointer. The pointer can initially be set to interrupt to the dynamic linker. The first time you call a procedure in the module, the call fails because the indirect pointer is not set. This starts up the dynamic linker, which links the module into the program, loads it into memory from the disk, and fixes the indirect pointer so that, next time, the procedure will be called without an interrupt.

This means that you defer loading until you actually need the module. But how is this an advantage? It seems like it will take the same amount of time to load the module, no matter when you load it. You are not really saving load time, but just moving it around.

Let's take a specific example to explore the issues. Suppose you have a program that has 1M of base code and uses five library modules, each taking 200K. Suppose further that the program always uses the code in all five library modules. With dynamic linking, the program will start up twice as fast. The initial delay will be less, but there will be five more small delays distributed throughout the execution of the program as the five modules are loaded. Often this, in itself, is an advantage. People will notice an extra three-second delay at startup, but may not notice six half-second delays at various places during program execution.

In addition, with static loading the program requires 2M bytes to run during its entire execution, but with dynamic linking the program will use less memory for a while, until all five modules are loaded. If some of these modules are not used for a while, then it will not request that memory until it is actually needed.

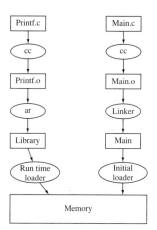

Figure 10.12 Dynamic linking of modules

But dynamic linking might actually save loading a module, as well as saving memory space throughout the execution of the program. Suppose that each run of the program only uses one or two of the library modules—different ones each time, depending on the input data to the program. In this case, dynamic linking is more efficient. The loading takes less time, since only one or two modules are loaded instead of all five.

Finally, dynamic linking always loads the most recent version of the module, since it is not searched for until it is actually needed. This is especially true if we compare it with static loading without load time dynamic linking. A load module might have been linked several months ago, and some of the modules may have newer versions.

Static loading takes a little bit less time, but dynamic loading saves memory during execution, allows faster startups, and always gets the most recent version of modules. All in all, dynamic linking has a lot to recommend it.

Figure 10.13 shows the difference between these techniques by showing the three different times (and two different places) the library routines are copied to. The following table summarizes the these techniques:

Method	Link Time	Load Time	Use Time
Static linking	Copy in libraries.	Load in the executable.	—
Load time dynamic linking	Remember where libraries are.	Load in executable. Copy in libraries.	—
Run time dynamic linking	Remember where libraries are.	Load in executable.	Copy in libraries

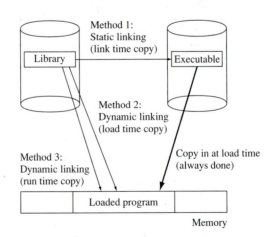

Figure 10.13   Static and dynamic linking

DESIGN TECHNIQUE: STATIC VERSUS DYNAMIC

We saw how run-time dynamic linking has several advantages over static linking. The static versus dynamic tradeoff is a common one in operating systems and in computer science in general. Programs are static and processes are dynamic. Compilation is static and interpretation is dynamic. Memory in a program can be allocated statically or dynamically.

In many cases, static solutions are faster and dynamic solutions are more flexible, but this is not always the case.

Dynamic solutions are a form of late binding.

To read more about static versus dynamic tradeoffs, see Section 13.3.

We can do some simple computations to see the tradeoffs between these methods. Suppose we have the following parameters:

- Program size: 1 Mbyte.
- Library modules: 4 modules of 1/2 Mbytes each.
- Total program size: 3 Mbytes.
- Time to load 1 Mbyte: 1 second.
- Time to invoke the loader: 100 milliseconds.

The following table breaks down the delays in each case.

Method	Disk Space	Load Time	Run Time (4 used)	Run Time (2 used)	Run Time (0 used)
Static linking	3 Mbytes	3.1 sec.	0	0	0
Load time dynamic linking	1 Mbyte	3.1 sec.	0	0	0
Run time dynamic linking	1 Mbyte	1.1 sec.	2.4 sec.	1.2 sec.	0

Dynamic solutions are better when the demand is uncertain. Static solutions are better when the demand is known.

10.4 WHY USE DYNAMIC MEMORY ALLOCATION?

Why does a program need to allocate memory while it is running? In fact, most programs do not, but many do. For some programs, the amount of memory they will need is not known until run time. Let's take a simple example of a program that reads in the description of a large graph, and decides whether the graph is connected or not.

The graph can be represented with a linked network of node structures. Suppose the node structure is 16 bytes long, and there is one for each node in the graph. We will not know how many nodes the graph contains until we read in the description of the graph. There might be 1,000 nodes or there might be 500,000 nodes.

Suppose we tried to avoid dynamic memory allocation for graph nodes. If we assume a maximum graph size of 500,000 nodes, we would have to allocate (16 × 500,000) 8,000,000 bytes for graph nodes each time we run the program. Since most graphs will be smaller than that, some or most of this space will be wasted most times the program is executed. It is more efficient to allocate node space as we need it.

This is a simple case because all the nodes are the same size. If all the memory requests are for the same size of block, then the dynamic memory allocation problem is very simple. In this case, we would take all of the free memory and divide it up into 16-byte blocks. We would link these blocks into a linked list, and allocate nodes from the list as needed. In some graph problems, nodes are deleted, so we might free up graph nodes. In this case, they would be linked back on to the list of free nodes.

This situation (where all the blocks required are the same size) is the simplest dynamic memory situation and, in this case, dynamic memory allocation is easy. But this is not a typical situation. Usually, a program will need to allocate different types of structures of different sizes. In this case, the solution to the problem is more complicated. In the next sections, we will characterize the problem in a general way, and then look at some solutions.

*10.5   THE MEMORY MANAGEMENT DESIGN PROBLEM

The design problem we are presented with is illustrated by Figure 10.14, and can be summarized as follows:

- We have a large block of memory, say N bytes.
- Requests for subblocks of the large block come in at unpredictable times.
- All requests are for from 1 to N bytes of memory.
- All requests must be satisfied eventually.
- When a memory block is available, we allocate it to some request. The memory block is in use for a while, and then returned to the system.
- The goal is to have the average amount of memory allocated over some time period that is as large as possible.
- A constraint is that the memory allocation algorithms should not use too much processor time or memory space to run.

We start with a large chunk of memory. We will receive a series of requests for blocks of the memory. A request can be satisfied with a block of memory that is at least as large as the size requested (it can be larger, but the excess will be wasted until the block is returned to the allocator). Once the request is satisfied, the memory is in use for a while, and then it is returned to the allocator. We assume that there will usually be a queue of

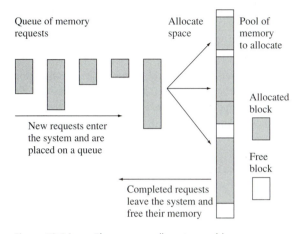

Figure 10.14   The memory allocation problem

memory requests, that is, that there is more demand for the memory than memory available. The goal is to use the memory as efficiently as possible, that is, to have as much of the memory in use at a time as possible. We also want to be sure that no request has to wait forever because a sufficiently large block of memory never becomes available.

*10.6   SOLUTIONS TO THE MEMORY MANAGEMENT DESIGN PROBLEM

As in most design problems, there is not one best solution for all cases, but rather a range of solutions, each with its good and bad points and each of which is best in some situations. In any particular design situation, there will be a best solution for that situation, but often it is hard to determine which is best without implementing several and testing them.

There are two major issues in a memory allocation algorithm: memory organization and memory management. Memory organization is how the block of memory is divided up into subblocks for allocation. You can divide up the memory once and for all, before any bytes are allocated (the static method), or divide it up as you are allocating it (the dynamic method). Memory management (or allocation policy) is the decisions about which to allocate to a request.

10.6.1   STATIC DIVISION INTO A FIXED NUMBER OF BLOCKS

Suppose the large block of memory we are allocating is 500,000 bytes long, and we know that half of the requests will be for 50,000 bytes and half will be for 200,000 bytes. We divide the memory into two blocks of 200,000 bytes and two blocks of 50,000 bytes. We will keep two queues, one for each size of block. Incoming requests will be put on the queue corresponding to the number of bytes they need. As you can see, the implementation of this method is very easy. Figure 10.15 shows this solution.

Two Queues or One?   But what if there are requests for 50,000 bytes waiting, no waiting requests for 200,000 bytes, and one of the 200,000 byte blocks is unused (as shown in Figure 10.16)? Should we allocate a 200,000-byte block to a 50,000 byte request? If we do, the other 150,000 bytes will be unused since we cannot change the size of the blocks dynamically. If we do make such an allocation, and the next millisecond a 200,000 byte request comes in, then it will have to wait for the small request to finish using the large block. If we do not make such an allocation, then maybe no large requests will come in, and the small request will have to wait unnecessarily.

Variable-Sized Requests   This two-size scenario is unlikely to occur. Normally, we do not have such exact knowledge of the sizes of incoming requests. A more typical

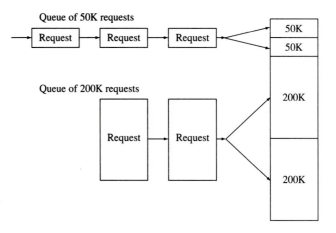

Figure 10.15   Allocation with a queue for each size of block

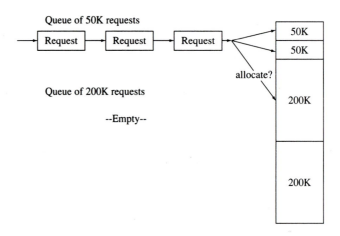

Figure 10.16   Allocate a large block to a small request?

situation is that the requests are for sizes varying over a large range. For example, maybe they are normally distributed around 100,000 bytes (see Figure 10.17.) In these cases, you have to pick a few sizes and hope they work out. You must have a partition big enough for the largest request you expect to get. If a few requests are very large, then you must allocate at least one very large block.

Static division is:

- Easy to implement.
- Good when:
    -There are only a few different request sizes, or
    -When the range of the request sizes is small.

- Bad when:
    -The range of the request sizes is large, or
    -Some requests are very large.

10.6.2   BUDDY SYSTEMS

We have already noted that, when all requests are for the same size block, then the memory allocation problem is easily solved. You statically divide up the memory into blocks of that size and keep them on a list.

If you have two different sizes of requests and you have some idea of the distribution of the requests for the two sizes, you can statically divide up the memory into blocks of two different sizes and keep a list for each one.

A problem with this technique that we mentioned before is that you might have a large block and a small request, and you have to decide whether to allocate the large block to the small request or not. There is a class of solutions, called buddy systems, to deal with this problem.

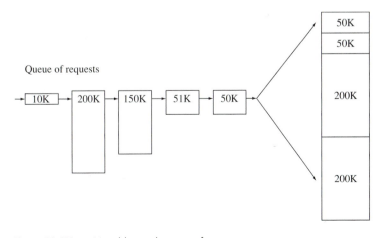

Figure 10.17   Variable-sized requests for memory

Suppose we have 500,000 bytes of memory, and requests of sizes 50,000 bytes and 100,000 bytes. We divide the memory up into five blocks of 100,000 bytes, and put them on a list. We create another list of free blocks of 50,000 bytes, which will start out empty. When a request comes in for a 50,000-byte block and the 50,000 byte list is empty, we look at the 100,000-byte block list. If there is a free block on that list, we divide it up into two blocks of 50,000 bytes, allocate one to the request, and put the other one on the 50,000-byte block list. When a 50,000-byte block is returned, we check to see if the other 50,000-byte block that made up the 100,000-byte block is also free. If so, the two are taken off the 50,000-byte block list, joined again, and the resulting block is put on the 100,000-byte block list. Figure 10.18 shows a series of block allocations and frees.

buddy system

This method allows us to use larger blocks to satisfy smaller requests without wasting half the block. The generalization of this technique is called a *buddy system*. In the buddy system, there is a free block list for each power of two. Say we have 512,000 bytes. Then there will be free block lists for block sizes 512,000 bytes, 256,000 bytes, 128,000 bytes, 64,000 bytes, 32,000 bytes, 16,000 bytes, 8,000 bytes, 4,000 bytes, 2,000 bytes, and 1,000 bytes.[5] They all start off empty except for one block on the 512,000 byte block list. When a request is received, you round it up to the next power of two and look on that list. For example, a request for 25,000 bytes will be satisfied with a block of size 32,000 bytes. If that block list is empty, then you try the next-larger power of two, and divide a free block there into two blocks. If you fail to find a block in that list, you keep going up until you do find one, or until you run out of lists, in which case the request must wait.

This method allows you to keep the simplicity of the statically allocated blocks, but handles the difficult cases of large requests and of running out of blocks of a certain size. One problem is that you can waste a lot of space rounding up to the next power of two. For example, a block of 10,000 bytes requires a block of 16,000 bytes, and so 6,000 bytes (37.5 percent) are wasted.

A buddy system is a combination of static and dynamic decisions. We decide statically which sizes of blocks to allow (powers of two), and we decide dynamically how many of each size to have.

The buddy system is clever, but it turns out that dynamic storage allocation, as discussed in the next section, is no harder and is more effective in allocating memory.

10.6.3   POWERS-OF-TWO ALLOCATION

powers-of-two allocation

There is a simpler variation of the buddy system that is called *powers-of-two allocation*. This is like the buddy system, except that you do not split and combine blocks. If you are out of blocks of a certain size, you wait for one to be freed, or else you use a larger block (without splitting it).

---

[5]We will not go below 1,000 bytes, but if we had to satisfy a large range of request sizes, we could continue down with smaller and smaller blocks, down to just a few bytes.

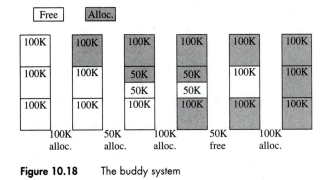

Figure 10.18   The buddy system

The powers-of-two method is not a good system for general dynamic memory allocation, but it becomes useful when combined with a paging system (see Chapter 11). We will look at it again in Section 10.10.

*10.7   DYNAMIC MEMORY ALLOCATION

Since we cannot predict the sizes of processes, the static solution is not a good one for the management of memory within a process, or for the management of process memory in an operating system. So we have to dynamically divide the memory into blocks in response to the requests that come in. This is an interesting problem which we will examine in this and the next two sections.

Dynamic memory allocation is a classic problem in computer science. It is a task of some complexity, but it is much studied and the techniques are well understood.

dynamic memory allocation

The basic idea is simple. We have a large block of memory. When a process needs some memory, we give it a small block of the big block of memory. When a process is finished, it returns its block of memory to the allocator. At any one time, the large block of memory is split up into many blocks; some are allocated and some are free. The allocator has to keep track of the allocated and free blocks. When a process requests a block of memory, the allocator picks one of the free blocks, gives the process all or part of it, and then records what it did. If it only allocated part of the free block, it divides the block into an allocated block and a free block. When a process finishes, it returns the block of memory to the allocator, which adds it to its set of free blocks available for allocation. Figure 10.19 shows the allocation of a block and the freeing of a block.

There are two key decisions in the design of a memory allocator:

- How do we keep track of the blocks, and
- Which block do we allocate from when a request comes in.

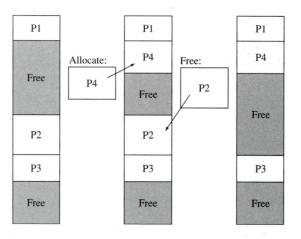

Figure 10.19   Allocating and freeing a memory block

fragmentation

An important issue in dynamic memory allocation is called *fragmentation,* that is, memory becoming divided up into so many small blocks that none of them are useful because they are all too small to satisfy any pending request. One simple precaution is to ensure that there are never two free blocks right next to each other. If this happens, the allocator will combine them into one bigger free block. The method we use to keep track of the blocks is usually responsible for doing this. Even doing this, there might still be lots of small blocks between allocated blocks.[6] We will come back to the fragmentation problem as we talk about allocation methods.

*10.8   KEEPING TRACK OF THE BLOCKS

There are two major methods of keeping track of blocks: a list and a bitmap. The list method is the most popular by far, and is also the most obvious.

10.8.1   THE LIST METHOD

block list

We keep a linked list of all the blocks of memory. We will call this the *block list*. When we need to allocate a block of memory, we go down the block list to find a suitable free block. Once we have found one, we either allocate the entire block, or divide it up into one block of the requested size and a free block containing the rest of the original block. When a block is freed, we change its status on the block list and combine it with the surrounding free blocks, if there are any. Figure 10.20 shows the list method of keeping track of memory blocks. Figure 10.21 shows the block list after block P5 is allocated, and Figure 10.22 shows the block list after block P3 is freed.

---

[6]Note, however, that there can be at most one more free block than allocated blocks, since two free blocks cannot be next to each other. We will come back to the fragmentation problem as we talk about allocation methods.

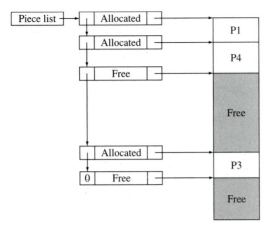

Figure 10.20   The block list method

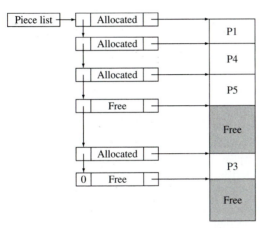

Figure 10.21   The block list after allocating P5

10.8.2 KEEPING ALLOCATED BLOCKS ON THE BLOCK LIST

It is not strictly necessary to include the allocated blocks on the block list since we never do anything with them. They are each allocated to a process and will be returned when the process completes (or sooner). However, we still want to keep the allocated blocks on the list for error checking. A program might erroneously try to free memory that has not been allocated to it. If the allocator believes the errant program, the block list will become inconsistent, and the same area of memory might be allocated twice at the same time. Some allocators do not check for this, and it is possible to crash them by improper memory freeing. It is best to avoid this problem and keep track of all blocks, free and allocated.

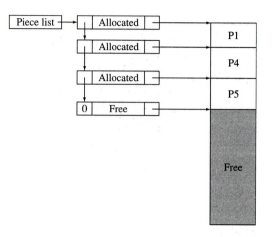

Figure 10.22   The block list after freeing P3

10.8.3   WHERE IS THE BLOCK LIST KEPT?

One important issue is where in memory the block list itself is kept. Just as we needed use of the processor to do processor allocation, we need use of memory to do memory allocation. This is an interesting design question, and we will examine it in some detail.

What we have is a recursive design problem. Our major problem is how to allocate memory in a process, and the solution we are examining is to use a block list. This solution requires that the block list nodes be allocated in some way, and so we have another memory allocation problem.[7]

As is usual when we encounter a recursive design problem, the recursive problem has different characteristics than the main problem. The general memory management problem had requests of widely varying sizes, but this problem has fixed-size blocks, that is, block list nodes. For fixed-size blocks, the memory allocation problem is easy: statically divide the available memory into fixed-size blocks and keep them on a stack.

But then the problem is how many nodes allocate to the block list, that is, how much available memory will there be? There must be a node for each block in the system, but the number of blocks in the system will vary widely depending on how big the memory requests are.

Figure 10.23 shows how this works. Part of the memory is reserved for the block list, and the rest of the memory is available for allocation to satisfy requests for memory.

The space for block list nodes must be taken from the free space for allocation. If we allocate too many block list nodes, then we may run out of memory while a lot of space is wasted on unused block list nodes. If we allocate too few block list nodes, then we may run out of block list nodes and be unable to allocate free memory even though it is available.

---

[7]We have seen a recursive design problem before, when we used messages or semaphores to implement process-level mutual exclusion, and then found we needed operating-system-level mutual exclusion to implement messages or semaphores.

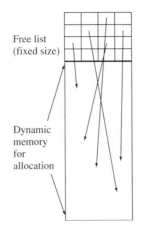

Figure 10.23   Reserving space for the block list

Again, the static solution requires accurate prediction of the behavior of the process (in this case, the number of blocks that will be allocated at one time). If this behavior is unpredictable, then the static solution will not be satisfactory.

10.8.4 USING BLOCK HEADERS AS BLOCK LIST NODES

For the special case of main memory, we have another solution that is commonly used. The blocks already consist of memory, and so we can take a little memory from each block to use as a block list node. This method puts a header structure at the front of each block, which is used as a block list node. It is like taxing each block by a fixed number of bytes to pay for the memory management space overhead. Figure 10.24 shows this structure.

This method uses part of the memory we are allocating to user processes for the block list. This header records the size of the block, the status of the block, and the list pointer(s). When the block is allocated, you give the process only the area after the header, since the memory allocator needs to maintain this header information even when the block is allocated. This is a nice method since it uses the same space for the blocks and the list nodes. Since we allocate all memory from the same pool, we will not run out of space until all the memory in the system is exhausted.

A variant of this method can also be used if the allocator does not keep track of allocated blocks. Then the block list only includes free blocks, and so the list headers use the first few words of the free block, space that is not being used anyway. When the block is allocated, it will no longer be free, and so the header is not required. This way, the entire block can be allocated to the requester. As we observed before, this assumes that the memory allocator trusts the requester to release memory correctly. If this is an operating system allocating blocks of memory to processes, the operating system will probably not be willing to trust the processes, and so this method cannot be used. But it is a possible solution with trusted

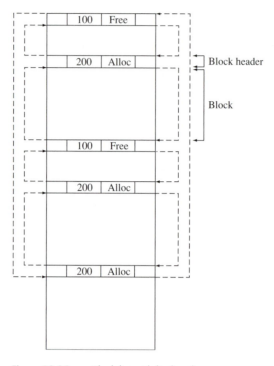

Figure 10.24   Block list with list headers

processes. For example, the other processes might be other parts of the operating system that the memory allocator trusts to work correctly.

10.8.5   THE BITMAP METHOD

In a big restaurant, they need to keep track of which tables are free and which are busy. Often they do this using a diagram of the restaurant showing each table. They mark the diagram to show what tables have people at them. This makes more sense than a list of free tables because it is faster to see if a table is free or busy.

bitmap

The list method is the most obvious way to keep track of free space. The *bitmap* method is a completely different approach to the problem, and is analogous to the restaurant diagram. The bit map is a long string of bits, one for each block of storage. Suppose you divide 4 Mbytes of storage into 128-byte blocks. This makes 32K blocks. A bitmap for this would have 32K bits (4K bytes). If the block is free then the corresponding bit is 1, else it is 0.[8] Figure 10.25 shows an example of a bitmap where each bit tells whether a block of 100 bytes is free or not.

We must allocate space in multiples of the unit of storage we have chosen for the bitmap, 128 bytes in this case. To allocate a block, we round up to the next multiple of 128 and divide by 128 to see how many blocks we need. Then we look through the

---

| [8]Of course, this is just a convention and we could do it the opposite, 1 for allocated and 0 for free.

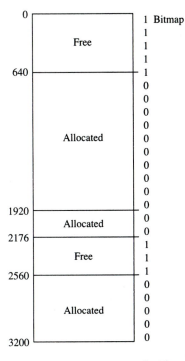

Figure 10.25   Bitmap method for memory allocation

bit map for a string of that many consecutive 1 bits. So, for 10,000 bytes, we need (10,000/128) 79 blocks of 128, or 79 consecutive 1 bits. We record the allocation by setting the bits to 0. Freeing storage is done by setting the bits back to 1.

The bitmap method is not commonly used for main memory allocation, but it is sometimes used to keep track of free space on a disk.

10.8.6   COMPARING METHODS

Here are the advantages of the list method:

- If there are few blocks, it uses very little space.
- The overhead (one block list node) is the same for all blocks, so this method is more attractive for large blocks.
- The space required for the list is independent of the size of the memory being allocated, and is only related to the number of blocks.
- The block list does not need to be in contiguous storage.
- It is fast to find free blocks.
- Blocks of any size can be allocated, so there is never any space wasted inside a block.

Here are the advantages of the bitmap method:

- The amount of space required is static and does not depend on the number of free blocks.

- Part of the bitmap can be used at a time because the parts do not depend on each other. That is, you can keep most of it on disk and only a portion of it in main memory.

- There is no need to combine contiguous free blocks explicitly. The method does that automatically.

- To avoid very large bitmaps, it is necessary to have a block granularity that is not too small (say, not less than 16–64 bytes).

*10.9   WHICH FREE BLOCK TO ALLOCATE?

When we allocate a block to a request, we can choose any of the free blocks which is big enough. When we allocate space from a free block that is larger than the requested size, we split up the free block into two blocks; one we allocate to the requester, and the other is a new (but smaller) free block. How do we decide which free block to allocate to a request?

The goal of any strategy for allocating free blocks is to minimize fragmentation. As we allocate memory, we accumulate free blocks that are too small to satisfy a request. These are spread between the allocated blocks and called *fragments,* and this process is called *fragmentation* or *checkerboarding.* We would like to allocate blocks to create the least fragmentation. Here are some possible strategies:

fragments
checkerboarding

first fit

- *first fit*—Choose the first block that is large enough. This avoids going through the entire list and does not favor large or small holes.

next fit

- *next fit*—Choose the next block that is large enough. This is the same as first fit, except it starts looking at the point in the free list where the last allocation was done.

best fit

- *best fit*—Choose the free block that is closest to the requested size. This creates small holes and preserves large holes.

worst fit

- *worst fit*—Choose the largest free block. This avoids creating small holes and uses up the large holes.

It is not obvious, a priori, which of these is better, but simulation studies by Shore (1975) and Knuth (1973) show that next fit is a slightly better method than best fit, in that it creates the least fragmentation. Worst fit does considerably worse.

Fragmentation means that memory is wasted, but how much? Knuth derived the "unused memory rule" which states that, if the average allocated block is of size s_0 and the average hole is of size ks_0 (where $0 < k < 1$), then the expected degree of fragmentation is the fraction $\frac{k}{k+2}$. Using this formula, we get the following table relating the ratio of the average free block to the average allocated block and the degree of fragmentation.

Average Free/Allocated Size	Space Lost to Fragmentation
1/2	.20
1/3	.14
1/4	.11
1/5	.09

So, in general, we can expect 10 percent to 20 percent of the storage will be lost to fragmentation. Using a fixed block size would, in most cases, waste even more space due to mismatches between the fixed block size and the different sizes requested.

The main problem in dynamic storage allocation is fragmentation, that is, getting too many small free blocks. There is really no way to avoid this problem, although you can avoid making it worse than it has to be. The problem with the best-fit method is that it produces more small blocks than necessary, and that is why it does not work as well as you would expect. You just have to accept that some storage will be wasted on small free blocks, and that is the price you pay for the advantages of dynamic storage allocation.

10.10 EXAMPLES OF DYNAMIC MEMORY ALLOCATION

The methods we have discussed so far are not used in modern operating systems for two main reasons. The first reason is that they do not solve the exact problem faced by modern operating systems. In Chapter 11, we will see how *paging* works. In a paging system, all of main memory is divided up into pages, which are usually about 4 Kbytes long. Paging is so useful that every modern operating system uses it. In a paging system, memory management is divided into two parts (see Figure 10.26). The first part is the page allocator that allocates physical memory in whole pages. The page allocator has two clients. The first client is the paging system, and the second client is the operating system memory manager. The operating system memory manager only allocates blocks smaller than one page. It allocates space for process descriptors, open file structures, strings, etc.

The operating system memory manager has a simpler job than general dynamic memory allocation since all the blocks it allocates are less than the page size (say 4 Kbytes) and it can always get more memory from the page allocator.

The second reason the operating system does not use one of the algorithms we mentioned so far is that they are too slow. The operating system needs faster memory management that does not require searching lists of unknown length.

A powers-of-two allocator is reasonable in an operating system because there will only be a few sizes to allocate. With 4K pages, we will have lists of blocks of sizes 2K, 1K, 512, 256, 128, 64, and 32 bytes. Each page consists entirely of blocks of one size. If a list is exhausted, then we can allocate a new page for it and divide it

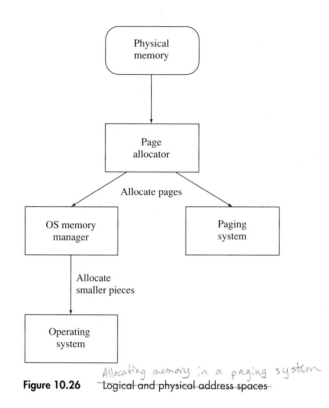

Figure 10.26   ~~Logical and physical address spaces~~ *Allocating memory in a paging system*

up into blocks of the required size. If there are lots of free blocks, we can try to find whole pages that are free and remove them from the free list they are on. This method does not require any searching of free lists. McKusick and Karels (1988) describe a powers-of-two memory allocator with these and other improvements.

The buddy system is used in UNIX System V release 4 (Barkley and Lee, 1989). They use a lazy version of the buddy system with bounded delays. Other examples are the zone allocator in Mach and OSF/1 (Sciver and Rashid, 1990) and the slab allocator used in Solaris 2.4 (Bonwick, 1994).

10.11   LOGICAL AND PHYSICAL MEMORY

We discussed the memory-mapping mechanism in Chapter 2, but let's review the terminology again so it is fresh in your mind. A computer system has *physical memory*, which is a hardware device. The physical memory is divided up into small units called *memory cells,* which we will normally assume to be eight-bit bytes. The physical memory cells are named with *physical addresses,* and these physical addresses together form the *physical address space*. The physical addresses are *contiguous,* meaning that each consecutive address refers to a cell. If

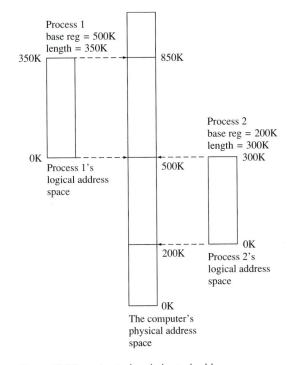

Figure 10.27   Logical and physical address spaces

there are 4 megabytes (2^{22} bytes) of memory, then the physical addresses will run from 0 to $2^{22} - 1$.

Physical addresses are only used in system mode. In user mode, *logical addresses* are used. When a user mode process accesses a byte using a logical address, the logical address is mapped into a physical address by the hardware. It does this by adding together the logical address, and the contents of the *base* register. So a user-mode program uses logical addresses, and they form the *logical address space*. The logical address space is also contiguous, using consecutive addresses from 0 to some upper limit.

A computer system has only one physical address space, but can have several logical address spaces (see Figure 10.27). The logical address 124 can refer to a number of different memory cells, depending on the current value of the *base* register, but the physical address 124 always refers to the same memory cell.

10.12   ALLOCATING MEMORY TO PROCESSES

Each process requires a certain amount of memory to run. The amount of memory required depends on how big the program and data it uses are. Processes vary widely in how much memory they require, from a few thousand bytes to millions of bytes. In most systems, the processes assume their logical memory is contiguous. Using simple memory mapping, with *base* and *bound* registers, the operating system must allocate contiguous physical memory in order to provide the user with contiguous logical memory.

Physical memory is a resource that we can divide up into blocks and allocate to the processes, but, as we just observed, each process needs a contiguous block of memory. We cannot load a process that takes 600 Kbytes into two separate 300-Kbyte blocks of memory. (Later, we will see that, with some help from the hardware, we *can* do this.) The problem the operating system has is how best to manage the memory resource, that is, how and when to divide the memory into blocks, and how and when to allocate the blocks to processes.

10.12.1   STATIC MEMORY MANAGEMENT

In our simple operating system, we divided up the memory statically (that is, before the operating system started running processes) into 20 blocks of 50 Kbytes each. These 20 blocks were permanently allocated to processes 0 through 19.

The first design decision to make in designing a memory management system is whether to divide up the memory into blocks statically or dynamically. We can, as we did in the simple operating system, decide before the operating system starts how many blocks there will be and how big each block will be. This means that no decisions about dividing up memory are made while the operating system is running. This strategy was sufficient for our simple operating system, where we were concentrating on process implementation and did not want to worry about memory allocation, but it is not a practical solution for a real operating system.

In addition to dividing up the memory statically into fixed-size blocks, we can also, as we can in our simple operating system, allocate each block to a specific process. Actually, we allocated it to a process slot. If the slot is unused, then the memory is unused and wasted. It might be better to only allocate memory to actual processes rather than process table slots.

What we could have done is to divide the physical memory into fewer but larger blocks, and allocate the blocks to processes as they are created. For example, we could have divided our 1 Mbyte of memory into five blocks of 200K each, instead of 20 blocks of 50K. The operating system gets one block, so user processes can use the other four blocks. When a process is created, it is allocated a block of memory. Figure 10.28 shows the original and revised versions.

But what happens after four processes have already been created and we want to create the fifth process? All the blocks of memory have been allocated to processes (remember that one goes to the operating system). What happens is that the fifth process must wait until one of the four existing processes exits and its memory can be reclaimed. Process create requests will be put on waiting lists until memory is freed to satisfy them.

But it is useless to allow for 20 processes when there are only four blocks of memory for processes to run in. A system that statically allocates memory blocks need only have one process slot for each block of memory.

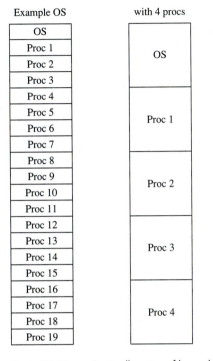

Figure 10.28   Static allocation of larger blocks

In other words, if you statically divide up the memory, there is no difference between static and dynamic allocation of memory to processes. There is a one-to-one correspondence between process table slots and memory blocks. In order to use dynamic allocation, we need to do dynamic division of memory.

10.12.2   HANDLING VARIABLE-SIZED PROCESSES

Now it is time to think about dynamically dividing the memory into blocks. There are several reasons why we want to do that.

In a typical operating system, we do not know how big the processes will be. Some will be small and some will be large. If we statically divide the memory into blocks, we would have to make the memory blocks big enough for the largest process we want to run. But then the memory would be largely wasted when we were running small processes.

An alternative solution would be to statically divide the memory up into different-sized blocks. A small process could run in any block (although we would prefer to give it a small block and save the larger blocks for larger processes), and a large program might fit into only one of the blocks. This makes the queuing of processes waiting to be created a little more complicated (but not much). This solution was tried in several early operating systems. It does work, but it is inflexible and does not lead to the efficient use of memory.

The solution used in most operating systems is to dynamically divide the memory into blocks. Then the operating system faces the same dynamic memory allocation problem we looked at in Section 10.7. Dynamic memory allocation works in an operating system in about the same way as it does within a process. One difference is that an operating system allocates much larger blocks and gets fewer requests than a per-process memory manager. The range of possible solutions is the same, but the best one to choose might be different because of the different conditions in the design problem.

So the solution to operating system memory management is dynamic memory management, but now we will go back and be sure that we really want to solve the problem. Do we really need to run more than one process at a time? This topic is discussed in the next section.

10.13   MULTIPROGRAMMING ISSUES

There are several reasons for wanting to run more than one program at a time. We have seen that people get interrupted during a task, and often want to suspend one process and run another one. Also, it is more efficient to run several processes at once. For example, we would want to be able to print a document while working on another document. Finally, it is often more convenient to break up a task into several distinct parts, and let one program handle each part. This increases the reusability of programs. The UNIX shell pipeline is an example of this. By packaging various functions into small programs that run in parallel as separate processes we can use a small set of programs to do a large set of useful functions.

So we need multiprogramming, the ability to run several programs at the same time, and to do this we need to have several programs in memory at the same time. Thus the task we are presented with is how to use the memory we have to the best possible advantage, that is, we want to have as many programs in memory as possible, and always the most useful ones.

But having more than one program in memory at a time presents some ancillary problems that we need to deal with. The two main problems are

- Memory allocation, and
- Memory protection.

With monoprogramming, the operating system could just allocate all the memory to the process that is running, sit back and wait for it to finish, and then reclaim all the memory to give to the next job. With multiprogramming, we have to do dynamic memory allocation, that is, we need to respond to a series of memory requests and be constantly allocating and freeing memory.

Since there is more than one process in memory, we have to be sure that one process does not read or write the memory of another process. Actually, this problem was present in monoprogramming as well, since we had to protect the operating system from the user process.

Multiprogramming improves hardware efficiency and user efficiency. It is worth the trouble.

10.14   MEMORY PROTECTION

memory protection

The *base* and *bound* registers described in Chapter 2 provide a satisfactory solution to the protection problem. A process cannot access any memory with lower addresses, since the hardware adds the relocation value to every address (using unsigned arithmetic), and it cannot access any memory above its allocation, since the limit register will prevent this.

We should note, however, that *base* and limit registers (or some generalization of them) are not required to implement memory protection. Another approach is to have some idea of the identity of a process and of ownership of parts of memory. For example, suppose each process had an eight-bit process number, and each 4K block of memory had an eight-bit owner register. A process can only access a block of memory if its process number is the same as the owner register of the block. In this case, all processes can address the memory of all other processes, but they cannot actually access the memory since the owner register and the process number will not match.

We might reserve some special values. A process number of 0 can be used by the operating system and represent a "skeleton key" that always matches. An owner number of 0 can represent public memory that any process can access, no matter what its owner number is. The IBM360 used this kind of memory protection scheme. Figure 10.29 shows the two forms of memory protection.

Note that *base* and *bound* registers solve the memory relocation problem as well as the memory protection problem, but lock and key systems only solve the memory

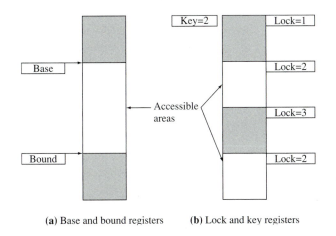

(a) Base and bound registers   (b) Lock and key registers

Figure 10.29   Two forms of memory protection

protection problem. On the other hand, lock and key systems allow for noncontiguous memory allocation.

10.15   MEMORY MANAGEMENT SYSTEM CALLS

memory manager

The part of an operating system that manages memory is called the *memory manager.* An important question to ask is, who are the clients of the operating system memory manager, that is, who makes memory requests? We have seen two examples of this in this chapter.

- When a process is created, memory for it is allocated, and the program it will run is loaded into that memory. So the first client of the operating system memory manager is the process creation module of the operating system.

- When a process is running and it runs out of free memory in its allocated memory, it asks for more from the operating system.

10.15.1   STATIC ALLOCATION OF MEMORY TO PROCESSES

In our simple operating system, there were no system calls to change the memory allocation of a process. In that system, the only time memory is requested is when a process is created. A process was created with an initial size, and the size never changes during execution. In a system with no system calls to change the memory allocation of a process dynamically, the create process procedure in the process manager is the only client of the memory manager.

Figure 10.30 shows the situation. The process manager requests a block of memory for the process whenever a new process is created. The request is queued until it can be satisfied. We are assuming that there is more demand for memory than there is memory available, so that the queue is not usually empty and a request usually has to wait for a while before it is satisfied. If this is not the case, then memory management is easy; just give out whatever memory the processes ask for. There was no queue in our simple operating system because there was no memory allocator at all.

This type of memory allocation is quite simple. First, process creation does not occur very often by computer standards, maybe 20 or 30 times a second, certainly not thousands of times a second or even hundreds of times a second. Second, the process manager is going to be asking for fairly large chunks of memory, enough to put a whole process in. This means sizes like 20K bytes, 100K bytes, or 2M bytes. Thus we have an easy dynamic allocation problem: infrequent requests (so allocation efficiency is not a big concern) for large blocks (so block overhead is not a concern).

10.15.2   DYNAMIC ALLOCATION OF MEMORY TO PROCESSES

So far, our system call interface does not include a system call to allocate more memory dynamically, but most real operating systems do allow this. This means that any process can request more memory, and so is a potential client of the memory manager.

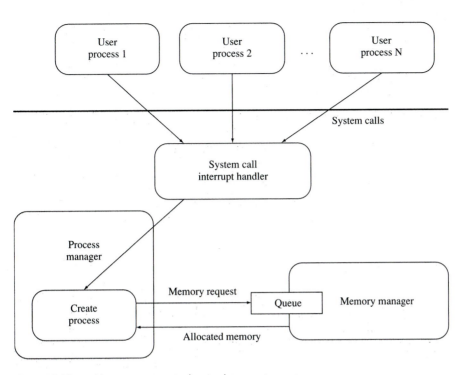

Figure 10.30   Memory requests in the simple operating system

The UNIX memory management system call is a good example to look at, since it has a very simple interface. When a process starts, it gets an initial allocation of memory. The highest memory address is called the "break" (for historical reasons). There is only one memory management system call. It requests that the value of the break be changed, that is, that the amount of memory allocated to the process be changed. This system call can be used to increase or decrease the amount of memory allocated to the process, but, in practice, in almost all cases an increase is requested.[9] Additional memory is added at the end of the previous memory allocation, so the user sees a larger address space.

The format of the system call is:[10]

```
int brk( char * addr );
```

This sets a new value for the break. It returns 0 on success and −1 on failure (if it could not allocate the memory).

---

[9]In fact, in UNIX, a process is not allowed to reduce its memory allocation below what it was initially allocated. It can, however, ask for more memory and later give it back.

[10]They used brk in UNIX instead of break because break is a reserved word in the C programming language.

As we see in Figure 10.31, the process's logical memory is divided up into five areas:

- *code*—the executable code created by the compiler.

- *static data*—data areas that are allocated when the program is loaded into memory and remain allocated the whole time the program is running. This includes both initialized and uninitialized data.

- *dynamic data*—data areas that are allocated during program execution via the `new` or `malloc` functions. Areas of this memory are allocated and freed during program execution. This is also called the *heap*.

- *unused address space*—free logical address space for use by either the dynamic data area or the stack area. This address space does not correspond to any physical memory.

- *stack*—the run time stack used by the programming language to hold procedure call stack frames.

The per-process memory manager allocates space to the running process from the dynamic data area. When the per-process memory manager runs out of dynamic data space, it expands the area by requesting more from the operating system. The stack can also grow during program execution by using more space in the unused logical address space.

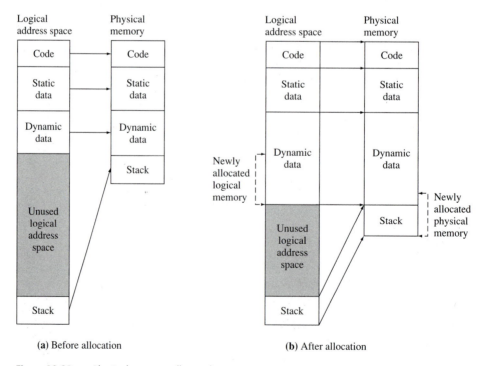

(a) Before allocation   **(b)** After allocation

Figure 10.31   Physical memory allocated to a running process

Figure 10.31 shows what happens when a process runs out of dynamic data space and needs to allocate more. These unused addresses form a reservoir of logical addresses to use for the newly added dynamic data area. This figure assumes a paging system (paging systems are discussed in Chapter 11), since this cannot be done with *base* and *bound* registers.

10.15.3 WHAT ABOUT **NEW** AND **MALLOC**?

Most programming languages allow dynamic memory allocation, that is, the programmer can request memory while the program is running. In C, the malloc library procedure is used, and in C++(and Pascal and Ada), the new construct is used. We have seen that dynamic memory allocation is handled by a memory manager that is part of the runtime control of the programming language. This memory manager acts as a middleman since it gets large blocks of memory from the operating system and then doles it out in smaller chunks to satisfy dynamic memory requests. The local memory manager in the process has a much harder job than the operating system memory manager since it gets many more requests for much smaller chunks of memory so the management problems are greater. An active program might make thousands or tens of thousands of dynamic memory requests a second, and the average request size might be only 10 or 20 bytes.

It is appropriate that these requests are handled by a memory manager internal to the process, since you would not want to pay the overhead cost of a system call for so many small memory requests.

10.15.4 FREEING MEMORY AT EACH LEVEL

As we have seen, the operating system manages its memory, allocates it to processes, and, later, processes free the memory. When a process exits, all the memory it has been allocated is freed, but a process can also free memory while it is still running if it no longer needs the memory.

Within each process, there is another memory manager, the new/malloc memory manager, that manages the dynamic data area for the process. Figure 10.32 shows the two levels of memory managers.

The per-process memory manager only manages the dynamic data area. The programming language runtime procedures manage the stack. The code and static data areas do not change size as the program executes. For the rest of this section, we will refer to the per-process memory manager as the *malloc* memory manager, or just *malloc*.

The two levels of memory management do interact. When *malloc* runs out of memory, it asks the operating system for more. But what happens when you free memory from a program? This frees the memory to *malloc*, but not to the operating system. If an area of memory at the end of *malloc's* area all becomes free, malloc *could* decide to free that memory and return it to the operating system. Figure 10.33 shows a situation where there is a large free area at the end of the dynamic memory area.

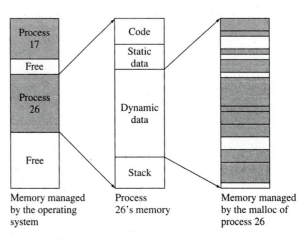

Figure 10.32   Two levels of memory management

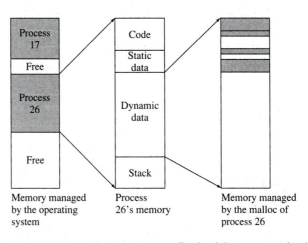

Figure 10.33   Free memory at malloc level, but not at OS level

In practice, however, very few, if any, per-process memory managers do this. The main problem is that the situation happens so seldom that it is not worth it to check for it. The free memory has to be at the end of the dynamic data area, and it has to be completely free. A single, small block near the end of the dynamic data area that is not free will prevent the entire area from being freed. So programs generally grow larger, but never grow smaller.

This effect is a consequence of our two levels of memory management. All design choices have advantages and disadvantages.

Remember, it is not that *malloc* cannot free memory, it is just that it probably will not. If you have a very long-running program that tends to allocate a lot of memory and then free it, you might want to have a custom memory manager for it that will free the memory back to the operating system when it is no longer being used. An example of a program like this would be an X server. If you load some fonts and bitmaps, they will take up memory. If you later unload them, the memory will not be returned to the operating system. The memory will be reused, of course, if you load some other fonts or bitmaps.

10.15.5   A Different Memory Management System Call

The UNIX *brk* system call was developed in a time when memory was always allocated in large contiguous blocks. In Chapter 11, we will see that modern memory management can easily deal with logical address spaces that are not contiguous. This allows us to use a more obvious system call for memory allocation. We can present the system call here, but you will have to wait until Chapter 11 to see how it could be implemented.

The format of our new memory allocation system call is:

```
char * AllocateMemory( int length );
```

This call allocates *length* bytes and returns the starting address of the the new memory. If the memory cannot be allocated, it returns an address of 0. This memory might not be contiguous with any other memory you have been allocated, so each block of memory you get is independent of all the other blocks.

This is certainly a more straightforward way to allocate memory. There is no need to move the stack or readjust any existing memory. Modern operating systems are more likely to have a memory allocation call like this.

*10.16   EXAMPLE CODE FOR MEMORY ALLOCATION

In this section, we will show some example code to explain in more detail how memory allocation in an operating system would be handled.

First, consider the data type and data object declarations. We need a queue (RequestList) of memory requests (struct MemoryRequest), which we will keep as a doubly linked list. It is initialized as an empty list. We also need a doubly linked list (BlockList) of blocks (struct Block).

The memory allocator is initialized (Initialize) by giving it a large chunk of memory to allocate. The block list starts out with one free block on it, which is the entire of chunk of memory that is being managed. Later requests will divide it up into smaller blocks.

MEMORY ALLOCATOR DATA

```
// The structure for memory requests
struct MemoryRequest {
    int size;           // in bytes
    Semaphore satisfied;    // signal when memory is allocated
    char ** startAddressSlot; // return block address to the caller here
    MemoryRequest *next, *prev; // doubly linked list
};

// The memory request list
```

```
// keep a front and back pointer for queue
MemoryRequest * RequestListFront, *RequestListBack;

// The structure for block list nodes
struct Block {
    int size;        // in bytes
    int isFree;        // free or allocated block
    char * start;      // where the block starts
    Block *next, *prev; // doubly linked list;
};

// The block list
Block * BlockList;

// The initialization procedure needs to be called before
// any requests are processed.
void Initialize( char * start, int size ) {
    RequestListFront = 0;
    BlockList = new Block(size, True, start, 0, 0);
}
```

The RequestABlock procedure is called to request a block of storage to be allocated. Along with the size of the request, the requester passes a semaphore for the memory allocator to signal when the request has been satisfied, and the address of a place to put the address of the allocated block.

MAKE AN ALLOCATION REQUEST

```
// The request procedure: request a block to be allocated
void RequestABlock( int size, Semaphore * satisfied,
    char ** startAddressSlot) {
    MemoryRequest * n = new MemoryRequest( size, satisfied,
    startAddressSlot, 0 , 0);
    if( RequestListFront == 0 ){ // list was empty
    RequestListFront = RequestListBack = n;
    } else {
    RequestListBack-> next = n;
    RequestListBack = n;
    }
    TryAllocating();
}
```

The TryAllocating procedure is called whenever something has changed that makes us believe a request might be able to be satisfied. It is called each time a new request comes in and each time a block of memory is freed. It looks through all the pending requests and checks if any of them can be allocated. If the request is allocated, then it is removed from the request queue.

TRY TO ALLOCATE TO A REQUEST

```
// The allocation procedure
void TryAllocating( void ) {
    MemoryRequest * request = RequestListFront;
    // look through the list of requests and satisfy any ones you can
    while( request != 0 ) {
        // can we allocate this one?
        if( CanAllocate( request ) { // yes we can
            // remove from the request list
            if( RequestListFront == RequestListBack ) {
                // it was the only request on the list
                // of the request list is now empty
                RequestListFront = 0;
                break; // no more requests
            } else {
                // unlink it from the list
                request->prev->next = request->next;
                request->next->prev = request->prev;
                MemoryRequest * oldreq = request; // save the address
                // get the link before we delete the node
                request = request->next;
                delete oldreq;
            }
        } else {
            request = request-> next;
        }
    }
}
```

The **CanAllocate** procedure checks to see if a specific request can be satisfied. It does this by looking through the block list for the first free block that is big enough. This is the *first-fit* algorithm.

If it finds a free block, it splits the free block up into an allocated block (to return to the requester) and a free block, which consists of the rest of the block that was not allocated. It passes back the location of the allocated block, and signals the semaphore to inform the requester that the request has been satisfied.

TRY TO ALLOCATE A BLOCK

```
// See if we allocate one request
int CanAllocate( MemoryRequest * request ) {
    int size = request->size;
    Block * p = BlockList;
    // go through the list of blocks
    while( p != 0 ) {
        if( p->size >= size ) {
            // this block is big enough to use, see what is left over
```

```
            int extra = p->size - size;
            if( extra != 0 ) {
                // split the block into two blocks
                Block * np = new Block;
                np->size = extra;
                np->isFree = True;
                np->start = p->start + size;
                np->prev = p;
                np->next = p->next;
                p->next->prev = np;
                p->next = np;
            }
            p->isFree = False;
            *(request->start) = p->start;
            SignalSemaphore( request->satisfied );
            return True;
        }
        p = p->next;
    }
    return False;
}
```

The **FreeBlock** procedure is called to free a block of memory after the requester has finished using it. It goes through the block list looking for the block (based on its start address). We merge free blocks with adjacent free blocks on either side, if possible.

FREE AN ALLOCATED BLOCK

```
// Free a block of memory
void FreeBlock( char * start ){
    Block * p = BlockList;
    // go through the list of blocks to find this one
    while( p != 0 ) {
        if( p->start == start ) {
            p->isFree = True;
            // merge with the next block( if it is free )
            Block * nextp = p->next;
            if( nextp != 0 && nextp->isFree ) {
                p->size += nextp->size;
                p->next = nextp->next;
                nextp->next->prev = p;
                delete nextp;
            }
            // merge with the previous block( if it is free )
            Block * prevp = p->prev;
            if( prevp != 0 && prevp->isFree ) {
                prevp->size += p->size;
                prevp->next = p->next;
```

```
            p->next->prev = prevp;
            delete p;
        }

        return;
    }
    p = p->next;
    }
// ERROR: returned block not found
}
```

10.17   SUMMARY

There are various ways to manage the memory resource in an operating system. Most processes do their own low-level memory management, and only rely on the operating system for allocating large chunks of memory. The study of memory management can be divided into two parts: the management of memory within a single process, and the management of memory between processes in an operating system.

A compiler generates an object module as the result of a compilation. Each object module is divided into a header, a machine code section, an initialized data section, an uninitialized data section, a symbol table, and a relocation section. Useful object modules are collected into libraries. A linker combines object modules and libraries into a load module that is ready to be loaded into the memory of a process. When a process is initiated, the run-time loader initializes the process's memory from the load module. The loading of library modules can be delayed until the process is executed (this is called load time dynamic linking). This saves disk space in storing the load module. The loading of library modules can be delayed until they are first used by the running process (this is called dynamic linking). This saves startup time and can sometimes avoid unnecessary loading.

Each process manages its own memory, and so must solve the general memory allocation problem. Static allocation of memory and static division of memory into fixed-size blocks does not work very well in general. The best solution is dynamic memory allocation. The basic algorithm is simple, but there are a number of design decisions to be made. You can keep a free list (the most common method) or use a bit map. You can keep the free list in a separate area or with the rest of the dynamically allocated memory. All dynamic memory allocation leads to fragmentation despite our best efforts to avoid it.

The dynamic allocation of more memory to running processes is important so that processes can efficiently use memory, but it makes memory management a little bit harder. The two levels of memory management (within a process and between processes) do not interact well, and, in particular, it is hard to free memory once it has been allocated at both levels.

10.17.1 TERMINOLOGY

After reading this chapter, you should be familiar with the following terms:

- best fit
- bitmap
- block list
- buddy system
- checkerboarding
- defined external symbol
- dynamic data
- dynamic memory allocation
- dynamic relocation
- external symbol
- first fit
- fragment
- fragmentation
- header section
- heap
- initialized data section
- library
- linker
- linking
- load module
- load time dynamic linking
- machine code section
- memory manager
- memory protection
- next fit
- object module
- powers-of-two allocation
- run time dynamic linking
- static data
- static relocation
- symbol table
- undefined external symbol
- uninitialized data section
- worst fit

10.17.2 REVIEW QUESTIONS

The following questions are answered in the text of this chapter:

1. Why are there two levels of memory management?
2. What are the two different kinds of external symbols and how do they differ?
3. Why do we distinguish between initialized and uninitialized data in an object module?
4. What is the purpose of the header section in an object module?
5. Describe the linking algorithm.
6. Describe the differences between linking and relocation.
7. Describe the format of a load module.
8. Describe the process of loading a load module for execution.
9. Give the relative advantages and disadvantages of load time dynamic linking and run time dynamic linking.
10. What is the dynamic memory allocation design problem?
11. What is the difference between powers-of-two allocation and the buddy system?
12. Give the advantages and disadvantages of keeping allocated blocks on the block list.
13. Compare the block list and bitmap methods of keeping track of free blocks.
14. What are the differences between first fit, next fit, best fit, and worst fit?
15. What is the difference between a logical address space and a physical address space?
16. Why is it better to allocate memory to processes dynamically?
17. Why is memory protection important in a multiprogramming system?
18. Compare the `brk` and `AllocateMemory` system calls described in the chapter.

10.17.3 FURTHER READING

See Korn and Vo (1985) for more information on new and more efficient `mallocs`. See Maccabe (1993, Ch. 10) and Stallings (1992, Appendix 5A) for more information on linking, loading, and object module formats. Knuth (1973) gives a derivation of the 50-percent rule and has a good discussion of dynamic memory allocation techniques. See Peterson and Norman (1977) for a complete discussion of buddy systems. More information about dynamic memory allocation can be found in Shore (1975, 1977), Bays (1977), and Beck (1977). Stephenson (1983) gives an improved version of first fit.

10.18   PROBLEMS

1. Give two reasons why every new or malloc request is not handled by a system call to the operating system instead of by a per-process memory manager.

2. Linking requires that we remember the places that need linking and do the linking once the symbol is defined. Describe the data structures that would be used to keep track of the information during the linking process and to make the links when the symbol is defined.

3. Consider the algorithm we gave for creating a load module. Modify this algorithm to reflect the fact that the code sections of all the object modules need to be loaded together, as do the initialized and uninitialized data sections.

4. Why do we want to keep the three sections (code, initialized data, and uninitialized data) separate in a load module?

5. Some systems guarantee that "uninitialized" data will be initialized to some value (usually zero). UNIX system do this. By "uninitialized," we then mean not initialized by the programmer. Other systems do not guarantee any initialization of this storage. Give arguments for and against both of these design choices.

6. Describe the object module format on a machine you use. Compile the C++ program in Figure 10.4 and look at the object module it produces. How does it differ from the example given in Figure 10.5?

7. A runtime loader usually reads the header of the load modules first, then it reads the rest of the load modules. Why does it do this? What does it do between the reading of the header and the reading of the rest of the load module?

8. What information must be kept about a load module after it is loaded if some parts of the load module will be dynamically loaded?

9. A linker must keep track of all references it sees to an external variable it sees until it sees the definition of the external variable. Then it must fill in the correct value for all the references. This involves going back to parts of the load module that have already been processed and patching them. The loader could do this in two ways: (1) it could thread a linked list through the places in the load module where the references themselves go; or (2) it could keep a linked list in its own memory of the location of all the references it needs to patch. Compare these two methods. What are the advantages and disadvantages of each one?

10. A linker will read library files and find modules that define external references that the linker has not found yet. Design a data layout for a library file that will facilitate this activity. Remember that a library is basically a collection of object modules. What tables and indexes, if any, will it have? Will these tables be at the beginning or end of the library file? How will they be sorted?

11. What is the purpose of the relocation information in the object module format? How might this information differ from architecture to architecture?

12. Often, different operating systems will run on the same hardware architecture. As an example, both UNIX and MS/DOS run on Intel 80x86 machines. Suppose we wanted to design a common object file format that would work for both operating systems. The idea is that a module compiled on one operating system could be run on the other. What are some of the problems you would encounter in doing this?

13. Suppose you keep a block list with both free and allocated blocks on it. What error checking would you do when a block is freed? Now suppose we only keep a record of free blocks. What error checking is possible when a block is freed?

14. Suppose we use a dynamic memory management scheme that requires 8 bytes per block in space overhead and requires 50 microseconds to respond to a request for memory. Suppose that the average request size is 256 Kbytes, and you get an average of 30 requests a second.

   a. What is the average space and time overhead for dynamic memory management?

   b. Now compute the average space and time overhead for dynamic memory management in a system where the average request is 40 bytes and you get an average of 2,000 memory requests a second.

   c. The first figures are more typical of the memory management demands on an operating system and the second are more typical of the memory management demands of a program doing a lot of dynamic memory allocation. What does this say about how each one should be designed?

15. Describe a dynamic memory management situation where you think the buddy system would perform very well, and one where you think it will perform very poorly.

16. Suppose you have 16 Mbytes of main memory. Using the list method, you have an overhead of eight bytes per memory block. Using the bitmap method, you use an allocation granularity of 128 bytes. How many blocks are there when the space overhead of both methods is the same? What is the average block size for this many blocks?

17. Suppose you were allocating 16 Mbytes (2^{24} bytes) of memory, and will use either bitmap allocation or list allocation. For the bitmap, you will use allocation units of 128 bytes (2^7 bytes, so there will be 2^{17} allocatable units). For the list system, you will thread the list through a block header at the beginning of each block (free or allocated). This header will take up 8 (2^3) bytes.

   Consider the situation where the average block allocated is 256 (2^8) bytes (some are larger and some are smaller, but the average is 256 bytes). Which method will use more storage for allocation system overhead, bitmap or list?

   Now consider the situation where the average block allocated is 64K bytes (2^{16} bytes). Which method will use more storage for allocation system overhead, bitmap or list?

   Show some figures (and explain them) to support each answer.

18. Write a program that allocates a block of memory dynamically every few seconds. Run it, and while it is running use an operating systems utility to look at how much memory it is using. Do this for various sizes of blocks. Report your results.

Hint: In C++, use new and delete, and in C, use malloc to allocate, say, 20,000 bytes at a time.

19. Write a program that allocates a lot of space, then deallocates it. Does the memory it uses go up and then down, or does it stay up? *Hint:* In C++, use new and delete, and in C, use malloc and free.

20. Give the advantages and disadvantages in using a doubly linked list for the free list.

21. Write a C++ subroutine that finds a block of *N* units in a memory allocation bitmap. Write a C++ subroutine that finds a block of *N* units of memory in a system that uses a free list and first fit. Compare the two procedures.

22. Explain why it is easy to dynamically allocate blocks of memory if all the blocks are the same size. Why don't we have to use a dynamic memory allocation algorithm in this case?

23. Describe a kind of operating system where it would be reasonable to assume that all processes were about the same size.

24. Why is the space allocated to a stack automatically increased when the stack overflows it? Why is there a limit to how much it can be increased altogether?

25. Describe an application that would be much easier to implement on a computer that used the lock/key form of memory protection than it would on a computer that used the *base/bound* register form of memory protection.

26. Design an extension of the lock/key method of memory protection that allows different protection for reading, writing, and executing in an area of memory. Can you think of a similar extension for the *base/bound* method of memory protection? Can it solve part of the problem, if not all of it?

27. Many modern OSs will dynamically load parts of the operating system. Give one example of a part of the operating system that would be a very good candidate for dynamic linking, and give one example of a part of the operating system that you would not want to dynamically load.

28. Consider the problem of dynamically loading operating system modules. What problems would you encounter? What would be the benefits of doing this?

29. Suppose you wanted to implement a per-process memory manager that returned excess unused space to the operating system. Say that, as soon as 75 percent of the dynamic memory was free, it would halve the size of the memory pool. What techniques would you use to accomplish this goal? How hard would it be? What kind of overhead would you incur?

30. Modify the code for memory allocation in Section 10.16 to use block headers at the beginning of each block rather than a separate list of block structures like it uses now.

31. Modify the code for memory allocation in Section 10.16 to use a next-fit algorithm rather than the first-fit algorithm it uses now.

32. Modify the code for memory allocation in Section 10.16 to use a best-fit algorithm rather than the first-fit algorithm it uses now.

11

Virtual Memory

In the last chapter, we looked at ways to allocate memory dynamically out of a pool of free memory. In this chapter, we will look at ways to divide a program into smaller pieces so they are easier to allocate and more programs will fit into memory at the same time. Then we will see how we can keep some of these small pieces on disk, and thereby fit even more program in memory at the same time.

11.1 FRAGMENTATION AND COMPACTION

compaction

There is a way to eliminate fragmentation after it occurs, and that method is called compacting storage, or *compaction*. You compact storage by moving all the allocated blocks to one end of storage to create one big block (see Figure 11.1). This eliminates all fragmentation, but it has one major problem: it is expensive to move all that memory around. With today's larger memories, compaction is even more expensive and less attractive.

11.2 DEALING WITH FRAGMENTATION

contiguous

We have observed that fragmentation is inevitable in dynamically allocated memory. What can we do to reduce the effects of fragmentation? The smaller the pieces we allocate, the easier it is to find space and the smaller the loss due to fragmentation. So far, we have assumed that a program runs in a big block of physical memory and that that memory was *contiguous*, that is, consisting of consecutive physical addresses. Compilers and linkers assume contiguous memory, but memory mapping has given

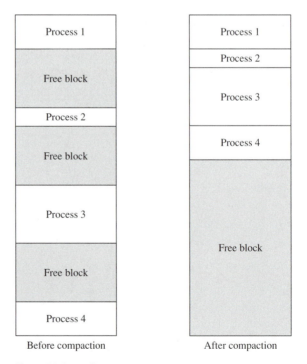

Before compaction   After compaction

Figure 11.1   Compacting memory

us some flexibility. We need the logical address space to be contiguous, but it is not necessary for the physical address space to be contiguous.

The operating system memory manager allocates physical memory space, not logical address space, so we can divide the program into several parts and put each part into a separate area in physical memory. Each part will be smaller and hence will fit into smaller free blocks, and so the effects of fragmentation will be reduced. We will need some hardware assistance to get this to work, but first we have to decide on what basis we will divide up the program into parts. We will provide a series of answers to this question.

11.2.1 SEPARATE CODE AND DATA SPACES

The processor knows when it is fetching an instruction and when it is fetching data (instruction addresses come from the program counter). So the processor can use two relocation registers, one for code addresses and one for data addresses. Figure 11.2 shows how the relocation works, and Figure 11.3 shows the two address spaces. This allows us to put the code and data parts of a program into two different blocks of physical memory, so it will be easier to find blocks that are large enough.

11.2.2 SEGMENTS

But what about programs where the data is much larger than the code, or the code is much larger than the data? In these cases, this split will not help much. Also, why stop at only two parts of the program? Why not more? This generalization is called *segmentation,* and Figure 11.4 shows how it would work with 16-bit addresses and four segments. In Figure 11.4, there are four segment registers, each with two parts:

segmentation

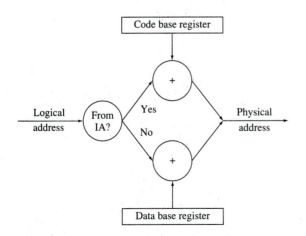

Figure 11.2   Memory relocation with separate code and data spaces

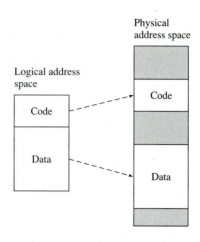

Physical
address space

Logical address
space

Code

Code

Data

Data

Figure 11.3 Separate code and
data spaces

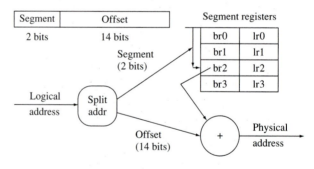

Segment	Offset
2 bits	14 bits

Segment registers

br0	lr0
br1	lr1
br2	lr2
br3	lr3

Segment
(2 bits)

Logical
address

Split
addr

Offset
(14 bits)

+

Physical
address

Figure 11.4 Four segments

segment register

bri is base register i and lri is length register i (where i is 0, 1, 2, or 3). The logical address is divided into two parts, a 2-bit segment number and a 14-bit offset within that segment. The segment number is used to choose one of the four relocation registers, called *segment registers*. A segment register contains a base register (which points to the beginning of the segment) and a length register (which records how long the segment is). Each segment register is, in effect, a *base* and *bound* register pair. The 14-bit offset part of the logical address is then added to the contents of the base register of the chosen segment register to get the physical address.

Segments need not be completely full, so the segment registers contain not only the base address of the segment but its length as well. When the segment is accessed, the offset is compared with the length of the segment, and, if the offset is larger (or equal), a segmentation fault is generated.

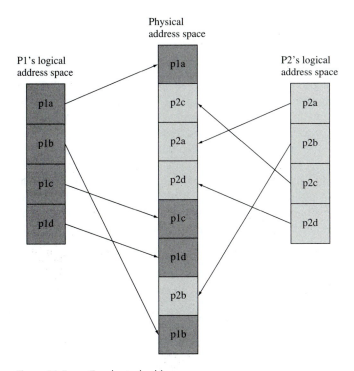

Figure 11.5   Two logical address spaces

This method has several advantages over the code/data split. First, we have divided the program into four pieces instead of just two, so each part will be that much smaller. Second, each piece can be the same size because the split is an arbitrary one by address, rather than being based on the content of the program (whether something is code or data).

Figure 11.5 shows the relationships between the three address spaces (two logical and one physical) and the two address maps. Process 1 and Process 2 each have an address space which is mapped into parts of the physical address space. Each logical address space is contiguous, but its image in the physical address space is not contiguous. The address map is defined by the values of the four base registers.

This method can be easily generalized to larger numbers of segments. The legendary DEC PDP11 used this method with 16-bit addresses and eight segments. This divided the 64K address space into eight 8K segments. Later, PDP11s also used a code/data split to get 16 8K segments. This was done, however, to increase the size of the logical address space rather than to improve memory allocation.

The logical memory of a process should be contiguous. The physical memory of a process does not need to be.

11.2.3 NONCONTIGUOUS LOGICAL ADDRESS SPACES

Segment systems always use base registers and limit registers in pairs, and hence allow segments of varying size. In Figure 11.5, we show each of Process 1 and Process 2 using the entire 16-bit (64K) address space. Suppose that a program was only 24K long. We could pack this into one full-length 16K segment and one half-length 8K segment. This would break the program up into two parts, and the logical address space would still be contiguous. See Figure 11.6.

But there are many other ways we could break up the program. We could break it up into four 6K pieces, and put one in each of the four segments. (See Figure 11.7.) Then we would only have to find four 6K free blocks instead of a 16K and an 8K free block, and it is easier to find small free blocks. But this would mean that the logical address space would no longer be contiguous. The table below shows the base and limit registers and the range of logical addresses that is mapped by each of the four segments.[1]

Segment	Base	Limit	Logical Addresses
0	100K	6K	0–6K
1	194K	6K	16K–22K
2	132K	6K	32K–38K
3	240K	6K	48K–54K

If a logical address of, say, 8K is generated, the two high-order bits (00) will place it in the first segment, but the 14 low-order bits will be larger than the limit register and so the address will be flagged as illegal by the memory mapping hardware. This is true of all logical addresses in the ranges 6K–16K, 22K–32K, 38K–48K, and 54K–64K. This is what we mean by the logical address space being noncontiguous— there are holes in the logical address space.

Unfortunately, it is unlikely that this kind of mapping will work if we use typical compilers and linkers. Compilers and linkers assume that the logical address space is contiguous, and are not set up to deal with gaps in the address space. Now it is possible that these tools could be modified to handle noncontiguous address spaces, but it would be a lot of work and extra complication. It is possible to use noncontiguous address spaces for dynamically allocated storage. We will discuss this more in Section 12.13.9.

So we are really not free to split up the program into pieces that are evenly distributed across the segments, but we must first fill up segment 0, then fill up segment 1, and so on. For a 16 bit (64K) address space, this is not a problem, since the 16K pieces are fairly small and most programs are larger than 16K. But suppose we want to move to a 32-bit (4Gbyte) address space and still use four seg-

[1]The base register values are chosen arbitrarily.

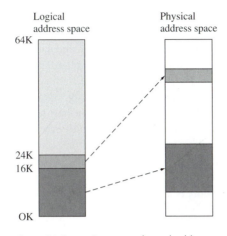

Figure 11.6   Contiguous logical address
spaces (uses two segments)

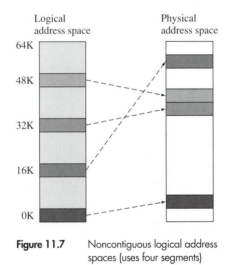

Figure 11.7   Noncontiguous logical address
spaces (uses four segments)

ments. Each segment would be 1 Gbyte of memory. Very few programs would fill up even one segment, and so the segmentation hardware would be essentially unused and no benefits would be gained from it.

Since we know the computer industry is moving to larger and larger address spaces, the only solution to the problem is to have much smaller segments that we can fill up completely (and many more of them, of course). But if we are going to fill up each segment, what do we need the length registers for? The answer is that we don't. We will call this new fixed-size segment a "page." The next step in breaking up our program into smaller pieces is to go from segments to pages.

11.2.4   PAGE TABLES IN HARDWARE REGISTERS

A segment has a base register and a length register, and can be any length from 0 up to some maximum. A *page* has a base register, but the page has a fixed length and so it does not need a length register. Thus pages are fixed-length segments. A *page table entry* (*PTE*) is a word of information about one page. A *page table* is a collection of page table entries. So far, our page table entries contain only the base address of the page frame that holds the page, but later we will see that a page table entry has other fields as well.

Let's look at an example so we understand this idea more easily. Suppose the logical address is 16 bits long. We will divide this up into 4 bits of page number and 12 bits of offset into the page. This provides 16 pages of 4Kbytes each. Figure 11.8 shows how the logical address is handled by the memory-mapping hardware.

With base/limit memory mapping, we had two hardware registers: a base register and a limit register. With our four-segment system, we had eight hardware registers: four segment base registers and four segment limit registers. With this paging system, we have 16 hardware registers: the 16 page base registers. Each time we switch between processes, we have to save the registers of the old process and load the registers of the new process.

Our original hardware had 2 memory management registers and 34 other registers to save and restore. With this paging system, there would be 16 memory management

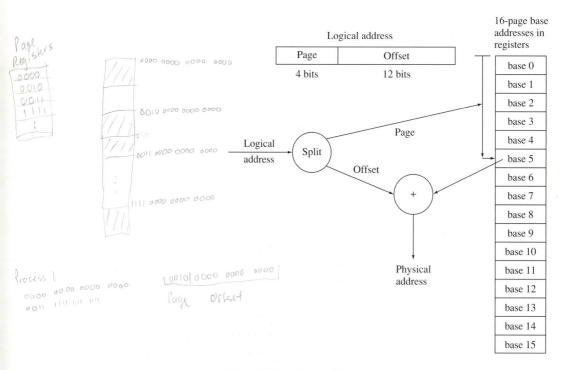

Figure 11.8   Page table in registers

registers. This is still a reasonable number, but if we are going to have very many more pages, then this will get to be an intolerable overhead on process switching.

For example, suppose we kept the 4K pages and decided to expand to a 20-bit (1 Mbyte) address space. This would require 256 page base registers. The hardware cost of providing 256 more fast registers is actually fairly small. The more significant cost is 512 memory accesses (256 stores of the old page registers and 256 loads of the new page registers) for every process switch.

11.2.5   PAGE TABLES IN MEMORY

We have to find some method of reducing the number of registers that we need to save and restore on a context switch. One solution is to store the page base addresses in main memory. We allocate 256 words of memory, and keep the page base addresses there. Page information in memory is also called a *page table*. Now we only need one hardware register—a page table base register which tells us where in memory to find the page table. Figure 11.9 shows how this changes the mapping. The only differences are the addition of the page table base register and the moving of the page table to memory. Figure 11.10 is a different view of the mechanisms of paging.

Suppose we extend our logical address space to 22 bits (4 Mbytes) and divide it into 10 bits of page number and 12 bits of offset into the page. This keeps the 4 Kbyte

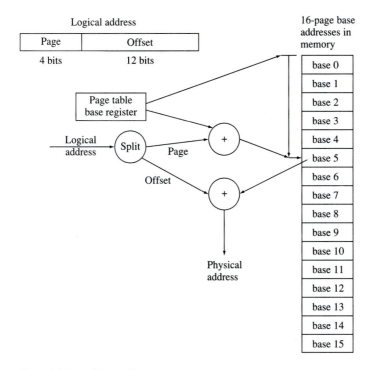

Figure 11.9   Page table in memory

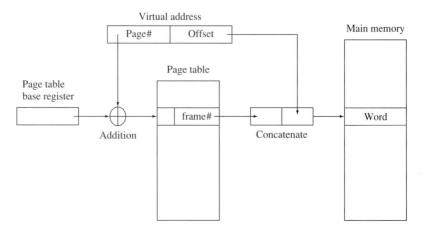

Figure 11.10   Another view of paging

pages we have been using, and makes the page table 1K entries long. Since each page table entry will be 32 bits (4 bytes), that means the page table will be exactly one page long also, which makes things neat and tidy.

What if a program does not take up the whole address space? Then some of the pages will not be needed. To handle this case, we can add one more hardware register, a page table length register, which records the number of valid pages in the page table. So a program must be an even multiple of 4K long, but it can be any length from 4K to 4M in 4K increments.

11.2.6   USING A PAGE TABLE CACHE

Putting the page tables in memory allows us to have page tables as large as we want without having to save and restore large numbers of registers. This means that switching processes will not be inefficient. Putting the page table in memory solves the slow context switching problem, but it causes a new problem, and that is an extra memory fetch on every memory access. Each time the program sends out a logical address, it will require a memory cycle, either a read or a write. But with the page table in memory, each memory read (writes are similar) will require one memory cycle to read the page base address from the page table in memory, and another memory cycle to read the word itself. Suddenly, we have doubled the number of memory cycles required. Since memory cycles are already the bottleneck in almost all programs, we have effectively halved the speed of execution of a program.

Clearly we cannot tolerate such a reduction in processing speed, so we must figure out a solution to this problem. The only way to avoid having to read the page base addresses from memory is to keep them in registers, so we will use the technique of caching.

The idea is that we keep, in processor registers, the last few page base addresses that we have looked up in the page table. Figure 11.11 shows a flow chart for caching of page table entries. The algorithm in C++ is shown in Figure 11.12. The hardware

Logical address

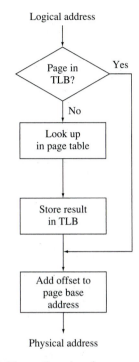

Physical address

Figure 11.11   Flow chart for paging with a TLB

will search the page table cache in parallel using associative registers, and so this operation is very fast. This cache is usually called a *translation lookaside buffer,* or *TLB.*

Figure 11.13 shows a block diagram of the TLB lookup. The page part of the logical address is isolated and used in two places. It is used to do a hardware parallel (hence very fast) search in the TLB to see if the page table entry (PTE) for this page is in the TLB. If so, then that PTE is used, and no memory fetch is required to get it. If the TLB search fails, then the PTE is fetched from the page table in memory. In that case, the newly fetched PTE is kept in the TLB (and some other TLB entry is evicted). In either case, the page base address is taken from the PTE and used to compute the physical address.

But suppose there are 256 pages and only 8 page cache entries. It would seem that we would find the page in the cache only $8/256 = 1/32$ or 3 percent of the time. But this is not generally the case. The fact is that most programs exhibit a high degree of locality. By *locality,* we mean that programs don't just jump all around their address space randomly, but rather they tend to concentrate in small areas of the program at a time. This might be a program loop, or some data that they are using heavily. The program code and data references tend to cluster around a few pages for a while, then they might move on to another few pages, and so on. The result is that only a few pages are in use at a time, and once they are loaded into the page table cache, you usually find the PTE on the cache.

translation lookaside buffer
(TLB)

locality

```
const int PageTableCacheSize = 8;
const int pageSizeShift = 12;
const int pageSizeMask = 0xFFF;

struct CacheEntry {
  int logicalPageAddress;
  int pageBaseAddress;
} PageTableCache[PageTableCacheSize];

extern int pageTableBaseRegister;
int LeastRecentlyUsedCacheSlot( void );

int LogicalToPhysical( int logicalAddress ) {
  int i;
  int logicalPageAddress = logicalAddress & ~pageSizeMask;
  // first see if this page is in the cache
  for( i = 0; i < PageTableCacheSize; ++i ) {
    // in the hardware, this lookup is done in parallel
    if( PageTableCache[i].logicalPageAddress == logicalPageAddress )
    return PageTableCache[i].pageBaseAddress;
  }
  // if not found in the cache we have to look it up in memory
  // first compute the address of the page table entry
  int pteAddress = pageTableBaseRegister
      + (logicalAddress >> pageSizeShift);
  // then fetch the page base address from the page table
  int pageBaseAddress = MemoryFetch( pteAddress );
  // now update the cache by replacing the entry that has not been
  // used in the longest time (the least recently used one)
  // with this new entry
  i = LeastRecentlyUsedCacheSlot();
  PageTableCache[i].logicalPageAddress = logicalPageAddress;
  PageTableCache[i].pageBaseAddress = pageBaseAddress;
  // and then return the physical address of the page
  return pageBaseAddress;
}
```

Figure 11.12   Caching the page table entries

cache hit
cache miss
cache hit rate

     Each time the page base register is found in the cache, we call it a *cache hit*. If it is not in the cache we call it a *cache miss*. The *cache hit rate* is the percentage of times we get a cache hit, so if the cache hit rate is 90 percent, then 9 memory accesses out of 10 we find the page base address in the cache. Thus the effective memory access time is $0.9 * 1 + 0.1 * 2 = 1.1$. In other words, the average memory access takes 1.1 memory cycles, so our effective slowdown is 10 percent, which is probably acceptable.

     We need to be sure to invalidate the cache when we change processes, since we will be entering a new logical address space and all the logical addresses will refer to different physical pages. The hardware does not normally keep an address space identifier in the page cache, and depends on the operating system to invalidate the cache when it does a process switch. Some modern memory management

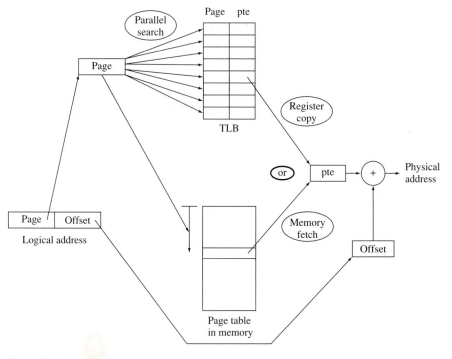

Figure 11.13   TLB lookup

chips actually do keep the address space numbers in their cache, and do not require invalidating the cache. This is especially useful for very large caches where entries might stay valid across several context switches.

Let's review what we did here. We found that it was too expensive (in context switch time) to keep the page table in hardware registers. When we moved the page table into memory, we found that it was too expensive (in extra memory cycles), so we moved some of the page table back into registers. But, we did not move all of the page table back into registers, only a small portion of it, and locality ensured that the effective memory access time was acceptable. The TLB is still a source of inefficiency in context switching, and modern processors have other techniques to deal with that problem.

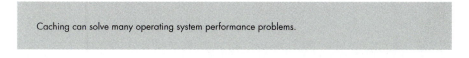

Caching can solve many operating system performance problems.

11.2.7   ANALYSIS MODELS OF PAGING WITH CACHING

Suppose we are going through a large array that covers several hundred pages, and that each page has 1024 array words in it (4 K byte pages). The first word of each page will cause a page cache miss, but the next 1023 words will have their page table entry in the cache. So over the 1024 words fetched, 1 will require two memory cycles (since we have to look up the page table entry), and 1023 will require only one memory cycle (since the page table entry will be in the cache). This totals to 1025 memory cycles to fetch 1024 words, or 1.001 memory cycles per word fetched, that is, about one-tenth of one percent speed decrease.

This is not even the best case, either, since a program loop will access the same code many times, and often access the same variables (such as the loop counter or an accumulator) many times also. So the overhead for keeping the page table in memory (as opposed to registers) is very low.

Let's try to think of the worst case. Suppose you have a program loop that accesses an array in a way such that each reference is to a new page. We will assume the entire code loop stays in the instruction cache memory and does not require any memory references. Each array reference will cause a TLB miss and require a page table lookup. Thus the effective memory access time will be doubled. Clearly this is a large slowdown, but the worst case will not occur that often. Figure 11.14 shows the worst and best cases for array access.

An important point here is that memory layout is an important factor in program performance. Modern computer systems are highly optimized with many caches. These caches generally assume good hit rates and high program locality. Programs that do not have high cache hit rates will still work, but can be several times slower than expected. When we start looking at virtual memory in the next chapter, we will see cases where program performance can be hundreds of times slower because of unexpectedly low hit rates.

11.2.8   MEMORY ALLOCATION WITH PAGING

Each program is divided up into pages, and each page is the same size, so memory management becomes almost trivial. All pages are the same size, and all programs will be allocated an integral number of pages. The extra bytes left over at the end of the last page are left unused. Physical memory is divided up into blocks of memory, called *page frames,* that can hold a page. A page frame is the size of a page, and is always at an even page boundary. For example, if the pages are 4K, then the page frames are at physical addresses 0, 4K, 8K, 12K, 16K, 20K, etc.

page frame

The advantage of paging is that a page can go into *any* page frame. All we have to do is set the base address in the page table. This means that memory is divided into a bunch of fixed-size blocks that are all the same. So memory management consists of keeping a list of the free page frames, handing them out when a page frame is requested, and putting them back on the list when a page frame is freed.

DESIGN TECHNIQUE: SIMPLE ANALYTIC MODELS

We did some simple calculations to determine the cost of paging with and without a TLB, and found that we needed a TLB with a 90 percent or better hit rate. We will do some calculations on page faults, and determine that we need a 99.9999 percent hit rate on page references. These simple models help us determine goals for our designs. Simple analytic models are useful in other parts of operating systems and computer science. To learn more about the use of simple analytic models, see Section 13.5.

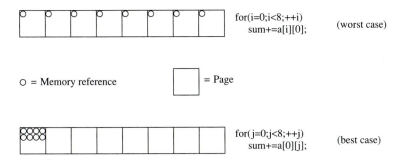

Figure 11.14   Worst and best cases for paging of array accesses

There is apparently no fragmentation at all, since all blocks are of fixed size, but this is a bit of an illusion. A problem that comes up with pages is *internal fragmentation,* that is, the wasted space at the end of the last page of a program. Pages tend to be smaller than segments to reduce internal fragmentation. internal fragmentation

The fragmentation in dynamic memory allocation is called *external fragmentation* since the fragments are external to the memory allocated to processes. The wasted space at the end of a program in a paging system is internal to the memory allocated to the program, and so this is called internal fragmentation. external fragmentation

Figure 11.15 shows internal and external fragmentation. When you allocate blocks of memory, then the holes in between are the external fragments. With paging, all the memory is allocated, but the last page of a process might not be filled and that creates internal fragments. This means that the amount of the internal fragmentation is fixed by the page size, and so goes down as a percentage of program size as programs get bigger. External fragmentation, on the other hand, tends to be a fixed percentage of the memory allocated.

11.2.9   TERMINOLOGY: PAGE AND PAGE FRAME

It is important to understand the distinction we are making between pages and page frames. A page is 4 Kbytes (or 1 Kbyte, or whatever the page size) of information. It is the same page whether it is stored on disk or in memory, since the page is the information, not the medium that holds the information. A page frame is 4K of physically contiguous bytes that start on an even 4K boundary, no matter what the content of that memory. A page frame is a container for a page.

> Pages are logical entities that contain information. Page frames are physical entities that contain pages.

11.2.10   PAGE TABLES

We have taken a simplified view of page tables so far, and viewed them as simply an array in memory of page base addresses. Actual page tables contain more information

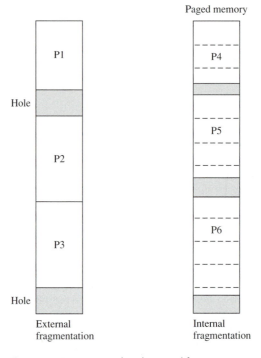

Figure 11.15 Internal and external fragmentation

about the page than the base address. A typical page table entry (see Figure 11.16) contains the base address where the page is located in memory and a *protection field* which describes the allowed uses of the page.

protection field

The base address always ends with a string of 0 bits, since page frames begin at multiples of the page size. It is not really necessary to store these zeros, because the hardware can put them back on when it uses the page table entry. So if we have, for example, 32-bit physical addresses and 12-bit page offsets (4K pages), then the page base address need only be 20 bits long. Figure 11.16 illustrates this idea.

The protection field tells how the page can be validly used. For example, there might be three bits in the protection field:

- *bit 0*—The page can be read.
- *bit 1*—The page can be written.
- *bit 2*—The page can be executed.

This allows eight possible protection values:

- *000*—The page cannot be used for any purpose.
- *001*—The page can only be read. This is used for read-only data.
- *010*—The page can only be written.
- *011*—The page can be read or written. This will detect invalid jumps into read-write data.

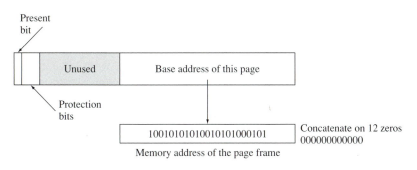

Figure 11.16 Page table entry

- *100*—The page can only be executed. This will detect code being used as data.
- *101*—The page can be read or executed. This will prevent the code from being written.
- *110*—The page can be written or executed. This is not likely to be used.
- *111*—The page can be read, written, or executed. This means there is no protection at all.

The protection information is a bonus we get from paging that allows extra hardware protection for the program. With page protection fields, it is not possible to write into the instruction area. Since the instructions are usually loaded first in memory, they occupy the low addresses, and those pages are set to execute only. This tends to find the use of 0-valued pointers (uninitialized pointers often have a value zero). It is also possible to ensure that constants are not written over by marking the pages they are in as read-only.

In Section 11.7.1, we will talk about the use of the "present" bit (but we will bet that you can guess what it is used for).

11.2.11 PAGING SUMMARY

With paging, the process sees a contiguous, linear address space that is easy to work with. The paging is transparent to the process in that the process does not have to do anything different than it would in a nonpaged system. The physical memory is divided up into a large number of small chunks (page frames) that are all the same size. These are simple to manage because no dynamic memory allocation (as described in Section 10.4 and following sections) is required, there is no external fragmentation, and everything fits in fixed-size slots.

Memory management has been made much easier. But we have had to get considerable hardware help to achieve this end.

We have done as much as we can with sharing memory space. If we want to increase the efficiency of memory use, we have to think about preempting memory like we did the processor, and that is what we will do in the next few sections.

Paging eliminates external fragmentation and the need to do dynamic memory allocation.

DESIGN TECHNIQUE: THE DESIGN PROCESS

Our presentation of the development of paging shows a typical example of a design process. Our initial goal was to ameliorate the effects of fragmentation. We went through a series of steps; each one solved a part of the problem, but caused another problem.

One does not generally arrive at a solution to a design problem in a single step. Instead, you go through a series of attempts, none of which quite work, but some of which have the seeds of the eventual solution. This is why it is recommended that you have a brainstorming stage during the initial stages of problem solving. It is important to come up with as many ideas as possible, even if some of them seem to be fatally flawed. Usually these solutions *are* fatally flawed, but some variant of them may not be.

Do not worry if your first solutions do not work. This is to be expected. Each solution that does not work teaches you a little more about the problem and helps you understand it a little better. Plan to iterate on solutions.

Iteration is a natural and necessary part of design.

*11.3   MEMORY ALLOCATION CODE WITH PAGES

In this section, we will redo the memory allocation code from the previous chapter, but with pages to show how much simpler memory allocation is when you have fixed-size pages instead of variable-sized segments.

The memory request structure is almost the same, except we keep the address of an array in which to put the base addresses of the pages allocated. The block list becomes a list of free pages. Initially, all the pages are in the free page list.

PAGED MEMORY ALLOCATOR: DATA

```
const int PageSize = 4096;

// The structure for memory requests
struct MemoryRequest {
    int npages;      // size of the request in pages
    Semaphore satisfied;    // signal when memory is allocated
    int * pageTableArray; // store page numbers here
    MemoryRequest *next, *prev; // doubly linked list
};

// The memory request list
// keeps a front and back pointer for queue discipline
MemoryRequest * RequestListFront, *RequestListBack;

// The structure for the free page list
struct FreePage {
    int pageNumber;
```

```
    FreePage *next;
};
// The free page list
FreePage * FreePageList;
int NumberOfFreePages;

// The initialization procedure needs to be called before
// any requests are processed.
void Initialize( int npages ) {
    RequestListFront = 0;
    NumberOfFreePages = npages;
    FreePageList = 0;
    // put all the pages on the free page list
    for( int i = 0; i < NumberOfFreePages; ++i ) {
        FreePageList = new FreePage( i, FreePageList );
    }
}
```

Memory requests are handled nearly the same way as before.

PAGED MEMORY ALLOCATOR: TRYALLOCATING

```
// The request procedure: request a block to be allocated
void RequestBlock( int npages, Semaphore * satisfied,
        int * pageTableArray ) {
    MemoryRequest * n = new MemoryRequest( npages, satisfied,
        pageTableArray, 0 , 0);
    if( RequestListFront == 0 ) {// list was empty
        RequestListFront = RequestListBack = n;
    } else {
        RequestListBack->next = n;
        RequestListBack = n;
    }
    TryAllocating();
}

// The allocation procedure
void TryAllocating( void ) {
    MemoryRequest * request = RequestListFront;
    // look through the list of requests and satisfy any ones you can
    while( request != 0 ) {
        // can we allocate this one?
        if( CanAllocate( request )  {// yes we can
            // remove from the request list
            if( RequestListFront == RequestListBack ) {
                // it was the only request on the list
                // of the request list is now empty
                RequestListFront = 0;
                // make sure we drop out of the loop
                request = 0;
            } else {
                // unlink it from the list
```

```
                    request->prev->next = request->next;
                    request->next->prev = request->prev;
                    MemoryRequest * oldreq = request; // save the address
                    // get the link before we delete the node
                    request = request->next;
                    delete oldreq;
                }
            } else {
                request = request->next;
            }
        }
    }
}
```

We free a page table by freeing each page.

PAGED MEMORY ALLOCATOR: FREEPAGES

```
// Free a set of pages
void FreePages( int npages, int pageTable[] ) {
    for( int i = 0; i < npages; ++i ) {
        FreePageList = new FreePage( pageTable[i], FreePageList );
    }
}
```

We allocate a request if there are enough free pages for it. We take the free pages off the free page list.

PAGED MEMORY ALLOCATOR: CANALLOCATE

```
// See if we allocate one request
int CanAllocate( MemoryRequest * request ) {
    if( request->npages >= NumberOfFreePages ){
        NumberOfFreePages -= request->npages;
        int * p = request->pageTableArray;
        for( int i = 0; i < request->npages; ++i ) {
            *p++ = FreePageList->pageNumber;
            FreePage * fpl = FreePageList;
            FreePageList = FreePageList->next;
            delete fpl;
        }
        return True;
    }
    return False;
}
```

*11.4   SHARING THE PROCESSOR AND SHARING MEMORY

In previous chapters, we have examined the processor resource as the primary *time resource* in a computer system. The processor is a serially reusable resource, that is, the processor can only be used by one process at a time. But the processor can be switched between processes rapidly and cheaply. This is called time-multiplexing. Managing a time-multiplexed resource only involves scheduling decisions, since keeping track of the resource is easy: you just remember who has it currently.

time resource

Memory, on the other hand, is a *space resource* that can be divided up into pieces and shared between several processes at the same time. This is called space multiplexing.

space resource

Of course, a space resource can also be time multiplexed. For example, a hotel is divided into rooms and can have a number of guests at one time, each in their own room (space multiplexing). (See Figure 11.17.) A guest in the bridal suite might be moved to another room when a newlywed couple comes to stay, and moved back in again when they have left (time multiplexing).

A space resource is more complicated to manage than a time resource, since both time and space multiplexing are possible with a space resource. In the last chapter, we looked at various techniques for sharing memory between processes, that is, space multiplexing of memory. But memory can also be time multiplexed, just like a processor. We preempt a processor by saving the processor state into memory. The state of memory is its contents. We preempt memory by saving the memory contents onto disk. In this chapter, we will look at techniques for time-multiplexing memory. We will start with the historical methods of swapping and overlays to set the scene, and then discuss the main topic of this chapter, virtual memory.

> Memory can be both time multiplexed and space multiplexed

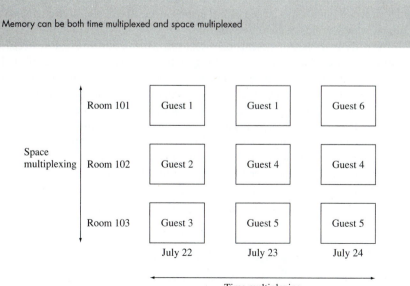

Figure 11.17   Time and space multiplexing of hotel rooms

DESIGN TECHNIQUE: MULTIPLEXING

Time and space multiplexing in general was discussed in Section 1.2.2., time multiplexing of the processor was discussed in Chapter 5, space multiplexing of memory was discussed in Chapter 10, and time multiplexing of memory was discussed in this chapter.

Multiplexing is common wherever resources are shared and used for multiple purposes. For example, we use time and space multiplexing when we use windows on the display screen.

For more discussion of multiplexing, see Section 13.1.

---

*11.5   SWAPPING

The first operating systems were batch systems that ran only one program at a time. The memories at the time were so small that it was not practical to have more than one program in memory at a time. But soon people starting thinking about time-sharing systems, and it became desirable to run more than one program at a time. Since it was not possible to fit more than one program in memory at the same time, it was necessary to time-multiplex the memory. Here is how they did it.

A program would be running and interacting with a user at a terminal. After that user's time allotment was up, the entire program was written out to secondary memory (tape or disk), and another user's program would be read back in from secondary memory. Then that user would run for a while. (See Figure 11.18.) This mechanism is called *swapping* because one process was "swapped" (exchanged) with another. It is really quite fast to write a job out and read another job in (a fraction of a second), and so this system works quite well. The first time-sharing system was CTSS at MIT, and it swapped out to tapes. Once disks became more affordable, swapping was done to disks, which are faster and more flexible.

The early time-sharing systems only kept one job at a time in memory because of memory limitations, but as memories got bigger, time-sharing systems were able to keep several programs in memory at the same time. Swapping was still used, however, since it increased the number of users that the system could handle. Interactive users are very slow, by computer standards, and very *bursty*, that is, they type for a while and then think for a while. Interactive users typically do not use a lot of processor time (many of them are editing, which is not computationally intensive), so you can serve a lot of them at a time.

At any one time, most of the users' programs are swapped out to disk. The main memory contains only the currently active users. When a user whose program is swapped out requests service (by typing something on the terminal), another user's program is swapped out and that user's program is swapped in.

swapping

bursty

Swapping allows you to keep the most useful processes in memory.

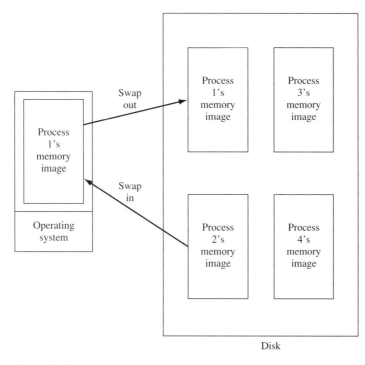

Figure 11.18   Swapping

11.5.1 EFFICIENT RESOURCE USE AND USER NEEDS

In swapping, we see an example of a technique that sacrifices efficient resource use to meet the needs of the users. Swapping jobs in and out of memory takes up resources without actually causing programs to progress, and so is not really an efficient use of resources. A batch system is more efficient in terms of use of the computer resources. However, users like interactive systems and feel it is worth it to sacrifice efficiency for convenience.

The history of operating systems has shown a steady trend away from a concentration on efficient resource use and towards ease of use. Today's workstations devote a tremendous amount of their resources to graphical user interfaces that are there because users like them. The concentration is on the efficiency of the human's resources, not the computer's resources.

There is another way to look at this which might be more illuminating. There are two important activities in the history of operating system design. The first is a continuous increase in services to the user. Operating system designers are always looking for new services they can provide that will help their users program and use applications. Once the desired functionality is settled, then the operating system designer tries to implement this functionality as efficiently as possible. As the services to users have gotten more elaborate, they have also gotten more resource-intensive to implement, and efficient implementation has remained very important.

DESIGN TECHNIQUE: PERSISTENT OBJECTS

Swapping pretty much requires dynamic relocation of processes. When a job is swapped out and later swapped in, it might be swapped into a different place in memory than where it was when it was swapped out.

What about extending the idea of swapping to data structures instead of entire programs? For example, suppose you had a large graph implemented as a linked structure. Each node in the graph is a C++ structure or class and is the linked list of arc nodes. Each arc node points to another node. Such a data structure can be used to represent general graphs with any number of outgoing and incoming arcs. Such a structure is also filled with pointers.

Suppose we were dealing with a large number of such graphs, and we wanted to be able to write them out to disk and read them in again later. Suppose we took the naive approach and just wrote out the nodes to disk, and then, later, read them in again. Well, unless we read each node into exactly the same place as it was before, the pointers would be all wrong. It is a bad idea to write pointers out to disk in any case.

Also, if we wanted to write out such a graph from one program and read it into another, there is very little possibility that the pointers will remain correct after doing this.

How can we be more clever about this? Well, one way is to convert the graph into a more portable form when we write it out. We can convert pointers into unique character string names, and write out pointers as strings. When we read the graph in again, we have to convert those strings back into pointers. This requires keeping a map of strings to pointers. This approach will work, but it involves a lot of processing.

Another strategy would be to use the technique used to relocate whole programs. In a program, every address is relocated with a relocation register. In the data structure, all addresses could be offsets from a base pointer that is some address below all the pointers in the graph. Each address in the graph would have to be relocated before use by adding in the base pointer. This would involve some inefficiency because we will not be able to rely on the hardware to do it for us.

But it would be very easy to relocate such a graph. We would write out the graph with just the offsets. When we read it in again, we would just have to set the one base register, and the entire graph would be relocated.

We could achieve this same effect by implementing the graph using an array of structures. Then all pointers are really array indices, and the entire array can be written out to disk and read in again later. The disadvantage of this approach is that we have to allocate the whole array at once and in contiguous storage.

We bring up this discussion since it relates to an issue that is assuming greater importance as object-oriented programming becomes more popular. This is the issue of **persistence** of objects. Normal data structures only exist as long as the program that defines and manipulates them exists. If you define a binary tree in a program, that tree goes away when the program exits. If you want to save any information, it must be saved as a file in the file system. Normally, the file system is the only means of persistent storage in the computer system.

But now databases also provide persistent storage of data, and, with the increase in interest in object-oriented programming, there has been an increase in interest in object-oriented databases. Now a true object-oriented database would allow you to store objects. But objects contain data and, usually, pointers. For example, a graph might be an object. Therefore, we have to find a way to store these data structures on persistent storage, and read them back in again later. Using the relocation technique would allow this to be done efficiently. This is an example of applying the relocation idea in another context.

persista

The important point to understand is that efficiency is not the most important criterion for what services to offer, but it is a very important criterion in deciding how to implement those services.

> User needs are the primary concern in designing what operating system services to offer. Efficiency is the primary concern in designing how to implement operating system services.

DESIGN TECHNIQUE: MULTIPLE DESIGN GOALS

We decided that we wanted to provide user processes with large virtual address spaces, and then we went to a lot of trouble trying to implement them efficiently.

All design projects have two steps, the design of the interface and the design of the implementation. The interface determines what functionality the system will have, and the implementation determines a good structure to implement that functionality.

When we are designing the interface, our primary duty is to the users of the interface. We want to make the interface as convenient to use as possible. We look at user needs and try to meet them. Once the functionality has been decided upon, we start designing the implementation. In this stage, our duty is to design as efficient an implementation as possible.

There are several caveats we have to add to this idealized view of design. First, "efficiency" is not a single concept. In implementing an interface, we might be concerned with any or all of the following forms of efficiency:

- How much space the programs uses.
- How much processor time the program uses.
- How much engineering time the development takes.
- How much computer time the development takes.

- How expensive it is to make changes in the product after it is delivered.
- How much delay there is until the product is ready.

In fact, the measure of efficiency we are interested in is probably some combination of these measures. We say this to emphasize that by "efficiency" we do not mean only how fast the program runs.

We described the process in two stages: first you design and specify the interface, and then you do the implementation. In real projects, it is not so cut and dried. If we find that a certain feature is very expensive to implement, we will probably go back to the interface design and see if we can modify it a little to something that is just as useful (or almost as useful), but easier to implement. User needs are the primary consideration, but not the only consideration. And besides, one of the things the user needs is likely to be a reasonably efficient implementation.

So, things are not as simple as we indicated, but the basic idea is still one to keep in mind: the two stages, interface design and implementation design, are logically separate and have different goals. There is mixing because that is how life is, but you should keep them separate as much as you can.

> Design goals critically affect design choices.

*11.6   OVERLAYS

Swapping was used to allow several programs to run at the same time, even though the memory was not large enough to hold several programs. But sometimes a single program by itself was too large to fit into memory, and that presented a more serious problem. Swapping is a convenience that saved time. It wasn't necessary because you could always run the programs one at a time, but if a single program was too large to fit into memory, then you could not run it at all.

Overlays

If the data area was too large, the program could read it in from disk (or tape or cards) in pieces and work on it a little at a time. But what if the program code itself were too large to fit into memory? *Overlays* were a solution to this problem.

To understand the idea of overlays, let's take a specific example. Suppose you have a statistical program that offers four different kinds of statistical tests. Each statistical test is independent of the others, and the user only asks for one at a time. Suppose the code for all four tests will not fit into the memory, but the code for each individual test will fit into memory. What you do is link the program so that the code for all four tests is placed in the same memory area. The program consists of a small core program that controls overlays and reads user input, and then a large overlay area for the code for a statistical test. The core code determines which test is needed, loads in that code, and then jumps to it. When the test is completed, the core code looks for the next test desired, loads in that code, and then jumps to it.

Figure 11.19 shows an example with four overlays. The core program takes 100K, and the overlays take 300K, 250K, 100K, and 300K. The full program is 1050K, but it will run in 400K.

Overlay facilities were developed that were generic, that is, that would work for any program. You just had to tell it which parts of the program should share the same memory areas, and the overlay loader would take care of everything. Each time a procedure call was made to an overlay area, the code would check to see if the correct overlay was present. If not, it would read in the correct code and then make the call.

More complex programs had a tree of overlays, and it was often quite difficult to design the overlay structure for a program, even when the overlay system was handling the mechanics of overlaying.

The overlay technique worked, but it was a lot of effort for the programmer to figure out how the overlay structure should work, and there was a lot of run time overhead to getting overlays to work. But the idea was very good. In the next section we will look at virtual memory, which is a more general and more effective solution to this problem.

Overlays allow you to run a program that is larger than the address space you are running it in.

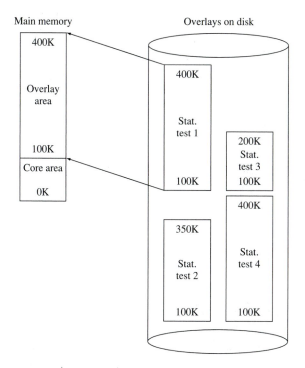

Figure 11.19   Overlays

11.6.1 OVERLAYS IN PCS

IBM PCs (and their clones) did not have enough memory for some programs. The problem was not that the memory was too expensive, but that the architecture of the 8086 and 8088 machines did not have a large enough logical address space. The total logical address space was 1 Mbyte (20 bit addresses), but even that was hard to use because of the awkward segment architecture it used. The IBM PC architecture allowed programs to use 640 Kbytes, and reserved the rest of the 1 Mbyte for hardware devices such as video boards that had frame buffers in the address space.

As PCs became more powerful, this memory limitation became very constraining, and it limited what could be done on PCs. PC vendors looked for ways around the problem. One method was overlays. Overlays are the traditional software method of running a large program in a small address space. Many popular programs used overlays.

But overlays were not the only solutions to the memory problem that was used in PCs. There were also more hardware-oriented solutions. The traditional hardware solution was the idea of *bank switching*. In bank switching, you have two memories that both are set to the same addresses. For example, you might have two memories that cover the range from 768K to 896K. There is an instruction to switch them, that

bank switching

is, to indicate which one you want active. This way, you can have more available memory, but not all at the same time. The form of bank switching that became popular on PCs was called *expanded memory*. (See Figure 11.20.)

The memory area from 640K to 1M was reserved for hardware devices, but not all of it was actually used by the hardware devices on any one system. With expanded memory, a program would find those areas in memory between 640K to 1M that were unused, and do bank switching on those areas. This method was good for things like disk buffers that did not all have to be in the address space at one time. The vendors developed a bank switching standard, many boards were sold, and many software vendors modified their products to use expanded memory. Expanded memory could be used by any PC with the addition of an expanded memory board.

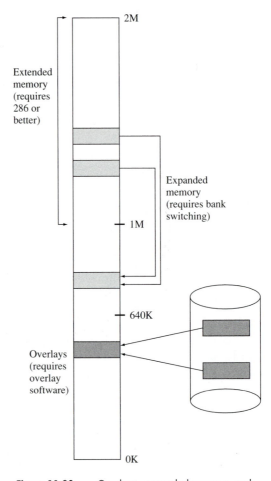

Figure 11.20   Overlays, expanded memory, and extended memory in PCs

The other method used to increase the address space in PCs was called *extended memory.* Extended memory was just memory whose physical addresses were above 1 Mbyte. This meant that it was not accessible to 8086 machines, but it could be addressed by 80286 machines. The problem was that DOS required the 80286 machines to run in 8086 mode while doing DOS system calls. So systems were developed where the machines would run in 80286 mode while in the user program, and then switch back to 8086 mode when making DOS system calls. This method was complicated by the awkward way that 80286 machines would switch modes. Figure 11.20 shows the three methods.

11.7 IMPLEMENTING VIRTUAL MEMORY

Swapping is a good solution because it allows a number of programs to run at the same time and it is handled entirely by the system. But swapping only applies to whole programs, and so we cannot be selective enough about what we keep in memory. Overlays are a good solution because they allow us to move small parts of program in and out of memory. But overlays require the programmer to design the overlay structure. What we would like is a method that combines the good features of both ideas, but without their problems. There is such a method, and it is called *virtual memory.*

virtual memory

We almost have virtual memory already in our paging system. The paging system divides the program up into a number of small parts, and this division is done based purely on logical addresses so the programmer does not have to make any decisions about how to divide up the program. In fact, paging is entirely transparent to the programmer. The hardware is already checking each memory reference and picking up the page base address to use. Using the protection bits, it is already checking each page reference for validity. To achieve virtual memory, we simply need to drop the requirement that every page be in memory while a program is running. When a process references a page that is not in memory, an interrupt is generated. This interrupt does not end the program: instead, it is intercepted by the operating system. The operating system figures out which page was found to be missing, reads it in from disk, changes the page table to indicate that the page is now in memory, and restarts the program at the instruction that caused the exception. The program does not even know that this happened. From the point of view of the process, all the pages are in memory, and that is why it is called *virtual* memory.

Virtual memory combines the good points of swapping and overlays. It is like overlays in that only part of the program is in memory at any one time, and the rest of it is out on disk. It is like swapping in that the missing parts of the program are brought in automatically by the system, and the programmer does not have to worry about how this happens or how to logically divide up the program.

Figure 11.21 show the components of a virtual memory system. The user sees a large linear virtual address space. Only parts of the virtual address space are in physical memory. The rest of it is "virtual" and is kept on the disk until needed. The disk contains an image of the entire virtual address space, even the parts that are in

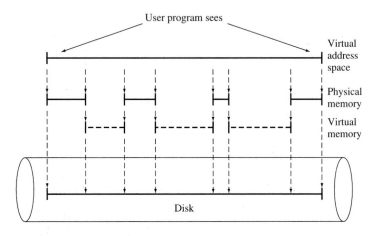

Figure 11.21   Virtual memory

physical memory. The virtual memory system module of the operating system maintains the illusion of the virtual memory by moving pages from disk to physical memory when they are needed.

> With virtual memory, some of the memory is simulated with disk.

11.7.1   HARDWARE REQUIRED TO SUPPORT VIRTUAL MEMORY

To implement virtual memory, we will add a new field to each page table entry. This field will be a single bit, and it will be called the *present bit*. If the present bit is 1, the page is present in memory and the base address field is valid. If the present bit is 0, the page reference is a legal program reference but the page is not currently in memory. When a page is accessed, the hardware checks the present bit, and if the present bit is 0 it generates an interrupt, usually called a *page fault interrupt*. The operating system handles the page fault exception by reading in the page and fixing up the page table.

    To make this clearer, let us first look at the algorithm the hardware will implement for making memory accesses. The following code gives the algorithm that the hardware uses.

present bit

page fault interrupt

THE HARDWARE VIRTUAL MEMORY ACCESS ALGORITHM

```
const int LogicalPages = 1024;
const int ByterPerPage = 4096;
const int OffsetShift = 12;
```

```
const int OffsetMask = 0xFFF;
const int PhysicalPages = 512;
enum AccessType { invalid = 0, read = 1, write = 2, execute = 3 };
struct PageTableEntry {
    int pageBase : 9;
    int present : 1;
    AccessType protection : 2;
    int fill : 4; // fill to 16 bits;
};

PageTableEntry UserPageTable[LogicalPages];

int MemoryAccess( int logicalAddress, AccessType how, int dataToWrite
= 0 ) {
    int page = logicalAddress >> OffsetShift;
    int offset = logicalAddress & OffsetMask;
    PageTableEntry pte = UserPageTable[page];
    // check if the access is valid
    if( how != pte.protection ) {
        // you CAN read a read/write page
        if( !(how = read && ptr.protection = write) ) {
            // otherwise it is a protection violation
            CauseInterrupt( ProtectionViolation );
            return 0;
        }
    }
    if( pte.present == 0 ) {
        GenerateInterrupt( PageFault, page );
        return 0;
    }
    int physicalAddress = (pte.pageBase << OffsetShift) + offset;
    switch( how ) {
        case read:
        case execute:
            return PhysicalMemoryFetch( physicalAddress );
        case write:
            PhysicalMemoryStore( physicalAddress, dataToWrite );
            return 0;
    }
}
```

First, the algorithm checks if the access is a valid one according to the protection bits, and if not, it causes an interrupt. Then, it checks if the page is present in memory, and if it is not, it causes a page fault interrupt. Otherwise, it executes the appropriate memory operation.

11.7.2 SOFTWARE REQUIRED TO SUPPORT VIRTUAL MEMORY

The operating system will reserve an area on disk to hold the image of the virtual address space of each process. This is called the *swap area*. Some (or all) of the pages in the swap area will be in memory at any one time.

swap area

There are four times when an operating system has to consider page tables and page faults.

- When a process is created.
- When a process is dispatched.
- When a page fault occurs.
- When a process exits.

Figure 11.22 show the parts of the virtual memory system that are affected by each event, and the sections below describe in detail how each event is handled.

Process Creation   To create a process P, the operating system must:

1. Let $N =$ the size of P in bytes (which is obtained from the load module). Round N up to the next highest multiple of pagesize.
2. Allocate N bytes for P in the swap area on disk.
3. Allocate space in main memory for P's page table. This will require $N/pagesize$ page table entries.
4. Initialize the swap area by copying in the machine code and initialized data sections from the load module.
5. Initialize the page table by marking all the pages as not present and setting the protection bits appropriately for each page (execute-only for code, read-only for constant data, read/write for other data).
6. Record this information in the process descriptor (the location in memory of the page table and the location in the swap area of the program image).

Process Dispatch   To dispatch process P, the operating system must:

1. Invalidate the TLB (since we are changing page tables).
2. Load the hardware page table base register with the address of the process's page table (kept in the process descriptor).

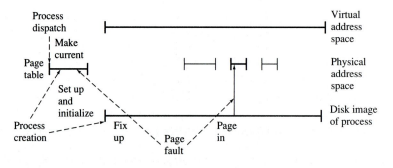

Figure 11.22   Virtual memory events

Page Fault   To handle a page fault for process *P,* the operating system must:

1. Let *K* = the number of the page that caused the fault (the hardware will provide this information with the page fault).

2. Find an empty page frame. This involves finding a page to replace, and writing it out to the swap area (*if* it has been changed since it was read in from the swap area).

3. Read in page *K* from disk (it will be on the swapping disk at disk location `SwapOrigin(process P) + (K*pagesize)`.

4. Fix up the page table entry by: (1) setting the present bit to 1; and (2) setting the frame number to the address of the newly allocated frame.

5. Restart the instruction that caused the page fault (the hardware will have already undone any effects of the partial execution of that instruction, so it will be safe to reexecute it).

Process Exit   When a process exits, the operating system must:

1. Free the memory used by its page table.

2. Free the disk space used by its memory image.

3. Free the page frames the process was using.

As you can see, the basic idea and implementation of virtual memory is quite simple. The hard part is deciding which page to evict from memory when a page fault requires you to bring in a new page. We will spend a considerable amount of time on that question, since it is the critical issue in the design of a paging system. But first we will look into whether virtual memory is a practical idea or not.

> The events important in virtual memory are: process creation, process dispatching, page fault, and process exit.

11.8   WHAT IS THE COST OF VIRTUAL MEMORY?

We do not want to get a page fault on every memory access, or else the program would be hideously slow. The percent of memory references that causes page faults is called the *page fault rate*. The page fault rate must be very low for paging to be a practical method.   page fault rate

Let's do some calculations to see what a reasonable page fault rate would be. Suppose a memory cycle normally takes 200 nanoseconds if the page is in memory. If we get a page fault, we will need to execute a few hundred to a few thousand instructions to handle the page fault interrupt, and we will have to read in the page from disk. On a 50 MIPS machine, 2000 instructions takes 40 microseconds. Reading 4K from disk will take, say, 20 milliseconds. The 20 milliseconds dominate the page fault time, so let's ignore the other delays. This means that an instruction that normally takes 200 nanoseconds will take 20 milliseconds, or 100,000 times longer.

Obviously, we don't want to have very many page faults, or the program will be slowed down by a huge factor. If one instruction out of 100,000 caused a page fault, then the average memory access time would be double what we would get if there were no page faults, since 100,000 memory accesses would take 200,000 memory cycle times. This would cause the program to run at half speed, but even this is an unacceptable speed penalty. Suppose we wanted to run only 10 percent slower than unpaged memory. To achieve this, we would need to limit the average page fault rate to, at most, one page fault for every 1,000,000 memory accesses.

The following table shows a range of page fault rates and the corresponding slowdown they will cause. If a slowdown factor is 2, that means that the average memory access will take twice as long as it would in an unpaged system (where the entire program is in memory).

Page Fault Rate	Slowdown Factor
$1/1,000,000$	1.1
$1/100,000$	2
$1/10,000$	11
$1/1,000$	101
$1/100$	1001
$1/10$	10001
1	100001

The higher page fault rates and slowdowns (like a slowdown factor of 1001) are clearly in the unacceptable range.

11.8.1 PAGING MORE THAN ONE PROCESS

In the calculations in the previous section, we assumed that the paging disk was free to read in the page we needed. If there are other processes being paged, then the slowdown due to paging will be even greater.

Sometimes paging is done to a disk that is dedicated to paging, but if this is not the case then other disk I/O will also interfere with paging and increase the slowdown even more.

11.8.2 LOCALITY

Now let us suppose, for purposes of argument, that page references were uniformly distributed throughout the address space. This would mean that each time an address is generated, all possible addresses are equally likely. In order to achieve a page fault rate of one in 1,000,000, we would have to keep 999,999 out of every 1,000,000 pages in memory.

This would not give us much of an advantage over unpaged memory, but fortunately our supposition that page references are uniformly distributed throughout the address space is very far from being true. In fact, page references are extremely nonuniform. It is intuitively obvious why this would be so. After we execute an instruction, the next sequential instruction is almost always executed next. This instruction is almost certainly on the same page, and so the page references for instructions will almost always be the same page as the previous instruction. Even when you do not execute the next sequential instruction, you are branching at the end of a loop, and branching to a nearby instruction that is also probably on the same page.

Sequential instruction execution generates a type of locality called *spatial locality* because the next reference is spatially close (close in address) to the previous reference. Instruction loops generate a type of locality called *temporal locality* because the next reference to an instruction word is temporally close (close in time) to the previous reference to the same word. The loop executes the same set of instructions over and over. Spatial locality means that words near each other tend to get accessed in a short space of time, and temporal locality means that the same word will be accessed more than once in a short space of time. Since a page contains a large number of words that are close in address and are in memory for a period of time, paging benefits from both kinds of locality.

spatial locality

temporal locality

Data references are similar. If you are accessing an array sequentially, you will almost always be accessing a data word on the same page as the last word. Thus, data references exhibit spatial locality. In addition, programs tend to access the same data items over and over, that is, data references also exhibit temporal locality.

We saw this concept of locality before, when we talked about translation lookaside buffers (TLBs) in Section 11.2.6. The same locality that ensures that instruction and data references cluster in a few pages also ensures that the page table entry for these few pages will be in the TLB.

Since both instruction and data references exhibit a high degree of locality, we can expect that almost all page references will be to a few pages.

But how far is it from the vague "almost all" in the previous paragraph to the 999,999 in 1,000,000 that we need to make paging practical? Experience has shown that, for typical programs, if you have from 25 percent to 50 percent of the pages in memory at any one time, you will get acceptably low page fault rates, that is, on the order of one in a million.

So we see that virtual memory is not magical. With virtual memory, we can fit two to four times as many programs into memory. But we cannot normally fit 10 times as many programs in memory. On the other hand, a program might use a large data area that is used in a very localized fashion. Such a program might be able to have only a few percent of its data pages in memory at a time, and still have a fairly low paging rate. Such programs exist, but they are special cases and are not typical.

DESIGN TECHNIQUE: LOCALITY

The locality principle is used many times in these chapters. Locality allows TLBs to work, and it allows paging to work.

In fact, it is a generalization of the locality principle that is the basis behind any system that uses caching. Caching works because questions are not asked randomly. The same question, or closely related questions, are asked in clumps. Caching works be-cause it takes advantage of this knowledge about the questions that will be asked.

The current directory concept allows the use of short file names in the most common cases. It works because the files asked for are localized, usually in the same directory as the previous file asked for, or at least in a nearby directory.

DESIGN TECHNIQUE: LATE BINDING

With virtual memory we do not bind pages to page frames until the first time the page is used. This is a form of lazy creation where the page in memory is not created until it is first needed. In programming languages we do not allocate stack space for a procedure until it is called. These are both examples of late binding. Early versus late binding is an example of the static versus dynamic tradeoff.

To learn more about late binding see Section 13.2.

Page fault rates must be very low. Locality makes this possible. Programs with low locality should not be paged.

11.9   VIRTUAL MEMORY MANAGEMENT

We will talk about page replacement algorithms in the next chapter. In this section we will discuss the modules and tables that must exist in an operating system in order to implement virtual memory. Figure 11.23 shows a block diagram of the data structures of a virtual memory subsystem. The data structures shown are:

- *Page frames*—This is the part of physical memory reserved for user pages. These are the page frames the virtual memory manager is allocating.

- *Page tables*—These are the page tables for all the processes in memory.

- *Free page frame list*—This is a list of all the page frames that are not currently in use by any process.

- *Modified free page frame list*—This is a list which contains the free pages whose current contents need to be written out to disk.

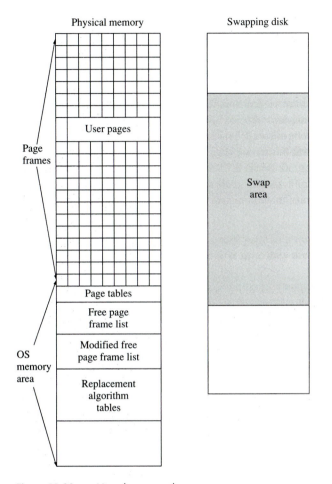

Figure 11.23   Virtual memory data structures

- *Replacement algorithm tables*—All page replacement algorithms keep tables of information about the pages. They use this information to decide which pages to replace.

- *Swap area*—This is the area on disk where pages are written when they are removed from memory. A complete image of the memory for every process is kept in the swap area.

Figure 11.24 shows a block diagram of the data structures, the procedures that use and modify them, and the events that cause these procedures to be executed. Events that cause changes in the tables are named with bold text. There are three such events: a page fault exception, a timer interrupt, and a create process system call interrupt. Memory management procedures are drawn as rectangles with rounded corners. Data tables are shown as rectangles.

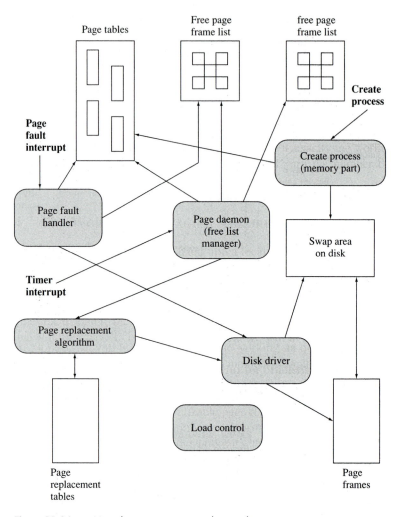

Page tables

Free page frame list

free page frame list

Create process

Page fault interrupt

Page fault handler

Create process (memory part)

Page daemon (free list manager)

Swap area on disk

Timer interrupt

Page replacement algorithm

Disk driver

Load control

Page replacement tables

Page frames

Figure 11.24   Virtual memory events and procedures

When a create process system call is made, the create process procedure is called. It sets up the page tables and the swap area for the process.

When a page fault occurs, the page fault handler is called. This examines the page tables and figures out which page needs to be read in. It allocates a page frame and calls the disk driver to read the page into the page frame.

An operating system may not wait until a page fault occurs to look for a page to replace. Operating systems often keep a pool of free page frames so a page fault can immediately be granted a page frame. There is a *paging daemon* that wakes up every so often and makes sure there are sufficient page frames in the free page frame pool. The paging daemon will call the page replacement algorithm to determine which pages to replace.

paging daemon

Every so often, a timer interrupt activates the paging daemon. It is the job of the paging daemon to make sure that there are always some free page frames to use when a page fault occurs. If the free page frame list gets low, the paging daemon calls the page replacement algorithm to pick some pages to replace.

The page replacement algorithm will consult its tables and determine the best pages to replace. Some of these pages will have been modified, and so the copy on disk is no longer correct. Before the page can be used by a new process, its current contents have to be written out to the swap area. The page replacement algorithm calls the disk driver to do this write, and places the page on the modified free page frame list. When the disk write completes, the page frame will be removed from the modified free page frame list and put on the free page frame list.

When a page fault occurs, the page fault handler will look in the free page frame pool to see if the page it needs happens to be already there. This would happen when a page fault occurs on a page that was replaced but is still in a "free" page frame. It still contains the page data, and so it can be "rescued" from the free page frame pool and used again. If the page is not found on the free list, then the page fault handler must get a free page and read the faulting page into it.

> An operating system is largely a table manager. It responds to events by looking things up in tables and changing table entries.

11.10   DAEMONS AND EVENTS

Operating systems respond to events—a system call interrupt, a device interrupt, the arrival of a message over the network, etc. An operating system is principally made up of event handlers that are activated by these events. As such, the operating system is a passive entity that does not initiate actions on its own, but only responds to the actions of devices and the processes it is running.

The model of an operating system as an event manager is a good one, but it does not tell the entire story. Sometimes the operating system does do things on its own, instead of in response to external events. One example is the paging daemon we discussed in the last section. The operating system knows that free pages will be required because processes get a continual stream of page faults. So it prepares for this by keeping a pool of free pages to use when a page fault occurs. The paging daemon wakes up every so often and makes sure that the free page pool has enough free pages in it. If the pool is too low, then it starts freeing some pages.

Technically, the paging daemon is responding to a timer interrupt. But this is just so it can gain control periodically and fit into the interrupt-driven model of the operating system.

DESIGN TECHNIQUE: SYSTEM MODELS AND DAEMONS

Operating systems are essentially reactive systems, that is, they react to events. They are not proactive, in the sense that they do not go out looking for things to do where they can be useful.

Operating systems react to interrupts. But, if we include timer interrupts, then an operating system process can be activated every so often and go looking for useful things to do. The timer allows us to add proactive elements to a basically reactive operating system.

The concept of a daemon is a proactive part of an operating system. A daemon might wake up at 3 A.M. every night and see if parts of the disk need optimizing (to move files into contiguous blocks). Another daemon might wake up every 30 seconds and make sure there are enough free pages in the free page pool.

There are advantages to both the reactive and the proactive models, and you get the best of both worlds by combining them.

User interfaces are another example of this. The way user interfaces are implemented in graphical user interface systems is reactive. The interface consists of a number of screen objects which react to user input by calling parts of the application. So the application becomes a reactive system that reacts to user input. Generally this is a very good model and corresponds to the accepted user interface principle that the user should feel in control of the interface. But some things do not fit into this model, such as receiving messages from other parts of the system. In fact, a recent trend in user interfaces is the idea of an *agent*, that is, a daemon that is given a general task and goes off on its own, and is proactive in achieving its goals.

DESIGN TECHNIQUE: POLLING, SOFTWARE INTERRUPTS, AND HOOKS

There is another issue with daemons, and that is how one process can know when some event of interest had occurred. There are two general approaches to that problem: polling and interrupts. In the polling approach, you check over and over again to see if the event has occurred. Often you use a timer, and check at periodic intervals. For example, our paging daemon woke up every so often and checked to see if there were enough free page frames. A scheduling daemon might wake up every so often and examine the performance statistics to see if there is a need to change the scheduling parameters of the system.

Suppose you have a program that is displaying a directory. You would like the display to be kept up to date, even when other programs change the directory by deleting or adding files. One solution is to check every few seconds and see if the directory has changed. This is easy in UNIX because it keeps a time of last modification for each directory.

The interrupt solution would be a mechanism that would allow you to register interest in the directory, so that the operating system will inform you when a

change has been made to it. This assumes that the operating system has a facility that allows you to register interest in a directory. Few operating systems have such a facility, and so you are usually stuck with the polling solution.

The ability to register interest in certain events is often called a **hook**. The idea is that any event in a computer system is caused by the action of some software, or else some software detects and handles the event. Since this code is executed anyway, it is handy if it can send a message to any interested processes that the event has occurred. This allows any process to get control when the event occurs.

This idea can be used inside a single program as well. For example, the emacs text editor defines a number of useful hooks. You can, for example, say you want a certain procedure to be called whenever a file name lookup fails. This gives you a chance to find the file in some other place and allows the file name lookup to succeed. Or you can get control when a file is written, and do the writing yourself in some special way.

Continued

hook

The hook idea allows you to get control when certain events happen, and is a form of **software interrupt.** Hooks are more efficient than polling, and more flexible, too, since they allow you to get control before an event happens and to change the system's response to the event.

Notice that the direction of the call is reversed with a hook. Normally, the entity that is interested in the event would make the call, but with a hook, the entity that causes the event makes the call. This is useful since that is the entity that knows when the call should be made.

Hooks are a form of software interrupt.

It is called a *daemon* because it acts on its own and does things, instead of responding to specific events. Modern operating systems have dozens of different daemons.

daemon

11.11   FILE MAPPING

A virtual memory system allows you to have a larger logical address space than physical address space. A copy of the process's logical address space is kept on disk because it may not always be in physical memory. Another way to look at virtual memory is that it creates a logical address space out of data stored on disk, and takes care of moving the parts of the address space that you are currently using into memory.

If you think about it for a moment, you will see that file I/O does exactly the same thing. Parts of the data on disk are moved into the logical address space so they can be used in the computation. File I/O is not as convenient as virtual memory because the user has to worry about when the data needs to be brought in memory and when it needs to be written back out again.

Virtual memory, as we have defined it, only maps process images from the swap area into memory. It will not map a file into virtual memory. It would simplify the operating system and the job of the user process to extend the virtual memory system to allow it to map any file into the virtual address space. Most newer operating systems allow this and the facility is called *file mapping*. Another name for file mapping is *memory-mapped files*. Once this is done, then all file reading and writing is accomplished with ordinary memory operations. That is, changing the file data in the virtual memory is like writing to the file, and reading the file data in virtual memory is like reading the file. This means that no special I/O operations are necessary; they are subsumed by ordinary memory operations.

file mapping
memory-mapped files

Figure 11.25 shows a file mapped into the virtual address space. Assume that the C++ pointer file refers to the beginning of the file when it is mapped into the address space. Then you can access the file with array operations:

- x = file[912]; // file read
- file[912] = 12; // file write

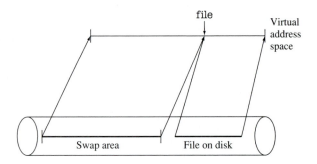

Figure 11.25   Mapping a file into the virtual adress space

Normally, we would map the file into a part of the virtual address space that is not used, for example, into the address space after the end of our program, data, and stack areas. The file-mapped area will not be copied to the swap area, like the other parts of the address space, because the file on disk acts as the disk backup for that part of the virtual address space.

File Mapping the Code Space   When we described how a process is loaded in a virtual memory system, we noted that the code is copied from the load module into the swap area before we began execution of the program. If we have file mapping, we can avoid that step and use the load module itself as the disk backup of the program code. The code does not change, so we do not have to worry about damaging the load module by writing changes to it. If we already have the mechanism for file mapping, then any parts of the load module that are read-only can use this facility, and do not need to be copied into and take up space in the swap area. This will speed up loading because it avoids a disk-to-disk copy.

11.11.1   THE SYSTEM CALL INTERFACE

Let us look at what the system call interface to file mapping would look like. There will be two system calls:

- int MapFile(int openFileID, char * startAddress = 0, int startOff-set = 0, int length = 0)—The open file openFileID is mapped into the caller's virtual address space. All or part of the file might be mapped in. The first byte in the file to be mapped is at file offset startOffset (this is usually 0), and length bytes will be mapped. If length is zero, then the rest of the file (from startOffset to the end of the file) is mapped in. The selected bytes of the file are mapped in the caller's virtual address space, starting at virtual address startAd-dress and continuing for length bytes. If startAddress is 0 (the default), then the operating system picks the virtual address where the file will be mapped. If the return value is negative, then an error occurred. Otherwise the return value is the virtual address the file is mapped into. Possible error returns are:

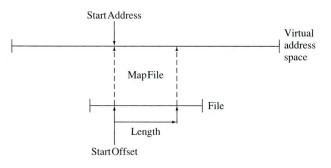

Figure 11.26   The effect of the MapFile system call

-1 $\Rightarrow$ fileName could not be found.

-2 $\Rightarrow$ startAddress is not a legal address.

-3 $\Rightarrow$ the file would not fit in the allocated address space (from startAddress to the end of your allocated address space).

Figure 11.26 shows the effect of the MapFile system call.

- int UnMapFile(char * startAddress)—The mapped file is unmapped.

You map a file with MapFile, read and/or write the data, and then UnMap-File will unmap it.

11.11.2   AN EXAMPLE OF USING FILE MAPPING

As an example of how you would use the file-mapping interface, suppose we had a file that contained some text, and you wanted to count the number of lowercase 'a's in the text. The program in Figure 11.27 shows how you would use file mapping to do this.

The MapFile call allows you to specify a length and an offset in case you want to map the file in pieces. It is simpler to map an entire file, but sometime you will want to do it in pieces. This makes the mapping more like I/O, and is useful for very long files.

File mapping is most useful with very large address spaces where you can afford to use up address space for large files. It is likely it will be more used with the new generation of hardware with address lengths over 32 bits.

11.11.3   ADVANTAGES OF FILE MAPPING

File mapping means that the user does not have to do explicit I/O, and so the interface to the operating system is easier. You access and modify data in memory on disk the same way.

File mapping is more efficient than file I/O. Ordinary I/O requires a system call for every I/O operation. With file mapping, there are only two system calls. All file access is handled by the virtual memory system.

```
int CountLetter (char * fileName, char letter ) {
   int fid = open( fileName, Reading );
   char * fileArea = MapFile( fid );
   int fileLength = GetFileLength( fid );
   int letterCount = 0;
   for( int i = 0; i < fileLength; ++i ) {
      if ( fileArea[i] == letter )
          ++letterCount;
      }
   }
   UnmapFile ( fileArea );
   return letterCount;
}
```

Figure 11.27   Count letters

Another advantage of file mapping is that it reduces the number of copies of the data in physical memory. Figure 11.28(a) shows what happens normally. When a process reads a page of file data, it is first read into the operating system address space (we'll see this in Chapter 16). Then it copies the data into the user's address space. If two users read the same data, there will be two copies. Since normally address spaces do not share pages, there will be three copies of the page in physical memory.

Figure 11.28(b) shows what happens with file mapping. The page is brought into memory once, and mapped into the virtual address space of the process that mapped the file. The operating system never needs to map it. If a second process maps the same file, it will see the same physical page as its copy of the file.

This example shows one difference between the semantics of file mapping and ordinary file I/O. Changes to the file are seen immediately by all processes mapping the file. Ordinarily, a process would have to read the data in to see any changes in the file. With file mapping, you have a "live," shared copy of the file.

Even with file mapping, you still need the normal file I/O operations. One advantage of file I/O is that it is atomic. While you are reading or writing, the file is locked, and no other process can read or write the file at the same time. In addition, you need ways of increasing or decreasing the length of a file.

File mapping integrates virtual memory with the file system and allows you to place any file on disk into your address space.

11.11.4   MEMORY AND FILE MAPPING ON THE IBM 801

The IBM 801 was the first RISC computer, and it was innovative in a number of ways, both in hardware and software. The designers of the 801 system used a segmented virtual memory that supported file mapping.

The virtual address space in the 801 consists of up to 2^{36} segments, where each segment can be up to 2^{28} bytes long. The IBM PC/RT used 4096 segments, so we will assume that number for the rest of the next few paragraphs. Each segment is mapped

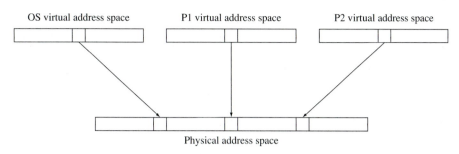

(a) Each process has a physical copy of the data

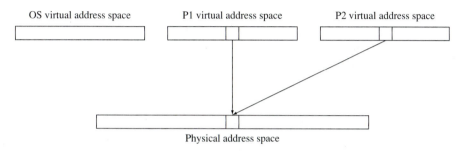

(b) The processes share a physical copy of the file data

Figure 11.28   Multiple copies of file data in memory

with a page table. There is a systemwide segment table containing 4096 entries. Each entry in the segment table is a segment descriptor which contains the protection bits and a pointer to the page table for the segment. So the virtual address space consists of up to 2^{40} bytes (2^{12} segments of 2^{28} bytes each). This virtual address space is common to all processes running in the system (including the operating system). The protection bits in the segment table entries protect the segments from unauthorized use. Figure 11.29 shows the memory addressing and file-mapping facilities of the IBM 801 computer and operating system.

A running process does not have immediate access to all 4096 segments in the virtual address space (even if it does have the proper permissions). Virtual addresses on the 801 are 32 bits long. The 801 has 16 hardware segment registers, and the high-order four bits of a virtual address are the number of the segment register to use. The segment registers contain copies of the segment descriptors for 16 segments. Modifying the contents of the segment registers is a privileged operation, so if a user process wants to access a new segment, it must ask the operating system to do it.

So we have an interesting situation here that is different from the virtual memory systems we have seen before. First, there is only one address space for all processes, instead of each process having its own address space. All the segments are shared by all the processes. We depend on protection rather than different address spaces to limit access. Each process can only access a small portion (2^{32} bytes out of

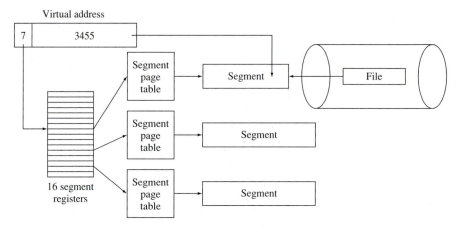

Figure 11.29   Virtual memory in the IBM 801

2^{40} bytes) of the address space at any one time, but can access all of it by asking the operating system to change your segment registers.

The IBM 801 architecture allowed for large numbers of segments. For example, it could expand the address space from 40 bits to 48 bits. This would allow 2^{20} or 1M segments, and a total address space of 2^{48}. With this many segments, it would be necessary to page the segment table.

File I/O is done by mapping a file into a segment and then accessing the memory in that segment. This means that you can only access, at most, 16 files at a time directly, although you can access more by changing segment registers.[2] File segments are automatically shared because all segments are shared.

11.11.5   FILE MAPPING EXAMPLES

File mapping has so many benefits that almost all modern operating systems use it. This includes OS/2, Windows NT, Mach, OSF/1, SVR4, and most other versions of UNIX. In Section 12.13, we will discuss the virtual memory system of several operating systems, and there is more discussion there of file mapping in a range of operating systems.

11.12   SUMMARY

Memory allocation is harder when we have to find physically contiguous space for the whole program. Compaction creates a large, physically contiguous block, but it requires a lot of processor time. There are a number of ways to divide a program into

---

[2]Actually, the maximum will be smaller than 16 because you must use a few of your segment registers to map your code, data, and stack.

smaller pieces so that it is easier to find space for the pieces. Segments are one way to do this, but they create pieces that are too big and of varying sizes. It is easier to divide a program into many small, equally sized pieces called pages. This requires a page table to map logical to physical addresses. For small address spaces, the page table can be kept in hardware registers. For large address spaces, the page table is large and must be kept in memory. This requires a page table cache, called a translation lookaside buffer or TLB. Page table entries also have protection bits which allow us to limit access to pages in various ways.

Virtual memory means that you keep some of the logical address space of a process on disk. This idea was started in the early days of computing with the methods of swapping and overlays. Modern virtual memory systems use paging, where some of the pages are on disk and some are in memory. The operating system has a number of duties in a virtual memory system. It must manage the virtual address space of the process when it is created, when it is dispatched, when it gets a page fault, and when it is destroyed. This management function consists mainly of looking things up in various tables and making changes to tables as circumstances change. Extensive hardware support is also required for a virtual memory system.

Locality is the tendency of a program to use some parts of its logical address space over and over again. Locality is the result of sequential program execution, loops, and program modularity. It is locality that makes paging a practical method, and very low page fault rates are required for paging to be fast enough.

Most newer operating systems allow you to map files into the virtual address space. This makes for convenient I/O, allows the operating system to unify virtual memory and I/O, and have a single system for disk access.

11.12.1 TERMINOLOGY

After reading this chapter, you should be familiar with the following terms:

- bank switching
- bursty
- cache hit
- cache hit rate
- cache miss
- compaction
- contiguous
- daemon
- external fragmentation
- file mapping
- hook
- internal fragmentation
- locality
- memory-mapped files

- overlay
- page
- page fault interrupt
- page fault rate
- page frame
- page table
- page table entry (PTE)
- paging daemon
- persistent objects
- present bit
- protection field (in a PTE)
- segmentation
- segment register
- software interrupt
- space resource
- spatial locality
- swap area
- swapping
- temporal locality
- time resource
- translation lookaside buffer (TLB)
- virtual memory

11.12.2   REVIEW QUESTIONS

The following questions are answered in the text of this chapter:

1. What are the benefits of compaction?
2. Compare segments and pages.
3. How can the logical address space be contiguous if the physical address space is not contiguous?
4. Compare segment registers to base and limit registers.
5. What are the problems with noncontiguous logical address spaces?
6. Compare page tables in registers with page tables in memory.
7. What is the purpose of a TLB?
8. Why do programs exhibit locality?
9. What is the relationship between program locality and the TLB hit rate?
10. Why does paging make memory allocation easier for the operating system?

11. What is the difference between a page and a page frame?

12. What is the difference between internal fragmentation and external fragmentation?

13. What is the purpose of the protection bits in the page table entry?

14. Why does design require iteration?

15. Compare swapping and overlays.

16. Why is it called *virtual* memory?

17. Describe the hardware changes required to switch from a base/limit register system of memory mapping to a paging system.

18. Describe the actions an operating system must take when a page fault interrupt occurs.

19. What is a typical page fault rate?

20. What is a paging daemon? What does it do?

21. Relate the terms daemon, polling, interrupts, and hooks.

22. What is a page replacement algorithm?

23. How does file mapping make using files easier and more efficient?

11.12.3 FURTHER READING

See Satyanarayanan and D. Bhandarkar (1981) for a discussion of TLB design trade-offs. See Section 12.15.3 for references on virtual memory systems.

11.13 PROBLEMS

1. In the chapter, we talked about the idea of compacting memory in the physical address space. Consider compacting memory in the virtual address space. Can you think of a situation where you might want to do this?

2. Suppose you have a memory of 128Kbytes, and you can move a word (four bytes) of memory every microsecond.

   a. If memory is 80 percent full, how long will it take to compact it? (Assume you have to move all allocated memory.)

   b. Do the same calculation with a memory of 32Mbytes and assuming that you can transfer 64 bytes per microsecond.

   c. Now suppose that a system contains, on the average, three processes, and processes execute an average of 10 seconds. How long will it be until the next process completes (on the average)?

   d. Redo the calculation with 100 jobs that complete in 3 seconds (on the average).

3. A linker knows how to combine object modules together into a single linear address space. It knows how to resolve external references, find object modules, and read libraries. It knows how to read and write object modules and load modules.

   Suppose you wanted to modify such a linker to link modules into an address space that was not contiguous. For example, suppose the logical address space consists of 1 Mbyte in 16 segments of 64K each. For each program, you want to divide it up into 16 pieces, one in each segment, where all the pieces are approximately the same size. Describe some of the tasks and problems you would encounter in modifying the linker to do this. How would the load module format have to change in order to support this?

4. What TLB hit rate would be required to achieve an effective memory access time in a paged system only 1 percent slower than the equivalent unpaged system?

5. Suppose we have a paging system with 10 pages, and the likelihood that a page is referenced is based on the exponential probability distribution. We can simulate the page number of the next memory reference by generating a uniform random number, x, between 0 and 1, and then computing $10e^{-10x}$ and rounding it down to the nearest integer. Most of the time you will get 0, implying that page 0 is referenced. Some of the time you will get 1, less often 2, less often 3, etc. Suppose you have a TLB of 2 pages. When you have a TLB miss, you must replace one of the pages in the TLB. There are three strategies you can use for this. First, you can replace a random page (get a uniform random integer from 0 to 1). Second, you can replace them in order: first slot 0, then slot 1, then slot 0 again, then slot 1 again, etc. This is called first-in, first-out (or FIFO). Third, you can replace the one that has not been used for the longest time. This is called least recently used (or LRU). That is, when you get a TLB hit, you exchange it to the first slot (if it is not already there). Assume the slots start out with pages 0 and 1 in them.

   Write a simulation program that computes the TLB hit rate for this system.

6. Suppose that the average amount of external fragmentation in a dynamic memory allocation system is 20 percent of the space. Suppose that 70 percent of the blocks are allocated and 30 percent are free, and that the average free block size is one-half of the average allocated block size. In a paging system, the average internal fragmentation is one-half of a page. Suppose the average allocated block is 100Kbytes. At what page size will the internal fragmentation and the external fragmentation be (about) equal?

7. Suppose we have a multiprogramming operating system, and a process asks for more memory while it is running. It is possible that you will have to move the process around in physical memory to satisfy that request. Explain why this is. Explain why it depends on the kind of memory mapping you use (*base/bound*, code/data split, segments, pages).

8. Explain the differences between logically contiguous memory (that is, memory that is contiguous in the logical address space) and physically continuous memory.

9. Can pages overlap? Can page frames overlap? Why or why not?

10. State and explain two major advantages of paged virtual memory over the base/limit register method of memory mapping.

11. Some computers have several possible page sizes. Do you think it is possible to switch between two processes that use different page sizes? That is, is it possible to have page size a parameter that changes as you switch processes? If it is not possible, explain why. If it is possible, explain what problems the operating system would face in dealing with it.

12. Explain why small page sizes necessitate keeping the page table in memory rather than in hardware registers.

13. With page tables in hardware registers, you have to copy the page table registers each time you switch processes. With page tables in memory and using a TLB, you also have a "register filling" overhead when you switch processes. Explain why that is. Explain why there is no "register saving" overhead in this case.

14. What changes would be required in the program in Figure 11.12 to change the page size from 4 Kbytes to 1 Kbytes?

15. Is it reasonable for segment tables to have the same kind of protection bits as page tables (as shown in Figure 11.16)?

16. Could we keep the segment table in memory, as we did the page tables? Why or why not? Would there be any difference in how they were handled?

17. Bank switching is the hardware equivalent of overlays: both place two (or more) parts of a program in the same addresses. Suppose a typical instruction takes 1 microsecond, the bank switching hardware instruction takes 10 microseconds to switch banks, and bringing in an overlay takes 100 milliseconds. We want the program to run at no more than 110 percent of the speed it would run with no swapping or bank switching. What percent of instructions can require an overlay to achieve this? What percent of instructions can require a bank switch to achieve this?

18. Suppose it takes a disk an average of 10 milliseconds to get to a specific sector, and that, once it is there, it can transfer 2Mbytes per second, and that the average job is 300,000 bytes long. How long does it take to swap one job out and another job in?

19. Suppose we wanted to design an automatic overlay system. This system would lay out the overlays and ensure, at run time, that the right overlay was always in memory. It would do this based on a specification by the programmer. The programmer would provide a list of the procedures and global data structures that would go in each overlay. What code needs to be added to each procedure call for this to work? Where would this code be placed? What data is kept by the overlay system? What are we assuming about the use of global data by procedures? Decide what computations can be done at compile (or load) time, and which ones have to be done at run time.

20. Suppose we had an extremely fast paging device that took only 2 milliseconds to store or fetch a page. Redo the calculations in Section 11.8 based on this new paging device. Do the calculations one more time for a paging device that can read or write a page in 200 microseconds.

21. Rewrite the hardware virtual memory access algorithm (in Section 11.7.1) to use a TLB.

22. Procedure calls will reduce the locality of a program. How can the linker reduce this loss of locality?

23. Most programming languages allocate procedure activation records (the record of the saved registers, local variables, parameters, etc.) on the stack rather than allocating them from the per-process memory manager. Which method would cause more program locality, using the stack or the memory allocator? Explain your reasoning.

24. Suppose we have an average of one page fault every 100,000 instructions, a normal instruction takes 1 microsecond, and a page fault causes the instruction to take an additional 10 milliseconds. What is the average instruction time, taking page faults into account? Redo the calculation assuming that a normal instruction takes 0.5 microseconds instead of 1 microsecond.

25. Using the same assumptions as we gave for the previous problem, suppose we used a paging algorithm that took an additional one millisecond per page fault, but decreased the page fault rate to one in 120,000 instructions. Would this result in an increase in overall performance or not? Explain your reasoning.

26. Three things take up time in a swapping system: (1) swapping out the old job, (2) swapping in the new job, and (3) running the new job. When the new job is ready to be swapped out again, it becomes the old job, and the cycle starts over again. If we can overlap these activities, we can speed up the system. There are three levels of overlap:

   a. No overlap.

   b. You can overlap running a program with either swapping in or swapping out (but not both).

   c. You can overlap all three things.

   Suppose we have a computer system where each job is 200Kbytes long, the CPU can execute 1M instructions per second, the I/O channels can transfer 1Mbytes per second, and a job runs exactly 300K instructions before being swapped. (K=1024; M=K*K) We only consider the CPU time spent on running the jobs to be useful. The *effective computation rate* is the ratio of useful computation time to total time. So if the CPU was busy only half of the time, the effective computation rate would be 0.5. For each of the three overlap cases above, compute the effective computation rate. Now assume that you can speed up either the CPU or the I/O channels by 100 percent (double their speed). For each of the three overlap cases, indicate which one would be better to speed up (you can speed up only one, not both) and how that speedup will affect the effective computation rate. If your results seem anomalous, explain why.

27. Explain how the UNIX process system call `exec` could be used to implement overlays. Would it be the same as the kind of overlay system described in Section 11.6?

28. Consider the following structure for a page table entry and skeleton of the C function to translate addresses:

```
struct pte {
    int present          : 1; /* = 1 if page is in memory */
    int readAllowed      : 1; /* = 1 if the page can be read */
    int writeAllowed     : 1; /* = 1 if the page can be written */
    int executeAllowed   : 1; /* = 1 if the page can be executed */
    int unused           : 12; /* unused bits */
    int pageFrame        : 16; /* page frame number (if present=1) */
};

struct VirtualAddress {
    /* 32 bit virtual address with 16K pages */
    /* physical addresses are also 32 bits */
    int pageNumber       : 18;
    int pageOffset       : 14;
};

/* global variable that contains the physical address of the first */
/* level page table for the running process */
struct pte * PageTableBaseAddress;

/* accessType is (one of) 1 for read, 2 for write and 4 for execute */

/* This procedure will translate the virtual address AND fetch the */
/* word addresses Assume no translation lookaside buffer */
int mmu( struct VirtualAddress va, int accessType ) {
    /* algorithm for translation of the virtual address and fetch */
    /* of the word addresses */
    /* use the procedure "fetch(physicalAddress)" to fetch a word */
    /* from the physical memory. use this to fetch page table entries */
    /* and data words */
}
```

Complete the mmu procedure to do the address translation.

29. Do pages and page frames have to be the same size? Why or why not?

30. In a paged OS, any allocation whose size is a page or greater is allocated by whole pages. So dynamic memory allocation is only used for blocks whose size is less than one page (say 4 Kbytes). Explain why this fact makes a buddy system allocator more attractive than it would be if it were doing all allocations.

31. Consider a system call that will insert N pages of virtual memory at a specific virtual address. What are the problems in implementing such a system call? What uses would it be put to? What happens to all the virtual addresses after the addresses are inserted?

32. Suppose we had 30 Gbytes of disk storage on our computer. How large a virtual address (in bits) would it take to map the entire file system into your virtual address space? Then do the same calculation for 250 Gbytes of disk storage.

Now suppose there are 15,000,000 computer installations in the world, and each has 20 Gbytes of disk storage. How much virtual address space (in bits of virtual address) would be required to map all of that storage into your virtual address space?

33. The IBM 801 has only 16 segment registers, even though 4096 segments are possible. Give some reasons why they did not provide more segment registers.

34. Suppose you wanted to extend the file mapping interface to allow you to modify the length of a file that is mapped. What would you add to the existing system calls, and what new system calls would you add to do this? Be sure it is clear how they are used to change the length of a mapped file.

chapter
12

Virtual Memory Systems

In the last chapter, we looked at the mechanisms of virtual memory in an operating system. In this chapter, we will look at page replacement algorithms and at some extensions and variations of the paging idea.

12.1 PAGE REPLACEMENT

placement

replacement

page replacement algorithm

In a dynamic memory allocation system, the principle problem was *placement*—where would we allocate a block. In a paging system, placement is trivial, since all page frames are the same size and interchangeable. In a virtual memory paging system, the principal issue is *replacement*—which page should we remove from memory so we can bring in a new page. What we need is a *page replacement algorithm,* an algorithm that will tell us which page to replace. A large number of page replacement algorithms have been proposed and investigated over the years.

local replacement

global replacement

An important early decision to make in deciding on a page replacement algorithm is whether it would replace only another page belonging to the process that needs the new page, *local replacement,* or should all the pages in memory be considered for replacement, *global replacement.* Global replacement is simpler and is more commonly used, so we will discuss it first.

12.2 GLOBAL PAGE REPLACEMENT ALGORITHMS

12.2.1 MEASURING THE PERFORMANCE OF A PAGE REPLACEMENT ALGORITHM

We are going to look at several page replacement algorithms, and so the question comes up, how do you decide among them? The main performance measure is the number of page faults they generate. To compare two algorithms, you compare them on a particular sequence of page references and see which one produces fewer page faults. Of course, you have to do this for a range of page reference sequences that are typical of the processes you want to run under this paging algorithm. Unfortunately, there is a wide range of paging behavior among programs, and it is hard to say what typical behavior is.

Another performance question is not how two page replacement algorithms compare with each other, but how an algorithm compares to the best that can be done with this particular page reference sequence. This brings us to our first page replacement algorithm.

12.2.2 OPTIMAL PAGE REPLACEMENT

optimal page replacement algorithm

In order to make judgments on the effectiveness of a page replacement algorithm, it is useful to have a bound on how well any algorithm can do. So we want to think about an *optimal page replacement algorithm,* that is, an algorithm that produces the fewest possible page faults.

We claim that an algorithm that replaces the page that will not be used for the longest time is an optimal algorithm. The way to reduce the page fault rate is to increase the average time between page faults. The optimal algorithm puts the page fault on the page being replaced as far in the future as possible.

Replacing the page that will be unused for the longest time is the optimal algorithm, but this is not a generally useful algorithm since it requires knowledge of the future behavior of the program, and we do not generally have that knowledge.

Sometimes, however, we might actually have that knowledge. If we run a program once and observe its page reference sequence, then we can predict the page reference sequence the next time we run the program. So, in certain special cases, we might have future knowledge.

The optimal algorithm is still interesting, however, because it gives us a lower bound on page faults and allows us to see how well another algorithm is doing compared to the optimal one. If we have an algorithm that is within a few percent of the optimal algorithm, it may not be worth our trouble to try to find a better one.

> Optimal page replacement is not realizable but is a standard to compare other page replacement algorithms against.

12.2.3 THEORIES OF PROGRAM PAGING BEHAVIOR

All global page replacement algorithms try to emulate the optimal algorithm and replace the page that will not be used for the longest time; in other words, all page replacement algorithms try to predict the future. They do this by looking at the past behavior of the programs running in the system, and use this information to predict future behavior. Each page replacement algorithm embodies a theory about how programs behave. The theory says that if a program has been acting a certain way in the past, it will act a certain way in the future. If the theory is accurate, then the page replacement algorithm will work well; otherwise it will not.

theory of program behavior

When discussing each algorithm, we will discuss its theory of program behavior.

> Page replacement algorithms have a theory of how past program behavior predicts future program behavior.

12.2.4 RANDOM PAGE REPLACEMENT

The optimal algorithm required knowledge of the future to work. The other extreme would be an algorithm that requires no knowledge at all (of the future or of the past) to work. The *random page replacement algorithm* is such an algorithm. It does not take anything about the program's paging behavior into account, but simply picks a page at random to replace. Figure 12.1 shows one view of random page replacement.

random page replacement algorithm

The theory of the random page replacement algorithm is that the past is of no use in predicting the future and should not be considered.

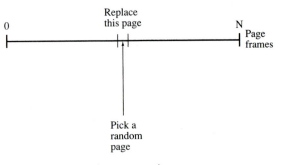

Figure 12.1   Random page replacement

This algorithm is easy to implement and is not the worst possible page replacement algorithm. One advantage of random page replacement is that its performance is predictable. Other algorithms make some assumptions about how programs will behave. If those assumptions are valid, the algorithm will work well, but if they are not valid, then the algorithm will work badly, worse than random replacement. Let's think of this in another way. Suppose the program deliberately tries to make the paging algorithm perform badly. It does this by accessing pages in such a way that the page replacement algorithm's choices always turn out wrong. In other words, it acts as an adversary. But a program cannot do this against random page replacement because its choices are unpredictable and there is no way for the program to "defeat" the random page replacement algorithm. There is no algorithmic way a program can act to make random page replacement do any worse than it would with a well-behaved program.

Just as the optimal algorithm is the upper bound on algorithm performance, the random replacement algorithm should be the lower bound of performance. It is possible for algorithms to be worse than the random algorithm, but any one that is should not be used.

> Random replacement is useful where you think that worst cases are likely.

12.2.5   First-In, First-Out Page Replacement

FIFO page replacement

In *first-in, first-out (FIFO) page replacement* you replace the page that has been in memory the longest. The implementation is easy: you just keep a pointer that starts at the first page frame and continually cycles through all the page frames, replacing each page as the pointer passes it.

The theory behind FIFO is that old pages are not referenced as much as new pages, that programs keep moving on to new program and data areas and do not go back to old code or data that much. This theory does not seem to be true in practice, and the FIFO page replacement algorithm works poorly. The problem is that

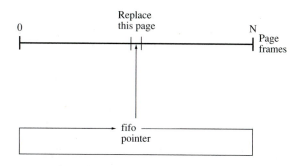

Figure12.2   FIFO page replacement

programs tend to have certain pages of instructions and data that they use over and over all through the execution of the program. Even though these pages are heavily used, under FIFO they eventually get old and are paged out. Generally they get referenced again very soon, and so the page written out has to be read in again right away. Figure 12.2 shows one view of FIFO page replacement.

Many stores are stocked using a FIFO theory. Take a bookstore for example. When someone wants to buy a book, it is probably a book that was published recently. If you wanted to buy an old book, you probably would have bought it already, so most customers want new books. Therefore, bookstores stock mostly books that have been published recently.

FIFO is not a good paging algorithm.

12.2.6   LEAST-RECENTLY USED PAGE REPLACEMENT

Least-recently used (LRU) page replacement keeps track of the last time each page was accessed and replaces the page that has not been accessed in the longest time.

The theory behind LRU is that pages are in active use for a while, and once they stop being actively used they are not used for a long time. Another way to say this is that the recent past is a good predictor of the near future. LRU predicts that the future will be a reflection of the past around the present. That is, recently accessed pages will be accessed again soon, and pages that have not been accessed for a while will not be accessed for a while in the future. Figure 12.3 shows this idea pictorially. In the extreme, the optimal page to replace, the one that will not be accessed for the longest time in the future, is the page that has not been accessed for the longest time in the past. Pages that have been used recently will be used again soon, and pages that have not been used recently will not be used again soon.

LRU is a very good theory and is one of the best global paging algorithms. Simulation studies (Coffman and Varian, 1968) have shown LRU to be within 30 percent

LRU page replacement

to 40 percent of optimal. The problem with LRU is that it is expensive to record the necessary information. To implement LRU, you need to record the access time of the accessed page on every memory reference. Clearly, this is impossible in software, and it is even expensive in hardware.

Recording the time of last access of each page is only feasible if the page table entries are in registers since it is too slow to read, modify, and write the page table entry in memory on every memory reference. But the active pages will be in the translation lookaside buffer, which is kept in hardware registers, so this approach is possible but it requires a fair amount of hardware.

Figure 12.4 shows one view of LRU page replacement. We keep a list of the page frames in order of their most recent use. A page reference moves a page frame to the front of the list (and moves the other page frames down one slot). On a page fault, the last page frame in the list is removed from memory.

Any software implementation must be an approximation of LRU.

LRU is an excellent paging algorithm, but it must be approximated by the implementation.

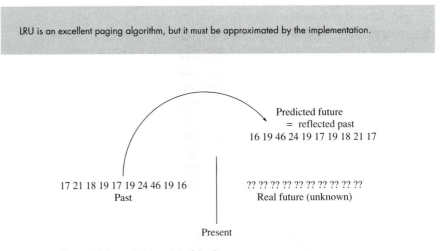

Figure 12.3   LRU model of the future

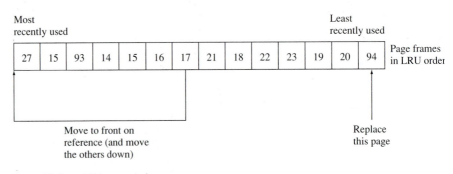

Figure 12.4   LRU page replacement

12.2.7   APPROXIMATIONS OF **LRU**

Most LRU approximations use a combination of software and hardware. They use some simple hardware mechanism to provide the basic information, and then use software to develop approximate LRU information.

The hardware required most often is a bit that tells you whether a page has been referenced or not. We call this bit the *referenced bit*. The referenced bit is a field in the page table entry that is set to 1 by the paging hardware whenever that page is accessed. There are machine instructions to read the referenced bit and to set it to zero.

referenced bit

Here is how our first approximation of LRU works. Every time we get a page fault, we can scan the pages and see which ones have their referenced bit set. These pages have been referenced recently. We pick a page to replace that has a referenced bit of 0, and then set all the referenced bits back to 0. The referenced bits serve to divide the pages into two groups, those that have been reference since the last page fault and those that have not. This is a very crude approximation of LRU.

We can improve the approximation with more effort in the software. Suppose we keep a counter for each page. This counter is initialized to zero. Every so often (say every second), an LRU daemon will wake up and check the referenced bit of all the pages in memory. For each one that has been referenced in the last second, it will reset the counter back to zero, and for the other pages it will increment the counter by one.

When we get a page fault, the counter for each page tells you how many seconds have gone by since the page was referenced. We pick the one with the highest count as the least-recently used page. Typically this counter will be small, say only eight bits. When it gets to 255, we just leave it there and lump all pages that have not been referenced for 255 or more seconds in the same group.

In true LRU, each page has a unique reference time, and so all pages are ordered from most-recently used to least-recently used. If there are N pages, there are N categories. Our first LRU approximation reduced the number of categories to only 2. All pages referenced since the last page fault were in one category, and all the pages that were not referenced since the last page fault were in the other category. Our second approximation of LRU divided the N pages into 256 categories, which should provide a much closer approximation of LRU. Figure 12.5 shows the LRU approximations.

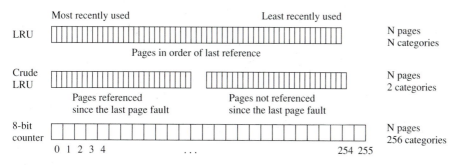

Figure 12.5   LRU and its approximations

12.2.8   CLOCK ALGORITHMS

clock algorithms

There is a class of page replacement algorithms called *clock algorithms* that have a pointer that points to each page frame in turn, looking for a page to replace. The name comes from the visualization that all the page frames are arranged in a circle (like the numbers on a clock face), and the pointer moves around the page frames like the hand of a clock. (See Figure 12.6.)

The FIFO Clock Algorithm   The clock algorithms vary according the how they decide whether to replace a page or not. The simplest clock algorithm always replaces the page the clock hand is pointing at, and then moves on to the next page. This is identical to the FIFO algorithm. This is not ordinarily considered a clock algorithm, even though it fits the clock model. It is a degenerate case of the clock algorithm.

The Basic Clock Algorithm   The simplest "real" clock algorithm looks at the page the clock hand is pointing to and, if its referenced bit is 0 (that is, if it hasn't been referenced recently), the page is replaced. If its referenced bit is 1, then the referenced bit is set to 0, the page is passed by, and the clock hand is moved to the next page. To keep from getting replaced, the page has to get referenced at least once every revolution of the clock hand.

This also is a rough approximation of LRU. It divides the pages into two groups. The first group is those pages that have been referenced, but the clock hand has not passed them yet. They have a reference bit of 1. The second group is those pages that have a referenced bit of 0 and will be replaced when the clock hand gets to them (unless they are referenced before then). These are the same two groups as the simplest LRU approximation, except that the clock algorithm adds a total ordering of

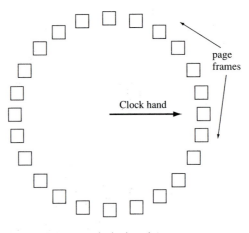

Figure 12.6   A clock algorithm

these pages induced by their location around the clock face. This ordering means that you do not replace a random page that has not been referenced recently, but you replace the one that has had the longest time to get referenced.

The basic clock algorithm is really a modified FIFO algorithm. In fact, when it was first developed, it was called first-in, not-used, first-out (FINUFO). It is also called *not recently used (NRU)*.

not recently used

Just to give you a rough idea of the scales involved, experiments have shown that one clock algorithm had to look at an average of 13 page frames in order to find one to replace.

Using Modified Bits   Besides a referenced bit, most paging hardware supports another bit in the page table entry called the *modified bit*. This bit is set to 1 whenever the page is written into. This bit is sometimes called the *dirty bit*.[1]

modified bit
dirty bit

The modified bit is important since a page that has been modified must be written out to disk before it can be replaced. If a page has not been modified, then the copy in the swap area is still correct and there is no need to write it out. Replacing a modified page takes twice as long since there is a disk write to write the old page out, and then a disk read to read the new page in. Because of this, some page replacement algorithms try to avoid writing out modified pages. There is a variation of the clock algorithm that does this. It is shown in Figure 12.7 and described below.

This clock algorithm looks at the page under the clock hand and looks at both its referenced bit and its modified bit. If the referenced bit and the modified bit are 0, then the page is replaced. If the referenced bit is 1, it is set to 0 and the page is passed over and given another chance. If the referenced bit is 0 and the modified bit is 1, then the modified bit is set to 0, the transfer of the page to disk is begun (or at least requested), and the page is passed over.

How can a page be modified and not referenced? Well, normally it can't, but if a page is modified and referenced and the clock hand passes over it the referenced bit is set to 0. The next time the clock hand passes the referenced bit is 0 and the modified bit is 1 (unless it is read or written in the meantime).

Another problem here is that if you set the modified bit to 0, how will you know the page has been modified when it comes time to replace it? There are two solutions to this problem. One is to keep a separate bit array which contains the "real" modified bit. When you set a hardware modified bit to zero, you set the modified bit in this array to remember that the page really has been modified. A second solution is to initiate a transfer of the page to disk as soon as you set the modified bit to zero. This will ensure that the dirty page is written out to disk. When we start the transfer of the page to disk, we remember that this transfer is in progress, and we do not reallocate the page until the transfer is completed.

This clock algorithm variation is also called the *second chance algorithm* since modified pages are given a second chance (that is, a second revolution of the clock hand) to get referenced before they are replaced.

second chance algorithm

---

[1] Not to be confused with Monty Python's concept of the "naughty bits."

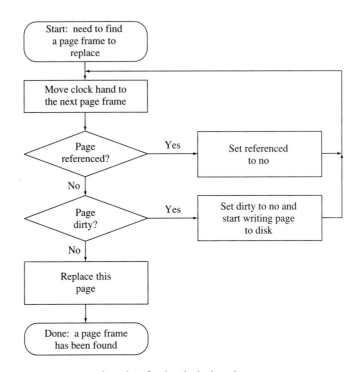

Figure 12.7   Flow chart for the clock algorithm

Here is a description of the general clock algorithm:

1. Test the page frame pointed to by the clock hand.
2. If it fails the test, then replace this page and the algorithm is completed.
3. If it passes the test, then:
   a. Modify the page frame information.
   b. Move the clock hand to the next page frame.
   c. Go back to step 1.

This is the algorithm for all the clock variations. Here is a table of the appropriate test and modification for each specific clock algorithm.

Variant	Test	Modification
FIFO	always fail	none
Clock	ref=1?	ref←0
Second chance	ref=1 or mod=1?	if ref=1 then ref←0 else mod←0

Clock algorithms are versatile and effective.

12.3 PAGE REPLACEMENT EXAMPLES

A typical program will have hundreds or thousands of pages. Pages are referenced at least once each instruction (one for the instruction fetch and another for the data fetch, if any), so a typical program execution will contain many millions of page references. Page faults only occur about once every million page references. Because of these large numbers, it is difficult to give realistic examples of page replacement. Instead, we will give radically simplified examples which show the basic idea of the page replacements but which do not represent real program behavior. Since we want to show page replacement in response to page faults, our examples will have lots of page faults, like one every two or three page references. A real program that page faulted at that rate would run 50,000 times slower than it would with real memory.

In the following page fault diagrams, we will show the same page reference string and number of page frames for five algorithms: optimal, LRU, clock, FIFO, and random. The labels on the left side are page frame numbers, and the labels on the top are the page reference numbers. The items in the matrix are the page numbers in each page frame *after* the page reference and subsequent page replacement (if any). An entry is followed by an asterisk if there was a page fault and this was the page just brought in. An entry is followed by a plus sign if the page was referenced and was found in memory. Thus each column has either an asterisk or a plus following one of the page numbers in that column.

The page fault count following the name of the page replacement algorithm does not include the initial four page faults to fill the available page frames with pages.

Let's take a page reference string and see how it would be handled by our different page replacement algorithms. Suppose we have a program that consists of eight pages and we have four page frames of physical memory for it. This means that half of the program will be in memory at any one time. The page reference string will be 1232563463731536342434451. Here are the results:

Optimal (7 page faults)

	1	2	3	2	5	6	3	4	6	3	7	3	1	5	3	6	3	4	2	4	3	4	5	1
0	1*	1	1	1	1	1	1	1	1	1	1	1	1+	1	1	1	1	1	2*	2	2	2	2	1*
1	-	2*	2	2+	2	6*	6	6	6+	6	6	6	6	6	6	6+	6	4*	4	4+	4	4+	4	4
2	-	-	3*	3	3	3	3+	3	3	3+	3	3+	3	3	3+	3	3+	3	3	3	3+	3	3	3
3	-	-	-	-	5*	5	5	4*	4	4	7*	7	7	5*	5	5	5	5	5	5	5	5	5+	5

LRU (10 page faults)

	1	2	3	2	5	6	3	4	6	3	7	3	1	5	3	6	3	4	2	4	3	4	5	1
0	1*	1	1	1	1	6*	6	6	6+	6	6	6	6	5*	5	5	5	5	2*	2	2	2	2	1*
1	-	2*	2	2+	2	2	2	4*	4	4	4	4	1*	1	1	1	1	4*	4	4+	4	4+	4	4
2	-	-	3*	3	3	3	3+	3	3	3+	3	3+	3	3	3+	3	3+	3	3	3	3+	3	3	3
3	-	-	-	-	5*	5	5	5	5	5	7*	7	7	7	7	6*	6	6	6	6	6	6	5*	5

Clock (10 page faults)

	1	2	3	2	5	6	3	4	6	3	7	3	1	5	3	6	3	4	2	4	3	4	5	1
0	1*	1	1	1	1	6*	6	6	6+	6	6	6	6	5*	5	5	5	5	2*	2	2	2	2	1*
1	-	2*	2	2+	2	2	2	2	2	2	7*	7	7	7	7	6*	6	6	6	6	6	6	5*	5
2	-	-	3*	3	3	3	3+	3	3	3+	3	3+	3	3	3+	3	3+	3	3	3	3+	3	3	3
3	-	-	-	-	5*	5	5	4*	4	4	4	4	1*	1	1	1	1	4*	4	4+	4	4+	4	4

FIFO (12 page faults)

	1	2	3	2	5	6	3	4	6	3	7	3	1	5	3	6	3	4	2	4	3	4	5	1
0	1*	1	1	1	1	6*	6	6	6+	6	6	6	1*	1	1	1	1	1	2*	2	2	2	2	2
1	-	2*	2	2+	2	2	2	4*	4	4	4	4	4	5*	5	5	5	5	5	5	3*	3	3	3
2	-	-	3*	3	3	3	3+	3	3	3+	7*	7	7	7	7	6*	6	6	6	6	6	6	5*	5
3	-	-	-	-	5*	5	5	5	5	5	5	3*	3	3	3+	3	3+	4*	4	4+	4	4+	4	1*

Random (12 page faults)

	1	2	3	2	5	6	3	4	6	3	7	3	1	5	3	6	3	4	2	4	3	4	5	1
0	-	-	3*	3	5*	5	3*	3	3	3+	7*	3*	3	3	3+	3	3+	3	3	3	3+	3	3	3
1	-	-	-	-	-	-	-	-	-	-	-	-	-	5*	5	5	5	4*	4	4+	4	4+	5*	1*
2	-	-	-	-	-	6*	6	4*	6*	6	6	6	6	6	6	6+	6	6	6	6	6	6	6	6
3	1*	2*	2	2+	2	2	2	2	2	2	2	2	1*	1	1	1	1	1	2*	2	2	2	2	2

Naturally, the optimal algorithm is best. The LRU and clock algorithms are the same, but for longer sequences we would expect LRU to be better than clock. FIFO is a little worse, and for longer sequences it will be much worse. Random is the same as FIFO on this short example, but for typical longer sequences, random will be much worse than any of the others.

12.4 LOCAL PAGE REPLACEMENT ALGORITHMS

We observed that each page replacement strategy has a theory of how programs behaved. So far, we have looked at the quite simple theories used by FIFO and LRU. In order to develop better page replacement algorithms, we will need more sophisticated models of how programs behave. In this section, we will develop the working set model of program behavior.

Each global page replacement algorithm assumes a theory of process behavior, but the global algorithms do not treat each process individually. Instead, they lump them all together in one group and look at the paging characteristics of the entire group together. We can do better page replacement if we treat each process individually.

Researchers have been working on developing more accurate models of program paging behavior since the 1960s. This development is an excellent example of the *science* in computer science. At each stage, a mathematical model of program behavior was proposed. Then the model was validated by comparing it to the behavior of real programs. Usually the model was found to be insufficient to explain the behavior of real programs, and so a more complex model was tried. The currently accepted model of program behavior is a phase model of working sets.

12.4.1   What Is a Working Set?

At any one time, a process is only using a subset of its pages. This is the principle of locality that makes paging feasible. Intuitively, the *working set* of a process is the set of pages that it is currently using. If all these pages are in memory, then the process will not get any page faults. This description of the working set is vague, and since it is the set of pages a process is currently using, it involves predicting the future again. To formulate the concept into something we can compute, we will have to define the working set in terms of past page references. To do this, we will need the concept of *virtual time* in a process. Each page reference is one unit of virtual time, and we will number the time units from 1 to T (the present time). At each unit of virtual time, the process makes a reference to a page. The *reference string* is the sequence of pages $r_1, r_2, r_3, \ldots, r_T$ where r_t is the page referenced at virtual time t. We will look back at a certain number, θ, of page references, and the set of pages referenced in that interval will be the working set. So the working set is:

working set

virtual time

reference string

$$W(T, \theta) = \{p \mid p = r_t \quad \text{where} \quad T - \theta < t \le T\}$$

[handwritten annotations: "element of the set", "time", "page ref", "$p \in W(T, \theta) = \{253, 142, 130, 163\}$"]

Like LRU, the working set model uses the theory that the recent past will be like the near future, that is, the set of pages that have been recently used is the set of pages we will be using in the near future.

The working set theory is that a program needs all the pages in its working set in memory in order to run efficiently, and so the operating system should only run a process when all the pages in its working set are loaded into memory.

12.4.2   Program Phases

A working set is, informally, the subset of its pages that a program is currently using and, formally, the subset of its pages that has been referenced in the last θ page references. In each case, the important fact is that the working set is a subset of the process' pages. Since a program will, in most executions, reference all its pages, this implies that the working set will change as time goes on.

Originally, researchers held the idea that the working set of a program slowly changed over time as the program entered new phases of its work. Measurements of real program behavior have shown that this "slow drift" model of program phase changes is incorrect. Instead, programs change phases abruptly, and the working set changes radically in a short time. Each working set is called a *program phase*. Each transition between phases causes a lot of page faults.

program phase

The currently accepted model of program behavior is that a program goes through a series of phases. Within each phase, the working set is fairly stable, and page-referencing behavior can be modeled with any one of several simple probabilistic models of program behavior. But the transitions between these phases are short and sudden.

Measurements show that 95 percent to 98 percent of the virtual time of a process is spent in phases where the working set is stable for a period of time. Hence, only 5 percent to 2 percent of a process' time is spent in transitions between phases. However, 40 percent to 50 percent of the page faults occur in these transitions, and page fault rates are 100 to 1000 times higher in the transitions than they are within the phases.

Let's take a specific example of a program with phases. We will use a program that has very distinct phases to make the ideas show up clearly. Suppose a program has three arrays and it is going to sort them one after the other. Each array uses 10 pages of memory and it takes 200,000 page references to sort one of the arrays. We will use a value of $\theta = 1000$, that is, we will look at the last 1000 page references to compute the working set. We will only look at references to data pages, not program pages.

The following table shows the real working set for this program and what is computed by $W(t, \theta)$.

t	Number of Pages in the Working Set	Number of Pages in $W(t, 1000)$
0–199,999	0–9	0–9
200,000–200,999	10–19	0–19
201,000–399,999	10–19	10–19
400,000–400,999	20–29	10–29
401,000–599,999	20–29	20–29

We see that $W(t, \theta)$ is a good approximation of the working set except in the transitions between phases where W takes too much of the past into account. The measured working sets in the transitions are twice as big as the stable working sets within phases. All of the page faults will occur in these transitions.

During the transition period the process may reference a lot of different pages before it settles down into the new working set. The size of the computed working set, as measured by W, increases sharply during phase transitions. This is due to two factors. Most of the increase in the working set size is due to the fact that W is looking too far back and is getting too many pages from the previous phase, that is, most of the increase is due to inaccuracies in how W measures the true working set of the program. Another factor is that the working set really is larger between phases, since the program is often using pages from the previous and the next phase at the same time. These two factors combine to cause a large increase in the size of W and the number of page faults during the transition. Figure 12.8 shows the general trend of the working set sizes as a program moves through three phases. Figure 12.8 is not based on real data, but the graphs produced from measurements of running programs look quite similar to this figure.

12.4.3   VARIABLE RESIDENT SET SIZES

The set of pages that a process currently has in memory is called its *resident set*. The resident set should be the current working set of the program. If it does not include part of the working set, then excessive page faults will be generated. If it includes

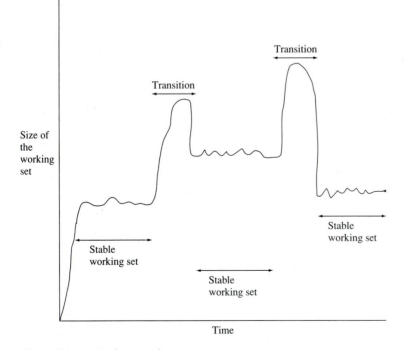

Figure 12.8   Working set phases in a program

more than the working set, then those extra pages will not be referenced and that memory is not used productively.

Since working sets change as the program makes a transition to another phase, the size of the working set, and hence the resident set, should change during the execution of a program. So the size of the resident set should change as the program changes phases.

The global page replacement algorithms do change the resident set size of the programs, but in an indirect way. A more direct approach is to directly measure the working set of a program and make sure the resident set is exactly the working set. This means that a local page replacement scheme will vary the number of page frames allocated to a process as its working set changes.

12.4.4   THE WORKING SET PAGING ALGORITHM

working set

The *working set* concept can be translated into a local page replacement algorithm. We monitor the working set for each process by computing W as described above. For each process, we keep its working set in memory while it is running. As the computed working set (determined by W) changes, we will change the resident set of the process to reflect those changes. Sometimes we will increase the size of the resident set and sometimes we will reduce it. By implication, a process cannot be run unless its entire working set will fit into memory. If the working set of a process will not fit into memory, then the process is removed from memory completely until its working set will fit.

The working set algorithm is a very good algorithm, and some believe (Denning, 1980) that it is close to the optimal realizable page replacement algorithm. Unfortunately, it is hard to implement the working set algorithm efficiently.

The problem with implementing the working set algorithm comes down to computing W. Computing W is theoretically possible, since it does not require predicting the future, but practically it is not feasible to compute W directly. It is like LRU in that to compute it would require extensive hardware support. What is generally used is a software approximation of W.

12.4.5   APPROXIMATING THE WORKING SET

One hardware requirement for implementing the working set algorithm or an approximation of the working set algorithm is a timer that records the virtual time of each process. Fortunately, the process management part of the operating system is probably already doing this. When a process is dispatched, the dispatcher notes the time on a high-resolution (one microsecond or shorter) timer. When the process is interrupted, the elapsed time is added to the accumulated total execution time in the process descriptor. The accumulated total execution time is used as the virtual time of the process. This will not be exactly the reference number used in defining the working set, but it is sufficient for our purposes.

Here is an algorithm that will approximate the working set page replacement algorithm.

DESIGN TECHNIQUE: WORKING SET CONCEPT

Some ideas from operating systems have close analogies in other areas of computer science or even beyond. For example, the idea of *thrashing* is familiar to all of us who have too many things to do. We find that the overhead of switching between tasks ends up taking up a lot of our time, and we find it more efficient to go hide somewhere and get one task done without interruption.

The working set model has been applied to user interfaces in an interesting way. A working set is the minimum number of page frames a program needs to run without excessive page faulting. The idea can be applied to screen space and windows. Certain tasks require information from several sources and so need a window on each source. If the screen space is not sufficient to display all these windows, then the user will waste a lot of time switching between and rearranging windows. This idea was used to develop the idea of multiple workspaces, each of which holds the working set of windows for a particular task.

Anyone who has tried to get certain types of work done on an airplane will have experienced the same phenomenon. The tray table is quite small, and if you have several documents to work on, you will end up spending a lot of time switching documents and trying to figure out where to put a document you are going to need again in a minute.

Here again, we use models to inspire ideas rather than to prove them. The idea of working sets and thrashing (when the working set is not present) can inspire the idea for a window manager with multiple workspaces, each holding the working set of windows for one task. This analogy does not prove that the multiple workspace idea is a good one. This is proved by trying it out and seeing if it improves the way people work with windows.

> Models and analogies are for inspiration, not proof.

---

1. When a page fault occurs, scan through all the pages that process has in memory.

2. If the referenced bit is set, then set the "time of last use" of that page to the current virtual time of the process.

3. If the referenced bit is not set, then check the "time of last use" field of the page. If the page has not been used within θ (the working set parameter) time units, then remove the page.

4. Bring in the new page and add it to the resident set of the program.

Step 3 removes a page from the resident set if it has not been used within the working set window (θ). Step 4 adds a new page to the resident set since the page fault indicates that it is now part of the working set. So the size of the resident set (that is, the measured working set) may move either up or down or may stay the same after each page fault.

This algorithm requires a scan of all the resident pages each time there is a page fault. This could be a large overhead, and so even this approximation of the working set algorithm may be too slow for practical use.

12.4.6   WSClock Paging Algorithm

There is a variant of the clock algorithm that does a good job of simulating the working set algorithm and is very efficient as well. The algorithm is based on the observation that a page is in the working set of a process if it has been referenced in the working set window. When we look at a page, we see if it has been referenced in that window, and remove it from memory if it has not.

WSClock algorithm

Here is the *working set clock (WSClock) algorithm.*

1. Examine the referenced bit of the page frame the clock hand is currently pointing to. Say page N is in this page frame.

2. If the referenced bit is on, then:
   a. Turn off the referenced bit.
   b. Set LastUsedTime(N) to the virtual execution time of the process that owns the page.
   c. Move the clock hand to the next page frame.
   d. Go to step 1.

3. If the referenced bit is off, compare (where P is the process the page belongs to):

$$CurrentVirtualTime(P) - LastUsedTime(N) < \theta$$

   a. If the difference is less than θ (the size of the working set window), then:
      (1) Move the clock hand to the next page frame.
      (2) Go to step 1.
   b. If the difference is more than θ and the page is not modified, then use this page frame to hold the page that the process just faulted on.
      (1) Remove this page from the resident set.
      (2) Use this page frame to hold the page that the process just faulted on.
      (3) Exit the algorithm.
   c. If the difference is more than θ and the page is modified, then:
      (1) Schedule the page for page out and continue looking for a page to replace.
      (2) Go to step 1.

The page frames are in a circular list, as they are in all clock algorithms. When you need to find a page to replace, you look at the next page frame. If the referenced bit is on, then you turn it off and record the virtual time of the process that owns that page as the "last used time" of the page. This saved time is an approximation of the last time the page was referenced. If the referenced bit is off, then you compare the current virtual process time with the saved "last used time" for the page in that page frame. If this difference is larger than the working set window size, then we can conclude that the page has not been referenced in the working set window and so is not in the working set, so we replace it. Otherwise we move on to the next page frame. We may examine pages from several different processes while looking for a page to replace.

The important difference between this algorithm and the working set approximation we described above is that we do not scan all the resident pages when we get a page fault, but just enough of them to find a page to replace. We may not remove pages from the resident set as quickly as the original working set algorithm, but we do remove them when we need a new page.

The working set clock algorithm looks like a global algorithm, but we are keeping information about the working set of each process. The thing that is "global" about the algorithm is that we decide on a global basis which pages to look at to test whether they are within the working set window for their process.

If all the page frames are examined and none can be replaced (even after waiting for modified pages to be paged out), then memory is overcommitted. We pick a process to swap out and reclaim all of its page frames. This is how WSClock ensures that processes are only run if their entire working set can be resident. WSClock works even better with LT/RT load control (see Section 12.6.6).

This is an efficient and reasonably accurate approximation of the working set algorithm, and simulations (Carr and Hennessey, 1981) show it performs as well as working set.

*12.5 EVALUATING PAGING ALGORITHMS

Now that we have seen several paging algorithms, we need a way to compare them and decide which one to use. As we noted before, each paging algorithm is based in a model of program paging behavior, and if that model is accurate the algorithm will perform well. The problem is that an operating system runs a lot of different programs with different paging behaviors. An operating system will use a single paging algorithm, and that may work well on some programs and poorly on others. We want to use an algorithm that will work well on the largest range of programs.

There are three approaches to the evaluation of paging algorithms: measurement, simulation, and mathematical modeling. In the measurement approach, you implement the algorithm in an operating system and measure its performance while programs are running. This approach is quite expensive and lengthy. More commonly, the measurement approach is used to get example page reference traces to use in simulation approaches to the evaluation of paging algorithms.

The mathematical modeling approach involves finding a mathematical model that describes the behavior of a computer system doing paging. This requires a model of program behavior. We have already seen some models of program behavior. The problem with the mathematical model approach is that models that are simple enough to be able to be analyzed mathematically are usually not accurate enough in the way they model program behavior. We will discuss the simulation approach in the next section.

12.5.1 METHODOLOGY FOR PAGING SIMULATION

In the simulation approach, we use simulation techniques to measure the performance of paging algorithms. Figure 12.9 shows the stages you have to go through in order to do paging simulation experiments.

The first thing to do in using simulation is to get a suite of "typical" programs, that is, programs that represent the kind of programs that you will be using. In addition to

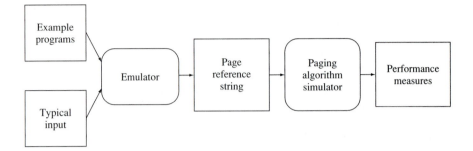

Figure 12.9   Steps in the simulation analysis of page replacement algorithms

getting typical programs, you need to get typical input data to drive the programs. This is not an easy thing to do, and what is typical changes over time anyway, but there is no other way to proceed.

Then you run each program with one or more sets of typical data, using a program that records the address reference string of the program. Such a program will contain an *emulator* for the hardware architecture the program is compiled to run on. The emulator will interpret and execute each machine instruction and record all the page references. Emulation of this sort causes a slowdown of from 50 to 500 times, so gathering this data requires a lot of machine time. Since programs make many millions of memory references, this trace data is very large and requires a lot of disk space to store it.

A *page reference string* is the sequence of pages a program references during a particular execution. It contains one reference for each memory reference the program makes. The result of the emulator step is a number of page reference strings representing typical program behavior.

The next tool you need is a program that can read in a page reference string and compute how many page faults a particular paging algorithm would generate with this reference string. That is, you simulate the operation of the paging algorithm. By examining the page reference string, you can figure out which pages would be in memory, when page faults will occur, and what page will be replaced. You must write a simulator for each paging algorithm you want to evaluate and compare the number of page faults each algorithm generates.

The problem with this comparison is that there are three variables you need to consider. For each test run, you have to specify:

- The page reference string to use.
- The size of the page.
- The number of page frames available.

You want to use representative page reference strings. That means very long strings, and a wide range of them. Each simulation runs a long time, and you have to run a lot of them to get representative results. You will want to repeat all these runs

emulator

page reference string

for a range of page sizes and numbers of page frames. It should be clear by now that the simulation approach is very resource intensive, but this is generally true of all uses of simulation.

12.5.2   SOME PAGE SIMULATION RESULTS

The simulation approach is the one most commonly used to evaluate paging algorithms. We have quoted a number of results about page replacement algorithms in the text already and most of these have come from simulation experiments. One of the surprising things is that most of the paging algorithms that have been proposed perform about the same. The graph in Figure 12.10 shows the ranges of performance that you typically see. There are two things to note about this chart. The first is that all of the "reasonable," realizable algorithms perform about the same, and pretty close to the optimal algorithm. The second thing to observe is the sharp "knee" in the chart. If a process does not have enough page frames, then it will fault excessively no matter what page replacement algorithm you choose. Conversely, if a process has enough page frames, then all of the page replacement algorithms will perform well.

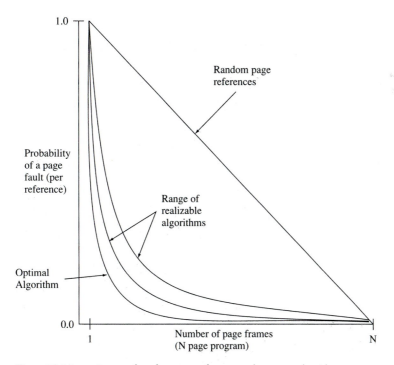

Figure 12.10   Range of performance of page replacement algorithms

The point here is that there are two things a paging system must decide: how many page frames to give a process, and what pages to keep in those page frames. Figure 12.10 indicates that the second decision is fairly easy to make (since the algorithms do not vary much) and the first decision is critical to performance.

The way to ensure that processes have enough page frames to run efficiently (without excessive page faulting) is to be sure that there are not too many processes in memory at the same time. Deciding how many processes to have in memory is called load control, and we will discuss it in the next section.

12.6   THRASHING AND LOAD CONTROL

Early paging systems experienced a form of catastrophic performance failure called thrashing. It was caused by incorrect load control.

12.6.1   HOW THRASHING OCCURS

One purpose of paging is to pack more processes into memory so that there will always be some process ready to run and not waiting for I/O. This way we keep the CPU busy. In the early paging systems, keeping the CPU busy was an important goal, and so they were set up to detect when the CPU busy percentage got too low. When CPU use went down below some threshold, say 25 percent busy, then they would try to load another process into memory to increase the CPU use rate.

This was an early form of what we now call *load control,* which is the operating system policy that tries to determine how many processes the operating system should be running. Unfortunately, this load control policy led to an unexpected and disastrous phenomenon called *thrashing.*

thrashing

If the processes in memory started getting more page faults, then the CPU use would go down because processes were frequently waiting for pages. This caused the load control mechanism to try to load another process into memory. This new process caused the competition for memory to increase and so caused the page fault rate to increase. This caused the CPU use rate to go down still further, and that caused the load control mechanism to try to load still another process into memory.

This phenomenon, called a positive feedback loop, caused the system to load so many processes into memory that none of them had enough memory to run. The page fault rates went up so high that no process could run more than a couple of hundred instructions before it got a page fault. We observed before that you have to have a very low page fault rate for paging to be acceptably fast. If the page fault rate increases to, say, once every 1000 instructions, then the program will run 1000 times slower than expected. This meant that jobs were running thousands of times slower than they would with low page fault rates, and the system was spending all its time servicing page faults and waiting for pages to be read in. The word "thrashing" describes the situation quite well, and one has images of dinosaurs caught in the tar pits whose thrashing around to get free just caused them to sink more rapidly into the tar.

12.6.2   LOAD CONTROL

What was learned from observing the phenomenon of thrashing was the necessity for better *load control,* that is, the operating system has to monitor the paging rate and reduce the level of multiprogramming if the paging rate is too high. Virtual memory is not magic, and you cannot run as many programs as you want simultaneously or else thrashing will occur. The early systems had a form of load control, but it was based on CPU utilization, which is the wrong measure. Load control must be based on the paging rate.

load control

  The idea of load control is quite simple. You monitor the page fault rate by incrementing a counter every time there is a page fault. Every second or so, you check the page fault rate to see if it is over some threshold. If it is, you remove one process from memory, that is, you swap it out and give all its page frames to other processes. A new process can be started or a swapped-out process can be swapped in only if the page fault rate is low enough.

  Figure 12.11 shows the difference between the tasks of a page replacement algorithm and a load control algorithm. They do logically different things, but they are closely enough related that they have to communicate with each other (load control uses information that the page replacement algorithm collects). The working set algorithm is a page replacement algorithm that includes load control.

12.6.3   SWAPPING

We talked about swapping early in this chapter as a predecessor of paging. Paging was supposed to replace swapping. We have seen that this is not entirely true. A paging system needs a load control mechanism, and it sometimes needs to remove processes from memory completely until more memory is available.

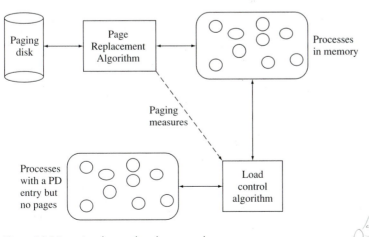

Figure 12.11 Load control and page replacement

In swapping, we write the entire process out to disk. In a paging system, a copy of the process is already on disk. To swap a process out, all we have to do is to release all the page frames it is using, and mark it "swapped out" in its process descriptor. This will cause the dispatcher to ignore it, and it will stop getting processor time. Its page frames can be used by other processes. To swap a process in, it is only necessary to change its status in its process descriptor to runnable again. Soon the dispatcher will dispatch it, and it will start running again and competing for page frames with the other processes.

12.6.4 SCHEDULING AND SWAPPING

Swapping creates a scheduling problem. You have to decide which programs should be in memory, when they should be swapped out, and what other program(s) should be swapped in. The memory scheduling has to be coordinated with the processor scheduling.

What you need is a two-level scheduling system where the levels are called short-term scheduling and medium-term scheduling. The *medium-term scheduler* (or memory scheduler) decides what jobs will be in memory, and the *short-term scheduler* (or processor scheduler) decides which of the jobs in memory will get to use the processor. (See Figure 12.12.) These two schedulers have to be coordinated since it is important that, as much of the time as possible, at least one of the processes in memory be able to use the processor. That way, at least one process will be making progress. In general, the medium-term scheduler should schedule a mix of processes into memory that will utilize all the resources of the system.

medium-term scheduler

short-term scheduler

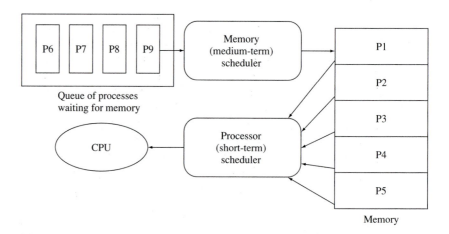

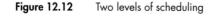

Figure 12.12   Two levels of scheduling

12.6.5   LOAD CONTROL AND PAGING ALGORITHMS

Generally load control is an additional mechanism that we add to a page replacement algorithm. The page replacement algorithm is in charge of trying to keep the most useful pages in memory, and the load control algorithm is responsible for deciding how many processes should be in memory. The two mechanisms are independent, but they do interact.

Some Measures of Load   Some of the paging algorithms we have encountered have natural load measures. The clock algorithm has a clock hand that moves around to all the page frames. If the clock hand is moving at a low rate (in revolutions per second), then either there are not many page faults or the clock hand does not have to move very far to find a page to replace. In this case, more processes should be brought into memory. If the clock hand is rotating quickly, then there are too many page faults or it is too hard to find a page to replace. This means the memory is overcommitted and we should remove a process from memory.

Page Fault Frequency Load Control   If we do not want to use some load measure from the page replacement algorithms (or it does not have any natural ones), we can do more generic load control by monitoring the overall page fault rate to determine whether the load is too high. This is called *page fault frequency load control*. The purpose of load control is to keep the page fault rate at a reasonable level, and so a direct measurement of the page fault rate seems like a good measure. When the page fault rate gets too high, we reduce the level of multiprogramming by swapping out a process.

> page fault frequency load control

But how do we decide what paging rates are "too high"? One measure that has been proposed is the $L = S$ criterion. We define L as the mean time between page faults and S as the mean time to service a page fault (assuming no waiting for other processes to use the disk or other time in queues). The $L = S$ load control method tries to keep L equal to S. If L gets higher than S, then a process is swapped out. If L gets lower than S, then a process is swapped in (if there are any waiting to be swapped in).

? higher / lower ?

The logic behind this is intuitive. If those two rates are equal, then the swapping system can exactly keep up with the page faults.

> Load control is necessary in any paging system.

12.6.6   PREDICTIVE LOAD CONTROL

In the previous sections, we described how to add load control to any page replacement algorithm—monitor the page fault rate and swap out a process if it gets too high. This is a form of reactive load control (also called adaptive load control)

predictive load control

where we detect that the load is too high and reduce it. The working set algorithm is a *predictive load control* method. It tries to predict what loads will be too high and prevents them from happening. One would expect that predictive load control would be better (if it predicts accurately) because it will not have to suffer reduced performance until the overload is detected.

There is a predictive method of load control that can be added to any paging algorithm, and it is called LT/RT (load time/run time) load control. The idea is based on the facts about phase transitions we talked about in Section 12.4.5. We observed that the page fault rates for programs in transition were hundreds to thousands of times higher than for programs within a program phase. The most predictable transition is when a program is first loaded (or swapped in after being completely swapped out). Then it has to load in all the pages of its working set.

The LT/RT algorithm divides processes into loading processes and running processes. Any process that has just been activated and whose paging rate is still high is called a loading process. The load control strategy is to only allow one loading process (per paging disk) to be executing at a time.

If two loading processes are competing, then the loading phase of each one of them will be lengthened. During this longer loading phase, other programs may finish and allow even more programs to start. This positive feedback can cause the paging device to be saturated, even though memory is not really overcommitted. Page faults during loading indicate loading problems, not too little memory allocated to the process. Page fault frequency load control can be fooled by loading processes.

LT/RT load control has been shown in simulation studies (Carr and Hennessey, 1981) to be very effective—more effective than the working set load control.

12.6.7   PRELOADING OF PAGES

A swapped-out process will lose all its page frames, and so when it is swapped back in again it will get a page fault on every page. It seems like we might as well bring in some of its pages right away, rather than have a flurry of page faults while it loads in the pages it needs.

demand paging

Up to now, we have used only what we call *demand paging,* which means that we do not read in a page unless we get a page fault on the page. This is generally a good strategy, since it avoids bringing in pages before they are really needed. An al-

prepaging

ternative policy is called *prepaging,* which involves reading in pages before they are requested by the program. We only want to prepage a page if we have a good reason to believe it will be accessed in the very near future.

But how can we predict which pages will be used? Well, the page replacement algorithms have been doing that all along, and we can use their predictions for prepaging. When a process is swapped out, we remember which pages it had in memory. These are the pages the page replacement algorithm thinks it needs. When the process is swapped in again, we prepage in all the pages it had before.

It is harder to prepage a new process because we have no idea which pages it will need.

12.7   DEALING WITH LARGE PAGE TABLES

In early paging systems, the logical address space was small enough that they could have the page table entirely in hardware registers. This became infeasible with larger address spaces, and so the page tables were moved out of hardware registers into memory to avoid the problems of saving and restoring so many registers. What happens when the page tables get so big they do not easily fit into physical memory? We have organized our paging hardware on the premise that the page tables are always in memory. This is not really feasible, even with 32-bit logical address spaces. We will look at some solutions to this problem.

12.7.1   WHAT IS THE PROBLEM?

First, let's look at the extent of the problem. Suppose we have a 32-bit address space (which is pretty much the standard these days) and 12-bit page offsets (4 Kbyte pages). This leave 20 bits of page number, over one million pages. Each page table entry takes four bytes, so 4 Mbytes of memory is required to hold a full page table. This is for a process that is as large as possible, 4 Gbytes. Few processes will be that big, but programs are getting larger and larger and the sum total of the page tables for 100–200 processes can add up to many megabytes, even if none of them used the total address space possible. As programs get larger, we will have to do something about the size of the page tables.

12.7.2   TWO-LEVEL PAGING

One solution is to reuse the paging idea and page the page tables themselves. This idea is called *two-level paging*, and it is an elegant solution to the problem of large page tables. We will start with an example of a specific two-level paging system.

two-level paging

Suppose we have a 32-bit virtual address. This will be divided up into 10 (high-order) bits of *master page number,* 10 (middle) bits of *secondary page number,* and 12 (low-order) bits of offset into the (4 Kbyte) page. The hardware page table register points to a master page table containing 1024 entries.(See Figure 12.13.) The master page table is also called the *primary page table*. Each entry is four bytes, and so the master page table is 4 Kbytes long (which conveniently fits exactly into one page frame). The master page number is used to look up the entry in the master page table. The master page table entry contains the address of a secondary page table, which also contains 1024 entries and is 4 Kbytes long. The secondary page number is used to look up an entry in the secondary page table. The secondary page table entry contains the base address of the page, which is added to the offset to get the physical address of the word being accessed.

master page number
secondary page number

primary page table

Figure 12.14 gives another visualization of two-level paging. Both of these diagrams only show one secondary page table, but you should note that there will be many secondary page tables, one for each entry in the master page table.

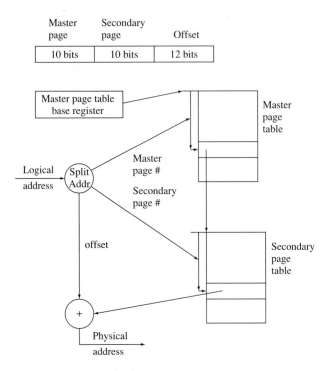

Figure 12.13   Two-level paging

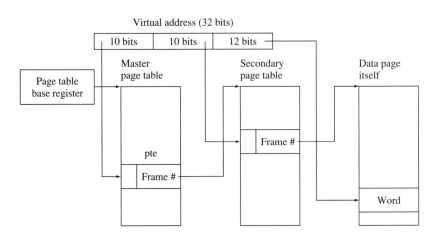

Figure 12.14   Two-level paging (another view)

Each secondary page table entry maps one 4K page, so an entire secondary page table maps 4 Mbytes of memory. One master page table entry maps one secondary page table, or 4M of memory. Thus a program of 4 Mbytes or less will only require two pages of page tables, a one-page master page table and a one-page secondary page table. In general, page tables in a two-level paging system are one page larger than they would be in a one-level paging system.

12.7.3   BENEFITS OF TWO-LEVEL PAGING

If we use two-level paging, small programs will still have small page tables and large programs will still have large page tables, but we are better off for two reasons. First, the page pages do not have to be in contiguous physical memory. The master page table and the secondary page tables are all one page long and they can be anywhere in memory.

The second benefit of two-level paging is that we can allow page faults when fetching the secondary page tables. That is, the master page table must always be in memory, but we can page the secondary page tables in and out as needed. So a program with a very large page table need not have the entire page table in memory at one time. Because of locality, we can afford to keep a substantial portion of the secondary page tables on disk without generating excessive page faults.

The main benefit of two-level paging comes in larger programs. A large program will only need to have part of its page tables in main memory, and the page table of an inactive program (large or small) will be paged out to disk and use very little main memory (only a page frame for the master page table). We are again exploiting the locality of page references in typical programs.

This method is especially good if we have lots of inactive processes. A process that is not active for a long time will have all of its secondary page tables paged out, and so will consume very few system resources. It is handy for users to keep lots of inactive processes around because it is easy to start them up again. Two-level page tables mean that they can do this without putting much of a load on the system memory.

Another benefit of this organization is that we can have large holes in the logical address space. For example, suppose we call the 4 Mbytes of address space mapped by one secondary page table a *segment*. We could have the code in one segment, the data in another segment, and the stack in another segment. If each segment begins on a 4M boundary, we will have one master page table entry and one secondary page table for each segment. The invalid pages between the segments would allow the hardware to detect when we overran a segment (like the stack).

12.7.4   PROBLEMS WITH TWO-LEVEL PAGING

One problem with two-level paging is that you have to look up in two page tables for every memory reference. Without caching hardware, that would mean three memory cycles for each memory access. Clearly, a translation lookaside buffer is necessary to avoid these extra memory references.

But, more importantly, two-level paging does not solve the other problems of very large address spaces: the page tables still have to be initialized and the pages still have to exist on disk. Such large page tables will take a long time to initialize, and the large address space will consume a lot of disk space. Finally, two-level paging still does not handle really large address space such as the 64-bit address spaces that are now becoming more prevalent.

If the address space is *really* large, we could go to *three-level page tables,* which extends this idea in the obvious way. (See Figure 12.15). With address spaces this large, we might go to other methods such as inverted page tables. We will look at this in the next section.

12.7.5   SOFTWARE PAGE TABLE LOOKUPS

Paging is normally handled by paging hardware. The operating system sets up the page tables and the appropriate hardware registers, and the hardware handles the page table lookups. As we have observed, however, the hardware does not usually have to look in the page table for the page table entry. Instead, the hardware will normally find the page table entry in the translation lookaside buffer (TLB). Only when the page is not in the TLB does the hardware have to do an actual lookup in the page tables. We want this to happen very seldom, since it requires an extra

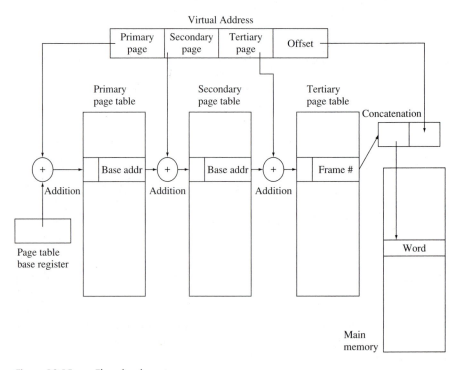

Figure 12.15   Three-level paging

memory cycle (two with two-level paging and three with three-level paging) to fetch the page table entry. If we have a large TLB, we might be able to get the cache miss rate down very low.

So there are three levels of performance and they are shown in the following table which shows the time penalties of three events in four paging schemes.

Event	1-Level Paging	2-Level Paging	3-Level Paging	Software Paging
TLB hit	1	1	1	1
TLB miss	2	3	4	10–50
Page fault	100,000	100,000	100,000	100,000

If the page table entry is in the cache, then the memory word is fetched directly by the hardware and it takes one memory cycle to get the word. If the page table entry is not in the cache, the hardware looks it up in the page table (in memory) and then fetches the memory word. This is called a cache miss, and it takes two memory cycles to fetch the word (three in a two-level paging system). If the page itself is not in memory, then a page fault occurs, and the operating system software takes care of reading the page into memory. This third case takes a very long time because it requires disk I/O. The first two cases are handled by the hardware because both cases are common enough so that they have to be handled very quickly. Page faults are rare enough that we can afford to let the software handle them.

If we provide a large enough TLB, we can reduce the cache miss rate so that cache misses are uncommon. In this case, we could afford to let the operating system software handle cache misses as well as page faults, and the hardware will be simplified. In addition, we can use more sophisticated methods that would be too complex, too expensive, or too experimental to put into hardware. This idea is called *software page table lookups*.

software page table lookups

So here is the idea. The hardware looks up the page in the TLB and fetches the word if it finds the page. If not, the hardware generates a TLB miss interrupt, which is handled by the operating system. The operating system finds the correct page table entry, loads it into the TLB, and restarts the instruction. (See Figure 12.16.) The hardware does not have to handle page table lookups and it does not have to handle cache management.

Inverted Page Tables   Since the hardware does not handle paging, it does not dictate the structure of the page tables, so the operating system is free to use any data structures it wants to represent the page tables. A structure that works very well for very large address spaces is an *inverted page table*. An ordinary (noninverted) page table has an entry for each page in the virtual address space and is used to look up the page frame that that page is in. With extremely large address spaces, this becomes a very sparse table since physical memories are not as large as virtual address spaces. An inverted page table has one entry for each page frame in physical memory and is used to look up which virtual page is in the page frame.

inverted page table

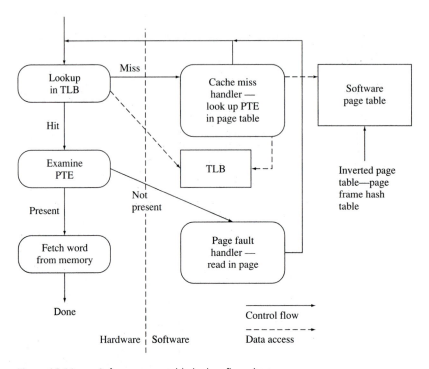

Figure 12.16   Software page table lookup flow chart

This type of page table is "inverted" because it is indexed by the physical page number and contains virtual page numbers, while an ordinary page table is indexed by the virtual page number and contains physical numbers.

The problem with an inverted page table is that it is not fast in the direction we want to go. It is easy to find out which page is in a page frame with an array access, but to find out which page frame a particular page is in requires a search of the entire table. The cache miss will tell us which virtual page is needed, and we have to find the page frame (or really the page table entry). But there are standard data structures to handle lookup problems like this (for example, hash tables, skip lists, binary trees). We can keep a hash table and look up a virtual page very quickly (in constant time).

Figure 12.17 shows normal paging with very large address spaces. Each process has a page table that contains mostly invalid entries that do not provide any information. That is because, with a very large address space, most of it is not in physical memory. The page tables are indexed by the incoming virtual page numbers, and their entries in the page table contain a physical page frame number. The entire page table lookup and access are done in hardware.

Figure 12.18 shows inverted page table paging. There is one inverted page table for the entire system, which is shared by all processes. The virtual page number is found in the inverted page table using a hash table lookup. (This figure shows one re-hash to find the virtual page number.) Once this is found, the index of the inverted page table where the virtual page number is found is the physical page frame number

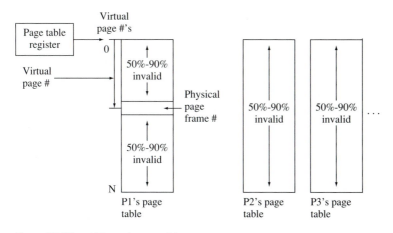

Figure 12.17   Normal page tables

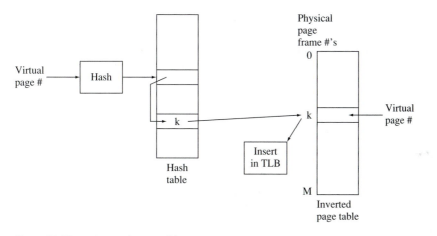

Figure 12.18   Inverted page table

we are looking for. The PTE is reconstructed (from the physical page frame number and the protection bits which are also kept in the inverted page table) and put in the TLB. Then the access is attempted again, and this time there will be a TLB hit. This entire process can be handled in software, although some machines implement hardware lookup in the inverted page table.

Efficiency of Inverted Page Tables   Page fault rates have to be extremely low since a page fault requires a disk access which takes a very long time. With software page table lookups, a TLB miss traps to the operating system, which then does the page table lookup. This does not require a disk access, and can be done in less than 50 instructions instead of a few hundred thousand instruction times (like a disk access). So if the TLB miss rate is, say, 0.1 percent, we will have about a 10 percent slowdown.

DESIGN TECHNIQUE: CHANGING WITH TECHNOLOGY

Software page table lookups are a good example of how the design of operating systems has changed with the technology to support it. The original paging systems had small TLBs whose hit rate was not high enough. For these systems, handling TLB misses in software would be too expensive, and therefore the hardware had to handle the mechanics of page tables. But with newer TLBs with high ($>$ 99 percent) hit rates, we can afford to handle the TLB misses in software. This simplifies the paging hardware (since it does not have to do page table lookups) and frees up space on the chip for other uses (like bigger caches). It also allows more experimentation with page table structures and more sophisticated structures (like inverted page tables).

Periodically reexamine and update your design assumptions because conditions change.

When the hardware was accessing the page tables, they had to be in the format the hardware understood. This was determined by the paging hardware and could never be changed. If the operating system is going to be handling page table lookups, it can use any data structures it wants to represent the page tables. Since the hardware does not do page table lookups, it does not restrict how the page tables can be structured.

Inverted Page Tables in Hardware   We have presented inverted page tables as a method that causes a fault when there is a TLB miss and the operating system software does the page table lookup. It is also possible to use this method where the hardware does the hash table lookup and finds the correct PTE. The IBM 801 memory management does this. Hash table lookup is a fairly simple technique and can be easily implemented in the hardware.

By implementing the inverted page table in hardware, we do not have to reduce the TLB miss rate so much, since a miss will be handled quickly in hardware. We still get the main advantage of inverted page tables, that is, much smaller page tables. But doing the page table lookup in software has some additional advantages. First, we simplify the hardware, freeing up chip area for more caches or other speedups. Second, we can experiment more easily with different page table organization, different hashing algorithms, different TLB replacement algorithms, etc.

---

*12.8   RECURSIVE ADDRESS SPACES

Two-level paging works very well, but it is not the only way to apply the idea of paging to page tables. The DEC VAX system used a method that is similar to two-level paging but is different in several crucial respects.

The idea is as follows. The operating system runs in virtual memory also. The virtual memory system creates an address space for each process and one for the the operating system. The page tables should only be accessible to the operating system, and so should be in the address space of the operating system. Normally, the page tables are kept in the physical address space (which is only accessible to the operating system), but we can instead keep the page tables in the virtual address space of the operating system. Let's examine exactly how that works first, and then we will compare it with two-level paging.

The operating system's virtual address space is mapped with page tables that exist in physical memory. The process's virtual address space is mapped with page tables that exist in the system's virtual address space. The crucial difference is that the hardware page table base address register for a user process contains a virtual address in the system's virtual address space. See Figure 12.19. This idea is called a *recursive address space*.

recursive address space

Figure 12.20 shows a representation of the two different ways of applying the paging idea twice. In both cases, each process has its own address space. With two-level page tables, the master pages are in the physical address space. Each master page table maps a secondary page table address space, one for each process. These are little address spaces that are only seen by the operating system and the paging

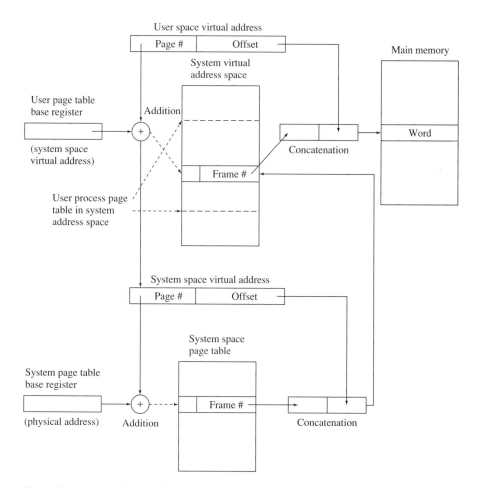

Figure 12.19   Two levels of virtual memory

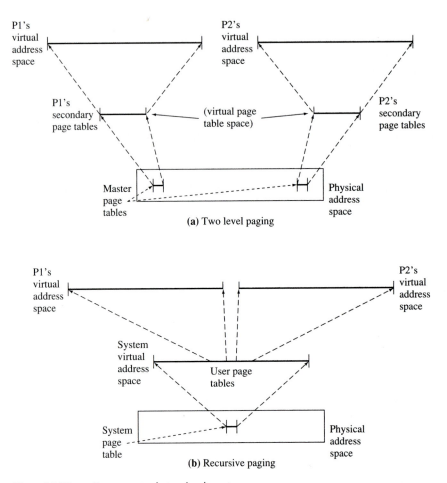

Figure 12.20   Two ways to do two-level paging

hardware. In recursive paging, the page table for the system address space is in physical memory and the process page tables are in the system address space (along with all the rest of the system code and data). In recursive paging, all the page tables are in the same address space, whereas in two-level paging each process's secondary page tables are in their own little address space.

12.9   PAGING THE OPERATING SYSTEM ADDRESS SPACE

Note that the operating system itself is paged when we organize things this way. Of course, we could have paged the operating system even with one-level paging. Since each process has its own address space, we only have to add one more address space for the system and run the operating system with paging on. Since the operating system can modify its own page tables, it will still be able to access any physical address it wants, although it may have to go to a little more trouble to do so.

But what if we get a page fault and go to the page fault handler, and it gets a page fault? It would seem that we would get into an infinite cycle, and indeed we would. The solution to the problem is "Don't do that." That is, we make sure that certain crucial code, like the page fault handler, never gets paged out. Paging systems provide a way to lock pages in memory and prevent them from being paged out. This might be a flag in the page table entry, or it could be kept in a separate table maintained by the paging system.

What parts of the operating system need to be locked into memory? The paging code, of course, and usually all the interrupt handlers since they need to run quickly and cannot afford to wait for a page to be read in. In general, the critical parts of the operating system that we want to run quickly will be locked in memory.

12.9.1 LOCKING PAGES IN MEMORY

There are other reasons you might want to lock pages in memory as well. For example, suppose that the I/O hardware uses physical addresses and so does not go through the page table. This is the way I/O hardware usually operates. Suppose we wanted to transfer a disk block directly into the address space of some user. We would translate the logical address of the I/O buffer to a physical address and give the physical address to the I/O controller. We need to lock the pages comprising the buffer in memory because we do not want those pages to be paged out and assigned to another process. If that happens, the I/O controller would transfer the data into the memory of another process.

Another reason to lock pages in memory is when the process is high priority and we want it to finish as quickly as possible. By locking its pages in memory, we prevent page faults that would slow the program down.

*12.10   PAGE SIZE

An important decision in a paging system is what page size to use. There are factors that encourage large page sizes (pages of 8 Kbytes or more) and factors that encourage small page sizes (pages of 1 Kbytes or less). As a consequence, most paging systems use some middle-sized page (like 4 Kbytes) as a compromise. Some paging systems allow two (or more) page sizes. This allows the system to be configured according to its expected workload.

12.10.1 REASONS FOR A LARGE PAGE SIZE

There are two reasons for having a large page size. The first has to do with the characteristics of the disks that are used for paging. As we will see in the next chapter (see Section 14.4), the bulk of the time to read in a page is the time to get to where the page is stored on disk. The time to transfer the data is a small part of the access time.

So it is better to move a lot of data in one access than to have several disk accesses. This consideration might change if we are paging to different devices that have different access time characteristics.

A second reason for large pages is that it takes fewer page faults to bring in a substantial portion of the program. We have observed that half of the page faults occur in loading the working set back again after a process has been swapped out or when a program changes phase to another working set. With large pages, there are fewer page faults to get the working set read in.

12.10.2   REASONS FOR A SMALL PAGE SIZE

There are two reasons for choosing a small page size. The first is internal fragmentation. On the average, half of the last page will be lost to internal fragmentation. If the page size is small, then this loss is small. On the other hand, smaller pages mean larger page tables, and we get what is sometimes called *table fragmentation,* that is, space wasted on tables.

For example, suppose the average program size is 300 Kbytes. If the page size is 1 Kbyte then the average program will have 300 pages. Each page table entry is four bytes, so the page table will take 1200 bytes. The total fragmentation consists of internal fragmentation (which is, on the average, half the size of the page at the end of each program) plus table fragmentation (which is the size of the page table of the average program). The table in Figure 12.21 shows the internal, table, and total fragmentation for a range of page sizes. Since the two factors vary inversely, we have a minimum. In this case, the smallest total fragmentation is with a 1K or 2K page. Remember that this table only figures in these two kinds of fragmentation, and there are other factors that are affected by the page size.

The second reason for small pages is that they allow us to only have the parts of the process that are really necessary in memory. Suppose you have a 4 Kbyte page which holds two 2 Kbyte procedures, and that one procedure is being heavily used but the other is not being used at all in this phase of the process. The 2 Kbytes occupied by the unused procedure are wasted and should not be in memory. If we used a

Page Size	Internal Fragmentation	Table Fragmentation	Total Fragmentation
8K	4K	150	4.2K
4K	2K	300	2.3K
2K	1K	600	1.6K
1K	512	1200	1.7K
512	256	2400	2.7K
256	128	4800	4.9K

Figure 12.21   Internal and table fragmentation for a range of page sizes

2 Kbyte page, then we could have the useful procedure in memory and the other one could be paged out. Smaller pages allow exactly the parts of the address space we are using to be in memory. Experiments have shown that if the page size is halved, then the average amount of memory required to hold the working set of the program is reduced by 10 percent.

Small pages are good for programs with long phases since we can get the exact working set in memory. Large page sizes are better for programs with short phases since they lower the cost during initial loading and phase transitions. Simulations (Coffman and Varian, 1968) indicate that increasing the number of pages is more effective at reducing page faults than increasing the size of the page.

12.10.3   CLUSTERING PAGES

One problem with paging is that, when a program is started, it gets a lot of page faults while it is loading in its pages. This also happens when a process is swapped in after being completely swapped out. In these cases, it has to reload its entire working set into memory. One way to avoid this is to bring in more than one page after a page fault. This idea is called *clustering,* With clustering, we bring in several (two to eight   clustering or more) pages at every page fault. The pages around the faulting page are part of the same *cluster,* and they are brought into memory all at the same time. The idea behind this is that page references are localized, and so the pages around a faulting page are likely to be in the working set of the program as well. This is a guess that usually turns out to be correct, and it saves page faults when processes are loading.

Clustering only affects the loading of pages. The pages are not paged out in a cluster. If we always move the pages in and out in a cluster, we are effectively increasing the page size of the system. This is a different technique (although it is also called clustering) and is used when the page size is too small.

12.11   SEGMENTATION

We have used the word "segment" several times, and now it is time to define it more carefully and discuss the use of segments in memory management.

12.11.1   WHAT IS A SEGMENT?

Paging is an arbitrary division of the logical address space into small fixed-size pieces. Instead of using pages, we could divide the address space of a process into pieces based on the semantics of the program. Such pieces are called *segments.*   segment For example, we could put each procedure or module, array, matrix row, or linked list in a segment. A segment is a division of the logical address space that is visible to the programmer. *Segmentation* leads to a *two-dimensional address space*   segmentation because each memory cell is addressed with a segment and an offset within that   two-dimensional address space segment. Segments are the size of the logical object they hold, and so are not of any fixed length.

12.11.2   VIRTUAL MEMORY WITH SEGMENTATION

Segments can be used as a basis for a virtual memory system that is similar to paging. Figure 12.22 shows segmented virtual memory. Instead of a page table, we have a segment table. Since segments can be of variable length, the segment table entry must contain a length field as well as the segment base address (in addition to protection and presence information). The virtual address is divided into a segment number and an offset into the segment. The segment number is used to index into the segment table to retrieve the segment table entry. The offset is added to the segment base address, and also checked against the segment length. The resulting address is used to access the word in memory. As you can see, the mechanism for segmentation is nearly the same as that for paging.

Segment table entries have a present bit which allows some segments to be kept on disk until they are needed and allows the use of segments for virtual memory.

Segment table entries also have protection bits like page table entries, but they are more useful with segments since everything in a segment is logically related (all

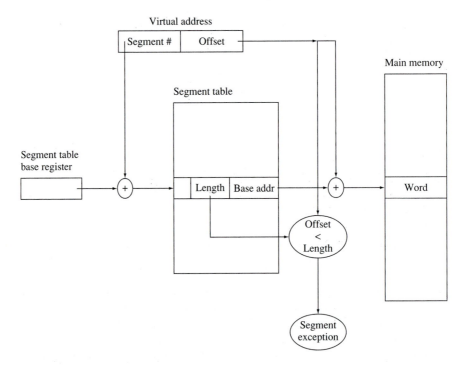

Figure 12.22   Segmentation

one procedure, one array, one list, etc.) and so they will all have the same protection status. In a paged system, a single page may contains parts of two different arrays which should be protected differently.

Are Segments Contiguous to Each Other?   Suppose you have a paging system with 1024-byte pages. If you are at byte 1023 of page 12 and you move one byte higher, you get to byte 0 of page 13. Now suppose you have a segmentation system with 64 Kbyte segments, you are at byte 64K-1 of segment 12, and you move one byte higher. In a "true" segmentation system, you will get a segment overflow because the segments are logically distinct and are not contiguous with each other. Segments create a two-dimensional address space where you have a number of linear address spaces. This is what makes the protection of segments work well.

12.11.3   SEGMENTATION WITH PAGING

Segments can be of different lengths, so it is harder to find a place for a segment in memory than a page. With segmented virtual memory, we get the benefits of virtual memory but we still have to do dynamic storage allocation of physical memory. In order to avoid this, it is possible to combine segmentation and paging into a two-level virtual memory system similar to two-level paging. Each segment descriptor points to a page table for that segment. This gives you some of the advantages of paging (easy placement) with some of the advantages of segments (logical division of the program). The problem is that it requires you to use large segments (a number of pages), and that reduces the usefulness of segments to divide the program into logical pieces.

The Burroughs 5000 and 6000 machines had a segmented virtual memory and the average segment size on them was less than 50 bytes. Clearly, paged segments would not have been useful there.

12.11.4   HISTORY OF SEGMENTATION

In the early days of virtual memory, both paging and segmentation were considered reasonable ways to implement virtual memory. In fact, computer scientists often preferred segmentation because it divided the program into logical segments. This followed the natural partitioning of the program and allowed for more precise protection of the parts of a program.

But segmentation was only used on a few commercial machines, mainly the ones from Burroughs, and pure segmentation is no longer used in any commercial machines. There are several reasons why this is so.

First, paging is transparent to the user, so you can add a paging system to a computer without changing any programs. Paging divides up the logical address space into pages without the user knowing anything about it. Segmentation changes the addressing structure that is visible to the program. All the compilers have to be rewritten to accommodate segmentation. This made it much easier to change to paging.

Second, segmentation requires dynamic allocation of variably sized blocks, which led to external fragmentation and extra time and complexity for the operating system. Paging divides physical memory into equally sized page frames and makes dynamic allocation of space simple.

The only commercial systems using segmentation now are systems that use paged segments. But paged segments nullify some of the advantages of segmentation. You can achieve nearly the same result with two or three levels of page tables.

12.11.5   SEGMENT TERMINOLOGY

So far, we have used the word "segment" in several different ways. This section talks about the classical use of the word segment, as in a segmented virtual memory. These segments are of varying length and contain some logical program unit. In Section 12.7.3, we used the word "segment" to refer to the 4 Mbyte block of memory mapped by a master page table entry. This was a fixed-length segment, but in the spirit of the word since we talked about putting some logical unit of the program (like the stack) in a segment and isolating it from other parts of the address space using

---

DESIGN TECHNIQUE: FIXED- AND VARIABLE-SIZED OBJECTS

Dynamic storage allocation works, but it loses some of the space to external fragmentation and it is fairly complex. Because of these problems with dynamic storage allocation, we went to a lot of trouble to reduce the problem to that of allocating fixed-size pages. This illustrates a basic truth of programming: fixed-size objects are easy to deal with, and variable-sized objects are hard to deal with. It is always to your advantage to use fixed-size objects if you possibly can. For example, dynamic allocation of fixed-size objects is trivial, but for variable-sized objects it is much harder.

It is worth your while to convert variable-sized objects into fixed-size objects. If your operating system uses objects of size 30 bytes and size 50 bytes, it might be better to always allocate 50 bytes and just not worry about the wasted 20 bytes in the smaller structures.

Suppose you are allocating strings of variable size and they will vary from 1 to 5000 bytes long. You might consider a block method. Have blocks of 32 bytes—28 bytes of string and four bytes of pointer. The pointer is to the next block in the string. You break the string up in 28-byte sections, and store one section in each block. You will waste an average of 14 bytes (half a section) for each string (unless there are many short strings, in which case you should choose a smaller block size), and you will waste the four bytes of pointer in each string. But you will gain overall because you will be allocating fixed-size objects. You will not have to worry about reclaiming the space of freed strings. All the free blocks can be on a list. You free blocks by adding them to the list, and allocate blocks by removing them from the list. There will be no external fragmentation of storage. The simplicity of the storage allocation may be worth the extra storage used by this method (due to internal fragmentation and pointers).

Avoid variable-sized objects if at all possible.

DESIGN TECHNIQUE: ALLOCATION OF MEMORY FOR OBJECTS

Many library functions return an object of unpredictable length, for example, the system call that returns the full path name of the current working directory. This path name could be quite long or it might be fairly short. The question is, where does the memory come from to hold the path name? There are three possible strategies to use:

- The library routine can allocate the storage, and the caller is responsible for freeing the storage when it is no longer needed. In this case, the call would look something like

  ```
  char * getcwd( void );
  ```

  and a pointer to the current working directory is returned.

- The library routine can have one static block of storage where it puts the path name. In this case, the call would look something like

  ```
  char * getcwd( void );
  ```

  The call looks the same, but the semantics are different. The storage where the path name is kept is not owned by the caller, and another call to getcwd will overwrite it.

- The user can provide the storage and pass it to the library function. In this case, the call would look something like

  ```
  int getcwd( char * buffer, int sizeOf-
  Buffer );
  ```

In this case, the user sends in the storage and indicates how long it is. The return value is used for error codes. One possible error would be that the storage provided was not long enough to hold the entire path name.

Each of these methods has good and bad points. The method where the library function allocates the storage means that you do not have to allocate it yourself. The defect is that you have the responsibility of freeing the storage. The other problem is that you might only want to look at the string and not save it, and so you will free it immediately. This incurs the overhead of a dynamic storage allocate and free for no purpose. The static string method is the fastest, since no storage allocation needs to be done. The problem is that, if you need to keep a copy of the string, it involves one copy into the static area and then another copy into an allocated string. This method will only work if there is a known maximum size that strings can be, since the space must be permanently allocated and be enough for all situations. The third solution is more trouble for the system caller since it has to provide the storage. This storage can be static, global, local, or dynamically allocated, so this option is the most flexible for the system caller.

Of course, in a language with garbage collection this would not be an issue, since deallocation is automatic and not the responsibility of the programmer.

---

unmapped addresses. In Section 11.2.2, we used the word "segment" to refer to a variable-sized chunk of the logical address space. When you hear the word "segment," you can be sure that it refers to a part of address space that is either a logical part of a program or is variable in length (sometimes both).

Names and Concepts   Often you will have systems that are called "segmentation" systems where the segments are contiguous. The point here is not whether it is valid to use the name "segment" for these objects. The point is that there are two logically different ways to handle segments, contiguous and noncontiguous. Whether you call them by the same name or different names will not change the fact that there are two different concepts, each having its own advantages and disadvantages. When you hear the word being used, do not assume either one, but find out which it is.

12.12   SHARING MEMORY

Our basic memory model so far has been to give each process its own address space. This is consistent with the virtual processor model we have been using. Each process is running in its own virtual computer that is separate from all the other virtual computers. Processes that want to communicate do it through an IPC protocol like messages that is similar to two computers communicating over a network.

But sometimes it is convenient for two processes to share memory. We have seen one example of that with the idea of threads, where two threads share the same address space. But we would like to do this with parts of the address space instead of the entire address space.

There are several reasons why we would like to share memory. One is space efficiency. Suppose two programs were each using a word processor. It would be nice if they could both share the code but each have their own data space. Or two programs working on the same data might want to share the data but use different code.

There is no reason why the same page cannot be mapped into two different address spaces. The page is in a page frame, so we just point two different page table entries to that page frame. This works especially well if the pages are code pages that are not modified. If data pages are shared, the two processes have to worry about conflicting changes and may need mutual exclusion protocols. Figure 12.23 illustrates the idea. This figure shows two processes sharing the word processor code, but each process has its own data page. They are running the same program, but on different data.

If the pages are mapped into the same page numbers in both processes, then things will work fine. Even if the pages are mapped into different page numbers in the two processes, things will be fine unless the pages contain addresses. Then the question is, do they contain the correct addresses for the first process or for the second

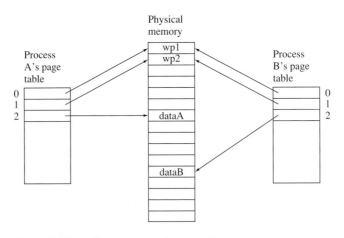

Figure 12.23   Two processes sharing code

process? Most computer architectures allow code to be written so that it is *position independent,* that is, all absolute addresses are kept in registers and not in the code so the code can be moved around in the address space and still work.

Segments are also easy to share. The same addressing problems can come up if the segment is mapped into two different segment numbers in the two processes sharing the segment, and the same set of solutions are possible.

12.12.1 REASONS FOR SHARING MEMORY

There are two main reasons for sharing memory. The first reason is to save space in memory by avoiding having two copies of shared pages in memory. If executable code is shared, then we can have one copy of it in the physical memory, and those pages can be mapped into the address space of all the processes that are executing that code. It is mainly code that is shared, but it is also possible to share data. If the memory is writable, then sharing is often not possible since each process needs its own copy.

The second reason to share memory is to transfer large amounts of information between processes. In this case, we usually have read-write memory being shared. Normally it is written by one process and read by the other. It is faster to pass information in shared memory than to send it via messages. Passing information by shared memory does not require any copies.

Some message systems allow you to pass a section of memory along with a message to avoid copying data for large messages. The memory can be mapped into the receiver's address space. Actually, there are two possible ways a large message could be passed. It could be passed as shared memory, or the memory could be unmapped from the sender's address space and mapped into the receiver's address space. The second alternative would transfer the memory, and so it would never be shared simultaneously by the sender and receiver but rather it would be shared serially.

Some instances of shared memory can be handled with threads. To do this, we combine the two processes into one process with two threads. The thread alternative is not always the best solution, since often the two processes are logically separate and only want to share some memory, not all their address space. Also, this cannot be easily done if the two processes are on different machines in a network. So threads and shared memory are two solutions to the problem of sharing large amounts of data, and there are situations where each is preferable.

12.12.2 SHARED MEMORY SYSTEM CALLS

Let us look at some typical system calls to use shared memory. The first issue to address is how to identify shared memory. A section of shared memory is similar to a message queue or pipe, and we have the same naming options:

1. System-assigned names that are returned by a system call and must be passed to other processes by some form of IPC or to child processes.

2. User-assigned names that are arbitrary integers. The sharing processes must agree somehow on the identifier. This method is used in the UNIX shared memory system calls.

3. Shared segments that are named by the file-naming system.

The second and third options are similar. The main difference is whether the name is a character string or an integer. Let us assume the second method.

- `void * AttachSharedMemory( int smid, void * smaddr, int flags )`—This call creates a section of shared memory with identifier `smid` (if one does not exist already). If a section with this identifier already exists, then that one is attached. The memory is placed at the address `smaddr` in the address space of the system caller. If `smaddr` is 0, then the system will decide where it should be placed. In either case, the address of the shared memory is returned by the system calls. The `flags` determines whether the shared memory is read-only and other details of the mapping.

- `void * DetachSharedMemory( void * smaddr )`—This call detaches the shared memory from the process. The shared memory is freed when the last process detaches it.

Two processes wishing to share memory will attach the memory using the same shared memory identifier. Then the memory is in both address spaces until they detach the shared memory segment.

Processes sharing memory might also need semaphores or messages to synchronize the use of the shared memory.

12.13   EXAMPLES OF VIRTUAL MEMORY SYSTEMS

Some of the concepts we have discussed so far have been simplifications to make the explanations easier to understand. Real operating systems use many optimizations when these ideas are implemented.

In this section, we will discuss the virtual memory systems of several existing operating systems. Some features will be present in two or more of these systems, and in those cases we will discuss the feature in general first and then refer to that discussion when we talk about individual operating systems.

12.13.1   SWAP AREA

swap area

A *swap area* is a part of a disk reserved solely for swapping. It is not managed by the file system. This makes swap I/O faster since the file system creates overhead on I/O requests.

The swap area is usually two or three times the size of main memory. A new process cannot start unless there is available swap space for it. That is why you sometimes get an "out of memory" message from a virtual memory system. This message really means "out of swap space."

Some systems will reserve main memory for processes and not require swap space. The idea is that the memory is always filled with pages, and so those pages do not need swap space. This allows the system to runs more processes in the same amount of swap space. This is called *virtual swap space*.

virtual swap space

It is also possible to swap to a regular file instead of to a special swap area. This is not as efficient, since it incurs file system overhead, but it does not require the system to reserve a lot of swap space that cannot be used for other purposes. Many systems allow swapping to a swap area or to ordinary files. This allows them to use an optimistic strategy for swap space management. If they run out of swap space, they can swap to a file instead.

12.13.2 PAGE INITIALIZATION

A process starts with no pages in memory, and so it will page in a number of pages very quickly. Pages are often treated differently the first time they are paged in than other times.

For example, the code pages will usually be read in directly from the load module. This avoids the step of copying the code pages from the load module to the swap area. The first time a code page is swapped out, it can be written to the swap area. This is not necessary, however, because it can always be read in from the load module. Most modern systems read initially from the load module, but some swap code to the swap area because it is faster to swap in pages from the swap area than from a file. If file mapping is used, the load module will always be the disk backup for the code pages.

The same thing is true of initialized data pages, although they have to be in the swap area unless they are read-only.

The uninitialized data and stack pages are initially marked as *zero-fill* pages, meaning that the first time they are used, a page frame is allocated and filled with zeros. The first time they are paged out, they are written to the swap area.

Figure 12.24 shows how pages are initialized. Code and initialized data are initialized from the load module. Other pages are just allocated as zero-filled free pages. So none of the pages actually have to be initialized in the swap area. They only go into the swap area after the initial page-out.

12.13.3 PAGE SHARING

If a process runs a program that another process is also running, they can share all the read-only pages. This includes all the code pages and the read-only data pages as well.

It is even possible to share writable pages (at least for a while) with a technique called *copy-on-write*. Suppose a process calls `fork`. This requires the operating system to create an exact duplicate of the address space of the process. This can be a lot of copying if the process is large. One solution is to just copy the page table, that is, to share all the pages. But in both page tables, the writable pages are marked as read-only. If a protection violation occurs on one of these pages, we detect that this is a

copy-on-write

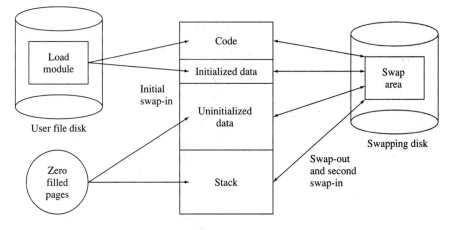

Figure 12.24   Initialization of process pages

write to a copy-on-write page. Then we copy this one page and fix up both page tables so they each point to their own copy of the page, and both are writable. If we are lucky, we will only have to copy a few pages and we will avoid copying the entire address space.

The copy-on-write technique is most useful for efficiently implementing the UNIX `fork` system call, but it can be used in other places where you want to avoid copying of an object as long as possible. The technique is also known as a *lazy copy.*

Figure 12.25 shows how copy-on-write works. In Figure 12.25(a), there is a process with four pages, two of which can be written. After it forks (Figure 12.25(b)), the child process has its own page table but shares all the pages. All the pages have been changed to read-only, so we can detect writes into copy-on-write pages. Somewhere else (not shown in the figure), the operating system remembers that those pages are copy-on-write pages that are supposed to be read-write. When the child writes the stack page, it will get a protection interrupt. The operating system will see that it is not a real protection violation, but a write to a copy-on-write page. At that point, the operating system will make a copy of the page and fix up both page tables. The parent's page table entry is set back to read-write, and the child's page table entry is set to point to the copy of the page and is set to read-write.

12.13.4   TWO-HANDED CLOCK ALGORITHM

The clock algorithm is a commonly used page replacement algorithm in real operating systems. This approximates LRU and does pretty well. Some operating systems use a *two-handed clock* where the second hand follows the first hand by some distance and allows pages to be reclaimed sooner than waiting for a full revolution of the clock hand. Figure 12.26 shows how a double handed clock works.

lazy copy

two-handed clock

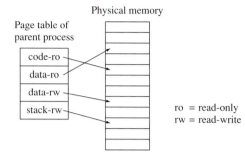

(a) Before the fork

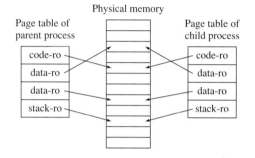

(b) After the fork

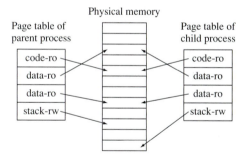

(c) After the child writes the stack

Figure 12.25   Implementing copy-on-write

12.13.5 STANDBY PAGE LISTS

Many operating systems keep several lists of page frames. Figure 12.27 shows these lists. First they keep track of which pages are dirty (modified) because they cannot be allocated immediately. Dirty pages are scheduled for cleaning and moved to the clean page list after they have been written out.

Some free page frames come from processes that exit or are swapped out. These page frames will not be used again. These page frames are allocated first when a free page frame is needed.

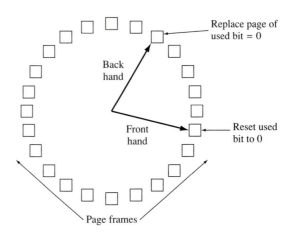

Replace page of
used bit = 0

Back
hand

Reset used
bit to 0

Front
hand

Page frames

Figure 12.26   Two-handed clock

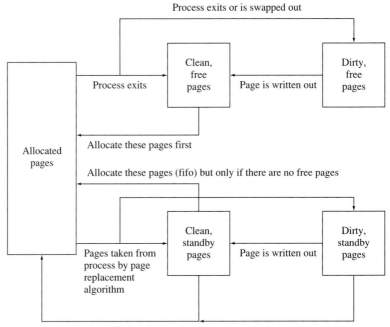

Process exits or is swapped out

Clean,
free
pages

Dirty,
free
pages

Process exits   Page is written out

Allocate these pages first

Allocated
pages

Allocate these pages (fifo) but only if there are no free pages

Clean,
standby
pages

Dirty,
standby
pages

Pages taken from
process by page
replacement
algorithm

Page is written out

Rescue page if it is referenced

Figure 12.27   Standby page lists

Some page frames are taken from processes by the page replacement algorithm. These page frames might be used again soon. These pages are put in a standby list. When a page frame needs to be allocated to a process and no free pages are available, then a page is taken from the standby list. Pages on the standby list are used in a first-in, first-out order so that a page may remain on this list for some time. If a page on the standby list is referenced while it is on the list, then it is "rescued" by removing it from the standby list and giving it back to the process that referenced it. In this case, we will get a page fault, but we will not have to read in a page since it will already be in memory.

Usually about 1 percent to 2 percent of the page frames will be on the standby list. There is a paging daemon that periodically chooses enough pages to replace to keep this many pages in the standby list. The standby list acts as a buffer where pages that have been chosen for replacement wait for a while to see if they are referenced again. This buffer means that we have an approximation of the working set algorithm, since pages in the working set will usually be rescued. Note that we get this working set effect no matter what actual page replacement algorithm is used to choose pages to go into the standby list. What this means is that the actual page replacement algorithm used is not really that important. It is just the first of two mechanisms that cooperate to choose which pages to actually reuse. In fact, several operating systems use the FIFO algorithm, which is known to be a poor page replacement algorithm. The use of the standby list transforms this into a very good page replacement algorithm.

Another advantage of keeping a number of pages in the standby list is that you can write out a number of dirty pages at a time. This makes for more efficient I/O transfers (see Chapter 14). This requires disk drives that can do scatter/gather transfers (which most of them can do), and it requires that pages are dynamically allocated space in the swap area. This is because, for an efficient transfer, the pages have to go to the same place on the disk.

In an actual operating system, the clean and dirty pages might actually be on the same list, and status flags show whether they are clean or dirty.

12.13.6   CLUSTERING PAGES

As we observed in Section 12.10.3, it is useful to cluster pages for swap-in so that a process loading its working set will not incur so many page faults. Most of the operating systems we will survey use clustering to speed process loading.

12.13.7   FILE MAPPING

We discussed file mapping in Section 11.11. File mapping has so many advantages that almost all modern operating systems use it. One important benefit of file mapping is that the virtual memory system takes care of disk caching (see Section 15.7).

12.13.8   PORTABLE VIRTUAL MEMORY SYSTEMS

It is desirable for an operating system to run on several different hardware platforms. There is not just one dominant computer architecture, and an operating system that can run on all the major ones has an advantage. Because of this, designers have tried to make operating systems portable between architectures. One aspect of this is to make the virtual memory system portable. This has been hard to do since the virtual memory hardware varies widely, even within the same processor architecture. But over the years, operating system designers have developed techniques that allow them to write portable virtual memory systems.

The main technique used for portability is to specify a small abstract machine that is similar to most real hardware. Most of the virtual memory system is written assuming this abstract machine and the set of operations it supports. To move the operating system to a new machine, it is necessary to implement this small abstract machine on this new hardware. This is the only part of the virtual memory system that is hardware dependent, and so once this is written the rest of the virtual memory system will work on the new hardware.

12.13.9   SPARSE ADDRESS SPACE

In Section 11.2.3, we noted that it is inconvenient for a process to be given a non-contiguous logical address space. But this applies only to the initial address space used for the code and initialized data because this is laid out by the compiler, and the compiler assumes the address space is contiguous. It is no problem for dynamically allocated storage to be noncontiguous with other storage; in fact, it can be an advantage. Suppose we allocate a large array of, say, 1,000,000 integers taking 4 Mbytes. If we allocate the array in some remote region of the address space and make sure that the address space around it is not allocated, then we will be able to tell if we try to go beyond the bounds of the array because we will get an unallo-

region

cated memory error. We will use the term *region* for a contiguous span of pages in the address space.

The stack should be a region, but it does not have to be contiguous with any other region. In fact, we want to leave a lot of unused address space at the end of the stack so we can expand it into contiguous addresses. Some systems have a special

guard page

kind of page, called a *guard page,* which they put at the end of a region. If we access the guard page, we get a memory protection interrupt, and that signals the operating system that the region has to be expanded. In this case, when the stack overflows, it will hit the guard page and be automatically expanded.

This shows a good reason for noncontiguous allocation—to save address space so a region can be extended with contiguous addresses.

12.13.10   OS/2 VERSION 2.0

OS/2 2.0 uses 4 Kbyte pages and 32-bit virtual addresses. It uses two-level page tables. When a process is swapped out, even its master page table is swapped out.

OS/2 uses a single-handed clock for page replacement, and replaced pages are put on a standby list. Dirty pages that are passed over by the clock hand are scheduled for swap out. The pages in the standby list are used in FIFO order, and pages that are used while on the standby list can be reclaimed for the process.

The virtual address space does not have to be contiguous. Virtual address space is allocated in two stages. First you reserve the virtual addresses without committing any swap space or physical memory. Later you commit the virtual addresses, and this allocates swap space for the pages and will assign physical page frames to the pages when it gets page faults on them.

OS/2 uses copy-on-write pages to do lazy copies (for example, on forks). Pages from executable files are marked swap-on-write, meaning that they will not be swapped to the swap area unless they are written into. They are always fetched directly from the executable file.

OS/2 uses scatter/gather I/O to write out a number of dirty pages at a time. It uses a bit map to keep track of free page frames in the swap area. A page is not necessarily swapped out to the same place each time it is swapped out. It goes into the most convenient page frame in the swap area. This way, it can swap out a number of pages at the same time to consecutive page frames in the swap area.

12.13.11 Windows NT

Windows NT uses a 4 Kbyte page and 32-bit virtual addresses. It uses two-level page tables.

Windows NT uses the same two-stage allocation of memory as OS/2, that is, a process can reserve virtual address space without reserving swap space for it. Later the process can commit the memory, and this allocates swap space for it. Windows NT does not allocate page tables for uncommitted memory. It uses a tree structure to keep track of the parts of the virtual address space that have been reserved but not yet committed.

Pages are replaced using a local FIFO strategy, but replaced pages are not swapped out and reused immediately but placed in a standby list. If a page in the standby list is accessed, it is rescued from the standby list and no swap in is necessary.

The main virtual memory structure is a section. A *section* is a range of virtual addresses that is backed either by space in the swap area or by a file. A section backed by a file is used for file mapping. A section can be mapped into the virtual address space of a process. A process can map in a *view* of the section, that is, part of the section. Two processes can share memory by mapping the same section into each of their virtual address spaces. Sections are used to map the code and data from load modules into a process. The code and data sections are mapped in using copy-on-write status so that they can be shared until a process modifies them.

Indirect page table entries are used for shared pages. The page table entries for shared pages point to one shared page table entry. This allows a shared page to be swapped out without having to change the page table of every process that is sharing the page.

Processes with special privileges can set the protection on their own pages and can lock pages into memory.

Windows NT uses demand paging, but it clusters pages on initial swap in so that the initial loading of the memory for a process will go faster and not require as many page faults.

Windows NT is built on a *hardware abstract layer* (a small abstract machine) for easy portability.

12.13.12 MACH AND OSF/1

The Mach operating system has an interesting memory architecture that has been influential in UNIX and other operating systems. In this section, we will present the main ideas of the memory system in Mach.

Goals of Mach Memory Architecture   Mach had several goals for its memory system:

- *Flexible sharing*—Mach was intended to be a distributed system and they wanted to have two ways of sharing: copy-on-write sharing for fast copies, and read-write sharing for shared memory. They also wanted to be able to share memory between machines.

- *Large, sparse address space*—They wanted to support a large address space and allow memory to be placed anywhere in the address space.

- *Memory-mapped files*—They wanted to be able to map files into the address space.

- *User control of page replacement*—They wanted to allow processes to control their own paging if they felt they could do better than the system.

Basic Objects   Mach is an object-oriented system, and so everything in Mach is an object. A *port* is a message queue to send requests to an object. The messages sent to the port are equivalent to method invocations on the object. Objects are implemented by object managers which maintain object state and handle messages on the ports that represent the objects.

port

A *memory object* is a specific source of pages. A memory object can be a file on the local machine, but it could be a file an another machine, space in the swap area, another process, a frame buffer, etc. A *pager* manages a memory object and handles messages from the memory object's port. These messages tell it to get certain pages and read them into memory or to write out a page in memory. An *internal pager* is implemented by Mach and an *external pager* is implemented by a user process. The internal Mach pager allows memory objects that are backed by swap space or by files. The pagers cache some of the pages of a memory object in memory page frames, and these are the resident pages. A *virtual memory object* or *VM object* manages a region of virtual memory in an address space. The VM object sends messages to the pager to read and write pages from the memory object. The address space of a process (called a *task* in Mach) is a collection of regions, each controlled by a VM object.

memory object

pager

virtual memory object

Using the Basic Objects   Each region is a set of contiguous pages in the address space, but the regions can be anywhere in the address space. So the region concept allows for a large, sparse address space. A memory object can be a file, and so that allows for memory-mapped files. An external pager allows a user process to manage its own page replacement. If two processes both map a region into their address space, then they are sharing the memory. A VM object can implement copy-on-write sharing of a region of memory. An external pager could synthesize the pages when they are requested or get them from another node in the network. This allows the implementation of shared memory distributed over two or more nodes in a network.

Each process has an address space made up of several regions. Each region has an inheritance attribute that can be do-not-share, copy-on-write-share, or read-write-share. When a process forks, the parent and child will share the regions marked read-write-share. The copy-on-write-share segments will be shared until they are written into by either process. The do-not-share regions are not copied at all.

The Mach Memory System   Mach uses global FIFO replacement, but, like Windows NT and OS/2, replaced pages are placed on a standby list where they can be rescued if they are accessed before they are reused. Mach tries to keep 1.25 percent of the page frame free (in the free or standby lists).

The Mach virtual memory system is mostly portable and tries to isolate all machine dependencies in part of the code.

Mach uses copy-on-write to avoid copying whenever possible (for example, for forks).

Pages are clustered into groups of 1, 2, 4, or 8 for faster page in when a process is starting up.

SVR4 UNIX has copied most of the features of the Mach memory system. OSF/1 is derived from Mach and uses the same memory system. Windows NT has a concept of sections which is similar to Mach regions.

12.13.13   SYSTEM V RELEASE 4

SVR4 uses a two-handed clock for page replacement. Replaced pages are put at the end of the free list and can be rescued if they are accessed before being reused.

The virtual address space is made up into *segments*. The segment types are text segment, data segment, stack segment, shared segment, and file mapped segment. Pages are swapped from a local file, a swap area, a remote file (over the network), or a frame buffer. A swap area can be a device or a regular file. Segments allow for mapped files.

The SVR4 virtual memory system is largely hardware independent.

SVR4 also clusters pages for faster process startup.

12.13.14   OTHER SYSTEMS

4.3 BSD uses a two-handed clock page replacement algorithm.

The 4.4 BSD virtual memory is based on the Mach virtual memory architecture.

The DEC VMS operating system uses local FIFO with a standby list.

The Macintosh operating system uses the second-chance clock algorithm.

IBM's MVS uses 4 Kbyte pages and three-level paging. The lowest level consists of segments of up to 256 pages (1 Mbyte). The intermediate level consists of segment tables which are paged by the top level. It uses an LRU approximation for page replacement. At fixed timer intervals, it increments counters for each page that has not been referenced in the last time interval.

12.14   VERY LARGE ADDRESS SPACES

The new generation of processors allows for virtual address spaces larger than 32 bits, and most of them allow for a 64-bit virtual address. This change is necessary because 32 bits is getting too small for some very large programs. There has been speculation on how this change will affect operating systems, and the dominant opinion is that operating systems for very large address space processors will use a single address space for all processes. This will abandon the paradigm of a separate address space for each process and the idea of combining protection with the address space. The result will be that there will be only threads, all sharing the same (very large) address space.

All code and data will appear only once in the address space, and they will never move once they have been placed in the address space. Naturally, the address space will be very sparsely populated.

There are many issues and problems to be worked out for this kind of operating system. See Chase et al. (1994) for more information.

12.15   SUMMARY

The page replacement algorithm is responsible for deciding which page to replace when we need to bring a new page into physical memory. In order to maintain high page hit rates, the page replacement algorithm must pick pages that are not going to be used for a long time. Page replacement algorithms decide which page to replace by looking at the past page use behavior of the process and using that to predict the future page use behavior of the process. The least recently used (LRU) algorithm seems to be the most successful at this prediction, but it is hard to implement. The most common page replacement strategies are approximations of LRU. The clock algorithms are intended to act similarly to LRU and work very well. Both algorithms use the referenced bit to discover when pages are used.

A paging system must avoid high paging rates, and so it must avoid putting too many processes into memory. We can do this by detecting overloading when it occurs or by predicting it and avoiding it. A load control method decides how many processes should be in memory. The working set strategy tries to predict memory overloading and prevent it. It works by trying to predict the pages a program needs to run, that is, the program's working set. It is a very effective page replacement and load control method, but is also very hard to implement and so is usually approximated. The WSClock page replacement algorithm is a good approximation of the working set algorithm. There are also other methods of load control. An effective method is to limit the system to one loading process.

Paging is a good idea, but it starts breaking down with very large address spaces since the page tables start using too much physical memory. Some ways of dealing with the problem are two-level paging, three-level paging, recursive address spaces, and inverted page tables.

Paging is not the only way to achieve virtual memory; segmentation is another method. But segmentation implies that you have to deal with dynamic memory management and fragmentation, and so paging is much more popular.

12.15.1 TERMINOLOGY

After reading this chapter, you should be familiar with the following terms:

- clock page replacement algorithm
- clustering
- copy-on-write
- demand paging
- dirty bit
- emulator
- first-in, first-out (FIFO) page replacement algorithm
- global replacement
- guard page
- inverted page table
- lazy copy
- least-recently used (LRU) page replacement algorithm
- load control
- local replacement
- master page number
- medium-term scheduler
- memory object
- modified bit
- not recently used (FINUFO) page replacement algorithm
- optimal page replacement algorithm
- page fault frequency load control
- page reference string
- page replacement algorithm
- pager
- placement
- predictive load control
- prepaging
- primary page table
- random page replacement algorithm
- recursive address space
- referenced bit
- region
- replacement
- secondary page number
- second chance page replacement algorithm

- segment
- segmentation
- short-term scheduler
- software page table lookups
- swap area
- theory of program behavior
- thrashing
- three-level paging
- two-dimensional address space
- two-handed clock
- two-level paging
- virtual memory object
- virtual swap space
- working set
- WSClock page replacement algorithm

12.15.2   REVIEW QUESTIONS

The following questions are answered in the text of this chapter:

1. What is the difference between placement of a block of allocated memory and replacement of a block of allocated memory?

2. Compare local and global page replacement. What are the advantages of each?

3. What is a theory of program behavior? Give two examples.

4. Explain why the best, worst, and average cases for the random page replacement algorithm are all the same.

5. How would you implement FIFO page replacement?

6. Describe an approximation of LRU.

7. Why is a modified bit useful in a paging system?

8. Describe the general clock algorithm.

9. Contrast resident set with working set.

10. Describe the working set algorithm.

11. Why does the working set algorithm require you to swap out a process completely if all of its working set will not fit into memory?

12. Why do you need page reference strings to evaluate page replacement algorithms? What do you do with them?

13. Why do you need to emulate a machine's instruction set in order to generate page reference strings?

14. Why is load control important?

15. Explain how load control is a form of scheduling.

16. When would the preloading of pages be useful?

17. Describe two-level paging.

18. What problem is two-level paging trying to solve?

19. What are the advantages of an inverted page table?

20. Compare two-level paging with recursive address spaces.

21. What are the advantages and disadvantages of paging the operating system address space?

22. Give a reason to lock a page in memory.

23. Give some arguments for a large page size. Give some arguments for a small page size.

24. Compare paging and segmentation.

25. Why would we want to share memory between address spaces?

12.15.3   FURTHER READING

Denning (1970) provides a review of virtual memory techniques. See Belady (1966), Hatfield and Gerald (1971), Hatfield (1972), Morrison (1973), Mattson et al. (1970) and Coffman and Varian (1968) for studies of page replacement algorithms. See Aho et al. (1971) and Prieve and Fabry (1976) for a discussion of optimal paging algorithms. Goldman (1989) discusses the use of a clock algorithm in the Macintosh operating system. See Madison and Batson (1976) for a discussion of program locality. See Carr and Hennessey (1981) for a discussion of the WSClock page replacement algorithm.

See Denning (1968) for the original paper on the working set model and a discussion of thrashing. Denning (1980) is an excellent review of the development of the working set model over 10 years. Madison and Batson (1976), Denning and Kahn (1975), and Batson (1976) discuss program locality and the program phase model. Chu and Opderbeck (1977) discuss the PFF (page fault frequency) algorithm.

See Chu and Opderbeck (1974) for a discussion of the effects of varying page size. See Batson (1970) for a discussion of average segment size measurements.

Chang and Mergen (1988) discuss the use of inverted page tables in the IBM 801.

Carr and Hennessy (1981) discuss the simulation of paging algorithms and present an improved method of using traces.

12.16   PROBLEMS

1. Explain why we use the word "global" when we talk about global page replacement.

2. Give some reasons why local page replacement is better than global page replacement.

3. Give some reasons why you think LRU is a good page replacement algorithm. Why is its theory correct?

4. Compare the clock page replacement algorithm with the FCFS algorithm with a free page list that is used FCFS. (It acts as a buffer and delays replacement a lot like the clock algorithm does.)

Consider the average time a page stays in the free page list (before being rescued or reused). Would this be a good load control measure?

5. Consider a variation of the clock algorithm called the "counting" clock algorithm. Each page frame has a counter. The algorithm takes a parameter N. N is in the range 1 to 10.

Here is the algorithm: Look at a page frame. If the referenced bit is 1, then set it to 0 and set the count to N. If it is 0, then decrement the count. If the count is zero, then replace the page.

Give your analysis of this paging algorithm. Is it better than clock? Is it a generalization of clock?

6. Consider each of the global page replacement strategies we looked at in this chapter: optimal, random, FIFO, LRU, clock, and second chance. Think about converting each one into a local page replacement strategy. First say if it is makes sense at all to convert it to a local strategy. Then decide whether it would be better, worse, or about the same as a local strategy (compared to the same page replacement algorithm as a global strategy). Give arguments to support your answer. Remember that a local page replacement algorithm has to make decisions about how many page frames a process should be allocated.

7. What would be the worst possible page replacement algorithm? Suppose that the optimal algorithm gives a page fault rate of one in a million for a program with 20 pages and 10 page frames. Estimate the page fault rate of your worst possible page replacement algorithms on this same page reference string. *Hint:* It is not possible to get the page fault rate up too high because of program locality. Remember that a page is replaced only when there is a page fault.

8. Suppose that the hardware keeps an eight-bit shift register for each page frame, and there is a single hardware instruction that would shift the referenced bit for each page frame into the high-order bit of its associated shift register (the low-order bit is discarded). There are instructions to read and set these shift registers. How would you use this hardware to implement an approximation of LRU? Do you think this would be better than the approximations described in the chapter? Why or why not?

9. Suppose you are writing an emulator and you are at the point where you want to emulate a single instruction, one that adds two hardware registers together. Estimate the number of machine instructions that it would take to emulate this instruction.

Then estimate the number of instructions that one iteration of the basic fetch-execute loop would take. This iteration would fetch the next instruction, increment the PC, decode the instruction, and jump to the code that emulates that instruction.

Assume that the emulator emulates memory with a large array, the registers with a small array, and the PC with an integer variable. To do the estimates, write the C++ code to do it and then estimate the number of machine instructions each C++ statement will take.

What does this say about the speed of emulation?

10. Suppose we have a 48-bit virtual address space. Design a two-level paging system for this. How big are the master page tables, the secondary page tables, and the page frames? How many pages total will there be in the logical address space, and how much memory will the page tables take for a program that used the entire address space?

11. Suppose your paging system uses inverted page tables, and you are using a hash table to find the page frame a specific page is in. Assume the hash table takes an average of two probes to find the page or discover that it is not there. Estimate how many machine instructions it will take to handle a TLB miss when the page is in the page table. Be sure to include the time for the TLB replacement algorithm.

12. Suppose we have a computer system with a 44-bit virtual address, page size of 64K, and 4 bytes per page table entry.

   a. How many pages are in the virtual address space?

   b. Suppose we use two-level paging and arrange for all page tables to fit into a single page frame. How will the bits of the address be divided up?

   c. Suppose we have a 4 Gbyte program such that the entire program and all necessary page tables (using two-level paging as in part *b*) are in memory. (*Note:* It will be a *lot* of memory.) How much memory (in page frames) is used by the program, including its page tables?

13. Suppose we have a computer system with a 38-bit virtual address, 16K pages, and 4 bytes per page table entry.

   a. How many pages are in the virtual address space?

   b. Suppose we use two-level paging and arrange for all page tables to fit into a single page frame. How will the bits of the address be divided up?

   c. Suppose we have a 32 Mbyte program such that the entire program and all necessary page tables (using two-level paging as in part *b*) are in memory. How much memory (in page frames) is used by the program, including its page tables?

14. Suppose you have a two-level paging system where the first level uses 10 bits, the second level uses 10 bits, and the page offset uses 12 bits. If you have a program that uses 18 Mbytes of memory, how many page frames will it use for the program and page tables if everything is in memory?

15. Suppose you have a two-level paging system where it takes 10 milliseconds to service a page fault and a regular memory access takes 200 nanoseconds (1/5 microsecond). An average instruction takes 500 nanoseconds. The translation lookaside buffer hits 90 percent of the time, and the user page fault rate is one page fault every 100,000 instructions.

   a. What is the average time for a memory fetch where there are no page faults?

   b. What is the average instruction time for all instructions, including the ones that cause page faults?

16. Suppose a given program consists of a main program which fits into one page, and a long series of procedures which each fit on a page. The main program is a loop that calls several of these procedures each time through the loop, but a different set each time through so no one procedure is called very frequently. The procedures very seldom call one of the other procedures. The main program and the procedures frequently reference global data, which also fits on one page. Suppose a number of processes with these characteristics run simultaneously. (*Note:* They are not running the *same* program, and there is no sharing of pages between processes. They are running programs that *act similarly.*) Consider each of the three page replacement algorithms:

    a. First-in, first-out.

    b. Least recently used.

    c. Clock.

Discuss what kind of performance each algorithm would give, given this group of programs. Assume a global page allocation policy.

17. In this problem, you have to make up some page reference strings that are good for one paging algorithm and bad for another paging algorithm. Come up with two different page reference strings and a page fault chart for each. Here is an example of the format you should use:

Page ref	1	2	3	2	4	2	5	2	3	4	
Page 0	1*	1	1	1	4*	4	4	4	3*	3	FIFO
Page 1	-	2*	2	2	2	2	5*	5	5	4*	8 page
Page 2	-	-	3*	3	3	3	3	2*	2	2	faults
Page 0	1*	1	1	1	4*	4	4	4	3*	3	LRU
Page 1	-	2*	2	2	2	2	2	2	2	2	7 page
Page 2	-	-	3*	3	3	3	5*	5	5	4*	faults
Page 0	1*	1	1	1	4*	4	5*	4	4	4	OPT
Page 1	-	2*	2	2	2	2	2	2	2	2	5 page
Page 2	-	-	3*	3	3	3	3	3	3	3	faults

The first line has the page reference string. The next section has a line for each page frame. (Note the label says "Page" rather than "Page frame." This is just to save space.) Each column lists the page that is in each page frame *after* the page fault (if any) for the reference has been handled according the page replacement algorithm being shown. An asterisk ("*") is placed after the page if there was a page fault on that reference and this was the new page brought in as a result of that page fault. The next section is the same, except it is for the LRU paging algorithm. And the final section is for the optimal page replacement algorithm. On the right, each section is labeled and the total number of page faults is given.

Make up two such charts that each compare LRU, FIFO, and OPT. On the first chart, show a page reference string that is good for LRU and bad for FIFO. On the second chart, show a page reference string that is good for FIFO and bad for LRU. OPT, of course, will always be the best. The main problem here is to make up these page reference strings. Think of the premise of each algorithm and try to make up a reference string that follows one premise but not the other. For each example use three page frames and a reference string of at least nine references. The first three references on each chart should be exactly the same as in the example above. This is the filling of the pages, and it should be the same for each algorithm. The page frame numbers start at 0 and the pages start at 1. Follow this convention in your charts. You should include a sentence or two explaining what you wanted the reference string to do, that is, how it works well with or interacts badly with the paging algorithms.

18. Suppose an instruction takes $1/2$ microsecond to execute (on the average), and a page fault takes 250 microseconds of processor time to handle plus 10 milliseconds of disk time to read in the page. How many pages a second can the disk transfer? *100*

Suppose that $1/3$ of the pages are dirty. It takes two page transfers to replace a dirty page. Compute the average number of instructions between page faults that would cause the system to saturate the disk with page traffic, that is, for the disk to be busy all the time doing page transfers.

19. Why might it be bad for the page fault rate to be too low?

20. The concept of virtual memory depends on locality. If a program uses a lot of pages, the virtual memory will not work no matter what page replacement algorithm you use. For example, suppose that a program has 5000 (4K) pages ($= 20$ Mbytes), and goes into a loop where it references one word in page 0, then one word in page 1, then one word in page 2, and so on over and over. It will access all 5000 pages every 5000 instructions. This program requires 20 Mbytes of memory, and no page replacement algorithm can improve that.

A program with locality, however, will not access a lot of pages in a short period of time, but will restrict itself to a few pages. A page replacement algorithm tries to guess which pages the program will access in the future, and keeps those pages in memory.

For each of the following page replacement algorithms, describe the characteristics of the programs that make that algorithm behave very poorly, that is, describe the worst case for each algorithm. Your programs should *not* just be programs that access a lot of pages; no paging algorithm can handle that. Instead, come up with programs that would work well with the optimal paging algorithm but would work much worse with the page replacement algorithm you are constructing a worst case for. *Hint:* Each algorithm makes certain assumptions about how programs behave. The worst-case program will act in exactly the opposite way.

a. First-in, first-out.

b. Least recently used.

c. Clock.

d. Second chance.

e. Working set.

21. Rewrite the hardware virtual memory access algorithm (in Section 11.7.1) for a two-level paging system.

22. Rewrite the hardware virtual memory access algorithm (in Section 11.17.1) for a system where the page tables are paged (as in Section 12.8).

23. Describe the response of the operating system to the four paging-related events (as is done in Section 11.17.2), but for a two-level paging system.

24. Some paging systems use *clustering* when loading pages. This means that, whenever they get a page fault, they load the page that was faulted on and also some other nearby pages (unless they are already loaded). Paging out is not changed by clustering, that is, we use any of the page replacement algorithms with no changes. For example, we might load the faulting page and the next three pages when we get a page fault.

   a. Give one advantage of clustering.

   b. How can it be the case that some of the pages in the cluster might already be loaded, since they are all loaded together?

   c. Why would clustering be hard to implement if we were using an inverted page table?

25. What would be a good load control measure for each page replacement algorithm?

26. Paged segments would seem like an ideal solution that combines the advantages of pages with the advantages of segments. Explain why this is not so.

G 1 - 4,5,25
*** 2 - 1,2,16
    3 - 3,6
    4 - 12,15
    5 - 7,19

1 - 8,10
2 - 11,13
3 - 14,18
4 - 20
5 - 24,26

chapter
13

Design Techniques III

13.1 MULTIPLEXING

13.1.1 OVERVIEW

Multiplexing is a way of sharing a resource between two or more processes. In space multiplexing, you give each process part of the resource. In time multiplexing, you give each process the resource part of the time.

13.1.2 MOTIVATION

Let us take display screen space as an example of a scarce resource. Anyone who uses a window system wishes they had a larger screen; there never seems to be enough space to show all the things you want to show. We can space multiplex the screen by having several windows on the screen at the same time (but not overlapping one another). For example, we might be editing three files at the same time. See Figure 13.1 for an example.

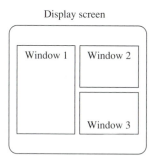

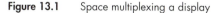

Figure 13.1   Space multiplexing a display

547

multiplexing

Most window systems allow windows to be overlapped. Overlapping windows is a method of time multiplexing the display. In Figure 13.2(a), window 1 is using most of the screen area, but if we move window 2 to the front, as in 13.2(b), then window 2 is using most of the screen area. By combining time and space multiplexing, we can achieve efficient use of the screen space resource.

Actually, the situation in Figure 13.2 is a little more complicated than we indicated. The window in back is not completely hidden and is still using some screen space. Suppose we reduced the back window into an icon, as in Figure 13.3. The screen is divided into two areas, the window area and the icon area. These two areas space multiplex the screen. The window area is time multiplexed between

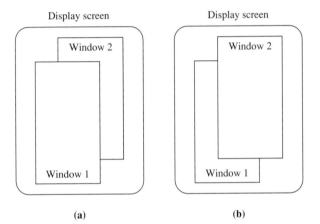

Figure 13.2   Time multiplexing a display

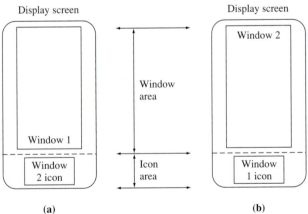

Figure 13.3   Time and space multiplexing a display

windows 1 and 2, and the icon area is time multiplexed between the icons for windows 1 and 2.

In a window system, the display is the most important resource, and so both time and space multiplexing are used to ensure that the most important windows are visible at any point in time.

13.1.3 OPERATING SYSTEM EXAMPLES

Windows   Windows are both space multiplexed and time multiplexed.

Overlapped and Tiled Window Managers   Some window managers will only tile windows and will not allow overlapping windows. The idea is that the window manager takes more control of the screen space and iconizes windows when necessary. In other words, it handles most of the time and space multiplexing for the user. In an overlapped window manager, the user is responsible for all time and space multiplexing decisions. Which is better depends on how well the tiled window manager handles your windows. If it always does the right thing, then it is better, but if it makes wrong decisions, then it is worse. The issue is not really tiled versus overlapped, but system control versus user control.

Virtual Memory   An operating system that runs more than one process at a time is space multiplexing the memory. With virtual memory, you move processes between memory and disk to achieve time multiplexing of memory.

13.1.4 COMPUTER SCIENCE EXAMPLES

Message Acknowledgments   Some message systems require that each message be acknowledged by an acknowledgment message which confirms that the message was received. This is like a registered letter. The problem with this is that it doubles the number of messages that have to be sent. If messages are going both ways, one solution is to combine a message with an acknowledgment. This is an example of space multiplexing the message.

Satellite Communications Links   Satellites are used for long-distance communications. They are expensive to put in orbit, and so satellite time is a scarce resource. Each satellite has hundreds of channels, so the link is space multiplexed (actually, it is called frequency multiplexing in this case, but it is conceptually space multiplexing). In addition, each channel is time multiplexed. You might have 100 phone connections time multiplexed on 50 channels. (See Figure 13.4.) When a person is not talking, their connection is used by another phone connection. When a person starts talking again, the system quickly finds a free channel to use. This is why the beginning of your first word is sometimes clipped. The system could not find a channel fast enough to transmit the beginning of the word.

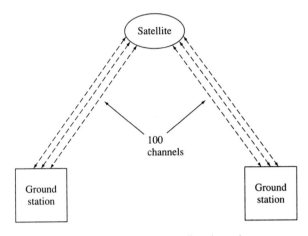

Figure 13.4   Time multiplexing satellite channels

13.1.5   APPLICABILITY

Whenever you have to share a resource, you can do it with time or space multiplexing.

13.1.6   CONSEQUENCES

- Multiplexing allows you to share objects and get more use out of them.
- Time multiplexing allows you to share an object that cannot be shared by two processes at the same time.

13.2   LATE BINDING

13.2.1   OVERVIEW

late binding

Late binding is a way to gain flexibility by delaying a decision as long as possible. The later you make a decision, the more information you have about what is the best decision.

13.2.2   MOTIVATION

Virtual memory is an example of late binding. We do not bind a page to a page frame until the page is referenced. Demand paging is late binding, and prepaging is earlier binding. We only use prepaging if we have some reason to believe we can predict future page use (for example, if we have computed the working set of an application that was swapped out).

We know only a small part of the program will be used at any one time (the principle of locality tells us this), but we do not know which parts in various stages in the program. So we use late binding, and only load pages when they are requested.

13.2.3   OPERATING SYSTEM EXAMPLES

Virtual Memory   The Motivation section discussed virtual memory in terms of late binding.

Network Routing   In a store-and-forward network, the path a message will take is not determined ahead of time. When a message arrives at a node, the node decides where to route it next. This way, they can take advantage of information about the load on links and about whether certain links are down.

13.2.4   COMPUTER SCIENCE EXAMPLES

Binding Time   The concept of binding time comes from programming languages. For example, a static variable is bound to its storage when a program begins execution (early binding), and a local variable in a procedure is bound to its storage when the procedure is called (late binding). Most languages bind procedure arguments to their values when the procedure is called (early binding, also called *eager evaluation,* but some wait until the variable is used for the first time (late binding, also called *lazy evaluation* or call-by-need).

eager evaluation
lazy evaluation

Lazy Creation   If an object is expensive to create, we would like to avoid creating it until it is actually needed. If it is never needed, then we avoid the overhead of creating it. This is called *lazy creation,* and it is an example of late binding.

lazy creation

Programs that use a lot of windows often use lazy window creation. Windows are not created when the program starts but when they are first requested. Thus the program starts up faster, but small delays are experienced the first time you use each window.

Stack Allocation   The local variables in a procedure are allocated on the stack when the procedure is called. This is a later binding than allocating variables statically when the program is started.

Key Encoding   Encoding keys with key numbers rather than ASCII characters is an example of late binding. We do not commit ourselves as to which character the key will represent until as late as possible. This allows flexibility that would be lost with early binding. For example, we can easily change a keyboard into one with a different key layout (such as the Dvorak keyboard) just by moving the key caps around and changing the key number to ASCII character mapping in the terminal software.

By sending the raw "key down" and "key up" information rather than the processed "key typed" information, we extend our flexibility in several ways. First, it allows us to make any key a "shift" key, that is, a key that is held down and affects the interpretation of other keys. Second, it allows us to autorepeat any key and with any parameters. In the days of terminals, some keys autorepeated and some didn't—it depended on the terminal.

just-in-time

Manufacturing   In the field of manufacturing, the current trend is for *just-in-time* inventory of raw materials. Rather than have a large inventory of materials for the manufacturing process, you arrange for them to be delivered to the factory just as they are needed. Then you do not pay the capital cost of having the inventory, and you need less space to hold the inventory. This is late binding of resources.

13.2.5   APPLICABILITY

A computation consists of evaluating a function with some arguments. The function can be evaluated any time from the first time all the required inputs are available to the time when the result is needed. The time we choose to evaluate the function is called the *binding time*. *Early binding* means that it is evaluated early in this time period, and *late binding* means that it is evaluated towards the end of this time period.

13.2.6   CONSEQUENCES

- When you delay a decision or computation, you will know more about it when you finally have to do it.
- Sometimes you can delay a computation and it will never be needed. Then late binding is more efficient.
- Sometimes you have to repeat a late binding each time it is used. Early binding is often more efficient since you only have to do it once.
- Early binding can do all the bindings at one time and get some economies of scale. For example, you can load the compiler into memory once and compile everything.

The main advantages of early binding are efficiency and economies of scale. For example, a compiler binds source code to object code before execution (early binding) and can do this very efficiently by translating the entire program at once. An interpreter binds source code to execution as the statements are executed (late binding).

In the case of an interpreter, the translation of a statement is sometimes done each time the statement is executed. Here we have an example of work being done only once in the early binding situation and many times in the late binding situation. However, this is not a necessary consequence of late binding. It is possible for an interpreter to translate source code into object code as a statement is first executed, and reuse the object code the next time the statement is executed. More normally, an interpreter will translate into a parse tree the first time a statement is executed, and then save that for the next time.

Binding is the connecting of the name of an object to the object it refers to. Early binding is more efficient, if we can predict the needs of the system accurately. It is generally more efficient to bind early, but not if the binding turns out to be not needed at all. In systems where you can predict future demand, early binding is more efficient, but if there is uncertainty about the demand, then late binding is better.

13.2.7 IMPLEMENTATION ISSUES AND VARIATIONS

Reservations   *Reservations* are, in general, a method of early binding. They are a   reservations
means of predicting the future more accurately by scheduling certain events to occur at specific times. This reduces the uncertainly of predicting the future. Reservations are used when the costs of underused capacity or denial of service because of overloading are high. We reduce our freedom in order to avoid these costs.

But what if the reservations are not kept? This increases the uncertainty and reduces the effectiveness of reservations. In order to avoid this, some systems use penalties to reduce the likelihood a reservation will not be kept. For examples, often professionals (doctors, lawyers, etc.) will charge you for an appointment whether you keep it or not. Airlines hedge their bets because it is not certain that people will keep their reservations and there is no penalty for missing a reservation. They compensate by over-reserving and depending on a certain number of no-shows.

Lazy Binding and Multiple Binding   There are two significant variations of late binding. The first variation we will call lazy binding. In lazy binding, you delay a binding (or a computation) until it is needed for the first time. Then you do the computation and save the result. This requires that you get control on the first use of the object so you can do the binding.

The second variation occurs when you redo the binding (or computation) each time it is requested. For example, an interpreter may parse a line each time it is executed.

The first variation is more time efficient because it only does the computation once no matter what. It may be less space efficient because it has to save the result of the computation (as would early binding).

The second variation is better if the result of the computation might change after it is computed. Take network routing, for example. You want to redo this each time because conditions on the network are constantly changing.

Efficiency and Binding Time   One advantage of a connection protocol is that the file name is looked up once during the connection (the open) and is converted to an internal name (often a table index). This file name lookup involves reading the disk (maybe several disk reads) and could take a long time. If we have to do a file name lookup for every read and write, the connectionless protocol would be much less efficient.

We can make the connectionless protocol more efficient by the use of caching. When we look up a file name, we remember the results of the lookup in a cache table for later use. The next time we look up the same name, it is found in the cache table, and the name lookup for a connectionless protocol becomes nearly as efficient as the table lookup for a connection protocol.

In the study of programming languages, we encounter the concept of binding time, which can be applied to the connection-versus-connectionless discussion. By *binding time* we mean the time that a name is connected with a value. In the file case, the name is the file name and the value is the file information on disk. A connection protocol uses an *early binding time,* meaning that the file is looked up as soon as you know you want to use the file. A connectionless protocol uses a *late binding time,* meaning that the file is not looked up until you are ready to read or write it. In this case, we have to do the lookup each time we read or write the file because there is no place to store the looked-up value.

It is a common case that early binding is done just once and late binding is done each time the value is used. For this reason, early binding is usually more efficient than late binding. But caching can make the lookup fast enough to make late binding competitive with early binding.

13.2.8 RELATED DESIGN TECHNIQUES

Late binding is a variant of the static/dynamic split. Early binding is static and late binding is dynamic. But with binding we often have more than two choices; we have a whole range of binding times from early to late.

Late binding is often a variant of the space/time tradeoff as well. We accept extra processing to save space. Virtual memory is a perfect example of this. The program runs a little slower and the hardware is more expensive, but we save memory space.

> Late binding is more flexible but sometimes more expensive.

13.3 STATIC VERSUS DYNAMIC

13.3.1 OVERVIEW

We can perform a computation once at the beginning of an activity in the expectation that the result will be needed. Or we can wait until we actually need the result done and compute it then.

13.3.2 MOTIVATION

We discussed dynamic loading in Section 10.3.2 and saw the advantages of doing things dynamically.

13.3.3 OPERATING SYSTEM EXAMPLES

Program and Process Programs are static and processes (program executions) are dynamic.

Relocation   We can statically relocate code by systematically changing addresses in the code. Or we can dynamically relocate code by changing each address as it is used.

Dynamic Linking   In dynamic linking, you delay the linking and loading until the module is used at run time. Linking and loading a program is a costly process, with lots of processing and lots of I/O time. With load time dynamic linking, we move the time that the modules are linked in (that is, bound) until load time. This saves disk space. With run time dynamic linking, we move the link and load time to the time of the first use. This will be more efficient if several of the modules are not used in a typical execution of the program. Even if all the modules are eventually loaded, dynamic linking will save memory space during program execution (before all the modules are loaded in).

Static Process Creation   Almost all operating systems allow the dynamic creation of processes, but a few do not. We have the usual tradeoff, that is, static is more efficient but less flexible. But the efficiency edge for static process creation is very small, and few operating systems use static process creation. We might stop to consider when a real operating system would use static process creation.

The only operating systems that use static process creation are *real-time operating systems*. A real-time operating system is one that must react to inputs and respond to them quickly. An example is the operating system for a flight control computer on an advanced jet airplane. The fastest planes these days are inherently unstable while flying and require constant adjustment of the flight surfaces (things like ailerons) in order to avoid going out of control. These adjustments must be made so rapidly that it requires a computer to do them. If the adjustments are not made quickly enough, it will be too late because the airplane will already be out of control. This is the essence of a real-time system; the responses must be on time or they are useless. Compare this with a timesharing system where a user is waiting for a window to open. If the system is slow, the user may be irritated but nothing terrible will happen and the window will still be useful to the user.

real-time operating system

Static Scheduling   A real-time system cannot afford to be late with a response to an event. Hence one must be able to prove that a certain response time is guaranteed. An easy way to do this is to have a fixed number of processes and fixed scheduling. Say you have five processes and you give each one a time slice of 100 milliseconds in rotation. Each process will get a time slice every 500 milliseconds and so is guaranteed to be able to respond to an event within 500 milliseconds. Access to other resources can also be guaranteed when there are a fixed number of processes. Figure 13.5 shows fixed scheduling of five processes.

So the reason for static resource allocation in a real-time operating system is not efficiency but predictability in the operating system.

We should note that static scheduling is the norm. Things are usually scheduled days, weeks, or months in advance. Think about airplane schedules, performances, store hours, etc. Predictability is more highly valued than efficiency.

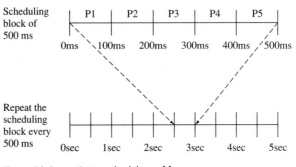

Figure 13.5   Static scheduling of five processes

13.3.4   COMPUTER SCIENCE EXAMPLES

Memory Allocation   Static storage allocation is done before the program begins, and dynamic storage allocation is done during program execution.

Compilers and Interpreters   One example of early and late binding is compiling and interpreting programs. We generally expect the entire program to be executed, and so compiling is more efficient. If we are debugging and expect that the program will fail early in the execution, then interpretation will be more efficient since there is no need to translate the entire program.

Typing Checking   Compilation is static translation of program source code, and interpretation is dynamic translation. Compilers generally do static-type checking, but array bounds are checked dynamically unless we can prove (statically) that they will not go out of range.

Static Variables   In C++, local variables can be given the `static` attribute, and this will cause them to be allocated statically. The practical effect of this is that they will retain their values between calls to the procedure, and they can be used to remember the state of the procedure. A typical example is a random number generator which needs to remember the last number it generated in order to generate the next number.

Instruction Counting   Suppose you are evaluating a new computer architecture and you want to know how often programs use integer division so you can decide how much hardware to devote to that operation to make it fast. You can analyze programs and find out the *static frequency counts* of integer division, but this does not tell you what you want to know. You want to know how much program *execution* will be slowed down by a slow integer division. What you want are *dynamic frequency counts*. To get this, you have to run the program under a simulator and count how many integer divides are actually executed, that is, you must measure the number of divisions in the process, not the program.

The static frequency counts are much easier to obtain (you only have to read and analyze a bunch of programs), but they are not useful. Getting dynamic frequency counts is much harder (it involves using a simulator and actually running the programs with typical inputs), but the results are more useful.

13.3.5 APPLICABILITY

You can do things either statically or dynamically when you have a choice about when you can perform a computation, that is, when the inputs are known before the output is required.

13.3.6 CONSEQUENCES

• Static solutions are often faster because you do something only once instead of every time it is needed.

• Dynamic solutions can be faster if you do not need to do the computation at all.

The static-versus-dynamic decision is one of the most fundamental design decisions. A lot of other design decisions come down to static versus dynamic if you look at them the right way. Connection-versus-connectionless protocols are one example of a static-versus-dynamic tradeoff.

In general, it is faster to perform activities once before a program begins than to do it while the program is running. For one thing, you can do all of them together, loading the processing program only once instead of each time.

Static is better when this is the case and you know you will actually have to do these things. A classic example is compiling versus interpreting. Compiling is the static solution when we translate the program once before it begins execution. Interpreters wait to translate statements until they are about to be executed. If you are debugging and the program fails in the first few hundred statements, then an interpreter will be faster since it is faster to interpret a few hundred statements than to compile tens of thousands of statements. But once the program is working and it runs to completion each time, then compiling is faster.

Dynamic solutions are flexible and are used when you cannot predict how things will go. Static solutions are efficient and are used when you can predict how things will go.

This tradeoff represents something very basic in all fields of human endeavor. In language we have nouns and verbs, which represent things and actions. This seems to be what the world is made up of. Static is related to things and represents creating on object (usually a data structure) that we will need later; it represents storage. Dynamic is related to actions and represents computing an object when it is required; it represents computation.

In many (but not all) instances of this tradeoff, static actions are done only once but dynamic actions are done repeatedly during program execution. If local memory for a procedure is allocated statically, then it is allocated once before program execution begins. If it is allocated dynamically, then it is allocated each time the procedure is called.

Doing things statically is generally faster, since we only do them once instead of many times. Doing things dynamically often saves space, since we do not need to keep a record of them except when they are being used. Let's take the allocation of local storage for a procedure as an example again. Static allocation is done once and takes up space all the time. Dynamic allocation is done each time the procedure is entered and so takes up more time, but the space is only used while the procedure is active.

In the usual tradeoff, static things are done only once and hence are more time efficient, and dynamic things are done more than once and are less time efficient. With the proper data structures, it is usually possible to ensure that even dynamic things are only done once, but they still tend to be less efficient because static things are done in a batch and dynamic things are done one at a time, which tends to be less efficient.

Sometimes doing things dynamically is actually more efficient. Later we will see cases where static things are done once and dynamic things are done either once or not at all.

13.3.7   IMPLEMENTATION ISSUES AND VARIATIONS

Static and Dynamic Tradeoffs   It is much more efficient in memory use to allow processes to request additional memory while they are running. If you must request all memory when the program begins, then you have to allow for the worst case. This means that, in the average cases, you will have requested too much memory, and the extra memory will be unused and wasted. If you can request memory dynamically, then you can request the minimum initially and only get extra memory as you need it.

We have seen static/dynamic tradeoffs before, but the tradeoffs in the case of dynamic memory allocation are a little different. In a connectionless protocol, the tradeoff was flexibility versus efficiency. A connectionless protocol required longer requests and each one had to be set up each time, but successive requests could be handled by different file servers with no trouble. A connection protocol was faster to execute because of the saved state information, but it doesn't handle failure of file servers or multiple file servers as easily. One can make a good case with both connection and connectionless protocols.

With dynamic loading you have the typical tradeoff that the dynamic alternative was less time efficient but more space efficient. The space efficiency depends on how many of the library modules are called by the running program and when they are called during program execution. Since most programs use all their code, the space savings for dynamic loading are generally small. One can make a good case with both static and dynamic loading.

With dynamic memory allocation, the space efficiency advantage is so great that only a special-purpose operating system would not have dynamic memory allocation. Real-time systems, which generally use static resource allocation, would be the only class of operating system that you would not expect to allow dynamic memory allocation.

	Processing Time	Memory Space	Complexity
Connection Protocol	Low	High	High
Connectionless Protocol	High	Low	Low
Static Memory	Low	High	Low
Dynamic Memory	High	Low	High
Static Allocation	Low	High	Low
Dynamic Allocation	High	Low	High

Dynamic Storage Allocation   In some ways, however, this is a bad example because local variables for procedures are allocated on the stack. While this is actually dynamic storage allocation, stack allocation is so efficient that it is hardly any slower than static allocation. Stack allocation is a very clever technique that is very efficient in both space and time. Allocation of all the local variables for a procedure is done by simply subtracting a constant from the stack pointer, and deallocation is done by adding a constant to the stack pointer. The only defect of stack allocation is that the storage has to be released in the reverse order of allocation. This works perfectly for conventional procedures, which always have to return in reverse order of the calls.

Unfortunately, the efficiency of stack allocation has prevented compiler writers from using any other methods, and so languages have been restricted to conventional procedures. This has inhibited languages from making procedures into first-class objects (that can be returned as values of functions and stored in variables) and has also prevented the wider use of coroutines.

Stack allocation is so efficient that it is not even called dynamic allocation. The term dynamic allocation is usually restricted to the allocation of memory explicitly at the programmer's request. This is the new function in C++. This form of allocation is more typically dynamic in that it takes a fair amount of time and is definitely much slower than static allocation.

Predicting the Future   A key feature of the static-dynamic tradeoff is how well you can predict the future. Static solutions generally involve doing some work early, before the results are required. This work pays off if the results really are needed in the future. When you have certain knowledge of the future, you can do work in advance and know it will not be wasted. But if the future is uncertain, then you may do work that is unnecessary.

Deciding between static and dynamic solutions to a problem is a matter of how accurately you can predict the future. If you have a very good idea of what will happen, then the static solution is usually the best. For example, if you know a graph will require 5000 nodes, you should allocate them all at the same time, at the beginning.

If you have no idea about the future, then you should do things dynamically so you can adjust to circumstances as they develop. For example, if you have no idea whether a graph will contain five nodes or 500,000 nodes, you should allocate the nodes dynamically as you find that you need them.

> Dynamic solutions are for unpredictable situations, and static solutions are for predictable situations.

> In some situations, the dynamic solution is necessary because the static solution is too restrictive.

Terminology   In everyday English, static means fixed or stationary and dynamic means active or forceful. These meanings are very close to their technical meanings in mechanics (a branch of physics), where statics is the study of systems where the forces are in equilibrium and there is no motion, and dynamics is the study of systems where the forces are not in equilibrium and hence are causing motion to occur.

The terms *static* and *dynamic* have technical meanings in computer science that are somewhat different than their meanings in everyday English or mechanics. In computer science, we think of static and dynamic in terms of a process execution. Static activities are done before the process begins execution, and dynamic activities are done after the process begins execution. See Figure 13.6. The execution of a program is the analog to motion.

Generalizations   Actually, the words *static* and *dynamic* are used in computer science in a slightly wider context than we have presented so far. Before, we defined static activities as ones that take place before program execution has begun. We can replace "program execution" with any activity that has a definite beginning and ending. For example, we can think of the connection-oriented protocol as a static

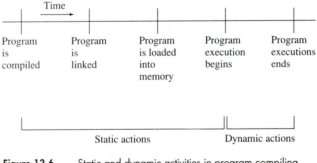

Figure 13.6   Static and dynamic activities in program compiling, linking, loading, and execution

solution since the route finding and lookups are done before the communication is established. We can think of a connectionless protocol as the dynamic solution since all the computation is done as needed during the progress of the communication and might have to be done several times. In a connectionless communication, the route from one end to the other has to be found for each message, but in the connection-oriented protocol, the route is found once (statically) before the communication begins and the same route is used for the entire communication.

This brings up another advantage of dynamic solutions, and that is that they tend to be more flexible. With a connection-oriented protocol, you must use the same route throughout the communication, even though that route might have gotten very busy or might even have been broken. With a connectionless protocol, you can use the fastest route for each message, and each message might go on a different route.

So, to summarize, static solutions generally take less time and more space and are less flexible, while dynamic solutions take more time and less space and are more flexible in responding to changing conditions.

> The static/dynamic distinction is a part of almost every design decision. It is your most powerful source of useful tradeoffs.

Computation on Demand   In dynamic solutions, you do not perform a computation until it is needed. But what if the result of the computation is needed more than once, maybe many times? Some forms of dynamic solutions perform the computation each time it is requested. Dynamic relocation is an example of this. Another solution is to perform the computation the first time the result is needed but save the result. All later requests will use the computed result and are equivalent to the static solution.

This second form of dynamic solution can be nearly as efficient as static solutions in all cases, and more efficient in the cases where the result is never needed.

13.3.8   RELATED DESIGN TECHNIQUES

Static solutions use early binding and dynamic solutions use late binding.

13.4   SPACE-TIME TRADEOFFS

13.4.1   OVERVIEW

Save processing time by using more space (by using more-redundant data structures), or save space by using more time (by recomputing redundant data).

13.4.2 MOTIVATION

Suppose we want to count the number of one bits in a large array of 32-bit words. Here is the first version of the bit counting program.

BIT COUNTING — ONE AT A TIME

```
inline int CountBitsInWordByBit( int word );
int CountBitsInArray( int words[ ], int size ) {
    int totalBits = 0;
    for( int i = 0; i < size; ++i ) {
        totalBits += CountBitsInWordByBit(words[i]);
    }
    return totalBits;
}
enum{ BitsPerWord=32 };
inline int CountBitsInWordByBit( int word ) {
    int bitsInWord = 0;
    for( int j = 0; j < BitsPerWord; ++j ) {
        // Add in the low order bit.
        bitsInWord += word & 1;
        word >>= 1;
    }
    return bitsInWord;
}
```

How can we trade space for time in this program? We are looking at the bits one at a time. Let's try looking at them four at a time.

BIT COUNTING — FOUR AT A TIME

```
enum{ HalfBytesPerWord=8, ShiftPerHalfByte=4, MaskHalfByte=0xF };
// Here is the number of 1 bits in the first 16 integers (in binary)
// 0000=0 0001=1 0010=1 0011=2 0100=1 0101=2 0110=2 0111=3
// 1000=1 1001=2 1010=2 1011=3 1100=2 1101=3 1110=3 1111=4
int BitsInHalfByte[16] =
    {0, 1, 1, 2, 1, 2, 3, 3, 1, 2, 2, 3, 2, 3, 3, 4 };
inline int CountBitsInWordByHalfByte( int word ) {
    int bitsInWord = 0;
    for( int j = 0; j < HalfBytesPerWord; ++j ) {
        // Use the low order 4 bits as an index into the table.
        bitsInWord += BitsInHalfByte[word & MaskHalfByte];
        word >>= ShiftPerHalfByte;
    }
    return bitsInWord;
}
```

We precomputed the number of 1 bits in all possible four-bit integers and saved them in an array. Then we look at the word four bits at a time, and look up the number of 1 bits in the array. This should cut the running time by nearly three-quarters, since most of the cost would be in the bit counting itself and that computation is dominated by the number of loop iterations. The two loops are the same, except that the second one has one addition and index operation that the first one does not have.

We can gain another 50 percent by going to full bytes, but then precomputations become more tedious since we have to precompute 256 subtotals. The standard way to handle this is to write a program to do the precomputing.

BIT COUNTING — EIGHT AT A TIME

```
inline int CountBitsInWordByByte( int word );
int CountArrayInitialized = 0;
int CountBitsInArray( int words[], int size ) {
    int totalBits = 0;
    if( !CountArrayInitialized ) {
        InitializeCountArray();
        CountArrayInitialized = 1;
    }
    for( int i = 0; i < size; ++i ) {
        totalBits += CountBitsInWordByByte(words[i]);
    }
    return totalBits
}
enum{ BytesPerWord=4, ShiftPerByte=8, MaskPerByte=0xFF };
int BitsInByte[256];
void InitializeCountArray( void ) {
    for( int i = 0; i < 256; ++i ) {
        BitsInByte[i] = CountBitsInWordByBit( i );
    }
}
inline int CountBitsInWordByByte( int word ) {
    int bitsInWord = 0;
    for( int j = 0; j < BytesPerWord; ++j ) {
        bitsInWord += BitsInByte[word & MaskPerByte];
        word >>= ShiftPerByte;
    }
    return bitsInWord
}
```

We use our first version of the bit counting function to initialize the counts in the array for this version. This is an example of another common design technique, that is, reduce one version of the problem to a simpler version. We want to count bits quickly, and we do it by using precomputed counts. Since there are only a few counts to precompute, we can do that computation by the simple, slow method.

This technique also assures that the counts are correct. It is easy to make a mistake in entering items into a table.

13.4.3   COMPUTER SCIENCE EXAMPLES

Caching   Caching uses more space to speed up a calculation.

In-line Procedures   By making a procedure we save code space since it only occurs once, but we add execution time because we incur the overhead of passing the arguments, making the call, saving registers, restoring registers, and returning the argument.

In some cases, we have to use very small procedures. Object-oriented programs often require this to keep a strict separation between the clients of the object and the implementation. In these cases, we can use in-line procedures to trade back the other way. When a procedure is in-lined, it takes more space (assuming it is called more than once) but less time.

Why not just move the code in line textually? Because we like procedures not so much for the space/time tradeoff but for their program structuring benefits. Subroutines were originally devised strictly to save space in the program since memories were very small. Gradually it became apparent that their advantages for program structuring and reusability far outweighed their space savings.

With the possibility of in-lined procedures, we can logically structure our programs independently of the time and space efficiency decisions involved in whether they make a procedure in-line or not.

> In-line procedures give you a choice between time and space.

Encoded Fields   Suppose we have a structure with eight boolean fields. We could encode each boolean field in a byte by itself or encode all eight of them in one byte. The encoded method saves seven bytes on each record, but it uses more execution time because it takes more machine instructions to extract bits from a byte than to just fetch a byte.

Let us assume that the compiler will handle all the work in getting at the bits (as C++ does), so the only issue is data space versus execution time (and not code complexity). If there were only a few instances of the structure, then we would probably choose to use whole bytes for booleans. But if this was an array of thousands of such structures, we would probably choose to encode the boolean fields in a single byte.

We could also consider hybrid tradeoffs if we had information about how often the boolean fields would be used. If two of the fields are used a lot and the rest infrequently, we could encode those two in their own bytes and encode the rest in a single byte.

A specific example of this is found in the file descriptor used in UNIX. The file descriptor contains all the information the system keeps about the file, and this includes a number of boolean fields (in particular, the owner-group-other, read-write-execute fields comprise nine boolean fields). Since this disk contains tens of thousands of these records, the UNIX designers decided to encode these boolean fields into a single word. Since these fields are infrequently used, there is no problem.

Preprocessing Data   Now let's consider another variation on the problem. Suppose you have a database of 1,000,000 records containing many boolean fields. Naturally, you would encode the boolean fields in this case. Suppose the processing was such that you read a few records and then did a lot of processing on the records, with many accesses to these boolean fields. Here is a case where some preprocessing would be appropriate. The structure on disk would have encoded boolean fields, but when you read a structure into memory you would convert it to decoded fields (one byte per boolean field). This would take a little processing time, but this would be made up in faster access to the fields.

> Some ways of trading time for space are:
> - In-line procedures.
> - Encoded fields.
> - Preprocessing data.

Redundant Data   In a doubly linked, circular list, half of the link fields are redundant since you can get to all the records in either direction. The double links use extra space to save processing time. Compare a binary search tree with a simple linked list. Both can be used to search for a node, but the binary search tree uses extra fields to achieve faster search times.

Postscript   Postscript describes images as a program. It takes time to run the program, but the program is usually smaller than the bitmap of the image.

Database Indexes   In a database, we can keep many indexes to the data and look things up quickly, but the indexes take space.

13.4.4 APPLICABILITY

Use a space-time tradeoff when you want to be able to adjust the resource requirements of a program.

13.4.5 CONSEQUENCES

You can save space and lose time, or vice versa.

13.4.6   IMPLEMENTATION ISSUES AND VARIATIONS

Control and Data   Time and space are the two fundamental components of any computation. To compute, we need a processor (time) and memory (space). We sometimes call them control and data. It is not too surprising that we can trade one for the other.

Time and Space   One of the pervasive dichotomies in life is that of time and space. Our world is spatial, and we are quite familiar with the three dimensions of space and how things move around in them. Time, though, is more mysterious. It seems to run in only one direction, and you cannot move about in it at will. It seems to be an essentially different sort of thing than space. The difference shows up clearly in operating systems where there are time resources and space resources, which are managed quite differently.

This dichotomy is also ubiquitous in computer science. The following table shows some of the places that this dichotomy shows up in computer science.

Time	Space
Dynamic	Static
Processor	Memory
Code	Data
Compute	Look up (cache)
Postscript	Bitmap
Sound	Image

Processor and memory are the two main resources in a computer system. A program consists of executable code and data that the code operates on. It is often the case they you can choose to use more memory and save computation (the classic time/space tradeoff). For example, you can keep several indexes in a database. They take up memory, but they make finding things faster. A binary search tree takes more space than a list of items, but can be searched much more quickly. We can cache the results of computations that we expect to do again. A graphical figure can be kept as a bitmap, which takes a lot of space but is fast to display, or as a Postscript program, which usually takes less space but takes more time to execute and generate the figure.

A sound is everywhere in space but only at one point in time, while an image is in one point in space but continues to exist as time goes on. At the user interface we can present an image that takes up screen space but can exist in any range of time, or we can output a sound which takes up no screen space but is gone once it is played.

13.4.7   RELATED DESIGN TECHNIQUES

Notice that trading space for time is really another example of the static/dynamic tradeoff. We statically precompute some data and save them, and then we do not have to do it dynamically.

You can usually trade off execution time for memory space. This is a static/dynamic tradeoff.

13.5   SIMPLE ANALYTIC MODELS

13.5.1   OVERVIEW

Often you can look at simple analytic models of a system and gain useful insights, even if the models are very abstract.

13.5.2   MOTIVATION

Let us think about the efficiency increases that multiprogramming will provide. Suppose we have a program that computes half the time and does I/O half the time, and runs for one minute. If we had two such programs to run and we ran them serially, they would take one minute each for a total of two minutes.

Now suppose we ran them together in a multiprogramming system. It would be nice if one program was computing while the other program was doing I/O so they both finished after one minute. Things do not ordinarily work out this way because programs do not compute and do I/O in completely regular ways. For example, suppose each program did all its computing in the first 30 seconds and all its I/O in the second 30 seconds. When the two programs started together, say one gets started computing and continues for 30 seconds. The other program has not gotten to the stage where it can use the I/O devices, and so it just waits for 30 seconds. When the first program finishes its compute phase and starts doing all I/O, the second program can compute while the first program is doing I/O for the next 30 seconds. Here is where you are getting the advantage of multiprogramming. After one minute, the first program completes, and the second program has finished its computer phase and will finish after 30 more seconds of I/O. The total time is 90 seconds—better than the two minutes serial execution would take but not as good as the one minute that perfect sharing would take. This example it typical; we cannot expect two processes to overlap computing and I/O perfectly.

Let's look at this in a different way. At any moment in time, there is a 0.5 chance that the first program will need to do I/O and not be able to use the processor. During the time the first program wants to do I/O, the second program will also want to do I/O with a 0.5 chance, so the chance that they both want to do I/O at the same time is $0.5 * 0.5$ or 0.25. If they both want to do I/O, then neither will be using the processor. But the rest of the time $(1.0 - 0.25$, or 0.75 of the time), at least one program will want to be using the processor, so there is a 0.75 chance that the processor will be executing. This means the processor will operate at 75 percent efficiency, and so 60 seconds of processing (30 seconds for each program) will take 80 seconds.

In general, if each program does I/O P of the time, then two programs will both need to do I/O $P * P$ of the time, and so the processor will be busy $(1 - P * P)$ of the time.

Suppose each program needs the processor 25 percent of the time. The following table show the processor use efficiency with respect to the number of such programs running together:

Number of Programs	Percent Processor Use	Percent Gained
1	25%	—
2	44	19%
3	58	14
4	68	10
5	76	8
6	82	6
7	87	5

We can see that the gains in efficiency get less and less as we pack more and more programs into memory.

13.5.3 OPERATING SYSTEM EXAMPLES

TLB   We formulated a simple model of the TLB to give us some idea of the slowdown of address translation with a TLB.

Virtual Memory   The working set model and program phase model are simple models of program paging behavior.

Disks   In Chapter 15, we looked at several models of disk-seek performance.

Scheduling   Queuing theory models are used in scheduling.

13.5.4 APPLICABILITY

Simple analytic models should be used whenever you can find one. But you have to be careful how you interpret the results. A model that is too simple will ignore important aspects of the problem, and so the results will be of no use. A model should be used to give you insights, but you should test those insights independently to be sure they really hold.

13.5.5 CONSEQUENCES

A simple analytic model can give you insights into the system that are hard to come by looking at the real system because it is too complicated.

13.5.6   IMPLEMENTATION ISSUES AND VARIATIONS

Accuracy of Models   The simple mathematical model of multiprogramming shows the way these models should be used in design. This model is not intended to be numerically accurate. The model is far too simple to be able to give accurate predictions in a complicated situation like multiprogramming a computer system. If we were looking for accurate predictions, we would probably have to use a simulation model, and that would take a tremendous amount of effort and require a very complex simulation model to achieve accurate results.

The purpose of models like this is insight, not accurate prediction. What insights does this model give us? First, it tells us that increasing the level of multiprogramming will increase processor utilization. Second, it tells us that this increase is subject to the law of diminishing returns, and we should take this into account in our implementation. We gain a lot in average processor use when we add the first few programs, but after that the percent gain gets smaller and smaller.

We will encounter other simple mathematical models in the course of studying operating systems, and generally they will help us develop intuition about the design situation rather than predict specific outcomes.

The Law of Diminishing Returns   ~~We see from the above model~~ that the more programs you have in memory, the less you gain from each one in terms of additional processor use efficiency. This is an example of the ubiquitous law known most widely in its manifestation in economics as "The Law of Diminishing Returns." It states that the average return on investment gets smaller (is diminished) as the investment is increased.

This law shows up everywhere. Suppose you decided to buy a rototiller for $300. If you share it with your neighbor, then you each pay $150 and you save $150. If you share the expense with two neighbors, then you each pay $100 and you save $200, $50 more than before. The following table shows the savings.

Number of Sharers	Dollars Saved	Additional Dollars Saved
1	—	—
2	$150	$150
3	200	50
4	225	25
5	240	15

Adding the first neighbor saved $150, but adding the fourth neighbor saved only $15. As you can see, the returns do diminish rapidly. Considering the problems of sharing with too many neighbors, you will probably decide to share it with just one or two others.

In computer science, we have something often called "The 80/20 Rule," which has several different versions. The program optimizer finds that 20 percent of the code in a program accounts for 80 percent of the execution time. A software manager finds that 20 percent of the code takes 80 percent of the time to write. A program debugger finds that the last 20 percent of the bugs take 80 percent of the time to find.[1]

This rule is generally a good thing in computer science and makes it easier to find efficient algorithms. We will see a good example of that later in this chapter when we talk about the *locality* of memory accesses, which is just another example of the 80/20 rule or the law of diminishing returns.

13.6   SUMMARY

Multiplexing is a basic technique in resource management. We have seen numerous examples of it before this. In this chapter, we saw how it applied to windows in a window system where screen space was the resource that was being multiplexed.

Many tradeoffs are possible by moving the binding time, that is, the time we make a decision or perform a calculation. Late binding allows us to make better decisions and is the basis of many useful features and optimizations in systems. For example, lazy creation allows us to defer work until later. With luck, we will never have to do the work at all.

The static/dynamic tradeoff is closely related to binding time. The classic example is compilers (static) and interpreters (dynamic). The key insight was that if you could predict the future accurately, then static solutions were better; otherwise, dynamic solutions were better.

You can often use extra space to hold redundant data that will save processing time. This is called the time/space tradeoff. Similarly, you can often eliminate redundant data to save space, and recreate the data when it is needed using extra computation. This is the most common and most useful tradeoff in programming.

Simple analytic models can often be used to gain insight into complex systems.

13.6.1   TERMINOLOGY

After reading this chapter, you should be familiar with the following terms:

*   binding time
*   eager evaluation
*   just-in-time
*   late binding
*   lazy creation
*   lazy evaluation

---

[1] Sometimes you hear this called "The 90/10 Rule," indicating even more concentration. The exact figures are not the point; the point is that a small fraction of the code/bugs takes a large fraction of the time.

- multiplexing
- real-time operating system
- reservations
- space-time tradeoff

13.6.2 REVIEW QUESTIONS

The following questions are answered in the text of this chapter:

1. Why is virtual memory a form of multiplexing?
2. Why is lazy creation useful?
3. Give some examples of late binding.
4. Why are reservations an example of early binding?
5. Why is static scheduling used in most cases?
6. Why is predicting the future important in deciding a static versus dynamic tradeoff?
7. What are some possible meanings of *efficiency*?
8. Why are variable-sized objects hard to deal with in a program?
9. What is the "Law of Dimishing Returns"?

13.7 PROBLEMS

1. Database systems have to deal with variable-sized objects all the time. They use a process called *normalization* that involves factoring out variable-sized lists from database records. Explain how this works.

2. MS Windows uses a technique called *multidocument architecture* where some subsystems put up a window that contains other windows and icons. It is basically a recursive desktop. What design techniques does this idea involve?

3. Many windows managers implement virtual desktops that are larger than the physical screen. They also implement multiple desktops that you can switch between. Describe these features in terms of multiplexing.

4. For each of the following program events, indicate whether they are done always statically (AllStat) (before execution begins), always dynamically (AllDyn) (after execution begins), either statically or dynamically depending on the compiler and the execution (Either), or both in the same execution (Both).

    a. The multiply in the statement "int x = 60*24;"

    b. The multiply in the statement "x = 60*y;"

    c. Allocation of storage for a global variable.

    d. Allocation of storage for a static variable.

    e. Allocation of storage for a variable local to a procedure.

    f. Allocation of storage for the code for a procedure.

    g. Allocation of space to pass arguments to a procedure.

    h. Searching the C library for a string function.

5. Give an example of a program whose total storage needs are completely predictable, and one whose total storage needs are unpredictable and will vary greatly from execution to execution. Discuss how each program should allocate its storage.

6. Discuss buses and taxis in terms of multiplexing. Discuss computer buses in terms of multiplexing.

7. Discuss how doctors make appointments in terms of early and late binding and the efficient use of resources.

14

I/O Devices

The two essential resources necessary for computation are a processor and memory, and these are the resources we have studied up to now. If, in addition to doing computations, you want to get programs and data in and out of memory, you need some input/output (I/O) capability. In this chapter, we will discuss the typical I/O devices and controllers you find in a computer system, and in the next chapter we will discuss the device drivers that control them.

14.1   DEVICES AND CONTROLLERS

input device

output device

I/O devices

An *input device* is an electromechanical device that generates data for a computer to read. An *output device* is an electromechanical device that accepts data from a computer. Many devices are both input and output devices. Collectively, all the devices (input, output, and input/output) are called *I/O devices*. Here are some examples of devices:

- *Input-only devices*—mouse, trackball, keyboard, CD-ROM.
- *Output-only devices*—printer, graphics display screen, plotter.
- *Input/Output devices*—disk, tape, writable CD, network, terminal, modem.

A terminal is really an input-only device (a keyboard) and an output-only device (a screen) packaged together in the same box.

14.1.1   DEVICE CONTROLLERS

device controller

I/O devices do not usually communicate directly with the computer system. Instead, there is an intermediate electronic device called a *device controller*. A device controller is primarily an interface unit. On one side, it knows how to communicate with an I/O device, and on the other side, it knows how to communicate with the computer system (usually over the system bus). A device controller can usually control several I/O devices, although it is most common for a device controller to control only a single device. Figure 14.1 shows the connections between the I/O devices, the device controllers, and the system bus. Typically, the controller is on a card that plugs directly into the system bus, and there is a cable from the controller to each device it controls.

There are several advantages to splitting the "transfer data" functionality of an I/O device from the "interface to the computer" functionality of an I/O controller. There is the possibility of sharing the controller among several devices. It is typical for

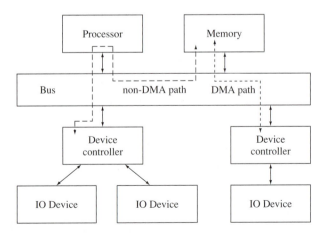

Figure 14.1   Device controller and I/O devices

many terminals or telephone dial-up lines to be controlled by a single controller. You can upgrade one without upgrading the other. For example, you might put a faster or bigger disk for use on the same controller. You can buy the two components from different manufacturers, and this allows increased competition and choice for the buyer.

The operating system will communicate directly with the device controller and indirectly with the I/O device (through the controller). A device controller is really a special-purpose computer with a very limited instruction set, limited to input/output control. Also, a device controller is not usually a stored program computer. Instead, the processor gives it one instruction at a time. When the device controller completes that instruction, the processor gives it another instruction. Some device controllers do know how to execute programs of more than one instruction. Then they are called *I/O processors* (IOPs), or sometimes *channels*.

I/O processors
channels

Most controllers have *DMA* (direct memory access) capability, meaning that they can directly read and write the memory in the system. (See the "DMA path" in Figure 14.1.) A controller without DMA capability provides the data (or accepts the data) one byte or one word at a time, and the processor takes care of storing it in memory (or reading it from memory). (See the "non-DMA path" in Figure 14.1.) DMA controllers can transfer data much faster than non-DMA controllers. These days, nearly all controllers have DMA capability.

DMA

*14.2   TERMINAL DEVICES

A terminal is a device that allows a user to communicate with a computer. It consists of a screen for output from the computer and a keyboard for input to the computer. The name "terminal" comes from the fact that a terminal is at the terminal, or end, point of a communication path.

14.2.1   BASIC TERMINALS

The basic terminal has a screen that can only display characters (not graphics) and a keyboard. Figure 14.2 shows the main parts of a terminal. In this diagram, components that are memories are shaded grey.

The terminal communicates over a serial line, one bit at a time, with a serial port. A *serial port* (see Section 14.3.1) is a connection which allows communication (in both directions) of a stream of bits. The bits are grouped into groups of 10 bits that encode 8-bit bytes. The serial port is the terminal device controller. The serial port sends commands to the terminal on the serial line going from it to the terminal, and it receives data from the terminal on the serial line going from the terminal to the controller.

serial port

The most common terminal command will be to display a character on the screen. The display-a-character command is represented by the ASCII code of the character to be displayed. For example, the one byte display command 65 is the ASCII representation of the character 'A' and tells the terminal to display an 'A'. There is a

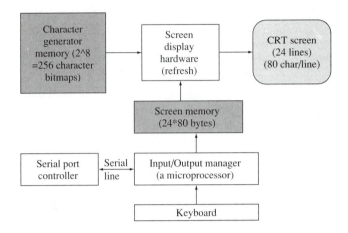

Figure 14.2   A basic terminal device

microprocessor in the terminal that reads the 'A' from the serial port and places it in the screen memory.

The screen has a fixed number of lines and columns, typically 24 lines of 80 characters each. There is a byte of screen memory for each character position on the screen. For a 24 line by 80 column terminal, that would require $24 \times 80 = 1960$ bytes in the screen memory. The screen display hardware is continually refreshing

refreshing

the screen. By *refreshing,* we mean the hardware is rewriting the image on the screen based on the contents of the screen memory. The screen is refreshed from 30 to 60 times a second, and so any changes in the screen memory will be reflected on the screen in no more than 0.033 seconds (with a refresh rate of 30 times a second). The screen needs to be refreshed because the image on the screen is created by aiming a

phosphor

beam of electrons at a special chemical (called a *phosphor*) on the inside of the screen that glows for a short time after it has been hit by the electron beam. If not continually refreshed, the image on the screen will fade away in a fraction of a second. This may seem like an inconvenience, but it is also an advantage since you never need to erase anything. Instead, you just write something new and the old image fades away.

The display is a glass tube (called a cathode ray tube or CRT). The electron beam that writes on the screen is generated at one end of the tube and then aimed by electrodes which produce a magnetic field (see Figure 14.3). The beam does not draw the characters directly, but instead traverses the screen in a fixed pattern as shown in Figure 14.4. It starts out in the upper left corner and moves to the right horizontally. This horizontal line is called a *scan line*. There are a fixed number of

scan line

dot positions along the horizontal line, and a dot can be written or not in each posi-

pixel

tion by turning the beam on and off. Each dot position is called a *pixel*. When it gets to the right end of the horizontal line, the beam is turned off and is moved back to the left side of the screen a little below where the previous scan line started. This is

horizontal retrace

called the *horizontal retrace.* Then the beam writes another scan line of dots. It does this for a number of scan lines until it gets to the bottom of the screen. When it gets

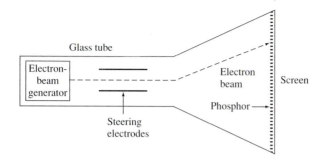

Figure 14.3   Electron beam drawing on a CRT

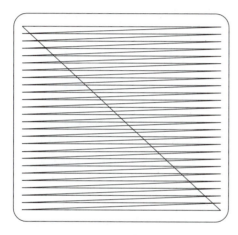

Figure 14.4   The trace of the electron beam on the screen

to the lower right corner, it moves back up to the upper left corner (with the beam turned off). This is called the *vertical retrace*. A terminal might draw 400 scan lines with 640 bit positions (pixels) in each scan line. A graphics display device might draw 1024 scan lines of 1280 dot positions.

vertical retrace

The characters on the screen are made up of arrays of these small dots written by the electron beam. A character might be 8 dots wide and 14 dots high, for a total of 112 dots. Figure 14.5 shows how the letters 'A' and 'B' might be represented in an 8 by 8 and an 8 by 14 pattern of dots. The *character generator memory* is memory in the terminal that converts an ASCII character (from the screen memory) into an array of 8 by 14 dots that can be written on the screen.

character generator memory

You can change the shape of the characters that are written to the screen by changing the contents of the character generator memory. In most terminals, this is done by replacing the ROM chip that holds the memory, but some terminals have a writable screen generator memory that allows you to send commands that will change the contents of the character generator memory. This allows you to define your own characters, which is useful for many purposes (such as international

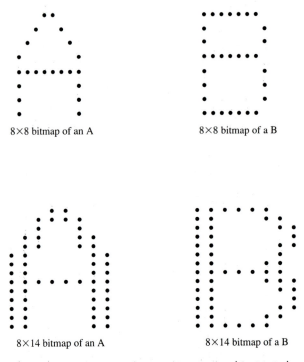

8×8 bitmap of an A

8×8 bitmap of a B

8×14 bitmap of an A

8×14 bitmap of a B

Figure 14.5 Bit patterns for A and B in 8×8 and 8×14 pixels

character sets). Note that the same contents in the screen memory can display differently on the screen if the character generator memory is changed.

This organization means that you can display nice-looking characters but not use too much memory. A character on the screen requires one byte of display memory, but would require 112 *bits* = 14 *bytes* (for an 8 × 14 pixel character) to store the bit pattern. The limitation of this memory-saving technique is that you can only display the characters in the character generator memory. Terminals were made this way because memory used to be much more expensive than it is now, and it was not feasible to have lots of memory in a reasonably priced terminal.

ASCII codes are really only 7 bits long, and the screen memory uses 8-bit bytes. So you have 128 character codes that are not used by the ASCII character set. In addition, only 95 of the 128 ASCII characters are printable characters. The rest are control codes (like tab, ring the bell, carriage return, line feed, delete, device control, etc.). So this gives us 128 + 33 = 161 unused character codes which can be used for other bit patterns that you want to display. For example, you can include a set of line parts that allows you to draw boxes on the screen. These characters are also used for international characters to accommodate languages with slightly different alphabets.

A terminal that displays graphics is quite a bit more work. We will talk about such terminals in Section 14.2.11.

The keyboard generates character codes for the keys that are typed, and these character codes are sent on to the device controller. We will talk more about this after a section about display commands.

14.2.2 DISPLAY COMMANDS

A terminal can be thought of as a special-purpose computer for entering and displaying characters. Until about 1975, terminals did not have microprocessors in them, but handled all the commands with logic circuits. This limited the size and complexity of the command set. Once the terminal manufacturers started using microprocessors, it was much easier to add more complicated commands to the command set of a terminal, and terminal command sets got more complicated.

The most important terminal command is the command to display a character on the screen. This command is the same for every terminal; it is one byte long and is the ASCII representation of the character to display.[1] The location on the screen to display the character (line and column position) is not part of the command; the command is just the single ASCII character. The location is implied, and is called the *cursor position.* The single ASCII character command causes the terminal to place   cursor position
that character in the screen memory at the cursor position. The screen refresh logic then takes care of displaying the character on the screen. Then, the cursor position is advanced one character to the right so successive characters are written, left to right, along a single line, just as you would expect. If the cursor position is already at the rightmost character position in a line, then it might stay there after writing or it might move down to the next line. Terminals differ on which action is taken. The terminal usually has several commands that set the cursor position. The cursor position is usually shown visually on the screen by marking the position with a box or underline (sometimes blinking).

Early terminals were basically electric typewriters and could only print a character in the "next" position. The carriage return and line feed commands moved back to the left margin and down to the next line. Some early CRT terminals mimicked this behavior and only allowed writing characters on the bottom line of the terminal. They responded to a line feed command by scrolling up all the lines and starting a new blank line on the bottom of the screen. These were sometimes called "glass TTYs" and were rapidly replaced by terminals with commands to place the cursor anywhere on the screen.

Two commands (set cursor position and display character) are sufficient to write any pattern of characters that you want on the screen, but most terminals have other commands that allow you to move around the screen quickly and write the text you want without using so many command characters. This was important in the early terminals since the serial port was not very fast and its speed was a limitation on terminal performance. These lines were as slow as 10 to 30 characters a second. At 30 characters a second, it would take $1920/30 = 64$ seconds, or over a minute, to write a full screen. Later terminal rates went up to 120, then 960 characters a second, and now they are even faster.

The carriage return character moves the cursor position to the beginning (the leftmost character) of the line it is currently on. The line feed character moves the cursor position down one line. These reflect the commands available on early printing terminals that were modified electric typewriters. The line feed moved the

---

[1]Some terminals used to use character representations other than ASCII, but ASCII is now the standard.

platen[2] up one line and the carriage return "returned" the carriage,[3] that is, moved it to the left as far as it would go. Even though most terminals became cathode-ray tube (CRT or TV-like) terminals, they kept the terminology and commands of the electric typewriter terminals. Sometimes, there was a command that combined the carriage return and the line feed. This was called a new line command.

Different operating systems use different conventions for lines. UNIX uses the line feed character to terminate a line. Macintosh systems use the carriage return character to terminate a line. PC systems tend to use a carriage return and a line feed to terminate a line.

All the commands we have discussed so far are a single character (a letter, digit, carriage return, etc.). For more complex commands, terminals use sequences of characters that form a single command. The ASCII escape character (decimal 27) is often used as a lead-in to a multiple character command. The next few characters indicated the command and the parameters to the command. A useful command is one that would set the cursor position to any line and column value. This allows you to write any character on the screen quickly. First, you issue the move current position command, and then you write the character.

Other useful commands insert and delete characters in a line or lines on the screen, scroll the entire screen (or parts of it), etc. Another command might control which character generator memory that was used (some terminals had two or more of these). This would allow you a character set larger that 256 characters. Many other commands are available in terminals.

Once terminals got the commands that would allow random access to the screen, a whole new class of programs was possible that used the full screen instead of just the bottom line of the screen. The first of these were the "full screen text editors." Almost all text editors are of this type these days, but when they first became common they were a huge improvement on the line editors that were previously the standard.

14.2.3   EXAMPLE DISPLAY COMMANDS

Let's look at some specific examples of terminal display commands. We will start with the VT100 terminal. This was a very successful terminal that was built by Digital Equipment Corporation. Its display command set has been widely copied and has become the standard for terminal emulators (see Section 14.2.15). The terminal has 24 lines of 80 characters each.

As our example, we will use the display version of the well-known C "Hello, World" example. We want the terminal to:

1. Clear the screen

2. Go to line 12, character 30

3. Write "HelloWorld"

---

[2] The *platen* is the cylinder that the paper was wrapped around and that moved the paper up and down.
[3] The *carriage* is the mechanism that prints characters on the paper and can move left and right along the platen.

4. Go to line 12, character 35

5. Insert "," (changing it to "Hello, World")

The VT100 commands to do this are given below. The string <E> is a single escape character (which is the decimal number 27).

1. <E>[;H,<E>[2J (8 bytes—clear screen and home cursor)

2. <E>[13;30H   (8 bytes—go to line 12 character 30)

3. HelloWorld   (10 bytes—ASCII characters)

4. <E>[13;35H   (8 bytes— go to line 12 character 35)

5. , World   (7 bytes—ASCII characters
                    —changing it to "Hello, World")

The lines are numbered from 1 on the VT100, so we used line 13 instead of 12. The VT100 does not have an insert character command or mode, so we have to rewrite the rest of the line after the inserted characters. The VT200 has an insert character mode, and so for a VT200, line five would be:

5. <E>[4h, <E>[4l (10 characters)

We go into character insert mode, insert the two characters, and then exit insert mode. The rest of the characters on the line are moved over to make room and are not written over. This command is actually longer, but that is only because the line we have to write over again ("World") is so short. Usually the insert character command is shorter than rewriting the rest of the line.

Just to see how another terminal would encode this, let's look at a Televideo 950 terminal.

1. <E>*   (2 bytes—clear screen and home cursor)

2. <E>=, >   (4 bytes—go to line 12 character 30)

3. HelloWorld (10 bytes—ASCII characters)

4. <E>=,C   (4 bytes—go to line 12 character 35)

5. <E>q, <E>r (6 bytes—insert mode, ", ", end insert)

This command encoding is more compact than the VT200, with a total of 26 bytes for the Televideo 950 as opposed to 44 bytes for the VT200. The move cursor command is encoded in a different way here. In the VT100 and VT200, it was encoded as a number in ASCII digits. In the Televideo 950, you take the row number and add it to the numerical representation of a blank. The blank (or space) is the lowest-numbered printable character, so if we add a number in the range 0 to 23 to it, we will get another printable character. The column number is encoded similarly. This allows the row and column number to take only two characters, and the command string is always printable ASCII. A space is 32, a comma (,) is 44 (32 + 12), a greater-than symbol (>) is 62 (32 + 30), and an upper case C (C) is 67 (32 + 35). The = is the mark of the move cursor command, so <E>=,> says to move the cursor to row 12, column 30.

These commands are not complicated, but their encoding is not obvious. It is difficult to do the encoding by hand, but computers, of course, do it easily.

14.2.4   Keyboard Events

The keyboard is the input device that is packaged with the screen output device in a terminal. When you press a key, it sends a code that represents that key to the device controller. The early terminals mapped keys directly into ASCII codes and sent the ASCII code itself down the serial line, but later people realized that the key should just send a code (a unique key number) and the software can interpret that key any way it chooses. This allows you to, for example, change the keyboard to a Dvorak keyboard (which arranges the letters in a pattern that is more efficient for typing) by moving the key caps and changing how the software interprets the key codes.

It is important to note here that the keyboard and the display are independent devices. When you press a key, it does *not* display the character on the screen. Instead, it sends the key code to the software, which then may decide to write the character on the screen by sending a display character command to the display. This allows a program to use letters for commands. The letters are not typed on the screen, but instead cause the display to be scrolled, a menu to pop up, a mode to be entered, etc. It is this logical separation of the two devices (keyboard and screen) that allows the use of key codes instead of ASCII characters.

It turns out that it is even more flexible if the keyboard reports not just keys typed but when a key is pressed (key down) and when it is released (key up). If the software gets a shift-down code, then an 'a'-down code, then an 'a'-up code, and finally a shift-up code, it knows that it is seeing a shifted 'a' and reports that an 'A' was typed. The software receives four events and two keys were pressed, but the single character 'A' is reported as typed. Reporting key down and key up means that any key can be a "shift" key and that the software can control things like automatic repeating of characters if they are held down for a certain length of time. This used to be handled in the terminal by hardware (or firmware—microprocessor code in ROM in the terminal), and so could not easily be changed.

The terminal device driver is the part of the operating system that talks to the device controller and will handle this processing. See Section 15.1.1. Let's look at an example of how the terminal device driver would handle a specific series of events from the keyboard. The table in Figure 14.6 shows a sequence of events over 1.8 seconds (this is a fast touch typist). We started the times at one second (1000 ms) so they would all be four digits and line up nicely. The times are shown in milliseconds, and we show the event that occurs at each time, the state of the software shift variable, the "typed" character produced by the event (if any), and a comment on what is happening.

A character is generated every time a nonshift key is pressed. When a key (other than a shift key) is pressed, the software also starts a timer. If the key remains pressed for the autorepeat initial delay (300 ms in this case), then the key starts autorepeating. The repeats happen faster (every 100 ms in this case) than the initial delay. This is the way people expect autorepeat keys to work. The software monitors the state of the shift key and automatically produces uppercase characters when the shift key is depressed.

Time (ms)	Event (Key Code)	Shift State	Output	Timer	Comments
1000	14⇓	unshifted	a	on	a (14) down
1200	14⇑	unshifted		off	a up
1350	92⇓	shifted		—	Shift (92) down
1450	14⇓	shifted	A	on	a down
1650	14⇑	shifted		off	a up
1750	15⇓	shifted	B	on	b (15) down
2050	timer interrupt	shifted	B	on	autorepeat on b
2150	timer interrupt	shifted	B	on	autorepeat on b
2200	15⇑	shifted		off	b up
2400	92⇑	unshifted		—	Shift up
2600	15⇓	unshifted	b	on	b down
2800	15⇑	unshifted		off	b up

Figure 14.6   Interpretation of a sequence of keyboard events

14.2.5 TERMINAL CAPABILITY DATABASES

As terminals got more popular and powerful, each terminal maker developed an instruction set for its terminal, and they were not generally the same. An ASCII character command always meant to display that character, but beyond that there was no standardization. The commands were conceptually the same (move cursor, insert line, clear screen, etc.), but the exact byte sequences that encoded the commands were different for each terminal.[4]

One way to deal with this is to have a database that describes how each terminal encoded a set of general commands available on most terminals. This is called a *terminal capability database* and allows a program to interact with a large number of terminals easily. The `termcap` and `terminfo` databases and the *curses* screen management system in UNIX use this idea. The BSD flavor of UNIX uses `termcap` and the System V flavor of UNIX uses `terminfo`. We are using the `termcap` data since it is easier to get in ASCII form.

terminal capability database

curses

To give you an idea of what the entries in a terminal capability database look like, Figure 14.7 shows the one for the VT100. The first line gives the various names for the terminal and the following lines give its capabilities. The actual encoding is not important here, just the idea of defining a set of common operations and mapping those common operations into specific command sequences for each terminal. If you are interested in what the encodings mean, you can look at the `termcap` man page on a (BSD-flavored) UNIX system.[5]

---

[4]Some manufacturers would use the command set of a successful terminal by another manufacturer. This would allow them to sell terminals to the (already proven) market for that terminal.

[5]Just to whet your appetite, we'll give you a few: do=down one line, cl=clear screen and home cursor, li=number of lines on screen, mb=turn on blinking attribute.

```
d0|vt100|vt100-am|vt100am|dec vt100:\
    :do=^J:co#80;li#24:cl=50\E[;H\E[2J:sf=5\ED:\
    :le=^H:bs:am:cm=5\E[%i%d;%dh:nd=2\E[C:up=2\E[A:\
    :ce=3\E[K:cd=50\E[J:so=2\E[7m;[se=2\E[m:us=2\E[4m:ue=2\E[\[m:\
    :md=2\E[1m:mr=2\E[7m:mb=2\E[5m:me=2\E[m:is=\E[1;24r\E[24;1H:\
    :rf=/usr/share/lib/tabset/vt100:\
    :rs=\E>\E[?31\E[?41\E[?51\E[?7h\E[?8h:ks=\E[?1h\E=:ke=\E[?11\E>:\
    :ku=\EOA:kd=\EOB:kr=\EOC:k1=\EOD:kb=^H:\
    :ho=\E[H:k1=\EOP:k2=\EOQ:k3=\EOR:k4=\EOS:pt:sr=5\EM:vt#3:xn:\
    :sc=\E7:rc=\E8:cs=\E[%i%d;%dr:
```

Figure 14.7   The TERMCAP entry for a VT100 terminal

DESIGN TECHNIQUE: ESCAPE CODES

The technique used to encode display commands (by preceding them with an escape character) is a standard way to compress a sequence of items. Suppose the longest command was 4 bytes. We could encode all display commands (including display a single character) as four-byte commands and avoid the use of escape codes. But since almost all commands are character display commands, that would be grossly inefficient in use of space since the command sequences would be nearly four times longer than they would be if we used escape codes.

We use escape codes in character strings as well, but for different reasons. In character strings, we use escape codes for characters that are hard or impossible to represent in the string. For example, if we use the double quote character as the string delimiter, then there is no way to include a double quote character in the string. We solve this problem with escape characters. We assign backslash as the escape character, and encode the double quote as two characters: the backslash and the double quote. This technique can be used to encode other special characters such as newlines. We might also use it to encode the tab character, not because we can't just put a tab in a string (we can do this) but because it is hard to "see" a tab in a string because it acts differently depending on where it occurs. Figure 14.8 shows an encoded string with escape characters and the "real" string it represents.

These days, many people are concerned with internationalization of computer software. One aspect of this is being able to handle languages with much larger character sets than the 26-letter English alphabet. For example, many Asian languages have very large character sets. In order to accommodate this, we have to allot 16 bits for each character. This allows for 64K characters in the alphabet. But this also means

Encoded string (23 bytes)

Decoded string (19 bytes)

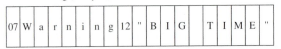

Figure 14.8   String with escape characters

Continued

that character strings are twice as big, even when they only contain English characters. The solution is a variation of the one we used for terminal display commands, and it also uses the idea of escape code. When we are reading a character string, we are always in some alphabetic mode. The mode tells us which alphabet we are using. Some of the alphabets will be 8 bit and some will be 16 bit. In each alphabet, there is an escape character that allows us to change the current alphabet. Suppose we use up to 256 alphabets. We reserve 256 codes out of the 64K codes of each alphabet to be alphabet change codes. These are escape codes. For the eight-bit alphabets, we reserve one code to be the alphabet change code, and the 8-bit character after it indicates which alphabet to change to.

Figure 14.9 shows a string that is a mixture of an 8-bit ASCII alphabet and a 16-bit Arabic alphabet.

Summary   Let's review the three variations of the escape character idea that we have just seen.

- *Display commands*—The escape character was the lead-in to a command of variable length. Either the command code implied the length, or the command had a special termination character that indicated the command was ended and to go back to reading single characters to display.

- *Encoded strings*—The escape character was the lead-in to a single character that specified one special character.

- *Mixed character sets*—The escape character changed the mode (the alphabet in use), and the new mode stayed in effect until there was another mode change.

The encoded string example is a special case of the mixed character set example because it changes the character set mode, but just for the one following character. After that, the mode goes back to the original mode.

The escape code idea is related to the design principle of "Win big and then give some back" as we discussed in Section 9.3.

Relation to Caching   Caching is a time optimization where you optimize the most common cases instead of making all the cases fast (which often is not possible anyway). Escape codes are a space optimization where you make the most common cases short instead of making all the cases short (which is impossible anyway due to information theory considerations). They are complimentary methods, one optimizing time and the other optimizing space but both doing it by optimizing the most common cases.

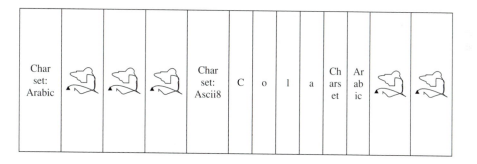

Figure 14.9   Mixed 8- and 16-bit alphabets

14.2.6 VIRTUAL TERMINALS

The capability database and the `curses` subroutine package are good examples of an idea we will see again in the next chapter, that is, the virtualization of I/O devices. The program that uses a terminal communicates with the command set of the "curses" terminal. This is a generalized terminal that has all the capabilities of typical terminals. It is a *virtual terminal* because it is not a real hardware device, but instead is created   virtual terminal with software (the curses subroutine library) and data structures (the internal curses data structures and the termcap database).

Before the program starts, a terminal type is chosen (via the TERM external shell variable). The curses subroutine package uses the termcap database to translate virtual terminal commands into the corresponding commands for the terminal chosen.

Figure 14.10 shows the flow of commands. This figure shows the program communicating with two different terminals. This is to show that the virtual terminal can be converted in different actual terminal command sets. The program would be connected to only one terminal at a time.[6]

Here is the way you would display "Hello, World" using curses.

1. erase();   (clear screen and home cursor)
2. move(12,30);   (go to line 12 character 30)
3. addstr("HelloWorld")   (write ASCII characters)
4. move(12,35);   (go to line 12 character 35)
5. insch(','); insch(' ');   (insert ',' then ' ')

Note that curses is a set of procedures callable from a C program. You do not send the curses virtual terminal an encoded string of characters. The curses procedures, however, will send an encoded string of characters to your real terminal.

device virtualization

We will see this same process of *device virtualization* done with tapes and disks and other devices in the next chapter. The pattern will always be the same: a generalized, virtual interface will be used to communicate with a range of similar devices,

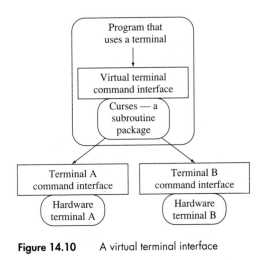

Figure 14.10   A virtual terminal interface

---

[6]Actually, there is nothing to prevent a program from connection with two different terminals using *curses* at the same time. Few programs do, however, since there is seldom a need to do so.

DESIGN TECHNIQUE: REUSING OLD SOFTWARE

It is a generally accepted idea that our best hope for improving software productivity is reuse of software. The fastest way to write something is not to write it at all. Reuse can happen at many levels. We can reuse procedures, objects, libraries, etc., that is, parts of programs, or we can reuse entire programs. One problem with reusing an old program is that the old program assumes an environment that no longer exists. The best example of this is the emulation of old machines. When the IBM 360 came along (around 1964), there were a lot of useful and debugged programs that were written in the assembly language for the IBM 1401 computer. The 360 had a mode where it could emulate the 1401 instruction set, and this allowed these old programs to be used on the newer (and much faster) 360s. The 1401 environment was simulated for these programs.

When graphical user interfaces came along, there was a large body of software written for terminals.

One could have rewritten all these programs to use a graphical user interface, but that is a lot of work and many bugs would creep in during the rewriting. A better solution is to use a terminal emulator that emulates a terminal on one side and uses the graphical user interface on the other side. In X windows, it is still the case that a lot of the software people use was written for terminals.

Such emulations can extend the useful life of software and increase its reusability.

When you make a change in a system, it is a good idea to support old versions as much as possible. This support can take several forms. You can support old data formats. You can recognize old formats and automatically translate them into the new formats. You can provide utilities that allow users to translate their files from the old format to the new format.

Go to some effort to support old versions.

and a combination of software and a database translates to the device interface of the specific device.

Virtual devices allow the operating system to provide a nicer device interface to the user.

14.2.7 TERMINAL INTERFACES

We have seen that there are a number of different interfaces between a program and a terminal. Figure 14.11 shows the succession of interfaces that the communications between a program and a terminal go through. The program communicates with curses, which communicates with the terminal device driver, which communicates with the (hardware) terminal controller (a serial port), which finally communicates with the terminal itself. To the program, however, it seems as though it is communicating directly with the terminal. The succession of interfaces insulate it from the variations in type of terminal, controller, and device driver.

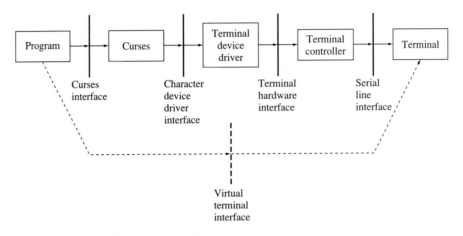

Figure 14.11   Interfaces to a terminal

14.2.8   MOUSE DEVICES

relative device

Another common device is a mouse. Sometimes a mouse is connected to the keyboard and sometimes a mouse is connected directly to the computer by its own serial port (or it may even have a controller of its own). A mouse provides two types of input. When the mouse is moved, it reports the movements as they happen. A mouse is a *relative device* so it reports the change in position in the two directions, not an absolute position on the mouse pad or in some other frame of reference. A mouse also has one or more buttons, and it will report when the buttons are pressed and released.

The mouse will report the movement, button press, and button release events in a sequential stream as they happen. These are coded as multibyte records. The first byte is the event type, and the following bytes are the particulars of the event (which button, whether it was a press or a release, or, for mouse movement events, the vertical and horizontal change).

14.2.9   EVENT STREAMS

event model

If the mouse is connected to a keyboard, then the keyboard will report mouse events and keyboard events in a combined stream of event records. But if the mouse and keyboard are separate, then they each will report a stream of events. There may be other input devices (dials, digitizing tablets, eye gaze trackers, etc.) that will also be reporting events. Usually there will be software that will combine all the input events into a single stream of event records. Each record will have a time stamp (when the event occurred), an event type, and some event details. We call this the *event model* and it allows us to combine the inputs of several devices into a single stream of input events. This makes things easier for the software that processes input.

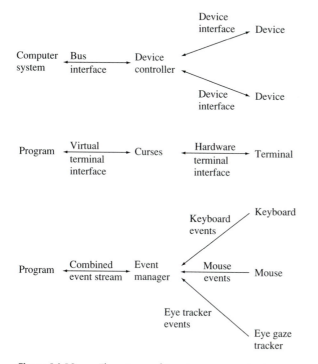

Figure 14.12   Three types of two-stage communication

14.2.10 VARIETIES OF TWO-STAGE PROCESSING

We have just seen three different situations where communication was done in two stages. It will be useful to consider how they are similar and how they are different. Figure 14.12 shows the three situations.

In the case of device controllers, we were separating two necessary stages to improve the modularity of the system. It was necessary to do the actual I/O (the device does this) and to transfer data over the bus of the computer system (the controller does this). The controller in the middle acts to translate between different interfaces.

The case of the virtual terminal is the same in the sense that the curses program (in the middle) translates between interfaces. But in this situation the middle step is not strictly necessary. The program could have communicated directly with the terminal using the terminal's interface. (In fact, that is how programs did it before curses was developed.) Another way of saying this is that a device interface and a bus interface are very different and require substantial conversion, but the virtual and real terminal interfaces are nearly the same. The two stages are for portability between terminals. curses can talk to all terminals. A device controller can only talk to one kind of device.

In the third case, we are combining event streams so that the knowledge of the details of how each event is reported is hidden from the program. It is most like the curses case since it is translating events from one representation to another, but

DESIGN TECHNIQUE: TWO-LEVEL IMPLEMENTATIONS

We first talked about two-level implementation in Section 4.4, and we have seen a number of examples of two-level implementations since then:

- Two levels of memory management (in each process and in the operating system).
- Two-level paging.
- Device controllers and devices.
- Virtual terminals and real terminals.
- Multiple-events streams into a single-event stream.

We will see more examples in Chapter 15:

- Two levels in a device driver (upper and lower level inside a single device driver).
- Logical and physical disks.
- Two levels of device driver (disk device driver communicating with a SCSI device driver).

The method used for memory management with the `brk` system call and a local memory manager (provided by the programming language) demonstrates the general design technique of implementing a service on two levels. The first (lower) level is usually implemented in a simple, straightforward way, and the second (upper) level is implemented by using the lower level, but with more sophisticated algorithms.

In the case of dynamic memory allocation, the operating system handles the relatively infrequent allocation of large blocks of storage to processes. Each process gets large chunks of memory from the operating system, and then reallocates it in smaller pieces during process execution. This level of allocation is of much smaller pieces and is much more frequent, and more complex algorithms are used.

We also saw this technique in the implementation of critical sections. We used a simple technique to implement the critical section needed to imple-

ment semaphores. This technique is used only in the operating system, and was either disabling interrupts or using a test-and-set instruction in a spin lock. Semaphores were then used to implement the second level of critical sections. The lower level used busy waiting because the critical section times were very short. The upper level used waiting queues and worked well with longer critical sections.

In two-level paging, we do not have two actual levels of implementation, but rather two uses of the same idea (paging) in a single implementation. This comes under the category of using the same idea twice.

This is a very effective strategy for complex problems. We use two-level implementation for several reasons:

- To separate two necessary levels that are conceptually different (e.g., device controllers and devices, two levels of a device driver, logical and physical disks, two levels of device driver). This improves the modularity of the system.

- To add a level of indirection to increase flexibility (e.g., virtual terminals and real terminals, multiple events streams into a single event stream).

- To allow one component on one level to serve or use several components at the other level (e.g., device drivers and devices, virtual terminals and real terminals, multiple events streams into a single event stream, logical and physical disks).

- To allow us to defer design decisions as long as possible (late binding) (e.g., little languages, policy/mechanism splits).

- To divide the problem and solve it with two more specialized solutions instead of one general solution (e.g., two levels of memory management).

- To apply the same idea twice (e.g., two-level paging) and enjoy the benefits twice.

Two-level implementations are effective in many design situations.

the representations are similar and the purpose for the transformation is standardization and portability.

> Two-level implementations are more modular and more flexible than a combined implementation, but they usually are slower. Sometimes speed is more important than modularity and flexibility, but usually it is not.

14.2.11   GRAPHICS TERMINALS

Terminals that display only characters are cheap and fast, but sometimes we want to display graphics on our screens. For a long time, graphics terminals were very expensive, but these days the technology is so advanced that very good graphics terminals are quite inexpensive.

There are two major ways to draw graphics on a screen. You can actually draw the lines on the phosphor on the screen by moving the electron beam in the shape of the figure you want to draw, literally writing with the beam. This is called *vector graphics*. The other way is to always move the beam across the screen in lines in a fixed pattern over and over again, as we saw in Figure 14.4 and talked about in Section 14.2.1. This second way is called *raster graphics* and it is the technology used by television. For a variety of reasons, the raster graphics model has pretty much taken over, and almost all graphics terminals use raster graphics.[7]

    vector graphics

    raster graphics

A graphics screen has a large number of scan lines (say 1024), and each scan line is a series of potential dot positions across the line from left to right. Each individual dot is called a pixel and can be individually turned on or off. So all graphic images are made up of dots. This is, in fact, how pictures are printed in a newspaper or a book. If you have enough pixels, you can get very realistic-looking graphics.

Raster graphics screens are controlled in much the same manner as the character screens we described above, except that pixels replace characters. There is a screen memory which has a bit for each pixel on the screen. There is screen display hardware that reads the contents of this memory 30 to 60 times a second and writes the pixel pattern on the screen. You draw pictures by storing ones and zeros in the bit positions in the screen memory. This screen memory is often called a *frame buffer*. The frame buffer memory is contained in the graphics device controller, which is on the memory bus of the computer system. You can draw graphics by writing into the frame buffer memory.

    frame buffer

A character terminal does not have a frame buffer. Instead, the character generator memory determines the pixels that are turned on. In a graphics terminal, each pixel is addressable and can be turned on or off individually. This provides the power to display any possible graphical image.

---

[7]There are a few very-high-end graphics systems that use vector graphics.

14.2.12   COLOR AND COLOR MAPS

Most graphics terminals allow you to draw in color. All this requires is to allocate more than one bit in the frame buffer for each pixel. If each pixel has one byte, then the value in the byte can indicate one of 256 different colors to draw the dot in. Before, the bit indicated whether the pixel was on (lighted) or off (dark). Now it indicates which color the pixel is to be, with white (lighted) and black (dark) still possibilities.

There are millions of colors when you consider all the shades and mixtures of color possible, and so 256 seems like far too few colors. Color is usually specified with 24 bits. These 24 bits can be encoded in various ways, but in any case they allow for 2^{24} or about 16 million colors. Some color terminals have 24 (or 32) bits per pixel, but this is expensive, and many color terminals use only 8 bits per pixel and use a color map to map the 8-bit colors to 24-bit color specifications.

color map

A *color map* is a set of 256 24-bit registers which map 8-bit color identifiers into 24-bit color specifications. When a pixel is drawn, the 8 bits for the pixel are used to look up the color in the color map, and the resulting color specification is used to generate the color of the pixel. This allows a choice of millions of colors but only 256 distinct colors in use at a time.

Entries in the color map become a resource that must be managed. The color map is usually managed by the window manager.

14.2.13   COMMAND-ORIENTED GRAPHICS

In the model we just described, the user of the graphics terminal draws by writing bit patterns into the frame buffer. This model is quite different from the terminal model we described before, since here we can write directly into the frame buffer, where in a terminal we could only write indirectly through commands issued to the terminal. Some graphics terminals use this command model also. In these terminals, the frame buffer is not directly available to users of the device, but instead they issue commands to the device to draw graphic objects. This arrangement makes it easier to optimize the drawing of graphics because users say what they want at a higher level, for example,"I want a circle at (200,200) with radius 50 and colored green." The hardware can then decide the fastest way to do this.

Figure 14.13 shows the two models for graphics controllers.

14.2.14   X TERMINALS

X terminals are very common these days. The architecture of the X window system is quite involved, but we can explain X terminals without getting into too much detail about X itself.

An X terminal is a command-oriented graphics terminal. It is like a character terminal, except that it has a much richer set of instructions. Instead of just having instructions to display characters and move the cursor position, an X terminal has a full

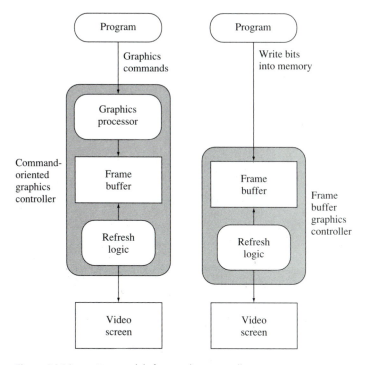

Figure 14.13   Two models for graphics controllers

set of commands to draw graphics images. For example, it has commands like draw circle, draw circle filled with a certain color, draw a bitmap, draw a line (of various thicknesses and colors), draw text, etc. In addition, there are commands to manage areas on the screen (called windows). Finally, the X terminal has a keyboard and mouse and reports a unified stream of input events.

The computer system communicates with the X terminal over a communication line, gives it commands, and receives an event stream from it. The program writing to an X terminal does not have direct access to the frame buffer but must draw using the graphics commands provided. Figure 14.14 shows the communication in an X system.

14.2.15 TERMINAL EMULATORS

Over the years, a large body of terminal-oriented software has been written. Many programs use the curses interface, which will work with just about any terminal. Most computers have a capability to connect terminals and allow access to computing over serial lines connected to serial ports. Some of these serial ports are connected to modems, which can communicate over phone lines to other modems. The computers assume that the device attached to the modem on the other end is a terminal.

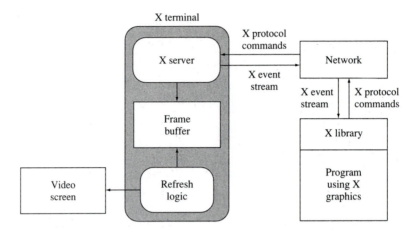

Figure 14.14   Communications in the X window system

But over the past several years, terminals have been slowly being replaced by workstations, PCs, and X terminals. Terminal capability databases allow a computer to connect to a wide variety of terminals, but a PC is not a terminal, and does not act like a terminal. A PC is a full computer, however, and can run programs to make it act any way you want it to act. So the solution to this problem (that a PC is not a terminal) is to write a software program that communicates with a modem over a serial port on the PC and pretends that it is a terminal. Such a program is called a *terminal emulator.*

terminal emulator

A terminal emulator detects typed characters from the PC keyboard and sends them via the modem to the host computer. It monitors the receiving end of the serial line for terminal display commands and parses and executes those commands. A terminal emulator will mimic some particular terminal and react to its display commands by writing on the PC's display. Most terminal emulators can mimic several types of terminals, but nearly all of them can mimic a VT100. There are very few real VT100s left anymore (they have been obsolete for several years), but there are millions of terminal emulators that can mimic the VT100 display command set. Figure 14.15 shows a terminal emulator.

An X window is not a (regular) terminal either, in that it does not understand the command set of any terminal in the terminal capability database. But we can use the same technique in an X window that we did with PCs. We can write software that puts up an X window. The X window can display text and accept keystroke inputs. The software translates these into the protocol of some type of terminal (probably a VT100). Anyone can write such an emulator. The most common one used in X windows is called **xterm**. Figure 14.16 shows how an xterm acts as a terminal emulator. Normally, a program that runs on a terminal will communicate through a software device driver and a hardware device controller to the hardware terminal device. With an xterm, the program will communication through a pseudo-tty driver (see Section 15.6.5). The pseudo-tty is really a pair of software device drivers, with one end acting like a regular terminal device driver and the other end for the terminal emulator. The xterm connects to this end and emulates a terminal.

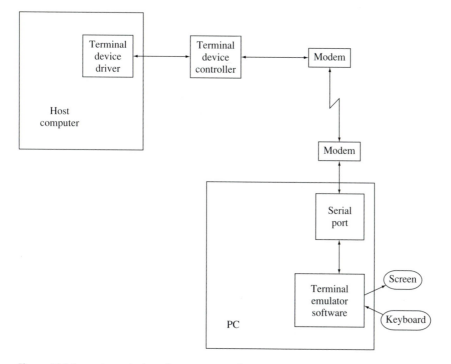

Figure 14.15   A terminal emulator over a modem

(a) vi editor running on a hardware terminal

(b) vi editor running on an xterm

Figure 14.16   An xterm as a terminal emulator

It is not hard to write a terminal emulator, but it is somewhat tedious. You must be able to parse and interpret a large number of terminal commands. But one advantage of the terminal emulator being in software is that you can add additional capabilities that would be too difficult or expensive to put in a terminal. For example, almost all terminal emulators will save lines that scroll off the top of the screen and allow you to scroll back and look at them later for reference. They also contain code to make it easy to transfer data between the host computer and the PC running the terminal emulator.

14.2.16   VIRTUAL TERMINALS AND TERMINAL EMULATORS

Suppose we are using a terminal emulator with a program (like vi) that uses a curses library. The program sends commands to a virtual terminal, which converts the commands into byte sequences that are sent along the serial line. At the other end of the serial line, these byte sequences are interpreted by the terminal emulator software and converted to screen display commands, for example, X library calls.

So we have a virtual device talking to another virtual device using the language of a long-obsolete VT100 terminal. The two concepts (the curses virtual terminal and the terminal emulator) work together with no problems, and this allows old software (like vi) to run on modern window systems without any changes.

If virtual systems are well designed with clear interfaces, they can be easily combined and the usable life of the software is increased.

14.2.17   PPP: A NETWORK EMULATOR

A workstation is usually connected to a network directly. This means that an X server running on the workstation can be on the network and, for example, display windows from X programs running on other machines on the network. If you are dialing up from a modem, you are connected to the workstation and not directly to the network. So an X server on your terminal or PC is not connected to the network and so cannot display X windows from other machines.

We can solve this problem with a strategy similar to terminal emulators. Figure 14.17 shows the components required. The *PPP* network emulator on the PC side acts like a network interface, so the X server thinks it is communicating with a network. The *PPP* network emulator connects to the host computer (the workstation) through a serial line and a modem (as we have seen before). On the workstation end, it then connects to a corresponding PPP network emulator running on the workstation. Network requests are passed from the PPP network emulator on the PC to the one on the workstation, which puts them on the real hardware network. Similarly, network messages to the X server on the PC are received by the PPP network emulator on the workstation, passed on to the PPP network emulator on the PC, and then to the X server.

This is the same idea that was used to implement remote procedure calls in Section 8.13.4. The idea is to have a pair of modules on the two machines that work together to create the illusion that the two machines are one machine.

14.2.18   MODEMS

In the last section, we showed modem devices. In this section, we will talk briefly about how they work.

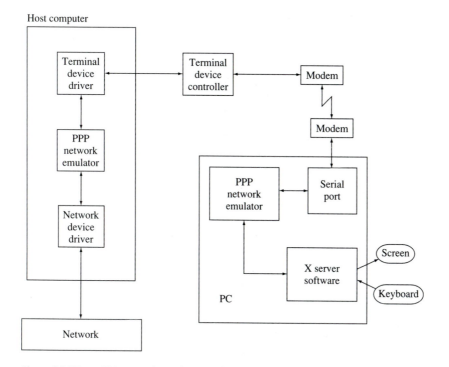

Figure 14.17   PPP network interface emulation

The goal of communication in a computer is to send bits from one place to another. The data communicated is a string of bits, say 01101001. It does not matter how these bits are represented; what is important is the bits themselves, the information. At various points in a computer system, bits might be represented as:

- The state of a flip-flop in a register.
- The voltage level on a wire.
- The polarity of the magnetization on a disk surface.
- The frequency or phase of a tone.

A telephone line can only be used to communicate electrical signals that represent sound, so to communicate over a telephone line you must communicate with sound. Computers use variations in the sound signal to communicate bits of information. The process of converting bits to sound is called modulation, and the reverse process is called demodulation. The hardware device that knows how to do this is called a *modem* (modulator-demodulator).

modem

Modem devices are always paired because signals are modulated on one end and demodulated on the other. Signals go both ways, and so each modem does both modulation and demodulation. The result is that an electrical signal is converted from a voltage level from a serial port on one side to a voltage level to a serial port on the other side. This allows communication between the two serial ports and, hence, between the computers they are connected to.

This is a similar idea to that used in RPC and PPP, that is, a pair of devices or modules work together to communicate between two systems.

*14.3 COMMUNICATION DEVICES

There is a class of devices that pass data from one place to another, and we call these communication devices. Serial ports, parallel ports, and networks are the most common examples.

14.3.1 SERIAL PORTS

Terminals are devices and require a terminal device controller. Terminals are usually connected to a serial port controller, which acts as terminal device controller.

serial port controller

A *serial port controller* connects to the system bus and provides one or more (often as many as 16) serial ports for devices. Each serial port has the capability of sending a stream of bytes in both directions, to and from the device. Normally a terminal is connected to a serial port, but any device that can receive or send a stream of bytes according to the serial port protocol can be connected to a serial port. Thus a serial port is a generic interface for communicating bytes of information to and from a computer. For example, a printer can be connected to a serial port. Mouse devices on PCs are often connected to a serial port.

Figure 14.18 shows how serial ports fit into a computer system. The serial port controller is connected to the system bus and so can communicate with the computer. The serial port device driver is the software in the operating system that communicates with the serial port device controller. The serial port device driver is often called a terminal device driver since the most common device on a serial port is a terminal (or something that acts like a terminal). The serial port device controller in the figure controls three serial ports which can connect to a variety of serial devices. In the figure, we show it connecting to a modem, a terminal, and a printer. The modem is connected to another modem over a phone line, and so the terminal connected to that modem is communicating over that serial port to the serial port device driver.

It is called a *serial* port because it sends the bits in the characters one at a time (that is, serially). A serial port has only one wire for sending data (and another one for receiving data). The eight bits of the byte are sent out one at a time. Usually, two extra bits sent with the byte to help in the control and timing of the communication.

Serial ports are useful to connect many kinds of devices to a computer. Suppose you wanted to control an electric train layout with a computer. One approach would be to build (or better yet, buy) an electronic device that will send commands to the engines, switch switches, and detect when trains pass over specific points in the track. This device could communicate with the computer over a serial port. It would accept commands as sequences of bytes over the port, and report on events as messages over the serial port. It would be easy to connect such a device since it would have a cable that would plug into one of your serial ports. Then you load some software (provided by the company that makes the device) that communicates with the device through the

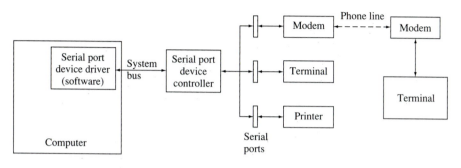

Figure 14.18   Serial ports

serial port, and you are ready to automate your train layout without having to buy any other special interface hardware and without the train controller device manufacturer having to know any details of your computer configuration.

14.3.2 PARALLEL PORTS

The one-bit-at-a-time nature of a serial port limits the speed at which it can transfer data. An alternative is a parallel port, which is like a serial port in many ways except that it has an interface designed for higher-speed transfer of information. A parallel port has 8 or 16 lines for communicating information, and so can transfer 8 or 16 bits at a time.

A *parallel port controller* is connected to the system bus and provides one or more parallel ports. Printers are often connected to parallel ports since they can accept data at high speeds.

parallel port controller

Figure 14.19 shows how a parallel port device controller fits into a computer system. It is similar to the setup of a serial port device controller, except the parallel ports have multiple lines. We show four parallel lines to a port in the diagram, but eight is the most common width of a parallel port. We show a model train layout connected here also. The higher speed will allow better control of the train layout.

The four parallel lines can be thought of as a four-bit binary number. A D/A (digital to analog) converter will convert such binary numbers to 16 levels of voltage on a circuit, and so the signal can be used to control a speaker or other analog audio device. If we had 16 bits, we could specify 64K levels of voltage and we could play music quite accurately. Similarly, an A/D converter can digitize voltages into binary numbers and transmit them to a parallel port. This would allow us to digitize sounds, store them in the computer, and play them back later. If this were connected to a telephone line, you could implement an answering machine entirely in software.

14.3.3 ETHERNET DEVICES

A serial or parallel port connects one device to a computer. A network connects several computers or devices together using a single, shared connection. An ethernet is a widely used technology that allows you to connect a number of computers together. Figure 14.20 shows three computers and a laser printer connected with an

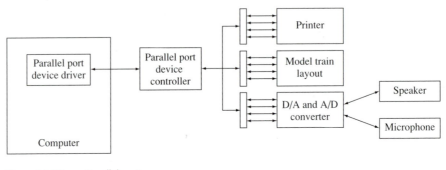

Figure 14.19   Parallel ports

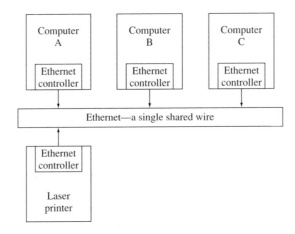

Figure 14.20   An ethernet configuration

ethernet. An ethernet is really just a single wire (a coaxial cable or other technology, maybe not even a wire) that is the "device." Several ethernet device controllers connect to a single ethernet. Computers and other devices can then be connected to an ethernet controller.

This setup is different from the devices and controllers we have seen so far, since a network is a different type of device. Most devices are connected to only one controller but the purpose of a network "device" is to communicate between computers and so a number of controllers connect to the single network device. The network device does not do anything with the data stream; it just transfers it around. An ethernet is a bus-type or broadcast network in that all communications go to every controller on the network.

When computer A wants to communicate with computer B via the ethernet, it sends data to its ethernet controller, which sends it over the ethernet, and it is read by the ethernet controller belonging to computer B. In effect, computer A treats computer B like a device that is connected to its ethernet controller. The network is an intermediary in that it presents a device interface to both computer A and computer B.

Information is transferred on an ethernet in *packets,* which are packages of bits   packets
(up to several thousand bytes of information) that are transferred in a unit. The operating system software gives a packet to the ethernet hardware with the address to
send it to, and the hardware handles the transfer. On the other end of the transfer, the
ethernet hardware will read the packet, store it in memory, and interrupt the processor, telling it that a packet has arrived.

14.3.4 OTHER NETWORK DEVICES

There are many other network technologies, but they are pretty similar to ethernets
from the operating system's point of view. They all transfer information between
computers, in packets, over some network medium. They vary in dimensions, such
as the packet sizes allowed, the time it takes to transfer data, the reliability, the cost
of the media and the controllers, etc.

14.4 DISK DEVICES

Disk devices allow long-term storage of data in a computer system. They read and
write data in fixed-sized *disk blocks* (also called *sectors*). Disk blocks vary in size   disk block
from 512 bytes to 16K or more, but 4K is fairly typical these days (in 1995). Fig-   sector
ure 14.21 shows the basic disk mechanism and a view of a single disk platter from
the top.

A disk is made of one or more platters. Each platter is a metal[8] disk that is covered with magnetic material (like what is used on audio and videotapes). A platter is
from 2 to 8 inches in diameter. All the platters are fastened to a central spindle that rotates. When operating, the spindle (and the attached platters) spins at 3600 to
7200 rpm. How fast is this? Suppose we have a platter that is 5 inches in diameter and
is spinning at 5400 rpm. The circumference is $\pi \times d \approx 16$ inches, or about $1\frac{1}{4}$ feet.
Spinning at 5400 rpm means that a point on the outside edge is moving $5/4$ feet $\times$
$5400 = 6{,}750$ feet per minute, or about a mile a minute, 60 miles an hour, or about 100
kilometers per hour (at the outside edge of the disk platter).

Each platter has a number of concentric *tracks*. Each track is a circle around the
platter and can be used to record data. The data is recorded bit serial, that it, as a
string of bits around the circular track. The track is divided up into *sectors,* each of
which is a disk block. There are typically about 50 Kbytes on a track, or 50 1K
blocks. A platter has from 500 to 5000 concentric tracks.

Each platter in the stack has tracks in the same positions. The tracks that are at
the same position on each platter form a group that is called a cylinder because the
tracks form an imaginary cylinder through the platters.

Each disk block has an address that tells where it is on the disk. The address has
three parts: cylinder, track, and sector. The cylinder indicates which track on the

---

| [8]Some disks are made of other materials than metal.

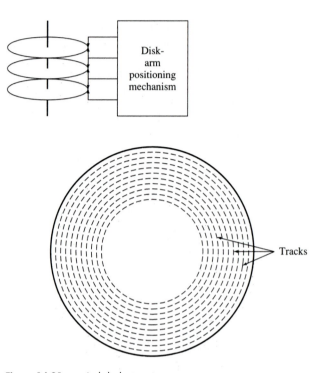

Figure 14.21   A disk device

platters it is. This is a number between 0 and the maximum number of tracks on a platter (minus 1 since we started counting at 0^9). Once we have specified the cylinder, we have to specify which platter (and which side of the platter) the track is on. We call this platter number the track number (or head number, or surface number). Finally, we have to specify which sector in that track we are referring to.

We can think of all the sectors on a disk as being in one long sequence of sectors by (figuratively) laying the tracks out one after the other. We start with cylinder 0 (the one nearest the outer edge of the platters. We start there from track 0, then track 1, track 2, etc., until we have used all the tracks in that cylinder. Then we go to the next cylinder and do the same thing. We number the sectors as we encounter them, and get a large sequence of sectors. If we have three platters, six tracks per cylinder, 1600 cylinders and 32 1-Kbyte sectors per track, then we have:

- 1 Kbytes per sector.

- 32 sectors or 32 Kbytes per track.

- Three platters with both sides of each platter used.

---

[9]Computer scientists habitually number things from 0. Anyone who has written programs knows that starting from 0 is easier for most loops and the mathematical equations that they are derived from. Unfortunately, starting counting at 0 makes it harder to talk in natural language about things. We get anomalies like the fact that item 3 is really the fourth item. This issue is this: Which do we do more, and in which place are errors more critical?

- Six tracks, 192 sectors, or 192 Kbytes per cylinder.
- 1600 cylinders, 307,200 sectors, or 307.2 Mbytes per disk unit.

We can think of the sectors as being numbered from 0 to 307,199. Some newer disk controllers use this linearized sector number as a sector address, instead of the three-part (cylinder, track, sector) address. This makes things a little bit easier in the software and allows the disk controller to manage the disk in more efficient ways (like having more sectors on the outer tracks, which are physically longer since their radius is larger).

14.4.1 Timing of a Disk Access

There are a number of delays that make up the time to access the data on the disk. Figure 14.22 shows these delays and their relative magnitude. The three factors are seek time, latency time, and transfer time.

In order for the disk to read (or write) a sector, the sector must move under the read-write heads. There is a read-write head for each track in a cylinder, and they all move together. Once you move to a cylinder, you can read (or write) all the tracks in the cylinder without moving the read-write heads. Moving the heads to a cylinder is called a *seek*. A seek takes from 1 to 30 milliseconds, depending on the speed of the disk and the number of cylinders to seek over. Typical values today (in 1995) for the average seek for a disk are from 5 to 15 milliseconds.

Once the read-write heads are at the correct cylinder, you still have to wait until the sector you want to read (or write) moves under the heads. This time is called the *latency time*. For three disk revolution speeds, we have:

- 3600 rpm = 60 rps = 1/60 sec/revolution = 16.7 ms/revolution.
- 5400 rpm = 90 rps = 1/90 sec/revolution = 11 ms/revolution.
- 7200 rpm = 120 rps = 1/120 sec/revolution = 8.3 ms/revolution.

On the average, we have to wait for one-half of a revolution, so the average latency time for rotation rates of 3600 to 7200 rpm is 8.4 to 4.2 milliseconds.

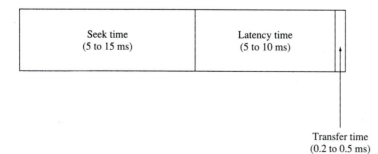

Figure 14.22   Delays in accessing a disk sector

transfer time

Once the sector is at the read-write heads, it will take $1/32$ of a revolution to read the disk block. This is called the *transfer time*. At 11 milliseconds per revolution, that is $11/32$ or 0.344 milliseconds. (For 3600 rpm, $16.7 \text{ ms}/32 = 0.52 \text{ ms}$, and for 7200 rpm, $8.3 \text{ ms}/32 = 0.26 \text{ ms}$.)

So the average total time to read a disk block at 5400 rpm is 8 ms + 5.5 ms + 0.344 ms, or about 14 ms. The transfer time is negligible, and the seek and latency times are about the same, each about half of the total access time.

14.4.2 FLOPPY DISKS

The disks we have been discussing up to now are called *rigid* disks because they are made out of a rigid material (usually metal). The read-write heads on these disks "fly" above the rotating disk. Rigid disks are best for maximum speed and capacity, but they are expensive and the media are not removable. Floppy disks were developed to meet the need for disks that were cheaper and allowed you to remove the disks from the disk drive. Floppy disks are called "floppy" because they are made of a material that is not rigid (usually soft plastic). When the disk is spun, the centripetal force makes the disk flat.

Other than differences in technology that lead to differences in speed and capacity, floppy disks are not much different from other disks. Some of the details of dealing with floppy disks might be different[10] but basically you treat them the same.

From the operating system's point of view, the only difference in dealing with a floppy disk is that the disk may be removed and replaced by another disk. In this respect, floppy disks are similar to tape devices, which also have removable media.

14.4.3 RAID DEVICES

Hardware engineers are constantly trying to improve disks by increasing their performance, reliability, and capacity. By performance we mean higher transfer rates and faster access times. The methods they have used to improve performance have been to increase the rate at which disks spin (reducing transfer and latency times), packing bits more densely along a track (increasing capacity and transfer times), and packing tracks closer together (increasing capacity). As disks get faster and bigger, it gets harder to make improvements, and so engineers have looked for other methods for improving the performance of disks.

When it got harder and harder to make faster processors, engineers turned to parallelism to get speed increases, and this led to multiprocessors and multicomputers. We can do the same things with disks, and this method has come to be called *RAID* or *redundant array of inexpensive disks*.

RAID

| [10]For example, you cannot leave floppy disks spinning when not in use because it wears out the disk.

Let's start with an example to see how one kind of RAID works. Suppose we have a disk like the one specified in the previous section, a 307 Mbyte disk with tracks containing 32 1-Kbyte blocks which makes one revolution in 20 ms and can transfer a block in 0.344 ms. We take two of these disks, and put them in the same enclosure. This two-disk RAID unit will have blocks of 2 Kbytes which will consist of the matching blocks (the ones with the same block number) on the two disks. The access time for a block on this RAID unit will be the same as for the disks that go in it, but the capacity will be double and, more importantly, the transfer rate will be doubled since we can now deliver a 2 Kbyte block in 0.344 ms. The transfer rate has increased from $1K/0.000344 = 2.98$ Mbytes/second to $2K/0.000344 = 5.95$ Mbytes/second.

Clearly we could increase the transfer rate more by using even more disks in parallel. We can increase the reliability of the RAID unit by including spare disks to be used when a disk fails. We could also include paired disks and write everything twice to get improved reliability. The same RAID unit can be used different ways by changing the software that controls it.

RAID units allow very large blocks and high transfer rates, but most operating systems are not designed for such units and cannot use them effectively. New hardware devices require new operating system structures to put them to the best use. In the case of RAID, there are now types of file systems, called log structured file systems, that are designed to use RAID units. We will talk about these in Section 17.8.3.

Figure 14.23 shows a RAID unit and several different ways to use it. We could record the same sector on two disks for reliability, and we could spread a logical sector over four disks for increased transfer rate. We can have spare disks to swap in when one of the disks fails.

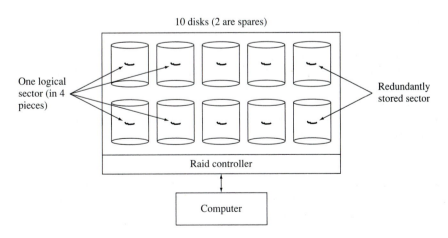

Figure 14.23   A RAID unit

DESIGN TECHNIQUE: THE POWER OF PARALLELISM

We almost always want things to go faster: compilers, processors, algorithms, translations, user interfaces, disk access, printing, etc. Usually there are ways to make things faster by using more resources. We can use more-complex algorithms that are faster, we can use more-expensive electronics that are faster, we can use more-expensive components in printers to make them faster, we can spin disks faster, we can use more-expensive mechanisms that position disk heads faster, etc. But as we get faster and faster, it becomes more and more expensive to make things faster. This is called the **Law of Diminishing Returns.** In this situation, we can turn to parallelism to make things faster in a different way.

Suppose we have a situation where the printer is always backed up and there are always many print jobs ahead of you in the queue when you try to print. We can use parallelism effectively in this situation by buying more printers. The queues will be spread over more printers and the time to get your job printed will go down.

But suppose the problem is that you are printing out a 1000-page manual, and at 20 pages a minute it takes 50 minutes to print the manual. Getting another printer will not help at all in this situation unless we break up the manual into sections and print sections on different printers. Doing this takes some effort.

The point is that parallelism can improve bandwidth (or throughput), but not latency. It can get more jobs through per unit of time, but it cannot get one job finished any faster (unless the job can be split into multiple jobs).

With multiple processors we could run several jobs at the same time, but we could not run one job any faster. With RAID devices we could get larger disk blocks in the same amount of time, but we could not reduce the time it takes to get a single disk block.

Parallelism can improve bandwidth but not latency.

14.5   DISK CONTROLLERS

Law of Diminishing Returns

Disks are connected to a disk controller, which then communicates with the rest of the computer system. The program sends commands to the disk controller, which relays them to the disk devices. When a disk is reading data, it is transferred from the disk device to the disk controller and then to the memory. Several disks can be attached to a single disk controller, but only one of them can be transferring data at a time. If you need data on two different disks connected to the same disk controller, then you must read them one at a time.

But, as we have seen, the bulk of the time in accessing a disk block is the seek and latency times. A disk controller can start a seek on one disk and then transfer data from another disk while the first disk is seeking. This is called overlapped seeks and it serves to increase the overall rate at which you can access data from a set of disks. Figure 14.24 shows a disk controller with two disks that is transferring from one disk while it is seeking on the other disk.

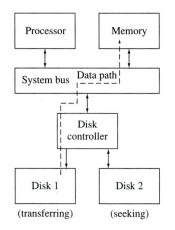

Figure 14.24   Overlapping data transfer and seeking

*14.6   SCSI INTERFACES

An interesting and important variation of the device controller idea is called the *SCSI* (small computer system interface) (pronounced "scuzzy") controller. A SCSI controller connects directly to the computer bus (see Figure 14.25) on one side and controls another bus (the SCSI bus) on the other side. The SCSI bus is a bus designed for connecting devices to a computer in a uniform way. The important thing about the SCSI bus is that there is a standard protocol for sending device control messages and data on the bus. Each device connected to the SCSI bus has a SCSI interface that knows about the bus protocol. There are chips that you can buy inexpensively that will handle this.

In effect, the SCSI controller is a generic device controller. You can connect any SCSI device to any SCSI bus. It means you can add devices without opening the computer box and installing a device controller on its internal bus. SCSI controllers do for general device interfaces (to disk and tapes and the like) what serial ports do for serial devices, that is, they are generic device controllers.

Figure 14.25 shows a SCSI bus. The SCSI controller is connected to the computer's bus and can communicate with the processor and memory. The SCSI controller also controls the SCSI bus, and various devices can be connected to the SCSI bus. A device just needs a standard SCSI interface (a single chip) in order to be connected to a SCSI bus.

SCSI started out on smaller computer systems, where the main advantage was to have a single device controller controlling several devices, and it was advantageous to be able to install one SCSI bus and then the system owner could buy any SCSI device to put on it. But the advantages of a common interface soon became apparent in all sizes of systems, and newer versions of SCSI have much higher data rates and are used in high-end systems.

SCSI

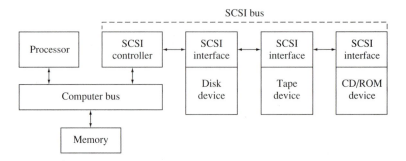

Figure 14.25   A SCSI bus configuration

*14.7   TAPE DEVICES

In the "old days" (say, until the early 1980s), most computer tape devices were large, open-reel units. But, as it did with audiotapes, the advantages of cartridge tape units became apparent, and these days nearly all computer tape units are cartridge units of various sizes. They all act in a similar way, however, and we will start by speaking of them generically.

tape drive

A *tape* consists of a long reel of magnetic tape, pretty much like an audio or videotape (see Figure 14.26). The *tape drive* can read the tape sequentially. The most natural way to use a tape is to start out at the beginning and read or write straight through to the end. Once a tape is written, you normally cannot rewrite parts of it; you must rewrite the entire tape. You can read a tape randomly, but it is not an efficient operation since you have to reel the tape back and forth looking for things. So tape is not for constantly changing data (like disks), but for archival data that you write once and keep and do not read much. In short, tape is ideal for backing up the information on disks, and that is principally what tape is used for.

A tape (see Figure 14.26) is a long (hundreds or thousands of feet) strip of plastic tape coated (on one side) with magnetic material (basically very finely ground iron filings) that can be magnetized to record data, and the magnetization can be detected to read the data. The read/write heads do the magnetizing and the detecting of magnetic charge. Of course, it would be too messy to keep the tape as a long strip, so it is rolled onto a spool and encased in a cartridge.

DAT

The most common form of tape these days is the *DAT* (digital audiotape) that uses the same tapes and technology as is used in DATs for music. There is a strong tendency to say "DAT tape," but this is technically redundant since the "T" in "DAT" stands for "tape."

Tape is a continuous medium, and a tape drive will usually allow you to write blocks of any length on a tape. Disk drives, you will recall, would only write in disk block units. Most tapes are written in very long blocks because it is more efficient to do it that way.

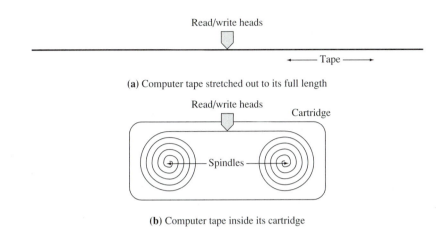

(a) Computer tape stretched out to its full length

(b) Computer tape inside its cartridge

Figure 14.26   A tape device

Tape I/O is fairly easy: you give commands to read or write tape blocks. There are additional commands to rewind the tape or skip over blocks on the tape.

*14.8   CD DEVICES

The *CD* (or compact disk) is a newer medium for computers and has just become common in the 1990s. Logically, the CD is a cross between a tape and a disk. It is like a disk in that direct access is quite efficient, so it can be used for data that will be accessed in unpredictable ways (like a database). It is like a tape in that it is intended to be written once and mostly read thereafter. So it is suitable for information that does not change rapidly (or at all). The big advantage of CDs is that they hold a lot of information (around 600 Mbytes) on a small, durable and inexpensive medium.

CD

The CD/ROM (CD/read only memory) is a write-once medium that can only be written by special machines that are fairly expensive. But they can be read by very inexpensive readers. Once written, CD/ROMs can only be read and are useful for the distribution of information. Computer documentation is now commonly distributed on CD/ROM.

There are two types of writable CDs. The first is the WORM (write-once, read-many) drive that uses a technology that can be written only once but read any number of times. Once it has been written, it essentially becomes a CD/ROM. The difference between a WORM drive and a CD/ROM drive is that the WORM drive can write one time, that is, the end user of the WORM media can write it once without special, expensive equipment.

There are also writable CDs which can be written a large number of times. These are like disks, but much cheaper. Generally, the access times to writable CDs are much slower than disks, and sometimes it takes much longer to write them than to read them.

The interface to CDs is quite similar to the interface to disks. They have tracks and sectors just like disks.

14.9   SUMMARY

Terminals used to be a very common device in most operating systems, but now they are being superseded by PCs and X terminals. Still, the basic ideas of terminals are part of how we interact with computers. Terminals are special-purpose computers that know how to display characters. They have an instruction set and a complex internal architecture. Most operating systems virtualize terminals in order to deal with the large number of different terminal types. A mouse is often associated with a terminal and provides its own set of events. Graphics terminals can display graphics and have very extensive command sets. These days, terminals are often emulated and are realized as windows in a window system. This requires a terminal emulator program.

Some devices exist only to transfer data between parts of a computer (serial or parallel ports) or between computers (ethernet and other network devices).

Disk devices are the main storage for a computer system. Disks are getting faster all the time, but they are very slow by computer standards and a lot of work is done in the operating system in order to make disk access as quick as possible. RAID devices are parallel arrays of disks intended to speed up disks using the same basic disk technology.

All devices need device controllers to interface them with the computer system bus. Controllers are like little computers and contain all the "intelligence" in the I/O hardware. Serial ports are terminal controllers. Disks require disk controllers. A SCSI controller is a generalized and standardized device controller that can be used as the interface for all SCSI devices.

14.9.1   TERMINOLOGY

After reading this chapter, you should be familiar with the following terms:

- CD (compact disk)
- channel
- character generator memory
- color map
- curses
- cursor position
- DAT (digital audio tape)
- device controller
- device virtualization
- direct memory access (DMA)
- disk block
- event model
- frame buffer

- horizontal retrace
- input device
- I/O device
- I/O processor
- latency time
- Law of Diminishing Returns
- modem
- output device
- packets
- parallel port controller
- phosphor
- pixel
- PPP
- RAID (redundant array of inexpensive disks)
- raster graphics
- refreshing
- relative device
- scan line
- SCSI (small computer system interface)
- sector
- seek
- serial port
- serial port controller
- tape drive
- terminal capability database
- terminal emulator
- transfer time
- vector graphics
- vertical retrace
- virtual terminal

14.9.2 REVIEW QUESTIONS

The following questions are answered in the text of this chapter:

1. Why are I/O devices important in a computing system?
2. Why is it useful to put I/O devices and I/O controllers in different hardware units?
3. What is the main function of a device controller?
4. Why is DMA useful?

5. How does a terminal know where to display a character that is written?

6. What is the purpose of the character generator memory?

7. Why is it sufficient to place the character into the screen memory in order to get it displayed on the screen?

8. Why do CRT screens need to be refreshed?

9. Why is the electron beam turned off during retraces?

10. Why do characters displayed by a terminal have to be represented as a pattern of dots?

11. Why is it important to be able to change the cursor position in a terminal?

12. What is the advantage of sending key-down and key-up signals from a keyboard instead of a code each time a key is pressed and released?

13. What is the use of a terminal capability database?

14. What is the purpose of a frame buffer?

15. Compare vector graphics with raster graphics.

16. Compare using 8-bit color with a color map with 24-bit direct color.

17. Compare the two types of graphics controllers: command-oriented and frame buffer.

18. Explain how an X terminal is a command-oriented graphics terminal.

19. Explain the similarities and differences between terminal emulators and PPP network emulators.

20. Why is a modem necessary? Why do we always use modems in pairs?

21. What is the difference between a serial port and a parallel port?

22. Compare a serial port controller to a SCSI controller. How do they have similar purposes?

23. What is the "device" in an ethernet?

24. How many tracks are there in a cylinder in a single-platter disk?

25. Contrast seek time and latency time.

26. Name three different ways to use a RAID device with 20 disks.

27. Which of these does RAID improve: seek time, latency time, transfer time?

28. What are the advantages and disadvantages of connecting four disks to a single disk controller?

29. What are the advantages of SCSI controllers over regular disk controllers?

30. Why are tapes good for backing up disks?

31. Compare a magnetic disk with a CD.

14.9.3 FURTHER READING

Sierra (1990) is a good survey of disk technology. Patterson et al. (1980) discuss RAID systems. Also see Reddy and Banerjee (1989).

14.10   PROBLEMS

1. The color map registers can be time and space multiplexed. Explain how each one would work in a window system with multiple windows on the screen.

2. Why does the curses virtual terminal have a procedure call interface, but the real terminal it controls has an interface consisting of strings of ASCII characters?

3. Consider the two sequences of display command to write "Hello, World" on the terminal (one for a VT100 and one for a Televideo 950). Compute how long each sequence will take at the following baud rates:300, 1,200, 9,600, and 28,800.

4. Suppose you have a graphics terminal with a frame buffer. You cannot use it as a character terminal by writing ASCII characters into the frame buffer. Why not? How can you use it as a character terminal?

5. What does a character terminal do if the character in its screen memory is not a valid ASCII character?

6. When you write a character to a terminal, it writes the character at the cursor position and moves the cursor position one to the right. What should the terminal do if the cursor position is already at the right-hand position on the screen? What should it do if the cursor position is at the lower right-hand character position on the screen? Give reasons for your answer in terms of what the programmer and the terminal user will expect, what seems to make the most sense, and what makes the terminal easiest to use.

7. The commands to a terminal to print an ASCII character contain only the characters, and do not say where to place the character on the screen. Why did they design it like this?

8. Give two advantages of a DMA device controller over a non-DMA device controller.

9. Consider a terminal that refreshes the screen 60 times a second. How long should it take for the phosphor to fade out after it has been written? Give a range of possible values and give arguments for a specific value. Do the same calculation for a screen that refreshes 30 times a second.

10. Suppose each scan line is 15 inches across and contains 1024 pixels. There are 1024 scan lines that are evenly spaced over 15 inches down the screen. Assume that the electron beam travels at a constant rate the entire time it is drawing on the screen (including the horizontal and vertical tracebacks). Compute how fast the beam must move and the time required to write a single scan line for a horizontal retrace and for a vertical retrace. Assume the display refreshes 30 times a second.

11. Suppose we have a scan line of 1024 pixels that is 15 inches long. How far apart are the pixel centers on the scan line? Give a range of possible values for the diameter of each pixel (assuming it is a circle) and argue for one specific value. Consider whether it would be a good idea or not for the pixels to overlap, and, if so, by how much.

12. Suppose you had a terminal with 1024 scan lines (down the screen) and 768 pixels (across the screen) per scan line. It has 64 Kbytes of writable memory that can be used as either screen memory or character generator memory (you can split it up any way you wish and change the split at any time). It can generate characters of sizes 8×8, 8×14, and 12×20. Figure out how many characters will fit on the screen using the

three character sizes and how much screen memory and display memory will be needed at each size.

13. Suppose you had a terminal which could use several different sizes of character, and had writable character generator memory so you could define your own character sets. Design a specific command set that will allow the use of these facilities. Make it look generally like one of the display command sets we saw examples of in the chapter.

14. Suppose we have a keyboard with a mouse attached, and it will report the stream of key down, key up, mouse move, and mouse button down and up events. All events *should* shown indicate the state of the shift keys (shift, control, and alt). Design a message format for reporting a unified stream of events from this keyboard (and mouse).

15. Suppose you had a disk which rotated in 10 milliseconds and had 50 sectors per track. The seek time for N cylinders is $3 + N/10$ milliseconds. Suppose the disk is currently at cylinder 0. Compute the expected time it would take to read to 10 consecutive sectors from cylinder 100, and the expected time to read one sector from each of the following cylinders: 10, 20, 30, 40, 50, 60, 70, 80, 90, 100.

16. Suppose we have a 5-inch disk with 50,000 bits per track. What is the bits-per-inch for a track at the edge (assume a diameter of five inches and a track with a diameter of two inches?

17. Some disks can be connected to two disk controllers at the same time. These are called *dual-ported* disks. Why would this be useful? Compare connecting two disk controllers to a dual-ported disk to connecting two ethernet controllers to an ethernet. Are we doing a similar kind of thing or are the two situations fundamentally different?

18. In the previous question, we talked about dual-ported disks. This could lead to some synchronization problems between the two disk controllers. What are those problems and what is a solution to them?

19. Compare a serial port controller with a SCSI controller. What are the similarities and the differences between them?

20. Serial port controllers can be connected to many different kinds of devices (terminals, modems, printers, etc.), but disk controllers can only be connected to disks. Explain why this is.

21. Suppose you have a disk whose total radius is $5\frac{1}{4}$ inches, and circular tracks on the disk range from the outermost track (with a radius of five inches) to the innermost track (with a radius of three inches). Compute the length of the innermost track and the outermost track. Compute how much of the total disk surface area is being used for tracks. If we assume that each track holds 64K bits, what is the density (in bits per inch) of the inner track and the outer track? If we have 1000 tracks on the disk, what is the density of tracks (in tracks per inch) on this disk? Which is closer, two bits on the same track or two tracks that are next to each other?

22. Consider our example disk in Section 14.4. Suppose that disk was spinning at 7200 rpm. Compute the average latency and transfer rate for the disk.

23. Suppose a DAT holds 5 Gbytes of data in records of 5 Kbytes each, and the tape can read a record in three milliseconds and skip over a record in one millisecond. How many records are on the tape? Assume no space is taken up for the gaps between records on the tape. How long does it take to read the entire tape? Suppose you want to get to a random record on the tape and you are at the beginning of the tape. How long, on the average, will it take to skip to that record and read it?

chapter

15

I/O Systems

The *I/O system* is the part of the operating system that controls input/output (I/O) devices. The main components of the I/O system are device drivers, which are the modules that control I/O devices. In this chapter, we will discuss the I/O system.

15.1   I/O SYSTEM SOFTWARE

In Chapter 14, we discussed some of the devices that are connected to a computer system. Now we are ready to talk about how the operating system deals with these devices and how they are presented to the user of the operating system.

15.1.1   DEVICE DRIVERS

Devices are, in general, complex and hard to use. Devices are controlled by communicating with device controllers through device controller registers, or sending them commands in the format of a message (e.g., SCSI devices). Each device controller has its own layout for its control registers or command messages. Any two disk controllers have essentially the same set of instructions (seek, read, and write), but the instructions are issued in different ways, have different operation codes, and go into different registers. Disk operations have the same kinds of errors, but they are signaled in different ways and with different codes in each disk controller.

No particular device is *that* complicated, but a computer system must be prepared to deal with hundreds of devices, and a lot of the complexity is because there are so many different devices to deal with. In order to manage this complexity, we create a module for each device controller whose job it is to communicate with that particular device controller. Everything that the system needs to know about that device controller and the devices attached to it is contained in this module. The module is called a *device driver.* The device driver will know the details of how the device controller works (addresses of the controller registers, bit layouts in the registers, the format of the command messages, error codes, operation codes, etc.).

device driver

A device driver knows how to control one device controller (and the devices connected to it), and it also knows how to communicate with the rest of the operating system. The interface to the rest of the operating system tries to hide the complexity and variety of devices, and instead presents a simple, uniform interface to the rest of the system.

A device driver is an interface module that communicates in the device's language on one side and the operating system's language on the other side. It is the software equivalent to the device controller, and that is why there is a device driver for every device controller.

Figure 15.1 shows the relationship between the devices, device controllers, device drivers, and the rest of the operating system. Each device controller is connected to one or more devices. There is a device driver for each device controller, and the device drivers constitute the I/O subsystem of the operating system.

The primary components of the I/O system are the device drivers.

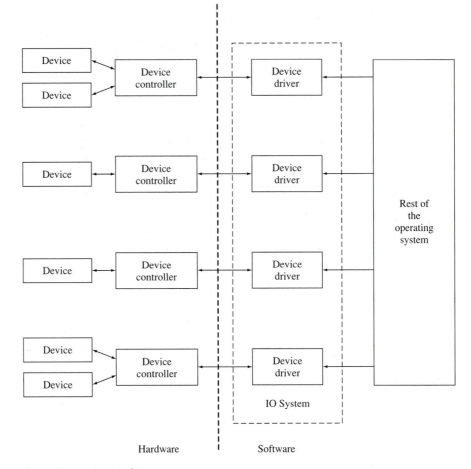

Figure 15.1   Device drivers in an operating system

15.1.2   DEVICE DRIVER INTERFACES

A device driver is a software module that defines an interface, that is, a set of procedures that can be called. We want to unify the device driver interfaces so that they all have the same procedures with the same parameters. Then we can treat the device drivers, and hence the devices, in a uniform way. Unfortunately, it is not feasible to do this, but we can reduce the number of device driver interfaces to just two types.

First let us look at the two functions that are common to all device drivers. They are:

- `int deviceDriver.open ( int deviceNumber )`—This call is made once before the device is used and allows the device driver to do any necessary initialization on the device. The `deviceNumber` indicates which device is to be opened if the device driver is handling more than one device. In many devices (disks, for example), this procedure does not do anything since no initialization is necessary. But other devices (for example, some printers) require an initialization sequence when they are powered up. The returned value is the success code for the open, which could fail because the device number is invalid or the device is not ready to use, for example, if the device is a floppy disk drive but no floppy disk has been inserted into the drive.

- int deviceDriver.close (int deviceNumber)—This call is made once when the system is finished with the device. For most devices, the close will not do anything, but some devices might require some cleanup activities. For example, a close on a tape device might rewind and eject the tape, or a floppy disk drive might eject the floppy disk.

The deviceNumber is necessary since a controller might control more than one device and each must be opened individually. If a device has removable media (for example, a floppy disk drive, a tape drive, or a CD/ROM drive), then it might be opened each time a new disk, tape, or CD is inserted and closed before one is removed.

15.1.3 THE TWO CATEGORIES OF DEVICE DRIVERS

Some storage devices have addresses for the data they contain. For example, a disk drive contains a number of sectors: each one has a unique address, and you can read and write data by address. Other disk-like devices such as CDs also have addresses. Some types of tapes also have addressable data where each tape record has a number or address. In almost all cases, the addressable blocks are all of the same size. We refer to the category of devices with fixed-size, addressable blocks as *block devices,*   block device and their device drivers will all have the same interface, which we will call the *block device interface.*

We will classify all other devices as non-block devices. They will also have a common interface. These are devices that send or receive data in streams of bytes, with no addresses associated with the bytes and usually with no fixed block size. For example, a terminal keyboard produces a sequence of keystrokes, but they do not have addresses and they do not come in fixed block sizes. This class of devices will be called *character devices,* and they will all use the *character device interface.*   character device

Both of these interfaces have an *open* and a *close.* We will discuss the rest of each interface in the next two sections.

15.1.4 THE BLOCK DEVICE INTERFACE

The disk is the archetypal block device. Disks differ in details, but they all do basically the same thing, read and write fixed-size blocks of data at specified addresses. Hence they have three procedures:

- int deviceDriver.read (int deviceNumber, int deviceAddress, char * bufferAddress)—This call reads a block of information from address deviceAddress and writes it into memory at address bufferAddress.

- int deviceDriver.write (int deviceNumber, int deviceAddress, char * bufferAddress)—This call reads a block of information from memory at address bufferAddress and writes it to the disk block at address deviceAddress.

- int deviceDriver.seek (int deviceNumber, int deviceAddress)—This call moves the read/write heads to the correct cylinder to read the block at address deviceAddress.

The seek is not strictly necessary, since the read and write operations will seek if necessary.

Having a common interface means that the rest of the operating system can treat all disks uniformly and use the same code to access any disk. This simplifies things considerably. The file system, for example (see Chapter 16), will read and write blocks on all the disks, but it does not need to know what kinds of disk the blocks are on because all disks have an identical block device driver interface.

In most systems, disks are the only block devices. Other block devices are either basically disks (like CDs, compact discs) or tapes with addressable blocks. In later sections, we will sometimes talk specifically about disk drivers rather than block device drivers, since disks are the dominant form of block device and other block devices can be treated as disks.

15.1.5 THE CHARACTER DEVICE INTERFACE

Character devices all read and write streams of bytes, but they also vary considerably (since this is really the catch-all group of devices that are not block devices). We need basic read and write calls, but we also need some way to deal with the specifics of each individual device. We will add a generic call to perform device-specific operations. So the character device interface is:

- int deviceDriver.read (int deviceNumber, int numberOfBytes, char * bufferAddress)—This call reads numberOfBytes bytes from the character stream of the device and writes them into memory at address bufferAddress.

- int deviceDriver.write (int deviceNumber, int numberOfBytes, char * bufferAddress)—This call reads numberOfBytes bytes from memory address bufferAddress and writes them to the character stream of the device.

- int deviceDriver.DeviceControl (int deviceNumber, int controlOperationCode, int operationData)—This call performs some device-specific action. The controlOperationCode indicates the type of operation, and operationData is the data to use, if necessary (not all operations require data).

The read and write are what you would expect. To write characters on a terminal, you write the characters to it. Similarly, you read keystrokes from the keyboard with the read procedure.

Data from character devices does not have an address. Character devices read or write the "next" data.

The DeviceControl procedure is general, in that every character device driver has one, but device specific since the meaning of a call to DeviceControl will differ from device to device. Each device driver will implement a set of DeviceControl commands. For example, a tape drive might have commands to rewind the tape or skip a file on the tape. A terminal device driver might have commands to ring the bell, change the character coding, set whether characters are echoed or not, etc.

The DeviceControl call is common to all character device drivers in name only. The syntax of the call is the same for each character device, but the semantics of the call can be different for each driver.

> Unified device driver interfaces (block device and character device) make it easier for the rest of the operating system (and the users) to use devices.

15.2   DISK DEVICE DRIVER ACCESS STRATEGIES

If a disk device driver gets several requests in a short time, it will keep them on a queue while they wait to be serviced. When the disk becomes free and several requests are waiting, the driver can choose any one of them to service next. Disk device drivers use a scheduling strategy for ordering requests that will use the disk as efficiently as they can. Since the difference between reads and writes is small and the controller itself will handle the seeks, a disk device driver will have a simpler interface that just accepts disk requests for its queue. This is called the strategy routine:

- int strategy (int deviceNumber, int readOrWrite, int deviceAddress, char * bufferAddress)—This call queues the disk request. The request will be removed from the queue and serviced in the order the disk access strategy dictates.

15.2.1   HANDLING DISK REQUESTS EFFICIENTLY

The disk driver can handle the requests in its queue in any order it wants, so this leads to a scheduling problem. It is analogous to the processor scheduling problem but with one big difference, and that is that the disk cannot be preempted. Once a request is started, it must be allowed to run to completion.

Our goal is to maximize the effective use of the disk, that is, to maximize the number of disk requests that are processed in a time period. The time taken by a disk request consists of these parts: the seek time, the latency time, and the transfer time. The transfer time is fixed for all blocks and cannot be improved upon, but we can reduce seek and latency times by careful scheduling.

Until recently, the seek time dominated the access time, and disk scheduling methods tried to minimize seek times. But as we have seen, the latency times are about the same as the seek times on modern disks, and so both must be considered for maximum efficiency. For now, however, we will just consider optimizing seek times, as this makes the problem simpler. In a later section, we will consider how to optimize latency times.

15.2.2   DOUBLE BUFFERING—AN ASIDE

double buffering

Some programs have to read and process a large file residing on disk. Often the processing takes a lot of time. If we read a block, process it, read the next block, process it, etc., then the program will have to wait for the disk I/O. This is shown in Figure 15.2(a). It would be faster to process one block while reading the next block. This technique is called *double buffering* because it requires two disk buffers, one to hold the disk block being processed and one to hold the disk block being read. When the program finishes with a block in one buffer, it starts the disk I/O on the next block to go into that buffer, and then switches to the other buffer. Figure 15.3 gives a flowchart for double buffering.

Double buffering saves time (see Figure 15.2(b)) in the sense that the job is completed in less clock time. The same I/O time and processing time is used, but some of the I/O time is overlapped with the processing time.

One characteristic of double buffering is that a process using it will always have an outstanding disk request. As soon as a buffer is emptied, the next block is requested. The program will start out by requesting a block in both buffers.

If a program is reading a file and writing out a modified version of the file, then it will use double buffering on the input side and on the output side, and hence will use four buffers. It will have at least two disk requests outstanding at any one time.

15.2.3   A DISK SCHEDULING EXAMPLE

Suppose we have a disk with 100 cylinders numbered 0 (the outermost cylinder at the edge of the disk) to 99 (the innermost cylinder nearest the spindle). The read/write heads are currently at cylinder 50, and there is a queue of disk requests for the

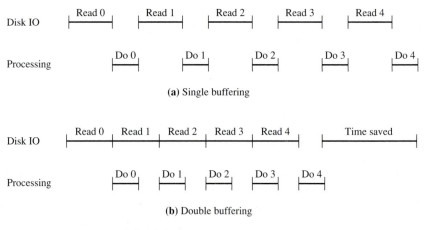

Figure 15.2   Single and double buffering

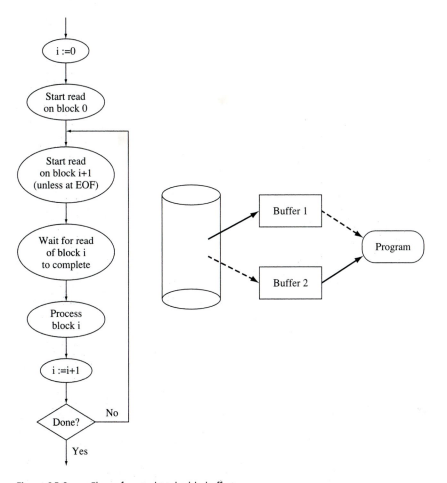

Figure 15.3   Flow of control in double buffering

following cylinders: 30, 15, 40, 43, 38, 77, 58, 14, 90, 5, 88, 27. The queue is listed so that the first request (for cylinder 30) came in first, and the rest are in order of arrival. Let us look at some possible scheduling strategies to decide the order in which to service these requests.

First-Come, First-Served   One possibility is to service the requests in FIFO order, that is, in order of arrival. This strategy is called first-in, first-out (FIFO) or first-come, first-served (*FCFS*). The table in Figure 15.4 gives the number of cylinder   FCFS
seeks this requires.

FCFS has the advantage that all requests are treated equally, which means that the average response time will be the same for all requests. Another advantage is that it is not possible for a request to wait forever. The big disadvantage is that there is a lot of unnecessary seeking. This is shown dramatically when we go to cylinder 90, then to 5, and then back to 88.

Start At	End At	Cylinders Moved
50	30	20
30	15	15
15	40	25
40	43	3
43	38	5
38	77	39
77	58	19
58	14	44
14	90	76
90	5	85
5	88	83
88	27	61
Total		485

Figure 15.4   FCFS disk head scheduling

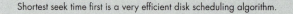

First-come, first-served is an obviously fair scheduling method, but it is usually not resource efficient.

Shortest Seek Time First   We might try to minimize seeking by always picking the request that is closest to the current position of the read/write heads. In the study of algorithms, this is known as a *greedy algorithm*. Greedy algorithms are usually pretty good. This strategy is called shortest seek time first (*SSTF*). The table in Figure 15.5 gives the number of cylinder seeks this requires.

SSTF

You can see how SSTF dramatically decreases the number of cylinders we have to seek over, from 485 to 130.

Shortest seek time first is a very efficient disk scheduling algorithm.

Problems with SSTF Scheduling   SSTF is very efficient, usually optimal, but it has a serious problem that FCFS does not have, and that is that some requests can wait a much longer time than others. This happens if the disk head stays in one part of the disk servicing requests, and does not service requests from more remote cylinders.

Let's take a specific example. Suppose you have just two processes, P1 and P2. P1 requests cylinders in this order: 40, 41, 42, 43, 44, 45, and so on. P2 requests cylinders in this order: 80, 81, 82, 83, 84, 85, and so on. Each process uses double buffering, that is, they process one block while requesting the next one. We assume

Start At	End At	Cylinders Moved
50	43	7
43	40	3
40	38	2
38	30	8
30	27	3
27	15	12
15	14	1
14	5	9
5	58	53
58	77	19
77	88	11
88	90	2
Total		130

Figure 15.5   SSTF disk head scheduling

that the processing does not take as long as the time to access a block, so the process will always have a pending disk request. If both processes begin at the same time, then P1 will request cylinders 40 and 41, and P2 will request cylinders 80 and 81. Suppose the disk heads are at cylinder 50, and so they go to cylinder 40 first. P1's request completes, and the disk scheduler chooses its next request (for cylinder 41) first, since it is closest (only one track away). Since its first request is completed, P1 now requests cylinder 42. P2 is still waiting for its first request (for cylinder 80). When P1's second request completes, its request for cylinder 42 is already in the queue and will be chosen, since it is the closest. P1 then issues another request for cylinder 43. Things go on like this as long as P1 can keep the disk busy.

This is not a far-fetched example. Something like this could easily happen. It is unlikely any request will wait for hours, but it could wait for tens of seconds or even minutes. This would make the response time very unpredictable.

> All scheduling, other than first-come, first-served, favors some users and discriminates against other users.

*SSTF with Aging   Because of this problem, SSTF is not an acceptable disk scheduling method if we expect heavy loads and we cannot allow some requests to wait a long time. But SSTF is so much more efficient than FCFS that we would like to find a compromise method that is still fast but doesn't ignore requests for a long time, like SSTF can do. The crux of the problem here is that some disk requests are being passed over in the queue too many times, that is, we strayed too far from FCFS in the quest for efficiency. There is a standard technique for handling situations like this, and it is called *aging*. Because aging is such a generally useful technique, we will present it first, and then look at another solution that handles the problem in a different way and is more commonly used in disk head scheduling.

Aging solutions all have the same general pattern. The age of a request is the time it has been waiting to be serviced. (FCFS scheduling always chooses the oldest request.) As time goes on, a request that hasn't been satisfied will get older. The priority that determines which request is chosen next is a combination of the priority of the algorithm we are adding aging to (in this case, we use the SSTF priority of the number of cylinders away the request is), and the age of the request. The priority is figured so that, as a request gets older, its priority increases, and after a certain age it will be guaranteed to have the highest priority.

For example, we could compute the SSTF with aging priority as the number of cylinders it would require us to move minus the number of tenths of a second the request has been waiting. The request with the lowest priority would go first. After a few seconds, the priority of a request would become negative and no new request could go ahead of it, even if it were for the same cylinder the disk is currently at. In the previous example, it would take about four seconds, and then P2's request would have aged enough to be chosen.

Let's take an example similar to the one in the previous section and see how aging will affect it. We will change things a little to make the computations easier and to show the effect better. P1 will ask for some sector in cylinder 0 in each request, and P2 will always request a sector in cylinder 20. Each process will make 10 requests. A seek of 20 cylinders takes 20 time units, and it takes 10 time units to service a request once you have reached the right cylinder. (These time units are about one millisecond each.) The read/write head starts at cylinder 0.

First let's see how SSTF handles this example. SSTF will always choose P1's requests for cylinder 0 over P2's requests for cylinder 20, so all 10 of P1's requests will be serviced first. This will take until time 100. Then SSTF will seek to cylinder 20 and handle P2's 10 requests. It will take 20 time units to do the seek and another 100 to service P2's 10 requests. SSTF will complete the requests in 220 time units.

Suppose we add an aging factor to the priority. The new priority is half the number of time units the request has waited, minus the number of cylinders to seek.[1] The request with the highest priority number is chosen. In case of a tie, the one with the shortest seek time is chosen. This SSTF with aging algorithm will handle the requests as shown in Figure 15.6. In Figure 15.6, each process always has two outstanding disk requests (except at the end, when P1 is on its 10th request). For each request, we show the age and the priority. The two request columns on the left are for P1's requests, and the two on the right are for P2's requests. Requests shown in **boldface** are picked for service at that time. The line below it is a new request and will always have age 0.

---

[1] We are subtracting the number of cylinders to seek so that higher numbers will mean higher priority.

aging

		P1's Requests				P2's Requests			
Time	Cylinder	Wait Time	Priority	Wait Time	Priority	Wait Time	Priority	Wait Time	Priority
0	0	**0**	**0**	0	0	0	−20	0	−20
10	0	0	0	**10**	**5**	10	−15	10	−15
20	0	**10**	**5**	0	0	20	−10	20	−10
30	0	0	0	**10**	**5**	30	−5	30	−5
40	0	**10**	**5**	0	0	40	0	40	0
50	0	0	0	**10**	**5**	50	5	50	5
60	0	10	5	0	0	**60**	**10**	60	10
90	20	40	0	30	−5	0	0	**90**	**45**
100	20	50	5	40	0	**10**	**5**	0	0
110	20	**60**	**10**	50	5	0	0	10	5
140	0	0	0	**80**	**40**	30	−5	40	0
150	0	**10**	**5**	0	0	40	0	50	5
160	0	–	–	10	5	50	5	**60**	**10**
190	20	–	–	40	0	**60**	**40**	0	0
200	20	–	–	50	5	0	0	**10**	**5**
210	20	–	–	**60**	**10**	10	5	0	0
240	0	–	–	–	–	**40**	**0**	30	−5
270	20	–	–	–	–	0	0	**60**	**10**
280	20	–	–	–	–	**10**	**5**	0	0
290	20	–	–	–	–	–	–	**10**	**5**
300	20	–	–	–	–	–	–	–	–

Figure 15.6   SSTF with aging disk scheduling

P1 gets six requests serviced before the aging kicks in and lets P2 get three requests in. After that they will alternate, each getting three requests in a row and then the other process gets three requests. The third request in each group is a priority tie, and so the request on the same cylinder gets to go first.

In this example, P1 finishes after the first request in its second group of (what could have been) three, and so the last four requests are from P2. The total time taken is 300 time units, which is about 36 percent slower than the 220 time units for straight SSTF.

We can compute the average slowdown for longer strings of requests. The first six requests always go to P1 and take 60 time units. After that, they are serviced in groups of three that take 50 time units (20 for the seek and 30 for the transfers). Of that, SSTF would have to do the transfers but not the seek, so the average slowdown for aging is $50/30 = 1.67$, or a 67 percent slowdown.

If we wanted larger groups than three, we could reduce the amount of priority per unit of age. If we arranged for groups of 10, then the average slowdown would be $120/100 = 1.2$, or 20 percent. In general, we can adjust the aging parameters to achieve a continuum of scheduling strategies from FCFS (if age was the entire priority) to straight SSTF (if age did not count at all).

As a check, let's see what FCFS would do with this. FCFS would seek with every request since it would alternate between P1 and P2, so each of the 20 requests would take 30 time units (20 for the seek and 10 for the transfer). This would be 600 time units—actually 580 since P1's first request will not require a seek. So we have 220 for SSTF, 300 for SSTF with aging, and 580 for FCFS. Even with aging, SSTF is almost twice as fast, and if we adjust the aging parameters we can get it even closer to SSTF.

There are many variations of aging. We can parameterize the aging algorithm by how fast the request ages. We could age requests faster by counting the number of 20ths of a second, for example. Another variation would be to have a threshold age. For example, we could schedule a request using SSTF, unless some request is over three seconds old; then, only requests over three seconds old would be considered, and they would be serviced, oldest first, until they are all completed, then we would go back to SSTF.

Aging solves the problem with SSTF; a request that ages awhile is sure to be picked, and no request can wait too long. This change makes SSTF a little less efficient, but it is worth it to remove the serious flaw in plain SSTF.

> Aging can be added to any scheduling algorithm to prevent some requests from waiting too long.

The Elevator Algorithm   If you look at SSTF in action, you will see that it usually goes in one direction until there are no more requests in that direction (or the next one is far away), then it reverses direction and starts picking up requests in that direction. There is another disk scheduling algorithm that does that directly (rather than as a side effect), and it is called the *elevator algorithm* or the *scan algorithm*. It is called that because it mimics the algorithm used by elevators, which go in one direction until there are no more floor requests in that direction, and then reverse and go the other direction.

elevator algorithm
scan algorithm

Let's put that a little more precisely. Using the elevator disk scheduling algorithm:

1. Start at cylinder 0 and direction up.
2. Let N be the current cylinder.
3. If there are no requests at all, then wait until one arrives.
4. If the direction is up, then choose the closest request for a cylinder N or higher. If the direction is down, choose the closest request for a cylinder N or lower.
5. If no such request exists, then change the direction, otherwise service the request chosen.
6. Go back to step 2.

The elevator algorithm operates, in practice, nearly identically with SSTF. The elevator algorithm also has the same problem SSTF has, that is, it is possible that some requests will have to wait a long time. With SSTF, it happens when one request is far away from the others. With the elevator algorithm, it can only happen when there is a steady stream of requests for a single cylinder, so that the "elevator" does not move at all while servicing them. We could solve the problem with aging, as we did with SSTF, but there is a simple variation of the elevator algorithm that also solves the problem.

The Elevator Algorithm with Batching   The problem is that you might get a steady stream of requests for the same cylinder. The solution is to take the requests in batches. Use the elevator algorithm on each batch until all the requests are satisfied, and then go on to the next batch. This algorithm is called the *N-step scan algorithm*. N-step scan algorithm Suppose we start with some request in the waiting queue.

1. Start at cylinder 0 with direction up. Put all pending requests in the waiting queue.
2. Transfer all requests from the waiting queue to the elevator queue.
3. All newly arriving requests are put into the waiting queue.
4. Use the elevator algorithm on the elevator queue until it is empty.
5. Go back to step 2.

This N-step or *batching* technique could also have been used with SSTF to remove the problem of a request waiting too long. batching

> Batching is another way to modify a scheduling algorithm to prevent some request from waiting too long.

A small problem with the elevator algorithm is that the cylinders in the middle of the disk get better service since the scan passes over them more often than cylinders near the edge of the disk. A solution to this bias is to only sweep in one direction. Say you start at the outer edge of the disk and sweep in until there are no more requests in that direction. You then seek back to the outermost requested cylinder and start going in again. Since you always sweep in the same direction, all cylinders are treated equally.

15.2.4   SECTOR SCHEDULING WITHIN CYLINDER SCHEDULING

In the previous sections, we have looked at ways to optimize disk access by scheduling the order in which we visit the cylinders. This optimizes the seek time. Once we are at a cylinder, there may be several requests for sectors in the cylinder, so we should think about the optimal order to service the sector requests in a single cylinder. We do this by scheduling sector access within a cylinder.

When the disk is at a cylinder, the platter is rotating and the sectors come under the read/write heads in sequence. So the obvious thing to do is to sort the sectors in the order they are found on the cylinder, and service the requests in that order. This way, we might be able to handle all the requests in a single disk revolution. There are two factors to consider about this strategy.

Suppose the disk has three platters, so there are six tracks in a cylinder. There is a read/write head for each track (making six in all), and we can switch between read/write heads pretty much instantaneously because it only requires electronic switching (no physical motion is necessary). Even if sector 12 is on track 1 and sector 13 is on track 4, we can still read them one after the other on the same revolution.

But since there are several tracks in a cylinder, it is possible to have two requests for the same sector number. For example, we might have a request for sector 12 on track 1 and sector 12 on track 4. In this case, it is not possible to read them both on the same disk revolution because they pass under the read/write heads at the same time. It is only possible to read from one read/write head at a time because there is only one data path from the disk to the disk controller. In this case, we will have to take two disk revolutions to read the two sectors.

So here is our sector scheduling strategy. Order the requests by sector number. On each revolution, read (or write) one request from each sector as it comes under the read/write heads. If there are two or more requests for the same sector number, then it will take two or more disk revolutions to handle them all.

Sector scheduling is close, but not exactly analogous, to cylinder scheduling. In cylinder scheduling, we visit the cylinders in the order they are laid out on the disk. We stay at each cylinder until all the requests for that cylinder are satisfied. In sector scheduling, we visit the sectors in the order they are laid out on the disk. But we cannot stay at each sector until all the sectors at that sector number are read. We cannot do this because the disk rotates continuously, and it is not possible to stay at a sector.

15.2.5   COMBINED SECTOR AND CYLINDER SCHEDULING

In the special case we just discussed, we did sector scheduling within cylinder scheduling, that is, we decided which cylinder to go to first, and then, once we were there, we decided how to schedule the sectors for that cylinder. The two scheduling methods did not have to interact, and that made our life much easier. A more powerful scheduling method would consider cylinder and sectors together. It would go to the closest request considering both cylinder and sector information. If you have the necessary information, this is no more difficult than cylinder scheduling. You can use a shortest-access-time-first scheduling method, with batching or aging to prevent some requests from getting shut out.

The problem is that the operating system does not normally have the necessary information available at the right times. The disk controller will tell you what sector a disk is at, but the request goes from the disk driver, to the disk controller, to the disk, back to the disk controller, and, finally, back to the disk driver. This all takes a long time (in computer terms), and by the time you get the information, it will be out of date and you will have to model the disk to compute which sector it is currently at. This is all possible, but probably not worth the trouble. A better solution is to leave the scheduling to the disk controller. Many new disk controllers do not use cylinder, track, and sector numbers at the command interface. You simply provide an absolute sector number, and the disk controller figures out where that is. If you could submit a number of disk requests simultaneously, then the disk controller could do the scheduling. In this case, cylinder and sector optimization could be used, since the disk controller has fast access to the information necessary to do this scheduling.

15.2.6   REAL LIFE DISK HEAD SCHEDULING

Usually, disks are lightly loaded and there is only one or a few disk requests in the queue. In this situation, any scheduling method is fine. Sometimes the disk request queue gets longer when the disk cache flushes its modified blocks (see Section 15.7). In real systems, first-come, first-served disk head scheduling is only a little worse than other strategies.

*15.3   MODELING OF DISKS

In the previous section, we analyzed the effectiveness of several disk scheduling strategies, and found that SSTF was faster than FCFS, and that the scan algorithm was somewhere between them but closer to SSTF. To do this analysis, we used a model of how disk drives work. We assumed that the time to seek between two cylinders was proportional to the number of cylinders moved. This is a simple model that suffices for some purposes, but it does not accurately model seeking on real disks.

A seek on a real disk will start with a large movement to the approximate location of the cylinder it is going to. Then it will see what cylinder it is on, and make a small corrective move if it is not on exactly the right cylinder. This process is called *settling*. The settling process takes the same amount of time (on the average), no matter how many cylinders you seek.

settling

So a more accurate model of seek times is $T = c_0 + N \times c_1$, where N is the number of cylinders to seek. The constant c_0 models the fixed overhead on all seeks, and the constant c_1 models the time to move the heads over a cylinder. So the seek time for a disk might be $T = 3.0ms + Ncyl \times 0.04 \frac{ms}{cyl}$.

15.3.1   A DISK SCHEDULING ANOMALY

How does this more-accurate disk model affect our analysis of disk scheduling algorithms? Well, in practice, not at all. Our observations about the three algorithms are still correct. However, this new model does create the possibility of an anomalous situation where FCFS can be faster than SSTF. At first, it would seem impossible that this could happen, but it can. Let's look at an example and then see what makes it work.

Figure 15.7 shows the sequence of disk requests, giving their arrival time and service time. The service time is the rotational latency and transfer time after the heads are at the right cylinder. The disk starts out at cylinder 205 with no requests in the queue when the first request (for cylinder 185) arrives. We give a name to each request for use in the next two tables. The disk model is of an IBM 3330 disk, where the seek time is $T = 10ms + Ncyl \times 0.1 \frac{ms}{cyl}$.

Figure 15.8 shows how the FCFS algorithm would handle the series of requests, and Figure 15.9 shows how the SSTF algorithm would handle the series of requests.

The FCFS algorithm finished in 57.5 ms, and the SSTF algorithm finished in 67.5 ms, 10 ms or 17 percent slower. Why did this happen? Both algorithms seeked the same number of cylinders, but FCFS did it in two seeks and SSTF did it in three seeks. The 10 ms difference is the startup time on the extra seek. The problem was that SSTF went to cylinder 200 first and moved on to cylinder 210 before it saw the second request for cylinder 200. This caused it to have to seek back again to pick up the second request for cylinder 200.

Arrival Time	Cylinder	Service Time	Name
0 ms	185	8 ms	req1–185
13 ms	210	5 ms	req2–210
19 ms	200	2 ms	req3–200
35 ms	200	7 ms	req4–200

Figure 15.7   Disk request arrival and service times

Time	Cylinder	Events
0	205	req1–185 arrives; seek to 185 started
12	185	seek to 185 finishes; service of req1–185 begins
13	185	req2–210 arrives (still serving req1–185)
19	185	req3–200 arrives (still serving req1–185)
20	185	req1–185 completes; choose req2–210 seek to 210
32.5	210	seek to 210 completes; start serving req2–210
35	210	req4–200 arrives (still serving seq2–210)
37.5	210	req2–210 completes; choose req2–210 seek to 200
48.5	200	seek to 200 completes; start serving req3–200
50.5	200	req3–200 complete; start service of req4–200
57.5	200	req4–200 completes; Done

Figure 15.8   FCFS scheduling

Time	Cylinder	Events
0	205	req1–185 arrives; seek to 185 started
12	185	seek to 185 finishes; service of req1–185 begins
13	185	req2–210 arrives (still serving req1–185)
19	185	req3–200 arrives (still serving req1–185)
20	185	req1–185 completes; choose req3–200; seek to 200
31.5	200	seek to 200 completes; start serving req3–200
33.5	200	req3–200 completes; choose req2–210; seek to 210
35	200↦210	req4–200 arrives (still seeking to 210)
44.5	210	seek to 210 completes; start serving req2–210
49.5	210	req2–210 complete; start seeking to 200
60.5	200	seek to 200 complete; start serving seq4–200
67.5	200	req4–200 completes; Done

Figure 15.9   SSTF scheduling

15.3.2   CYLINDER CORRELATIONS

Besides the disk model, we make another assumption when we model a disk scheduling algorithm. That assumption is that the cylinders are accessed randomly. Some measurements of real systems seem to indicate that this is not so, and, in fact, the chance that two sequential requests are for the same cylinder is 2/3. The cylinders of successive requests are correlated with each other. This is some of the basis of the anomaly in the last section, where we had two sequential accesses to the same cylinder that FCFS handled without an extra seek.

We should not be surprised that this is the case. This is just another example of the principle of *locality*. Programs tend to read files sequentially, and operating systems try to keep file blocks on the same cylinder. So it is natural that successive disk requests should be for the same cylinder.

The moral is that any modeling makes assumptions about the system being modeled, and the results depend on the accuracy of these assumptions.

15.3.3   A MORE ACCURATE DISK MODEL

If we want to be even more accurate in our disk modeling, we can observe that the seek takes less time per cylinder for longer seeks, even after you factor out the startup and settling times. A better model is a function with several areas where you use one formula for different seek lengths. For example, we might use one formula for seeks of 50 cylinders or less, another for seeks of 50 to 150 cylinders, another for seeks of 150 to 400 cylinders, and another for seeks over 400 cylinders. Some simulations use such a disk model in order to get more accurate results.

15.4   DEVICE NUMBERS

Calls to a device driver included a device number. This was necessary because a device driver connects to a device controller, and the device controller might control more than one device.

The device number can be used to encode other information as well. For example, suppose we have a tape device. We can assign two different numbers to the same device, the difference being that when we use the second device number, then the tape is automatically rewound when it is closed. Or, if a tape can write at two different densities, it can have a different device number for each density. Or, we could do both, and have four different device numbers for the same tape device. This is information that we could send using DeviceControl for character devices, but with block devices this may be the only way to convey this information.

Device numbers are also used to define multiple logical disks on a single physical disk (see Section 15.6.1).

15.5   UNIFICATION OF FILES AND I/O DEVICES

We have simplified access to devices by classifying all devices as either block devices or character devices. All devices in the same class are accessed with the same interface. We have already seen (in Chapter 3) the interface to files that the operating system implements for users. We also saw in that chapter how devices could be accessed with the same file interface.

The file interface is a set of operations: open, read, write, seek, and close. This is quite similar to both the block device interface and the character device interface. The file system implements the file interface for files, and we will examine that in detail in the next chapter. The I/O system implements the file interface for devices with a fairly simple translation. The only change is that we export the DeviceControl interface to the user in the form of a DeviceControl system call that is only allowed for devices (the system call will return an error when used on an open file that points to a file and not a device).

Figure 15.10 shows the relationships between the parts of the operating system and the hardware. There are block devices connected to device controllers and managed by device drivers. All the block device drivers have the same interface (the block device interface). Similarly, there are character devices, controllers, and device drivers. All the character device drivers have the same interface (the character device interface). A block device can also be used as a character device. In the diagram, this is shown as a different driver. More likely, the same disk driver will export both a block device interface and a character device interface to the disk.

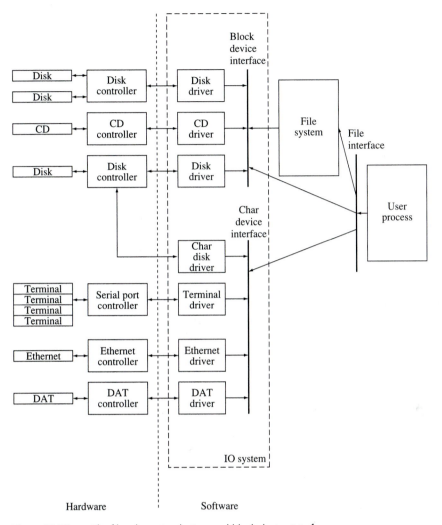

Figure 15.10   The file, character device, and block device interfaces

The file system uses the block device interface and exports the file interface for files. The I/O system uses the block device interface and the character device interface and exports the file interface for devices. The user only sees the file interface for both files and devices.

> The unification of file and device interfaces makes life easier for users and programmers, and makes the operating system easier to learn.

DESIGN TECHNIQUE: UNIFICATION OF CONCEPTS

UNIX and other operating systems unify the concepts of file and device. In Section 3.10, we described the unification of files and IPC (using pipes). These unifications reduce the number of protocols a user needs to learn, since the file access protocol is used for files, devices, and IPC.

If we see two similar sequences of code in a program, we unify them by writing a procedure and calling it twice. Object-oriented programming is based on the idea of the unification of concepts. A superclass represents a concept that unifies some aspects of its subclasses.

Unification of concepts simplifies a system and usually provides a deeper understanding of its structure.

See Section 18.5 for more examples and discussion of the unification of concepts.

15.6   GENERALIZED DISK DEVICE DRIVERS

The normal case is for a disk driver to talk to a disk controller which controls one or more disks. Each disk will have a separate device number and will look, to the file system, like a large array of N disk blocks numbered 0 to $N - 1$. But there are several possible variations on that arrangement, and we will look into some of them in this section.

15.6.1   PARTITIONING LARGE DISKS

Suppose we have a very large disk, say 8 Gbytes. With 4K sectors, this disk would have 2M blocks. Suppose we did not want to manage disks that large because our backup tapes only hold 5 Gbytes. What we can do is partition the disk up into two *logical disks* of 4 Gbytes of 1M sectors each. The disk driver assigns two device numbers to the single disk unit, say device numbers 0 and 1. When a disk request comes in for device 0, it accesses the disk in the normal manner using the sector number in the request. But if a request comes in for device 1, then the device driver adds 1 M to the sector number and then accesses the disk. (See Figure 15.11.)

The device driver is "pretending" that there are two 4-Gbyte disks out there, when there is really only one 8-Gbyte disk. Each portion the disk is divided into is called a *partition*. Of course, we can partition a disk into more than two parts. We could divide this disk into eight logical 1-Gbyte disks and use device numbers 0 through 7.

15.6.2   COMBINING DISKS INTO A LARGE LOGICAL DISK

When we partitioned a disk, we divided it up into two or more logical disks. Once we have the concept of logical disks that are different than the physical disks, we can also go in the other direction.

Suppose we had disks of 500 Mbytes, but sometimes we had files of more than 500 Mbytes to store. As we will see in the next chapter, file systems are structured to exist on a single disk. But this can be a single logical disk. Suppose we had two

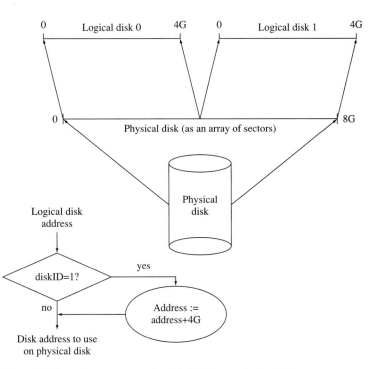

Figure 15.11   Partitioning a physical disk into two logical disks

500 Mbyte disks on a single disk controller. The disk driver could combine them into one logical disk of 1 Gbyte. Say each disk had 125K sectors (of 4 Kbytes each). The combined logical disk would have 250K sectors. A disk address to a sector from 0 to 125K would go to the first 500 Mbyte disk. If the device driver got a request for a sector from 125K to 250K, it would first subtract 125K from the sector number, and then access that sector on the second disk. Figure 15.12 shows how this would work.

Of course, you can combine any number of disks into a single large logical disk. The disks do not have to be all on one device controller, either. A single device driver can interface with two or more device controllers.

15.6.3 RAM DISKS

One normally expects a disk driver to store data on a disk, but this is not always necessary. As long as the disk driver acts like a disk, the rest of the operating system can consider it a disk. A *RAM disk driver* is a "disk" driver that allocates a chunk of memory, divides it up into sectors, and uses it like a disk. Suppose the RAM disk driver allocates 1 Mbyte of memory, starting at address baseAddress. It can divide this into 1000 1K blocks. A write request to block 200 would be written to address baseAddress + 1024*200. Figure 15.13 shows the RAM disk mapping with baseAddress = 3M.

RAM disk driver

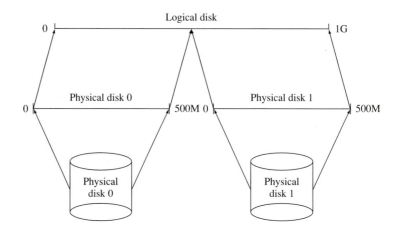

Figure 15.12   Combining two physical disks into one logical disk

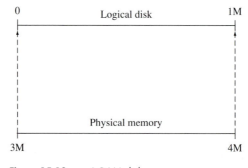

Figure 15.13   A RAM disk

The advantage of a RAM disk is that it is vastly faster than a real disk, probably something like 10,000 times faster. RAM disks have been used widely in PCs. On larger systems with more sophisticated operating systems, disk caching (see Section 15.7) is usually a more effective use of extra memory.

The RAM disk shows the power of the general device driver interface. Anything that implements the block device interface is essentially a disk device, and no real disk need be present.

A RAM disk driver implements the same interface as any disk driver, but a RAM disk is not identical to a disk in all respects. For example, it does not retain its contents if the computer is turned off.

15.6.4   MEMORY AS A DEVICE

memory as a device

In the last section, we saw how you can allocate memory as a RAM disk to get improved speed. Another variation of this idea is to consider all of the memory as a large "disk." We can write a memory device driver that can read or write any area of memory as if it

DESIGN TECHNIQUE: VIRTUAL OBJECTS

From one point of view, all a programmer does is design and implement virtual objects. This is the view taken by object-oriented analysis, design, and programming. By a virtual object, we mean a combination of data and procedures that simulates an object. Operating systems abound with virtual objects: virtual processors, virtual memory, virtual terminals, virtual printers, virtual disks, etc.

In previous chapters, we virtualized devices into generalized block and character devices, memory into virtual memory, terminals into virtual terminals, disks

into the virtual disks created by device controllers. Then these virtual disks were converted into files, which are really virtualized and idealized disks. In previous chapters, we virtualized the processor into a number of virtual processors.

The virtualization idea is very powerful and allows you to take the good characteristics of an object and eliminate some of the bad ones. For example, files provide persistent storage, like a disk does, but with a much nicer interface.

A lot of programming is the creation of virtual objects.

were a disk. Of course, such a device could be dangerous since it allows the reading and writing of any memory, so it would have to be carefully protected.

UNIX uses the memory device driver technique to read kernel tables and report system status (for example, a list of the active processes). Figure 15.14 shows the memory disk mapping.

Figures 15.13 and 15.14 look nearly alike, but their intent is very different. In Figure 15.13 we are simulating a disk with a RAM disk to get improved performance. In Figure 15.14 we are mapping the main memory of the computer into a "disk," so we can access memory using the familiar file interface. Since disk devices are named by the operating system, they use the same protection system as the operating system provides for files. This allows the operating system to give trusted processes access to main memory through the file interface, instead of changing the memory mapping for those processes.

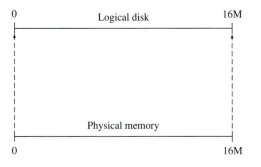

Figure 15.14   The memory "device"

15.6.5   PSEUDO-TTYS

We have seen how disk drivers can implement various kinds of logical disks from physical disks, and the RAM disk driver implements the disk interface with memory and no disk at all. Other device drivers can also simulate their devices, and the *pseudo-tty driver* is one example of that.

A terminal device driver (sometimes called a tty device driver since ttys were the first terminals) connects to terminals through a serial port device controller. Sometimes it is useful to simulate a terminal. For example, many programs are written to work on terminals (especially ones using the curses interface), and they will not run if they are not attached to a terminal. As we saw in Chapter 3, you can connect the standard input of a program to a file or a pipe instead of a terminal (which is the default). There is a DeviceControl call that will tell a program whether it is talking to a real terminal or to a file or pipe. Some programs will

> The device driver interface is very flexible and allows many interesting services to be provided in a simple framework.

refuse to run if they are not connected to a real terminal. For example, a program that reads a password may insist that it be talking to a real terminal and not to a file or through a pipe. Sometimes we want to trick such a program into thinking that it is talking to a real terminal even when it is not, and the pseudo-tty device driver will do that. The terminal emulator we discussed in Section 14.2.15 uses the pseudo-tty interface.

A pseudo-tty device driver is a device driver that pretends it is a terminal. If a process asks, via a DeviceControl, whether it is a terminal, it will say yes. But it is really connected through a pipe to another process. Pseudo-tty devices come in pairs; one end of the pair looks like a terminal, and the other end of the pair implements a pipe interface and is used by the program that wants to pretend to be a terminal. Figure 15.15 shows how this all works.

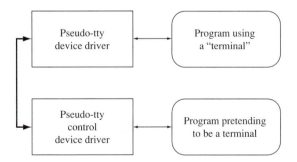

Figure 15.15   The pseudo-tty device driver

15.7 DISK CACHING

In Section 15.6.3, we saw that we can implement a disk in memory to get improved disk performance. There is another method of using memory to improve disk performance that is used in operating systems, and that is called *disk caching*.

In disk caching, the operating system allocates an area of memory to hold disk blocks that have been recently read or written. If a disk block is requested again while it is still in the disk cache, then no disk read is necessary; the copy of the disk block in the disk cache is used instead. This is a large improvement in performance, since a disk read takes about 20 milliseconds.

Figure 15.16 shows where the disk caching system fits in. Some part of the operating system (most likely the file system) requests a certain block from a certain disk. The `GetDiskBlock` module first checks to see if the disk block is already in the disk cache. If it is, then the disk cache buffer address is returned immediately, and no disk I/O is done. If it is not, then a buffer is allocated for this block in the disk cache. This will involve removing some other disk block from the cache. Typically, a least-recently-used replacement strategy will be used to select the block to replace. If the block to be replaced has been modified, then it will have to be written back to the disk. Then the new disk block is read in from the disk into the buffer in the disk

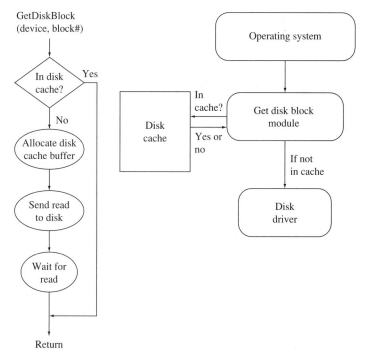

Figure 15.16   Disk caching

cache. The disk cache acts as a system buffer for I/O, as well as a cache for disk blocks.

Disk caching improves read performance the most. If two processes are reading the same disk blocks at about the same time, the disk blocks will only have to be read once. Some disk blocks are heavily used. The user's current directory, for example, is used by most programs that are run by that user. Commonly used commands, like the command to list a directory, are used so frequently that they will probably be found in the disk cache and will not be read from disk.

Caching does not improve disk writing performance because the disk I/O still has to be done. Caching just moves the write into the future. You get some speedup if a process is writing a disk block in small pieces. All the writing is done in the disk cache copy until the disk block is completely filled, and then it is written out to disk. But any program doing significant disk writing is probably already buffering whole disk blocks, so the disk caching system is not doing any good at all.

RAM disks are more effective for speeding up the writing of files. RAM disks work best with temporary files that are written once, then read once right afterwards, and then deleted. Such files never need to be written to or read from the disk.

RAM disks are analogous to swapping, and a disk cache is analogous to virtual memory. In fact, there are many similar problems and solutions in disk caches and virtual memory.

A large disk cache is so effective that disk reading ceases to be a significant factor in operating system performance and the biggest performance issue is disk writing. Disk cache hit rates in typical systems are 60 percent to 95 percent and mostly over 80 percent. (See Nelson, Welsh, and Ousterhaut (1988) and Smith (1985).)

Caching is an effective technique wherever locality is present. And locality is present in almost all streams of requests.

DESIGN TECHNIQUE: CACHING AND HINTING

A disk cache speeds disk access by saving blocks likely to be accessed in the near future. A TLB speeds up page table lookups by saving the results of page table lookups likely to be used again. Virtual memory saves page-ins by keeping in memory the pages most likely to be used again.

All of these are examples of caching. Caching can be used to speed up any process where the same computation is done over and over again. For more examples and discussion of caching, see Section 18.1.

A cache returns a correct answer quickly in some cases. There is a weaker form of optimization called *hinting* that returns an answer quickly in some cases (like caching), and the answer is likely to be correct but (unlike caching) not guaranteed to be correct. Hinting is used in place of caching in situations where cached values might be made incorrect because of changing conditions. Hinting requires a reliable method of testing whether an answer is correct. For more examples and discussion of hinting, see Section 18.2.

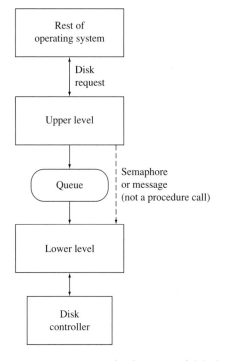

Figure 15.17   Two-level structure of disk drivers

15.8   TWO-LEVEL STRUCTURE OF DEVICE DRIVERS

We have seen that most disk device drivers have a **strategy** routine that accepts disk requests (reads and writes) and puts them on the disk queue. This part of the disk driver is often called the *upper half* of the disk driver. Its job is to implement the disk driver interface, that is, to interact with the rest of the operating system and place the requests on the disk request queue.

The *lower half* of the disk driver takes requests from the queue and translates them to disk block requests. The lower half of the disk driver handles the interface to the disk controller. Thus each half implements one side of the communication, and the two halves communicate through a queue. Figure 15.17 shows the two level structure of a typical disk driver.

15.9   SCSI DEVICE DRIVERS

Sometimes a request must go through two levels of device drivers. The *SCSI device driver* is an example of this. The reason we need two levels is that one device driver manages the SCSI device controller, and another device driver manages the SCSI device that

SCSI device driver

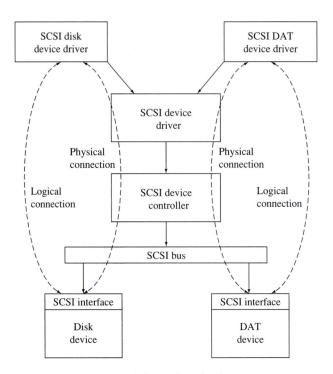

Figure 15.18   SCSI and device driver levels

is attached to the bus. Figure 15.18 shows the two-level structure of a SCSI device driver. The disk requests go to the SCSI disk device driver, which converts them to SCSI bus messages. It sends these to the SCSI device driver for transmission over the SCSI bus to the disk device. Logically, the SCSI disk device driver is talking directly to the disk, but physically the messages are going through the SCSI device driver and the SCSI device controller.

We could have used two levels of device drivers to implement the virtual disks we discussed in Section 15.6. Instead, we chose to have the single disk driver handle the virtualization of the disks and the disk interfacing.

15.10   EXAMPLES OF I/O SYSTEMS

The I/O structures described in this chapter are found in almost all modern operating systems. Most operating systems have the two classes of device drivers: character device drivers and block device drivers. This includes SVR4, other UNIX variants, MS/DOS, and OS/2. Windows NT unifies the two types of device drivers and has a single general device driver interface. Almost all modern operating systems unify device access and file access, both of which use the file access protocol. Most operating systems allow several levels of device drivers, and use this as a way of adding functionality. SVR4, most other modern UNIX versions, MS/DOS, OS/2, and Windows NT all allow dynamic loading of device drivers.

Most modern operating systems have eliminated the disk cache, and use file mapping to allow the virtual memory system to handle disk caching.

The elevator algorithm is the most common disk head scheduling algorithm.

15.11 SUMMARY

The I/O subsystem of an operating system is based on the idea of a device driver. A device driver generally communicates with a device controller. A device driver is an interface module that talks to a controller device on one side of the interface and to the rest of the operating system on the other side. We can simplify the operating system side by allowing only two classes of device driver interfaces. One class is the block devices, which consists of devices that transfer data in fixed-size blocks with addresses. The other class is character devices that transfer data in variable-sized streams of data where the data do not have addresses.

Disk device drivers have a difficult job since they must deal with complex device controllers and they are responsible for scheduling disk accesses for the most efficient use of the disk. The elevator (or scan) algorithm has been found to be a good disk head scheduling algorithm.

The I/O system provides direct access to devices and also serves the needs of the file system. The I/O system gives devices the same interface as those used for files.

We can generalize the concept of a device driver to allow for logical devices. For example, we can divide a single disk into several logical disks, combine several disks into a single logical disk, use RAM as a very fast logical disk, or simulate terminals with a process using a device driver that implements a logical terminal.

Device drivers usually have a two-level structure. The lower level interfaces with the device, and the upper level interfaces with the operating system. We can also layer device drivers into two or more levels. SCSI device drivers are an example of this, since the lower level of device driver manages the SCSI bus itself and the upper level of device driver manages the SCSI device that is on the SCSI bus.

The I/O system normally caches recently used disk blocks to speed up I/O. This works because disk access, like memory access, displays locality, and so the same disk blocks tend to be asked for over and over again.

15.11.1 TERMINOLOGY

After reading this chapter, you should be familiar with the following terms:

- aging
- batching
- block device

- character device
- device driver
- disk cache
- (disk) partition
- double buffering
- elevator algorithm
- FCFS (first-come, first-served) disk head scheduling
- I/O system
- logical disk
- memory as a device
- N-step scan algorithm
- pseudo-tty driver
- RAM disk driver
- scan algorithm
- SCSI device driver
- settling
- SSTF (shortest seek time first) disk head scheduling

15.11.2   REVIEW QUESTIONS

The following questions are answered in the text of this chapter:

1. What is the purpose of a device driver?
2. Describe the differences between block devices and character devices.
3. Why do character device drivers need a `DeviceControl` entry?
4. What is a strategy routine? What does it do?
5. What is double buffering? Why is it useful?
6. Does it make sense to use double buffering both on input and on output?
7. Why do we say that FCFS disk head scheduling is fair?
8. Why do we call the SSTF disk head scheduling algorithm a "greedy" algorithm?
9. Compare batching and aging.
10. Explain why aging works.
11. What do we mean by a disk model?
12. What is a device number? What are they used for?
13. Why do we want files and devices to have a unified interface?
14. Compare logical and physical disks.
15. What is the use of disk partitioning?

16. Why is a RAM disk good for temporary files that are written, read, and then deleted?

17. Why is it useful to be able to access memory as a device?

18. What are the advantages of accessing memory through the file interface?

19. Why is disk caching better for reading than writing?

20. What do we mean by the upper and lower levels of a device driver?

21. Why do SCSI device requests often have to go through two device drivers?

15.11.3 FURTHER READING

Teorey and Pinkerton (1972), Hofri (1980) Geist and Daniel (1987), Stevens (1989), Fuller (1974), and Wong (1980) discuss disk head scheduling policies.

See Chaney and Johnson (1984), McKeon (1985), Nelson et al. (1988), and Smith (1985) for studies of the effectiveness of disk caching.

Wilhelm (1976) describes the anomaly in disk head scheduling. Wilhelm describes a general disk model in (1977).

English and Stepanov (1992) describe a project that adds intelligence into the disk controller.

15.12 PROBLEMS

1. We noted that successive requests are likely to be for the same cylinder (we called this cylinder correlation). What does this imply about the expected performance of the FCFS and SSTF disk scheduling algorithms? Will they work better than we estimated, worse, or about the same?

2. Explain how to use a tape drive as a block device.

3. Give some possible meanings for different device numbers that refer to the same printer.

4. In Chapter 8, we discussed the shortest-job-first processor scheduling algorithm and the shortest-response-ratio-next variation on it. Shortest-response-ratio scheduling is a form of aging. Describe a variant of the shortest-job-first algorithm that uses batching to prevent long jobs from being ignored forever.

5. What is the maximum number of disk revolutions that the N-step elevator algorithm will spend at any one cylinder? Describe an algorithm to figure this out, using the list of requests for that cylinder.

6. Consider this variant of aging. Request priority is not affected by the age of the request until it reaches a certain cutoff age, say 10 seconds. When a request reaches the cutoff age, then the priority of each request is its age. This continues until there are no requests whose age is above the cutoff age. Then we go back to the original priority system. Will this variant also work, that is, will it prevent all requests from

waiting forever? How will it act differently than the aging algorithm we discussed in the chapter?

7. We noted that the I/O system translated the file interface into the device driver interfaces. What this means is that there is code in the I/O system to translate each file system call into the appropriate calls on the block or character device driver. Write the code that would do this. You will need two procedures for each file system call, one for block devices and one for character devices.

8. For each device discussed in Chapter 14, describe what should be done when it is opened and closed. *Hint:* For many devices, nothing will need to be done.

9. For each device discussed in Chapter 14, indicate whether it is a character device or a block device. Explain briefly why you made each classification.

10. Suppose we had access to three hardware registers which held the current disk cylinder, track, and sector, and that these registers were always up to date. We could use these to do more-effective disk head scheduling. Suppose we want to improve SSTF to SATF (shortest-access-time-first), where the shortest access time will take the rotation into account. To do this, we would need an accurate model of the disk, in particular, the amount of time it would take to go from (cylinderA, trackA, sectorA) to (cylinderB, trackB, sectorB). Give an example of what such a formula would look like. Use the following assumptions: 20 sectors around each track, 10 ms for the disk to spin one revolution, seek time for N cylinders is $2.0 + 0.2m * N$ ms. (ms = millisecond). Explain what changes to the SSTF algorithm are needed to make it into an SATF algorithm.

11. Consider triple buffering. Will this speed up the processing? Does it depend on the relative times of I/O and processing?

12. Why not have multiple disk drivers instead of using device numbers?

13. Why not combine all device drivers into one device driver, and use device numbers to differentiate between the various devices?

14. Suppose you have 64 Kbyte buffers, an input or output of a buffer takes 20 milliseconds, and it takes 1 millisecond to process one buffer. Make a table showing the memory use and the average time to read, process, and write out each buffer for three conditions:

   a. One buffer for input and output.

   b. One buffer for input and one buffer for output.

   c. Two buffers for input and two buffers for output. (This is the double buffering case for both input and output.)

15. Suppose you had immediate access (through a memory cell) to the current cylinder and sector of a disk. Suppose the disk has 400 cylinders and it takes one millisecond to seek over a cylinder. Suppose the disk has 32 sectors per track and it takes 0.5 milliseconds to spin over one sector. Write a unified shortest-access-time-first scheduling algorithm (not a program) for this disk. The algorithm should choose the closest request, taking both cylinder and sector into account. Assume you have a queue of requests, each with a cylinder and sector number.

16. What is the purpose of an aging algorithm? Does it make sense to use an aging algorithm with a preemptive scheduling algorithm?

17. Look up the `DeviceControl` interface to terminal devices on your system. How do you tell the terminal to not echo characters that are typed?

18. Devise a batching solution to the SSTF problem that gives results similar to the aging solution we used.

19. We used special device drivers to create logical disks that were part of a physical disk (partitioning) or that used several physical disks. We could have structured this with two levels of device drivers, as we did with the SCSI device drivers. Explain how this would work and compare it to the method we described in the book.

20. A disk block caching scheme speeds up file access by saving the recently accessed disk blocks in memory. Multiprogramming increases the overall work done in a computer system by having a number of programs in memory, so that when one program must wait for I/O another program can be run. Both of these methods for increasing the throughput of a computer system compete for main memory.

    Suppose you had a computer system where you could vary both the number of programs in memory and the size of the disk block cache at system startup time (but not dynamically). What measurements would you take of the running system to allow you to determine which factor to increase and which to decrease? Explain in some detail exactly how and where you would add measurement probes to the operating system to collect the data you need. How much data would you collect and how would you analyze it?

    Then devise a simple scheme to monitor these measurements while the system is running and to dynamically change these two factors depending on your measurements.

21. Assume the disk head starts at track 1; that there are 200 tracks; that a seek takes $(20+0.1*T)$ milliseconds, where T is the number of tracks to move; that rotational latency is 8 milliseconds; and that servicing the request itself takes 2 milliseconds. Here are the requests and the time they arrive (starting at time 0):

Arrival Time (ms)	0	23	25	29	35	45	57	83	88	95
For Track	45	132	30	23	198	170	180	78	73	150

    Compute the average time to service a request for the disk head scheduling algorithms in this chapter: FCFS, SSTF, and elevator.

22. Suppose we have a disk with 200 tracks. The disk head starts at track 100, and for the elevator algorithm, the disk head is moving up (to larger track numbers). Suppose the disk request queue contains the following requests in order at time 0: 27, 129, 110, 186, 147, 41, 20, 64, 120. Compute the average time to service a request for the disk head scheduling algorithms in the book: FCFS, STSF, and elevator.

23. Suppose we have a disk with 200 tracks. The disk head starts at track 100 and, for the elevator algorithm, the disk head is moving up (to larger track numbers). Suppose the disk request queue contains the following requests in order at time 0: 55, 58, 39, 18, 90, 160, 150, 38, 184. Compute the average time to service a request for the disk head scheduling algorithms in the book: FCFS, SSTF, and elevator.

24. Compare disk caching technique in Section 15.7 to a paged virtual memory system. In particular, construct an analogy between the two systems and say what the correspondences are. That is, indicate which things in the disk caching system correspond to things in the paging system, such as (but not limited to): page, page frame, TLB, page table, page replacement algorithm, etc. Consider how they are the same and how they are different.

25. Device drivers are usually structured in two levels.

  a. Explain exactly what is meant by a "two-level device driver."

  b. What are the advantages of structuring a device driver in two levels?

  c. What are the disadvantages?

26. Suppose we have a system and we have 1 Mbyte of memory to use. We can use it either for a 1 Mbyte RAM disk or 1 Mbyte of disk cache. The system currently has no disk cache and no RAM disks. Characterize the situations where the RAM disk will give better performance and the situations where the disk cache will give better performance. By "characterize the situations," we mean give the file reading and writing patterns of a process or set of processes.

27. Suppose you have a disk with 400 cylinders, 6 tracks on each cylinder, 60 sectors (disk blocks) on each track, and 1024 bytes per sector. The disk controller has two registers described in C as follows:

```
struct DiskCommandRegister { // write only and at address 0x800000100
        int Command : 4;
            // command = 1 == > read a sector
            // command = 2 == > write a sector
        int Cylinder : 9; // cylinder number    (0–399 are legal)
        int Track : 3; // track in cylinder (0–5 are legal)
        int Sector : 6; // sector in the track (0–59 are legal)
        int EnableInterrupt : 1; // if =1 then controller will cause an
                                 // interrupt when it completes an operation
        int Unused : 13; // to fill it out to 32 bits
}
struct DiskAddressRegister { // write only and at address 0x800000104
        // where in main memory to put the data or get the data from
        int BufferAddress;
}
struct DiskStatusRegister { // read only and at address 0x800000108
        int Busy : 1; // if =1 then the controller is busy
        int Status : 4; // Result of last command
            // status = 0 ==> command completed okay
            // status = 1 ==> disk address was illegal
            // status = 2 ==> memory address was illegal
```

```
        // status = 3 ==> sector read error
        // status = 4 ==> sector write error
    int Unused : 27; // to fill it out to 32 bits
}
```

You give commands to the disk by generating a command word in an integer and writing it to the disk command register. Each command is to read or write a sector. Before you issue the command, you must write the address of the buffer to read from or write to in the disk address register. The disk controller will cause an interrupt when the operation completes. The operation may have completed successfully, or some error may have occurred. Write the two parts of the disk driver for this disk. The C prototypes for the two parts are given below:

```
struct request {
    int readCommand;
    int logicalSectorNumber;
    char * bufferAddress;
};

Queue<request> diskQueue;

int UpperDiskDriver(
    int readCommand, // =1 if read sector, =0 if write sector
    int logicalSectorNumber,
    char * bufferAddress )
{
    struct request req;
    req.readCommand = readCommand;
    req.logicalSectorNumber = logicalSectorNumber;
    req.bufferAddress = bufferAddress;
    Insert( diskQueue, req );
    LowerDiskDriver();
}
int LowerDiskDriver ()
{
    // will be called by the upper disk driver and the disk interrupt
    // handler. Whenever it is called it must figure out what
    // happened and then retry the operation, go on to the next
    // request or just exit.
}
```

The upper disk driver handles disk sector read and write requests and puts them in a queue. Assume there is a queue abstract data type with operations insert and remove.

The lower part of the disk driver will be called from the upper part when it puts something on the queue. It will also be called when the disk controller interrupts, indicating the end of a disk operation. When the lower disk driver is called, it must check the disk to see if it is busy. If the disk is busy, the driver just exits. If the disk is not busy, then the driver checks on the last disk operation (if one just completed) and possibly starts a new operation. If a sector read or write fails because of a read or write error, then you should retry the operation. Retry an operation three times, and then give up on it. When an operation completes, go to the queue and get the next disk request (if any) and start on it. Do whatever other error checking is possible, such as validating the disk sector number.

Note you have not been asked to signal the rest of the OS when a disk request has completed. Ordinarily, the disk driver would do this, but we will just ignore that for this problem. *Hint:* You can write and read from a specific address with the constructs:

```
*(char *)(0x800000100) = n;
n = *(char *)(0x800000100);
```

You can write the driver in C or any other well-known language, or you can use a pseudo-language as long as it is readable. Remove items from the disk queue with the construct:

```
ret = Remove ( diskQueue, &req );
```

You pass the address of a place to put the request. `ret` is 1 if a request was returned and 0 if the queue is empty.

28. The upper and lower parts of the disk driver (in the previous question) communicate by the upper part directly calling the lower part. Change this so that they communicate via semaphores. Show the changes required by giving an outline of the new version of the upper and lower parts. Use comments to describe the parts that stay the same, and only include the things that are different. Also indicate what code in the old version is deleted in the new version.

3 - 10,12,13
4 - 21
*** 5 - 8,9,26

16

File Systems

The fourth main resource in a computer system is persistent storage, that is, a file system. By *persistent storage,* we mean storage that will continue to exist (and, of course, retain its contents) after the program that uses or creates it completes. The main memory allocated to a program is returned to the operating system after the program execution completes and the contents are lost. Persistent storage allows a program to create persistent data.

The most common hardware device that offers persistent storage is the magnetic disk. Other hardware devices also provide persistent storage (ROM, tape, CD). A file system provides an improved version of disk devices. A file system is not strictly necessary for computation, but it makes it much more convenient. There are some special-purpose operating systems that do not have a file system at all (for example, an operating system on a computer aboard a satellite).

16.1   THE NEED FOR FILES

16.1.1   USING DISKS DIRECTLY FOR PERSISTENT STORAGE

What is a disk like as a hardware device? Well, first of all, it *is* persistent. The data written on a disk is still there after the process that writes it has completed and been destroyed. The data written on the disk stay there indefinitely after it is written and does not require continuous power.

We saw in Chapter 15 that disks store data in large, fixed-size blocks that are addressed numerically as triples (cylinder, track, sector) or with a sector number. The disk is controlled by writing words into its control registers. Disk errors are uncommon but not rare, and so errors must be dealt with. The error reporting and recovery is complex.

Overall, the only nice thing about a disk is that it provides persistent storage. Everything else about it is complex and hard to use: the units of reading and writing are too large, the addressing and the operations are too complex, and the reliability is too low.

In order to make up for the poor user friendliness of disks, the operating system abstracts the disk resource into a much nicer persistent storage resource. This new resource will allow reading and writing in arbitrary, variable-sized units; it will have more convenient names (character strings); it will provide some structure to the storage, including concepts of ownership of storage and protection; it will provide reliable data storage; and it will provide simple, easy-to-use operations to access the data.

16.1.2   FILES

What we are talking about is a file system which implements files using disks. The basic concept in the file system is that of the file, which is a collection of information. A *file* is a sequence of bytes of arbitrary length (from 0 to a very large upper limit). Each file is owned by some user and is protected from unauthorized use by other users. Each file has a name, which is a character string and which shows where the file fits in to a hierarchical structure.

> Files are implemented by the operating system to provide persistent storage.

16.1.3   LEVELS IN THE FILE SYSTEM

Figure 16.1 shows the levels of the file system abstraction. There is the logical specification of the system call interface to the file system objects and operations, there is the implementation of the file system interface on the I/O system interface, and there is the implementation of the I/O system interface on the disk hardware. We

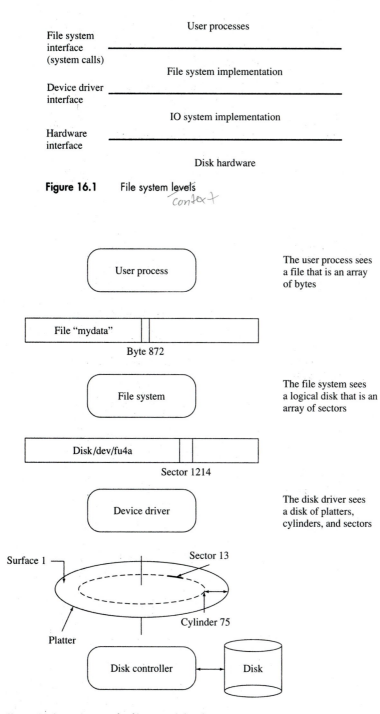

File system
interface
(system calls) —————————————————

File system implementation

Device driver
interface —————————————————

IO system implementation

Hardware
interface —————————————————

Disk hardware

Figure 16.1   File system levels

The user process sees
a file that is an array
of bytes

The file system sees
a logical disk that is an
array of sectors

The disk driver sees
a disk of platters,
cylinders, and sectors

Figure 16.2   Views of a file at each level

have already seen, in Chapter 15, the I/O system abstraction and the implementation of that abstraction. In this chapter, we will look at the file system abstraction and the implementation of that abstraction. We will discuss these two aspects of file systems separately. Figure 16.2 shows the views of files at each of the levels of file system abstraction.

First we will talk about the file system interface, that is, how the file system appears to processes. There are many possible variations in how the file abstraction can be presented to the user processes, and there are many important design issues in file system interface design. Some of these we have already discussed in Chapter 3.

After we discuss the file abstraction, we will talk about the implementation of file systems. Here, too, we will look at many design decisions and the different ways we can solve each design problem. We will see that the implementation of files has some similarities to the implementation of virtual memory.

16.2   THE FILE ABSTRACTION

There are two important aspects of a file system. The first is the files themselves, and the second is the method by which files are named. These are logically distinct services. In some distributed systems, they are totally separated, even being implemented on different machines.

Figure 16.3 shows the two parts of the file system. The file naming system takes a user-oriented file name (a meaningful character string) and returns an internal name for the file (a binary number) called a file identifier. The file identifier can then be used to access the file data.

16.2.1   VARIATIONS ON THE FILE ABSTRACTION

The basic concept of a file is pretty much the same in every operating system. A file is a named (almost always named by a character string), sequenced collection of information that has some structure, is composed of atomic units (usually a single byte), and has some associated meta-information about the file itself.

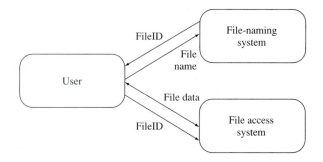

Figure 16.3   The two major parts of a file system

We will look at the file abstraction first, looking at each aspect of the file concept to see the possible variations in how it can be presented to user processes. Then we will turn our attention to the naming of files.

16.2.2   LOGICAL FILE STRUCTURE

What do files look like to processes? First we need to decide what kind of internal structure files will have. There are three possible forms of atomic units in a file:

- Bytes,
- Fixed-length records, or
- Variable-length records.

Figure 16.4 shows the three forms of record structure in a file.

The simplest atomic unit an operating system can provide is files that are simply a sequence of bytes. This is sometimes called a *flat file* because it has no internal record structure.   flat file

Many older operating systems required files to be divided into fixed-length records. Each record is a collection of information about one thing, and is analogous to a C++ structure. A record might represent an employee, a vehicle, a building, a city, an invoice, etc.

Fixed-length records are easy for an operating system to deal with, but do not reflect the realities of data. Students have taken different numbers of courses; invoices have different numbers of items; employees have different lengths of work history. To meet these needs, most operating systems also provide variable-length records.

One problem with a record structure is that it is hard to find anything unless you know where it is in the file, that is, which record it is in. For example, suppose we had a file where each record was an employee, and we wanted to find the record for Rita Mondragon. If we did not know which record it was in, we would have to search the entire file until we found it. To deal with this problem, some operating systems have a form of file called a *keyed file*. Each record has a specified field (a   keyed file
field is a part of a record, like a component in a C++ structure or class) that is the key

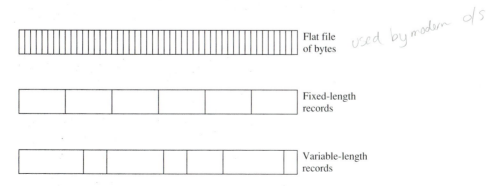

Flat file of bytes   *used by modern o/s*

Fixed-length records

Variable-length records

Figure 16.4   Record structures in a file

field. You can request a record by key rather than record number, and the operating system will find the record for you. Various search data structures have been used by operating systems to implement keyed files. B-trees are the most common.

Gradually, designers realized that data management was a complex and sophisticated problem that should not be solved in the operating system itself but in a separate program called a database management system. All record structuring is handled by the database management system, and it is only necessary for the operating system to provide basic, flat files for the database management system to build on.

As a consequence, most modern operating systems provide files that are simply a sequence of bytes, and the application programs, not the operating system, imposes structure on the files. Figure 16.5 shows the levels involved. The operating system provides flat files, and the database management system builds complex data structures on top of that. In some cases, the operating system will provide a more efficient, lower-level interface to the disk. Since the performance requirements for database management systems are very high, in some cases it might be allocated an entire disk or disk partition and be given direct access to the disk device driver interface. That way it can avoid the overhead of the file system.

> Most operating systems implement flat files, which are essentially arrays of bytes stored on the disk.

16.2.3   FILE SIZE AND GRANULARITY

An operating system designer would like to allow files to be of any length, with no fixed maximum size. Normally this is too difficult to implement, and so they settle

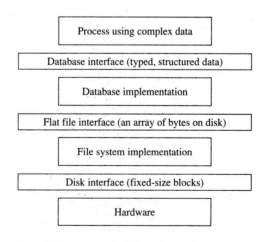

Figure 16.5   Levels of data abstraction

for a very large maximum file size. For example, the standard UNIX file system has a maximum file size of 1 billion blocks. With 4K disk blocks, that would be a maximum file size of 4 trillion bytes (4 Tbyte). This is the theoretical maximum, however, since the file pointers are 32-bit integers on most UNIX systems and they only go to 4 billion bytes (4 Gbyte). As 64-bit architectures become common and languages start using 64-bit integers, this size limit will be eliminated. It is fairly easy to implement a very large maximum file size, and so file size limits are not a problem in modern operating systems.

Granularity of Files   Some file systems to not allow files of just any length, but only in some fixed units such as disk blocks. This reflects the inherent granularity of the disks themselves. But most operating systems hide this granularity from the user and allow files of any size from 0 bytes on up.

16.2.4   FILE META-DATA

A file contains information, but the file system also keeps information about the file, that is, meta-data (information about information). A file system will keep track of things like:

- The name of the file.
- The type of the file.
- The size of the file.
- The owner of the file.
- The group(s) of users that have special access to the file.
- What access to the file is allowed to various users.
- The last time the file was read.
- The last time the file was written.
- The time the file was created.
- Which disk the file is stored on.
- Where the file is stored on disk.

There is generally a system call that will return all the meta-data about a file, and a command to display this information. In UNIX, the `stat` and `fstat` system calls return the meta-data about a file. The `ls` command makes this system call and will display the file meta-data. Looking at the various options of `ls` will show you the meta-data UNIX keeps on files.

Files contain data and have associated meta-data describing the file data.

16.3　FILE NAMING

Files in an operating system are generally named using a hierarchical naming system based on directories (as described in Section 3.2.2). Virtually all modern operating systems use a hierarchical naming system. In such a system, a *path name* consists of a series of *component names* separated with a *separator character*. In UNIX the separator is the slash ("/") character, and in MS/DOS the separator is the backwards slash ("\") character.[1]

path name
component name
separator character

16.3.1　COMPONENT NAMES

There are two main issues about the component names:

• What characters are allowed to be in the name?

• How long can the name be?

Most naming schemes have some disallowed characters. For example, it is inconvenient to allow the separator character to be in a component name. Sometimes spaces are not allowed because they are used as separators when file names are used on command lines.

Naturally, we would like component names to be as long as the user wants, but most systems place limits on the length because it takes a lot of programming to handle names of unlimited length. UNIX used to have a limit of 14 characters, but now allows longer names (from 28 to 255 characters depending on the UNIX version). The Macintosh OS allows names of up to 31 characters. MS/DOS limits names to 11 characters in length.

16.3.2　DIRECTORIES

We talked about hierarchical file systems and directories in Section 3.2.2. In that terminology, a directory is a name space, and the associated name map maps each name into either a file or another directory. We will see later that directories are usually implemented as files, and so there is not really a distinction between files and directories from the operating system's point of view. But users do think of them differently, and so it is useful to consider them as separate kinds of objects.

16.3.3　PATH NAMES

absolute path name

An *absolute path name* is a name that gives the path from the root directory to the file we are naming. This is an unambiguous way to name files, but absolute path names tend to be long. When you use a hierarchical file system to classify your files, you find that you create many levels of subdirectories, and hence your path names become long.

---

[1]In some operating systems, the delimiter between components is not the same for every level. VMS and MS/DOS are examples of this. The reason for this is generally because the system is an extension of a simpler naming system.

In actual practice, however, people tend to use files in one directory together. This means that you generally have one directory that you are working in. Most operating systems have a concept of a *working directory* (sometimes called the *current directory*), that is, the directory that you are currently most interested in. The working directory allows the use of relative path names. A *relative path name* is a path name that starts at the working directory rather than the root directory. Files in the working directory have short names and are easy to work with.

working directory

current directory

relative path name

This is an example of the *locality principle,* that is, that use tends to cluster in a small set of objects rather than being uniformly distributed over the set of all the objects you might be using. We saw in Section 11.8.2 that the locality principle applies to the use of memory also.

Figure 16.6 shows a directory tree. This directory tree could appear in a number of operating systems, but the path names would look slightly different from each other. The file represented as a black circle in Figure 16.6 would be named as follows in several operating systems:

- `/nfs/chaco/u1/crowley/os/book/ch02`—UNIX: full path name.
- `/nfs/chaco/u2/maccabe/osbook/Ch2`—UNIX: full path name of the alias to the file.
- `book/ch02`—UNIX: relative path name.
- `E:\u1\crowley\os\book\ch02`—MS/DOS: full path name (assuming the disk mounted from chaco is disk E).

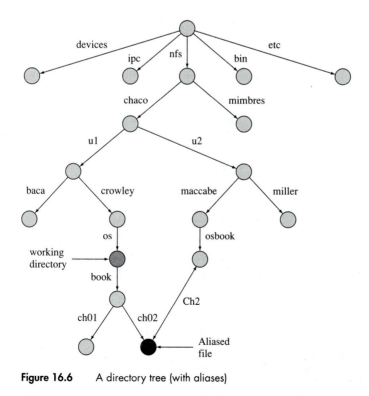

Figure 16.6　　A directory tree (with aliases)

- `os\book\ch02`—MS/DOS: relative path name.
- `Users:u1:crowley:os:book:ch02`—Macintosh OS: full path name (assuming the disk mounted from chaco is disk "Users").
- `chaco:[crowley/os/book]ch02`—VMS: full path name.
- `[book]ch02`—VMS: relative path name.

UNIX has a regular path structure and / is always the delimiter. MS/DOS uses the back slash (\) as the delimiter, and Macintosh uses a letter and colon notation to describe different disk volumes. VMS has special delimiters for the directory part of the name.

> Path names provide unique names for files. They are made up of component names, where each component is in the directory named by the path that precedes it.

16.3.4 VARIATIONS AND GENERALIZATIONS

A hierarchical name space is structured in a tree. A tree is a directed graph with no cycles, such that there is only one path from any node to the root. We can relax the conditions requiring unique paths, and allow two path names to map to the same object as long as the object is not a directory. This allows the leaves of the tree to be shared, thus allowing us to place a file in two different places in the hierarchy at the same time. This is useful because files often fit in more than one category.

We can relax this condition one more step, and allow two names to map to the same directory. This has the same advantages of allowing files to be in two different places in the hierarchy. But doing this makes some things (like traversing all the files in the hierarchy exactly once) a little harder to do.

Finally, we can remove the restriction against cycles and allow general graphs. There is still a directory where path names start (a "root" directory), but cycles are allowed. This also creates problems—for example, just traversing the whole file system without getting into an infinite loop takes some care. This degree of generality is not necessary and not used in file systems.

Figure 16.7 shows the three levels of generalization that we have discussed for directory graphs.

One problem with hierarchical file systems is that path names can get to be very long. One way to ameliorate this problem is to have a special designation for the current directory. Some path names are relative to the current directory, meaning that the first name is looked up in the current directory and not the root directory. Since most names a user uses are in the same directory or in directories close together in the hierarchy, these relative path names tend to be quite short.

The user always has the option of using an absolute path name (starting at the root directory) instead of a relative path name. In UNIX, a path name that starts with a slash is considered an absolute path name, and all other path names are relative.

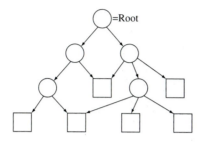

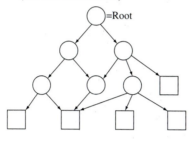

(a) Files can be in several directories
(tree with shared leaves)

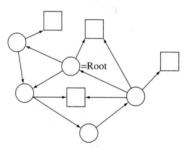

(b) Directories can be in several directories
(directed acyclic graph)

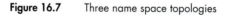

(c) Cycles are possible (general graph)

Figure 16.7   Three name space topologies

16.3.5   FILE NAME EXTENSIONS

File names are often ended with suffixes that indicate the type of file that they are.
Some examples (from several systems) are:

- file.c—a C program file.
- file.txt—a text file.
- file.s—an assembly language file.
- file.obj—an object file (in MS/DOS).
- file.o—an object file (in UNIX).

DESIGN TECHNIQUE: HIERARCHICAL NAMES

All modern file systems use hierarchical names, but hi-erarchical names are used in many other areas of computer science as well. Internet domain names and IP addresses are hierarchical names. Most programming languages use hierarchical names.

Hierarchical naming systems use compound names with several parts. Each part is looked up in a flat name space, usually called a directory. If this lookup leads to another directory, then the next part of the compound name is looked up in that directory.

The main advantage of hierarchical name space is that it is easy to assign unique names in a decentralized fashion. Adding a unique name to a directory guarantees that the object has a unique local name. Name lookup is also decentralized in a hierarchical naming system. Each directory can have its own lookup method. This makes it easy to combine name spaces that are implemented in different ways.

For more discussion of hierarchical names, see Section 18.3.

- file.exe—an executable file (in MS/DOS).

- file.wk1—spreadsheet worksheet.

- file.tex—tex or latex (a text formatter) file.

- file.mif—Framemaker interchange file.

- file.scm—Scheme program file.

- file.tmp—a temporary file.

file extension

The *file extensions* are sometimes part of the file naming scheme(as in MS/DOS), and sometimes merely a set of conventions whose use is not required by the operating system.

File extensions have several advantages. They provide an easy way for users to see the type of a file at a glance. They provide a way to group files so they can be moved, copied, or deleted as a group. They provide a way to form a family of files with a base name and several extensions (e.g., `prog.c`, `prog.h`, `prog.obj`, `prog.exe`).

> File name extensions are a means of indicating the type of the file. They also allow families of related files.

16.3.6 ALIASES

Hierarchical directory systems provide a means for classifying and grouping files. All the files in a single directory tend to be related in some way, but sometimes a file is related to several different groups and it is an inconvenient restriction to have to place it in just one group. This problem can be handled with the concept of a file alias. A *file alias* is a file name that refers to a file that also has another name. This means that a file will have two or more absolute path names (one for the original name and one for each alias). Aliases are shown in Figure 16.6.

file alias

Every file has a "real" path name, that is, a path name that leads directly to the file descriptor. Most systems implement aliases as a file that contains the real path

DESIGN TECHNIQUE: NAMING

Naming of objects is an important part of operating systems and programming languages. There are various types of names and methods of naming. A naming system has to have a way of assigning unique names and a way of determining the object referenced by a name (called *name resolution*).

Internal names are assigned by the system and are generally integers. External names are assigned by users and are generally character strings.

There are two methods of generating unique names. In the uniqueness check method, you propose a name and ask if it is unique. In the name assignment method, you request a unique name from the naming system.

For more discussion of naming, see Section 18.4.

---

name of the file. The file also needs some indication that it is an alias so that the file system will jump to the real file whenever the alias file is opened. In this case, one of the names is the real path name, and the other names are aliases and are treated differently in some cases. This is true of aliases in the Macintosh operating system, and it is true of *symbolic links* in UNIX.

symbolic link

UNIX does not keep the file descriptor in the directory entry for a file, so it can have a different kind of link that is called a *hard link*. With hard links, all path names are "real" and there is no difference between a file name and an alias. Because of the way they are implemented, hard links are only possible within a single disk partition, and so are not as useful as symbolic links.

hard link

> Aliases allow you to place files in more than one location in the file naming hierarchy.

16.4 FILE SYSTEM OBJECTS AND OPERATIONS

We have seen that the basic abstraction provided by the operating system is the file, that is, a named array of bytes on disk. For operating on files, we will add a second abstraction which we will call an open file. An *open file* is a source of bytes (for a file opened for reading) and a sink for bytes (for a file opened for writing). The open command creates an open file object that is attached to the file that was opened. Bytes read from the open file object come from that file, and bytes written to the open file object go to that file.

open file

An important reason for making the distinction between files and open files is to allow us to generalize this concept and allow for an open file that is attached to a terminal keyboard, an output window, a network connection, etc. (We saw how this worked in Chapter 3.) That is, anything that is a source of bytes or can accept bytes can be connected to an open file object. This simplification makes I/O more consistent.

So the file system will implement three objects:

* Files—that hold persistent data.
* Open files—that allow access to files.
* Directories—that name the files.

Each object has some data associated with it and some operations that can be performed on it. The file data consist of the contents of the file itself and the meta-data that the operating system keeps about the file. The open file data consists of the file it is associated with (or the device or other object, in the case of our extended open files) and the file pointer (or the current location we are reading from or writing to). The directory data is the list of names in the directory and the objects they refer to (or a pointer to the object they refer to). File names will not be objects in and of themselves. They are constructed out of sequences of directory entries.

Now we will look at the operations possible on these objects. We will take as an example the UNIX system call interface, since it is representative of the types of file system operations. Figure 16.8 is a table of UNIX operations applicable to files.

The *open* and *create* (creat in UNIX) calls prepare to access the contents of the file.[2] The *status* (stat in UNIX) call reads the meta-data about the file, and the *change owner* (chown in UNIX) and *change mode* (chmod in UNIX) change parts of the meta-data about the file (the owner and access permissions respectively). Some of the meta-data is changed implicitly by other operations. For example, opening a file will change its time of last access.

Figure 16.9 is a table of UNIX operations applicable to open files. The *read* and *write* calls read and write the file contents. The *seek* call sets the file location for the next read or write. The *close* call breaks the connection between the open file and the file, and destroys the open file. The *duplicate* call is necessary only because of the way UNIX passes open files to child processes and its convention that standard input and output are open files 0 and 1.[3] The *file lock* (flock in UNIX) call ensures exclusive access to the file. In this case, the file system is providing process synchronization operations. The *file control* (fcntl in UNIX) call controls various aspects of using the open file, such as whether reads from the open file are blocking or nonblocking. The *file sync* (sync in UNIX) call is related to the file system implementation and ensures that all important information about the file is written to permanent storage on the disk. The *file status* (fstat in UNIX) call has the same functionality as the one for files. It is useful when you have an open file but do not know the name of the file it is associated with. Finally, the *pipe* system call sets up a form of interprocess communication. It is included here only because pipes merge IPC into the file access protocols.

Figure 16.10 is a table of UNIX operations applicable to directories and file names. The file naming system is logically separate from the file storage system. However, directories are usually implemented as files, so their implementations are intertwined. These operations allow you to attach an alternative name to a file (*link*), unattach a name from a file (*unlink*), change the name of a file (*rename*), and create

---

[2]Actually, in UNIX, file creation is done using the *open* system call, with a flag telling it to create the file.
[3]Note that it is the open file that is duplicated, not the file itself.

Operation	Arguments	Return Value	Comments
Open	File name	Open file	Creates an open file attached to this file
Create	File name	Open file	Creates a new file and an open file attached to it
Status	File name	File info	Returns the file's meta-data
Access	File name, access type	Legal?	Checks if the access violates the protection rules
Change mode	File name, new mode	Success?	Changes the file's protection
Change owner	File name, new owner	Success?	Changes the file's owner and group

Figure 16.8   Operations on files in UNIX

Operation	Arguments	Return Value	Comments
Read	Open file	Success	Reads the file
Write	Open file	Success	Writes the file
Seek	Open file	New position	Changes the file pointer
Close	Open file	Success	Destroys the open file and updates the attached file
Duplicate	Open file	Success	Makes a copy of the open file
File lock	Open file	Success	Locks or unlocks the file the open file is attached to
File control	Open file	Success	Various control operations
File sync	Open file	Success	Write out file data to disk
File status	Open file	File info	Returns the open file's meta-data
Pipe	—	Two open files	Creates two open files that are attached to each other

Figure 16.9   Operations on open files in UNIX

Operation	Arguments	Return Value	Comments
Link	File name Alias name	Success	Create a directory entry that points to a file
Unlink	File name	Success	Remove a directory entry that points to a file
Rename	Old name New name	Success	Change the name of a file in a directory
Make dir	Dir name	Success	Create a directory
Remove dir	Dir name	Success	Remove a directory

Figure 16.10   Operations on directories in UNIX

(*make directory*—mkdir in UNIX) and destroy (*remove directory*—rmdir in UNIX) directories.

The *create* call creates a new file and also adds its name to the file name system. It was listed as a file operation, but it also affects a directory.

> Like all the parts of an operating system, the file system implements objects and operations on those objects.

16.5   FILE SYSTEM IMPLEMENTATION

To implement the file system, we have to implement the three objects the file system provides for users: files, open files, and directories. Each one will be implemented as a data structure and a set of procedures to manipulate the data structure.

16.5.1   FILE SYSTEM DATA STRUCTURES

Figure 16.11 shows the main data structures in a file system and how they are connected to each other.

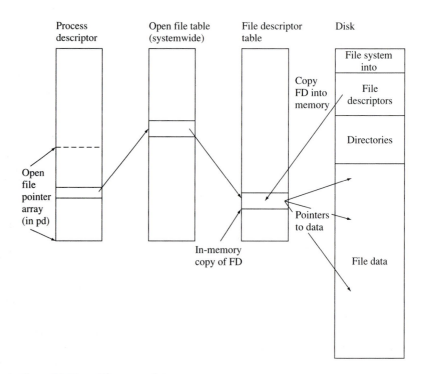

Figure 16.11   File system data structures

Now the task is to get
tem disk buffers are actua
module checks to see if th
the address of the disk buf
it is not, then a disk cache
is evicted from the cache),
disk to memory.

The logical file system
tem in order to satisfy one

The file naming system
ing a name search. A name
ries may involve the readir

A write system call is
data is going in the other
block is written, then the c
the parts that are written to
is necessary since the disk

(Forke
duplic
open f

Figure

The file system is implemented
system.

PD
wri

File
pointer
array

Figure 16.1

The duplica
initializes it to poi
shows the effect of

The pipe sy
structure. This is a
instead represents
the file system dat

The file-related syst
and write system co

16.5.3 CONNECTING

A remaining question is how
Devices are identified by a d
device switch, which is an
structures in the device swit
includes the entry points for

If the file system has th
switch and get the address o
scriptor contains the device
device driver to call. Figure

Remember that *specia*
vices rather than files. So t
do three things:

1. Load the device driver
2. Put an entry into the de
3. Put a name in the file s
   entry for the device in

Steps 1 and 2 are usually d
done dynamically by dynam
switch. Once this is set up, t

The *open file table* contains a structure for each open file. An open file structure contains the following information:

- The current file position (the location in the file of the next read or write).
- Other status information about the open file—whether it is open for reading or writing, the type of open file (file, device, pipe), whether the file is locked, etc.
- A pointer to the file descriptor for the file that is open (or to the device driver if the open file is connected to a device, or to a pipe data structure if the open file is connected to a pipe, etc.).

An open file is connected to a data source or data sink. Normally that is a file, but it can also be a device or a pipe, or possibly something else. Open files are created when an **open** or **creat** system call is made, and destroyed when a **close** system call is made. These calls allocate and free open file data structures. The diagram shows them in an array, but they may be in a linked list or other data structure.

A file is opened by a process and is connected with that process. When a file (or device or pipe) is opened, the open file structure is allocated and a pointer to that structure is placed in a table in the process descriptor of the process opening the file. This is called the *open file pointer table,* or sometime the *per process open file table,* and consists of an array of pointers to open file structures. The file identifier returned by the **open** system call is an index into that array. So when you use the file in a **read** system call, the system will index into the array and get a pointer to the open file structure.

Most open files are connected to files. Files exist on disk and consist of two parts. The first part, the data structure that represents the file, is the *file descriptor,* and it contains all the meta-data about the file. The second part is the file data itself, kept in disk blocks. Some of the items in the file descriptor point to the file data. A file descriptor data structure contains the following information:

- The owner of the file.
- File protection information.
- Time of creation, last modification, and last use.
- Other file meta-data.
- The location of the file data—this includes the device the file is stored on (that is, which device driver to use to read and write the file blocks) and the disk block addresses on the disk where the file data is located.

Principally, the file descriptor contains all the file meta-data. In addition it contains information about the location of the data in the file. This will consist of the addresses of one or more disk blocks. We will see later (in Section 17.3) how this information is stored. For now, we will just assume that the information is sufficient to find that file data.

Files are persistent, and so the file descriptors must be kept on disk along with the file data. But when you access a file, you have to refer to the information in the file descriptor over and over again, and so it is more efficient to store it in memory while the file is open. So, when a file is opened, the file descriptor is read into memory and put in a file descriptor table. This is shown in the diagram as an array, but it

open file table

open file pointer table

per process open file table

file descriptor

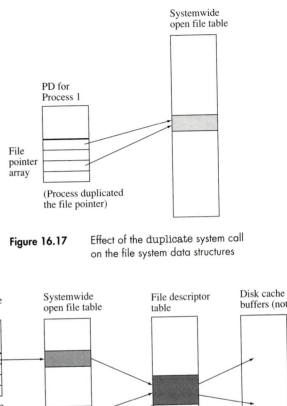

Figure 16.17   Effect of the duplicate system call on the file system data structures

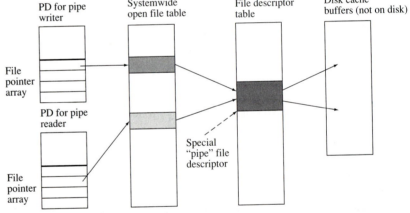

Figure 16.18   Effect of the pipe system call on the file system data structures

16.5.6   AVOIDING COPYING DATA

Using the method of implementing read (and write) by using disk cache buffers implies a memory-to-memory copy of the data (from the disk cache buffer to the user's I/O buffer). We could avoid this copying by writing data directly into the user's buffers, or we could use the virtual memory system to move the data from the system's address space to the user's virtual address space by just changing the user's page table, without any data movement. Figure 16.19 shows these two ways of avoiding copying. These techniques can only be used for full disk blocks.

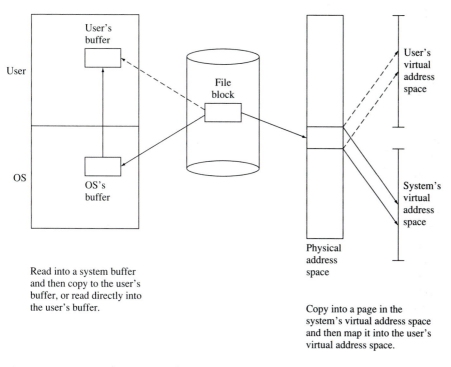

Read into a system buffer
and then copy to the user's
buffer, or read directly into
the user's buffer.

Copy into a page in the
system's virtual address space
and then map it into the user's
virtual address space.

Figure 16.19   Avoiding copying of I/O data

16.5.7 DIRECTORY IMPLEMENTATION

A directory is a table that maps component names to file descriptors. In some file system organizations, the file descriptors are in the directory, and in some file system organizations, the directories contain pointers to the file descriptors. We will examine the tradeoffs of this issue in Section 17.2.1. In either case, the directory might have only a few names in it, or it might have thousands. We cannot predict how large it will be, so it is difficult to allocate the space for the directory. It turns out that the easiest way to implement directories is by keeping each directory in a file.

We will assume that the directory contains a table of component names and a pointer to the file descriptor the name identifies. We keep this information in a file, and we look up a name in a directory by reading the file. This way, we can use all the mechanisms for handling files that we are going to need anyway to implement files.

Figure 16.20 shows the flow chart for a path name lookup, and the algorithm presented next describes the process in words.

1. If the path name starts with the '/' then let FD be the root directory and move the name pointer past the '/'. Otherwise, let FD be the current working directory and start at the beginning of the path name.

2. If we are at the end of path name, then return FD.

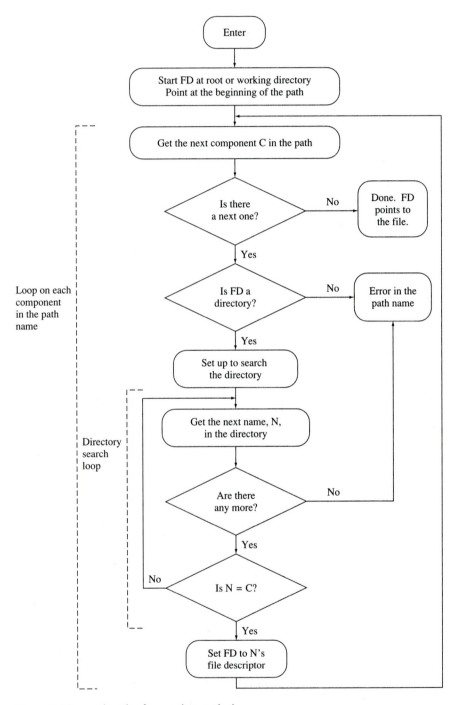

Figure 16.20   Algorithm for a path name lookup

3. Isolate the next component in the path name and call it C. Move past the component name in the path name.

4. If FD is not a directory, then return an error.

5. Search through the directory FD for the component name C. This involves a loop that reads the next name/fd pair and compares the name with C. Loop until a match is found or the end of the directory is reached.

6. If no match was found, then return an error.

7. If a match was found, then its associated file descriptor becomes the new FD. Go back to step 2.

The outer loop of the process goes through the path name one component at a time. Each component name is looked up in a directory, so there is an inner loop that searches through the directory looking for the component name. If some component (other than the last) is not a directory or if the component name is not found in the directory, then a bad path name error is returned.

Directories are usually implemented as files.

---

*16.6   AN EXAMPLE FILE SYSTEM IMPLEMENTATION

In this section, we will look at some of the code necessary to implement a file system. We have explained the principles behind the code already, and this should help in understanding the code.

16.6.1   SYSTEM CONSTANTS AND GLOBAL DATA

First we need a few more constants and type definitions. The ones shown here are used in several places in the file system code. Other constants and type definitions are made in later sections, so they will be closer to the code that uses them.

SYSTEM CONSTANTS AND GLOBAL DATA

```
const int BlockSize = 4096;
// only one disk for now
const int DiskNumber = 0;
// type for a disk block in memory
typedef char * BlockBuffer[BlockSize];
// type for block numbers = disk block addresses
typedef int BlockNumber;
```

We will write the code to allow for more than one disk, but whenever a disk number is required we will just use the constant `DiskNumber` because our hardware has only one disk. The `BlockBuffer` type defines a disk block in memory. Block numbers are usually 16- or 32-bit integers. This type will apply to both logical block numbers and to physical block numbers. It would probably be useful to distinguish between them in the type system. In C++, this would require us to define a class for each.

16.6.2   DISK CACHE

We will keep a cache of recently used disk blocks in memory. This is called the *disk cache*. The disk cache buffers will also serve as I/O buffers to read in and write out disk blocks.

DISK CACHE

```
const int DiskCacheSize = 200;
const int BlockBufferHashTableSize = 200;

// type for a disk block header
struct BlockBufferHeader {
    int useCount; // how many processes are using this block
    int wasModified; // indicates the buffer has been written since
                 // it was read from disk
    BlockBuffer * block; // the buffer itself
    int DiskNumber; // the disk it comes from
    BlockNumber blockNumber; // the block number on the disk
    BlockBufferHeader * next; // the hash table link
};
// the disk cache
BlockBufferHeader diskCache[DiskCacheSize]; //the buffers
int nextHeaderToReplace; // for FIFO replacement of cache buffers

//the hash table for looking up disk blocks quickly
BlockBufferHeader * blockBufferHashTable[BlockBufferHashTableSize];

int
HashBlockAddress( DiskNumber dn, BlockNumber pbn ) {
    return (dn + pbn) % BlockBufferHashTableSize;
}

BlockBufferHeader *
LookUpInDiskCache( DiskNumber dn, BlockNumber pbn ) {
    int hash = HashBlockAddress( db, pbn );
    BlockBufferHeader * header = blockBufferHashTable[hash];
    // get the linked list for this hash bucket and search it
    while( header != 0 && (header->bn != pbn || header->dn != dn) ) {
        header = header->nextHeader;
    }
    return header;
}
```

```
BlockBufferHeader *
FindCacheBufferToReuse( void ) {
    for( int i = 0; i < DiskCacheSize; ++i) {
        if( ++nextDiskCache >= DiskCacheSize )
            nextDiskCache = 0;
        if( diskCache[nextDiskCache].useCount == 0 )
            break;
    }
    if( diskCache[nextDiskCache].useCount != 0 )
        return 0; // no free cache buffers to reuse
    else {
        BlockBufferHeader * header = &(diskCache[nextDiskCache]);
        if( header->wasModified )
            DiskIO( WriteDisk, header->blockNumber, header->buffer );
        return &(diskCache[nextDiskCache]);
    }
}


BlockBufferHeader *
GetDiskBlock( DiskNumber dn, BlockNumber pbn ) {
    // See if the disk block is already in the disk cache
    BlockBufferHeader * header = LookUpInDiskCache( dn, pbn );
    if( header == 0 ) {
        // It's not in the disk cache so read it in.
        header = FindCacheBufferToReuse();
        header->useCount = 0;
        header->dn = dn;
        header->pbn = pbn;
        DiskIO( ReadDisk, pbn, header->buffer );
    }
    ++header.useCount;
    return header;
}


void
FreeDiskBlock( BlockBufferHeader * header ) {
    --header->useCount;
}
```

We need to keep some meta-information about each disk block buffer, so we define a **BlockBufferHeader** structure. It will contain a pointer to the actual disk buffer. It also contains the disk number and block number of the disk block contained in the buffer. We also have to keep track of whether the buffer has been modified since it was read from the disk. If so, we will have to write it out again before we reuse the buffer.

The disk cache will contain the most recently used blocks. Some of these blocks will be in active use and some will not. The ones that are not in active use are kept in the disk cache in case they are needed again soon. We only replace a block in the disk cache when we need to make space for another block that is needed immediately. We keep a use count to keep track of the buffers that are in active use and cannot be replaced.

When a kernel-mode process needs to use a disk block, it will call **Get-DiskBlock**. **GetDiskBlock** will return after the disk block is in memory (in a disk block buffer). The kernel-mode process will use the block for a while, and then indicate that it is done with the disk block by calling `FreeDiskBlock`. We maintain a use count of how many kernel-mode processes are actively using the disk block. While this use count is positive, we will not reuse the buffer.

`GetDiskBlock` will first check to see if the requested block is already in a buffer. This is done by the procedure `LookUpInDiskCache`. We use a simple hash table to make this search faster. A hash table entry contains the address of a linked list of buffers that hash to that value. This simple scheme makes block lookup in the cache quite fast.

If the block is not found in a buffer, then we have to choose a buffer to reuse for this block. This is done by the procedure `FindCacheBufferToReuse`. We use a first-in, first-out scheme and look for a buffer whose use count is zero.

Once we have a buffer to read into, we call the disk driver, `DiskIO`, to read in the block. `DiskIO` will not return until the block transfer is complete.

`FreeDiskBlock` only has to decrement the use count. The block will be reused when needed if the use count is zero.

16.6.3 FILE DESCRIPTORS

File descriptors are kept on disk with the file data, but when a file is in active use we read the file descriptor into memory and keep it in a table of active file descriptors. We could read it in each time we needed it, but this would be very slow.

File descriptors are usually kept in a special area of the disk. This special area will start with physical block 2 of the disk. File descriptors do not use an entire disk block each, but are packed (in this system) 32 to a block. We will learn more about how file systems are structured in Section 17.1.2.

FILE DESCRIPTORS

```
const int DirectBlocksInFD = 10;
const int NumFileDescriptors = 100;
const int BlockNumberSize = sizeof(BlockNumber);
const int BlocksMappedByIndirectBlock = BlockSize/BlockNumberSize;
const int BlocksMappedByDouble IndirectBlock
    = BlocksMappedByIndirectBlock * BlocksMappedByIndirectBlock;
// type for indirect blocks which are an array of disk block numbers
typedef BlockNumber IndirectBlock[BlocksMappedByIndirectBlock];

//type for a file descriptor in memory
struct FileDescriptor {
    int length; // length of the file in bytes
    int nlinks; // number of links to the file
    BlockNumber direct[DirectBlocksInFD]; // direct blocks
    BlockNumber single_indirect; // single indirect block
    BlockNumber double_indirect; // double indirect block
    // we won't use these fields but they are typically present
    int owner;
    int group;
    int time_created;
```

```
    int time_last_modified;
    int time_last_read;
    int pad[13]; // to pad it out to 128 bytes = 32 words
    // The following fields are not part of the file descriptor as it
    // is kept on disk. They are only used for the in-memory version.
    int useCount; // how many open files point to this file descriptor
    int disk; // disk number the file descriptor comes from
    int fd_number; // file descriptor number of the disk
};
const int FileDescriptorSize = 128;
const int FileDescriptorsPerBlock = BlockSize / FileDescriptorSize;

// the in-memory table of file descriptors
FileDescriptor fileDescriptor[NumFileDescriptors];

FileDescriptor *
GetFileDescriptor( int disk, int fd_number ) {
    // find the fd (or a free slot) the file descriptor table is in
    int i;
    free_slot = -1;
    for( i = 0; i < NumFileDescriptors; ++i ) {
        if( fileDescriptor[i].disk == disk
            && fileDescriptor[i].fd_number == fd_number ) {
            ++(fileDescriptor[i].useCount);
            return &(fileDescriptor[i]);
        }
        if( free_slot < 0 && fileDescriptor[i].useCount == 0 )
            free_slot = i;
    }
    if( free_slot < 0 ) {
        return 0;
    }
    // find the physical block the file descriptor is in.
    // the 2 + is because the file descriptor blocks start after 2 blocks
    int fd_block = 2 + (fd_number / FileDescriptorsPerBlock);
    int fd_offset
        = (fd_number % FileDescriptorsPerBlock) * FileDescriptorSize;
    BlockBufferHeader * fd_buffer = GetDiskBlock( disk, fd_block );
    FileDescriptor * fd = (FileDescriptor *)&(fd_buffer->block +
    fd_offset;
    MemoryCopy( (char *)fd, (char *)&(fileDescriptor[free_slot]),
        FileDescriptorSize);
    FreeDiskBlock( fd_buffer );
    fd->useCount = 1;
    return fd;
}
void
MemoryCopy( char * from, char * to, int count) {
    while( count-- >0 ) *to++ = *from++;
}

void
FreeFileDescriptor( FileDescriptor * fd ) {
    --(fd->useCount);
}
```

A file descriptor contains everything that we need to know about the file. This includes where on the disk the data blocks are located. We will defer the explanation and use of this part of the file descriptor until the next chapter, after we discuss a range of strategies for keeping this information.

The in-memory version of the file descriptor will contain three extra fields not contained in the disk version of the file descriptor. Two of these record the disk number and the file descriptor number. Naturally, these are not needed in the disk version because you need these to find the disk version. We also keep track of how many open files are using this file descriptor. Normally this use count is 1.

`GetFileDescriptor` fetches file descriptors from the disk and puts them in the in-memory table of active file descriptors. The first thing it does when it gets a request is to see if the file descriptor is already in the table. It does this with a linear search. If you expected a large table, you might use a hash table search like we used for the disk cache buffers.

While it is looking for the file descriptor, it also looks for free slots in case it does not find the file descriptor and has to read it into the table from the disk.

If the file descriptor is not found in the table and no table slots are free, then we return an error. This should not happen. Normally, we find a free slot and read the file descriptor into it.

We figure out the physical block number of the block that contains this particular file descriptor and read in that block. This uses the same `GetDiskBlock` procedure that is used everywhere in the file system to read disk blocks. Then we copy the file descriptor into the table.

We keep a use count for each file descriptor so we know when we can replace it if we need a table slot.

16.6.4   OPEN FILES

This code maintains the systemwide open file table and the per-process open file tables.

OPEN FILES

```
const int NumOpenFiles = 150;
const int OpenFilesPerProcess = 20;
// type for the open file table entries
struct OpenFile {
    int useCount;
    int openMode;
    int filePosition;
    FileDescriptor * fd;
};
// openMode is one or more of these ORed together
const int ReadMode = 0x1;
const int WriteMode = 0x2;

// the in-memory table of open files
OpenFile openFile[NumOpenFiles];

// some new fields in the process descriptor
```

```
struct ProcessDescriptor {
    // ... all the fields we had before plus:
    OpenFile * openFile[OpenFilesPerProcess];
        //these are all initialized to 0
    int currentDirectoryFD;
};

int
GetProcessOpenFileSlot( int pid ) {
    for( int i = 0; i < OpenFilesPerProcess; ++i ) {
        if( pd[pid].openFile[i] == 0 ) {
            return i;
        }
    }
    return -1;// no free open file slots left to allocate
}

int
GetSystemOpenFileSlot( void ) {
    for( int i = 0; i < NumOpenFiles; ++i ) {
        if( openFile[i].useCount == 0 ) {
            return i;
        }
    }
    return -1;// no free open file slots left to allocate
}
```

The open file structure has four fields. Like we do for all these structures, we maintain a use count for open file table entries so we know when we can replace them. We remember the mode the file was opened in so we can check later reads and writes to be sure they are allowed. We also keep the file position here and a pointer to the file descriptor of the file that is open.

Each process contains an array of pointers to open file table slots. The index into this array is the file identifier used by processes.

GetSystemOpenFileSlot finds a free slot in the open file table.

16.6.5 DIRECTORIES

A directory, in this file system, is a file that contains directory entries. Each directory entry contains the name and the number of the file descriptor of the file the name refers to. We are allowing for a maximum of 60 characters in a file name and 250 characters in a path name.

We record the file descriptor number of the root directory.

DIRECTORIES

```
const int FileNameSize = 60;
const int MaxPathNameSize = 250;
// type of a directory entry
```

```
struct DirectoryEntry {
    int FDNumber;
    char name[FileNameSize];
};
const int DirectoryEntriesPerBlock = BlockSize / sizeof(DirectoryEntry);

int rootFD = 0;// the first FD is always the root directory
```

16.6.6   FILE SYSTEM INITIALIZATION

We need to initialize the various tables we use, mainly setting all the use counts to zero.

INITIALIZATION

```
void
FileSystemInitialization( void ) {
    int i;

    // initialize the disk cache
    for( i = 0; i < DiskCacheSize; ++i ) {
        diskCache[i].block = &(diskBuffer[i]);
        diskCache[i].blockNumber = −1;
        diskCache[i].useCount = 0;
    }
    nextHeaderToReplace = DiskCacheSize;
    // initialize the file descriptor table
    for( i = 0; i < NumFileDescriptors; ++i ) {
        fileDescriptor[i].useCount = 0;
        fileDescriptor[i].fd_number = −1;
    }
    // initialize the open file table
    for( i = 0; i < NumOpenFiles; ++i ) {
        openFile[i].useCount = 0;
    }
}
```

16.6.7   FILE-RELATED SYSTEM CALLS

Now we are ready to implement the file system-related system calls. Here are the new cases in the case statement of the **SystemCallInterruptHandler** procedure.

SYSTEM CALL INTERRUPT HANDLER

```
void SystemCallInterruptHandler( void ) {
    // . . . initial part as before

    case OpenSystemCall:
```

```
    char * fileName; asm { store r9,fileName }
    int openMode; asm { store r10,openMode }
    pd[current_process].sa.reg[1]
            = Open( current_process, fileName, openMode );
    break;

case CreatSystemCall:
    // . . . Not implemented in this code
    break;

case ReadSystemCall:
    int fid; asm {store r9,fid }
    char * userBuffer; asm { store r10,userBuffer }
    int count; asm { store r11,count }
    pd[current_process].sa.reg[1]
        =Read( current_process, fid, userBuffer, count );
    break;

case WriteSystemCall:
    // . . . not shown, nearly the same as read

case LseekSystemCall:
    int fid; asm { store r9,fid }
    int offset; asm { store r10,offset }
    int how; asm { store r11,how }
    pd[current_process].sa.reg[1]
        =Lseek( current_process, fid, offset, how );
    break;

case CloseSystemCall:
    int fid; asm { store r9,fid }
    int ret_value;
    OpenFile * of = pd[pid].openFile[fid];
    if( of==0 )
        ret_value = -1;
    else {
        if(--(of->useCount) == 0 ) {
            --(of->fd->useCount);
        }
        ret_value = 0;
    }
    pd[current_process].sa.reg[1] = 0;
    break;

}
Dispatcher();
}
```

Most of these cases just get the arguments and call a procedure. The close file system call is so short we put it in line in the switch statement. The close decrements the use count of the open file. If this use count goes to zero, we also decrement the use count of the file descriptor it is pointing to.

16.6.8   SYSTEM CALL PROCEDURES

Now we will go through each of the procedures implementing a file system-related system call. We will start with the Open procedure.

OPEN FILE

```
int
Open( int pid, char * fileNameIn, int openMode ) {
    // find slots in the per-process and systemwide open file tables
    int process_ofslot = GetProcessOpenFileSlot(pid);
    if( process_ofslot < 0 ) return −1;

    int ofslot = GetSystemOpenFileSlot(pid);
    if( ofslot < 0 ) return −2;

    char fileName[MaxPathNameSize];
    CopyToSystemSpace( pid, fileNameIn, fileName, MaxPathNameSize );

    char * current_path = fileName;
    int fd_number;
    if( *fileName == '/' ) {
        fd_number = rootFD;
        ++current_path;
    } else {
        fd_number = pd[pid].currentDirectoryFD;
    }

    // This is the loop to look up the file in the directory tree
    while( 1 ) {
        // are we at the end of the pathname yet?
        if( *current_path == '\0' ) {
            // we are at the end of the path
            break;
        }
        // isolate the file name component
        current_component = current_path;
        while( 1 ) {
            ch = *current_path;
            if( ch == '/'|| ch =='\0' )
                break;
            ++current_path;
        }
        char save_char = *current_path;
        *current_path = '\0'; // temporarily put in end of string marker

        // get the file descriptor for the next directory
        FileDescriptor * fd = GetFileDescriptor( DiskNumber, fd_number );

        // search the directory for the name
        int dir_entry_number = 0;
        Directory Entry * dir_entry;
        while(1) {
```

```
        BlockNumber lbn
            = dir_entry_number / Directory EntriesPerBlock;
        // have we gotten to the end of the directory yet?
        if(dir_entry_number*sizeof(DirectoryEntry) >=fd->length ) {
            FreeFileDescriptor( fd );
            // the component name was not found
            return  -1;
        }
        BlockNumber pbn = LogicalToPhysicalBlock( fd, lbn);
        BlockBufferHeader * dir_buffer
            = GetDiskBlock( DiskNumber, pbn);
        int dir_offset = (dir_entry_number % DirectoryEntriesPerBlock)
            * sizeof(DirectoryEntry);
        dir_entry = (DirectoryEntry *)&(dir_buffer->buffer + dir_offset);
        // compare the names;
        if(strncmp(dir_entry->name,current_component,
            FileNameSize)==0)
            break;
        FreeDiskBlock( dir_buffer );
        ++dir_entry_number;
    }
    FreeFileDescriptor( fd );
    // pick out the fd number of this file
    fd_number = dir_entry->FDNumber;
    FreeDiskBlock( dir_buffer );
    // move to the next component of the name
    *current_path = save_char;
    if( save_char == '/' )
        ++current_path; // skip past the "/"
    }
    // read in the fd for this file and put it in the open file table
    fd = GetFileDescriptor( DiskNumber, fd_number );
    openFile[ofslot].fd = fd;
    openFile[ofslot].filePosition = 0;
    openFile[ofslot].useCount = 1;
    pd[pid].openFile[process_ofslot] = &(openFile[ofslot]);
    return ofslot;
a}
```

The first thing the open procedure does is allocate slots for the process in the open file table and in the systemwide open file table. If either of these allocations fail, then the system call returns an error.

Next we copy in the path name from the user's address space. If the name starts with a slash, then we start at the root directory; otherwise we start and use the current directory for the current process.

Now we can begin the major loop. In each iteration of this loop, we will process one component of the path name. We do this by searching for the name in the directory that the name is supposed to be in. The variable fd_number contains the file descriptor number of the directory we will search.

If we are at the end of the path name, then fd_number is the number of the file descriptor we are searching for. This might refer to a file or a directory.

If we are not at the end of the path name, then we isolate the string that is the next component of the path name. We do this by writing a null at the end of the name. We save (and later restore) the character we write over, so the file name is not permanently changed. This is not necessary in this code, because we do not use the path name for anything else.

Next, we have to search the directory for the component name. We get ready to do this by getting the file descriptor into the file descriptor table with **Get-FileDescriptor.** Then we enter an inner loop where we search the directory one entry at a time.

For each directory entry, we figure out which logical disk block it is in. Then we convert that into a physical block number. We will show this code in the next chapter. We get the block and compare the name in the directory entry with the component name we are looking for. If they match, we have found what we are looking for and we drop out of the loop. Otherwise we continue searching with the next directory entry. If we get to the end of the directory, we have an error in the path name, and so we return an error code.

Once we have found the component name, we get its file descriptor number, make that the new value of **fd_number,** and continue our major loop through the components of the path name.

When we get to the end of the path name, we have the file descriptor number of the file we want to open. We get this file descriptor and set up the various linked structures.

The next system call is the read system call. The process can read bytes from the file starting from any position, and can read as few or as many bytes as it needs. Since we have to read the disk in complete disk blocks, we have to do some buffering and adjusting. The read might begin in the middle of a disk block and end in the middle of a disk block. It might be entirely in one disk block, or it might span several disk blocks.

We handle this with a loop that reads the required disk blocks one at a time and transfers the data from each block.

READ FILE

```
int
Read( int pid, int fid, char * userBuffer, int count ) {
    OpenFile * of = pd[pid].openFile[fid];
    if( of == 0 )
        return -1;

    if( !(of->openMode & ReadMode) ) // check if the read is allowed
        return -2;

    int filepos = of->filePosition;

    // check against the file length and adjust if near EOF
    if( (filepos+count) > of->fd->length ) {
        count = (of->fd->length) - filepos;
```

```
    }
    if( count <= 0 )
        return 0;
    int bytesRead = 0;

    // Get the bytes one block at a time.
    // We may not use some bytes at the begining of the first block
    // and at the end of the last block.
    while( count > 0) {
        BlockNumber lbn = filepos / BlockSize;
        int offsetInBlock = filepos % BlockSize;
        int leftInBlock = BlockSize - offsetInBlock;
        int lengthToCopy;
        if( leftInBlock < count ) {
            lengthToCopy = leftInBlock;
        } else {
            lengthToCopy = count;
        }
        BlockNumber pbn = LogicalToPhysicalBlock( of->fd, lbn );
        BlockBufferHeader * header = GetDiskBlock( DiskNumber, pbn );
        CopyFromSystemSpace( pid, userBuffer, (header->block) +
            offsetInBlock, lengthToCopy);
        FreeDiskBlock( header );
        filepos += lengthToCopy;
        userBuffer  += lengthToCopy;
        count -= lengthToCopy;
        bytesRead += lengthToCopy;
    }
    return bytesRead;
}
```

The read starts with some error checking. It is legal for a process to try to read past the end of the file. That is why the read system call returns how many bytes it actually read. If the process is trying to read past the end of the file, we adjust the count to read to the end of the file exactly.

If there is nothing to read, we return immediately. Otherwise, we start a loop which will perform one iteration for each disk block we need to read.

We figure out which disk block we need, where in the block to start reading, and how many bytes to read from this block. This code takes care of the special cases with the first and last block. Then we convert the logical block number to a physical block number. (This procedure is defined in the next chapter.) Then we read the block and copy the parts we need. This copy involves a transfer between the system's address space and the user's address space, and so must be done by a procedure that knows how to do that. Finally, we adjust all the counts for the loop, and iterate until there are no more bytes to read.

The write system call is similar, but actually a bit more complex. This is because it may have to write a partial block. To do this correctly, it has to first read the block in and then change part of it. Other than this, read and write are just about the same.

The final system call we will show is the seek system call. This call adjusts the value of the file pointer.

LSEEK

```
int
Lseek( int pid, int fid, int offset, int how ) {
    OpenFile * of = pd[pid].openFile[fid];
    if( of == 0 )
        return −1;
    switch( how ) {
        case 0: // from beginning of file
            // nothing to do, offset is what we want
            break;
        case 1: // from current
            offset += of->filePosition;
            break;
        case 2:
            offset += of->fd->length;
            break;
    }
    // do not allow negative file positions
    if( offset < 0 )
        return −2;
    of->filePosition = offset;
    return offset;
}
```

The adjustment of the file pointer depends on the how argument. It can be from the beginning of the file, from the current file pointer, or from the end of the file. File pointers are not allowed to be negative, so if this change would make that happen, it is rejected and an error code is returned. Otherwise, the value of the new file pointer is returned.

16.7   SUMMARY

It is very useful to have persistent storage in a computer system that stays around even after the process that created it has exited. Disks provide persistent storage, but with an inconvenient user interface. A file system is an abstraction implemented by the operating system on top of the logical disk system. A file system provides a user-friendly interface to persistent storage. File systems provide reliable, convenient access to files of arbitrary length, which are named with a hierarchical naming system. The principal objects in a file system are files, open files, and directories.

All file systems provide the same general types of objects and operations, but there are many possible ways to present this functionality to the user. Most operating systems provide flat files (arrays of bytes on disk) and leave file structuring to database management systems and other application programs.

Files are generally given path names in a hierarchical system of directories. The syntax of a path name varies greatly between systems, even though the semantics are about the same. Many file systems provide for file aliasing, which allows you to place a file in several places in the name hierarchy.

The file system is implemented with several linked data structures, basically a table for each kind of object. There is a table of descriptors for open files and another table of descriptors for files. The file descriptors are stored on disk but are cached into the operating system's memory, while a file is open (attached to an open file).

The file system contains several levels. The logical file system is concerned with the file abstraction and logical blocks. The physical file system is concerned with how file blocks are stored on disk. The I/O system is concerned with disk I/O. The device number in the file descriptor connects the file system to the I/O system through the device switch. In addition, there is a file-naming system which handles directories and path names. Directories are usually implemented as files which only the operating system can write.

16.7.1 TERMINOLOGY

After reading this chapter, you should be familiar with the following terms:

- absolute path name
- component name
- current directory
- device switch
- file
- file alias
- file descriptor
- file extension
- flat file
- hard link
- keyed file
- open file
- open file pointer table
- open file table
- path name
- per process open file table
- persistent storage
- relative path name
- separator character
- symbolic link
- working directory

16.7.2   REVIEW QUESTIONS

The following questions are answered in the text of this chapter:

1. Why do we need files in an operating system?
2. Why don't operating systems implement files with records any more?
3. What are the advantages of a keyed file?
4. Relate the following terms: component name, directory name, absolute path name, relative path name, working directory, root directory.
5. Why are directories implemented as files?
6. What are the uses of file name extensions?
7. What are the uses of file aliases?
8. What are the three main objects in a file system?
9. What are the main operations on a file?
10. What are the main operations on an open file?
11. What are the main operations on a directory?
12. What are the main file system data structures (in memory)?
13. Describe what happens during an open system call.
14. What are the duties of the logical and physical file systems?
15. Describe what happens during a read system call.
16. Why are special files treated differently by the read system call?
17. What are two ways to avoid copying during disk I/O?
18. Describe the path name lookup algorithm.

16.7.3   FURTHER READING

See *Further Reading* at the end of the next chapter (Section 17.12.3) for references on file systems.

16.8   PROBLEMS

1. The file descriptor table is essentially a cache for the file descriptors on disk. Suppose we decided to trust our disk cache and read the file descriptor each time we need to use it. We expect that each time we read it, we will really get it from the disk cache, and so no disk I/O will be required. Compare this scheme with the original one with a file descriptor table in memory. How will this scheme be different? Will it be faster or slower? Will it use more or less memory?

2. Suppose the granularity for file length was 512 bytes, that is, all file lengths had to be a multiple of 512. What problems would this cause? What could you do about them?

3. Suppose we have a flat name space, but names can be of any length. How can we use names to divide our files into logical groups in such a system?

4. Suppose we have a flat file system with one directory and 1000 file names in the directory, and that we can read 10 names from a directory with one disk read. How many disk reads, on the average and in the best and worst cases, will it take to find a file in the directory if we know its name? Assume that file names are kept in directories in no particular order (that is, not sorted).

Now suppose that we have a hierarchical directory system with 10 names in each directory (including the root directory) and two levels of subdirectories. This means that there are 1000 files (10 subdirectories, 100 sub-subdirectories, and 1000 files in those sub-subdirectories). How many disk reads will it take, on the average and in the best and worst cases, to find a file in this system given its path name?

Now assume the names are sorted in the flat file system directory so you can use binary search to find the name. Redo the first calculation (average, best, and worst-case search times) under this assumption.

Now redo your first calculation assuming that we can read 100 file names in a disk read instead of just 10 (but the file names are unsorted again). *Note:* This will not affect the second calculation, since no directory has more than 10 names in it.

5. In the text, we looked at hierarchical file systems that used trees of directories to name files hierarchically. Suppose we generalized this to allow the directories to form a general directed graph. (See Section 16.3.4.) That is, each g-directory (for graph-directory) contains pointers to files and to other g-directories. But cycles are allowed, and, in fact, any directory can connect to any other directory. We will specify some g-directory as the "starting directory." Path names that start with a "/" will start at the starting directory and follow a path to the graph. What would be the advantages and disadvantages of this scheme over a hierarchical directory system.

6. File aliases are usually implemented by keeping the path name of the real file in the alias file. But this can lead to "dangling references," where the path name in an alias file is not valid. Explain how this can happen. Give a possible solution to the problem.

7. You can buy white boards that will make a copy of what is written on them on a piece of paper. Relate this to the idea of persistent and nonpersistent storage.

8. It is not really possible to implement a file system on a tape. Explain why not.

9. Find out the types of files that your operating system provides.

10. Find out what meta-data your operating system keeps about files.

11. Find out what characters are allowed in component names in your operating system.

12. Consider the file system data structures we discussed in Section 16.5.1 (and shown in Figure 16.11). What if we decided to combine the open file table and file descriptor table into a single unified table? Each table entry would have the combined file descriptor and open file data structures. What things would be harder to do with this data structure? How important is this loss of functionality? *Hint:* Consider the case when two processes have the same file open.

13. Consider the file system data structures we discussed in Section 16.5.1 (and shown in Figure 16.11). Suppose we did not have a systemwide open file table, but kept the open file records in a per-process open file table in the process descriptor. What things would be harder to do with this data structure? How important is this loss of functionality?

14. Suppose we decided to prevent extra copying when reading and writing files by requiring that user I/O buffers be on page boundaries, and move the data between the user's buffers and the system's buffers by changing the page tables rather than actually moving the data in memory. Explain exactly how this would work and what changes in the interface the process would see if we used this method.

15. Add code for the write system call to the example file system implementation.

17

File System Organization

17.1 FILE SYSTEM ORGANIZATION

17.1.1 WHAT IS A FILE SYSTEM?

So far we have files, open files, and directories as file system objects. These objects are represented by descriptors. But where do these objects reside? It is convenient to have an overall object that holds them, and we will call this object a file system. The file system object will have its own descriptor. A **file system** is a collection of files, blocks, directories, and file descriptors, all on one logical disk.[1]

There is a possible confusion here between the general term "file system" for the part of the operating system that implements files, and this "file system" that is a collection of files and directories. We will try to be clear on which is meant if there might be a confusion.

> A file system is the largest unit of structure placed on disks.

17.1.2 FILE SYSTEM STRUCTURE

A file system is stored on a logical disk. As we saw in Chapter 15, this might be a physical disk, part of a physical disk, or several physical disks. A disk is essentially a large array of disk blocks, so we have to lay out the parts of the file system on this array of disk blocks. Figure 17.1 shows an example file system layout. We will examine this layout first, and then think about the variations that are possible.

---

[1] Open files are not part of the "file system" that is the data structure on disk, but they are part of the "file system" that is the part of the operating system that implements files.

file system

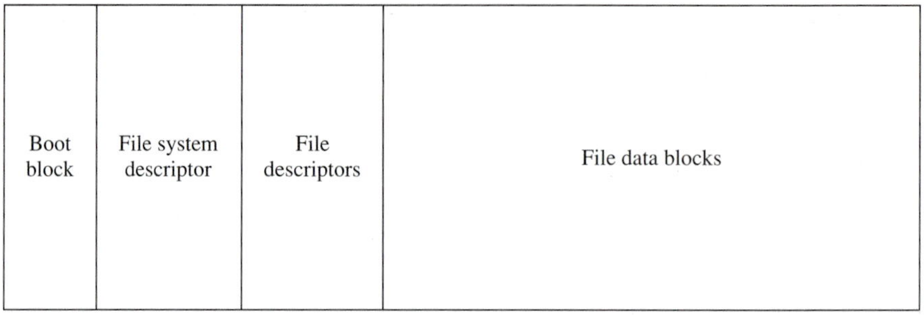

Boot block	File system descriptor	File descriptors	File data blocks

Figure 17.1   Layout of a file system (not to scale)

Usually, the first block of a disk is reserved as a boot block. We will talk more about this in Section 17.7. For now, we will just reserve block 0 for that purpose, and start the file system in block 1.

The entire file system is an object itself and needs a data structure to represent it. So we will reserve block 1 for the file system descriptor. We will examine the contents of the file system descriptor in Section 17.1.3.

It is common to keep the file descriptors in a special place on the disk, so we will allocate the next part of the disk for file descriptors. File descriptors are generally smaller than disk blocks, so several file descriptors will fit into each disk block in this section. Let us suppose that eight of them fit into each block, and we allocate 1000 blocks for this purpose. This gives us a maximum of 8000 files on this disk.

Since the file descriptors are all in one place, we can address them with numbers. File descriptor 0 will be the first one in block 2, file descriptor 1 will be the second one in block 2, file descriptor 8 will be the first one in block 3 and so on. This gives us nice short addresses for file descriptors. Alternatively, we could use a pair <disk block address, fd number (0 to 7)> to address file descriptors. The address of the file descriptor is the internal name of the file. We will examine file descriptors in more detail in Section 17.2.

The rest of the disk is allocated to blocks that will hold all the file data. Directories are implemented as files, so each directory will have a file descriptor in the file descriptor area and some data blocks in the data block area. There is not a special area in the file system for directories.

free block

Free Blocks   Some of the data blocks will be allocated and some will be free. All the allocated blocks will be linked to a file descriptor, so we could find a free block by following all the pointers in the file descriptors, finding all the allocated blocks, and assuming that all the rest of the blocks are free. This is, in fact, what we do if we are reconstructing a damaged disk, but for normal operation we will want to keep a list of free blocks for easy and fast allocation of blocks.

All disk blocks are the same, and so we just keep them in a single list. Typically, the list will be kept in some of the free blocks, themselves. Each block contains a number of addresses of free blocks, and the last address is the address of the free block that contains the next block of free block addresses.

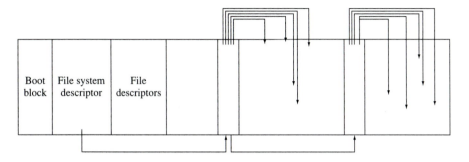

Figure 17.2   Free list organization

Figure 17.2 shows how the free list would be stored in a file system. The head of the free block list is in the file descriptor.

17.1.3   THE FILE SYSTEM DESCRIPTOR

Now we are in a position to define the contents of the *file system descriptor*: file system descriptor

- The total size of the file system (in blocks). This is the size of the logical disk the file system is stored on.
- The size of the file descriptor area.
- The first block on the free block list.
- The location of the file descriptor of the root directory.
- The time the file system was created, last modified, and last used.
- Other file system meta-data (e.g., if the file system is read-only).

We need the information about how the rest of the file system is laid out so we can find the file descriptors and the data block area. We need to find the beginning of the free list and the root directory. Often there is other information kept about the file system. For example, sometimes we have read-only file systems.

In UNIX, file system descriptors are called *superblocks*. superblock

17.1.4   VARIATIONS IN FILE SYSTEM LAYOUT

We might decide to keep the file descriptors in ordinary data blocks, instead of in a special place in the file system. The problem here is how to name them. If we only have one file descriptor per block, we can name it with the number of the disk block it is in. But then we will use an entire disk block for each file descriptor. Alternatively we could pack several file descriptors into one disk block and give it a two-part name: block number, and file descriptor number within that block.

In UNIX, the first file descriptor is always the root directory. This avoids having to record that information in the file system descriptor. MS/DOS allocates a special file system layout area in the file system layout for the root directory. This means that there is a limit on the number of files that can go in the root directory (the limit is 512).

Some file systems keep track of free blocks using a bit map. In that case, the bit map will be in a special place in the file system layout.

Some file systems (like MS/DOS) use an inverted table (see Section 17.3.14) to keep track of allocated disk blocks. There is only one such table, and it is allocated a special area on the disk. This is called *file allocation table (FAT)*. The MS/DOS file system is sometimes called the *FAT file system*.

file allocation table (FAT)

Some file systems keep several copies of critical data areas (such as the file system descriptor or the inverted table in MS/DOS), so if a part of the disk is damaged, the rest can still be recovered.

If the file descriptors are at one end of the disk, they might be far away from the file data blocks they point to, and this leads to long seeks. The Berkeley Fast File System (FFS) divides the disk into a number of "cylinder groups." Each cylinder group has a copy of the file system descriptor (called the superblock in UNIX), a file descriptor space, and a data block space. This way the directories, file descriptors, and the file are close together on the disk. In addition, this provides multiple copies of the superblock in case the master copy is damaged.

17.1.5   FILE SYSTEMS IN DISK PARTITIONS

We have been talking about the file system being on a disk, but all we have assumed is that the disk is a large array of disk blocks. Often a file system is in a partition of a disk, and not a whole disk. Or we could use a device driver that combined several disks into a large logical disk, and put a large file system on the logical disk.

Sometimes different types of file systems will be in the different partitions of a disk. This allows you to run more than one operating system (with differently structured file systems) from the same physical disk.

Also, some operating systems support several types of file system. For example, one partition might hold an ordinary file system, and another partition might hold a mirroring file system that makes two copies of all data and provides higher reliability.

17.1.6   COMBINING FILE SYSTEMS

Modern computers do not have just one disk and often have dozens of disks, so it is necessary to have files on several disks. The file system layout we described is intended to exist on a single disk. This is a logical disk, so it can be part of a disk or several disks. However, it is not convenient to combine all your disks into a single large logical disk. It makes backups (see Section 17.9.1) harder to do. It makes it harder to add disks and remove disks, and a failure in any one disk will bring down the entire file system. So we need a way to combine file systems into a single name space while keeping each file system separate from the others.

The first issue is the naming system. A simple solution taken by MS/DOS is to give each disk a letter name, so there are disks 'A,' 'B,' 'C,' etc. A file name is a disk letter followed by the path name in that file system, for example C:\usr\bin\ls. The problem with this is that the naming system is nonuniform: we have letters and then file names.

Another solution it to use a concept called *mounting*. If you have a directory in a file system, you can mount another file system on that directory. You are essentially splicing one directory tree onto a branch in another directory tree. mounting

There is a system call called *mount* which takes two arguments. The first argument is the *mount point,* that is, a directory in the current file naming system. The second argument is the file system to mount at that point. This file system will be located on a logical disk, so the form of the second argument will be the name of the logical disk the file system is on.

When we get to a mounted-on directory in a path name search, we jump to the root directory of the mounted file system and continue the search from there. Figure 17.3

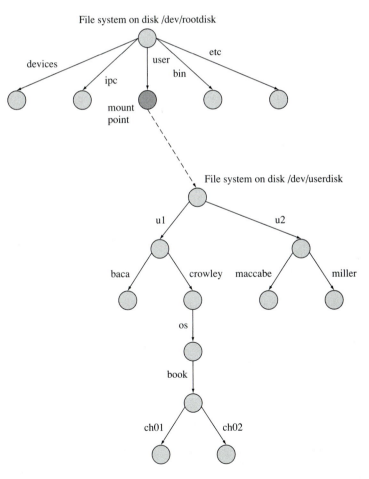

Figure 17.3   Mounting a file system

shows how this would work. The file system on the disk `/dev/rootdisk` is the root file system, and it is the only file system accessible when the operating system starts up. During the system initialization process, the user file system on device `/dev/userdisk` will be mounted on the `/user` directory in the root file system. The user tree is grafted on to the root tree at `/user`. This combines the two directories into a single directory.

The path name search algorithm has to be modified slightly to handle mounted file systems. Here is the new algorithm for looking up a path name.

1. If the path name starts with the '/' then let FD be the root directory and move the name pointer past the '/'. Otherwise let FD be the current working directory, and start at the beginning of the path name.

2. If we are at the end of path name, then return FD and stop.

3. If FD is not a directory, then there is an error, stop.

4. Isolate the next component in the path name and call it C. Move past the component name in the path name.

5. If FD is mounted on, then switch to the file system that is mounted on FD and make FD the root directory of this file system.

6. Search through the directory FD points to for the component name. This involves a loop that reads the next name/fd pair and compares the name with C. We loop until we find a match.

7. If no match was found, then there is an error, stop.

8. If the match was found, then its associated file descriptor becomes the new FD, and we go back to step 2.

The only change is that step 5 is new and handles mounted file systems.

A computer system might have a large number of file systems on its disks, but it is easier for users to see a single file directory tree. Mounting allows you to combine any number of file systems into a single directory tree and all the files into a single, uniform naming system. The user does not need to know anything about file systems or which disks the files are actually on.

It is possible for a single path name search to go through several mounted directories and to switch file systems (and hence logical disks) before the specified file is found.

Mounting changes the way the file system looks, and so it must be a protected operation. Normally, users cannot mount file systems.

17.1.7   NETWORK MOUNTING OF FILE SYSTEMS

In a network, we have a number of computer systems, and each one will have its own directory tree. It is convenient if each user on the network can see all the public files in the network using a uniform naming system. To achieve this, we can extend the mounting facility to allow you to mount a file system on another machine.

The mechanics of how this is done involve many details, but the basic idea is just the same as for a single file system. When a path name search reaches a mounted file system, it moves to the root directory on the mounted file system. If that file system is on another machine, then it will have to communicate with the other machine in order to complete the path name search. See Section 17.11.1 about the vnode/vfs architecture which supports network mounting.

> Mounting allows you to logically combine the naming systems of a collection of file systems.

17.2   FILE DESCRIPTORS

A file is an abstract object implemented by the operating system, and we will implement it in the usual way, with a data structure that records the information we keep about the file and with a set of procedures that operate on the data structure and hence the file. This file data structure is called a file descriptor. The file descriptor is where the operating system keeps all the meta-information about the file.

One of the items of meta-information about a file that must be kept in the file descriptor is where on disk to find the contents of the file. There are many ways in which we can maintain this information, and in the next section we will go over them.

In UNIX, file descriptors are called *inodes* (from index node).   inode

17.2.1   WHERE TO KEEP FILE DESCRIPTORS

There are three possible choices for the location of file descriptors. They can go with the file names in the directories, they can be kept in a special area of the disk, or they can be kept in regular disk blocks.

The most obvious place to keep file descriptors is in the directory along with the name. Then there is no additional disk read to find the descriptor. This is the simplest method and is used in many operating systems.

UNIX places the file descriptors in a special area on the disk, and the directory entries point to the file descriptors in this area. This makes UNIX links easy to implement. It also makes directories smaller and faster to search.

17.3   HOW FILE BLOCKS ARE LOCATED ON DISK

The user of the file abstraction sees a file as an array of bytes of any length. We need to figure out how to store such a file on a physical disk. A disk can only store data in fixed-size blocks, so we have to break the file into blocks and store these blocks on the disk.

Figure 17.4(a) shows a logical file that is 6,658 bytes long. Suppose we have a disk that reads and writes in blocks 1K (1024 bytes) long. The first step in storing the file on disk is to divide it into pieces that are one block long. Figure 17.4(b) shows the same file divided into seven 1K blocks. The last block is only partially filled, but the file descriptor will keep track of how long the file really is, and the extra bytes will be ignored by the operating system. Each of these disk blocks will be stored somewhere on the disk, and we need to be able to find all the blocks in a file.

logical blocks
logical block numbers
physical blocks
physical block numbers

These blocks will be called the *logical blocks* of the file. They are numbered from 0 with *logical block numbers*. We shall see that these blocks will be stored on the disk in *physical blocks* with *physical block numbers*. When we get a request to read a specific byte in the file, we are given its logical byte number in the file. We convert this to the logical block number it is in (by dividing it by the block size), and then we have to find the physical block number of the physical block that is holding this logical block.

17.3.1 THE BLOCK MAPPING PROBLEM

Here is the problem we need to solve. When we create a file, we need to allocate space for it on the disk, and we need to keep track of the space. When a file is created, the creating process might not have any idea how big the file will eventually get. For example, most operating systems keep various "log" files that record system activities, such as all logins, all commands, all file accesses, etc. These files keep growing steadily as events occur. We would like to be able to create a file without giving a maximum length, and just have the file grow as we write data into it.

When we read from the file, we give a logical byte offset to start reading from and a length. We need to be able to convert a logical block number to a physical block number. So we have to decide:

- How to store logical file blocks on the disk.
- How to allocate space to files as they grow.
- How to find a logical file block on the disk.
- How to record the necessary information in the file descriptor and other disk blocks.

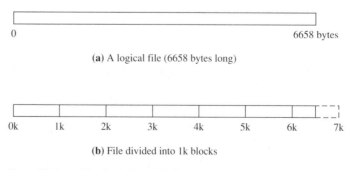

(a) A logical file (6658 bytes long)

(b) File divided into 1k blocks

Figure 17.4   File divided into blocks

17.3.2   Contiguous Files

The simplest solution is to keep the files contiguously on disk. The file descriptor only needs to keep the address of the first disk block, and the file length will tell us how many disk blocks it uses. Figure 17.5 shows a *contiguous file*.   contiguous file

Contiguous allocation makes it very efficient to read (and write) in the file. Disks can read physically contiguous sectors at maximum disk speed. Contiguous organization is very good for data that must be read or written at a high rate of speed, such as video data.

This speed comes at a high price in terms of disk space management, however. Contiguous files on disk are even more difficult to deal with than contiguous blocks of memory. One reason is that disks are much slower than memory, and rearranging files on a disk is a very slow operation indeed. There are two problems. The first is fragmentation. Often it will be hard to find enough contiguous space to put a file. Since we really cannot make a process wait for a file to be freed and space to become available, we would have to rearrange the existing files on the disk to coalesce the empty space into one large enough.

File systems have another problem, and that is that we usually do not know how long a file is going to be when it is created. The user creates the file and writes that data to it a little at a time. We could make the user state ahead of time how much space the file will require, and, in fact, some early operating systems did do that. But this is quite an inconvenience for the users because often they will not know how long a file is going to be. Often files are extended even after they have been created and closed for the first time. In these cases, we would have to make extra space at the end of the file, or else move the file to a bigger hole. For example, in Figure 17.6 we can extend File1 and File4 without moving them, but to extend File2 or File3 we would have to move the file or the one next to it.

These problems are serious enough that contiguous allocation of file blocks is only used in special cases where maximum speed is required. It is not really a feasible method for a general file system.

Note that this is similar to the decisions we made in memory management when we decided not to store a process's memory in physically contiguous memory, but to

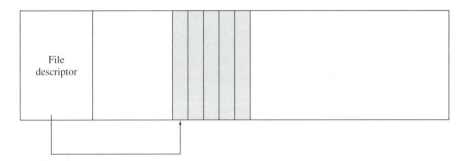

Figure 17.5   A contiguous file

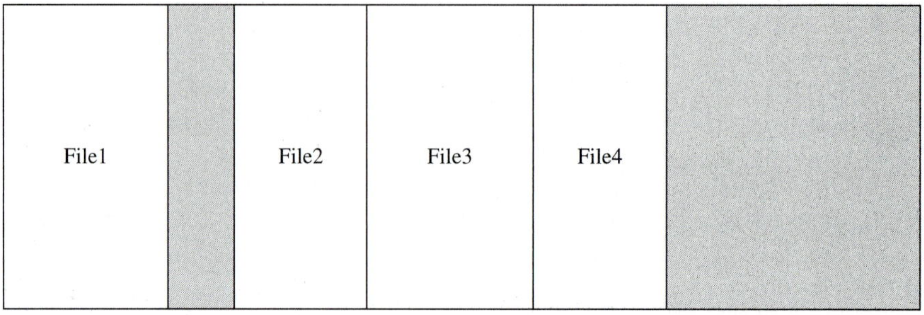

Figure 17.6   Extending contiguous files

divide it up into several pieces. This made the management of memory space much easier, just as it makes disk space management much easier.

Also, even if we allow files to be stored in separate pieces, there will be no rule against keeping them physically together for those files that require this. There are programs called *disk compactors* that do exactly this. We'll talk more about this in Section 17.3.17.

> Contiguous files are fast to read and write, but difficult to allocate.

17.3.3   INTERLEAVED FILES

interleaved files

Instead of keeping files in physically contiguous disk blocks, we can instead keep them in every other disk block or maybe every third disk block. This may seem silly, but in fact there used to be a good reason for storing files this way. The reason was that, with many disk controllers, it is not easy to read two consecutive disk blocks because, by the time you get the disk interrupt that the first one had been read, figure out that you want to read the next one, and issue the next disk request, the disk head will have already passed the beginning of the next sector and you will have to wait for an entire disk revolution before you can read the next disk block. This completely nullifies the speed advantage of contiguous allocation, and, in fact, it is the worst case because we have to wait an entire disk revolution for each block read. As recently as the 1980s, PC disk systems used interleaved files to deal with this problem. Modern disk controllers have local memory to buffer the next block and give the operating system enough time to request it.

Figure 17.7 shows two interleaved files.

In Chapter 15, we discussed rotational optimization to improve disk performance. We tried to service disk requests to reduce the rotational latency waits. If we place files in an interleaved fashion, we will be able to read them faster and avoid extra rotations. We mentioned that many modern disk controllers will read additional

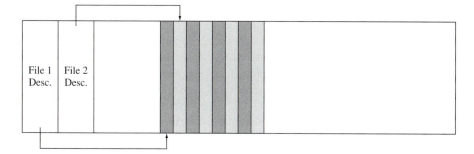

Figure 17.7   Two interleaved files

blocks and buffer them in case they get a request for them. The Berkeley Fast File System (FFS) tries to lay out file blocks so that they can be accessed in the least number of disk rotations. Sometimes it is not possible to store blocks sequentially on a disk. In these cases, the FFS tries to place the block in the next free space rotationally. This might be on a different track in the same cylinder. In this case, we have to interleave because even a smart disk controller cannot know which track to buffer. So they leave in enough rotational time to allow the file system to get the request out to the disk and for the disk to switch read heads.[2]

We bring up the topic of interleaved files here for another reason. There are two separate advantages of contiguous allocation. The first is reading and writing speed, and the second is the fact that you only needed the address of the first block to know the addresses of all the blocks in the file. Interleaved files also share this second advantage. The issue is that, in these cases, there is an algorithm to find the physical block number of logical block $N + 1$ if you know the physical block number of logical block N. We will see in the next section that losing this algorithm means that we have to expend a fair amount of time and space to keep track of where the disk blocks are.

> Interleaved files are best when there might be a delay in requesting logically consecutive blocks in a file.

17.3.4   KEEPING A FILE IN PIECES

The alternative to contiguous (or interleaved) files is to keep the file in several pieces at different places on the disk. The pieces could be a fixed size or they could be of variable size. For now, we will assume that the file is kept in pieces consisting of single disk blocks. These have a fixed size, which is convenient for space allocation, and

---

[2]Often a disk can switch heads in essentially zero time, but some controllers do have a small delay for head switching.

they are small, which prevents excessive internal fragmentation. After we explore this solution to this problem, we will look into variations that use larger pieces and variable-sized pieces.

If each logical block can be anywhere on the disk, we will need a physical block number to locate each logical block. We will call this physical block number the *disk block pointer* or *disk address* of the logical block. A large file will have many logical blocks and hence many disk block pointers, one for each logical block. We do not want to keep these disk block pointers in the file descriptor since we are not allowing a variable-sized file descriptor. So the first question is where do we keep these disk block pointers?

disk block pointer
disk address

17.3.5   WHERE TO KEEP THE DISK BLOCK POINTERS

There will be one disk block pointer for each disk block. If we assume that disk blocks are 4K long and disk addresses are 4 bytes long, then the list of disk block addresses will be about 0.1 percent as long as the file itself. So a 2 Mbyte file will require 2 Kbytes of file pointers. This presents us with a recursive file storage problem: where do we put all these file pointers on disk? This is recursive because the problem we were trying to solve was where to put the disk blocks of the file on the disk. We have reduced the problem to one that is 1024 times smaller (assuming a 4 Kbyte disk block and 4 byte disk pointers), so we have made some progress.

There are a number of possible solutions which we will go through in the next few sections. We will go through a logical sequence of solutions where the problems in one solution lead us to the next solution. This is what we did with memory management. Most of the solutions will not be practical for real file systems, since they will be too inefficient in time or space, but it is useful to go through the complete sequence so we can see how the practical solutions were developed.

17.3.6   DISK BLOCK POINTERS IN THE FILE DESCRIPTOR

We could keep all the disk block pointers in the file descriptor. The problem with this is that the file descriptor would be of variable size. This is not a feasible solution because it is too much trouble to keep track of variable-sized file descriptors.

Figure 17.8 shows file pointers kept in the file descriptor.

17.3.7   DISK BLOCK POINTERS CONTIGUOUSLY ON DISK

We could keep the disk block pointers in a "mini-file" that is kept contiguously on disk. This has all the problems of contiguous files, albeit to a lesser extent because these files are much smaller. But modern file systems hold larger and larger files, and the problems will quickly recur if we choose this solution.

Figure 17.9 shows file pointers kept in a contiguous area of the disk.

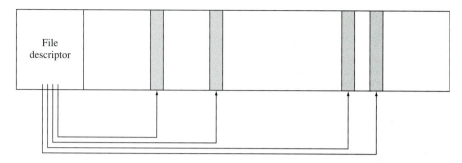

Figure 17.8   Block pointers in the file descriptor

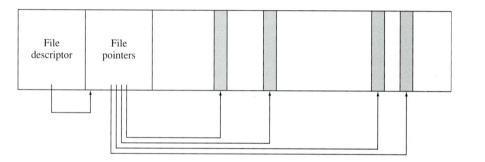

Figure 17.9   Block pointers in contiguous disk blocks

17.3.8   DISK BLOCK POINTERS IN THE DISK BLOCKS

A simple solution is to keep the pointer to the first logical block in the file descriptor, and, for each logical block in the file, the pointer to the next logical block in the current block. (See Figure 17.10.)

This method is simple, but it has several problems. The first problem is that you are taking four bytes away from each disk block. In memory, buffers will be the full disk block size, but four bytes will not be used. Users will have to remember that all the disk blocks are a word short. This is inconvenient, but not really that serious.

The second problem is much more serious. With this organization you must read the file sequentially, starting from the beginning, each time you use it. If you want to append to the end of the file (a common thing to do), you have to traverse the entire file to find the end. Random access to a file organized this way would be extremely expensive in terms of the number of disk block reads required.

Let's make some assumptions to get an idea of how inefficient it would be. Suppose it takes 10 milliseconds to read a disk block (this is very fast, even for the most modern disks). Suppose disk blocks are 4 Kbytes and we want to append to the end of a 300 Kbyte file. This will require reading 75 disk blocks (the entire file) and will take three quarters of a second, not that slow by human standards but very slow by computer standards. If the file is 3 Mbytes, then we get 7.5 seconds. Remember, it is not just the one process that is delayed this amount of time, but the disk drive and controller are used this entire time so no other programs or users can access this disk or any other disk on the same controller.

Random access is infrequent, but not really rare, and the penalty here for random access is way too high to be tolerable. This method is not really feasible for a general-purpose file system.

17.3.9   INDEX BLOCKS IN A CHAIN

We can save some time by collecting these block pointers together in a single disk block. Figure 17.11 shows how this would work.

In our running example with 4-byte disk block numbers and 4 Kbyte blocks, we can fit 1024 disk block numbers in a disk block. The file descriptor contains the address of the *index block* which contains the addresses of 1024 disk blocks. This allows for 1024 * 4K = 4 Mbytes of file.

Very few files are longer than 4 Mbytes, but it would be restrictive to have such a low limit on file size. How can we extend the file size? Well, again we have a recursive problem: How do we store this file of index blocks? We can think about the

index blocks

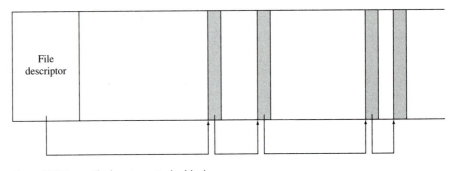

Figure 17.10   Block pointers in the blocks

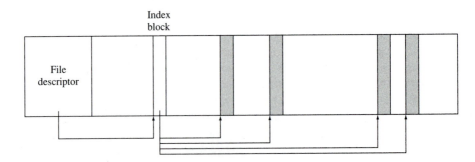

Figure 17.11   Block pointers in index blocks

linked blocks scheme in Section 17.3.8 again because this time it doesn't matter much if the blocks are a word short, since only the system will be using them, and only for lists of block pointers. The sequence of index blocks is going to be much shorter than the chains of data blocks for real files, and so the sequential access problem will not be that serious.

So the new scheme is like this: The file descriptor contains two words, the block number of the first index block and the number of blocks in the file. This second number can be computed from the file length, which we must also keep, so it does not really involve any more space. We go to the first index block to get the block number of the first 1023 blocks. If the file is longer than this, the 1024th block number points to a second index block. This gives us another 4 Mbytes (almost, because we lose one word from each index block for the next block pointer). If this isn't enough, we go to a third disk block, and so on. Figure 17.12 shows this idea with a chain of two index blocks.

What about really large files? Let's compute the number of disk block reads it takes to read the last byte of a file of various lengths using this scheme.

File Size	Block Reads
0–4M	2 (1 index + 1 data)
4M–8M	3 (2 index + 1 data)
8M–12M	4 (3 index + 1 data)
100M	26 (25 index + 1 data)
500M	126 (125 index + 1 data)
1G	251 (250 index + 1 data)
10G	2,501 (2,500 index + 1 data)
100G	25,001 (25,000 index + 1 data)

The growth is linear in the size of the file. One Gbyte is a really huge file by anyone's standards, and it takes 251 disk block reads, which is not too bad.

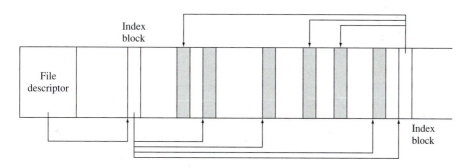

Figure 17.12   A chain of index blocks

There are ways we could improve this scheme with a little extra effort and storage. If appending to the end of the file was a common operation, we could keep another pointer to the last block in the chain. This would make appending very fast, no matter how large the file was. As another optimization, we could keep the index blocks on a doubly linked list and keep a pointer to the last index block we used. If file accesses show locality, then we can start from there and find new blocks without traversing the chain over from the beginning.

Linked index blocks is a practical method, but it is rarely used. The reason is that there are other schemes which are just about as simple and work better for very large files.

> Index blocks collect the next-block pointers in one disk block.

17.3.10   TWO LEVELS OF INDEX BLOCKS

double index blocks

Chained index blocks were a solution to the recursive problem: How do we store the "file" of index blocks on disk? To solve the problem, we went back to a previous solution, that is, chained block files. We could also solve the recursive problem by reusing the index idea again, that is, by using two levels of index.

The file descriptor contains a pointer to the primary index block. The primary index block contains the addresses of (up to) 1024 secondary index blocks. Each secondary index block contains the addresses of 1024 data blocks. (See Figure 17.13.)

Let's compute the maximum file size: 1024 primary index blocks * 1024 secondary index blocks * 4096 bytes in a data block = 4 Gbytes. This is a very large file and is an acceptable maximum size. In fact, if we use 32-bit unsigned words as file byte pointers, we can only have files 4 Gbytes long, so this is enough until we start using 64-bit integers for file pointers.

But even if we wanted a larger file size, we can chain the primary index blocks to get files of unlimited size. Let's look again at the number of disk block reads it takes to read the last byte of a file of various length using this new double-indexed scheme.

File Size	Block Reads
0–4G	3
10G	5
100G	26

It will be a long time before 100 Gbyte files are common.

Another strategy is to have more than one primary index block pointer in the file descriptor. By keeping 16 such pointers, we can have a maximum file size of 64 Gbytes without going to the extra complexity of chained index blocks.

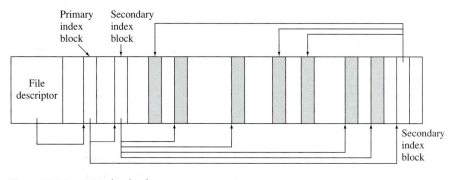

Figure 17.13   Two-level index

17.3.11   LARGE AND SMALL FILES

Well, along the lines of "if some is good, more is better," we can go to three lev-   triple index block
els of index blocks. This gives us a maximum file size of 4 Tbytes, very large
indeed. But more levels of index mean that the minimum time to access any data at
all is longer. With triple index blocks, it will take four disk reads just to read the first
byte of the file.

   The problem here is that we are serving two masters. We want to be able to have
very large files and access them efficiently, and we want to access small files
quickly. All studies of file sizes in typical computer installations (see Section 17.6)
show that small files predominate. In fact, the most common file size is one disk
block. So, if we do not handle small files quickly, we will be giving up a lot of
efficiency.

17.3.12   HYBRID SOLUTIONS

In this case, we can have the best of both worlds by combining these methods. Let us
take the UNIX file organization as an example. The file descriptor contains 13 block
addresses. The first 10 are direct block addresses of the first 10 data blocks in the file.
The 11th address points to a one-level index block. The 12th address points to a two-
level index block. The 13th address points to a three-level index block. Figure 17.14
shows the structure of UNIX files.

   This provides a very large maximum file size with efficient access to large files,
but also small files are accessed directly in one disk read (we assume the file descriptor has already been read).

Hybrid solutions are the best when the range of file sizes is very large.

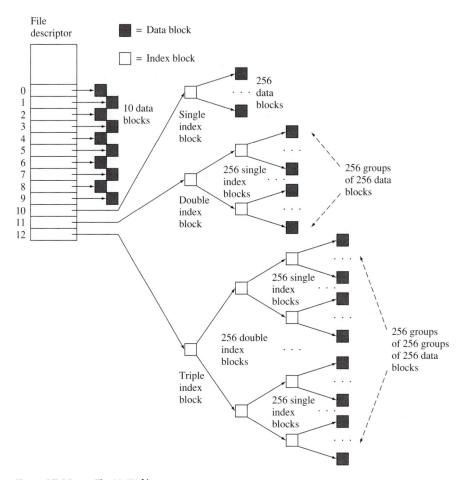

Figure 17.14   The UNIX file pointer structure

17.3.13   ANALOGY WITH PAGE TABLES

You may have already noticed the analogy of these solutions with page tables in virtual memory systems. The reason for this is that disk block mapping and page mapping are solving the same problem, that is, keeping a list of addresses to the parts of a large amount of storage that is kept in small pieces.

In memory management, we considered and rejected contiguous storage just as we did for disk files. The drawbacks of contiguous storage allocation are just too great. The fact of fixed-size disk blocks leads us to paging-like solutions, and we tried one- two-, and three-level indexes, just as we tried one- two-, and three-level page tables. We have not tried variable-sized pieces, as we did in memory management, but we will explore that idea in a later section.

We did not try chaining solutions in page tables since random access is too common in page tables, and the overhead of walking the chains would have been way too high.

There is one solution that we used in page tables that we have not tried for disk block pointers, and that is the idea of an inverted page table. The next section discusses that idea. This idea was developed long before inverted page tables were tried, but they both represent the same design approach to the problem.

17.3.14 INVERTED DISK BLOCK INDEXES

Up to now, we have been committed to the idea of keeping the file pointers for each file separate. Another plan would be to keep all the file pointers together in one big file. How big does this file have to be? Let's think of it this way. Suppose we think back to the linked file block idea. Each disk block contained the pointer to the next disk block in the file. There is exactly one block pointer for every disk block. Suppose the disk contains 10,000 blocks. Then we will have a file of 10,000 block numbers. This file will never change in size since it is based on the size of the disk itself, not the size of any particular file on the disk. If we have 4 Kbyte blocks and require 4 bytes for each block pointer, we can fit 1024 block pointers in one block, and so these 10,000 block numbers will fit in 10 disk blocks.

inverted disk block indexes

So here is the plan. The first 10 disk blocks contain all the next-block pointers for all the blocks on the disk. We still have to chain through the disk blocks sequentially to get to the end of the file, but all the disk blocks are together so this will take no more than 10 disk block reads. In fact, we can keep these 10 disk blocks in memory, and all file pointer chaining will be done by following pointers in memory. Compared to disks, main memory is very fast, so this will take almost no time at all.

Figure 17.15 shows the structure of an inverted disk block index. The inverted index is on disk and consists of a large array containing one disk block pointer for each (allocatable) disk block. We chain disk blocks together in a list by chaining their corresponding disk block pointers in the inverted index. In Figure 17.15, we show the chain for one file. The file contains five disk blocks. It starts at the block labeled *bof* (beginning of file) and ends at the block labeled *eof* (end of file).

This approach is very good for small disks but it breaks down for larger disks. Let's do some calculations. Suppose we have 4K disk blocks and 4-byte block numbers (as usual). Here is a table of the amount of memory and the number of disk blocks required for various sizes of disk:

Disk Size	Memory	Disk Blocks
40 Mbyte	10K	3
240 Mbyte	60K	15
4 Gbyte	1M	256

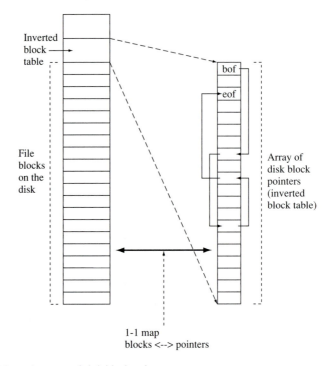

Inverted
block
table

File
blocks
on the
disk

bof

eof

Array of
disk block
pointers
(inverted
block table)

1-1 map
blocks <--> pointers

Figure 17.15   An inverted disk block index

The disk space overhead is always 0.1 percent, which is acceptable and in fact quite good. But the memory use goes up too quickly. For this method to work well, the inverted block table must be in memory (or mostly in memory). The reason for this is that our old friend locality is not present in this case. It is not usually the case that logically consecutive disk blocks are in physically consecutive disk blocks, and so we will jump all around the inverted index when following the blocks of a file.

Now 10K of memory for a 40M disk is acceptable, and even 60K for a 240 Mbyte disk given the large memories available today. But suppose we have three 4-Gbyte disks on a file server. This means that 3 Mbytes of memory is taken up for the inverted indexes. This is too much memory to allocate to this use because main memory is the most critical resource in modern computer systems. There are lots of better uses for that memory, since the other disk organizations we discussed work just as well (or better) and do not demand so much memory space.

What is the problem here? Why is locality not helping us? The reason is that this method ignores the critical locality that we need to take advantage of. This method does not discriminate between files that are currently being used and those that are not. The index block methods will keep block indexes in memory also, *but only for files that are currently open*. This makes all the difference because a computer system typically has lots and lots of files, but only a tiny fraction of them are open at any one time. It is this locality that the other disk organization methods are able to take advantage of and give fast disk access with a minimal use of main memory for file pointers.

The inverted disk block index method is used in the MS/DOS file system. MS/DOS system started out as a floppy-disk-oriented system. This method works very well for floppy disks, since they are small. A 360K floppy with 512-byte sectors will have 720 blocks. Since two bytes is enough per block, we need only a little over 1K to hold the inverted block index. Also, MS/DOS combined disk blocks to get an effective block size of 4K and reduced the size of the inverted block index by a factor of 8.

17.3.15　Using Larger Pieces

Up to now, we have assumed that the pieces we break the file up into are the same size as the disk blocks defined by the disk itself. There are three ways we can move beyond this:

- Use larger blocks.
- Allocate blocks several at a time.
- Use variable-sized pieces.

We can ignore the block size of the disk and use some multiple of it. For example, suppose that the disk had 1K blocks but we wanted to use 4K blocks. We could always read and write blocks four at a time, and act as if the block size of the disk was 4K. Many operating systems will do this when using disks with small block sizes. This technique is known as *clustering*.

clustering

It is more efficient to read disks in larger units. We discussed this in Section 14.4.1. The layout and access characteristics of disks imply that it only takes a little longer to read four disk blocks than it takes to read one disk block. For example, it might take 20 milliseconds, on the average, to read one disk block, and only 22 milliseconds to read four disk blocks. The actual transfer time is only a small part of the total disk access time.

A variation of this idea is still to read and write single disk blocks, but to allocate space on the disk in multiples of two or more blocks. For example, we might use 1K disk blocks, but always allocate disk space in units of four blocks at a time. This ensures that each four-block chunk will be allocated to consecutive disk blocks and will be fast to read. Note that disk blocks still take the same amount of space in main memory. We are simply ensuring that consecutive disk blocks will be read quickly from the disk.

Figure 17.16 shows the three ways to use larger pieces of the disk than a single disk block. In Figure 17.16(a), we combine pairs of 1K physical disk blocks into 2K logical disk blocks. All reading, writing, allocation on disk, and disk buffers are 2K long. In Figure 17.16(b), we keep the logical block size at 1K, the same as the physical block size, but we allocate physical blocks two at a time. Disk buffers are still 1K long, and reads and writes can be 1K or 2K long. This allows us to read files two blocks at a time for higher-speed access.

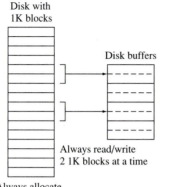

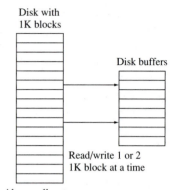

(a) Logical disk block of 2K

(b) Logical disk block of 1K
(allocate in 2K pairs)

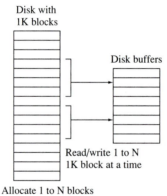

(c) Allocate in variable sized extents

Figure 17.16   Three ways to use larger pieces than one block

17.3.16   Variable-Sized Pieces

Another way to use larger pieces is to allow variable-sized pieces on disk. In a variable-sized piece scheme, we would not just keep a list of block addresses, but a list of pairs: block address and number of blocks. We would use as many contiguous blocks as we could for each piece. Variable-sized pieces are also called *disk extents*.

disk extent

In Figure 17.16(c), we show extents where we allocate in units of 1 to N disk blocks (as many as we need and can find together). Disk buffers are still 1K, the physical block size. But we can read and write 1 to N blocks at a time.

The advantage of this method is that we could keep files physically sequential for longer sequences, and enjoy the faster disk access this implies. Also, we would need fewer descriptors if each one described more of the file.

Unfortunately, there is a problem with this method (isn't there always something?). The problem is that, in order to access the file randomly, you have to go through all the pieces and count up the blocks. You must do this because each extent may have a different size. Also, space management is harder because we need to detect and allocate consecutive sectors whenever possible. As a consequence, the method of variable-sized extents is rarely used.

The following code demonstrates this problem by showing the two versions of the function that converts a logical block number to a physical block number, one using single blocks and one using variable-sized extents. The array that does this conversion (for the case where we allocate single blocks at a time) is scattered around the disk in index blocks and whatnot. To make the algorithm simpler, we are assuming that this array exists as a single array in memory. This makes it easier to compare the single-block method with the extent method. If we used extents, then the extent array would also be scattered around the disk. Again, we assume it is in a single array available to the translation function.

First, we present the algorithm for fixed-sized extents.

RANDOM ACCESS WITH FIXED-SIZED EXTENTS

```
// Assume some maximum file size
#define MaxFileBlocks 1000
// This is the array of logical to physical blocks
DiskBlockPointer LogicalToPhysical[MaxFileBlocks]
// This is the procedure that maps a logical block number into a
// physical block number.
DiskBlockPointer LogicalBlockToPhysicalBlock (int logicalBlock) {
    // Just look the physical block number up in the table.
    return LogicalToPhysical[logicalBlock];
}
```

The procedure consists of just a return statement that does an array access. And now we present the algorithm for variable-sized extents.

RANDOM ACCESS WITH VARIABLE-SIZED EXTENTS

```
// Assume some maximum file size
#define MaxFileBlocks 1000
// This is the type for extent structures
struct ExtentStruct {
    DiskBlockPointer baseOfExtent;
    int lengthOfExtent;
```

```
};
// This is the table of extents.
ExtentStruct Extents[MaxFileBlocks];
// This is the procedure that maps a logical block number into a
// physical block number.
DiskBlockPointer LogicalBlockToPhysicalBlock( int logicalBlock ) {
    // Compute the logical block number of the first block of each extent.
    int lbOfNextBlock = 0;
    // Loop through the extents.
    int extent = 0;
    while( 1 ) {
        // Figure out the logical block number of the first block of
        // the NEXT extent (not this one).
        int newlb = lbOfNextBlock + Extents[extent].lengthOfExtent;
        // If the next extent is too far then the logical block we
        // are looking for is in this extent, so exit to loop.
        if( newlb > logicalBlock )
            break;
        // Move to the next extent.
        lbOfNextBlock = newlb;
        ++extent;
    }
    // The physical block is an offset from the first physical block
    // of the extent.
    return Extents[extent].baseOfExtent + (logicalBlock - lbOfNextBlock);
}
```

Notice that the first case is very easy. It is a table lookup with no loop. The second case is harder because we have to loop through the extents until we find the one our block is in. As we loop through, we keep a running block count.

Note that looking through all the extents each time not only takes processor time, but it means that the entire extent table needs to be in memory all the time.

17.3.17 DISK COMPACTION

Several of these variant techniques we have been considering have one purpose: to get the blocks in a file in physically consecutive sectors on the disk. Our basic method allocates disk blocks one at a time anywhere on the disk. When it comes time to allocate another block, it is unlikely that you will allocate the physically consecutive one even if it was free (which it probably isn't). This means that files are scattered around the disk, and it takes longer to read a file sequentially, which is the usual mode of file access.

But although the method does not require logically consecutive blocks to be physically consecutive, it does not prevent this either, and this provides us with a way to improve access speed. Suppose one night we rearrange the disk so that all the files are in physically consecutive blocks. This is easily done by reading blocks, buffering them in memory while the disk is rearranged, and rewriting files out in physically consecutive blocks. This will take a while, but once we have done it, these files will stay physically consecutive (unless they are extended). If you do this every night, most of the files that stick around will be physically consecutive and will be quick to read.

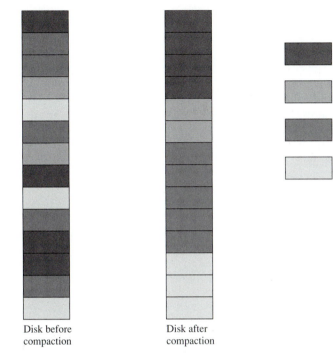

Disk before compaction

Disk after compaction

= File 1

= File 2

= File 3

= File 4

Figure 17.17   Disk compaction (for four files)

This process is called *disk compaction* and is commonly done in file systems. It only helps with files that stay around for a while, but that includes a lot of the file traffic (include files, system binaries, libraries, etc.). So again we are getting the best of both worlds: a file implementation that allows disks blocks to be anywhere on the disk and where allocation is easy, and a system where the most commonly used files are kept in consecutive blocks.

disk compaction

Figure 17.17 shows how disk compaction works. The four files shown have their blocks scattered around the disk. After compaction, the blocks of a file are always contiguous and so can be read very rapidly.

> Disk compaction can get the benefits of contiguous files within most file organizations.

17.4   REVIEW OF FILE STORAGE METHODS

Here is the sequence of attempts we made:

1. *Contiguous files*—Keep all data blocks contiguously on disk.
    a. Good points:
        (1) Fast access.

   (2) Simple to find any block.
  b. Bad points:
   (1) Fragmentation on disk.
   (2) Hard to extend files.

2. *Interleaved files.*
  a. Good points:
   (1) Fast access with noncaching disk controllers.
   (2) Simple to find any block.
  b. Bad points:
   (1) Fragmentation on disk.
   (2) Hard to extend files.

3. *File pointers in the file descriptor.*
  a. Good points:
   (1) Simple to find any block.
   (2) Easy to extend files.
  b. Bad points:
   (1) Variable-sized file descriptor (or severe limit on file size).

4. *Contiguous file pointers.*
  a. Good points:
   (1) Easy to find any block.
   (2) File descriptor needs only one pointer.
  b. Bad points:
   (1) Same problems as contiguous data block storage.

5. *Chained data blocks.*
  a. Good points:
   (1) Easy to allocate disk blocks.
  b. Bad points:
   (1) Slow to find random blocks.
   (2) Disk block pointers use up space in data blocks.

6. *Chained single index blocks.*
  a. Good points:
   (1) Fairly fast to find random blocks.
   (2) Files can be any size.
   (3) Block allocation is easy.
  b. Bad points:
   (1) Slow random access for large files.
   (2) All accesses take two disk block reads.

7. *Double index blocks.*
  a. Good points:
   (1) Fast access for large files.
  b. Bad points:
   (1) Limited file size.
   (2) All accesses take three disk block reads.

8. *Triple index blocks.*
   a. Good points:
      (1) Large maximum file size.
   b. Bad points:
      (1) All accesses take four disk block reads.

9. *Hybrid solutions.*
   a. Good points:
      (1) Uses the appropriate technique for each file size.
      (2) Fast for all sizes of files.
      (3) Large maximum file size.
   b. Bad points:
      (1) None.

We had to go through a number of versions, but we finally found a solution that is very good. It is fast for small files, efficient for large files, has a large maximum file size, and caches well into memory.

---

*17.5 IMPLEMENTATION OF THE LOGICAL TO PHYSICAL BLOCK MAPPING

In Section 16.6, we showed most of the the implementation of the file system. The only thing we did not show was how to map a logical block number into a physical block number. Now that we have seen a range of possible data structures to record this mapping, we can show an implementation of the mapping. We will use a simplification of the hybrid system used in UNIX. In this example, though, we will not have a triple indirect block.

The file descriptor contains `DirectBlocksInFD` (defined to be 10) direct block numbers which are the physical block numbers of the first `Direct-BlocksInFD` logical blocks in the file. Then it contains the physical block number of an indirect block. The indirect block contains the physical block numbers of the next `BlocksMappedByIndirectBlock` logical blocks in the file. Finally, the file descriptor contains the physical block number of a double indirect block, which contains the physical block numbers of `BlocksMappedByIndirectBlock` single indirect blocks.

LOGICAL TO PHYSICAL BLOCK NUMBER MAPPING

```
Block Number
LogicalToPhysical( BlockNumber lbn, FileDescriptor *fd ) {
    // lbn = logical block number
    BlockBufferHeader * header;
    BlockNumber pbn; // physical block number

    // first see if it is in one of the direct blocks
    if( lbn < DirectBlocksInFD ) {
```

```
            // if so return it from the direct block
            return fd->direct[lbn];
    }

    // subtract off the direct blocks
    lbn -= DirectBlocksInFD;

    // check if it is in the indirect block
    if( lbn < BlocksMappedByIndirectBlock ) {
        header = GetDiskBlock( DiskNumber, indirect );
        // are we past the end of the file?
        if( header == 0 ) return 0;
        // treat the block as an indirect block
        pbn = ((IndirectBlock *)(header->buffer))[lbn];
        FreeDiskBlock( header );
        return pbn;
    }

    // subtract off the single level indirect blocks
    lbn -= BlocksMappedByIndirectBlock;

    BlockNumber ibn, dibn;// indirect block number and double indirect bn
    // fetch the double indirect block
    header = GetDiskBlock( DiskNumber, doubleIndirect );
    if( header == 0 ) return 0; // past end of file?

    // figure out which indirect block in the double indirect block
    ibn = lbn / BlocksMappedByIndirectBlock;

    // get the number of the indirect block
    dbn = ((IndirectBlock *)(header->buffer))[ibn];
    // we got the number so we are done with the double indirect block
    FreeDiskBlock( header );

    // fetch the single indirect block
    header = GetDiskBlock( dbn );
    if( header == 0 ) return 0; // past end of file?

    // figure out the offset in this block
    lbn -= ibn * BlocksMappedByIndirectBlock;
    // equivalently: ibn = ibn % BlocksMappedByIndirectBlock;
    pbn = ((IndirectBlock *)(header->buffer))[lbn];
    FreeDiskBlock( header );
    return pbn;
}
```

If the logical block number is less than DirectBlocksInFD, then the address of the block is available directly in the file descriptor. If not, we adjust the logical block block number by subtracting DirectBlocksInFD. We do this because the indirect block will contain blocks DirectBlocksInFD to DirectBlocksInFD+BlocksMappedBy-IndirectBlock, and it is easier to factor out the DirectBlocksInFD from all further computations.

Next, we see if the logical block is mapped by the single indirect block. We know how many blocks it maps (`BlocksMappedByIndirectBlock`), and so we check by comparing this with the logical block number. If it is mapped by the indirect block, we get the indirect block and index into it to get the physical block number. The index is the logical block number (adjusted by subtracting `Direct-BlocksInFD`).

If the logical block is not mapped by the indirect block, it must be mapped by the double indirect block. If we had a triple indirect block, we would put another test here to see if it is in the range of blocks mapped by the double indirect block.

Again we adjust the logical block number to account for the block numbers mapped by the indirect block which we are skipping.

First we must fetch the double indirect block. We do a calculation to figure out which indirect block in the double indirect block that we need. We then extract the physical block number of that indirect block from the double indirect block. Then we get the indirect block and extract the physical block number from it.

This example shows how to handle direct blocks, indirect blocks, and double indirect blocks. Triple indirect blocks are done similarly. Other block mapping schemes use the same or similar techniques.

17.6   FILE SIZES

You might wonder how big files typically are in an operating system. This, of course, varies greatly from system to system depending on the users, but studies of file sizes in general-purpose computing systems consistently show that most files are small.

The tables in Figures 17.18 (Satyanarayanan 1981) and 17.19 (Mullender and Tanenbaum 1984) show the results of two of these studies.

Why are there so many short files? Since the file system is the only place to keep information that must be persistent, users and operating systems use the file system to remember things. For example, a common technique is to use an empty file to record a time that something has happened. You can write an empty file every time you print out all source code files in a directory whose latest version has not been printed out. Any source code files that are newer than the empty file have not yet been printed. File systems usually implement aliases by writing a path name in a file. Path names are rarely more than 50–100 characters, so this generates short files. Spoolers

File Size in Bytes	Percent of Files
< 0.5 K	24.5%
< 3 K	52.0
< 11 K	66.5
< 110 K	95.0

Figure 17.18   Distribution of file sizes

File Size in Bytes	Percent of Files
< 128	12%
< 256	23
< 512	35
< 1 K	48
< 2 K	61
< 4 K	74
< 8 K	85
< 16 K	93
< 32 K	97
< 64 K	99

Figure 17.19   Distribution of file sizes

use short files to record information about print requests. Users often write short shell files to do little jobs.

Strange (1992) notes that, on one user file system at UC Berkeley, 90 percent of the files were less than 5 Kbytes, and on another file system, 90 percent were less than 35 Kbytes. Even at Los Alamos National Laboratories, which is known for large codes and large data files, 50 percent of the files are less than 35 Kbytes (Powell 1977).

Most files are short.

*17.7   BOOTING THE OPERATING SYSTEM

An operating system can load a program into memory and run it, but what loads the operating system itself into memory and runs it? In this section, we will see how that happens.

Modern computers have some programs built into them. These are stored in read-only memory (ROM), which retains its contents even when the computer is turned off. This program is generally a small *ROM monitor* that can do simple things like reading and writing memory. The ROM monitor can also read one disk block into memory and transfer control to it. This is the hook we need to run the operating system.

First we write a short program that can search a file system directory tree, find the executable of the operating system, load it into memory, and then transfer control to it. We write this program so that it requires no relocation. We compile (or assemble) the program and place it in block 0 of a disk. Then we compile and link the operating system, and place it in the file system of that disk.

We load the operating system in two stages. We use the ROM monitor to read disk block 0 into memory and transfer to it. This will be our little loading program that will find the load module for the operating system, load it into memory, and execute it.

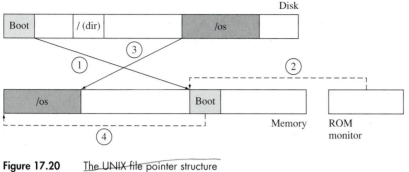

Figure 17.20   ~~The UNIX file~~ pointer structure
Booting on operating system

Figure 17.20 shows the steps of booting an operating system.

1. Read in the boot block with the ROM monitor.
2. Transfer control to the boot block loader.
3. The boot block loader finds and loads the operating system.
4. Transfer control to the operating system.

This process is usually called bootstrapping, or just *booting*. This is a reference   booting
to the old expression about lifting yourself up by your own bootstraps. It is, in fact,
not literally possible to lift yourself up by your own bootstraps, and, correspondingly,
the operating system is not really loading itself. Instead, we have a very simple
loader (in the ROM) that loads a more sophisticated loader (in the boot block on the
disk), which then loads the operating system (in the file system).

The bootstrap program must know enough about the file system organization
to find and read a file. This means a little of the file system code must be in the
bootstrap loader. Some UNIX bootstrap loaders only know how to search the root
directory of the file system, and so the load module for UNIX itself must be in the
root directory.

Once the operating system starts executing, it initializes itself and starts running
other programs.

*17.8   FILE SYSTEM OPTIMIZATION

The file system is usually the bottleneck of the operating system, and so it is essential that it be implemented as efficiently as possible. Basically, this means that we
want to make as few disk accesses as possible, and to make each disk access as fast
as possible. Disk accesses are made fast by reducing the seek times and the latency
times for each disk access.

The best thing for file access efficiency is to use physically sequential files for
several reasons:

• Sequential files do not require index blocks, and so we have fewer nondata disk
  accesses.

- With sequential files, we can read and write the files in larger units and reduce the number of disk operations.

- Seek time is reduced with sequential files.

But efficient use of disk space argues for files where each block can be anywhere on the disk:

- Fixed-size allocation units reduce external fragmentation to zero.

- Small block size reduces internal fragmentation.

So we have a conflict between time efficiency and space efficiency. But we saw in Section 17.3.17 that we can get the best of both worlds by compacting files that are heavily used so that they are physically contiguous. Physically sequential files can be read as much as 10 times faster than files whose blocks are scattered around the disk.

17.8.1 BLOCK SIZE

One important issue is what the block size should be. Large blocks are more efficient to transfer since they take fewer seek and latency waits to access. They also require smaller tables so that the direct access blocks contain more of the file and there are fewer index blocks. Experiments have shown that doubling the block size in a file system will nearly double the performance of the file system.

On the other hand, large blocks lead to fragmentation. We have seen in Section 17.6 that most files are quite small, and a large disk block size will be largely wasted on many files. The following table shows some measurements of a file system at the University of California, Berkeley. They examined the length of all the files and computed how much waste due to internal fragmentation would occur for a range of block sizes.

Block Size	Waste
512	6.9%
1024	11.8
2048	22.4
4096	45.6

As you can see, the internal fragmentation is a significant problem. This is because most files are short.

The arguments are nearly the same as for page size, and in the end we reach the same conclusion—that there are good arguments for both large and small file blocks. But we have some flexibility in file systems that we did not have in paging systems, mainly that we are operating on a much slower time scale and we can afford more computation with each disk access.

One solution that has been tried in several operating systems is to have two different file block sizes, one large and one small. For example, the Berkeley Fast File

System allows two file block sizes (typically 1 Kbyte and 8 Kbytes are chosen). The smaller blocks fit inside the larger blocks. There is some extra overhead for space management of small blocks inside of large blocks, but it means that small files can be in small (1 Kbyte) blocks and large files can be stored in large blocks.

17.8.2   COMPRESSED FILES

Large files take up a lot of disk space and take a long time to read. One way to reduce these overheads is to reduce the size of the file. But how can we do this? By asking users to use smaller files? No, but there is a way.

compressed file

There is a technique called compression that reduces information to a smaller size (in number of bits). Most files are not coded efficiently and are larger than they have to be. If we compress files, then we can reduce their size considerably. Using good compression methods over the mix of files you find in a typical computing system, you can reduce the average file size by one half with compression. This allows you to store twice as many files and read them twice as fast.

There is one problem with compression, and that is that it takes computing time to compress and decompress the files. In recent years, processor power has increased much more rapidly than disk sizes and speeds, and so users are willing to trade some of that processing power for faster file access and smaller file sizes. As a consequence, many computer systems routinely compress files before they write them to the disk and decompress them after they read them back in.

17.8.3   LOG-STRUCTURED FILE SYSTEMS

File system structures like those described so far have worked reasonably well in the past, but these file systems cannot use disk systems to their full capacity. The fastest possible use of a disk would have it constantly transferring data with no seek or latency delays at all. If we call this level of performance 100 percent, then typical file systems only drive the disks at 5 percent to 10 percent of their potential maximum.

One bottleneck is that it takes several disk accesses to access a file, and there is usually a seek between each of them. One problem with our organization is that the file descriptors and the file data are not kept together on the disk, and this guarantees a seek in accessing a file. An improvement is to place the file descriptors, the directories that point to them, and the file data itself close together on the disk. The Berkeley Fast File System tries to do this, and does increase the file system performance considerably. These improvements can get disk usage into the 10 percent to 20 percent range, but improvement beyond that will require a change in how the file system data structures are organized.

With the rapid increase in memory sizes (caused by the rapid decrease in memory costs), disk caches keep getting bigger. Disk caches are so effective that nearly all the disk I/O time in a file system is spent writing the disks.[3] Disk caching does not help writing speeds, and so writing has become the bottleneck in file system

---

| [3]This is disk O time rather than disk I/O time.

performance. The problem is that writes take place all over the disk and nearly always cause a seek.

The solution is to buffer the writes in memory and write the disk in very large sequential writes. The way to do this is a new file system organization called a *log-structured file system*. The implementation details of a log structured file system are somewhat complicated, but the basic idea behind it is simple to explain.

log-structured file system

The file system does not write data where it came from, but in the next sequential location on the disk. The file system writes out a *log,* a record of all the changes that have been made. When a block is changed, the new version is written out, not on top of the old version, but in the next sequential block on the disk. The file descriptor is updated to indicate that this is the current version of that block and the old block is freed. Then the new version of the file descriptor itself is written out, becomes the current version, and the space occupied by the old version is freed.

So the file system is just an ever-lengthening log of all the changes to the files and other data structures. It seems like this will take an unlimited amount of disk space, and it is avoiding this that makes the implementation of a log-structured file system hard. The solution is that the old parts of the log become invalid as new versions of the data are written. We reclaim the space taken by the old parts of the log by copying any valid data still there back into the new part of the log.

The log is buffered in memory and written in very large blocks (such as an entire cylinder) at a time to the disk. For such long writes, the transfer time dominates the seek and latency times, and we can run the disk to 65 percent to 75 percent of its possible capacity. Thus log-structured file systems perform about 10 times faster than conventional systems.

Log-structured file systems write the disk in large chunks and are ideally matched to RAID storage systems that implement very large blocks by spreading them over a number of disk drives.

17.9   FILE SYSTEM RELIABILITY

We started out the chapter with the idea that a file system provides *persistent* storage, that is, storage that lasts past the lifetime of the process that created it. The clear implication here is that someone wants to keep this information and use it later. So a file system must be *reliable*. It must store the data accurately and not lose any part of it.

The problem is that disk devices are not completely reliable and they occasionally lose data. The problem of creating reliable systems out of unreliable components is an old one in engineering, and the way to deal with the problem is well known. The answer is *redundancy,* that is, keeping more than one copy of the data you want to store reliably. Then if one copy is lost or altered, you can use the other copy. This is the idea of backups.

redundancy

17.9.1   BACKUPS

We back up a disk by making a copy of the data on the disk to a tape. We use a tape because the cost per bit of storage on a tape is much lower than on a disk. Data on tape takes longer to access, but, ideally, you will not have to read the backup tape at all since the disk version of the data will not be lost. In the rare cases where you have data loss, it is okay if it takes a little while to read the data off the tape.

While it is certainly possible to back up a disk to another disk (and some systems do this), it is an expensive way to make backups.

Usually an entire file system (here we mean "file system" as the object described in Section 17.1) is backed up to tape at once. There are two varieties of backup. In a *full backup,* you write all the file data in the file system to tape. Note that you do not have to copy the entire file system, including the directories and the file descriptors. Since you have the data on tape, you do not have to remember exactly where it was stored on disk. You do not have to store the directories because the full path names of the files imply the directory structure (except for empty directories, and you can handle this as a special case). And, of course, you do not have to back up the free space.

full backup

File systems are large and take a long time to back up fully, and so another type of backup, an incremental backup, is also used. An *incremental backup* does not back up every file on the disk, but only those files that have changed since the last time they were backed up.

incremental backup

For example, we might make a full backup of a file system every week and an incremental backup of the file system every day. This saves backup time and tape, since we do not back up files more than once. To restore a damaged file system, you start by restoring the most recent full backup. Then you go through the incremental backups taken after the full backup (in chronological order) and restore each one.

If we want greater reliability, then we use more redundancy, that is, we keep more than two copies of the data. The more copies you keep, the less likely you are to lose all of them.

If you have a disaster of some sort (a fire, a hurricane, etc.), then the disks and the backup tapes will both be destroyed. A common procedure to deal with this problem is to keep *off-site backups.* That is a backup that you store in another location than the computer system itself. By keeping backups at another location, you reduce the chance that the backups will be destroyed with the disks. For very important data (such as bank records), you would probably keep several copies in several different parts of the country to be assured that you will not lose all your copies.

off-site backups

Backups are not only for disasters and disk failures. Sometimes people mistakenly delete a file and then later realize that they really wanted it. The most common use of backups is to retrieve mistakenly deleted files.

CDs are more expensive than tape in terms of cost per bit of storage, but they are faster to access. They now sell devices that can hold a number of CDs in a sort of "juke box" that allows any of them to be accessed mechanically (with no human intervention required). With such a device, you can back up to CDs and people can retrieve old files without having to mount tapes or ask the system manager to restore the backed-up version.

17.9.2   CONSISTENCY CHECKING

A file system contains a number of interlinked data structures that should be consistent with each other. For example, the free list should contain exactly the blocks that are not allocated to any file. If some blocks are not allocated to a file and not on the free list, then they are lost to the file system and wasted. If a block is allocated to the

consistency checking

free list and also to a file, then it might be allocated again and exist in two different files. If a block is allocated to two different files, then they will conflict and data will be lost. Each file should be in some directory, and each valid directory entry should point to a valid file.

Sometimes the file system data structures become inconsistent. This could happen if the operating system crashed while it was updating the file system. In addition, parts of the file system can be lost due to failures in the disk media.

Since there is redundancy in the file system structures, it is possible to rebuild the file system and restore consistency. The most common case you want to do this for is when the operating system crashes unexpectedly. This might be caused by an error in the operating system, or a sudden loss of power due to a lightning strike, or for many other reasons.

Most operating systems have programs that will go through a file system, check it for consistency, and fix any inconsistencies. These programs are run periodically and whenever the system crashes.

> Backups provide redundancy to the file system level. Consistency checks take advantage of redundancy within a file system.

17.10   FILE SECURITY AND PROTECTION

Persistent information is often valuable information. We have seen the use of redundancy and backups to increase the reliability of the storage. We also need protection mechanisms so that users do not accidentally or deliberately destroy someone else's information. In addition, some information is private and should not be read by other people. Because of these needs, an operating system must provide means to protect the information in the file system.

But other things in the operating system might need protection as well. You probably do not want other users to alter the messages you send via the IPC system. You may not even want your messages to be read. You do not want other users to pretend they are you and send messages in your name. You do not want other users to destroy your processes or look inside your memory.

We will discuss file protection in Chapter 19 when we discuss other resource management issues.

17.11   EXAMPLES OF FILE SYSTEMS

Most operating system have file system data structures in memory that are similar to the ones we described in Chapter 16. In the discussions below, we will note when there are variations from this basic structure.

17.11.1   SVR4 AND SOLARIS

Many modern UNIX implementations use what is called the vnode/vfs file system architecture. A vnode (virtual inode) is similar to an inode in that it is a file descriptor. A vnode is a base class that is subclassed by each file system implementation. The vnode contains virtual operations for all the operations you might want to perform on a file: open, close, read, write, rmdir, mkdir, name lookup, ioctl, create, remove, link, rename, readdir, etc. A derived class (a subclass) will implement all these virtual operations for one type of file system.

A vfs (virtual file system) is the base class for a file system. It contains virtual operations for file system operations such as: mount, unmount, root, statfs, sync, etc. Each implemented file system will subclass the vfs class and implement these functions.

So an entry in the open file table will point to a vnode, which will really be a subclass of vnode for a particular file system implementation. A *virtual file system switch* is used to look up the appropriate operations.

The vnode and vfs objects represent that part of the file system that is independent of the particular file system organization. Each file system may maintain another file descriptor for information specific to that implementation. For example, an implementation of the standard UNIX file system will contain inodes.

But a vnode can also be an rnode (remote inode) which is managed by the Network File System (NFS). Or it can be a similar data structure for any number of file systems. SVR4 supports the following file systems through vnodes:

- *s5fs*—The original UNIX file system (as described in this chapter).
- *ufs*—UNIX file system (actually the Berkeley Fast File System).
- *hsfs*—High sierra file system (for CD-ROMs).
- *pcfs*—The MS/DOS FAT file system.
- *nfs*—Network file system.
- *rfs*—At&T's remote file system.
- And others.

Just as pseudo-device drivers could provide a device-like interface to something that is not really a device (like a pseudo-tty), vnodes can also point to data structures for pseudo-file systems. A pseudo-file system has the same interface as a file system, but it is not implemented on a disk device as most file systems are. Some examples are:

- *tmpfs*—A file system totally in virtual memory. This is used for temporary files (that is, /tmp). This is essentially a more efficient implementation of a RAM disk. It allocates space for the RAM disk as needed, instead of allocating it permanently to the RAM disk.
- */proc*—A file system that allows access to the memory of all running processes. File permissions prevent unauthorized access.
- */system/processors*—Information about the processors in the system.
- *loopback*—A way of extending an existing file system by adding a few new operations and letting the existing file system handle the rest of the operations.

- *fifo*—For fifos (an IPC method).
- *specfs*—For device files.
- *fdfs*—Holds file descriptors (e.g., `/dev/stdin`, `/dev/stdout`, `/dev/stderr`).
- *cachefs*—Provides generic caching facilities for other file systems.
- *namefs*—Provides generic naming facilities for other file systems.
- *tfs*—Translucent file system. This is used for keeping versions of source code trees. All copies are implemented as copy-on-write, so a new source tree only uses space for files that have changed.

The vnode architecture provides a nice way to structure and allow access to all these real and pseudo file systems.

17.11.2   WINDOWS NT

Windows NT supports multiple file systems using a technique called a *file system driver*. A file system driver implements one type of file system and has entry points (methods, since the file system is an object in NT) for all file system operations. Windows NT uses a unified driver model, where all device drivers and file system drivers have the same interface. A disk request generally goes through several levels of drivers. At the minimum, it goes through a file system driver and a device driver for the disk. If the disk is a partition of a larger disk, it will go through two device drivers. If the file system is built on another file system, it will go through two levels of file system drivers. The file descriptor indicates the file system driver to use, and so the disk request will start there.

This architecture makes it easy to add new file system organizations by adding a new file system driver. In fact, Windows NT allows you to dynamically load any driver, including a file system driver, so support for new file systems can be added dynamically.

Windows NT includes drivers for four file system organizations: FAT (MS/DOS), HPFS (OS/2), CDFS (CD-ROM), and NTFS (NT's own file system organization).

Windows NT uses an object naming system to name all objects in the system. When a file system is mounted, its file system driver handles name resolution for names within that file system.

The Windows NT file system is closely integrated with the virtual memory system, and it uses file mapping. The virtual memory system handles all disk caching.

17.11.3   MS/DOS

MS/DOS uses a FAT file system. The FAT is the file allocation table, which is an inverted block index. This kind of file system is not good for large disks.

The MS/DOS file naming system allows up to 26 block devices, named with driver letters A:, B: , . . . , Z:. Each drive has its own current directory and could be a partition of a disk.

Character device drivers are named with longer names like PRN:, LPT1:, and AUX:. The drivers for these devices are kept in a linked list, and the list is traversed to resolve a name into a device driver.

MS/DOS file names are in the 8.3 format, that is, eight characters of file name and three characters of file extension. The name and the extension are written separated by a period. Many operating systems use this name.extension convention for file naming, but in MS/DOS it is built into the system.

The layout of the MS/DOS FAT file system is as follows:

- *boot block*—This also contains information about the disk. The boot program branches around this information.

- *FAT*—The primary copy of the file allocation table.

- *FAT copy*—An extra copy of the file allocation table in case the first copy gets damaged.

- *Root directory*—The root directory can contain only 512 items because it has a fixed place and size in the file system layout. This makes it easy to find the root directory but limits the size of it.

- *Blocks*—This is the area where all file data is kept.

File descriptors are kept in the directories, so there is no separate area for them in the file system.

17.11.4   OS/2

OS/2 also uses the file system driver idea and allows file system drivers to be loaded dynamically. It supports the FAT (MS/DOS) and HPFS (OS/2) file systems. OS/2's HP (high-performance) file system allows file names up to 254 characters long, and the names are case sensitive.

OS/2 allows any number of attributes to be attached to a file in the form of [attribute-name,attribute-value] pairs. This allows the user to add any desired sort of meta-information to the file.

17.11.5   PLAN 9

The Plan 9 operating system for Bell Labs has an interesting file backup system. Every night it writes all files changed in the previous day to a WORM (write once, read many) drive. Actually, it is a *juke box* of hundreds of WORM CDs with a very large total capacity. The interesting thing about this is that all the backups become part of the file system. To see the backups made on March 15, 1995, you would execute the command cd /n/dump/1995/0315. All the files backed up that day would be there in their usual places in the files system (the directory structure is

---

operating sy
similar.

Each fil
cept of mou
erarchical n
hierarchy to

The file
of a file. The
are acceptab
method that

File sys
improving th
ter layout sc
tem is a radi
faster and to

17.12.1

After readin

- booting
- clusteri
- compre
- consiste
- contigu
- disk ad
- disk blo
- disk co
- disk ex
- double
- file allo
- file sys
- file sys
- file sys
- free blo
- full bac
- increm
- index t
- inode
- interle

- inverted disk block index
- logical block
- logical block number
- log-structured file system
- mounting
- off-site backups
- physical block
- physical block number
- redundancy
- superblock
- triple index block

17.12.2 REVIEW QUESTIONS

The following questions are answered in the text of this chapter:

1. Describe the layout of a file system.
2. How are free blocks kept track of in a file system?
3. What is a FAT file system?
4. What are the advantages of putting file systems in logical disks instead of physical disks?
5. What is the use of mounting?
6. How does mounting change the path name lookup algorithm?
7. Why do we need a function to map logical block numbers to physical block numbers?
8. What is the difference between contiguous and interleaved files?
9. Why can't we keep all the disk block pointers for the file directly in the file descriptor?
10. What are the main problems with the linked block method?
11. How do index blocks work?
12. How do inverted disks in a file system work?
13. Why are most files small?
14. Describe the boot process for an operating system.
15. Why are physically contiguous files faster to read?
16. What are the advantages and disadvantages of compressed files?
17. What are the advantages of a log-structured file system?
18. Why are incremental backups used?
19. What is the use of a file system consistency checker? When do you use it?

17.12.3 FURTHER READING

McKusick et al. (1984) describe the Berkeley Fast File System. Leffler et al. (1989) describe the file structures in 4.3 BSD UNIX. Grosshans (1986), Livadas (1990), and Harbron (1988) are book-length discussions of file system design and implementation. Golden and Pechura (1986) describe the file systems found in microcomputer file systems.

Rosenblum (1992) and Rosenblum and Ousterhout (1992) describe a log-structured file system.

Wiederhold (1987) discusses file system design from a database perspective.

See Satyanarayanan (1981), Strange (1992), Mullender and Tanenbaum (1984) and Powell (1977) for discussions of file sizes.

17.13　PROBLEMS

1. Describe some of the checks a file system consistency checker would make. Describe how it would go through the disk data structures and what tables it would create.

2. Write a program that will go through a directory tree, and create a histogram of the file sizes it finds. Divide the files into five categories: less than 512 bytes, less than 2.5K, less than 5K, less than 50K, and the rest. Run it on some directory trees and report your results.

3. Write a program that will go through a directory tree, and determine the internal fragmentation that would occur if the file block size were 1K and 8K.

4. Write a program that will go through a directory tree, and compute the average reduction gained by a compression program (like `compress` or `gzip`).

5. Extend the logical-to-physical block number mapping program in Section 17.5 to use the full UNIX method with a triple indirect block.

6. Extend the logical-to-physical block number mapping program in Section 17.5 to use 10 single indirect blocks and two double indirect blocks.

7. The UNIX hybrid method combines several of the methods we discussed in the chapter. What are all the methods that it is a hybrid of? Use the list of methods in Section 17.4. Explain your answer.

8. Compare *disk compaction* (Section 17.3.17) with memory compaction (Section 11.1). How are they the same and how are they different?

9. A *file system* is the data structure on a disk that holds files and directories.

   a. Is it possible to have two file systems on a single physical disk drive? Why or why not?

   b. Is it possible to have a file system than spans two physical disk drives? Why or why not?

   c. Is it possible to have a file that is not in a file system? Why or why not?

d. The *file descriptor* is the data structure that describes a file. Is there a corresponding *directory descriptor*? Explain your answer.

e. The *mount* operation allows you to graft the directory tree from one file system onto the directory tree of another file system. Does this mean that a file could span both file systems? Why or why not?

10. Suppose that the block size in a file system is 1 Kbyte, the average file is 512 bytes long, a file descriptor is 64 bytes long, and we allocate file descriptors in a special area of the file system. When we create the file system, we have to decide how much of the file system space to allocate for file descriptors. If we have a file system of 10,000 blocks, what percentage of it should be allocated to file descriptors?

We have not given you any information about the distribution of file sizes, only the average. You need to know the distribution to answer this question, so make some assumption about the distribution and state your assumption in your answer.

11. Give some reasons why it would be nice if users could mount file systems. Give some problems that it would cause.

12. Suppose we have a file system that uses 1 Kbyte blocks and 4 byte file pointers (so 256 fit in a block), and keeps the file descriptors of all open files in memory. Suppose we have a file of length 10,000 bytes. Make a table of how many disk block reads it would take to read the first byte of the file and the last byte of the file. Do this for the following methods of file storage: contiguous, interleaved, block pointers in the file descriptor, block pointer contiguously on disk, block pointer in the data blocks, index blocks in a chain, two-level index blocks, the UNIX hybrid method, and with an inverted disk block index. *Note:* Do not count the disk block read to read in the file descriptor: assume it is already in memory. Also assume that the entire inverted index is in memory.

13. Create the same table as described in the previous problem, with a file size of 100 bytes.

14. Create the same table as described in the previous problem, with a file size of 10,000,000 bytes.

15. Suppose we have 100 files of 5000 bytes each. Make a table of the amount of waste to internal fragmentation for these files for block sizes 512, 1024, 2048, and 4096.

Now suppose you have 50 files of length 100 bytes, and 50 files of length 9,900 bytes. The average file length is the same in both cases. Make the same table for this group of files.

16. Bit maps are not often used for main memory allocation because of the operation of finding K consecutive blocks. Bit maps are more commonly used for disk space allocation. Speculate on why this is so.

17. Some operating systems have file types. For example, MS/DOS differentiates between binary files and text files, and the file system operations treat them differently. Other operating systems treat all files alike, and let the application programs determine the file type based on the file contents. What are the advantages and disadvantages of each approach?

18. The UNIX system allows you to "link" to a file. UNIX does not allow ordinary users to link to another directory. Give some reasons why this restriction is made. How can linking directories cause problems for users and programs?

19. Consider a different method for implementing files. This file system uses 1 Kbyte blocks, and disk addresses are 4 bytes long. In this method, a file descriptor is kept in a disk block. The first 64 bytes of the block contain the status file information (everything except where the disk blocks are). Following these 64 bytes are 0 or more direct block addresses, that is, the addresses of data blocks. If there are more than 240 direct block addresses ($1024 - 64 = 960$, $960/4 = 240$), then the last disk block address is not a direct block but the address of another disk block of 256 direct block addresses. If this is not enough, then the 256th block is the address of another disk block of direct addresses. In other words, we use a linked list of disk blocks, each containing 239 or 255 direct block addresses. If the number of direct block addresses is less than 240, then the first few bytes of the file data are contained in the first disk block.

    This first 64 bytes also contains a count which gives the number of direct blocks. For example, a file containing 16 disk blocks would use 64 bytes for the file descriptor, $64 (= 16 * 4)$ bytes for direct block addresses, and the first 896 of data. Compare this implementation with the UNIX one as described in Section 6.5.

    How many disk blocks will be needed for a file of:

    a. 100 bytes.

    b. 10,000 bytes.

    c. 1,000,000 bytes.

    d. 100,000,000 bytes.

Count one disk block for the inode in the UNIX version. How many disk accesses will it take to read the entire file in each of those cases? How many disk accesses will it take to read the last byte of the file in each of those cases?

20. Suppose we have a disk with disk block addresses of two bytes, disk block size of 1000 bytes (not 1024, just for computation convenience), and a disk containing 65,000 disk blocks. Consider two different file system disk organizations for this disk:

    A. File descriptors take 100 bytes each. The first 500 blocks are used to store the file descriptors of all the files on the disk (10 file descriptors per block). Each file descriptor has 13 disk addresses:
       (1) The first 10 addresses are direct and address the first 10 data blocks in the file.
       (2) The 11th address points to an indirect block which contains the addresses of the next 500 blocks in the file.
       (3) The 12th address points to a double indirect block which contains the addresses of 500 indirect blocks.
       (4) The 13th address points to a triple indirect block which points to a block containing the addresses of 500 double indirect blocks.

    B. The directory entry points to the first block of the file. The file descriptor for a file is contained in the first 100 bytes of the first block of the file. If the file contains 900 bytes or less, these bytes are in the rest of the block. Otherwise, the first block of the file contains the addresses of the first 450 blocks of the file. If the file is longer than 450,000 bytes, then some of the 450 addresses point to indirect blocks (each of which then contains 500 data block addresses). The file descriptor indicates how many of the 450 disk addresses are direct (point directly to data blocks) and how many are single indirect (point to indirect blocks).

For each of the two file system organizations (*A* and *B* above):

a. What is the largest file that is supported by the system? Compute the theoretical largest file on any size disk. Do not consider the size of this disk.

b. What is the maximum number of files the system can support on this disk?

c. To access a file, we need to read the file descriptor and all the data blocks of the file. Indicate how many disk reads are required (in both file organizations) for a file of length:
(1) 500 bytes.
(2) 950 bytes.
(3) 10,000 bytes.
(4) 5,000,000 bytes.

Now consider three different situations:

i. Most of the files in the system are about 500 bytes.

ii. Most of the files in the system are about 5,000 bytes.

iii. Most of the files in the system are about 1,000,000 bytes.

For each of these situations, compare the two file systems and state if one would be better or they would be about the same (in terms of performance and efficiency).

21. Consider file system organization *B* in the question above.

a. How many disk accesses are required to read the last byte of the largest possible file?

b. Suppose we change the organization of the first file block as follows: Suppose we could have up to 450 double indirect block addresses after the file descriptor. What would be the size of the largest possible file?

22. Compare the bit map and hole list methods of keeping track of free space on a disk with 800 cylinders, each having 5 tracks of 32 sectors. How many holes would it take before the hole list would be larger than the bit map? Assume that the allocation unit is the sector, and that a hole requires a 32-bit word.

23. Suppose we used a bit map method for keeping track of free space on a disk with 10,000 disk blocks of 1000 words each. Each word is 20 bits long (not realistic, but it allows easy computations in this problem). How many disk blocks are required to hold the bit map?

Now consider three methods for free space:

a. The bit map method.

b. A method that keeps the free blocks in a linked list(as in the linked allocation scheme for file organization). That is, each free block points to the next free block.

c. A method similar to indexed allocation where there is a linked list of free blocks and each free block contains the addresses of 100 other free blocks. So the blocks on this chain are free, and they each point to 100 other free blocks and the next block on the chain of free blocks.

Compare these three methods.

24. Suppose we have an operating system where both the file system and I/O system are contained in separate processes. A user gets file services from the file system process by sending it messages. The messages are:

- `open(FileSystem, char * fileName);`—the file identifier for the open file (which will be an integer) is sent in a return message.

- `read(FileSystem, int fileID, int startAt, int length);`—the data read is sent in a return message.

- `close(FileSystem, int fileID);`—Return message just verifies that the close was done.

Note we are using a procedure call format to describe the messages. The procedure name (open, read, close) is the message type, the first argument is who the message is to, and the rest of the arguments are message parameters. Use this same convention for your messages.

When the file system receives one of these messages, it will do some of the processing itself, but it will have to ask the I/O system process to perform the I/O level functions, and may even have to ask the kernel to do some things for it. The I/O system will receive these requests, and will have to send messages to the kernel to get it to do things (like loading device registers). Assume that the system processes have no special privileges, that is, they cannot read or write device registers, change the memory map, etc.

For each of the three messages, show the sequence of events that happens starting when the message is sent to the file system and ending with the reply message to the user. This sequence of events will look something like this:

a. Message send: Client → File system—open (FileSystem, char * fileName).

b. File System: specify what processing is done.

c. Message send: File system → I/O system — specify message format.

d. I/O System: specify what processing is done.

e. Message send: I/O system → Kernel—specify message format.

f. Kernel: specify what processing is done here.

g. Interrupt to kernel: I/O interrupt.

h. Kernel: specify what processing is done.

i. Message send: Kernel → I/O system—specify message format.

j. I/O System: specify what processing is done.

k. Message send: I/O system → File system—specify message format.

l. FileSystem: specify what processing is done.

m. Message send: File system → Client—specify message format.

Notes: The purpose of this question is to determine whether you understand the sequence of events that occurs when you open (or read or close) a file, and if you understand what part of the operating system (file system, I/O system, or lower device driver) the events occur in.

Assume a file system organized exactly like the UNIX file system as described in the chapter.

18

Design Techniques IV

18.1 CACHING

18.1.1 OVERVIEW

Speed up a slow operation by remembering the result of previous invocations of the operation.

18.1.2 MOTIVATION

Suppose we use a connectionless form of file reading, where each read system call contains the path name of the file to read. It seems like we will have to look up the file name in the hierarchical directory system and find the file descriptor each time a read system call is made. Actually, the name-to-file lookup only has to be done once if we look it up the first time and save the result. The table of saved results then becomes a user-transparent version of an open file table. But it is different from an open file table in that, if the name is not found in the table, we know how to look it up. So we have a fast method that sometimes fails and a slower fallback method. This way we get a simple and robust system that is resistant to failures, but we still get speed in the common cases.

This is an example of the general technique of **caching.** Caching is applicable in any situation where a procedure is called repeatedly to do some computation, which is sometimes the same computation as a previous call and sometimes a new computation. After you compute a value, you save the computed result. The next time the procedure is called, it checks to see if it has already done the calculation, and, if so, it returns the saved answer rather than redoing the calculation.

Figure 18.1 shows a generalized caching system. It contains a module to compute $f(x)$, which is assumed to take a long time. When an input x comes into the system, it is looked up in the table of cached values. If it is found, then the cached value is returned (see

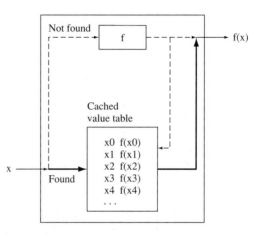

Figure 18.1   Generalized caching

the solid line path). If it is not found, then the value is computed and remembered in the cached value table (see the dotted line path).

18.1.3   OPERATING SYSTEM EXAMPLES

Virtual Memory   The operation is providing access to a page of the address space. The most used pages are cached in memory and are quick to access. The slow backup method is to get it from disk.

TLB   The TLB (translation lookaside buffer) is a cache for the page table in memory.

Path Name Lookup Cache   Some operating systems cache the results of path name lookups. This can be beneficial since a path name lookup might require a number of disk accesses.

File Descriptor Table   An operating system will keep copies of the file descriptors of all open files in memory. This is a cache of the file descriptors on disk.

Disk Block Caches   The most recently used disk blocks are kept in memory for fast access.

18.1.4   COMPUTER SCIENCE EXAMPLES

Memoizing a Function   In Scheme and Lisp you can easily put a wrapper around a function that remembers previous values. This is called *memoizing,* but is really caching. This can make very slow recursive solutions to problems much faster. The

memoizing

end result is a function that is as fast as the iterative version, and is clear and obviously correct as the recursive version.

Hardware Caching   The most common example of caching is in memory hardware. A memory module is repeatedly called to fetch words from its memory. Often the same word is fetched over and over again. If the memory module remembers the address and value of the last few words it has fetched, then it can avoid a memory cycle if it is asked for the same word again.

Modern computer systems make extensive use of caching to speed up processing. Memory boards often have cache memory associated with them. This is fast memory that remembers the last few thousand locations that have been requested. Processors usually cache both instructions and data in an internal cache on the chip. This is in addition to the memory cache.

18.1.5   APPLICABILITY

Use caching whenever you have to repeatedly compute a lengthy operation and where it is frequently called with the same arguments.

Caching is a method of taking advantage of knowledge about the distribution of questions you will be asked. If you tend to get asked the same question over and over again, then it pays to write down the answer instead of recomputing it each time. But if you rarely get repeated questions, then writing down answers will just waste space and the time to look through them.

Caching works if the questions are clustered, and doesn't work if the questions are all different.

18.1.6   CONSEQUENCES

* The average operation time is radically faster.
* It takes space to hold the previous answers.
* Caching may not help at all if you do not get asked to compute the function with the same argument frequently enough.

> Caching takes advantage of special information that some questions are asked more frequently and in clumps.

18.1.7   IMPLEMENTATION ISSUES AND VARIATIONS

Dynamic Programming   There is a technique called *dynamic programming*, which is a form of caching. Dynamic programming is applicable when you are computing a function that is defined recursively. Instead of computing it with a standard recursion,

dynamic programming

you build up a table of the values of the function for low values, and keep adding to the table for higher values.

Searching for Cached Answers   If you save a lot of answers, it may take a while to see if you have a saved answer. Hashing is generally used to speed up this search. In hardware, the search is done in parallel by parallel hardware.

Another solution is to only save one or a few previous answers. Often this is enough to achieve a high hit rate. This is an example of the Law of Diminishing Returns.

Cache Invalidation   An important issue in caching is when the cache entries become invalid. Suppose a memory module has a cache built into it. There is only one path to the memory, and that is through the cache. If a memory cell that is in the cache is written, the memory can either invalidate the cache or update it.

Now suppose that you have a multiprocessor system with one shared memory. Each processor will have a cache on the memory. When one processor writes the cache, it might invalidate entries in the caches of the other processors. But the situation is different here: the caches are not at the memory where changes are made. How can the caches know when changes are made and their cache has to be invalidated?

The solution in this situation is called the *snoopy cache*. Each cache watches all bus transactions and sees if any of the writes affect its entries.

But let's look at the situation more generally. A cache must arrange to be informed when events occur that will invalidate the cache. This is easier when there is only one hardware unit or software process that will make such changes.

Hooks   A hook is a mechanism whereby a process can register a procedure that will be called when an event occurs. The hardware or software process that causes the event also causes the registered procedure to be called. The classic example of a hardware hook is an interrupt. When an interrupt occurs the interrupt handler procedure is called. UNIX (and most other operating systems) has software interrupts whereby a process can register a procedure to be called when an event occurs. The events can be the pressing of certain keys, the occurrance of a hardware interrupt, the change in a window size, etc. Callbacks in GUI systems are also examples of hooks.

The hook is the ideal mechanism to handle cache invalidation. The process controlling the cache arranges to be notified whenever an event occurs that might change data held in the cache. When the event occurs the cache manager can invalidate or update the cache data. This will ensure the data in the cache is always up-to-date.

Static-Dynamic Hybrids   Caching is a dynamic method, but it has static elements in it. It is dynamic in that it is not done until run time, but it is static in that it uses static storage to save computations and avoid redoing work. With caching, we are in a mixed prediction situation. We cannot predict what data and instructions will be used, but once they are used, we can confidently predict that they will be used again in the near future. Caching is an adaptive solution that tries to combine the advantages of static and dynamic methods.

Caching can often be used to make dynamic methods faster. For example, in a connectionless file protocol you have to look up the file each time a read or write is done on the file. If you cache this information, you can make the file lookup so fast that the overhead for looking it up each time is very small. We see the typical technique of combining two methods to get some of the advantages of each.

> Caching is a dynamic solution with a nod to static.

Another example of this technique is the use of graphics contexts. Graphics calls often have a large number of parameters. For example, in drawing a circle you have the obvious parameters like the center and radius of the circle. Then you have graphics-related parameters like how thick the line drawing the circle should be, what color it should be drawn in, and whether the circle should be filled in and with what color.

These graphics parameters do not tend to change as much as the other parameters. If we draw 10 circles, they will all have different centers or radii, but they might all be in the same color with the same fill and line thickness. The solution to this problem is the concept of the *graphics context*. A graphics context is a collection of graphics parameters for all graphics operations. A graphics call specifies some parameters (like circle center and radius), and then a graphics context is used to fill in all the other graphics parameters. We set up a graphics context once and register it with the graphics engine. Then we can avoid sending the same parameters over and over again.

We set up a static graphics context rather than dynamically sending a full set of parameters each time.

graphics context

18.1.8 RELATED DESIGN TECHNIQUES

Caching is an example of trading space for time.

18.2 OPTIMIZATION AND HINTS

In general, optimizing depends on predicting the future. If you know what will be demanded of you, you can plan for it. Predicting the future requires a model of how things work. In paging, the best model was that the future will be like the past. In fact, this is the most successful model for all predictions of the future. You only deviate from this model if you have some good reason to do so, that is, if you have some information that circumstances have changed.

> Optimization depends on predicting the future.

18.2.1 OPTIMIZING AN ACTIVITY

There are two general approaches to optimizing an activity. You can optimize every instance, or you can optimize some instances. For example, suppose we are searching for an item in a sorted list using a sequential search algorithm. We can switch to a binary search and optimize every case, or we can add a cache of recently looked up items, and optimize only the cases where we get cache hits.

As another example, suppose our memory is not fast enough. We can use faster chips and optimize all the cases, or we can add a cache and optimize some of the cases.

18.2.2 HINTS

There is an important difference in these two cases. In the first case, the optimized method is *complete* in that it always answers the question. Binary search always finds the item (if it is there), and a faster memory will always return the stored value. In the second case, we add a method that is not complete, one that sometimes gives the answer (and quickly) but sometimes does not give the answer. When the new method does not give the answer, we revert to the older, slower method that is guaranteed to give an answer. By far, the most common method of the second type is caching.

hint

There is a related optimization method called a *hint*. A hint is an answer that might be correct but is not guaranteed to be correct. Let's take an example. Suppose you are on a network, and your files are kept on several file servers. When you access a file, your computer sends a message to a file server to access the file. But how do you know which file server the file is on? You can send a broadcast message to all of them asking if they have the file. It would be better to keep a record of where each file was the last time you asked for it. Then you can just go to that file server and ask for the file. If that file server does not have the file, then you can try the broadcast method.

18.2.3 DIFFERENCES BETWEEN CACHING AND HINTING

A method based on hints is different than caching. In caching, you know whether you have a right answer or no answer. You revert to the original method if there is no answer. With hints, you get an answer and check if it is correct. If it is not correct, then you revert to the original method. The key difference is, in a hinting scheme, you have to be able to check whether an answer is correct or not. Clearly, a hinting scheme would not make sense for a memory where there is no fast way to check if the answer is correct.

So, to summarize, there are three strategies for optimizing an activity:

- *Faster algorithm or faster hardware*—All cases are optimized.
- *Caching*—Some cases are faster; all the faster cases are correct.
- *Hints*—Some cases are faster; not all of the faster cases are correct.

18.2.4   WHEN TO USE HINTING INSTEAD OF CACHING

In caching, we have a fast method that sometimes works and a slow method that always works. The fast method always gives either the right answer or no answer, that is, a cache knows for sure what it knows and it knows what it doesn't know.[1]

In hinting, we have a fast method that sometimes works, a fast procedure to determine if a hint is correct, and a slow method that always works. The fast method can give either the right answer, a wrong answer, or no answer. The fast procedure can determine whether the hint is correct, and, if it is not, we use the slow method just as if there was no hint.

Why would a hint be wrong? In a dynamic situation, any information may become obsolete and incorrect. In dynamic situations, we cannot keep information in a cache and expect it to stay correct because things change all the time. This is the situation where you need to use hints rather than a cache.

18.2.5   HINTING EXAMPLES

Hinting is most useful in situations where we are looking for something, and we will recognize it when we see it. The prime example is networks. We often need to find out where a network service is located. For example, we might be looking for the location of a certain file or the print server or whatever. In a large network, we might be searching for the least-busy path between two points. The slow method of finding something on a network is to send out a broadcast message to every machine on the net, and ask if the thing you are looking for is there.

18.2.6   HINTS IN USER INTERFACES

Many programs remember where their window was placed the last time they were run. When started again, they put their window in the same place. This is a form of hinting. The program guesses where you want the window, based on the last place it was. If the hint is incorrect, the user can tell this and move the window.

18.2.7   OPTIMISTIC ALGORITHMS

There is a class of algorithms, called *optimistic algorithms,* that are related to the idea of hinting. The idea in an optimistic algorithm is to assume that things will work out correctly, and redo them if they do not. For example, in an Ethernet, a transmitter assumes that the transmission channel (the "ether") is free if it cannot detect a signal on it, and so it begins its transmission. If two transmitters begin at nearly the same time, they will both see a channel that is not busy and start transmitting. This is okay

optimistic algorithm

---

[1] We are reminded of the quote from Will Rogers, "It's not what you don't know that hurts you; it's what you know that ain't so."

because the transmitters will monitor the channel while they are transmitting, and they can detect the interference when two transmitters are broadcasting simultaneously. In this case, they each wait a random period and try again. In most cases, the optimistic assumption that no other transmitter is about to begin transmitting is true and the system works fine. If the channel is very busy and this optimistic assumption is no longer true, the Ethernet idea breaks down and the channel is poorly used.

The detect and recover method of handling deadlocks is an example of an optimistic algorithm. It assumes that deadlocks will not happen, but has a plan to fix things if they do. This is usually cheaper than trying to prevent deadlock.

There is an expression that people sometimes use: "It is better to ask forgiveness than permission." This summarizes the idea of optimistic algorithms. It is usually faster to fix errors occasionally then check for permission each time you want to do something. This assumes that fixing errors is possible and not too expensive. If this is not so, then optimistic algorithms are not appropriate.

18.2.8   VERSIONS OF FILES

These days, most of your files are not on your individual machine, but are on file servers that you access over a network. Some workstation operating systems will cache files, that is, when you open a file they will fetch a copy of the file from the file server and then access the local copy. These local copies stay around for a while, so if you open the same file later it may be the cached copy and avoid a network file transfer. This saves time for you in accessing the file and bandwidth of the network.

But how do you know that the file has not changed since you fetched it? You don't, and so this method is really a hinting method even though it is conventionally called file caching. In a hinting system, you need a way to know if the hint is correct. This can be done with modification dates. When you fetch a file, you remember when you fetched it, or you fetch its date of last modification along with the file. When you want to check the validity of a cached file, you go to the file server and get the current date of last modification for the file. If this is the same as the one you fetched, then the file is still valid. If not, you have to fetch it again.

Suppose you cannot get or do not trust the last modification dates. There are other methods you can use. You can make a 32-bit checksum of the file, that is, add up the entire file in blocks of four bytes used as 32-bit integers (ignoring overflow). This reduces the file to a 32-bit number. You compute this checksum on the file server, and locally for the cached file. If they are the same, you can be pretty sure they are the same file. How sure? Well, that's hard to say exactly. Almost any change in a file will change its checksum, but since there are only 2^{32} possible checksums and vastly more files, many pairs of (different) files have the same checksum. It is unlikely you will run into such a case, but there is chance. If files map uniformly into checksums (this is probably close to being true), then there is one chance out of 2^{32}, or about one out of four billion, that two particular files have the same checksum. We could go to a 64-bit checksum and be even more sure.

18.3 HIERARCHICAL NAMES

18.3.1 OVERVIEW

To make it possible to assign unique names in a decentralized way, use names that have parts (that is, internal structure). The parts correspond to levels in a hierarchy of name spaces.

18.3.2 MOTIVATION

Let's start with some useful terms and concepts. A *name* is an arbitrary identifier, usually an integer or a character string. An *object* is a thing that is to be named. Some typical objects are files, directories, devices, computers, etc. A *name space* is a collection of unique names. An *object space* is a collection of objects. A *name map* is a function from a name space to an object space. Figure 18.2 shows these concepts graphically.

name space
object space
name map

One interesting object that a name might map into is a name map. Suppose a name map maps some names into objects that are other name maps, and these other name maps map some names into still other name maps and so on (see Figure 18.3). This will create a directed graph of name spaces. The most useful such graphs are trees, and we call this a hierarchy of name maps, or a hierarchical name map. The root of the tree is the root of the hierarchical name map.

A *compound name* is an ordered sequence of names. To name objects in a hierarchical name map, we use compound names. We start at the root map of the hierarchical name map, and look up the first name in the compound name to get to the next name map. We look up the next name in the compound name in the current name map to get to the next name map. We continue this until we run out of names in the compound name. The object that we end up at is the object named by the compound name.

compound name

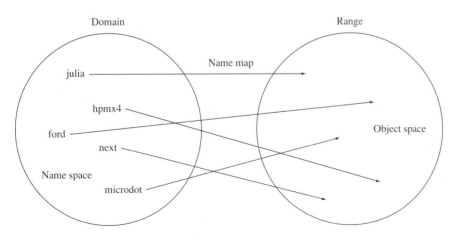

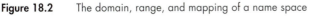

Figure 18.2   The domain, range, and mapping of a name space

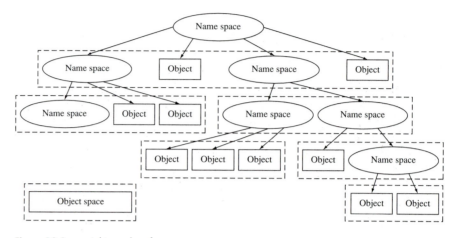

Figure 18.3   A hierarchy of name spaces

Hierarchy is an age-old technique for handling large and distributed systems, starting with the Egyptians or before. Most organizations are organized hierarchically. Computer scientists tend to use hierarchies whenever they can because they are so powerful and well behaved.

The use of hierarchy in naming is to have a multipart name, where each part is handled by one level of the hierarchy. At each level, we have a flat name space and require unique names, but a level does not have to be concerned about the names used in the levels above and below it.

This technique is so widely used that we hardly have to mention it here. In fact, a significant problem is the overuse of hierarchy, that is, trying to impose hierarchy on a system that is not naturally hierarchical, or imposing a single hierarchy on a system that has several natural hierarchies.[2]

We have seen hierarchical names used in operating systems to name files (see Section 16.3). We will see later that the hierarchical file naming system is also used to name other operating system objects (such as devices and pipes). Hierarchical names can be used to name all sorts of things. Let's look at some examples.

Examples of hierarchical name spaces are easy to find since the technique is so easy, useful, and powerful. Names of people form a two-level hierarchy. There is a family name that is given to all members of the family, and a personal name that is unique in the family. If two families each name a child Andrew, it is not a problem since the family name can serve to distinguish them.

Mailing addresses are typically in a multiple-level hierarchy. The highest level is the country (which is assumed to be the country you are in if country is not given). The next level is the state in the United States, the province in Canada, the region in France,

---

[2]Multiple inheritance in object-oriented programming languages was developed to handle situations where a single hierarchy was too restrictive.

the prefecture in Japan, or other similar political division. The next level is the city, then the street, then the street address, and finally the person. Figure 18.4 is an example.

Internet machine names use a hierarchical naming system. The highest level is the domain, which is one of com, edu, gov, org, net, or country name (Internet addressing is US-centric). The next level is the organization. Below that is zero or more levels of subnet, and then finally you get a single machine, and the lowest level is the login name on that machine.

These examples all show the advantages of hierarchical naming. Name generation can be localized and efficient, since all the components of a new name except the last one are fixed by the logical location of the object being named, and the last component only has to be unique in that small, flat name space. The names show the natural structure of the system, what family a person is in, what city a person lives in, or what organization a person works for.

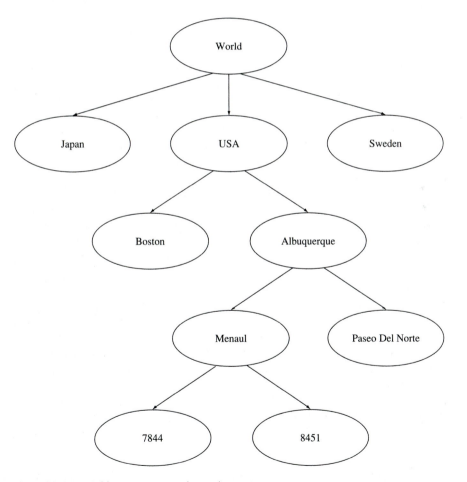

Figure 18.4   Address name space hierarchy

One problem with hierarchical names is that they tend to get long.[3] Since we are guaranteed uniqueness within each level of the hierarchy, we can often use defaults to shorten the most common uses of names. In a family, people are called by their personal names. In an address, the country is usually assumed. In an Internet address, any unspecified higher levels of the hierarchy are assumed to be those of the sender. In a hierarchical file system, a user has a "current directory" that is assumed to be the base of all relative addresses.

18.3.3   OPERATING SYSTEM EXAMPLES

File Naming   Almost all operating systems use a hierarchical naming system for naming files (and often for naming other operating system objects as well).

18.3.4   COMPUTER SCIENCE EXAMPLES

Internet Domain Addressing   Internet names, like `crowley@cs.unm.edu`, use a hierachical naming system. The machine names are a pure hierarchical system using a period as a delimiter between names. The most specific name is first, and the most general name is last. This is the opposite of file names, but the same as postal addresses. The login name on the machine is the most specific level of the hierarchy and is treated a little differently; in particular, the delimiter after it is an ampersand instead of a period.

IP Protocol Addresses   IP (Internet Protocol) addresses consist of 32 bits, divided into four octets. The high-order eight bits are the most general, and the low-order eight bits are the most specific.

Naming in Programming Languages   Programming languages for the naming of objects in nested structures are hierarchical.

Programming languages also use a related method called adjoined name space. This is discussed in the *Implementation Issues and Variations* section below.

18.3.5   APPLICABILITY

Use hierarchical names when you want to assign names locally and you want them to be unique globally. They work especially well when there is a natural hierarchy already present in the system.

18.3.6   CONSEQUENCES

- Unique names are only needed at each level, not throughout the system. Naming decisions are decentralized. Checking for uniqueness is fast.

---

[3]Actually, this is a problem with large names spaces in general, whether they are flat or hierarchical, but flat name spaces tend to be denser and hence typically do not grow as quickly.

- Names provide information about the object, such as its location or ownership.

- Names can get very long.

- The name space can be sparse in some parts of the hierarchy, and so the name space may be inefficiently used.

18.3.7 IMPLEMENTATION ISSUES AND VARIATIONS

Internal and External Names   In an operating system, there are two representations of names: character strings and integers (almost always unsigned integers). We will distinguish between *external names* that are chosen by the users of the operating system (people and programs) and *internal names* that are chosen by the operating system itself. In almost all cases, the users use character string names for external names, and the operating system uses integers for internal names.

external name
internal name

Flat Name Spaces   Each directory contains a set of unique, single-part names. This is called a *flat name space*. In a flat name space, all names are unique character strings with no internal structure.

flat name space

Flat name spaces have two problems. The first is an efficiency problem with large name spaces, since each candidate name must be compared with a large number of existing names to make sure it is not a duplicate. The second problem is that the names do not reflect the natural structure of the objects that exist in the system and to which the names refer.

Hierarchical name spaces were invented to solve these two problems with flat name spaces. But remember that hierarchical name spaces are built from flat name spaces (the directories).

Some operating systems restrict the number of levels of directories that are allowed. If only one level is allowed, then we have a flat naming system. More commonly, two levels are allowed—a directory of users, with each user having a directory of files. This restriction is now rare, since it is quite easy to implement hierarchical file systems with any number of levels.

> Each level of a hierarchical naming system is a flat name space.

> Use flat name spaces locally and hierarchical name spaces globally.

Assigning Unique Names   At any one level in a hierarchical name space, we have a flat name space that requires unique names. How do we ensure unique names? In a single-processor system, this is fairly easy; we try a name and make sure it is not a duplicate. Now that distributed systems are so common, the assigning of unique names is more complex. The only solution to this problem is to somehow simulate a single-processor system. There are two methods of doing this:

- A central naming authority, or
- A central name uniqueness checker.

In the first case, you apply to a central authority for a name, and it gives you one. In the second case, you present a candidate name to the central name uniqueness checker, and it either approves or disapproves of the name. If the name is approved, it is added to the list of names to check uniqueness against in a single indivisible action with the checking of the name. This is important to avoid two programs asking for the same name at the same time. Figure 18.5 shows the two alternatives.

An example of a name uniqueness checker is found in UNIX. Programs can run concurrently in UNIX, and it is possible for two processes to request a new name at essentially the same time. There is a form of open system call that requests that a file with a certain name be created, but the operation fails if the name already exists. It is an atomic operating system operation that checks for uniqueness and creates the new file. This is used to generate a file with a guaranteed new, unique name.

The phone company is a central naming authority for phone numbers. You apply for a phone and they give you a number.[4]

Unique Names in the C Library   The C library has several procedures to generate unique file names for temporary files. Here are two of them:

- char *tempnam (char *dir, char *pfx)—Generate a unique name for a temporary file. The file will be in directory dir and will start with the string in pfx.
- char *mktemp (char *template)—template is a file name with six Xs in it. It will be to a unique file name.

Both of these calls generate the file name, but do not create the file. The C library also has calls to generate a unique file name and open a file with that name (see tmpfile and mkstemp)

Adjoining Name Maps   We have seen the composition of name maps into hierarchical name maps. How else can we combine name maps into other name maps? One way is by *adjoining* two name maps, that is, look for a name in the first name map, and then, if not found, in the second name map. You can think of this as the sum of the two name maps. For any names that are mapped by both name maps, the first name map takes precedence over the second name map. We can generalize this process to adjoin any number of name maps. A name is looked up in the name maps, in order, until a name is mapped by one of the name maps.

adjoining name maps

Figure 18.6 shows the adjoining of two name maps. All the items in the first name map are unchanged in the adjoined name map. The entries for "guava" and "lemon" are *shadowed* in the secondary name map since the corresponding entries in the primary name map take precedence over them.

---

[4]Some years ago, it was possible to request specific phone numbers, and they would say yes or no. Even today, companies can often negotiate for specific phone numbers that are easy to remember.

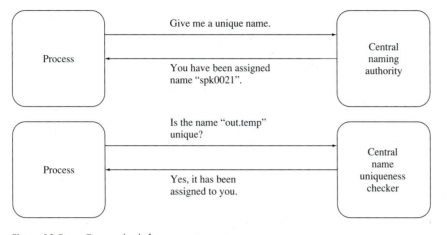

Figure 18.5   Two methods for generating unique names

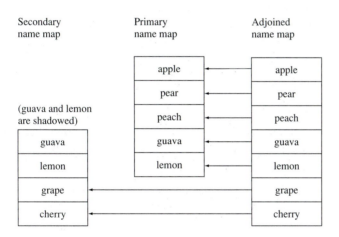

Figure 18.6   Adjoining name maps

UNIX has a concept of a *PATH*, which is a list of directories containing commands. We type a command to the shell the command name is looked up in the directories in the path until it is found and that command is executed.

The Plan 9 operating system uses a method to combine directories by adjoining to a composite directory. This generalizes the idea of PATHs so that an adjoined directory can be used any place a directory can be used, rather than just to look up command names in the shell.

18.3.8   RELATED DESIGN TECHNIQUES

Hierarchical names are an example of the divide and conquer design technique.

18.4   NAMING OF OBJECTS

The naming of objects is a critical issue in computer science. From the theoretical point of view, the ability to name objects and refer to them by name is the critical feature for a programming language and is the basis of its power. A well-known game in programming languages is to write a "self-reproducing" program, that is, a program whose output is an exact copy of the program source code. This can be done in most languages, and the trick is based on defining the appropriate string, giving it a name, and then printing out that string several times by repeating its name.

18.4.1   WHAT IS A NAME?

But what is a name? A name is an identifier that refers to a thing.[5] But that (admittedly vague) definition make a name sounds like a description. What is the difference between a name and a description? Actually, the distinction is not clear in many cases,[6] but we usually think of a name as an arbitrary string associated with an object. A name is of no use without a name mapping that associates the name with the object.[7] A description, on the other hand, stands on its own and does not need an associated mapping to find the thing, since a description is not arbitrary but is based on the attributes of the thing. If a description does need interpretation, then we do not consider it to be a very good description.

What is the purpose of a name? It is to be able to refer to an object without reproducing the entire object with each reference. A description always involves some reconstruction of the object, or else some search for the object based on its description. For example, suppose I have the string "/usr/local/bin/CC". I can describe it in several ways:

1. I can give the string itself, "/usr/local/bin/CC".

2. I can say it is the concatenation of the local bin path and the string "CC", that is, I can tell how to reconstruct it.

---

[5]Object-oriented programming has taken the formerly generic word "object" and given it a technical meaning in computer science. Window systems have appropriated the word "widget," a whimsical word that refers to an unspecified product or thing, and given it a technical meaning. So we will use the suspiciously vague-sounding old standby "thing."

[6]I was on a trip to Laguna Beach (CA) and was looking for a place to eat. I asked a clerk in a store for a recommendation and she said, "The place across the street from the Hotel Laguna is pretty good." Then, not knowing where the Hotel Laguna was, I asked, "Where is that?" and she replied, "Well, it's right across the street from the Hotel Laguna." After getting directions to the Hotel Laguna and thinking that the clerks in Laguna Beach were smart alecks, I walked down to the restaurant. When I turned the corner and saw the sign on the restaurant reading "The Place Across the Street From the Hotel Laguna," I realized that the clerk had really said, " 'The Place Across the Street From the Hotel Laguna' is pretty good," not "The place across the street from the Hotel Laguna is pretty good," and her second answer made perfect sense (at least to her).

[7]Note, however, that the same name mapping is associated with many names.

3. I can say it is the 24th string in the string table, that is, I can describe where to find it.

4. I can give its address in memory, which is another way to find it.

If I want to specify a file, I can

- Provide the (contents of the) file itself.

- Provide the path name of the file.

- Provide a procedure that will generate the file.

Reconstruction methods are not generally called names. Describing how to find the object is not usually called a name, but sometimes the address of an object is thought of as a name for the object.

We usually reserve the term *name* for an identifier that requires some lookup to find the object, and this lookup is in a *name table* and is done with a linear search, a binary search, a hash table, a binary tree, or other means. The important point is that this auxiliary name table is required, and the name is not sufficient to find the object without the name table. *(margin: name, name table)*

There are two important issues in naming: how names are assigned to objects (*name assignment*), and how names are used to find the objects (*name resolution*). We will not be much concerned with the issue of name resolution here, and will concentrate on how names are assigned to objects. *(margin: name assignment, name resolution)*

18.4.2 TYPES OF NAMES

There has to be some name authority that manages names. It may assign names or it may accept user-defined names. In this second case, it will also ensure that names are unique and reject names that are not. This name authority is usually also in charge of name resolution and, at least, it manages the name tables that are used for name resolution. In our case, we are discussing operating systems, and so it is the operating system that will be the name authority.

So the first issue we should consider is who assigns the name, the user or the operating system. (See Section 18.3.7 for a discussion of the assignment of unique names.) The operating system will generally assign a name that is convenient for itself, that is, one that is compact and that is easy to resolve. For this reason, an operating system often chooses numerical names. These are sometimes called internal names, with the connotation that their exact contents have no meaning to users. An address is an example of an internal name. Since it is an address in the system's address space, it has no meaning for a user and is just a number. For the operating system, however, such a name is very easy to resolve since it need just be used as an address to find the object or a pointer to the object.

When you open a file in UNIX, you get back a file identifier. This is a small integer (usually in the range 0 to 20 or 30). It has no meaning to the user, but to the system it is an index into the system-maintained, per-process-user open file table.

magic cookie

Such names are not examined by the user but just received, held, and presented back to the operating system when the object needs to be named. Sometimes the whimsical name *magic cookie* is used for such a name. The idea is that the user does not look at the contents of the name, but just uses it as a magic token that represents the object.

dense

Internal names are often integers and are often *dense* in the sense that they are consecutive integers. UNIX open file descriptors are consecutive integers. The advantages of consecutive integers are that they are easy to assign uniquely and it is easy to iterate over all the names.

If the users define the names, they generally choose character strings since they are easy for people to use. Character strings are not compact and generally not assigned densely, so they are not convenient from the system's point of view. But people like them very much, so they are widely used.

18.4.3   GENERATING UNIQUE NAMES

You can have as many files as desired in a directory by using different names. One issue that comes up immediately is how to ensure that the names are unique. The problem of generating unique names comes up frequently in computer systems. For example, a compiler often needs to create a temporary file. What should the file name be? A poor solution to this problem is to depend on the naming scheme of a hierarchical file system. File systems require that names in a single directory be unique, but the same name can be used in different directories and the file system hierarchy ensures that their full names are unique. If we assume there will never be more than one compile going on in a single directory, then we use a special name like **xxcompiletempxx**. One obvious problem is that you have to be sure that no one else uses that name. An ordinary user is very unlikely to use that name, but another compiler might. And are we absolutely sure that we do not want to do two simultaneous compiles in one directory?[8] Assumptions like this are a bad idea since they can cause systems to fail mysteriously, and they are often documented with buried comments in manual pages.

Another solution is to embed a number that is likely to be unique within the directory. For example, you might use the name $\text{TEMP}nnnn$, where $nnnn$ is the process identifier of the process creating the temporary file. The C library has functions that generate unique file names based on this idea. A variant of this idea is to use the current time and embed that in the file name.

All of these methods could, by chance, create a duplicate file name. The only way to be sure a file name is unique is to check if the name exists. Consider the following code:

CREATING A UNIQUE NAME

```
// generate a unique file name
char * name = "tempaaaa"
char * end = &name[7];
```

---

[8] I have run across this problem several times and been irritated at the restriction each time.

```
while( 1 ) {
   if( access(name,F_OK) != 0 ) // Does the file exist?
      break; // No, it is unique.
   while( 1 ) {
      if( *end < 'z') {
         ++(*end);
      } else {
         *end = 'a';
         -- end;
         // loop again to try the next position to the left
      }
   }
}
// "name" does not exist
fid = creat( name, MODE );
```

The problem with this code is that it contains a race condition. There is a delay between the time you check if the file exists and when you create the file with the unique name. UNIX contains a special form of open to deal with this situation. The code then becomes:

CREATING A UNIQUE NAME

```
// generate a unique file name
char * name = "tempaaaa"
while( 1 ) {
   fid = open( name, O_CREAT | O_EXCL, MODE );
   if( fid >= 0 )
      break;
   char * end = &name[7];
   while( 1 ) {
      if( *end < 'z' ) {
         ++(*end);
         break;
      else {
         *end = 'a';
         -- end;
         // loop again to try the next position to the left
      }
   }
}
// file with unique file name "name" has been created
```

The open is handled as an atomic action by the operating system, and so race conditions are avoided.

18.5   UNIFICATION OF CONCEPTS

18.5.1   Overview

Simplify a system by combining two concepts that are similar.

18.5.2   Motivation

We noted that it is common to name devices using the file naming system (see Section 3.5). There is no sense in having two naming mechanisms if one will do and the file naming system can easily be used to name things other than files.

But we took this one step further and unified the concepts of file and device under the concept of an open file that acted as a source or sink for data. Thus we have only one object that is a source of bytes, and that object is an open file. We have unified the concepts of device and file. The UNIX operating system has shown the power of unified concepts like standard input and output and pipelines.

18.5.3   Operating System Examples

Files and Devices   We can unify access to files and devices by accessing both of them using the file interface.

Device Drivers   We unified the interfaces to all block devices into a single block device driver interface. Similarly, the character device drivers all have a single character device driver interface.

Files and Interprocess Communication   We can unify access to files and communication between processes by accessing both of them using the file interface.

Virtual Memory and File I/O   We can access files using the virtual memory system by mapping the file into our virtual address space.

18.5.4   Computer Science Examples

Procedures   When you see two sections of code that are similar, you can often combine them into a single procedure where the parameters of the procedure allow you to change the things that vary between the two sections of code.

Super Classes   When you find two classes that have some commonalities, you can define the common data and methods in a superclass, and each subclass can inherit from it.

The idea of inheritance in object-oriented programming is an example of unification of concepts, and furthermore provides a powerful facility for partial unification. If two classes have anything in common, it can be factored out into a superclass. This way we do not have to fit two classes into exactly the same mold, but have a separate mold for the aspects they do have in common. Inheritance is a powerful technique for finding generalizations via the unification of concepts.

18.5.5   APPLICABILITY

Try to unify concepts whenever:

- Two concepts or interfaces are basically the same, and
- You do not lose functionality by combining them.

Whenever you have two objects in a system that act similarly, you should think about combining them into a single object. This is similar to the idea of procedures in programming. Whenever we see two sequences of statements that look similar, we think about combining them into a procedure. This serves two important purposes. First, code space is saved at a small cost of procedure calls. Second, and most importantly, it serves to identify important and recurring concepts in the system. It helps you to understand the system with fewer concepts. The complexity of the system is reduced, thus making the system more easily understandable. For example, we identified file access and device access as similar and recurring concepts: thus we were able to unify the concepts into the open file concept and so create a simpler system.

18.5.6   CONSEQUENCES

- There is only one concept to learn instead of two, so the system is simpler.
- There is only one concept to implement instead of two.
- The general concept may not exactly fit any of the particular cases, and so they will all be less efficient.

Systems with fewer concepts are easier to learn, use, and implement. Often the unified concept is easier to understand and more natural than any of the concepts it unified. If so, you have found a natural concept in the system.

The danger is trying to do this too much. Some concepts are different and should not be unified. For example, if a procedure has too many parameters, we suspect that we have not found the correct abstraction. If the unified concepts do not fit well, then the generalization will not work.

> Unify concepts with uniform interfaces.

18.5.7 RELATED DESIGN TECHNIQUES

Unification of concepts is a form of *generalization* or *abstraction*.

This is the opposite of *separation of concepts*. In unification of concepts, you have two concepts that do similar things and so can be combined. The combined concept does all the things you could do with either one. In separation of concepts, you have a single concept that comprises two parts. Each part could be used separately.

18.6 SUMMARY

Caching is a technique for trading space for time, and is useful whenever the same long computation is done more than once. Caching saves previous answers and can look them up without redoing the computation. Caching is the basis for many (maybe even most) optimizations.

Hinting is a variation of caching in a dynamic situation where previous answers might become invalid. It requires a method to check whether an answer is correct.

Hierarchical naming is useful in distributed systems. You divide the name up into parts and allow subunits control of subparts of the names. It is a way to ensure unique names with a minimum of central control.

Naming is an important issue in many parts of computer science. A naming system requires a way to assign names to objects and a way to resolve names into the objects they refer to.

Unifying concepts make for simpler systems. We have seen it with files, devices, and IPC. Object-oriented programming uses classes as a means of identifying unified concepts.

18.6.1 TERMINOLOGY

After reading this chapter, you should be familiar with the following terms:

- adjoining name maps
- caching
- compound name
- dense
- dynamic programming
- external name
- flat name space
- graphics context
- hint
- internal name

- magic cookie
- memoizing
- name
- name assignment
- name map
- name resolution
- name space
- name table
- object space
- optimistic algorithm

18.6.2 REVIEW QUESTIONS

The following questions are answered in the text of this chapter:

1. What makes caching work?
2. How does dynamic programming use caching?
3. How does memoizing use caching?
4. What are the differences between caching and hinting?
5. Why are hierarchical names useful?
6. What is the difference between an internal name and an external name? Which is more likely to be a string of characters?
7. Give an example of an adjoined name space. In the context of adjoined directories, what does shadowing mean? Give an example of shadowing.
8. What are the ways you can name an object?
9. How does object-oriented programming implement the unification of concepts?

18.7 PROBLEMS

1. The way that a text processor formats a page depends on what comes before it. For example, the current font is determined by the last command that changes the font. Suppose you have a text formatter that displays interactively the formatted form of the document (almost all of them do this). If we were to scroll up (towards the beginning of the document) and we encounter a font change command, then we have to scan back to the previous font command to find out what the font should be. For example, suppose the font is changed on pages 1, 4, and 15. If we are on page 15, and scroll up past the font change on page 15, we have to scan all the way back to page 4 to determine the correct font on page 14. This is also true of other formatting

states such as: left and right indent, next footnote number, page numbering style, etc. Think of a way to use caching to avoid unbounded scanning backwards in the file when you scroll up.

2. Consider the following recursive procedure to compute Fibonacci numbers:

```
int Fibonacci( int n ) {
    if( n < 2 )
        return n;
    else
      return fibonacci(n-1) + fibonacci(n-2);
}
```

This program is very short and clear, but it is very inefficient because it keeps re-computing the same function values. Change the program to use caching to avoid duplicate computation. *Hint:* Assume that the input n is less than 100.

3. Some file systems keep versions of files (that is, whenever a file is saved, the operating system preserves the previous version and does not store the new version over it). In such a file system, one can go back and access old versions of a file. Compare this with a text editor that keeps a history of all edits and allows you to undo edits. Describe the pros and cons of unifying these two mechanisms.

4. Consider the C++ programming language. What are the corresponding concepts in C++ to the following concepts: name, compound name, name space, object space, name map, flat name space, adjoined name maps, and hierarchical name map. For each one, give as many examples from C++ as you can think of. Is there anything like the example from Section 16.3.4 of name maps in a general graph?

5. Some naming systems *overload* names when they use adjoined name maps. This means that when you use a name, you might mean any of the matching names in all the adjoined name spaces (not just the first name found). Which name is used is decided by the data associated with the name after it is looked up in its name map. How does overloading of names affect the name lookup in adjoined name spaces? Does overloading make sense in a flat name space? Explain your answer.

6. Some naming systems implement *name completion*. This means that if you type a partial name and request name completion, it will give you all possible names in the naming system that start with that partial name. Explain how you would implement name completion in a hierarchical naming system. Explain how you would implement name completion in an adjoined naming system.

7. UNIX mail used to be addressed with a "path name" (that is, a list of machines to go through to get to where you want to go) rather than the hierarchical domain names that are used now. Why would these be easier to implement than hierarchical domain names? What problems would you encounter in implementing hierarchical domain names?

8. Name two places in a computer system where you get to choose names and two places where the operating system (or another program) chooses the names for you.

9. There are several common systems for naming books.

    a. Author–title–publisher–year—For example: E. D. Biggers–Behind That Curtain–Bobbs-Merrill–1928.

    b. Library of Congress—For example: QA76.3 B3412 1991.

    c. Dewey Decimal System—For example: 510.51.

    d. ISBN—For example: 02-43247834.

Compare these various naming systems. Are they flat, two-level, hierarchical, DAGs, or graph structured? Could some of them be considered to be in two or more of these categories? Are the names arbitrary or based on characteristics of the book itself? Are unique names assigned? How is uniqueness assured? Is there a central naming authority? Is there more than one naming authority?

19

Resource Management

We noted in Chapter 1 that there were two ways we could view the operating system, as a virtual machine manager and as a resource manager. In this chapter, we will concentrate on its role as a resource manager, that is, how it keeps track of the resources of the computer system, decides which processes should get to use them, and when they should get to use them.

19.1   RESOURCES IN AN OPERATING SYSTEM

19.1.1   HARDWARE RESOURCES

The presentation so far has been organized around the major resources of an operating system and the operating system subsystems that manage them:

*   *Processors*—Process management system.
*   *Memory*—Memory management system (including virtual memory).
*   *I/O devices*—I/O system.
*   *Disk space*—File system.

There is a major subsystem of the operating system concerned with each resource. We described how each subsystem takes a hardware resource and transforms it into another resource that is improved in one or more ways. These new resources are:

*   *Processes*—The virtualization of the entire computer, including a virtual processor that abstracts the hardware processor.
*   *Virtual memory*—The virtualization of physical memory.
*   *Logical devices*—The virtualization of the physical devices.
*   *Files*—The virtualization of disk space.

These resources are improved versions of the physical resources. (See Figure 19.1.) Processes are easier to use than the physical processors since their instruction set is extended with the system calls which perform a number of useful functions. In addition, there can be any number of processes, but there is only a fixed number of processors. Virtual memory can be larger than the physical memory, and there is a virtual address space for each process. Virtual memory is protected from incorrect use by protection fields in the page tables. Logical devices have uniform interfaces and are easier to use than the physical devices. A logical device can combine several physical devices or represent a part of a physical device. Files are easier to use than disks in terms of commands, naming, and reliability.

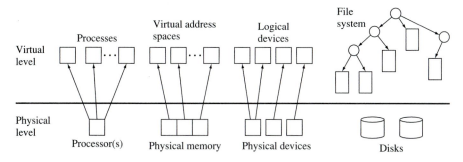

Figure 19.1   Physical and virtual resources in an operating system

19.1.2 SOFTWARE RESOURCES

There are other resources in an operating system that are not directly related to a specific hardware device. For example, the file system might allow a process to open a file with exclusive access, meaning that no other process can open the file until this process closes it. Exclusive access to a file is a resource. A message in a message queue is also a software resource. A process might need to read a message to continue, so the message is a resource.

Similarly, table space is a resource. An operating system might have a process table of fixed size, say 300 slots. This means that only 300 processes can exist in the system, and a process must obtain the process-table-slot resource in order to be created.

We will not look at the scheduling of software resources, but they will come up in our discussion of deadlock and starvation since these phenomena often arise out of competition for software resources.

19.2   RESOURCE MANAGEMENT ISSUES

19.2.1 MODEL OF RESOURCE MANAGEMENT

Figure 19.2 shows the model of resource management that we will be using. At various times in their execution, processes require the use of a resource controlled by an operating system resource manager. It goes through the following steps in using a resource:

1. The process requests the resource.
2. The process waits until the resource can be allocated to it.
3. The resource is allocated to the requesting process.
4. The process uses the resource.
5. The process returns the resource to the resource manager.

These steps are shown with the corresponding numbers in Figure 19.2. This figure also shows the tasks and goals of the resource manager. These will be discussed in the next two sections.

19.2.2 RESOURCE MANAGEMENT TASKS

A resource manager is responsible for a number of tasks.

allocation
- *Allocation*—It assigns resources to processes that need them.

accounting
- *Accounting*—It keeps track of the resources and knows which are free and which process the others are allocated to. It makes sure resources do not get lost or otherwise become unavailable.

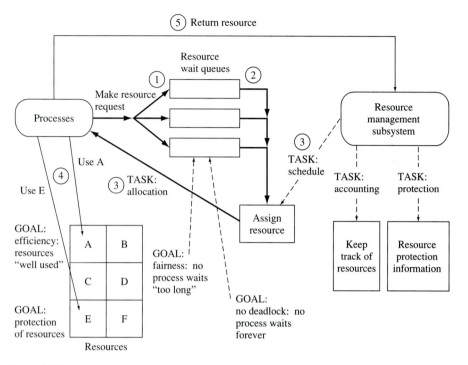

Figure 19.2   Resources in an operating system

- *Scheduling*—It decides which process should get the resource next when it be-   scheduling
  comes free.
- *Protection*—It makes sure that processes can only access a resource when the re-   protection
  source manager allows them to.

These tasks are shown in Figure 19.2.

Allocation and accounting are fairly simple. We will not discuss them in this chapter. Scheduling is the hard part of resource management. By "hard," we mean it is hard to make the right decisions to meet the goals listed in the next section. We have already discussed scheduling in several resource contexts. We will discuss protection later in this chapter.

19.2.3   RESOURCE MANAGEMENT GOALS

A resource manager controls the use of the resource. In doing this, the resource manager has several goals:

- *Efficiency*—The resources should be used as much as possible. A resource   efficiency
  should be used by the process that needs it the most.

- *Fairness*—Processes should get the resources they need.

- No *Deadlock* or *Starvation*—It should not be possible for a process to be blocked forever waiting for a resource.

- *Protection*—A process should not be allowed to access a resource without permission to do so from the resource manager.

These goals are shown in Figure 19.2.

The efficiency goal is somewhat hard to define exactly. Overall, we want processes to progress as quickly as possible. Processes need resources to progress, so we want to allocate resources so that processes can progress as quickly as possible. If we keep each resource as busy as possible, it will accomplish this goal, since processes need each resource for a certain amount of time and the more a resource is used the more processes will get their share.

Fairness is a notion that often conflicts with efficiency. Fairness means that all processes progress evenly so that no process is excluded. However, it might make sense to exclude a process that requires all of the memory, since then no other process can make progress.

The ultimate in unfairness is when a process never gets to finish, and that is the result of deadlock. Starvation causes a process to take a very long time and is also unfair. We separate out these two phenomena as extreme cases of unfairness.

We want to ensure that no process uses a resource unless the resource manager allows it to. If this is possible, then none of the other goals can be ensured. In addition, a process uses resources, and we want to ensure that no process can harm another process by obstructing its use of resources.

19.3   TYPES OF RESOURCES

19.3.1.   CONSUMABLE RESOURCES AND CAPITAL

The word "resource" is also used in economics, but there it has a somewhat different meaning. In economics, resources are *consumable*, meaning that when they are used, they are used up, and cannot (easily) be used again. Examples of resources are: timber, steel, oil, titanium, etc.[1] Resources like machine tools, factories, trucks, buildings, etc., are called *capital* in economics. The production process does not use them up, although they do wear out slowly.

The resources we have talked about are more like economic capital. When a process is done, we can use its memory and disk space over again and let another process use the processor and the I/O devices. None of the physical resources managed by an operating system is consumable,[2] but there are logical resources that are

---

[1] Of course, some of these resources are not literally used up and can be recycled. Some, like oil and natural gas, are actually used up.

[2] A possible exception is in portable computers, where the operating system might do power management to conserve battery power.

consumable. Messages, for example, are a resource in that a process may need to receive a message in order to continue processing. Once a message is read, it is gone and cannot be read again, so it is a consumable resource.

Capital resources are harder to manage than consumable resources, since you have to reclaim them and keep track of them, even after you have allocated them.

19.3.2 PREEMPTION OF RESOURCES

Time multiplexing a resource means that you switch it between two processes from time to time, but, at any one time, one process has complete control of the resource. One interesting question is when to switch the resource between processes. The simplest way to do it is to wait until one process is done with the resource, and then it is given to the next process. One would handle a printer this way, for example. When you use a printer, you print your whole document. You do not allow two processes to share a printer and alternate lines or pages—the output would be hopelessly mixed up.

Another possibility is to *preempt* the resource, that is, simply take a resource back from one process, even though the process has not finished using the resource, and give it to another process. The problem is that most resources have a "state" which the process using the resource depends on. When a resource is preempted, it is necessary to save the state of the resource so it can be restored when the resource is returned to the process it is being taken away from.

For example, when a process makes a system call, we switch the processor to another process. Before we do this, though, we save the current processor state in the process's save area. When the processor is given back to the process, the processor state is loaded back into the processor. The cost of saving and restoring state is the cost of preemption. The cost of preempting a processor is small. It consists of saving or loading a few dozen registers.

Since it is cheap to preempt a processor, we can afford to do it a lot. Typically, the processor is switched between processes many times a second. On the other hand, if the cost of preemption is high, then it may not be worth it to try to preempt the resource. Take main memory, for instance. The state of memory is its contents. In order to save the state, we would have to write out all the memory to disk, and then read it back in again to restore the state. This could take a lot of time. In fact, memory is preempted in this way, as we saw in Chapter 11, but one must do it very carefully to avoid unacceptably high overheads.

Another example is a tape drive. The state of the tape drive consists of which tape is in the tape drive and where on the tape it is going to be read or write next. For example, suppose the system is doing backups of user files on a cartridge tape when a user wishes to use the tape drive to load in a software package. We would have to eject the tape, have the operator remove it, and insert the new tape in order to switch contexts on the tape drive. This would take several seconds, a long time by computer standards. When the user finished, it would have to redo all these things. Clearly, this will not usually be worth the trouble—the cost of preemption is generally too high for tape drives.

> Preemption allows a resource to be switched between two processes so both can use it more or less at the same time.

19.4   INTEGRATED SCHEDULING

We have seen scheduling several times before in our discussion of the main subsystems of an operating system. In the simple operating system, we used round-robin scheduling where a process got to run until it made a system call or its time slice expired, and then the next (ready) process got to run. We looked at a number of processor scheduling methods in Chapter 8. In Chapters 10 and 11, we looked at swapping, which requires the scheduling of main memory. Virtual memory page replacement algorithms are also scheduling memory, but at a smaller resolution (a page instead of a whole process). We also looked at load control, which schedules processes into memory. Finally, in Chapter 15, we looked at the scheduling of disk heads to give the best service to disk transfer requests.

So a process will be served by several schedulers while it is running (see Figure 19.3). The memory scheduler decides which processes are resident in memory. The processor scheduler decides which processes are actively using a processor. The virtual memory scheduler decides which pages a process gets. The disk scheduler decides when a process's disk requests are served. Other I/O schedulers decide when a process can use various I/O devices.

Since all these schedulers are scheduling the same process and have some of the same goals, it would make sense for them to work together. In fact, we have seen some cooperation between schedulers. The virtual memory load-control mechanism works with the page replacement algorithm to be sure that memory is not overloaded. But beyond that, there is little coordination between schedulers in an operating system. There are several reasons why this is so.

The first reason is that the combined scheduling problem is quite complicated to solve, and most operating system designers do not want to go to that much trouble.

The second reason is that the expected gain is not that great anyway. Each scheduler locally optimizes the use of its resource, and the overall global effect is not bad in most cases.

The third reason is that the memory resource dominates the overall efficiency of the system. I/O scheduling is not really that important because processes do not wait for I/O devices much. I/O inefficiencies are concentrated in how you use the I/O device once you have control over it, and this is not a scheduling issue. Modern processors are very fast and are not generally that busy. Again, the large gains are in making a single process run faster, not in scheduling multiple processes. The real bottleneck is memory. There is never enough memory, and there are lots of useful things you can

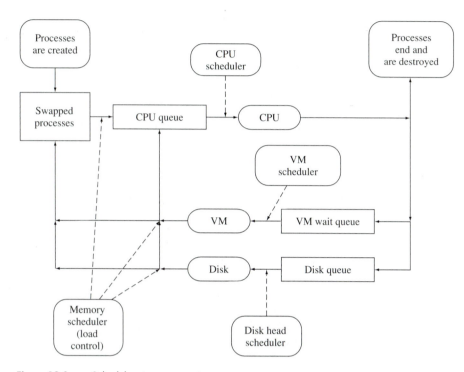

Figure 19.3   Schedulers in an operating system

do with extra memory (RAM disks, disk cache, trade time for space in an algorithm, etc.). The most critical scheduling task is that of scheduling memory, and that is done pretty well by the page replacement algorithm and the load control algorithm.

The fourth reason is that the trend these days is for more distributed systems, where the resources (and their schedulers) are distributed over a number of machines. This distribution makes central, integrated scheduling complex and unattractive. In these cases, local optimization of the use of a single resource is the best course.

19.5   QUEUING MODELS OF SCHEDULING

The scheduling problem can be characterized by a system of customers, servers, and queues (of customers). The terminology of "customer" is taken from the lines in stores. In the operating systems case, processes are "customers." Customers enter the system and are placed on a queue. When a server is free, it chooses a customer. The mathematical model of scheduling as a system of queues has been extensively studied and can be solved for many common cases. We will look at the model and some of the results that have been obtained.

We will start with the simplest form of the model, where there is one queue and one server and no preemption. Figure 19.4 shows the model. There are three parameters that

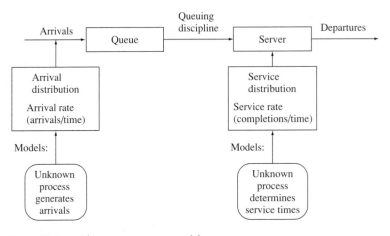

Figure 19.4   The queuing system model

must be provided for a specific instance of the model. They are:

- *Arrival distribution*—Including the arrival rate (the average number of arrivals per time period).
- *Service time distribution*—Including the service rate (the average number of customers serviced per time period).
- *Queuing discipline*—Often first-come, first-served.

Customers arrive from outside the modeled system, so we do not show the process by which they arrive. So we model customer arrivals with a probability distribution. Similarly, we do not know how customers are served, but instead give a probability distribution for the service times. Some possible probability distributions are:

- *Uniform*—There is a maximum and minimum, and each value in between is equally likely.
- *Exponential*—The probability of an interarrival time of x is $\lambda e^{-\lambda x}$. The parameter, λ, is the mean of the interarrival times.
- *Normal*—Interarrival times follow a normal (bell-shaped) distribution.

Figure 19.5 shows the three distributions. The horizontal axis of each graph is the interarrival time, that is, the expected time between two successive arrivals. The vertical axis is the probability of that interarrival time. The probability is 1 that an arrival will arrive some time, so the area under each curve must equal 1.

It turns out that the exponential distribution is the easiest to work with mathematically, and is also a reasonably accurate estimate of interarrival times and service times. So we have to specify the arrival rate (in arrivals per second) or the mean interarrival time (in seconds per arrival), and the service rate or service time.

We normally use a FIFO queuing discipline. Such a queue is called an $M/M/1$ queue (exponential arrival and service times, one server), and we specify two

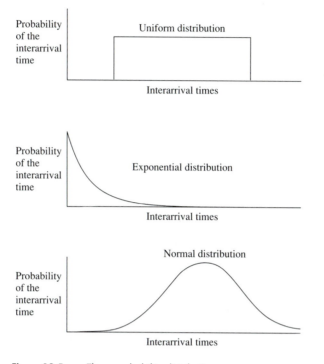

Figure 19.5   Three probability distributions

parameters: μ (the arrival rate in arrivals per second) and λ (the service rate in service completions per second). The ratio $\mu/\lambda = \rho$ is the load factor of the system.[3] ρ is the arrival rate divided by the service rate, and so if $\rho > 1$, then customers are arriving faster than they can be served. Such a queuing system is unstable, and the length of the wait queue and the average waiting time both will grow without bound.

$M/M/1$ system with $\rho < 1$ will stabilize, and we can predict the average time a customer will have to wait.[4] One might think that, since the service rate is faster than the arrival rate, customers would never have to wait, but this would only be true if customers arrived at a constant, steady rate. In reality, customer arrivals are not predictable, and often a clump of customers will arrive close together and so some will have to wait. At other times, there will be no customers and the server will be idle.

Mathematicians have analyzed $M/M/1$ queuing systems and found that the expected number of customers in the system (including the customer being served) is

$$N = \frac{\rho}{1 - \rho}$$

---

[3]Note that since μ and λ both have the same units, their ratio ρ is a dimensionless number.
[4]If $\rho = 1$, we also have an unstable system, and the average queue length and average wait time will grow without bound.

and the average time in the system (the sum of the waiting time and the service time) is

$$T = \frac{N}{\lambda}$$

The most interesting thing about these results is not the exact numbers they give in specific situations, but the general insights they give about how this queuing system acts. If ρ is close to one, then the average queue length

$$N = \frac{\rho}{1 - \rho}$$

saturated

will have a small denominator, and so N will get large. Figure 19.6 shows how the average line length grows as ρ approaches 1. A queuing system with ρ close to 1 is said to be *saturated.* A saturated system can be characterized as a system very sensitive to small changes in the load. If goes up even a little bit, the average wait time might go up a large amount. For example, if $\rho = 0.98$, the average queue length is 49. If $\rho = 0.99$, the average queue length is 99, more than double. A 1 percent increase in load doubles the queue length. The insight here is that it is not wise to run systems at close to their maximum capacity. Such systems will be unstable and unpredictable.

Little's Law

A useful result is *Little's Law,* which says that

$$N = \lambda T$$

where N is the total number of customers in the system, λ is the mean number of arrivals per second, and T is the average time a customer spends in the system. Little's Law is true for a wide range of queuing systems (not just $M/M/1$ systems). In fact, it is true for a wide range of systems where things arrive, stay a while in the system, and then leave. If the system is in balance and the number of customers in the system

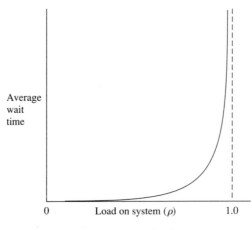

Figure 19.6   Waiting time as load increases

remains constant, then the arrival rate and the departure rate will be the same, and so either can be used in Little's Law.

Little's Law is basically intuitive, but it has many interesting applications. Suppose you are waiting in line in a restaurant that you figure holds 100 people, the average diner spends two hours in the restaurant, and there are 25 people waiting ahead of you. By Little's Law, the departure rate is 50 people an hour since

$$100 \ people = 50 \ \frac{people}{hour} \times 2 \ hours$$

so you can expect to wait about 30 minutes.

Suppose we wanted to estimate how many people died every year in a city that has a population of about one million. We assume that the city is a closed system with the same population(it changes so slowly that this is a reasonable assumption), and that the average person lives 70 years. So the average time in the system is 70 years, and if the system is in a stable state, then the arrival (birth) rate is the same as the departure (death) rate. So:

$$DeathRate \times AverageTimeInSystem = NumberInSystem$$

or

$$DeathRate \times 70 = 1,000,000$$

So the expected death rate is $1,000,000/70$, or about 14,000 people a year.

19.6   REAL-TIME OPERATING SYSTEMS

There are certain systems where a computer controls a process that is extremely time-sensitive, in that responses by the computer must be on time. Here are some examples:

- A computer is controlling the filling of a container. When the "container-is-nearly-full" interrupt comes, the computer must turn off the flow before the container overflows.

- A computer is controlling a screen used by an air traffic controller. When information comes in that shows an impending collision, the information must be shown to the air traffic controller in time to prevent the collision.

- A computer is reading data from a communication line, and the characters come at the rate of 500 characters a second. If the computer does not read a character from the line in time, it will be replaced by the next character and lost.

In general, a system is real-time when it is interacting with a real-world process that will move at a certain rate, and the system must match its speed to the speed of the process. Usually, a late response is of no use at all; the damage is already done.

An operating system that can handle real-time systems is called a *real-time operating system.* A real-time operating system must have a scheduling algorithm that ensures that responses to events happen on time. We can no longer depend on average response times since every response must be on time, so the scheduling algorithms we have considered so far will not be adequate for real-time systems.

Traditionally, such operating systems have used a deterministic scheduling system where each process has a guaranteed, fixed time slot. Let's look at an example. Suppose we are controlling four real-time processes.

- Process A needs 10 ms of processor time every 100 ms.
- Process B needs 10 ms of processor time every 100 ms.
- Process C needs 10 ms of processor time every 20 ms.
- Process D needs 20 ms of processor time every 100 ms.

We divide every 100 ms into 10 slots (0, 10, 20, 30, 40, 50, 60, 70, 80, and 90) and assign each slot to one of the processes as follows:

- Process A gets slot 0.
- Process B gets slot 40.
- Process C gets slots 10, 30, 50, 70 and 90.
- Process D gets slots 60 and 80.

Figure 19.7 shows the schedule.

This example shows you the idea. Each process has two parameters: the *duty cycle,* which is the time period in which it must respond to an event, and the *time required,* which is the maximum amount of time it will require to respond to an event. We guarantee the response times by using fixed allocation. A process gets the time it needs in every duty cycle.

It may take some calculation to come up with a schedule for an arbitrary set of processes, but there are algorithms to compute these schedules.

A real-time process cannot afford to wait for resources since it is working on a fixed schedule, so a real-time system must have enough resources (including processor time) to meet the maximum demand. The simplest way to ensure this is not

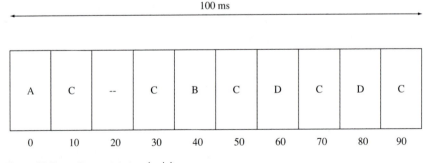

Figure 19.7   Deterministic scheduling

to share resources at all, but to have a permanent, fixed allocation of resources to processes.

Recent work has shown that it is possible to use more efficient nondeterministic scheduling algorithms and still ensure that all real-time demands are met. This is called rate-monotonic scheduling (Stankovic et al. 1995).

19.7   PROTECTION OF RESOURCES

In the previous chapters, we were concerned with showing how an operating system can provide services to user processes in the form of access to resources (both physical and virtual). In this chapter, we have looked at scheduling of resources where the operating system might withhold resources from a process until its turn comes up. Now we are going to talk about how the operating system will protect its resources from unauthorized use.

19.7.1   USERS AND PROCESSES

Up to now, the main active entities in a computer system were user processes (or threads) which caused things to happen by making system calls. Of course, user processes do not spring into existence on their own. There are people we usually call *users* who initiate user processes. It is the users whose interests and data we want to protect, and the user processes are acting as their agents. So while a user cannot really do much in a computer system except through a user process, we will sometimes talk about the user doing something and mean the user's process is doing something.

19.7.2   THE IMPORTANCE OF PROTECTION OF RESOURCES

The operating system must protect itself from interference by users, and it must protect users from each other. The operating system is in charge of managing the resources of the computer system. This means it decides who gets to use the resources and when. In order to do this, it must keep control of the resources and not allow them to be used without the approval of the operating system. The operating system must protect itself from damage so it can continue providing service to the users. In addition, the operating system must protect the interests of the users. This means that one user's processes should not be able to perform operations on other users' processes or data unless specifically authorized to do so.

19.7.3   RESOURCES THAT NEED PROTECTING

The resources of a computer system can be divided into two levels, hardware resources and software resources.

Hardware Resources   The hardware resources are the ones we have been discussing throughout the book:

- Processor
- Memory
- I/O Devices
- Disks.

We want to share the processor fairly, so each process gets its fair share. We want to protect the memory so that one process cannot read, write, or execute in the memory of another process (or the operating system) unless such sharing is explicitly allowed by the process. We want to be sure that a process has access to an I/O device (such as a terminal) only when it is allowed to by the operating system, and it is not allowed to interfere with other users' use of the I/O device. Finally, we separate out disks as a special case of an I/O device because that is where user files are kept. We want to make sure each user has a fair share of the disk, and that the information on the disk is protected from unauthorized destruction, modification, or disclosure.

Software Resources   The usual protection strategy used in an operating system is to protect the hardware resources by not allowing user processes direct access to them at all. Instead, they are given access to the virtualized versions of them (software resources). We discussed virtualization in Chapter 1 as a way of giving the user an improved environment to work in. Now we see it has another benefit because the virtual resources can be used to protect the hardware resources.

The software resources we are talking about are the virtualizations of the hardware resources, plus some other operating system resources that have no direct hardware equivalent:

- Processes.
- Virtual memory.
- Logical devices.
- Files.
- IPC objects: semaphores, message queues, ports.
- Shared memory.

19.7.4   WHAT WE ARE PROTECTING AGAINST

There are four types of protection failure that can happen to the resources in a computer system and that we would like to prevent:

1. *Unauthorized disclosure of information.* Information that is private is revealed to someone who is not authorized to have the information.

2. *Unauthorized modification of information.* Information is changed by someone who is not authorized to change the information. This includes: loss of data, modification of data, and falsification of data.

3. *Denial of service.* People who are authorized to use the computer are prevented from doing so. This includes: interruption of service, denial of service, slowing down of service.

4. *Unauthorized use of service.* People who are not authorized to use the service do anyway.

The first two problems have to do with the information in the computer system, and the second two problems have to do with the computing service itself.

19.7.5   AUTHORIZATION

In the previous section, we used the words "authorized" and "unauthorized" several times. The protection system will not prevent all processes from performing any operations. Each process is allowed to do some things (read some files, access its own memory, write to its own window, etc.), and it not allowed to do some things (write most other users' files, access the memory of other processes, write other processes' windows, etc.). The protection system will maintain a database of information that records the objects each user can access and what operations can be performed on them. For example, for each file, information is kept about who can read it, who can write it, and who can execute it. The job of the protection system is to enforce these constraints, that is, to allow authorized actions and to prevent unauthorized actions.

19.7.6   AUTHENTICATION

An authorization says that a certain user can perform certain operations on an object. An important part of protection is determining whether a user is really who she says she is. We call this process *authentication*. By far the most common method of authentication is a password system. A user signs on and claims to be a certain user, and proves this claim by providing a password that only that user should know. Each user is provided with an initial password, and users can normally change passwords at any time. For higher security, we sometime require that a user present a badge or key in addition to a password. For example, bank teller machines require a card with a magnetic strip and a password (called a PIN).

authentication

19.7.7   SECURITY AND PROTECTION ANALOGIES

In order to motivate how security and protection are implemented in operating systems, we can talk about security and protection in day-to-day life. Most people (these days) lock their houses when they are gone. Why do they do this? Because they do not want people getting into the house. What undesirable things happen when unauthorized people get into your house? They might steal things. This is the same as destroying things since you no longer have the use of them. They might also use up resources. For example, they might eat your food, use your hot water, make calls on your telephone, etc. These things will cost you money. They might look in your files and discover confidential information such as your credit card PIN number, your income tax returns, personal letters, etc.

There are several methods people use to prevent these things from happening. First, there is physical security. People use fences and walls to keep people out. They use locks on doors that are necessary to let some people in and out. The might have a guard to prevent unauthorized people from entering.

Imagine an office building with guards in the lobby who check everyone who tries to enter the building. The guards recognize some people on sight and allow them to enter. People they don't recognize must have badges. Once inside the building, all the offices have doors with locks, and so only people with keys can enter. Inside the offices, some doors have combination locks that require you to enter a combination on a keypad. Some offices will have safes that require a combination. Some safes might even require a key and a combination to open. All of these mechanisms (walls, doors, steel safes, alarms) serve to *authenticate* who the person is and whether she is one of the people who are allowed to enter the building. A person is shown to be authorized to enter by several methods. It might be related to the person herself (the guard recognized her), or something the person has (a badge or a key), or something a person knows (a combination). Sometimes two of these things are required (a key and a combination). These various techniques are used to authenticate people and give them access to offices, rooms, safes, etc.

Computer security is structured in a similar manner. The computer system has the equivalent of walls, doors, safes, and alarms that prevent people from getting access to computer resources without being authorized to do so. Authentication is done by something the person knows (a password) or something they have (a badge or card containing a microprocessor). Computer systems cannot reliably recognize faces and so that is not used as a method of authentication, but a few experimental systems will authenticate a user by hand geometry or retinal patterns.

Computer systems have protection mechanisms so that people will not use their resources in unauthorized ways. A person's files should be private. It should not be possible for someone else to read those files if the owner does not want them to. Also, other people should not be able to change existing files, add new files, or delete files unless the owner allows them to. A person should have an account on a system in order to use it, and should not be able to run programs or print documents unless they are authorized to do so.

19.7.8   GENERAL STRATEGY FOR PROTECTION

The first step in a protection system is to authenticate all users. This is usually done with a login process and typically requires a password. All processes initialized by the user or his processes are designed as acting for that user, and so have the privileges that user has (or maybe some subset of them).

The hardware itself provides protection mechanisms that can be used by the operating system to prevent direct access to the hardware resources. This means that a user process can only use the software resources provided by the system. The software (or virtual) resources can only be accessed through system calls. So it is necessary to add a processing step to each system call that verifies that the process making the system call is allowed to perform this operation on this object. The hardware protection ensures that all accesses to resources must go through these software checks.

19.7.9 PARTS OF A PROTECTION SYSTEM

The hardware protection mechanisms allow the operating system to prevent unauthorized access to hardware resources, so the only way they can be violated is by a process making system calls (e.g., open file, read file, remove file, etc.) to perform operations that they are not authorized to perform. The operating system provides certain logical objects (files, message queues, semaphores, threads, processes, shared memory, private memory, logical devices, etc.) and a set of operations on each object. A system call is a request by the process to perform some operation on some logical object. To provide protection, we need to do four things.

- First, we have to be able to know for certain which user each process represents.
- Second, we need to be sure that a process cannot affect any physical resource except by a system call that requests an operation on a logical object that is the logical version of that physical resource.
- Third, we need to keep information about what operations each user can perform on each logical object.
- Fourth, we need to be sure that the operating system code implementing each system call checks to be sure that the requested operation is an allowed operation on that object by that user.

The first point is the authentication problem. The second point is handled by hardware protection. The third point is the representation of protection information. The fourth point is the software protection mechanism. In the following sections, we will discuss each of these points in more detail.

19.8   USER AUTHENTICATION

In this section, we will look more closely at authentication and the various ways of authenticating a user.

19.8.1 PASSWORDS

Passwords are by far the most common method of user authentication, but they have some problems. If someone else finds out your password, then they can masquerade as you. There are two ways someone could find out your password: either they could discover it by some means, or they could guess it.

If you write down a password, then there is a possibility then someone will discover it. As a consequence, people are always admonished not to write down their password. But, if the password is hard to remember, then you are tempted to write it down. One "solution" is to use something that is easy to remember, like the name of your dog or the street you live on. But if you use a password like this, then it would be easy for someone to guess your password by trying the words they think you would find easy to remember. Many passwords have been guessed in this manner.

Many systems do not allow you to set your own password, but instead assign you a password. This makes it hard to guess, but also makes it hard to remember. One partial solution is to make the passwords *pronounceable,* that is, to form them according to the ways that regular English words are formed. The resulting passwords are nonsense, but nonsense that looks like English words.[5]

The second way a password could be obtained is to guess it by trying lots of different passwords until you guess the right one. The easiest way to do this is to guess words the person is likely to use. Then you only have to try maybe a few dozen potential passwords.

A more exhaustive approach might try all the words in the dictionary. Of course, this involves trying hundreds of thousands of potential passwords. Many systems will give you just three chances to sign on, and if you don't get the password right, they will drop the connection or otherwise cause some lengthy delay. This prevents people from trying passwords too quickly, and makes it less likely that a lengthy guessing attack will work.

In UNIX, however, the password guessing attack is more likely to work because the password file can be read by anyone, and contains all the passwords in encrypted form.

19.8.2 SYSTEM AUTHENTICATION

We have seen that it is necessary for the user to authenticate himself or herself to the operating system, but it is also sometimes necessary for the system to authenticate itself to the user. Let's look at an example to see why. Say you have a public room where people can use terminals to access the system. When you walk up to a terminal, it is displaying a login message or window, and you enter your user name and password. Suppose someone wrote a program that displays an exact copy of the system login message or window. They could start that program, and then leave the terminal. Someone else coming in later would think it was the system's login message, and enter their user name and password. The program could then save the user name and password, and then log the person in. Or, the program could just exit and the user would just think something had gone wrong and log in again.

The problem here is that the system did not authenticate itself to the user.

19.8.3 OTHER METHODS OF AUTHENTICATION

How do you know a person is who he says he is? There are three general approaches:

- Verify that a person knows some piece of information (such as a password).

---

[5]Of course, it could be French or Spanish also, but each language would have different rules about what words should look like. So the password generator would have to know your native language.

- Verify that a person has some object (such as a badge).
- Verify that a person has some physical characteristic (such as fingerprints).

We can base authentication on any of these methods or a combination of two or three. When you use an automatic teller machine, it authenticates you by something you have (your bank card) and something you know (your password or personal identification number (PIN)). You need both to use the automatic teller.

19.8.4 PASSWORD VARIANTS

We have mentioned various problems with passwords. There are variations on the password idea that are more secure. Basically, the password method of authentication is one that verifies that the person has certain information. But this information need not be only a fixed password. Maybe the information is a simple mathematical formula. For example, suppose the formula the person has to remember is $3 \times x - 12$. The system will provide a random number, say 62, and the person will respond with 174 ($= 3 \times 62 - 12$). We could expand on this method of "challenge and response" by having a large number of facts about the person. When the person tried to log in, the system could pick a random question to ask from the stock of questions for this person.

Another password variant is *one-time passwords*. These are safer because they are only used once. One-time passwords normally involve "smart" cards that can do the computations for you.

one-time password

19.8.5 IDENTIFYING OBJECTS

Another approach is to verify that a person has a certain object. This might be a badge, a card with a magnetic stripe of information, a "smart card" which contains a microprocessor and memory, a key, etc.

The problem is that such objects can be lost or stolen. A common solution is to combine something you have with something you know. As we observed, you need a cash card and a PIN number to obtain cash from an automatic teller.

19.8.6 IDENTIFYING A PERSON

Authentication can be based on the physical characteristics of the person wishing to be authenticated. This method is used when a guard recognizes you and allows you in. Automated methods include checking fingerprints, voice prints, the dynamics of how you sign your name, the pattern of blood vessels in your retina, the geometry of your hand, etc.

19.9 MECHANISMS FOR PROTECTING HARDWARE RESOURCES

Hardware mechanisms built into processors allow the operating system to keep control of and protect all of the hardware resources of the system. The primary mechanism provided for this is instruction protection, that is, preventing a process from executing certain instructions.

19.9.1 PROCESSOR MODES

A typical processor can run in two *processor modes:* system mode or user mode. In *system mode* (also called supervisor mode and privileged mode), all instructions are allowed. In *user mode,* any instruction that is used in the management of system resources is not allowed. If the process attempts to execute a privileged instruction in user mode, a protection interrupt is generated, the instruction is not executed, and the process is terminated. These are often called *privileged instructions.* Typical examples of privileged instructions are:

- Any instruction that changes the processor mode—This includes instructions that write directly into the mode bit in the processor status word, and the return from interrupt instruction.

- Memory management instructions—This includes instructions that set the page table base or the TLB.

- Timer instructions—This includes instructions that affect the operation of the hardware timer.

- Instructions that set other important hardware registers—This includes such registers as the one that sets the base for the interrupt vectors.

The basis of all hardware protection is the processor mode, so it is necessary to ensure that a user process cannot get into system mode. So any instruction that changes the mode must be protected. One exception to this is the system call or trap instruction. This instruction causes an interrupt which changes the processor mode to system mode and enters the operating system. This is allowed because it is a controlled entry into system mode. You must execute the operating system's system call handler, and so it cannot be used by a user process to execute its own code in system mode.

The processor mode is the basic hardware protection mechanism. It can be used to protect the resources of the system:

1. The processor mode itself;

2. The memory;

3. The processor; and

4. The I/O devices.

19.9.2 PROTECTING HARDWARE RESOURCES

The processor mode is the basic mechanism for hardware protection. In addition, there are other mechanisms that protect specific hardware resources.

Processor Protection   User processes are given direct access to the processor for executing instructions. If a user process goes into an infinite loop, then it will never release the processor back to the operating system. Operating systems use timers to prevent this. Before the operating system gives the processor to a user process, it will set the hardware timer for the timeout period (say 20 milliseconds). If the user process has not given up the processor during that period (via a system call), then the timer will interrupt it, and the interrupt will give control of the processor back to the operating system.

Memory Protection   Memory is protected by the protection bits in the page table entries. When the operating system sets up the page table for a process, it will only allow it access to its own memory. Instructions are marked as execute only, and some data is read only. This is done to help the process find internal errors (not for protection purposes). If two processes agree, then the operating system can set up their pages tables so that they share some of their memory.

The page tables themselves must be in the operating system's memory and not writable by any user process. This will prevent the user process from changing the memory protection for itself or another process. The hardware register that points to the page table must be protected or a user process could change its page table and get access to memory it should not have access to. If there are instructions that change the TLB, these have to be protected also, since they could be used to subvert memory management. This is the case in machines which use an inverted page table and have the operating system manage the TLB.

Device Protection   User processes should not be able to access any device they want. If the hardware has special I/O instructions, then these are privileged. More commonly, the devices are accessed through the device registers which are in the physical address space. The operating system will not normally provide any process access to the device registers, but instead will allow indirect access through system calls. For maximum speed, it may be desirable to allow a user process access to a device. This can be done by mapping the device registers of just that one device into the address space of the process. This allows the user process to do anything it wants with that one device.

Disk Protection   The disks are devices and are protected like all other devices. Access to the device registers of disks that have user file systems should never be given to a user process.

19.10   REPRESENTATION OF PROTECTION INFORMATION

In an operating system, we will have a collection of *objects* that we are protecting (these are the resources). For each object, there will be a set of *operations* that can be performed on that object. The *subjects* are the active entities that attempt to perform these operations on the objects. The subjects will be processes or threads. In order to perform a specific operation on a specific object, a subject must have a *right* (also called a *permission* or a *privilege*) to perform that operation on that object.

object
operation
subject

right
permission
privilege

19.10.1   OBJECT TYPES

There are several kinds of objects in an operating system:

- Processes (and threads if they are supported).
- Message queues (and other forms of IPC).
- Areas of memory (physical and virtual).
- Devices (physical and logical).
- Files (and directories).

19.10.2   OPERATIONS ON OBJECTS

Each object has several operations:

- *Processes:*
    - Create a process.
    - Terminate a process.
    - Read a process's memory.
    - Write a process's memory.
    - Send a message to a process.
    - Otherwise control a process (stop it, start it, send it an interrupt, etc.).
- *Message queues:*
    - Create a message queue.
    - Destroy a message queue.
    - Send a message to a queue.
    - Receive a message from a queue.
- *Areas of memory:*
    - Allocate an area of memory.
    - Free an area of memory.
    - Read from an area of memory.
    - Execute code from an area of memory.
    - Write to an area of memory.
- *Devices:*
    - Read from a device.
    - Write to a device.
    - Control a device (rewind, power down, change paper tray, etc.).
- *Files:*
    - Create a file.
    - Destroy a file.
    - Read a file.

-Write a file.

-Append to a file.

-Execute a file as a program.

Threads will have a set of operations similar to those of processes. Other forms of IPC (pipes and RPC) have operations similar to those on message queues. Pipes are often protected in the same way as files, and have the same operations.

19.10.3   THE PROTECTION DATABASE

The operating system must maintain data about what rights subjects have, that is, information about what operations each subject can perform on each object. We will call this the *protection database*. This information is not usually kept in one place, but kept in pieces around the system. The two most likely places to keep this information are with the subjects or with the objects. Each subject could have a list of all the objects it can use and what operations it can perform on them. This is called a *capability list*. Or each object could have an associated list that lists all the subjects that can access to the object and the operations they can perform on the object. This is called an *access control list*. Most systems use a combination of capability lists and access control lists.

protection database

capability list

access control list

19.10.4   ACCESS CONTROL LISTS

The most popular method of keeping protection information is the access control list. An access control list is a list of access control entries that is attached to an object. Each access control entry specifies a particular user or group of users and the operations they can perform on the object.

For example, suppose the object is file `PackageList`. There are five users: Alice, Brad, Cynthia, Devon, and Ella. Alice, Brad, and Cynthia are in the group SystemGroup. Here is an example access control list for the file `PackageList`.

1. User: Ella. Operations: Read, Write.

2. User: Brad. Operations: None.

3. Group: SystemGroup. Operations: Read.

Alice and Cynthia will be able to read the file because they are in the SystemGroup. Brad cannot read the file, even though he is in the SystemGroup, because there is a specific entry indicating that he cannot perform any operations, and that entry occurs before the entry for SystemGroup in the access control list. Devon cannot perform any operations because he is not listed in any access control entry. Ella can read and write the file, because she is listed in an access control entry with those operations.

Any security policy can be implemented with the access control list mechanism. In addition, the concept of an access control list is simple to understand, and it is easy to achieve the effects you want.

The only problem with access control lists is that it is tedious to specify an access control list for every object you create. The solution to that problem is to have a default access control list that is used as the initial access control list for an object, that is, a copy of the default list is used. If that is not quite right, then the creator of the object can modify the copy of the default list used initially.

19.10.5 CAPABILITY LISTS

A capability list contains some or all of the rights a process has. When a process wants to perform an operation, it will present a capability along with the operation request. You can think of a capability as a ticket. Suppose you are given a free pass to an amusement park. The ticket allows you to go to the park any time you want. Similarly, a capability allows you to perform any of a set of operations on a specific object.

Whereas access control lists are kept with the object and record who can access the object, capabilities are kept with the subject and record which objects the subject can access.

The page table of a process can be thought of as a capability list. It is a set of capabilities that allow the process to access certain pages in memory (and in the swap area on disk). Some of these are read-only capabilities, some are read-write, some are execute-only, etc. If some of these pages map into the device registers of devices, then they are capabilities to use that device.

Pure capability systems are unusual. There have been a few machines that use capabilities, but none of them has been widely used. Capabilities are more commonly used as a cache for information in access control lists.

19.10.6 MODIFYING THE PROTECTION DATABASE

Suppose a user creates a new file that she wants everyone to be able to read but that only she is able to write. This is easily expressed in an access control list with one entry for her and another entry for everyone else. This is much harder to express with capability lists. You would have to go to each user and add the capability to use that file to their capability list. This is a lot of work and not really a feasible solution.

But it is natural that access control lists would be good for adding new objects, since they are kept with each object. What if we want to add a new subject? This is also hard with capabilities, since you have to find all the objects that it should have access to and create a capability for each one. Adding a new subject is easier with access control lists, because they allow access control entries with wild card entries for subjects (like an entry for "all subjects"). This means that new subjects automatically get that access.

The difference is that we have not shown a way to use wild cards with capabilities. It is possible to develop such a system with capabilities, but it would be a lot of trouble.

Another problem with capabilities is the ability to revoke a capability. Suppose you wanted to revoke access to a file for a certain class of users. You would have to go to each user and remove the capability. This might be difficult if the operating system was running over a network and some of the nodes were down. With an access control list, you just have to change one entry.

For these reasons, capabilities are not widely used.

19.10.7 PROTECTION DOMAINS

Up to now, we have been associating capabilities directly with a user. That is, each user has a specific set of things he is allowed to do, and this does not change rapidly. All processes run by a user will inherit this set of capabilities. We will call a set of capabilities a *protection domain*. In these terms, each user has a protection domain, and all processes initiated by the user will have the same protection domain.

protection domain

But this model is too narrow for a full protection model. In military security, they often handle things on a "need-to-know" basis, that is, each person only knows what she needs to know to do her job. Obviously, she cannot know less or she would not be able to do her job. And knowing more is not necessary and limits the information disclosed if she is somehow induced to reveal what she knows. The process equivalent to this idea is the *principle of minimum privilege*. This principle says that a process should have only the capabilities it needs to do its job. This would argue that a custom protection domain be constructed for each process which has exactly the capabilities it needs to perform its functions.

principle of minimum privilege

It might be too expensive to construct a separate domain for each process, but there certainly will be a need for multiple protection domains in any case. For example, sometimes you would like to run a program that you do not fully trust. This might be a program you obtained over the Internet and you do not have the source code. The program purports to do something useful, but it is possible that it was written by someone who wanted to do mischief and it will try to delete all your files. The ideal solution is to run the program in a limited protection domain that only has capabilities related to the advertised functions of the program. This way, the program could not delete all your files even if it wanted to because the protection domain it runs in will not allow the deleting of any file it did not create itself.

There are several ways to implement protection domains. In a capability system, protection domains would be easy. It is only necessary to change the system so that sets of capabilities can exist independent of a process, and a process can run in a protection domain. There would be a capability to enter each protection domain, and only processes holding that capability would be allowed to enter. Actually, you might want to have some capabilities still associated with the process and some with the protection domain it is running in.

For access control lists, we could implement "subject" objects that are not associated with any user. The subject would be a protection domain and would have all the privileges that subject has in the access control lists. An operation on the subject object would be to allow the process to "become" that subject. Being that subject would be equivalent to being in that protection domain.

Notice that both implementations of protection domains involve a level of indirection. Instead of associating a capability list directly with a process, we associate it with a protection domain, and each process is associated with ("points to") a protection domain. Or instead of associating each user with a subject that is that user, we have subjects independent of users that have access privileges and associate each user process with a subject. The level of indirection means we can change protection domains by changing the process's link to the protection domain. This is not possible if the protection domain is part of the process.

Protection domains give an operating system a lot of flexibility in setting up protection for processes. They can be used with a user's own programs for error checking. If a process cannot perform any actions except those it is supposed to be doing, then errors in the program that do something wrong will be caught sooner. Protection domains are also useful when running other people's programs. They make sure that the program does not do things it is not supposed to do (either by mistake or by design).

19.10.8   PROTECTION IN DISTRIBUTED SYSTEMS

Protection is much harder in a distributed system since you probably cannot really trust the other machines and operating systems in the system, and you cannot be sure the communication lines are secure. This makes authentication harder. A message over the network might have been changed in transit, or it might be from a machine that cannot be trusted. There are methods to handle the authentication problem, but the need for authentication of every communication means that capabilities could be more efficient than access control lists. Of course, the problem shifts to authenticating the capability itself rather than the user identify. With a single operating system, the system can keep capabilities in its own memory, and prevent any tampering with or counterfeiting of capabilities. In a network, that is no longer possible. But it is possible to use cryptographic techniques to protect capabilities from being forged or changed. We will see these techniques in the section on cryptography.

19.10.9   CACHING PROTECTION DATA

Capabilities are efficient for checking access control lists because a capability is the right to perform a specific set of operations on one object. When you want to perform an operation, you can present a specific capability, not your whole capability list. So the protection monitor only checks that specific capability. With an access control list, the protection monitor has to look up the subject in the list each time. Because of this, most systems use capabilities as a cache for the protection data in the access control lists.

When you first access an object, you "open" it. This checks your access rights to the object and creates a capability that is a copy of those rights. This is basically an open file identifier. Each time you want to perform an operation on the object, you present the capability. This technique gives you the ease of use of access control lists and the efficiency of checking of capabilities.

19.10.10   Operations on Protection Objects

It is necessary that the protection system protect the protection database itself, as well as the objects. Another way of saying this is that the capability lists, access control lists, and protection domains are objects themselves, with operations and their own protection data. Here is a list of these protection objects and their operations.

*   *Access control list:*
    -Check access (of a subject for an operation).
    -Add an access control list element.
    -Remove an access control list element.
*   *Capability list:*
    -Use a capability (when requesting an operation on an object).
    -Add a capability list element.
    -Remove a capability list element.
*   *Protection domain:*
    -Enter the domain.
    -Create a new domain.
    -Destroy a domain.

19.11   MECHANISMS FOR SOFTWARE PROTECTION

Hardware protection mechanisms ensure that a user process cannot access a hardware resource directly. Instead, the operating system provides virtual resources that provide indirect access to the hardware resources. Virtual resources are accessed through system calls. To prevent unauthorized operations on virtual resources, the operating system must check every system call to be sure the operation is allowed. The mechanism that does these checks is called a *protection monitor.* There must be a protection monitor on the path to every operation on every resource.

protection monitor

19.11.1   File Protection Example

Let's take reading a file as an example. Figure 19.8 shows the protection monitors and data. When a user opens a file, a protection monitor for the file is invoked. It checks an access control list and finds that the user has read-only access to the file. This information is stored in the entry for this file in the open file table. When the user makes a specific I/O request to read the file, another protection monitor checks the access. It looks at the protection data in the open file table entry to be sure the read access is allowed. Note that we do not look up the user in the access control list on every read operation. This lookup is done once when the file is opened, and the protection data is copied into the open file table. The open file table

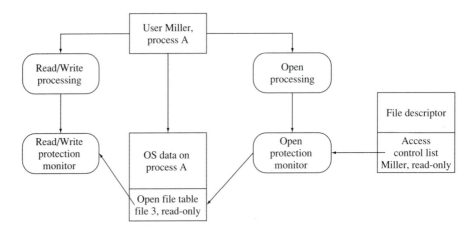

Figure 19.8   Protection monitors in file access

is also a capability list which is checked each time a read is performed. If the user attempts to write the file using that open file entry, the protection monitor will prevent the operation.

The model used here is a common one. The protection database is searched on the open command, and protection information is checked. This information is then converted to a capability, which is returned by the open and held by the process that called the open. All operations are checked against this capability. This is a much faster operation than looking up the protection information in the protection database for each operation. The capabilities are a cache for the protection information in the access control list.

Any object that is named in the file naming system can be protected using the same mechanism. An open command checks the protection and returns a capability, and the capability is used to check each operation on the object. For example, if a pipe is named in the file system, a process can open it for reading only if it has read permission to the name of the pipe.

19.11.2   IMPLEMENTATION OF PROTECTION

The computer hardware provides the basic mechanisms necessary to implement protection. The operating system uses these hardware mechanisms to maintain control of the computer system and to protect the hardware and software resources.

The basic principle of protection is that each operation on a resource is checked for validity by a protection monitor. That is, in every path from a process to a resource, there is an agent that checks the access. A system call is handled by the operating system by first dispatching it to the proper handler (figuring out what kind of system call it is). Then the specific handler performs the operation. Before it does this, it checks to be sure that the calling process has the right to perform the requested operation on the specified object. This involves looking up some protection

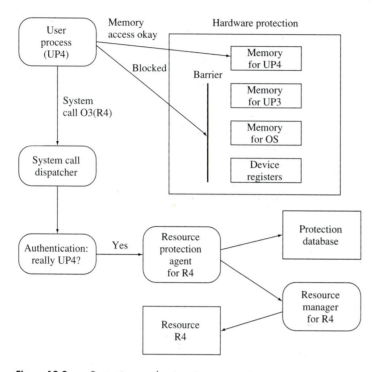

Figure 19.9   Protection mechanisms in an operating system

information in a database. The protection information has to be stored somewhere along the path between the process and the object. It can be stored with the process and passed to the protection manager, it can be stored by the protection manager, or it can be stored with the object. No matter where it is stored, the protection database itself must be protected from alteration by subjects. Figure 19.9 shows the protection mechanisms in an operating system.

The only operations that are not requested through system calls are operations on memory. It would be far too inefficient to require a system call every time a process wanted to store into its memory. The hardware acts as the protection monitor for memory, and it checks every access to memory using the protection information contained in the memory management system (typically in the page table entries).

19.11.3 PROTECTION MECHANISMS AND SECURITY POLICIES

The protection mechanisms we have described so far are general mechanisms that can be used in many different ways. Access control lists, for example, allow us to give read access to some users and read/write access to other users, but they do not tell us which users to give which permissions to. This is the role of a *security policy*.   security policy
A security policy is a specific way of using a protection mechanism. For example,

one policy might be to allow ourselves read-write access to all our files, and to allow everyone else read-only access to all our files.

A good protection mechanism will allow you to implement any security policy you want, but the best protection mechanism will not protect your data unless your security policy tells it to.

19.11.4 Variations in File Security

UNIX file security starts by classifying the user into one of there categories: the owner of the file, someone in the same group as the file belongs to, and all others. An obvious generalization is to increase the number of possible categories. Instead of the file belonging to just one group, the file could contain a list of groups, and each one could have a separate set of read-write-execute privilege bits. If the user was in any one of these groups, those permissions would be used.

Another generalization is to have more than three types of access. In addition to read, write, and execute, we could have:

- *Append*—The user could add information to the file, but not read or change any existing information.
- *Copy rights*—The user could pass on the access privileges he has to other users.
- *Expiring rights*—You could give a user privileges for a certain time period only.
- *Time-of-day rights*—You could give the user access rights that could only be used on certain days, or at certain times of the day.

19.12   EXAMPLES OF PROTECTION ATTACKS

In this section, we will go through some of the common methods used to attack the protection in an operating system, and the protection flaws that allow these attacks to succeed.

19.12.1 Browsing for Information

When a process gets memory from the operating system, it may have information in it that was written by the process that previously was using the memory. A process can browse through the new memory it gets looking for private data. The same is true for disk space. A process might be allocated a disk block for a file that contains old data.

The solution to this problem is to always write over memory or disk blocks before they are reassigned. This is how virtual memory systems normally work. When a page is allocated to a process, it is either loaded from disk or filled with zeros. Similarly, disk blocks allocated to a process must be written entirely before they are assigned to the user file.

19.12.2 Wiretapping of Communications Lines

It is common to communicate with a computer over communication lines that are not known to be secure. For example, we often call up a computer over a phone line. In addition, networks that run underground in tunnels can be wiretapped.

A person might just listen to the communications line browsing for information, like passwords. It is not uncommon to send passwords over communications lines. A more active intruder might change messages on the communications line, or forge messages and place them on the line.

The solution to this problem is to use cryptography to protect the information sent over the line, and to use cryptographic-based authentication techniques to ensure that messages cannot be modified or forged. We will discuss these techniques in Section 19.16.

19.12.3 TRIAL AND ERROR

Sometimes it is possible to guess a password by trying every possible password.

The solution to this problem is to make guessing take longer. The first line of defense is to use long passwords that contain upper- and lowercase, digits, and special characters. This makes it infeasible to try all possible passwords. The second line of defense it to not allow processes to guess passwords at a rapid rate. The operating system might only allow a process to try one password every five seconds. Or it might hang up on a dialup line that enters three passwords that are incorrect. These techniques serve to slow down the rate at which passwords can be tried, and makes it impossible to try all of them.

19.12.4 PASSWORD GUESSING

It is not necessary to try every possible password in order to guess a password. Instead, you can try to guess the password by trying passwords that the person is likely to pick. You might try passwords that contain the person's address, or phone numbers, or children's names, or pets' names, etc.

Another line of attack it to try all common words as passwords. For example, you might try every word in a dictionary.

The solution to this protection problem is to prevent users from using easily guessed passwords. A proactive solution is to encourage or require users to pick a password using a random password generator. These generators can be configured to generate passwords that are easily pronounceable in the person's native language. A reactive solution is to constantly test the passwords people have against words in the dictionary, or that appear in publicly available files about them. Another solution is to prevent a process from rapidly trying a lot of passwords (as was described in the previous paragraph).

19.12.5 SEARCHING TRASH

An external attack might involve going through a person's trash. Sometimes you can find modem phone numbers, user ids, and even passwords in the trash.

A solution to this problem is to shred all the trash before it leaves the building.

19.12.6 TRAP DOORS

Some programs contain code that will bypass some of their protection mechanisms. The most common reason for this is that it is code inserted while debugging the program. For example, a mail router program might allow a debugger to send a message under an assumed user id because this is necessary to test certain parts of the program. Or it might send back certain information about the message it is handling. Such code is called a *trap door.*

Sometime trap door code is left in a program after debugging. Sometimes this is an oversight, and sometimes it is deliberate. It is handy to have debugging trap doors in working programs to debug problems that arise while they are in use. The programmer might assume that no one will know about the trap door, and so it will not be used to subvert the program. But in many cases, other people find out about the trap door, and a few people will try to exploit it.

The solution to this problem is to establish procedures so that all trap doors that are inserted in a program during debugging are documented, and are disabled or removed before the program goes into general use.

There is another class of trap door which a programmer might put in a program because he wants to be able to get around the program's security when it is running. In other words, it is a deliberate trap door inserted for the purpose of breaking the security of the program. This is analogous to an employee leaving a small window open in a building so that he can later get back in and steal something.

The solution to this problem is harder because the programmer will try to conceal the trap door. There is no sure solution to this problem. Administrative procedures can be of some help. Procedures can be set up so that a single programmer cannot change the archived source code for a program. All changes must go through a formal change process, and at least one other person reviews all code changes. Even this will not catch all problems, but it can help.

19.12.7   RUNNING OTHER PEOPLE'S PROGRAMS

When a user runs a program, it is typical for that program to inherit all the privileges of the user running the program. This is not too much of a problem if it is the user's own program, because it will not do anything to harm the user except by mistake. A user will also run commercial software (compilers, database systems, spreadsheets, etc.), but these are usually from reputable companies which have reputations to preserve, and they are careful that their programs do not breach the user's security.

The problem comes when you run a program that you got from some other person that you do not necessarily trust. It might be a program you get from the Internet or a bulletin board. There are two problems that can occur in these situations. The program could do some things that it is not supposed to do. For example, a utility to reformat a program might delete some of your other files. This is called the Trojan horse problem. The second example is that the program could disclose information that it is not supposed to reveal. For example, a tax preparation program could send your tax data to the person who wrote the program. This is called the confinement problem.

The Trojan Horse Problem   In most systems all processes have the same privileges, and those are the privileges of the user running the program. If the user can delete files in a certain directory, then any program the user runs can delete files in that directory. The problem that can arise is that a program can delete files it should not be deleting.

For example, you get a program from the Internet that draws a cute cartoon. Hidden in the program is code that will delete a random file somewhere in your file tree. This is called the *Trojan horse problem.*

Trojan horse problem

We use the name Trojan horse for this kind of program because it is similar to the story (from Virgil's *Aeneid*) where the Greeks breached the security of Troy by hiding a few soldiers inside a large wooden horse that they left outside the gates. The Trojans brought the horse inside their walls and, at night, the soldiers got out and opened the city gates to the Greek army.

The solution to the Trojan horse problem is to use protection domains. Allow each program only the privileges necessary to do the job it is supposed to do. The problem with this solution is that it requires the user to be careful and set up a protection domain for each program. A simplified solution is to have one protection domain that is restricted to a certain part of your file tree and cannot enter other protection domains, cannot communicate with other processes, and has strict resource use limits. All foreign programs can be run in this protection domain. Any files it needs can be copied into the restricted file tree. This means that you only need the one protection domain for all foreign programs.

The Confinement Problem　　Suppose we are running a program in a limited protection domain. We have limited it so that the program cannot communicate outside of the domain. That is, it cannot write any files that are readable by other users, it cannot connect to the network, etc. You have attempted to confine the program and limit its ability to communicate with other programs. You might do this because the program is calculating your income tax and you do not want the information it uses revealed to anyone else. This is called the *confinement problem.*

confinement problem

You might think that a limited protection domain would solve the confinement problem, but the problem is more subtle than that. It is possible for a process to communicate information in other ways. Suppose, for example, the computer wanted to send a single character to another program. A character is seven bits long. Suppose at exactly 4 P.M. it starts varying how much processor time it uses every second, depending on the bits in the ASCII character. Suppose the character it wants to send is a. The ASCII representation of the character a is 1100001 in binary. So the first second the process uses the processor as much as it can, for example, running a tight computation loop. It does this again in the second second. The next four seconds it does not use any processor time at all, and in the seventh second it uses as much as it can. Another process would monitor the processor use (which is generally public information) during these seven seconds and figure out the character that the confined process was trying to send.

This may seem slow and error prone. The error-prone issue is not a problem because engineers have worked out effective ways of sending information over channels that have errors. It will take more time, but, if any information is being transmitted at all, you can transmit accurate information. The data rate certainly is slow, but it is possible that it might be improved. For example, we could reduce the bit interval from one second to one-tenth of a second.

Similarly, a process could manipulate its paging rate, and other processes might be able to get this information directly, or detect that the paging disk is loaded or not by monitoring its own paging.

Even though you might not be able to write to a file that other processes can read, you might be able to read or write to the same disk that other processes can also read or write. Again, you could manipulate the load on the disk as a means of transmitting information.

The moral here is that there are many ways to transmit information via so called *covert channels.*

covert channel

19.13   GOVERNMENT SECURITY LEVELS

The United States Department of Defense has established some standards for security in operating systems. They have several levels of security. The C2 level of security requires:

- *Secure logon facility:* A user ID and a password.

- *Discretionary access control:* A user can decide what access to allow for each of his files.

- *Auditing:* The system must detect and make a record of all security-related events. This audit log must include the user login ID of the user who caused the event.

- *Memory protection:* Memory must be able to be protected from unauthorized reading and writing. All memory must be reinitialized before it is reused so no record of its previous contents is left.

A secure login facility is what we have called user authentication. Discretionary access control is what we have called a protection mechanism, that is, a way for a user to decide who gets access to his files and what kind of access. We have also discussed auditing and memory protection as essential parts of a protection and security system for an operating system.

A higher level of security is the B2 level, which includes:

- *All C2-level requirements:* Secure logon, discretionary access control, auditing, and memory protection.

- *Mandatory access control:* The operating system must maintain a security level and compartment for each user and object. Information may not flow down to lower security levels.

19.14   PROTECTION EXAMPLES

19.14.1   PROTECTION IN WINDOWS NT

When a user logs on and provides a password, he is given an *access token* which identifies the user and the groups the user is in. Each object has an access control list that allows access based on the security ID and user groups in the access token.

All object access is through an *object handle*. An object handle is protected by the operating system and cannot be forged by the process. When an object handle is created (by an open), the access control list is checked, and the handle is created with certain access rights (the intersection of what is asked for and what is allowed by the access control list). All further accesses are checked against the rights in the object handle. The object handle is a capability for the object.

All resources in Windows NT are represented as objects under the control of the object manager and the security reference monitor. Even access to an object must go through the object manager, which uses the security reference monitor to check access rights.

When a new object is created, the default access control list is obtained from one of three places:

- If one is provided with the creation call, then it is used.

- If one is not provided by the call, and the directory the object is created in has an inheritable access control list, then that is used.

- Otherwise, the default access control list for the user is used.

19.14.2 Protection in OSF/1

OSF/1 uses access control lists and maintains audit logs.

19.14.3 Protection in UNIX

Authentication—Logging On and Passwords   In order to use a UNIX system, you first have to log on. You provide the system with a user name and a password, both of which are character strings. UNIX checks to see if you have given the right password for the user name. The user names are public in that it is not hard to find out the valid user names in a system, and users make no attempt to keep other people from finding them out. In fact, your user name is part of your E-mail address, so you generally want it to be widely known. You protect the password, however, and do not allow anyone else to see it.

UNIX keeps the user passwords in the password file, which is readable by anyone using the system. This is not the obvious security problem you might think, however, since the passwords in the password file are encoded with a "one-way" function so that it is very, very hard to determine the password from the encoded form.[6]

Once you have logged on, your user name is converted to an internal user number that is associated with all processes that you create. It is not possible to

---

[6]Having the password file publicly readable does make it easier for penetrators, though, and many newer versions of UNIX keep the encrypted passwords in a "shadow" password file that is not publicly readable. Some version of the password file must be publicly readable, since it is used to convert between user numbers and user names (among other things).

change your user number, so it acts as a reliable proof of your identity. UNIX implements this by keeping your user number in its own memory that users cannot access.

In addition to having a user name and corresponding user number, each user can belong to any number of *groups*. At any one time, you are associated with only one group and have a corresponding group number. You can move from group to group as you are working, but you are always in exactly one group.

File Access   Each file has an associated owner and group which are recorded as a user number and a group number. When you try to open a file, you are placed in one of three categories. If your user number is the same as the user number of the owner of the file, you are put in the "owner" category (which is always a category of exactly one member). If you are not the owner but your group number is the same as the group number of the file, then you are placed in the "group" category. If you are not the owner and not in the same group, then you are placed in the "other" category.

Your access to the file can differ according to which category you are in and the way you want to open the file. The three ways to open a file are for execution, for reading, and for writing. Each file has nine bits of protection information. These consist of read, write, and execute permission for the owner, members of the same group, and all others. The system will check whether users in your category have permission to perform the requested open on the file.

Once a file is opened, the system gives you an open file identifier which it keeps in a place that is accessible only to the operating system. This open file identifier allows you to use the file in the way you requested.

Notice that file access is accomplished in two steps. The first step is to open the file for a particular kind of use (read, write, execute, or read/write). The protection database for file opening is kept with the file.[7] Opening a file places an open file pointer in the process descriptor, and file read and write requests are checked by making sure the file was opened to allow that operation. Each file access is checked by using information kept with the process (the open file), not with the file.

So a file access is checked once (on open), and the open gives the process a "token" (the open file) which shows the process has permission to read and write the file.

Memory Protection   Each process has a private section of virtual memory that it can access, and that no other process can access. It is possible, by mutual consent, for two processes to set up an area of shared memory that both may read and write. Other than this, no process may read or write the memory of another process. The memory management hardware enforces this constraint.

Protection of Processes   Processes in UNIX can interact with each other using the "signal" mechanism. A signal is a special kind of message sent to another process. A process can exercise a fair amount of control over child processes. In particular, it

---

| [7]Actually, it is in the file descriptor.

can send signals to its child processes. You can use signals to terminate a child process. You can also go in and change the memory of a child process.

A process cannot send signals to any process that is not a child process, a child of a child, or so on. That is, protection is based on the process creation tree.

Protection of Interprocess Communication   Pipes form a main method of IPC in UNIX. Pipes are maintained in the file and I/O system, and are protected in the same way as files.

19.15   EXTERNAL SECURITY

So far, we have just looked at what we will call *internal security,* that is, security inside the computer system. A secure computing system also needs external security. By *external security,* we mean the ways of ensuring that the computing system and its data are secure against attacks from outside of the computer system.

internal security

external security

19.15.1   Physical Security

The first aspect of external security is physical security, that is, protecting the computer system itself. This security needs to prevent people from stealing or damaging the computer itself, or any other parts of the computer system. This also includes removable media such as CDs, tapes, and disks.

A computer system cannot be secure without physical security, but we will not say much more about this since techniques for physical security have been developed over thousands of years, are well known, and are outside the scope of this book.

19.15.2   Operational Security

In addition to protecting resources, there are some procedures that should be taken in the operation of an operating system to ensure security.

Backups   Files can be destroyed or modified because of disk failure, user error, system error, or malicious intruders. In any case, it is important to have backup copies of files so they can be restored when they are lost. We discussed file system backups at some length in Section 17.9.1. Here we will just note that frequent backups are an essential part of security in an operating system.

Of course, backup tapes (or disk) present another security problem because they could be read by people who are not supposed to read them. One solution is to rely on physical security to prevent unauthorized access to the backup tapes. Another solution is that used in the Plan 9 operating system, and that is to have the backup device protected in the same way as the regular file system (see Section 17.11.5).

Auditing   Another aspect of security is keeping accurate records so you can find out what happened if security was breached. An operating system should be able to detect and record every event that is related to protection or security. Security-related events would be any attempt to create, access, or delete any system resource. This process is called *auditing*. The audit record is called the *audit log*. The audit log will be kept on a file since it should be a permanent record (and because it will be large). Each entry in the log should record the time, the user who initiated the operation, the operation, and the object the operation was performed on.

auditing
audit log

19.15.3   NONTECHNICAL SECURITY THREATS

A common form of security violation involves tricking a person into revealing protected information. This is sometimes called *social engineering*. Social engineering techniques include calling employees up on the phone and getting them to reveal information, searching through trash, and getting a job at the company you want to infiltrate. If you call up a person in an organization and impersonate someone from personnel, computer security, or another employee, you can often get them to reveal access codes, modem phone numbers, etc. Passwords, employee numbers, and phone numbers can often be found in trash. Getting a job as a janitor can allow someone access to many areas of the company and allow the person to find out a lot of information.

social engineering

19.16   THE USE OF CRYPTOGRAPHY IN COMPUTER SECURITY

Cryptography has many uses in computer security. It can be used to keep communications secret by encoding them. Equally important, it can help users authenticate themselves to the system and help authenticate the system to the user.

19.16.1   WHAT IS CRYPTOGRAPHY?

Cryptography comes from the Greek word meaning "secret writing." It is the study of secret codes, that is, ways to encode messages so only you and your trusted associates can decode them. Cryptography has been used for thousands of years, principally for political and military communication. People have long had a need to communicate secretly and to write down information but prevent others from reading it.

The advent of computers revolutionized cryptography, and we often use the term *modern cryptography* for the computer-based cryptography that has been developed over the last 40 years or so. Modern cryptography has given us encoding systems that are, for all intents and purposes, unbreakable.

modern cryptography

19.16.2 SOME BASIC DEFINITIONS

We start with a *message, M*, which is a sequence of bits. Often, these bits are ASCII characters, allowing the message to be a textual document. The message is also called the *plain text,* meaning that it is not encoded but readable by anyone. We have an encryption function, *E*, which takes a message and an *encryption key, K_E,* and produces an encrypted version of the message, *C*, called the *cipher text:*

$$E(M, K_E) = C$$

The decryption function, *D*, reverses the process using a *decryption key, K_D:*

$$D(C, K_D) = M$$

We can put these together:

$$D(E(M, K_E), K_D) = M$$

to show clearly that when you encrypt a message and then decrypt it, you get the same message back. It is often the case that encryption and decryption can be done in either order, that is:

$$E(D(M, K_D), K_E) = M$$

It may seem strange to decrypt a message before you encrypt, but both the encryption and decryption functions basically convert one bit string into another (that is, a hashed-up version of the first bit string), and they both do about the same thing. We will see later that this property of applying encryption and decryption in either order is handy for implementing digital signatures.

19.16.3 PUBLIC AND PRIVATE KEY CRYPTOSYSTEMS

In many cases, the encryption and the decryption functions are the same, and the encryption and decryption keys are the same or very closely related. Let's look at some examples.

One method of encryption and decryption is to exclusive-or the message with the key. Say the key is 256 bits long and the message is 2048 bits long. We take the message 256 bits at a time, exclusive-or that part of the message with the key, and the result is 256 bits of encrypted text. Decryption uses the same process and the same key. If you exclusive-or a bit with another bit twice, you get the original bit back again, that is,

$$(A \; xor \; B) \; xor \; B = A$$

This is a simple and fast method of encoding but it is fairly easy to break because you are using the same key over and over again. The code breaker can use the statistical properties of the language you are encoding to figure out the key.

On the other hand, if you do not repeat using the key, that is, if the key is as long as the message, then this code is unbreakable. By unbreakable we mean that having the encoded text is of no use at all in discovering the message. The obvious problem

message

plain text
encryption key
cipher text

decryption key

here is that you need a very long key. How do you transmit the key to your intended receiver and how do you both protect it? Any code can be broken if the key is stolen, and large keys are harder to keep secret than small keys.

private key cryptosystem

public key cryptosystem

A cryptosystem where the encryption and decryption key are the same or easily derivable from one another is called a *private key cryptosystem* because it is necessary to keep both keys private in order to maintain security. Surprisingly, there is another kind of cryptosystem, called a *public key cryptosystem,* where only one of the keys need be kept private.

Now since the decryption key will decrypt messages encrypted with the encryption key, it is necessary that they have an algorithmic relationship, that is, it is always possible to compute one key if you know the algorithms and the other key. How then can we make one key publicly known? Because there is a difference between what is theoretically computable and what is practically computable.

In a public key cryptosystem, the encryption key is publicly known and can be sent without worrying about someone else reading it. We can publish it in the phone book, or in a newspaper, or on the Internet. The decryption key must remain private and must be guarded jealously. The computation required to compute the private key from the public key is possible, but would take too long to be practical.

The most well know public key cryptosystem takes advantage of the fact that it is hard to factor large numbers. Mathematicians have been looking for ways to factor numbers for a long time, and no one has found a fast method except for special cases. So if you have a 200-digit number that is the product of two 100-digit prime numbers, it is essentially impossible to discover the two prime factors of the number. The encryption key is then based on the 200-digit number and is publicly known, and the decryption key is based on the two 100-digit factors and is kept secret.

Public key cryptosystems were discovered fairly recently (in the 1970s), and most people were surprised that such a thing was possible. We will express the uses of cryptography in terms of public key cryptosystems because they are the easiest to explain. All of the things we talk about can be done with private key cryptosystems as well.

19.16.4   USING CRYPTOGRAPHY FOR PRIVACY

Certainly the obvious use of cryptography is to keep data private. We can encrypt a message before we send it out and prevent anyone else from discovering its contents. We can keep files encrypted in the file system and prevent anyone else from reading the real contents. The operating system can keep its password file encrypted to prevent anyone from discovering the passwords. This is particularly important in networks, where the messages go through many machines and it is not possible to trust them all to keep your message private.

19.16.5   USING CRYPTOGRAPHY FOR AUTHENTICATION

digital signature

Cryptosystems play an equally important role in methods of authentication. This is based on the idea of a *digital signature*. Signatures are used to authenticate documents, because it is very hard to duplicate how a person signs their name, but it is hard to see how we can "sign" a digital document. Signatures depend on how you use dozens of muscles in your hands and arms, and they are difficult to duplicate even with the help of computers. On the other hand, it is very easy to change the bits of a document. So how could we digitally sign a document?

The trick is to make all the bits in the document related to each other so that you cannot change just one or a few of them. We can do this with encryption because encryption takes the bits of a message and mixes them all up in complicated ways.

Suppose we have a public key cryptosystem and we have two people, A and B. A sends a message to B, and B wants to be certain that A sent the message. Person A has a public key Pu_A that is widely known, and a private key Pr_A that only A knows. Similarly, B has public key Pu_B and private key Pr_B.

A sends the message $D(M, Pr_A)$ to B. When B receives this message, he "encrypts" it with A's public key to get $E(D(M, Pr_A), Pu_A) = M$. B can be certain that A sent message M because only A knows Pr_A, and so only A could decrypt M with Pr_A. Someone else could send B a sequence of bits, Y, and say it was from A, but when B encrypts it ($E(Y, Pu_A)$), it will just be a meaningless jumble of bits. Finding a bit sequence Y such that $E(Y, Pu_A) = M$, for any given M, is computationally infeasible and is as hard as computing A's private key from his public key.

Now, of course, A would not only want to send an authenticated message to B, but A would also like to keep the message secret. So A would send the message $(A, E(D(M, Pr_A), Pu_B))$, that is, A would encrypt the authenticated message with B's public key so that only B could read the message. On receiving $(A, E(D(M, Pr_A), Pu_B))$, B would extract A, which says who it is (allegedly) from, decrypt it with Pr_B, and encrypt it with Pu_A to authenticate it.

19.16.6 AUTHENTICATING PUBLIC KEYS

This all seems very easy and neat, but there is still a problem. Public keys are obtained from public channels. How can we be sure that we are getting the right public key? Suppose that C arranged for B to believe that Pu_C was really Pu_A. He might do this by intercepting Bs messages to a public key source on the Internet. Then C can send messages to B of the form $D(M, Pu_C)$, claiming they are from A. B will check them by encrypting with Pu_C, which he thinks is Pu_A, and accept that the messages are from A.

The problem here is that it is hard to get started if you cannot trust anyone. You can get various public keys, but can you be sure that they are authentic? It seems that we have to solve the authentication problem in order to use public key cryptosystems to solve the authentication problem. In a way, this is true, but we can solve a much simpler form of the problem.

The idea is to have, in your network, a trusted public key server. Let's say that server is Z. Then all that is necessary is for you to know one public key for sure, and that is Pu_Z. If you know Pu_Z, you can communicate with Z and have it send you the public keys of anyone else you want to communicate with. So if A wanted to send an authenticated message to B, they would go through the following sequence of messages. Figure 19.10 shows the authentication process.

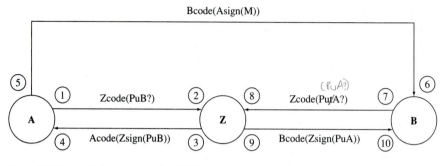

Figure 19.10   Authentication of public keys

1. A sends $E(M, Pu_Z)$ to Z, where M = "Send me B's public key." (A doesn't want other people to know what he is doing (so he encrypts it with Pu_Z), but does not sign the message since Z will hand out public keys to anyone; they're public, after all.)

2. Z receives $E(M, Pu_Z)$ and computes $M = D(E(M, Pu_Z), Pr_Z)$. (Z receives the message and decrypts it with its own private key, which Z, of course, knows.)

3. Z sends $E(D(M, Pr_Z), Pu_A)$ to A, where M = "B's public key is Pu_B." (Z sends out the public key of B and signs the message with its private key. Z also encrypts the message so that no one but A can read it.)

4. A receives $E(D(M, Pr_Z), Pu_A)$, decrypts it with his private key, authenticates that the message is from Z by encrypting it with Z's public key, and gets B's public key from the message. (The message is provably from Z, and Z is trusted to give out accurate public keys, so now A knows B's public key with certainty.)

5. A sends $E(D(M, Pr_A), Pu_B)$ to B, where M = "I owe you 100 dollars." (A sends a signed IOU to B.)

6. B receives $E(D(M, Pr_A), Pu_B)$, and decrypts it to get $D(M, Pr_A)$, which is allegedly from A.

7. B sends $E(M, Pu_Z)$ to Z, where M = "Send me A's public key."

8. Z receives $E(M, Pu_Z)$ and computes $M = D(E(M, Pu_Z), Pr_Z)$.

9. Z sends $E(D(M, Pr_Z), Pu_B)$ to B, where M = "A's public key is Pu_A" (Z sends out the public key of A and signs the message with its private key. Z also encrypts the message so that no one but B can read it.)

10. B receives $E(D(M, Pr_Z), Pu_B)$, decrypts it with his private key, authenticates that the message is from Z, by encrypting it with Z's public key, and gets A's public key from the message. (The message is provably from Z, and Z is trusted to give out accurate public keys, so now B knows A's public key with certainly.)

11. B can now verify that the message $D(M, Pr_A)$ really is signed by A.

Note that A cannot deny sending the message to B because only A knows Pr_A and could have signed the message. Of course, A could claim that someone stole Pr_A, but there are administrative ways to deal with that. A could also claim that Z sent the message, but we are assuming Z is trusted by all.

This all depends on two things. First, we need a trusted server that knows everyone's public key. It is not that hard to secure and trust a single machine: the problem is trusting every machine on the network. Second, we need to be sure we have an accurate Pu_Z. Since there is only one public key that we have to be sure of, it is easier to ensure this. We can get the key personally from someone we trust. Also, the key can be available on every machine, so you can ask a lot of different machines. On a larger scale, we could publish the public key in the newspaper. It would be hard to change every copy of the newspaper with a fake one(this assumes we trust the newspaper).

19.17   SUMMARY

Computer systems contain hardware resources and software resources. An important job of an operating system is resource management. The main parts of resource management are allocation, accounting, scheduling, and protection. The major goals of resource management are efficiency, fairness, no deadlock or starvation, and protection. A computing system has several resource schedulers: processor scheduler, memory scheduler, disk schedulers, etc.

Queuing theory can be used to guide the selection of scheduling policies. Real-time operating systems often use fixed scheduling to ensure that all scheduling goals are met all the time.

Protection in an operating system is necessary to protect the users from interfering with one another and to protect the operating system itself. There are hardware mechanisms to help the operating system protect the hardware resources. The basic hardware protection mechanism is the processor mode. Hardware resources can be managed only by processes running in system mode. Other hardware protection mechanisms are the timer and the paging system. The operating system creates software resources and protects them by checks during system calls.

The first step in protection is user authentication, which ensures that a user is who he says he is. Authentication is normally done with passwords.

The active entities in a system are called subjects, and they are authorized to perform certain operations on the objects in the system. The protection database records what subjects are authorized to perform what operations on what objects. A capability is the right to perform a certain operation on a certain object. A capability list is a list of capabilities that are all associated with a particular user or protection domain. An access control list is a list of records that is associated with an object, and indicates which subjects can perform which operations in the object. Most protection systems are based on some form of access control list. The protection database itself is a set of objects, which are also under the protection system.

A protection monitor is a mechanism that checks every requested operation in the protection database and ensures that only authorized operations are permitted to be completed. A protection system must ensure that every operation is checked by a protection monitor.

There are many possible protection attacks and problems. In this chapter, we discussed: browsing main memory and disk blocks for information left by previous users of the memory; wiretapping of communications lines to intercept private data and passwords; repeated trials—attacks that attempt to guess a password by trying every possible password; password guessing by trying words gotten from information about the user; trap doors, which are security holes left in a program from debugging Trojan horse attacks, where a program is advertised to do one thing but does something else (like delete all your files) in addition; and the confinement problem, where you try to prevent a program from disclosing private data that it is working on.

External security is concerned with the physical protection of the computing equipment and storage media. It includes physical security of the objects, backups, and auditing.

Cryptography is the use of code to protect the privacy of information. Modern cryptography is used to keep data secret, and also to authenticate users in networks.

19.17.1   TERMINOLOGY

After reading this chapter, you should be familiar with the following terms:

- access control list
- accounting
- allocation
- auditing
- audit log
- authentication
- capability list
- cipher text
- confinement problem
- covert channel
- deadlock
- decryption key
- digital signature
- efficiency
- encryption key
- external security
- fairness
- internal security
- Little's Law

- message
- modern cryptography
- object
- one-time password
- operation
- permission
- plain text
- principle of minimum privilege
- private key cryptosystem
- privilege
- privileged instruction
- processor mode
- protection
- protection database
- protection domain
- protection monitor
- public key cryptosystem
- real-time operating system
- right
- saturated
- scheduling
- security policy
- social engineering
- starvation
- subject
- system mode
- Trojan horse problem
- user
- user mode

19.17.2 REVIEW QUESTIONS

The following questions are answered in the text of this chapter:

1. Name the physical and logical resources in a computer system.
2. Describe how a user program interacts with the operating system resource manager.
3. What are the four main tasks of the resource manager?

4. What are the four main goals of the resource manager?

5. What is meant by preemption of a resource, and why is this important in resource management?

6. Name four different schedulers in an operating system and the resource they schedule.

7. Explain why all scheduling in an operating system is not done by a single, integrated scheduler.

8. What is a mathematical queuing system?

9. What is an arrival distribution?

10. What is a service distribution?

11. What are the three most common distributions?

12. What is an $M/M/1$ queuing system?

13. What is Little's Law?

14. Why do real-time operating systems often use fixed scheduling?

15. What is the relationship between users and processes in terms of protection?

16. Why is protection of resources important?

17. What are the four main threats in a computer system?

18. What is authentication?

19. What do we mean when we say an operation is "authorized"?

20. How are passwords used for authentication?

21. What are the dangers when a system does not authenticate itself to the user?

22. What are the three major types of authentication?

23. What is a one-time password?

24. Explain why processor mode is the cornerstone of hardware protection.

25. How does the timer help to protect the processor?

26. How does memory protection help to protect devices?

27. What is the protection database?

28. What is a capability?

29. What is a capability list?

30. What is an access control list?

31. Why are access control lists the most flexible way to keep the protection database?

32. What is a protection domain?

33. How do you construct a protection domain with capability lists?

34. How do you construct a protection domain with access control lists?

35. What is a security policy?

36. What is the confinement problem?

37. What is external security?

38. What is cryptography?

39. What is cipher text? What is plain text?

40. What is a public key cryptosystem?

41. What is a digital signature?

42. How can cryptography be used to implement digital signatures?

19.17.3 FURTHER READING

Stankovic et al. (1995), Liu and Leyland (1973), Abbot (1984), and Hong et al. (1989) discuss real-time scheduling.

See Saltzer and Schroeder (1975) and Popek (1974) for overviews of protection. See Lampson (1969) and (1971) for the original papers on the matrix model of protection. Popek (1974) has a survey of protection structures.

Morris and Thompson (1979), Seely (1989), and Lamport (1981) discuss password security. See Rubin (1996) for a discussion of one-time passwords.

Winkler (1996) discusses nontechnical threats to computer system security.

Lempel (1979) has a good review of modern cryptography. See Diffie and Hellman (1976) and (1979) for the original papers on public key encryption. See Rivest et al. (1978) and (1983) for the original papers on RSA encryption. See Akl (1983) and Davies (1983) for more information on digital signatures. Popek and Kline (1979) look at security in networks and the use of digital signatures.

19.18 PROBLEMS

1. Consider a library as a resource manager for books. Explain how it does each of the tasks of a resource manager and how it strives towards the goals of a resource manager.

2. Consider a hotel as a resource manager for hotel rooms. Explain how it does each of the tasks of a resource manager and how it strives towards the goals of a resource manager.

3. Suppose we wanted to integrate the memory scheduler and the processor scheduler. What information would they exchange, and how would they use that information?

4. Suppose we wanted to integrate the disk head scheduler and the processor scheduler. What information would they exchange, and how would they use that information?

5. Suppose we wanted to integrate the disk head scheduler and the memory scheduler. What information would they exchange, and how would they use that information?

6. Suppose we have a single processor system, and jobs arrive at a rate of 10 jobs a second. Suppose each job takes an average of 50 milliseconds to complete. Assume that both distributions are exponential. What is the expected number of jobs in the system and the average time in the system?

Repeat the calculation assuming an average processing time of 90 milliseconds, and then with an average processing time of 99 milliseconds.

7. Suppose you have a real-time system where process A needs 20 ms of processor time every 100 ms, process B needs 20 ms of processor time every 100 ms, process C needs 10 ms of processor time every 50 ms, process D needs 40 ms of processor time every 200 ms, and process E needs 10 ms of processor time every 100 ms. Figure out a fixed schedule for these processes that will meet all their needs.

8. Devise a program for the system to authenticate itself to the user each time the user logs on.

9. The cornerstone of hardware protection is the processor mode. If a user process can run in system mode, then all protection is lost. Explain why this is so, that is, explain how a user could access each hardware and software resource from system mode.

    Explain why memory protection is important in protecting processor mode, that is, explain how a process that can affect the memory protection can get into system mode.

10. Design the data structures for a system using access control lists. The system should protect the objects and operations discussed in the chapter. Describe a data structure that will record the information in the access control list. Be sure to allow for groups and wild cards so you can, for example, allow everyone read access to a file.

11. Design the user interface for a system using access control lists. The system should protect the objects and operations discussed in the chapter. Indicate how the items in an access control list would be displayed to the user, and how the user would edit the access control list.

12. Suppose we had a group TheGroup, and we wanted to allow anyone in the group add and delete file privileges in a directory. We also wanted to allow Dolores Supervisor this same access. All other users can read the file. Show how you would implement this protection using an access control list. Then show how you would implement this protection using a capability list.

13. Show how to implement protection domains with:

    a. Access control lists.

    b. Capabilities.

    c. The UNIX file protection system.

14. We have noted that protection systems can also protect themselves. Explain why there is no circularity in this. Do other protection system protect themselves? Use as examples: doors with locks, alarm systems, human guards, hardware protection (system mode, memory protection).

15. How would you implement the UNIX file system protection using access control lists? How would you implement it with capabilities?

16. Show how to use cryptography to solve the following problem: Create a message that can be read if any two of three people cooperate, but cannot be read by any one of them acting alone. Use only the public keys of the three people.

20

The Client-Server Model

In this chapter, we will explore the ideas that lead to distributed systems. We have mentioned networks a few times before, but in this chapter we would like to bring all the ideas together and show what is required for an operating system to run in distributed environment.

We will start with modularity in the operating system by moving some operating system functions out to user-mode processes.

20.1   THREE MODES OF COMMUNICATION

The way in which two entities communicate in the simple operating system depends on what each of the two entities are. We have seen three fundamentally different methods of communication. Within a single process, two procedures communicate with procedure calls. Between a process and the operating system, communication is with system calls. Two processes communicate with messages. (See Figure 20.1)

We can use syntactic tricks to make these methods of communication look similar. By using a system call library, we have made system calls look like procedure calls to the programmer. In Section 8.13.4, we saw a technique called *remote procedure calls* that made message communication look like procedure calls to the programmer. But on the implementation level, these three modes of communication are fundamentally different. In the next section, we will see how to merge system calls and messages.

20.2   SYSTEM PROCESSES

We will make two changes to the simple operating system. The first is to eliminate all system calls except those for sending and receiving messages. We will make it possible to send a message to the operating system, and so the effect of a system call can be achieved by sending a "system call" message to the operating system. We will create a message queue for the system. This will always be message queue 0. Messages to message queue 0 will be intercepted by the message sending code and handled directly by the operating system.

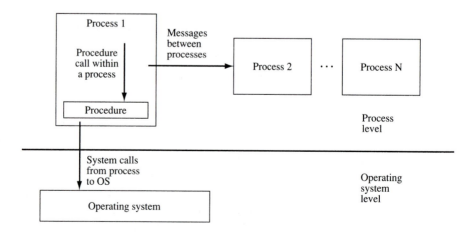

Figure 20.1   Three modes of communication in an operating system

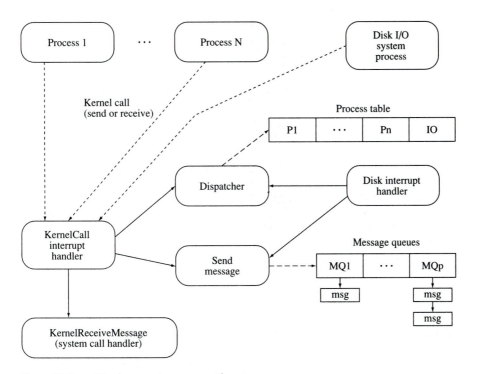

Figure 20.2   Simple operating system with system processes

The second change is to start moving parts of the operating system out to processes (which run in user mode). We will show how to move disk I/O out to a process. The same could be done with the rest of the I/O system (including the device drivers), the file system, the process scheduler, and most of the virtual memory system.

The simple operating system in Chapter 5, extended in later chapters, is implemented so that the entire operating system runs in system mode. It is possible to move some of the operating system functionality out of the operating system and into user-mode processes. These will be called *system process* because they are processes that are logically part of the operating system.   system process

20.2.1 OVERVIEW

Figure 20.2 shows the parts of the modified operating system. We moved the disk subsystem out of the operating system and into the process labeled "Disk I/O System Process" on the diagram. No internal detail is shown for the disk I/O system process, so the diagram looks simpler. The complexity of the disk subsystem is still there, but it is not part of the operating system. In a later section, we discuss why it is advantageous to structure things this way.

kernel

By moving the disk driver subsystem out of the operating system, we have made the operating system smaller and simpler. The word *kernel* is often used for such a simplified operating system. We will start using the term kernel for the operating system in some places. All kernels are operating systems, but not all operating systems are kernels. We will also use the term *kernel call* instead of system call.

Processes can exchange messages using the send and receive kernel calls. Disk interrupts are converted into messages to the disk I/O system process. Messages to the kernel are actually system calls and are handled by the system call handler.

20.2.2   THE INITIAL PROCESS

The code for the initial process starts the disk I/O system process, which is our first system process, that is, a process that runs as a user process but actually is performing operating system services.

THE INITIAL PROCESS

```
void main() {
    // start the disk driver process
    (void)CreateProcess( DiskDriverProcessBlock, DiskDriverProcessSize );
    // ... the rest is the same as in the simple OS
```

20.2.3   SYSTEM CONSTANTS

We need a few additional constants for this operating system.

SYSTEM CONSTANTS

```
enum Constants {
    // all the same constants as the simple OS
    // plus ...
    // kernel call call numbers
    SendMessageKernelCall = 1,
    ReceiveMessageKernelCall = 2,
    // message type numbers
    CreateProcessSystemCall = 1,
    ExitProcessSystemCall = 2,
    DiskReadSystemCall = 3,
    DiskWriteSystemCall = 4,
    ReadDeviceRegisters = 5,
    WriteDeviceRegisters = 6,
    SystemCallComplete = 7,
    //fixed message queue numbers
```

```
    SystemCallMessageQueue = 0,
    DiskDriverMessageQueue = 1,
};
```

20.2.4 INITIALIZATION

There are two message queues that are treated specially. Message queue 0 is reserved for messages to the operating system. Message queue 1 is reserved for messages to the disk I/O system process. We will create these during system initialization as queues 0 and 1 so processes can start using these message queue identifiers immediately, without having to create them.

SYSTEM INITIALIZATION

```
// This is the main program for the operating system. It is executed
// only once, when the operating system is initialized.
int main( void ) {
    // ... same as before

    // Create message queues 0 (for the OS) and 1 (for the IOP)
    for( i = 0; i < 2;++i ) {
        message_queue_allocated[i] = True;
        message_queue[i] = new Queue<MessageBuffer *>;
        wait_queue[i] = new Queue<WaitQueueItem *>;
    }

    // All the other message queues start out unallocated.
    for( i = 2; i < NumberOfMessageQueues; ++i )
        message_queue_allocated[i] = False;

    // Let's go!
    Dispatcher();
}
```

20.2.5 INTERRUPT HANDLING

In this version of the operating system, the "system calls" are really messages to the kernel and are not directly implemented with the system call instruction. To make a point of this difference, we will call the message send and message receive interrupts "kernel calls," and the messages to the kernel will usually contain system calls. It will be the same machine instruction; our change in terminology for it is intended to emphasize its new and different use. There will be fewer kernel calls than there were system calls. In fact, there will only be two kernel calls: send message and receive message. If a message is sent to message queue 0, it is handled directly by the kernel.

KERNEL CALL INTERRUPT HANDLER

```
void KernelCallInterruptHandler( void ) {

  // ... initial handling is as before

  // ... all the cases in the switch are eliminated
  // and these new ones are added.

  case SendMessageKernelCall:
    int * user_msg; asm{ store r9,user_msg }
    int to_q;asm{ store r10,to_q }

    // check for an invalid queue identifier
    if( !message_queue_allocated[to_q] ) {
        pd[current_process].sa.reg[1] = -1;
        break;
    }
    int msg_no = GetMessageBuffer();
    // make sure we have not run out of message buffers
    if( msg_no == EndOfFreeList ) {
        pd[current_process].sa.reg[1] = -2;
        break;
    }

    // copy the message vector from the system caller's memory
    // into the system's message buffer
    CopyToSystemSpace( current_process, user_msg,
                       message_buffer[msg_no], MessageSize );
    SendMessageFromOS( to_q, msg_no );
    pd[current_process].sa.reg[1] = 0;
    if( to_q == SystemCallMessageQueue )
        KernelReceiveMessage();
    break;

  case ReceiveMessageKernelCall:
    int * user_msg; asm{ store r9,user_msg }
    int from_q; asm{ store r10,from_q }

    // check for an invalid queue identifier
    If( !message_queue_allocated[from_q] {
        pd[current_process].sa.reg[1] = -1;
        break;
    }
    if( message_queue[from_q].Empty() ) {
        pd[current_process].state = Blocked;
        WaitQueueItem item;
        item.pid = current_process;
        item.buffer = user_msg;
        wait_queue[from_q].Insert( item );
    } else {
        int msg_no = message_queue[from_q].Remove();
        TransferMessage( mag_no, user_mag);
    }
    pd[current_process].sa.reg[1] = 0;
    break;
}// end switch
```

```
        Dispatcher ();
}
void SendMessageFromOS( int to_q, int msg_no ){
   if( !wait_queue[to_q].Empty() ) {
        // some process is waiting for a message, deliver it immediately
        WaitQueueItem item = wait_queue.Remove();
        TransferMessage( msg_no, item.buffer );
        pd[item.pid].state = Ready;
   } else {
        // otherwise put it on the queue
        message_queue[to_q].Insert( msg_no );
   }
}
```

Some of the send message processing is used in several places, so it is put into the procedure SendMessageFromOS.

20.2.6   HANDLING SYSTEM CALLS

System calls are handled differently in this system than they were in the simple operating system. When you execute a procedure call, control goes off to that procedure, it does its work, and returns control to the caller. When control returns to the caller, the requested work is completed. In the simple operating system, system calls acted very much like procedure calls. The process executed the system call instruction, and when it returned, the system call had been completed. For example, if the system call was to read a disk block, when the system call returned, the block had been read, and the contents were in the user's buffer.

In this operating system, a system call is a message. A message is a one-way communication. The return code for a message send just indicates whether the message was sent successfully, not whether it was received or replied to. So the message send will return, but the sender will not know the results of the system call.

When the kernel receives a system call message, it will start working on it. When the system call is complete, it will send a reply message back to the system caller. The system call message must include the number of a message queue to send the reply to. So, to the process, a system call now consists of a message send (of the system call request) followed by a message receive (of a notification of the completion of the system call). It is not necessary that the process execute the receive immediately after the send. Suppose the process wants to read and process 500 disk blocks. The process can start two disk block reads before it waits for the first one to complete. Then it can enter a loop where it waits for a disk block read to complete, starts another one, and then processes the disk block just read. This technique is called double buffering, and was discussed in Section 15.2.2.

By separating system call requests from system call completions, we have given the process this additional flexibility, but we have made the system call interface more complicated. Now all system calls are in two parts, and the system caller is not blocked after sending the system call request message. Before the system calls were *synchronous*, meaning that they completed before they returned,   synchronous and when they returned you knew they had completed. Now the system calls are *asynchronous* because they return immediately, and the system call will be executed some time later.

We have said that system calls from a high-level language are usually implemented by calling a short assembly language procedure that actually executes the system call. This is done because most high-level languages will not generate system calls, that is, there is no language construct that results in the generation of a system call instruction. We can use this fact to shield the high-level language user from the system call changes we have just made.

The read disk block system call from a high-level language will still call a short assembly language procedure. This procedure will send the system call message, and then immediately execute a receive message to wait for the reply. The high-level language user will see no difference in the way the system call acts. The disk read system call will still not return until the disk block is read. Of course, then the double buffering technique will not be available to the high-level language user.

Figure 20.3 shows how we have implemented system calls by creating, in effect, an "operating system process." The "operating system process" does not really exist as an actual process, but it seems to because user processes can send messages to it.

20.2.7   THE SYSTEM CALL HANDLING CODE

The kernel's system call handler is shown next. The CreateProcessSystemCall case calls the CreateProcess procedure to do the work, and then sends a System-CallComplete back to the system caller. The CreateProcess procedure is the same as in the first operating system and is not shown here. ExitProcessSystem-Call frees the process table slot and the message buffer.

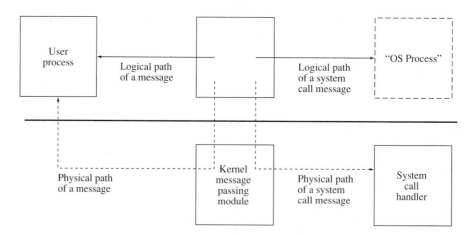

Figure 20.3   The "operating system process"

SYSTEM CALL MESSAGE HANDLER

```
void KernelReceiveMessage( int msg_no ) {
  int msg_no = message_queue[from_q].Remove();
  int * msg = message_buffer[msg_no];
  switch( msg[0] ) {
  case CreateProcessSystemCall:
    // Message format:
    //    msg[0] = CreateProcessSystemCall
    //    msg[1] = starting block number of the executable
    //    msg[2] = number of blocks in the executable
    //    msg[3] = message queue to reply to
    msg[1] = CreateProcess( msg[1], msg[2] );
    // reuse the same message buffer to send the reply message.
    // msg[0] = SystemCallComplete;
    SendMessageFromOS( msg[3], msg_no );
    break;

  case ExitProcessSystemCall:
    // Message format:
    //    msg[0] = ExitProcessSystemCall
    // free the process table slot
    pd[current_process].state = UnusedProcessSlot;
    FreeMessageBuffer( msg );
    break;

  case DiskReadSystemCall:
  case DiskWriteSystemCall:
    // Message format:
    //    msg[0] = DiskReadSystemCall or DiskWriteSystemCall
    //    msg[1] = block number
    //    msg[2] = address of buffer in user process
    //    msg[3] = message queue to reply to
    // forward the message to the disk I/O system process
    // convert to physical address
    msg[2] += pd[current_process].sa.base;
    SendMessageFromOS( IOSystemMessageQueue, msg_no );
    break;

  case ReadDeviceRegisters:
    // Message format:
    //    msg[0] = ReadDeviceRegisters
    //    msg[1] = message queue to reply to
    DiskCommandRegister reg2 = *disk_reg2;
    msg[0] = SystemCallComplete;
    msg[1] = (int)reg2;
    SendMessageFromOS( msg[1], msg_no );
    break;

  case WriteDeviceRegisters:
    // Message format:
    //    msg[0] = WriteDeviceRegisters
    //    msg[1] = control register
```

```
    //    msg[2] = memory address register
    // store the control words in the disk control register
    *Disk_memory_addr = msg[2];
    *Disk_control = msg[1]; // Load the control register last
                            // since it initiates the command.
    break;
  }
}
```

The last four system calls will be discussed in the next few sections.

20.2.8   USER KNOWLEDGE OF MESSAGE QUEUE IDENTIFIERS

The disk driver subsystem is no longer part of the kernel, and so these requests must be forwarded to the disk I/O system process. This is done by transferring the message to the message queue of the disk I/O system process.

You might wonder why we do this, rather than simply have the processes send disk I/O system calls directly to the disk I/O system process. The reason we choose to do it this way is so the user does not have to know the message queue identifier used for requests to the disk I/O system process. The message queue identifier of the kernel will always be 0, but the message queue identifier of the disk I/O system process might change as we add other system processes.

Registration of System Processes   An alternative solution would be to have the disk I/O system process register itself (using a system process registration system call) with the operating system when it starts up. The operating system can record that registration in a table, and we can add a get registration system call that will return the message queue identifier of the disk I/O system process to any user process. So to do disk I/O, you first ask the kernel for the message queue identifier of the disk I/O system process, and then send messages to it. Figure 20.4 shows the two main possibilities.

We can expand this facility when we have other system processes and have a system call that returns the message queue identifier of any registered system process. This is a good technique, and it is the basis for mechanisms to find processes in distributed systems, but we will have gone far afield from our simple operating system here if we use it. We will use the simple method of sending all system calls to the kernel, and having the kernel forward all disk I/O system calls to the disk I/O system process.

20.2.9   PROTECTION OF RESOURCES

It was necessary to add system calls to read and write the disk controller registers because the disk subsystem is in a process, and processes are not allowed access to the device registers. But the disk I/O system process is a special process that does need such access. We provide it by adding system calls to access the registers.

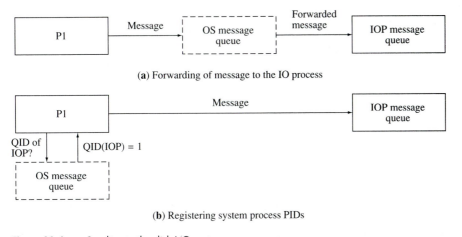

(**a**) Forwarding of message to the IO process

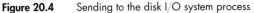

(**b**) Registering system process PIDs

Figure 20.4   Sending to the disk I/O system process

But this presents a problem, because now there is no protection on the ability to read and write device registers. This is a serious breach of protection since any process can write directly into the disk device controller's registers and interfere with the disk I/O system process. In a real operating system, there would have to be some protection. We could add protection by using a separate message queue and protecting access to this message queue via the protection system.

Before we moved the disk system out of the operating system kernel, we had no problem. The disk system ran in system mode, and had access to the device registers. Now that we moved it out of the operating system kernel, we have to provide it access to these registers, but in doing so we give any process access to these registers.

Another possibility is to have a system call to map the device registers into the address space of the disk I/O system process. This is a more efficient solution because it gives the I/O process direct access to the device registers. It is also less secure since the disk I/O system process can do anything it wants to the device with no chance for the kernel to check (or even record) each operation. This kind of tradeoff between efficiency and security is a common one.

> Moving operating system functions out of the operating system makes protection more complex and system calls more inefficient.

20.2.10   DISK INTERRUPT HANDLER

Disk I/O will be handled by a separate process, rather than in the kernel of the operating system. The operating system will forward disk interrupts to the disk I/O system process.

DISK INTERRUPT HANDLING

```
void DiskInterruptHandler( void ) {
  if( current_process > 0 ) { // was there a running process?
    // Save the processor state of the system caller.
    // ... as before
  }

  // send the message on to the disk I/O system process
  int msg_no = GetMessageBuffer();
  int * msg = message_buffer[msg_no];
  msg[0] = DiskInterrupt;
  SendMessageFromOS( IOSystemMessageQueue, msg_no );

  Dispatcher();
}
```

Note that disk interrupts are immediately converted into messages. This is another aspect of our converting everything into the client/server model. Processes communicate with messages, so we transform the low-level interrupts into high-level messages. Only a few parts of the kernel need to deal with hardware details; the rest of the system sees a collection of processes sending and receiving messages.

What we are doing here is moving between logical levels in the system. Disk registers and disk interrupts are at the lowest levels. We convert them to the the higher-level concept of messages. Figure 20.5 shows this pictorially.

20.2.11   DISK I/O SYSTEM PROCESS

The structure of the disk I/O system process is an infinite loop that first waits for a message and then executes a case statement based on the type of the message just received. This is the structure of what is called a *server*.

server

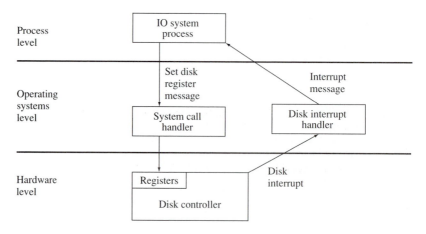

Figure 20.5   Logical levels in I/O processing

DISK I/O SYSTEM PROCESS

```
int message_queue_for_reply;
int DiskIsBusy = False; // initially false

struct IORequest {
    int operation;
    int disk_block;
    int buffer_address;
    int reply_queue;
    IORequest( int op, int db, int ba, int rq ) {
        operation = op; disk_block = db;
        buffer_address = ba; reply_queue = rq;
    }
};
Queue<IORequest *> * DiskQueue = new Queue<IORequest>;

void main() {
    int msg[8];

    // Begin a server loop
    while( 1 ) {
        ReceiveMessage( IOSystemMessageQueue, msg );
        switch( msg[0] )  {

        case DiskReadSystemCall:
        case DiskWriteSystemCall:
            // Message format:
            //    msg[0] = DiskReadSystemCall or DiskWriteSystemCall
            //    msg[1] = disk block number
            //    msg[2] = buffer memory address
            //    msg[3] = message queue to reply to
            DiskQueue->Insert(
                new IORequest( msg[0], msg[1], msg[2], msg[3]));
            break;

        case DiskInterrupt:
            DiskIsBusy = False;
            msg[0] = SystemCallComplete;
            SendMessage( message_queue_for_reply, msg );
            ScheduleDisk();
            break;
        }
        if( !DiskIsBusy && !DiskQueue->Empty()) {
            IORequest * ior = DiskQueue->Remove();
            DiskIO(ior->operation, ior->disk_block,
                ior->buffer_address);
            message_queue_for_reply = ior->reply_queue;
            delete ior;
        }
    }
}
```

Read and write requests are put in an internal disk request queue. Each time a message is received, the disk status and the queue are checked, and a request is started if possible.

The procedures DiskIO and ScheduleDisk are exactly the same as they were in the first operating system.

Since a user process cannot access the device registers directly, we cannot implement DiskBusy and IssueDiskCommand as we did in the first operating system.

For DiskBusy, we will assume that the disk I/O system process is the only process issuing commands to the disk, so we will just maintain a variable to remember whether the disk is busy or not. To actually communicate with the disk controller, we have to send a message to the kernel to do it for us. The procedure IssueDisk-Command builds the three register values and sends them to the kernel.

DISK I/O PROCEDURE

```
int DiskBusy( void ) {
    return DiskIsBusy;
}

void IssueDiskCommand( int rw_cmd, int block_number, char * buffer ) {
    DiskSectorRegister reg0;
    DiskCommandRegister reg2;
    int cylinder, track, sector;
    int msg[8];
    // get the disk address from the block number
    DiskAddress( block_number, cylinder, track, sector );

    // assemble the necessary control words
    reg0.sector = sector;
    reg0.track = track;
    reg0.cylinder = cylinder;
    reg0.disk = 0;
    reg2.command = rw_cmd;
    reg2.interrupt_enable = 1;

    // send the command to the kernel to put into the device registers
    msg[0] = WriteDeviceRegisters;
    msg[1] = reg0;
    msg[2] = buffer;
    msg[3] = reg2;
    SendMessage( SystemCallMessageQueue, msg );
    DiskIsBusy = True;
}
```

20.2.12 SERVER DATA STRUCTURES

This simple disk server has only one request in process at a time, so any disk interrupt message must be for that request. This allows us to keep a simple state (message_queue_for_reply) and a FIFO queue for requests. More complex servers might have several requests in service at a time (for example, a disk server that controls several disks), and it might want to schedule the disk requests in non-FIFO order. These servers will require more complex data structures to record what requests are in service and what requests have priority.

One problem that comes up is how to tell which request an incoming event message (like an interrupt message) is associated with. Many servers allow you to attach arbitrary identifiers with requests that will be returned to you when the request is completed. These identifiers can be used to match replies to requests.

20.3   MICRO-KERNEL OPERATING SYSTEMS

In the simple operating system we developed in Chapters 5, 6, and 8, all system services were provided by the operating system. Whenever a user process needed a service (like creating a new process or doing a disk read), it would make a system call to request the service from the operating system. In the operating system we described in the previous section, a user process sends a message to the operating system to request services, but not all services are provided by the operating system. Disk I/O services are provided by the disk I/O system process.

So now we have two service providers: the operating system and the disk I/O system process. There is no reason why we have to stop there. We can do this with all device drivers. The advantage of this is that it is easy to install new device drivers and change existing device drivers while the system is running. In addition, the device independent parts of the I/O system can also be moved into a system process. This process can communicate with the device drivers with messages. In fact, most of the operating system can be moved out of the kernel and into processes. This includes: the file system, many parts of the memory system, the policy part of the process scheduler, and even parts of the protection system.

Moving most of the functions out of the operating system reduces the size of the operating system. Because of this, the organization is often called the *micro-kernel* approach. The system processes that do much of the work for the kernel are called servers, and this type of system structure is also called the *client-server model*. Such a system consists of a number of server processes, which provide various services, and a collection of client processes that require services.

micro-kernel

client-server model

Figure 20.6 shows the internal structure of a server (a loop that reads messages and uses a `switch` statement to decide how to handle each message) and the communication between the server and its clients. In the client-server operating system, the communication is indirect since the service requests go first to the operating system and then are redirected to the server processes.

Sometimes these servers will have to defer calls until they can request services of other servers. This makes it convenient to structure servers with threads, as we saw in Section 6.7.4.

Figure 20.7 shows the structure of a micro-kernel-based operating system.

Processes that do operating-systems-like functions are called servers.

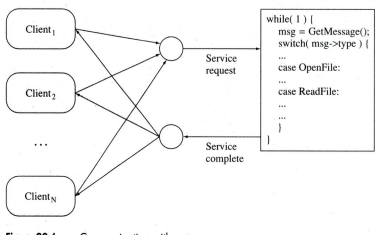

Figure 20.6   Communication with a server

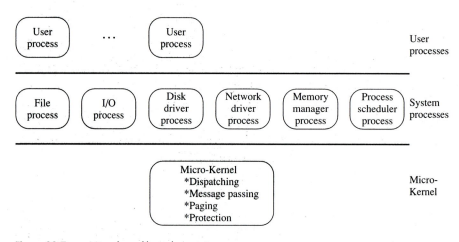

Figure 20.7   Micro-kernel-based operating system

20.3.1   TRADEOFFS OF THE CLIENT-SERVER MODEL

All processes are forced to use the operating system. There can be only one operating system on the machine, because the operating system controls all the resources of the machine. Thus, the processes have no choice about which operating system to use. If you want to test a new part of the operating system, you have to build the new operating system, stop the old operating system (and all the user processes running on it), and start the new operating system. Normal processes cannot run while a new operating system is being tested, unless they want to take a chance on the operating system failing and damaging their data.

The client-server model can improve both these problems. It is possible to have several server processes providing similar services in different ways. A process is free to deal with any of the servers, and can choose the one most compatible with its needs. For example, there might be a UNIX file system server and an MS/DOS file system server available. If you have a floppy disk, you can use either file system server to read it, depending on how it was written.

Suppose we want to test a new file system server. We can leave the existing server running and start a new file system server. We can send messages to the new server and test it while other processes continue to use the old server. If there is an error, only the new file system server process will fail, and other users will be unaffected. We can debug a new server without ever restarting the operating system, and so provide continuous service for the existing clients. When the new file system server is ready, we can begin rerouting file service messages to it, and gradually phase out the old file server, all without restarting the operating system.

Another advantage of the client-server model is that it fits in with a networked or distributed environment. If the operating system is one big program, it is not obvious how to distribute it over a number of machines. But if the operating system services are provided by a collection of five processes, we can easily distribute them over five machines. We can also have duplicate servers for some or all services, and have a system that is resistant to machine failures.

Another advantage of the client-server model is modularity. The operating system is in several smaller pieces instead of one large piece. This makes it easier to develop the modules, and makes it easier to test them and be confident of their correctness.

The principle disadvantage of the client-server model is speed. It is slower to send a message to another process and switch address spaces to that process than it is to make a procedure call on another module in the kernel. Client-server operating systems have not caught on as much as was expected because of this problem with efficiency. In every other way, they are an improvement on a monolithic organization, but the loss of speed seems to be larger than is acceptable to most users.

In the client-server model, we move some operating system services out of the operating system and into processes. Can we move all of the operating system services out of the operating system? No, we cannot, since something has to implement processes themselves. Process management is really the main thing that must be done by the operating system directly. This includes implementing processes, managing process data structures, and implementing message sending between processes. In addition, the operating system must maintain control over all the resources in the system and protect them from unauthorized use. These are the kernel of operating system services, and an operating system that only implements these services is usually called a *kernel*. In fact, over the years, the word kernel has been used in so many different ways that people now use the stronger term *micro-kernel* to mean an operating system that does only the essential services where the other system services are provided by server processes.

> The client-server model is a very popular way to structure operating system services, especially in distributed operating systems.

> The micro-kernel architecture moves as much of the functionality out to the servers as possible.

20.3.2   OBJECT-ORIENTED OPERATING SYSTEMS

In this book, we have taken the view that an operating system creates objects that processes (and threads) can use. Each object has a set of operations that are allowed on it. This point of view can be taken for any operating system, even though the system is not intended to be object oriented. You just interpret the system calls as operations on objects. Some operating systems, however, use this model explicitly and consider all operating system services to be structured as objects and operations on objects.

The client-server model is very close to the object model. Each server manages a certain type of objects, or a small set of objects. For example, the file server manages file system objects, directory objects, and file objects. But this structure is slightly different from the object structure you find in an object-oriented programming language. In a programming language, the model is that clients hold names or pointers to objects, and all operations are performed by sending messages to the objects using this name or pointer. The object performs operations on itself. In a client-server system, you send messages to the server, not the object. In the message, you give the name of the object you want to perform an operation on. The server manages the objects and resolves the names into objects.

20.4   THE DEVELOPMENTS TOWARDS A DISTRIBUTED SYSTEM

We can think of the developments towards a distributed system as a series of operating system models. Figure 20.8 shows a table of the operating system models that will be reviewed in this section.

In Chapter 5, we showed the simple operating system which had one processor. Communication within a process was by procedure calls, between processes was with messages, and to the operating system was with system calls. The only form of parallelism was the logical parallelism of processes interleaved on a single processor. This was shown in Figure 20.1.

In Chapters 6 and 8, we expanded the logical parallelism to include threads in user process and threads in the kernel. We allowed user processes to run in the kernel using kernel-mode processes. We added physical parallelism with multiple processors, and allowed the possibility of two or more threads running in parallel. This expanded model is shown in Figure 20.9.

	Logical Parallelism	Physical Parallelism	Operating System Structure
Simple OS (Chap. 5)	Processes	None	Monolithic
Threaded multiple processor OS (Chaps. 5 and 6)	Threads Kernel-mode processes	Multiple processors	Monolithic
Micro-kernel OS (Chap. 20)	Threads Kernel-mode processes	Multiple processors	Distributed in system processes
Network OS	Threads Kernel-mode processes	Multiple processors and systems	System processes on 1 processor
Distributed OS	Threads Kernel-mode processes	Multiple processors and systems	System processes on several processors

Figure 20.8   A sequence of operating system models

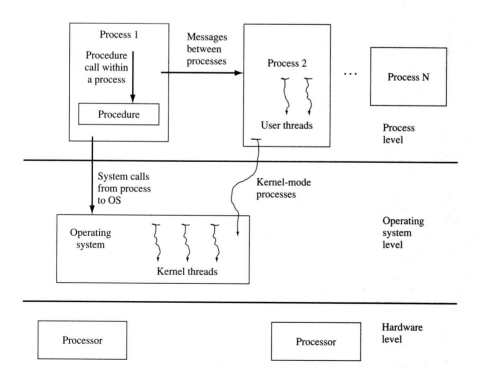

Figure 20.9   Expanded OS model

In both of these models, all of the functions of the operating system were performed by operating system code running in system mode. The operating system was one large program in a single address space. We use the term *monolithic* to describe this operating system organization because the system is one monolith.

In this chapter, we added system processes which allowed us to move parts of the operating system into user-mode processes. This allowed greater modularity in the system organization. This model is shown in Figure 20.10. We still show several processors, but there is just one shared kernel and the processes and/or threads will be physically parallel, but other than that they should not notice the multiple processors.

20.4.1   NETWORKED OPERATING SYSTEMS

Suppose we have two of these systems that are connected to a network. We could develop a system that looks something like Figure 20.11. This figure shows two separate operating systems on two separate computers that are connected on a network. The operating systems know about the network and use it to send messages to each other. We call this a *network operating system*. We show the connections between the processors with solid lines to indicate that this is the physical connection between the machines. The two kernels and processes on the two systems are connected with dotted lines to show this is a logical connection. The messages will be sent through the physical connection.

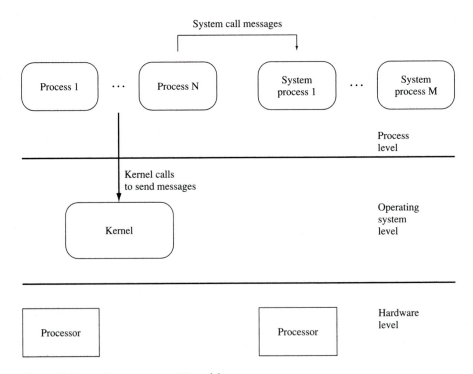

Figure 20.10   System process OS model

We can easily extend the message-passing model so that processes can send messages to processes on the other computer system. One way to do this is to have a pair of message queues, one on each system. Figure 20.12 shows how this works. Messages sent to a remote message queue are automatically forwarded (by the kernel) to the corresponding remote message queue on the other system. We will need a

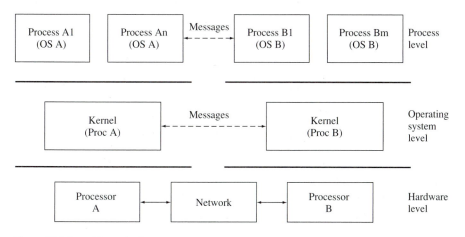

Figure 20.11   Networked operating system

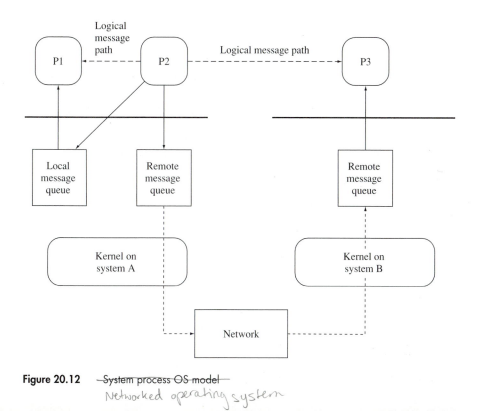

Figure 20.12   ~~System process OS model~~
Networked operating system

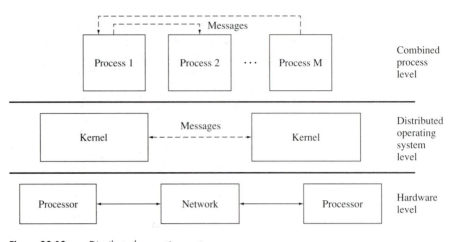

Figure 20.13   Distributed operating system

system call to set up such a shared message queue, and then processes on the two systems can communicate through it.

20.4.2 DISTRIBUTED OPERATING SYSTEMS

In a network of operating systems, each operating system runs independently of the others but will communicate with the others. If the two kernels cooperate closely, they can create the illusion that there is only one operating system running on the network. User processes do not need to know about where operating system objects reside. They have the illusion of a single operating system on a single machine. We call this a *distributed operating system*. Figure 20.13 shows a distributed operating system.

distributed operating
system

    Both user processes and system processes can run on any of the machines in a distributed system. This allows the operating system itself to be distributed over the network.

20.5 SUMMARY

Many newer operating systems use the micro-kernel approach. This means that the kernel of the operating system (the part that runs in system mode) is as small as possible. Most of the operating system functions are done by system processes which run in user mode. This leads to a more modular and more dynamic system, but it can cause performance problems. In this chapter, we showed how to move the disk driver out of the simple operating system. Another change we made was to convert system calls into messages to the kernel. Interrupts are converted to messages and sent to the relevant server process. Some of these are handled directly by the kernel, and some are forwarded to system processes.

Another way to look at this is that the operating system is made up of a collection of servers, each implementing an operating system object and the operations on the object. The kernel serves to connect the client processes to the server processes. This is the client-server model of an operating system. An operating system that knows about networks and communicates with other operating systems on the network is called a network operating system. If the operating system kernels cooperate closely, they can create the illusion of a single operating system. This is called a distributed operating system.

20.5.1 TERMINOLOGY

After reading this chapter, you should be familiar with the following terms:

*   asynchronous
*   client-server model
*   distributed operating system
*   kernel
*   micro-kernel
*   monolithic
*   network operating system
*   server
*   synchronous
*   system process

20.5.2 REVIEW QUESTIONS

The following questions are answered in the text of this chapter:

1. What are the three ways entities communicate in a computer system?
2. What is a system process?
3. How can messages be used to make system calls?
4. What do we mean by an "operating system process"?
5. Why do we have to add a system call to read and write the disk device registers?
6. Why does the kernel forward I/O requests to the disk I/O system process?
7. What do we mean by "registration" of a system process?
8. Why are the system calls to write device registers a protection problem?
9. Why are disk interrupts converted into messages?
10. Why does the disk I/O system process need an internal queue of disk requests?
11. What are the advantages of the client-server model?
12. What is the main disadvantage of the client-server model?

13. What is an object-oriented operating system?

14. What is a network operating system?

15. What is a distributed operating system?

20.5.3 FURTHER READING

There are many books on networked and distributed operating systems. Tanenbaum (1992) is a good place to start.

20.6 PROBLEMS

1. Consider some services that might be provided to a user process:

    • File system services.

    • Library to render 3D graphics.

    • Window system services.

    Each of these services could be provided by:

    a. Procedure call to a library linked in with the process.

    b. System call to the operating system.

    c. Remote procedure call to a server on another machine in the network.

    For each of these services, give the tradeoffs between the three methods of providing the service.

2. Suppose we wanted to add a file system process to this operating system. Show the changes that would be necessary to do this. You do not need to show the code for the file system process. Show the code you would add to the operating system to start the file system process, set up any message queues it needs, make sure the file system calls are forwarded to it, make sure it gets any interrupts it should get (if any), and get anything else you need to do to make it work. Just show two file system calls: open and read.

3. In the client-server model, the process server should make the scheduling decisions. The mechanism for switching processes will be in the kernel, but the policy decisions will be made by the process server.

    a. Where is the process table? In the process server or in the kernel?

    b. The kernel must be the one that actual switches to another process. How does it know which process to switch to?

4. The disk I/O system process keeps track of whether the disk is busy with an internal flag. This assumes that the disk I/O system process will be the only user of the disk. Because of this, the DiskBusy procedure does not actually look at the device registers, but uses the internal flag instead. Suppose we want to have DiskBusy actu-

ally read the device register and be sure of the disk's status. What changes would need to be made to the system to make this change? *Hint:* This is more involved than you might think. You will have to send a message to the kernel to read the disk status register, you will have to pick out the reply message from other messages to the disk I/O system process, and you will have to somehow delay the reply to the DiskBusy call to wait for the return message.

5. In this book, we talk about separating policy from mechanism. Suppose we do this by putting the mechanism in the operating system and the policy in special *system* processes that are not part of the operating system. For parts *a* and *b*, assume a single processor system with a micro-kernel.

    a. Suppose we wanted process scheduling policy to be handled by a system scheduling process (in a single-processor system). This can be done by having the kernel do the actual dispatching of processes based on a fixed scheduling algorithm, but having the scheduling process set policy by adjusting the parameters of the scheduling algorithm. That is, the kernel actually decides who goes next but it does it on the basis of scheduling parameters set by the scheduling process. So the kernel is not setting scheduling policy, it is just implementing the mechanism by which the scheduling policy is realized. What are the parameters (if any) of each of the following scheduling algorithms? Since algorithm is a scheduling mechanism, what are the the parameters that determine the policy each algorithm implements?

        (1) Round-robin.

        (2) Priority.

        (3) Multiple queues.

        (4) Shortest job first.

    b. In this structure, is the process table still kept entirely in the kernel, or are some parts of it kept in the scheduling process? What parts of the process table must be kept in the kernel? What parts should be kept in the scheduling process? Is your answer different depending on which one of the above four scheduling algorithms is used? How is it different?

    c. Suppose this is a distributed system using the micro-kernel-approach.

        (1) If it is a shared memory multiprocessor, will there be a micro-kernel for each processor or just one for all the processors? Will there be just one scheduling process or one for each processor? Explain your answers.

        (2) If it is a multicomputer with no shared memory, will there be a micro-kernel for each processor or just one for all the processors? Will there be just one scheduling process or one for each processor? Explain your answers.

6. In the procedure KernelReceiveMessage, the kernel changes the disk buffer address from a logical address to a physical address. Why can't the disk I/O system process do this itself? Specify a system call that would allow the disk I/O system process to do this translation itself. What extra information will it need to make this system call, and where will it get that information?

7. Specify a set of two system calls. The first is `RegisterSystemProcess`, which registers a system process with the kernel. The second is `GetRegistered-ProcessQID`, which returns the message queue of a registered system process. You will have to decide on a way of naming system processes.

8. The disk I/O system process has an internal queue of disk requests because disk requests and disk interrupts both are sent to its message queue. Devise a way for the disk I/O system process to use a message queue for disk requests, rather than having to use its own internal queue. Show the changes to the system required to implement this solution. You are not allowed to change the fact that all disk requests and interrupt messages go to the `SystemCallMessageQueue`. *Hint:* Use another message queue and forward to it.

9. It is a security problem to have a system call that allows any process to write the disk device registers. Develop and describe a solution to this security problem.

10. A device driver needs to be informed of device interrupts. Since it is a process, it cannot be an interrupt handler directly, so it must send messages when an interrupt occurs. In the operating system in this chapter, we automatically forwarded disk interrupts to the disk I/O system process. Specify a system call that a system process can make to request that it receive messages when a certain interrupt occurs.

11. Change the disk I/O system process so that it services requests using the shortest-seek-time-first algorithm. In this case, that means that it will take the request whose block number is closest to the block number of the last request serviced. You will have to change the internal queue to a data structure that allows more access to the items in the queue.

12. We used a system call `WriteDiskRegisters`. Why is this system call necessary? Why can't the disk I/O system process simply write the disk registers itself, instead of asking the operating system to write them for it?

13. Suppose we wanted to allow the disk I/O system process access to the device registers. Specify a system call called `MapDeviceRegisters` which would allow it to map the disk device registers into its address space.

References

C. Abbot. Intervention schedules for real-time programming. *IEEE Transactions on Software Engineering,* SE-10(3):268–274, May 1984.

A. V. Aho, P. J. Denning, and J. D. Ullman. Principles of optimal page replacement. *Journal of the ACM*, 18(1):80–93, January 1971.

A. Aho and B. W. Kerhighan. *The AWK programming language*. Prentice Hall, Englewood Cliffs, NJ, 1988.

G. Akl. Digital signatures: a tutorial survey. *Computer*, 16(2):15–24, February 1983.

T. E. Anderson, E. D. Lazowska, and H. M. Levy. The performance implications of thread management alternatives for shared-memory multiprocessors. *Performance Evaluation Review*, 17:49–60, [5] 1989.

Gregory R. Andrews and Fred B. Schneider. Concepts and notations for concurrent programming. *ACM Computing Surveys*, 15(1):3–43, [3] 1983.

M. J. Bach. *The Design of the UNIX Operating System*. Prentice Hall, Englewood Cliffs, NJ, 1986.

A. P. Batson. Program behavior at the symbolic level. *Computer*, 9(11):21–28, November 1976.

C. Bays. A comparison of next-fit, first-fit, and best-fit. *Communications of the ACM*, 20(3):191–192, March 1977.

R. V. Baron, D. Black, W. Bolosky, J. Chew, R. P. Draves, D. B. Golub, R. F. Rashid, A. Tevanian, and M. W. Young. *Mach Kernal Interface Manual*. Computer Science Department, Carnagie-Mellon University, January 1990.

L. L. Beck. A dynamic storage allocation technique based on memory residence time. *Communications of the ACM*, 25(10):714–724, October 1977.

L. A. Belady. A study of replacement algorithms for a virtual storage computer. *IBM Systems Journal*, 5(2):78–101, 1966.

M. Ben-Ari. *Principles of Concurrent Programming*. Prentice Hall, Englewood Cliffs, NJ, 1982.

M. Ben-Ari. *Principles of Concurrent and Distributed Programming*. Prentice Hall, Englewood Cliffs, NJ, 1990.

J. Bentley. *More programming pearls*. Addison-Wesley, Reading MA, 1988.

A. D. Birrell. An introduction to programming with threads. Technical Report 35, DEC Systems Research Center, January 1989.

A. P. Batson, S. Ju, and D. Wood. Measurements of segment size. *Communications of the ACM*, 13(3):155–159, March 1970.

R. E. Barkley and T. P. Lee. A lazy buddy system bound by two coalescing delays per class. In *Proceedings of the 12th ACM Symposium on Operating Systems Principles*, pages 167–176, Litchfield Park, AZ USA, December 1989. Published as ACM Operating Systems Review, SIGOPS, volume 23, number 5.

L. Bic and A. C. Shaw. *The logical design of operating systems*. Prentice-Hall, Englewood Cliffs, NJ, second edition, 1988.

A. D. Birrell and B. J. Nelson. Implementing remote procedure calls. *ACM Transactions on Computer Systems*, 2(1):39–59, [2] 1984.

J. Bonwick. The slab allocator: an object-caching kernel memory allocator. In *Summer USENIX Technical Conference Proceedings*, pages 87–98. USENIX, June 1994.

R. B. Bunt. Scheduling techniques for operating systems. *Computer*, 9(10):10–17, October 1976.

R. W. Carr and J. L. Hennessy. WSClock - A simple and effective algorithm for virtual memory management. In *Proceedings of the 8th ACM Symposium on Operating System Principles*, pages 87–95, Pacific Grove, CA, December 1981.

R. Chaney and B. Johnson. Maximizing hard-disk performance: how cache memory can drastically affect transfer rate. *BYTE*, 9(5):307–334, May 1984.

A. Chang and M. F. Mergen. 801 storage: Architecture and programming. *ACM Transactions on Computer Systems*, 6(1):28–50, [2] 1988.

J. S. Chase, H. M. Levy, M. J. Feeley, and E. D. Lazowska. Sharing and protection in a single address space operating system. *ACM Transactions on Computer Systems*, 12(3), April 1994.

W. W. Chu and H. Opderbeck. Performance of replacement algorithms with different page sizes. *Computer*, 7(11):14–21, November 1974.

W. W. Chu and H. Opderbeck. Program behavior and the page fault frequency algorithm. *Computer*, 9(11):29–38, November 1977.

E. G. Coffman and L. Kleinrock. Computer scheduling methods and their countermeasures. In *Spring Joint Computer Conference*, volume 32, pages 11–21, 1968.

E. G. Coffman et al. System deadlock. *ACM Computing Surveys*, 2(3):67–78, June 1971.

E. G. Coffman Jr. and L. C. Varian. Further experimental data on the behavior of programs in a paging environment. *Communications of the ACM*, 11(7):471–474, July 1968.

D. Comer. *Operating Systems Design: The XINU Approach*. Prentice Hall, Englewood Cliffs, NJ, 1984.

J. E. Coplien and D. C. Schmidt, editors. *Pattern Languages of Programs*. Addison-Wesley, Reading MA, 1995.

H. Custer. *Inside Windows NT*. Microsoft Press, Redmond, WA, 1993.

D. W. Davies. Applying RSA digital signature to emectronic mail. *Computer*, 16(2):55–62, February 1983.

H. M. Deitel and M. S. Kogan. *The Design of OS/2*. Prentice Hall, Englewood Cliffs, NJ, 1994.

Peter J. Denning. The working set model for program behavior. *Communications of the ACM*, 11(1):323–333, May 1968.

Peter J. Denning. Virtual memory. *ACM Computing Surveys*, 2(3):153–189, September 1970.

Peter J. Denning. Working sets: Past and present. *IEEE Transactions on Software Engineering*, SE-6(1):64–84, January 1980.

P. J. Denning and K. C. Kahn. A study of program locality and lifetime functions. In *Proceedings of the 5th ACM Symposium on Operating Systems Principles*, pages 207–216, Litchfield Park, AZ USA, November 1975.

W. Diffie and M. E. Hellman. New directions in cryptography. *IEEE Transactions on Information Theory*, 22(6):644–654, November 1976.

W. Diffie and M. E. Hellman. Privacy and authentication. *Proceedings of the IEEE*, 67(3):397–427, March 1979.

E. W. Dijkstra. Solution of a problem in concurrent programming control. *Communications of the ACM*, 8(9):569, 1965.

E. W. Dijkstra. *Cooperating Sequential Processes*, pages 43–112. Academic Press, 1968.

E. W. Dijkstra. Hierarchical ordering of sequential processes. *Acta Informatica*, 1:115–138, 1971.

Richard P. Draves, Brian N. Bershad, Richard F. Rashid, and Randall W. Dean. Using continuations to implement thread management and communication in operating systems. In *Proceedings of 13th ACM Symposium on Operating Systems Principles*, pages 122–36. Association for Computing Machinery SIGOPS, October 1991.

Robert M. English and Alexander A. Stepanov. Loge: A self-organizing disk controller. In *USENIX Conference Proceedings*, pages 237–252, San Francisco, CA, Winter 1992.

R. A. Finkel. *An Operating Systems VADE MECUM*. Prentice-Hall, Englewood Cliffs, NJ, second edition, 1988.

S. H. Fuller. Minimal total processing time drum and disk scheduling disiplines. *Communications of the ACM*, 17(7):376–381, July 1974.

E. Gamma, R. Helm, R. Johnson, and J. Vlissides. *Design patterns: elements of reusable object-oriented software*. Addison-Wesley, Reading MA, 1995.

R. Geist and S. Daniel. A continuum of disk scheduling algorithms. *ACM Transactions on Computer Systems*, 5(1):77–92, February 1987.

D. Golden and M. Pechura. The structure of microcomputer file systems. *Communications of the ACM*, 29(3):222–230, March 1986.

P. Goldman. Mac vm revealed. *BYTE*, September 1989.

B. Goodheart and J. Cox. *The Magic Garden Explained: The Internals of UNIX System V Release 4*. Addison-Wesley, Reading MA, 1992.

D. Grosshans. *File Systems Design and Implementation*. Prentice-Hall, Englewood Cliffs, NJ, 1986.

V. C. Hamacher, Z. G. Vranesic, and S. G. Zaky. *Computer Organization*. McGraw-Hill, New York, third edition, 1990.

P. Brinch Hansen. *Operating system principles*. Prentice-Hall, Englewood Cliffs, NJ, 1970.

T. R. Harbron. *File Systems*. Prentice-Hall, Englewood Cliffs, NJ, 1988.

D. J. Hatfield. Experiments on page size, program access patterns, and virtual memory performance. *IBM Journal of Research and Development*, 15(1):58–62, January 1972.

D. J. Hatfield and J. Gerald. Program restructuring for virtual memory. *IBM Systems Journal*, 10(3):168–193, March 1971.

J. W. Havender. Avoiding deadlock in multitasking systems. *IBM Systems Journal*, 7:74–84, 1968.

J. H. Herzog. *Design and Organization of Computing Structures*. Franklin, Beedle and Associates, Wilsonville OR, 1996.

Hewlett Packard. *PA-RISC Architecture and Instruction Set Reference Manual*. Hewlett Packard, Portland OR, third edition, 1994.

C. A. R. Hoare. Monitors: an operating systems structuring concept. *Communications of the ACM*, 17(10):666–677, October 1974.

M. Hofri. Disk scheduling: FCFS versus SSTF revisited. *Communications of the ACM*, 23(11):645–653, November 1980.

R. C. Holt. Some deadlock properties of computer systems. *ACM Computing Surveys*, pages 179–196, September 1972.

J. Hong, X. Tan, and D. Towsley. A performance analysis of minimum laxity and earliest deadline scheduling in a real-time system. *IEEE Transactions on Computers*, 38(12):1736–1743, [12] 1989.

J. H. Howard. Mixed solutions to the deadlock problem. *Communications of the ACM*, 16(7):427–430, July 1973.

J. J. Horning and B. Randell. Process structuring. *ACM Computing Surveys*, 5(1):5–30, March 1976.

S. S. Isloor and T. A. Marsland. The deadlock problem: an overview. *Computer*, 13(9):58–78, September 1980.

Donald E. Knuth. *Fundamental Algorithms*. The Art of Computer Programming. Addison-Wesley, Reading, MA, second edition, 1973.

M. S. Kogan and F. L. Rawson. The design of operating system/2. *IBM Systems Journal*, 27(2):90–104, 1988.

David G. Korn and Kiem-Phong Vo. In search of a better malloc. In *USENIX Conference Proceedings*, pages 489–506, Portland, OR, Summer 1985.

L. Lamport. A new solution to Dijkstra's concurrent programming problem. *Communications of the ACM*, 17(8):453–455, August 1974.

L. Lamport. Password authentication with insecure communications. *Communications of the ACM*, 24(11):770–772, November 1981.

B. W. Lampson. A scheduling philosophy for multi-processing systems. *Communications of the ACM*, 11(5):347–360, May 1968.

B. W. Lampson. Dynamic protection structures. *Fall Joint Computer Conference*, pages 27–38, 1969.

B. Lampson. Protection. In *Proc. Fifth Annual Princeton Conference on Information Sciences and Systems*, pages 437–443. Princeton University, 1971.

Samuel J. Leffler, Marshall Kirk McKusick, Michael J. Karels, and John S. Quarterman. *The Design and Implementation of the 4.3BSD UNIX Operating System*. Addison-Wesley, 1989.

A. Lempel. Cryptology in transition. *ACM Computing Surveys*, 11(4):286–303, December 1979.

A. M. Lister and R. D. Eager. *Fundamentals of Operating Systems*. Springer-Verlag, New York NY, 5th edition, 1995.

P. Livadas. *File structures: theory and practice*. Prentice-Hall, Englewood Cliffs, NJ, 1990.

C. L. Liu and J. W. Layland. Scheduling algorithms for multiprogramming in a hard real-time environment. *Journal of the ACM*, 20(1):46–61, January 1973.

Arthur B. Maccabe. *Computer Systems: Architecture, Organization, and Programming*. Irwin, Homewood, IL, 1993.

A. W. Madison and A. P. Batson. Characteristics of program localities. *Communications of the ACM*, 19(5):285–294, May 1976.

Brian D. Marsh, Michael L. Scott, Thomas J. LeBlanc, and Evangelos P. Markatos. First-class user-level threads. In *Proceedings of 13th ACM Symposium on Operating Systems Principles*, pages 110–21. Association for Computing Machinery SIGOPS, October 1991.

H. Massalin and C. Pu. Threads and input/output in the synthesis kernel. In *Proceedings of the 12th ACM Symposium on Operating Systems Principles*, pages 191–201, Litchfield Park, AZ USA, 1989.

Published as ACM Operating Systems Review, SIGOPS, volume 23, number 5.

R. L. Mattson, J. Gecsei, D. R. Slutz, and I. L. Traiger. Evaluation techniques for storage hierarchies. *IBM Systems Journal*, 9(2):78–117, 1970.

C. May, E. Silha, Simpson R, and Warren H. *The PowerPC Architecture: A Specification for a New Family of RISC Processors*. Morgan Kaufmann, San Francisco, second edition, 1994.

B. McKeon. An algorithm for disk caching with limited memory. *BYTE*, 10(9):129–138, September 1985.

Marshall Kirk McKusick, William N. Joy, Samuel J. Leffler, and Robert S. Fabry. A fast file system for UNIX. *ACM Transactions on Computer Systems*, 2(3):181–197, August 1984.

M. K. McKusik and M. J. Karels. Design of a general-purpose memory allocator for the 4.3BSD UNIX kernel. In *USENIX Conference Proceedings*, pages 295–303. USENIX, Summer 1988.

R. Morris and K. Thompson. Password security: a case history. *Communications of the ACM*, 22(11):594–597, November 1979.

J. E. Morrison. User program performance in virtual storage systems. *IBM Systems Journal*, 12(3):216–237, 1973.

S. J. Mullender and A. S. Tanenbaum. Immediate files. *Software—Practice and Experience*, 14(4):365–368, April 1984.

M. N. Nelson, B. B. Welch, and J. K. Ousterhout. Caching in the sprite network file system. *ACM Transactions on Computer Systems*, 6(1):134–154, [2] 1988.

Open Software Foundation. *Design of the OSF/1 operating system*. Prentice Hall, Englewood Cliffs, NJ, 1993.

J. Ousterhout. *Tcl and the Tk Toolkit*. Addison-Wesley, Reading MA, 1994.

David A. Patterson, Garth Gibson, and Randy H. Katz. A case for redundant arrays of inexpensive disks (RAID). In *Proceedings of the 1988 ACM Conference on Management of Data (SIGMOD)*, pages 109–116, Chicago, IL, June 1988.

G. L. Peterson. Myths about the mutual exclusion problem. *Information Processing Letters*, 12(3):115–116, June 1981.

J. L. Peterson and T. A. Norman. Buddy systems. *Communications of the ACM*, 20(6):421–431, June 1977.

G. J. Popek and C. S. Kline. Encryption and secure computer networks. *ACM Computing Surveys*, 11:331–356, December 1979.

G. Popek. Protection structures. *IEEE Computer*, 7(6):22–33, June 1974.

M. Powell. The DEMOS file system. In *Proceeding of the 6th ACM Symposium on Operating System Principles*, pages 33–42, Reading, MA, November 1977.

B. Prieve and R. S. Fabry. BMIN—an optimal variable-space page replacement algorithm. *Communications of the ACM*, 19(5):295–297, May 1976.

A. L. N. Reddy and P. Banerjee. An evaluation of multiple-disk I/O systems. *IEEE Transactions on Computers*, 38(12):1680–1690, [12] 1989.

R. L. Rivest, A. Shamir, and L. Adleman. On digital signatures and public-key cryptosystems. *Communications of the ACM*, 21(2):120–126, February 1978.

R. L. Rivest, A. Shamir, and L. Adleman. A method for obtaining digital signatures and public-key cryptosystems. *Communications of the ACM*, 26(1):96–99, January 1983.

M. Rosenblum and J. K. Ousterhout. The design and implementation of a log-structured file system. *ACM Transactions on Computer Systems*, 10(1):26–52, February 1992.

A. D. Rubin. Independent one-time passwords. *Computing Systems: The Journal of the USENIX Association*, 9(1):15–27, 1996.

M. Ruschitzka and R. S. Fabry. A unifying approach to scheduling. *Communications of the ACM*, 20(7):469–477, July 1977.

J. Saltzer and M. Schroeder. The protection of information in computer systems. *Proceedings of the IEEE*, 63(19):1278–1308, September 1975.

M. Satyanarayanan. A study of file sizes and functional lifetimes. In *Proceedings of the 8th ACM Symposium on Operating System Principles*, Asilomar, CA, December 1981.

J. V. Sciver and R. F. Rashid. Zone garbage collection. In *Proceedings of the USENIX Mach Workshop*, pages 1–15. USENIX, October 1990.

D. Seely. Password cracking: a game of wits. *Communications of the ACM*, 32(6):700–704, June 1989.

J. E. Shore. On the external storage fragmentation produced by first-fit and best-fit allocation strategies. *Communications of the ACM*, 18(7):433–440, August 1975.

J. E. Shore. Anomolous behavior of the fifty-percent rule. *Communications of the ACM*, 20(11):812–820, November 1977.

S. K. Shrivastava and F. Panzieri. The design of a reliable remote procedure call mechanism. *IEEE Transactions On Computers*, C-31(7):692–697, [7] 1982.

H. Sierra. *An introduction to direct access storage devices*. Academic Press, Boston, MA, 1990.

A. Silberschatz and P. B. Galvin. *Operating Systems Concepts*. Addison-Wesley, Reading MA, 4th edition, 1994.

A. J. Smith. Disk cache-miss ratio analysis and design considerations. *ACM Transactions on Computing Systems*, 3(3):161–203, August 1985.

SPARC International. *The SPARC Architecture Manual: Version 8*. Prentice-Hall, Englewood Cliffs, NJ, 1992.

William Stallings. *Operating Systems*. MacMillan, New York, 1992.

J. A. Stankovic, M. Spuri, M. DiNatale, and G. C. Buttazzo. Implications of classical scheduling for real-time systems. *IEEE Computer*, 44(6):16–25, June 1995.

C. J. Stephenson. Fast fits: New methods for dynamic storage allocation. In *Proceedings of the 9th ACM Symposium on Operating Systems Principles*, pages 30–32, Bretton Woods, NH USA, 1983.

Published as ACM Operating Systems Review, SIGOPS, volume 17, number 5.

W. Richard Stevens. Heuristics for disk drive positioning in 4.3BSD. In *Computing Systems*, volume 2, pages 251–274. USENIX Association, Summer 1989.

S. Strange. Analysis of long-range UNIX file access patterns for applicatio to automatics file migration strategies. Technical Report UCB/CSD 92/700, University of California, Berkeley Computer Science Devision, August 1992.

A. S. Tanenbaum. *Operating Systems: Design and Development*. Prentice Hall, Englewood Cliffs, NJ, 1987.

A. S. Tanenbaum. *Structured Computer Organization*. Prentice-Hall, Englewood Cliffs, NJ, third edition, 1990.

A. S. Tanenbaum. *Modern Operating Systems*. Prentice-Hall, Englewood Cliffs, NJ, 1992.

T. J. Teorey and T. B. Pinkerton. A comparitive analysis of disk scheduling policies. *Communications of the ACM*, 15(3):177–184, March 1972.

Avadis Tevanian, Richard F. Rashid, David B. Golub, David L. Black, Eric Cooper, and Michael W. Young. Mach threads and the UNIX kernel: The battle for control. In *USENIX Conference Proceedings*, pages 185–197, Phoenix, AZ, Summer 1987. USENIX.

U. Vahalia. *UNIX Internals*. Prentice Hall, Englewood Cliffs, NJ, 1996.

B. Welch. *Practical Programming in Tcl and Tk*. Prentice-Hall, Englewood Cliffs, NJ, 1995.

G. Wiederhold. *File organization for database design*. McGraw-Hill, New York, 1987.

N. C. Wilhelm. An anomoly in disk scheduling: a comparison of FCFS and SSTF seek scheduling using an emperical model for disk accesses. *Communications of the ACM*, 19(1):13–17, January 1976.

N. C. Wilhelm. A general model for the performance of disk systems. *Journal of the ACM*, 24(1):14–31, January 1977.

I. S. Winkler. The non-technical threaat to computing systems. *Computing Systems: The Journal of the USENIX Association*, 9(1):3–14, 1996.

C. K. Wong. Minimizing expected head movement in one-dimensional and two-dimensional mass storage systems. *ACM Computing Surveys*, 12(2):167–178, June 1980.

Glossary

A

absolute path name—An absolute path name is a path name that starts at the root directory. In UNIX, this means a path name that start with "/".

access control list—An access control list is a list of access control items associated with a object to be protected. Each access control item specifies a user or a group of users and a set of operations that user or group of users can perform on the object protected by the access control list.

accounting—Accounting is keeping a record of the resource use by users and processes. Accounting is done by a resource manager.

address space—An address space is a set of addresses each referring to a byte in physical memory or in another address space. The addresses in an address space are usually contiguous and usually start with 0.

adjoin—To adjoin two name spaces is to combine them into a single name space. A name is looked up in the adjoined name space by looking it up in the first name space and, if it is not found, looking it up in the second name space.

aging—Aging is a technique to avoid starvation in a scheduling system. It works by adding an aging factor to the priority of each request. The aging factor must increase the request's priority as time passes and must ensure that a request will eventually be the highest priority request (after it has waited long enough).

allocation—Allocation is the assignment of a resource to a process which made a request. Allocation is done by a resource manager.

architecture—The architecture of a system is the general structure of the system. The architecture describes the main components of the system, what the general function of each component is, and the relationship between the components.

asm block—An asm block is a block of assembly language code that is recognized by a C++ compiler and placed directly in the output assembly code at the point it occurs in the source code.

asynchronous—An asynchronous system call is a system call that returns immediately and does not wait for the activity initiated by the system call to complete. For example, an asynchronous system call to read a disk block will return after the block read is requested but before the block is actually read.

atomic action—An atomic action is an action by a process that completes without interruption by any other process.

audit log—An audit log is a record of all security-related events that occur in an operating systems. A security-related event is any event that accesses a system resource. The record of each event will include the operation requested, the object the operation is requested on, the user and process requesting the operation and the time of the request.

auditing—Auditing is the activity of keeping an audit log of all requests to access system resources.

authentication—Authentication is the activity of making sure that a user is really who he or she says he or she is. This usually involves giving a password.

B

bank switching—Bank switching is a hardware technique where two physical memories occupy the same addresses but at different times. It is a technique for allowing the use of more physical memory in a limited address space.

base register—A base register contains a base address that is added to each memory address generated by a process running in user mode. A base register is a hardware register that can only be written in system mode. Base registers are used for address mapping and memory protection. Also see bound register.

batch operating system—A batch operating system is an operating system that runs user jobs in "batches". Batch operating systems allow the use of faster I/O devices like tapes instead of card readers.

batching—Batching is a technique to avoid starvation in resource scheduling. A set of requests is collected into a batch and all the requests in the batch are serviced before any new requests are considered.

best fit—Best fit is a memory allocation algorithm where a request for a block of memory is always filled with the free block that is as small as possible and still satisfies the request.

binary semaphore—A binary semaphore is a semaphore where the count can only be zero or one.

binding time—The binding time of an attribute (of an object) is the time that the value of that attribute is determined. For example, the binding time of the address of a local variable is when the procedure it is declared in is called.

block device—A block device is an I/O device that works basically like a disk, that is, that reads and writes data in fixed size blocks, that has an address for each block, and that allows blocks to be read in any order, by address. The other type of device is the character device.

block list—A block list is a list of allocated and free blocks in a dynamic memory system. It is searched to satisfy a memory request and it is modified when a block is allocated or freed.

blocked—A process is blocked if it cannot continue executing until some event has occurred. Typical events that a process might be blocked waiting for are: the completion of an I/O operation, the arrival of a message in a message queue, the freeing of a block of memory, etc.

blocking send—A blocking send is a send that might block if a buffer is not available, the network is not available, the receiver is not ready to receive the message, or the receiver has not yet replied to the message.

booting—Booting is the process of loading the operating system into the computer memory and initializing the operating system.

bound register—A bound register is a hardware control register that can only be written in system mode. A bound register contains a limit that is compared with each memory address generated by a process running in user mode. If the address is at or above the limit then it is deemed to be an illegal address and the instruction that generated the address causes an interrupt. This is a method of memory protection. Also see base register.

buddy system—The buddy system is a method of memory management where all blocks come in pairs and bigger blocks are created by merging a block with its paired (or "buddy") block. All blocks can also be divided up into two paired blocks. The most common form of the buddy system is the binary buddy system where all blocks have a size that is a power of two and paired blocks are created by dividing a block into two equally sized pieces.

buffering—Buffering is the process of using memory to store output of a producer process until a consumer process is ready to read it. This allows the producer and consumer to operate at different rates.

bursty—A producer is bursty if it tend to produce data at an uneven rate, that is, it might produce a lot of data in a short time and then no data for a while after that.

busy waiting—A process or processor is busy waiting if it is waiting for an event to occur by inquiring, over and over again, if the event has occurred. For example, a processor can busy wait for a memory cell to become non-zero by reading it again and again and checking if it is still zero.

C

cache coherence problem—If a cache is recording some parts of a memory and it is possible for the memory to be changed without the cache being changed then steps must be taken to ensure that the cache is kept up to date with the actual contents of memory. This is called the cache coherence problem. This problem occurs when two processors share memory and each processor can modify the memory independently of the other processor. A popular solution to the cache coherence problem is the "snoopy" cache which watches all bus transactions to see if any of the memory cells it is caching are written into.

cache hit—A cache hit occurs when an item is found in the cache.

cache hit rate—The cache hit rate is the probability that a request will be found in the cache.

cache miss—A cache miss occurs when an item is not found in the cache.

caching—Caching is an optimization technique that is used whenever a process has to compute the value of a function over and over again and it is faster to remember previous values that to compute them over again. The caching technique remembers one or more previous values of the function and does not recompute them if they are requested again. The most common example of caching is a cache memory which consists of fast memory that remembers the values of some locations in a larger, slower memory. If the same location is requested a second time then it is fetched from the faster cache memory. This makes the effective access time of the memory smaller.

capability—A capability is the right to perform a specific operation on an object.

capability list—A capability list is a set of capabilities that is associated with a process or user. As such it represents the things that the process is allowed to do. A capability list defines a protection domain.

CD—A CD is a compact disk. It is used to store digital data. A CD is accessed in the same manner as a magnetic disk, that is, it has addressable sectors that are addressed by sector number or by a cylinder, track and sector number.

channel—A channel is an I/O processor that can transfer data to and from memory and can execute an I/O program.

character device—A character device is a computer device that reads or writes a continuous stream of data. It has no fixed block size and that data do not have addresses. The other type of devices is the block device.

character generator memory—A character generator memory is the memory in a terminal that determines the bit patterns that will be drawn for each ASCII character.

checkerboarding—Checkerboarding in another name for fragmentation, that is, a situation in dynamic memory management where many of the free blocks are too small to be allocated.

child process—A child process is a process that was created by, and is under the control of, another process (called the parent process).

cipher text—Cipher text is encoded text.

client process—A client process is a process that requests service from a server process.

client-server model—The client-server model is an architecture for operating systems or any systems of processes. In the client-server model, all system services are provided by a set of server processes, each of which provides a coherent set of operations. Client processes make requests for service to the server processes.

clock algorithm—A clock algorithm is one of a family of page replacement algorithms. A clock algorithm keeps a list of page frames and finds a page to replace by cycling through this list of page frames looking for a page frame that satisfies certain criteria. One possible criteria is that the referenced bit of the page is off indicating that the page has not been referenced recently.

clustering—Clustering is the grouping of a set of contiguous pages for some purpose. It is most often used for paging in where the entire cluster is paged in if any one of the pages gets a page fault. This causes new processes to load their working set with fewer page faults. The term clustering is also used for the technique of always moving a set of pages or disk blocks in and out of memory as a unit. This type of clustering is a way of increasing the effective page size or disk block size.

color map—A color map is a hardware device that maps from eight bit pixel values to 24 (or 32) bit color values. Color maps are used to reduce the size of the display memory needed in a frame buffer.

compaction—Compaction is a technique used in dynamic memory allocation for creating a large free block. In compaction all the allocated blocks are moved together and all the free blocks are collected into one large free block. Also see disk compaction.

component name—A component name is the name of an object in a directory. A path name or a compound name consists of a sequence of component names.

compound name—A compound name is a name that contains several parts. Each part is called a component name and is looked up in a directory or name space.

compressed file—A compressed file is a file that has been processed by a compression algorithm that reduces the amount of redundancy in the file and so reduces its size. Compressed files take up less space on a disk and are faster to send over communication lines.

condition variable—A condition variable is a variable used in a monitor to represent a condition or event. The two operations on a condition variable are wait and signal. A process that waits on a condition variable will be blocked until the next signal on that condition variable.

confinement problem—When a program runs and handles private data, the user might want to ensure that the program does not reveal the data to any other user. Making sure that a program does not do this is called the confinement problem.

connectionless—A connectionless protocol is one in which each message is independent of all other messages. A connectless protocol does not require a setup or open operation.

consistency checking—A file system contains redundant data that must be consistent. For example, no block can be both free and part of a file. Consistency checking is the process of going through a file system an making sure that the redundant data is consistent. Consistency checking is done after a system has crashed and there is a possibility that the file system data are inconsistent.

context—A context of a process is the information needed to start the process running on the processor. In other words, a process context is the set of values of all processor registers that affect the execution of the process.

context switch—A context switch is the activity of saving the context of a running process and restoring the context of another process.

contiguous—A set of memory addresses is contiguous if the addresses are in sequence with no missing addresses.

contiguous file—A contiguous file is a file that is stored in contiguous disk blocks, that is, disk blocks with contiguous addresses. Contiguous files can be read faster than files organized in other ways.

control register—A control register is a hardware register in a processor that controls the execution of the processor. The processor status word is an example of a control register. Control registers can only be written in system mode.

copy-on-write—A copy-on-write page in a virtual memory system is mapped into two (or more) virtual address spaces as a read-only page. If the page is written into in any of the virtual address spaces then a private copy of the page is made for that address space and marked read-write. Copy-on-write is a technique for doing lazy copies where the copy is not done until the last possible moment.

counting semaphore—A counting semaphore is the same thing as a semaphore.

covert channel—A convert channel is a means of transmitting information that is not intended for information transfer. An example is transmitting a bit of information by making a tape drive move or not.

CPU—A CPU is a central processing unit or processor. It is the part of a computer that can execute instructions.

critical section—A critical section is a section of code in a program that accesses a set of shared variables. It is necessary to maintain mutual exclusion of the critical section for a set of shared variables, that is, no two processes can be executing in their critical section at the same time.

current directory—The current directory (also called the working directory) is the starting point of relative path names. Usually a user is working with the files in the current directory.

curses—Curses is a library of functions that can control a wide range of terminal types by accessing a terminal control database.

cursor position—The cursor position in a terminal or text window is the place where text is inserted.

D

daemon—A daemon is an operating system process that wakes up periodically and performs some operation. For example, a paging daemon will wake up every do often and make sure there are an adequate number of free page frames.

DAT—A DAT is a digital audio tape. It is a means of storing digital data and is used in computer systems for disk backups.

database access and update—Database access and update is a pattern of interprocess communication where there is a database and readers and writers of the database. Readers can share the database but writers must have exclusive access to the database.

deadline scheduling—Deadline scheduling is a form of scheduling where each process has a deadline by which it must be completed. The scheduler tries to ensure that all processes complete by their deadline.

deadlock—Deadlock is a situation where a group of processes are all blocked and none of them can become unblocked until one of the others becomes unblocked. The simplest deadlock is two processes each of which is waiting for a message from the other.

deadlock prevention—Deadlock prevention is a technique for avoiding deadlock problems. A deadlock prevention technique makes rules so that deadlock is impossible. One technique for deadlock prevention is to require that all processes ask for all their resources in a single request, that is, a process is not allowed to request a resource while it is still holding another resource.

decryption key—A decryption key is a binary number that is the input for a decryption algorithm to decode a cipher-text message to a plain-text message.

defined external symbol—A defined external symbol is a symbol that is defined in a module and it declared external so that other modules can refer to it.

demand paging—Demand paging is the paging policy that a page is not read into memory until it is requested, that is, until there is a page fault on the page.

dense—A set of integers is dense if they are consecutive.

design problem—A design problem consists of a set of requirements (things to be accomplished) and a set of constraints (limitations on the possible solutions). The design problem is to find a solution that meets the requirements and satisfies the constraints.

design process—The design process is the set of steps to be taken in designing an artifact. The design process generally involves the stages of: stating the problem clearly, giving a description of the external appearance and behavior of the artifact, describing the internal structure of the solution, and implementing the artifact.

design space—The design space is the set of all possible solutions to a problem. Most of them will not meet all the requirements and constraints of the design problem.

device controller—A device controller is a hardware device that connects to the system bus of a computer and also connects to a device. It manages the communication between the device and the processor and memory of the computer system.

device driver—A device driver is a software component that communicates with a device controller and device. Device drivers present a uniform device interface to the operating system. Often there is a device driver for each device controller but it is possible for a device driver to communicate with several device controllers and several devices.

device independence—An operating system provides device independence if a program can read and write data from a range of devices and files with no changes to the program.

device switch—A device switch is a table in an operating system that converts device numbers into the addresses of entry points into the device driver for that device.

device virtualization—A virtualization of a device is a data structure and set of procedures (which use the data structure) that simulate the device being virtualized. The virtual device has a set of operations with the same overall functionality as the real device. Usually the virtual device is easier to use than the real device.

digital signature—A digital signature is a technique that "signs" a message so that a receiver can be certain who sent the message. It is the digital equivalent of a written signature on a document.

directory—A directory is a data structure in a file system that maps names into objects. The objects mapped are either files or other directories.

dirty bit—The dirty bit is a bit in the page table entry that indicates whether the page has been written to since the last time the dirty bit was cleared. Also see modified bit.

disk address—A disk address is the address of a disk block. It is either a sector number or a triple consisting of the cylinder, track and sector number of the disk block.

disk block—A disk block is the smallest unit which a disk can read or write. Each disk block has a disk address. Disk blocks are typically 512 bytes to 4 K bytes.

disk block pointer—A disk block pointer is an integer that contains a disk sector number. It acts as an address on the disk since it uniquely specifies a disk block.

disk cache—A disk cache is an area in memory that contains copies of the disk blocks that have been recently read or written. Disk caches save disk I/O because disk blocks that are in the cache do not need to be read from the disk.

disk compaction—Disk compaction is the process of moving the blocks on the disk around so that the blocks of a single file are contiguous and in order on the disk. After disk compaction it is faster to read files because there are no seek or latency delays.

disk driver subsystem—The disk driver subsystem is the part of the simple operating system that handles the system calls to read and write disk blocks.

disk extent—A disk extent is a sequence of contiguous disk blocks that belong to the same file. Some file systems store files in extents rather than in single disk blocks. This makes the files more contiguous and faster to read and write.

dispatch—To dispatch a process means to select it to be the next process to execute and the restore its execution context which starts it running.

dispatcher—The dispatcher is the part of an operating system that is called when the operating system has finished its work and it ready to run a process. The dispatcher picks a process to run and starts it running by restoring its execution context.

distributed operating system—A distributed operating system is an operating system that runs on a network of computers but gives the users the illusion that they are running on a single large system with one operating system. The users of a distributed system do not need to know where on the network their files or processes are.

DMA—DMA stands for direct memory access. A device controller is a DMA controller if it can read and write the memory over the system bus without the processor.

double buffering—Double buffering is a technique for speeding up the processing of a disk file by reading one buffer while processing another buffer (or writing one buffer while filling another buffer).

double index block—A double index block is a block that consists of the a series of disk block addresses of single index blocks. A single index block is a disk block that contains a series of addresses of disk blocks that contain file data.

dynamic data—The dynamic data area is the part of the memory of a running process that is used to satisfy requests by the dynamic memory allocator (the *malloc* or *new* allocator).

dynamic programming—Dynamic programming is a technique similar to caching where a problem is solved by building up a table of solutions to subprograms and use the table entries to solve larger and larger version of the problem.

dynamic relocation—Dynamic relocation is the relocation of memory addresses while the program is running.

E

eager evaluation—Eager evaluation is the computation of a function as soon as the arguments to the function are available. It is the opposite of lazy evaluation.

efficiency—Efficiency is a goal of a resource manager. An efficient use of resources is one where the least amount of the resource is used to accomplish the stated goal. Operating systems worry about efficient use of processor time and memory space.

elevator algorithm—The elevator algorithm is a disk scheduling algorithm where the disk head moves like an elevator in the building. The disk head moves in one direction (say towards in center of the disk) as long as there are requests in that direction. If there are no requests in a direction then it starts moving in the other direction.

emulator—An emulator is a program that implements (in software) the instruction set of a processor.

encryption key—An encryption key is a number that is the input to an encryption algorithm and is used to encode a plain-text message into a cipher-text message.

event model—The event model is used in graphic user interfaces (GUIs). In the event model, all events of interest to a process are combined into a single stream of events. Each event contains the type of the event, the time of the event and the parameters of the event. The main control loop of a process using the event model is a single loop which gets and then acts on events. Typical events are: keystrokes, mouse movement, mouse button clicks, input on a pipe, etc.

execv—The UNIX system call to run a new program in an existing process.

external fragmentation—External fragmentation happens when a dynamic memory allocation algorithm allocates some memory and a small piece is left over that cannot be effectively used. If too much external fragmentation occurs, the amount of usable memory is drastically reduced.

external name—An external name is a name intended for use by users of the operating system. External names are usually chosen by the user and are usually character strings.

external security—External security refers to security techniques not related the the operating system. This includes things like locks on the doors to the computer room.

external symbol—An external symbol in an object module is a symbol that is defined in this module and used in another module or defined in another module and used in this module.

F

fairness—A scheduling algorithm is fair if it treats all processes of the same priority equally.

FCFS—FCFS stand for first-come, first-served. It is another name for FIFO (first-in, first-out). In FCFS the job that has been waiting the longest is served next.

fifo—Fifo stand for first-in, first-out. In a fifo queue, the item that has been in the queue the longest is removed next. The term fifo is also used for a pipe that is named in the file naming system.

FIFO page replacement—The FIFO page replacement algorithm removes the page that has been in memory the longest.

file—A file is a collection of related information that is stored on a disk and that has a unique name.

file alias—A file alias is another name for a file. A file may have several aliases. File aliases allow a file to reside in more than one directory in the file system. This allows it to be classified in several ways. In UNIX a file alias is called a symbolic link.

file allocation table (FAT)—A file allocation table is an inverted disk block index.

file descriptor—A file descriptor is a data structure maintained by the operating system that contains all the meta-data the operating system needs to record about the file. File descriptors contain things like: the last time the file was read, the last time the file was written, the length of the file, the location of the file data on disk, the protection status of the file, etc. Another name for a file descriptor is a file control block.

file extension—A file extension is the part of the file name after a period and it indicates the type or use of the file.

file location—The file location is the offset into the file where the next read or write operation will start.

file mapping—File mapping is a technique where a disk file is mapped into the virtual address space of a process. File mapping can take the place of disk I/O.

file system—A file system is a data structure on a disk or disk partition. It contains files and directories. A file system is the largest unit of organization on a disk.

file system descriptor—A file system descriptor is a data structure on disk where the operating system keeps all the information it needs to record about the file system. Typical information kept in a file system descriptor is: the length of the file system, the lo-

cation of the root directory, the location of the file descriptors, the beginning of the chain of free blocks, etc.

file system layout—The file system layout is the way space is allocated in a file system. For example, the layout of the original UNIX file system contained: the boot block, the superblock (the file system descriptor), an area for inodes (file descriptors), and an area for data and index blocks.

filter—A filter is a program that reads a stream of ASCII characters, processes it in some way, and writes out a stream of ASCII characters.

first fit—First fit is a memory allocation algorithm where a request for a block of memory is always filled with the first free block in the block list that satisfies the request.

first-come, first-served scheduling—First-come, first-served scheduling always chooses the job that has been waiting the longest.

first-in, first-out—In a first-in, first-out queue, the item that has been in the queue the longest is removed next.

flat file—A flat file is a file that is simply a sequence of bytes with no larger structure. An example of a file that is not a flat file is a file with a record structure.

flat name space—A flat name space is a single list of names with no internal structure in the names. Each name in a flat name space must be unique.

fork—A fork is the UNIX method for creating a new process. The fork system call will create an identical copy of the forking process.

fragment—A fragment is a block of memory in a dynamic memory allocation system that is too small to satisfy any request.

fragmentation—Fragmentation occurs in a dynamic memory allocation system when many of the free blocks are too small to satisfy any request.

frame buffer—A frame buffer is a memory module that stores the image that is on a graphics display. The image on the display is refreshed from the frame buffer. The image is changed by changing the frame buffer. A frame buffer has from 1 to 32 bits per pixel on the graphics display.

framework—A framework is a shell of an application program that contains the major modules but does not contain any actual functionality.

free block—A free block is a piece of memory in a dynamic memory allocation system that is not currently in use and so is available for allocation.

full backup—A full backup of a file system is a copy (usually on tape) of every file in a file system.

full path name—A full path name is an absolute path name.

G

general purpose register—A general purpose register in a computer system is a register that can be used by the programmer for any purpose required. This is in contrast with a control register which can only be written in system mode and is used for on specific purpose.

global replacement—A global page replacement algorithm is an algorithm that looks at all the page frames in the system to decide which one to replace. This is in contrast with a local page replacement algorithm which will only replace pages that belong to the process the just had a page fault.

graphics context—A graphics context is a collection of information which gives the current default arguments to graphics operations. A graphics context contains things like: the background color, the foreground color, the fill color, the line width, the copy mode, etc.

guard page—A guard page is a page that is placed at either end of a data structure in virtual memory (for example, a stack, an array or a table). The guard page cannot be read or written and so if a process tries to write beyond the limits of the data structure it will get a protection fault when it tries to access the guard page. This can be useful in detecting array subscripts out of bound, stack overflow, table overflow, etc.

H

half context switch—A half context switch is either the saving or the restoring of the registers of a process.

handle—A handle is a,pointer to a pointer (which then points to the object). It is a form of indirection and makes it easy to move objects that there are many pointers to.

hard link—A hard link is a form of file alias used in UNIX that takes advantage of the fact the directory entries contain only inode (file descriptor) numbers and not the inodes themselves. So two directory entries can refer to the same inode. Each such entry is a hard link. Also see file alias.

hardware interface—The hardware interface is the collection of hardware items that are visible to the machine language programmer.

hardware resource—Hardware resources are: processor time, memory, device time and disk space. The operating system manages the hardware resources of the system.

header section—The header section is the part of an object module or a load module that comes at the beginning of the modules and describes the module and the layout of the rest of the module.

heap—A heap is a source of managed memory that is dynamically allocated.

hierarchical file naming system—A hierarchical file naming system is a system for naming files using a tree of files and directories. Each interior node in the tree is a directory and its children are the items in the directory. Hierarchical file naming system use path names to name files.

highest response ratio next scheduling—Highest response ratio next scheduling is a scheduling algorithm that always chooses the job with the highest response ratio. The response ratio of a job is the ratio of the waiting time plus the execution time divided by the waiting time. Highest response ratio next scheduling is really shortest job first with aging.

hint—A hint is the answer to a question that is likely to be correct but is not guaranteed to be correct.

hook—A hook is a mechanism that allows a user to get control when a specific event occurs.

horizontal retrace—The horizontal retrace is the time period where the electron beam in a cathode ray tube is moving from the end of one scan line to the beginning of the next scan line.

I

I/O address space—The I/O address space is an address space used to address I/O devices. It is separate from the memory address space and used by special I/O instructions (in computers that have I/O instructions).

I/O device—An I/O (input/output) device is an electro-mechanical device that converts digital data from internal, digital form to some external representation (magnetic variations, light, sound, inks marks on paper, etc.)

I/O processor—An I/O processor is a processor that can transfer data to and from memory and can execute an I/O program.

I/O system—The I/O system is the part of an operating system that handles I/O operations and devices. The I/O system consists principally of device drivers plus some device-independent code that manages I/O requests and device driver invocation.

implementation—The implementation of an interface is the code that performs each function and that contains entry points for all the functions of the interface.

incremental backup—An incremental backup of a file system is a copy of all the files in the file system that have changed since the last backup was made.

index block—An index block is a disk block that contains the addresses of other disk blocks. It is used by file systems to record the location of the disk blocks containing file data.

indirection—Indirection is the term for the process of getting from one place to another by going through an intermediate agent. A pointer to a pointer is the simplest example.

initial process—The initial process is the first process started by an operating system. It is the only process that is not created by a create process system call made by a running process.

initialized data section—The initialized data section is the part of an object module or load module that contains the data that is explicitly given an initial value by the assembly language source code.

inode—An inode is a file descriptor in UNIX.

input device—An input device is an I/O device that takes input from an external source and converts it to digital form for internal use in a computer system.

inter-process communication—Inter-process communication (IPC) refers to any method by which one process can communicate with another. Examples are: messages, pipes, ports, shared memory and RPCs.

interface—An interface is a contract between two software entities. One entity writes code using the functions specified by the interface and the other entity writes code that implements the functions in the interface.

interleaved file—An interleaved file is a file that is stored in every other disk block or every third disk block or in some regular pattern like those. If the location of the first block of an interleaved file is known then the location of all the other blocks in the file can be computed from it.

internal fragmentation—Internal fragmentation is the space wasted inside of allocated memory blocks because of restrictions on the allowed sizes of allocated blocks (that is, on the granularity of allocation).

internal name—An internal name is a name used mainly inside an operating system. Internal names are usually integers and are usually chosen by the operating system (not the user).

internal security—Internal security is the security involving the operating system. This is opposed to external security which does not involve the operating system.

interrupt—An interrupt is a hardware action taken in response to an event. The action the hardware takes is to interrupt the execution of the currently running program and jump to an interrupt handler. Interrupts are caused by device controllers (when they complete a I/O transfer), timers (when they count down to 0), system call instructions, instruction errors, etc.

interrupt vector area—The interrupt vector area is the area in memory where the hardware looks for interrupt vectors. An interrupt vector tells the hardware what routine to jump to when an interrupt occurs.

inverted disk block index—An inverted disk block index is an array of disk block addresses as long as the number of disk blocks on the disk. The value of the array entry for a disk block is the next disk block in the file. This means one can

chain through the file allocation table to find all the disk blocks in a file.

inverted page table—An inverted page table is a page table which is indexed by page frame number rather than by page number. Inverted page tables are better for very large address spaces where ordinary page tables would be too long.

IPC—IPC stand for inter-process communication. Some common forms of IPC are: messages, ports, pipes and RPCs.

J

just-in-time—A just-in-time strategy is a lazy strategy where an operation is not performed or a resource is not allocated until the time that it is actually needed.

K

kernel—The kernel is the essential part of the an operating system that performs the basic functions that every operating system must do: process dispatching, basic memory management, and protection.

kernel thread—A kernel thread is a thread that runs in kernel mode.

kernel-mode process—A kernel-mode process is a process that is running in system mode. A user-mode process changes to a kernel-mode process when it makes a system call (or gets an external interrupt) and starts executing in operating system code.

keyed file—A keyed file is a file of records which contain a designated field called a key. Records in the file can be accessed by giving the value of the key rather than the record number.

L

language interface—A language interface is an interface in the form of a language, that is, an interface in which one can write a program. The alternative is an interface that consists of a collection of procedures that one can call from a separate programming language. A separate programming language is not required to use a language interface.

late binding—When an attribute of an object is assigned a value we call that binding the attribute. If the binding is done very close to the last possible time it could be done then we call this a late binding. For example, demand paging is an example of late binding because we do not assign physical storage to a page until the page is first used, that is, at the latest possible moment.

latency time—The latency time of a disk transfer is the time taken up waiting for the disk platter to spin around so that the required data is under the read/write heads of the disk drive.

Law of Diminishing Returns—The law of diminishing returns says that the more you invest in something the lower the return on investment will be. For example, as you begin trying to debug a program you will find lots of bugs without much effort but as time goes on and your time investment in debugging goes up, the number of bugs you will find will go down. The reason is that there are fewer bugs to find and they are the harder ones to find because the easier one have already all been found.

lazy copy—A lazy copy is one that is done just by copying the page tables and setting the pages to copy-on-write status. Pages are copied as the they modified, that is, at the last possible moment.

lazy creation—Lazy creation is a technique where the creation of an object is delayed until the object is actually needed. For example, a graphical program will not create a window until a user action requires that the window be displayed.

lazy evaluation—Lazy evaluation is a way of implementing argument passing in a programming language. Arguments are not evaluated when they are passed but the first time they are used.

library—A library is a collection of object modules that can be included, as needed, in a program by a linker.

lightweight process—A lightweight process is a thread that is implemented by the operating system.

linker—A linker is a software tool that combines object modules and libraries into an executable load module. The principle activities of a linker are relocation and linking.

linking—Linking is the process of combining two or more object modules and fixing up the places where one modules calls a procedure in another module or accesses data in another module.

little language—A little language is a special purpose language that provides access to a set of functions. For example, the output formatting language of *printf* format strings is a little language.

Little's Law—Little's Law is a formula that is true in all system where objects enter the system, remain in the system for a while and then leave the system. Little's Law says that $N = \lambda T$ where N is the average number of objects in the system, λ is the arrival rate and T is the average time an objects spends in the system.

load control—A virtual memory system must not allow too many processes to be running and competing for page frames or else the system will thrash. So a virtual memory system must have a load control policy that makes sure that some processes are swapped out if too many are competing for memory.

load module—A load module is a file that contains a program that is ready to run and that can be loaded by the run-time loader of the operating system.

load time dynamic linking—Some linkers delay the linking of library modules until the program is being loaded for execution. This is called load time dynamic linking.

local replacement—A local page replacement algorithm is one that always replaces a page from the process that caused the page fault. The opposite of this is global replacement.

locality—Locality is the tendency of accesses to memory to be for the same memory locations (temporal locality) or nearby memory locations (spatial locality) that have been accessed recently.

log structured file system—A log structured file system is a file system that records all file system changes in a change log. The entire file system is the change log. This means that all writing is done in sequential locations in the log.

logical address—A logical address is an address that must be translated by memory management hardware into a physical address before it can be presented to the hardware.

logical address space—The logical address space of a process is the set of addresses that it uses internally. These addresses are translated to physical addresses by the memory management hardware.

logical block—A logical block is a block of information in a file. The logical block is the information not the storage medium where the information is kept.

logical block number—The logical block number of a block is the block number in the file.

logical disk—A logical disk is a software object that acts like a disk, that is, it is a sequence of disk blocks. A logical disk might actually be only part of a physical disk or it might actually span several physical disks.

logical parallelism—Logical parallelism in an operating system comes from time sharing. The processor is rapidly switched between processes and it gives the appearance of the processes actually running in parallel but logical parallelism does not involve any true, physical parallelism.

logical resource—A logical resource is a software object that acts like a physical resource.

LRU page replacement—The LRU page replacement algorithm always replaces the page that has not been used for the longest time.

M

machine code section—The machine code section of an object module or a load module is where the executable machine code is stored.

magic cookie—A magic cookie is a number that appears arbitrary to the process that holds it but has a meaning to the server process that it was obtained from and is sent back to with operations. An example would be an index into a table in the logical address space of the server process. This index has no meaning in another process but has meaning in the server process.

masked—Interrupts can be masked by the hardware so they will not be taken even if they are requested.

master page number—The master page number is the part of a virtual address that gives the offset into the master page table for the process. This is used in two-level (or more) paging systems.

mechanism—A mechanism is a means of accomplishing a task that does not dictate how to accomplish the task. For example, an access control list mechanism allows you to protect your files but it does not require you to, for example, make all your files read-only.

medium-term scheduler—A medium-term scheduler decides which processes should be in memory competing for page frames and which processes should be swapped out.

memoizing—Memoizing is the technique of speeding up a recursive function by keeping a memo table of previous arguments and values of the function. Memoizing is a form of caching.

memory address space—The memory address space is that part of the physical address space of a computer system that has physical memory assigned to it.

memory as a device—A device driver can act like a disk driver but actually access the physical (or a logical) address space when a process reads or writes the simulated disk. This is a good way to give some processes access to the physical address space and protect access with the file protection system.

memory manager—A memory manager is a software module that dynamically allocates memory.

memory mapped I/O—A system uses memory mapped I/O if the device registers are accessible through the physical address space.

memory object—An object in the Mach operating system that is a source of pages. Normally a memory object gets its pages from a file but the source could be a network connection or the memory object could generate the pages on demand.

memory protection—Memory protection is a hardware mechanism that allows the user or the operating system to decide who can access memory and how they can access it. Memory protection mechanisms are most commonly combined with memory mapping mechanisms but some, like lock and key systems, for example, are not connected with a memory mapping system.

memory-mapped file—A memory-mapped file is a file that is mapped into virtual memory. See file mapping.

message—A message is the content of a communication between two processes. Message passing is a common form of inter-process communication.

message queue—A message queue is a data structure that holds messages that have been sent but not yet received. Message queues are normally maintained by the operating system and kept in operating system memory.

meta-information—Meta-information is information about information. A file contains information that can be of any kind the user wishes. The meta-information associated with the file contains things like: the length of the file, the time the file was last opened for reading, the time the file was last opened for writing, who can access the file and how, where on the disk the file information is kept, etc. File meta-information is maintained by the operating system.

micro-kernel—A micro-kernel is a minimal operating system that performs only the essential functions of an operating system. All other operating system functions are performed by system processes.

model—A model is a representation of a system. For example, an equation can be a model for the motion of a rocket, a simulation program can be a model for a bank, and the client-server model describes the general architecture of a large class of systems of processes.

modem—A modem is a modulator-demodulator. It converts digital data into tones that can be send over a phone line (modulation) and converts tones back into digital data (demodulation). Modems allows the connection of a terminal to a computer over a phone line.

modern cryptography—Cryptography is the science of secret codes (creating codes and breaking codes). Modern cryptography is cryptography done with computers. The advent of computers allowed cryptographic techniques that would have taken too long without computers.

modified bit—The modified bit (also called the dirty bit) is a bit in the page table entry for a page that is set whenever the page is written into. This information is important to virtual memory systems since a page that has been modified must be written back out to the swap area before the page frame can be reused.

monitor—A monitor is a mechanism for process synchronization. It consists of a collection of procedures where the monitor enforces mutual exclusion between them, that is, the monitor only allows one process at a time to be executing in any of the procedures in the monitor. Monitors also provide condition variables to allow processes to wait for specific events.

mono-programming—Mono-programming is running only one program at a time in a computer system. Mono-programming was used in early mainframe computer operating systems and early personal computer operating systems.

monolithic—A monolithic operating system is one where all operating system code is in a single executable image and all operating system code runs in system mode.

mounting—Mounting is a technique whereby one file naming hierarchy is grafted on to a directory in another file naming hierarchy. Mounting is way of combining two (or more) file naming hierarchies that combines them into a single space of unique names. Typically a file system on a logical disk is mounted onto a directory in another file system. Mounting can be done between file systems on a single processor or between file system on different computer systems that are connected with a network.

multicomputer—A multicomputer is a computer system with two or more computers each with its own memory and with a communications network between the computers.

multiple queue scheduling—Multiple queue scheduling is a scheduling mechanism where there are several levels of queues from high to low priority. Processes move to lower priority queues as they use up their time slices on higher priority queues.

multiplexing—Multiplexing is a method of sharing a resource between processes by dividing it up into pieces or dividing the allocation up into small pieces of time. See space division multiplexing and time division multiplexing.

multiprocessing—Multiprocessing is the technique of running two or more processes in an operating system, in parallel, on two or more processors. Multiprocessing creates physical parallelism.

multiprogramming—Multiprogramming is the technique of running several programs at a time using timesharing. It allows a computer to do several things at the same time. Multiprogramming creates logical parallelism.

mutex—A mutex is another name for a binary semaphore. It is also a favored variable name for a mutual exclusion semaphore.

mutual exclusion—Mutual exclusion is a mechanism for avoiding race conditions by preventing two processes from running in their critical section at the same time.

N

N-step scan algorithm—An N-step scan algorithm is a batching variation on the scan (or elevator) algorithm where disk requests are taken in batches of requests and all the requests in a batch are satisfied before any new requests are considered. It is a way of avoiding starvation of some disk requests.

name—A name is an external identifier of an object. Names are normally chosen by the user and are normally character strings.

name assignment—Name assignment is the activity of assigning a name to an object. This might be done by the operating system or by the process creating the object.

name lookup—Name lookup is the activity of finding an object from its name. This often entails a table lookup or a series of table lookups.

name map—A name map is a function from names to objects. It is used in name lookup.

name resolution—Name resolution is another name for name lookup. It is the activity of finding an object from its name.

name space—A name space is a collection of unique names. A name space normally is associated with a name map that maps each name into an object.

name table—A name table is a lookup table for mapping names into objects.

network operating system—A network operating system is an operating system that is aware of the network it is on and can cooperate with other network operating systems on the network to pass messages and provide for a distributed file system.

next fit—Next fit is a memory allocation algorithm where a request for a block of memory is always filled with the next free block in the block list that satisfies the request.

nonblocking receive—A nonblocking receive is a message receive system call that will not block if there are no messages to receive but instead will return with an error code. Most receive system calls are blocking.

not recently used—Not recently used is another name for the clock algorithm. It is so named because it chooses pages for replacement if they have not been recently used.

O

object—An object is a resource that we are protecting in a protection system. Subjects are the active entities that request to perform operations on objects.

object module—An object module is the result of a assembly or compilation. It contains the machine code, the data, the relation information and the symbol table for the code module.

object space—An object space is a collection of objects that is the range of a name map.

off-site backup—An off-site backup is a set of backups (usually tapes) that is kept at a different location (off-site) from the disks that are being backed up. This means that a physical event, such as a fire or tornado, cannot destroy both the disks and the backups.

one-time password—A one-time password is a password that is used only once. One-time passwords are generated by an algorithm. The advantage is that a wire-tapper cannot reuse the password.

open file—An open file is an object implemented by the operating system that allows a process to read or write a file (or any other source or sink for data).

open file identifier—An open file identifier is an internal name given to an open file by the operating system. It is passed back to the operating system each time an operation on the open file is invoked. Usually it is an index into the open file pointer table.

open file pointer table—An open file pointer table is a table of all the files a process has open. It is maintained by the operating system. It is indexed by an open file identifier and contains pointers to entries in a system-wide open file table.

open file table—An open file table is another name for an open file pointer table.

operating system—An operating system is the software that controls the main resources of a computer system. It manages those resources and creates virtual versions of them.

operating system interface—The operating system interface is the set of system calls the operating system implements. Another view of these system calls is a set of object types that operating system implements and the operations on those objects.

operation—An operation is a function that can be performed on an object.

optimal page replacement—An optimal page replacement algorithm is an algorithm that always produces the fewest page faults for any page reference sequence.

optimistic algorithm—An optimistic algorithm is one that assumes the best (or a good) case and so can perform more efficiently when the assumption is valid. The algorithm can detect when the assumption is false and recover. For example, an optimistic mutual exclusion algorithm will assume that no other process is in its critical section or will start its critical section while this process is in its critical section.

output device—An output device is an I/O device that takes data from an internal, digital form and converts it to an external form.

overlay—An overlay is a module in a program that is brought into memory on demand, while the program is running. Two or more overlays will share the same memory addresses.

P

packet—A packet is the unit of data transfer in some networks (for example, in Ethernets). It is some data along with an address of the intended receiver.

page—A page is the contents of an area of virtual memory in a running process. All pages are the same size and are aligned on addresses that are multiples of the page size. The page is the information not the medium that records it so the same page can be in a page frame in memory or in a disk block on the disk.

page fault frequency load control—Page fault frequency load control is a method of load control that monitors the page fault rate. If the rate is too low then new processes are brought into memory and if the page fault rate is too high then one or more processes is swapped out of memory.

page fault interrupt—A page fault interrupt occurs when a memory reference is made to a page that is not in memory. The present bit in the page table entry will be found to be off by the virtual memory hardware and it will signal an interrupt.

page fault rate—The page fault rate is the number of page faults divided by the number of memory references. It is the likelihood that a memory reference will cause a page fault.

page frame—A page frame is an area of physical memory that can hold a page. The page is the information (the bits) and the page frame is the medium that stores the information. A disk block that can hold a page is also called a page frame.

page reference string—When a process is running it generates a series of memory references. If we take the page number that each reference refers to then the resulting sequence is a page reference string. Page reference strings are used as input to simulators that evaluate paging algorithms.

page replacement algorithm—A page replacement algorithm decides which page to replace when a free page frame is needed.

page table—A page table is an array of page table entries. A page number is derived from a memory address and that page number is used as an index into the page table to get the page table entry for that page. The page table entry is then used to find the page frame in memory where the page resides.

page table entry—A page table entry records the information about a page. This information includes: whether the page is in memory, the page frame where the page is located in memory and the types of operations allowed on the page (read, write, and/or execute).

pager—A pager is a software object in the Mach operating system that handles paging from a memory object into and out of memory.

paging daemon—A paging daemon is an operating system process that wakes up every so often and makes sure that the free page frame pool has not gotten too low. If it has, the paging daemon tries to free some page frames.

parallel port controller—A parallel port controller is a hardware device that connects to the system bus and also connects to one or more devices through a parallel port. The parallel port controller interfaces the device to the system bus.

parent process—A parent process is a process that has created one or more children and so is their parent. A parent process can usually control many aspects of its child processes.

partition—A partition is a area covering part of a physical disk. A partition can be configured as a logical disk.

path name—A path name is a compound name consisting of one or component names. Each component name can be looked up in a directory to find the directory in which to look up the next component name. The final name in the path name refers to the object that is named by the path name.

pattern—A pattern is an outline of a design that can be reused in several design situations.

per process open file table—The per process open file table is the list of open files that is associated with a process. It generally contains pointers to entries in a system-wide open file table.

persistent object—A persistent object is an object that will continue to exist even after the program that creates it has terminated. A file is the most common example of a persistent object.

persistent storage—Persistent storage is storage that will retain its value after the process that creates and writes it has terminated. A file is the most common example of persistent storage.

phosphor—A phosphor is a chemical that will glow for a short period of time after it has been hit with a beam of electrons. Phosphors are used in cathode ray tubes (like TVs and graphic displays) where an image is created by be making some parts of the phosphor coating of the tube to glow.

physical address—A physical address is an address that can be placed on the system bus and will be responded to be a hardware module on the bus (usually a memory module but possibly some other device).

physical address space—The physical address space of a computer system is the set of addresses that are valid on its system bus. Physical addresses do not require any translation before being used.

physical block—A physical block is a block on the disk. It is addressed with a physical block number.

physical block number—A file consists of a sequence of logical blocks which have logical block numbers. The disk block address of a logical block is called the physical block number of that block. In other words, the physical block number is the address of a block on the disk.

physical parallelism—Physical parallelism is parallelism caused by two (or more) processes each executing a process at the same time.

pipe—A pipe is a method of inter-process communication. It is accessed like a file. One process writes to the pipe and when another process reads from the pipe and it will read the same bytes, in the same sequence, that the first process wrote.

pixel—A pixel is a picture element. It is a dot on a graphic display screen that can be turned on or off. The patterns of pixels that are on creates the image on the graphics display.

placement—The placement problem in a dynamic memory system is the decision about where in memory to place a block. This is a problem in dynamic memory systems that use variable sized blocks but it is trivial in a paging system where all blocks are the same size and are always placed at addresses that are multiples of the page size.

plain text—A message is plain text before it is encoded. After encoding it is cipher text.

policy—A policy is a set of rules that is implemented by a mechanism. For example, a protection policy would be to only allow people in the Friends group to have read access to your files. The UNIX file protection mechanism could be used to implement this policy be setting the permission bits the right way.

policy versus mechanism—A mechanism is a means for implementing a policy. A policy is a set of rules for deciding what will be done and the mechanism is the means by which the rules are enforced.

port—A port is a message queue that only one process can read from. In the Mach operating system, a port represents an object. Operations on the object are performed by sending messages to the port. The process reading from the port is the server or manager for that object.

powers of two allocation—This is a method of dynamic memory allocation where all block sizes must be a power of two.

PPP—PPP stand for point-to-point protocol. PPP is a method of connecting to a network over a phone line. It consists of a process on one side that acts (to processes that want to use the network) like a network connection but really communicates over a phone line to another process. That other process is on a machine that is physically connected to the network and it performs the network operations for the other process.

predictive load control—Predictive load control is a form of load control where the algorithm tries to predict the load in the near future and takes steps to make sure it doesn't get too high or too low.

preemptive scheduling—Preemptive scheduling is a form of scheduling where the scheduler is allowed to allocate a resource to a process and then, later, take away the resource even though the process is not finished using it. Processor schedulers in computers are almost always preemptive schedulers whereas disk head scheduler almost never are.

prepaging—Prepaging is a paging strategy where the paging algorithm tries to predict which pages will be used in the near future and pages them into memory before they are requested, that is, before there is a page fault on them.

present bit—The present bit in a page table entry is a bit that indicates whether the page has been read into a page frame in memory or not. If a page is referenced when the present bit is off then a page fault interrupt will occur.

primary page table—The primary page table is the first page table used in a multiple level (usually two, three, or four level) paging system.

principle of minimum privilege—The principle of minimum privilege requires that a process should only have the privileges it needs to get its job done, and no more. It is used in protection systems to limit the damage when a program does not work correctly or is a Trojan horse program.

priority—The priority of a process is an indication of how important the process is. A priority scheduler will always favor higher priority processes.

priority scheduling—Priority scheduling is a scheduling method where, at all times, the highest priority process is assigned the resource.

private key cryptosystem—A private key cryptosystem is a system of encoding where the encoding key and the decoding key are the same or are easily computable from each other. In a private key cryptosystem both the encoding key and the decoding key must be kept private or the code will be compromised.

private scheduling queue—A private scheduling queue is a queue that only one process will ever wait on. The scheduler can always schedule that process by releasing any process waiting on the private scheduling queue. Usually this is the queue of a private scheduling semaphore.

privilege—A privilege is the right to perform a specific operation on a specific object. For example, a process might have the privilege of reading file *SecretData*.

privileged instruction—A privileged instruction is a hardware instruction that can only be executed when the processor is in system mode. Privileged instructions are instructions that affect the management of the hardware resources.

process—A process is an operating system concept that captures the idea of a program in execution. A process can hold resources (e.g., open files, address space, protection privileges, etc.) and it can be run by the dispatcher. In other words, it has resources to compute with and gets assigned a processor to do the computing. A process is always executing at some point in a program. A process has memory for its program and data. A process has a copy of the hardware registers that describe where in the computation it is.

process competition—Processes interact by competing when they are sharing resources that both of them need but only one can be using a time.

process cooperation—Processes interact by cooperating when they are working together on a task where each process is doing part of the task.

process descriptor—A process descriptor is a data structure in an operating system that contains all the information the operating system needs to record about the process. This information includes: the saved register state of the process, what memory is allocated to the process, where the process's page table is located, the groups the process is in, how much processor time and other resources the process has used, the files a process has open, etc.

process hierarchy—The process hierarchy is a tree where each process is a node in the tree. The child nodes of a parent node are the child processes of that parent process.

process management subsystem—The process management subsystem is the part of the simple operating system that implements processes. It does process creation, process dispatching and system call handling.

process state—While it is running, a process can be in one of several processes states. The minimal set of process states is: ready (to run), running (on a processor), and blocked (waiting for an event).

process table—The process table is a data structure in an operating system that contains the process descriptor of each process in the system. Any operation on a process will require that its process descriptor be looked up in the process table.

processor—A processor is the part of a computer system that executes instructions. It is also called a CPU.

processor mode—A processor is always running in a processor mode which determines which instructions are allowed to be executed. Most processors have two modes: user mode (where some instructions, called privileged instructions, are not allowed) and system mode (where all instructions are allowed).

processor sharing—Processor sharing is the theoretic limit of round robin where each ready process gets its share of the processor in all time periods, even very short ones.

producer-consumer—When two processes are cooperating on a task, it is common for one process to produce partially completed objects which are then passed on to the other process. We call the first process the producer, the second process a consumer and their relationship is called producer-consumer relationship.

program—A program is a set of instructions that can be used to control a process.

program phase—A program phase is a period of time in the execution of a program when the working set of pages changes slowly.

programming interface—A programming interface to a program is an interface where another process can invoke all the functions of a program. Some programs can only be controlled from the user interface.

protection—Protection is a mechanism in an operating system that checks whether a subject is allowed to perform an operation on an object.

protection database—A protection database is a database of all the protection information in a system. An important issue in the design of a protection system is how and where the protection database is stored.

protection domain—A protection domain is is set of privileges, that is, a set of rights to perform specific operations on specific objects. A process is always running in some protection domain. In some protection systems, a protection domain is a protected object and there is an operation to enter a new protection domain.

protection field—The protection field is in a page table entry and records the protection information for the page. Generally this is whether it is allowed to read, write and/or execute the page.

protection monitor—A protection monitor is a software module that checks the protection database to ensure that a requested operation is allowed.

pseudo-parallel—Two processes run in pseudo-parallel is they are timesharing a processor. Another term for pseudo-parallel is logically parallel.

pseudo-tty driver—A pseudo-tty driver is a device driver that pretends to be connected to a terminal but is really connected to a process.

public key cryptosystem—A public key cryptosystem is a system of encoding where the encoding key and the decoding key are different and the decoding key is not easily computable from the encoding key. In a public key cryptosystem only the decoding key must be kept private. The encoding key is the public key and can be widely disseminated.

Q

quantum—A quantum (or time slice) is the period of time a process is allowed to run before the operating system takes control back. This is enforced with a timer which is set before the process is started and causes an interrupt when the quantum is up.

R

race condition—A race condition is a situation where two processes either communicate or share memory while they are running and the output of one or both of the processes depends on the relative speed of the two processes. Race conditions are considered to be bad because computers should be deterministic. The reason the outputs are different depending on the relative speeds is because in some cases the output is wrong.

RAID—RAID stands for redundant array of inexpensive disks. A RAID device uses several disk drives in parallel to get higher transfer rates and/or more error correction.

RAM disk—A RAM disk is a disk driver that acts like a disk but actually stores the data on the "disk" in memory. The advantage of RAM disks is that they are much faster then regular disks. The disadvantage is that they are much more expensive than real disks and the data in them is not persistent between reboots of the operating system.

random page replacement—The random page replacement algorithm chooses a page to replace randomly when asked to select a page for replacement. It uses no information about past behavior of the program. Random page replacement is generally not a good page replacement algorithm but its worst case is the same

as its best case and so its worst case is better than most page replacement algorithms.

raster graphics—Raster graphics is a graphics technology where images on a display are produced from tiny dots on the display. The alternative to raster graphics is vector graphics which produces images by drawing them directly.

reactive system—A reactive system is a system that does not do things on its own but only to external events. User interfaces are mostly reactive in that they don't do anything unless the user initiates an action. Operating systems are basically reactive systems.

readers-writers problem—With a shared database it is generally acceptable to have several readers reading the database simultaneously but a writer must have exclusive access to the database. Maintaining these rules is called the readers-writers problem. Another name for this problem is the database access and update problem.

ready—A process is in the ready state if it is ready to run as soon as a processor is available. That is, the process is not waiting for an event such as the completion of a disk transfer.

ready list—The ready list is a list of all the processes in the system that are in the ready state. This list is a subset of the process table and is often a linked list running through the process table.

real-time operating system—A real-time process is a process that must respond to events within a certain time period. A real-time operating system is an operating system that can run real-time processes successfully.

recursive address space—A recursive address space is a virtual address space whose page tables are in another virtual address space.

recursive design problem—Often when you are trying to solve a design problem you will try a technique that leads to another instance of the same design problem. This is called a recursive design problem. Usually the recursive design problem will have different constraints than the original design problem and so different (and usually simpler) solutions are acceptable.

redirection—Redirection is the technique of changing the standard input or standard output of a process so that it gets its input or writes its output to a different place than normal. The normal place for input or output is the terminal running the program and it is redirected to or from a file.

redundancy—Redundancy is the technique of keeping more than one copy of data to protect against the data being lost.

reentrant program—A program is reentrant if it can be executed by two threads at the same time and it executes correctly for both threads. The thing that prevents a program from being reentrant is the use of global or static data. Another name for reentrant is thread-safe.

reference string—A reference string is a page reference string.

referenced bit—A referenced bit is a bit field in a page table entry that records whether the page has been reference since the last time the referenced bit was cleared. The paging hardware will set the referenced bit (for a page) every time it references a word on a page.

refreshing—Refreshing is the activity of continually rewriting the graphics image on a graphics display. Refreshing is necessary because the image on the display fades away rapidly after it is written.

region—A region is a contiguous span of pages in a sparsely populated virtual address space.

relative device—A relative device is a positioning device that returns relative movement rather than absolute locations. A mouse is a relative device whereas a touch sensitive screen is an absolute device.

relative path name—A relative path name is a path name that begins at the the current directory.

rendezvous—A rendezvous is a pattern of interprocess communication where two or more processes need to wait until they are all at a certain point in their respective programs.

replacement—Replacement is the problem of deciding which memory block to replace when making room for a new one.

reservations—Some scheduling systems allow a user to reserve a resource ahead of time. This is called a reservation. This is common in scheduling situations where the cost of waiting for a resource when it is needed is high.

resident set—The resident set of a process is the set of pages that are currently in memory.

resource management—Resource management consists of: accounting for a resource, scheduling the resource, protecting the resource, multiplexing the resource and transforming the resource.

right—A right is the ability to perform a specific operation on a specific object. Another name for a right is a permission.

round-robin scheduling—Round-robin scheduling is a scheduling method where each process gets a small quantity of time (called a quantum or time slice) to run and then it is preempted and the next process gets to run. This is called time sharing and gives the effect of all the processes running at the same time (this is called logical parallelism) albeit on much slower processors.

RPC—An RPC is a remote procedure call. RPC is a method of interprocess communication where one process communicates with another process by making a procedure call that crosses to the address space of that process and runs and the result is sent back to the address space of the caller. RPC is a method of transforming message passing so it looks like procedure calling.

run time dynamic linking—Run time dynamic linking is a technique where a library module is not linked and loaded until the first time it is called while the program is running.

running—A process is in the running state when it is executing on a processor. In a multiple processor system it is possible for two or more processes to be in the running state at the same time.

S

saturated—A queuing system is saturated if it is running near its maximum capacity and cannot absorb any more load.

scan algorithm—The scan algorithm (or elevator algorithm) is a disk scheduling algorithm where the disk head moves like an elevator in the building. The disk head moves in one direction (say towards in center of the disk) as long as there are requests in that direction. If there are no requests in a direction then it starts moving in the other direction.

scan line—A scan line in a CRT display is a horizontal line of pixels that represents one sweep of the electron beam across the screen.

scheduling—Scheduling is the activity of deciding when processes will receive the resources they request.

scripting language—A scripting language is a programming language intended mostly for interactive use and for one-shot programs that invoke the functions of other programs.

SCSI—SCSI stands for small computer system interface. SCSI is a bus standard that allows several devices of different kinds to be connected to a computer system through a single SCSI controller.

SCSI device driver—A SCSI device driver is a device driver than manages a SCSI bus. Sometimes more specialized device drivers (like disk drivers) will use the SCSI device driver to send messages on the SCSI bus.

second chance algorithm—The second chance algorithm is a form of the clock algorithm where pages that are modified but that have not been used in one clock hand rotation (hence their used bit is 0) are given one more clock hand rotation to be accessed again before they are removed. This second clock hand rotation is their second chance.

secondary page number—The secondary page number is the part of the virtual address that gives the page number of the page in the secondary page table. The secondary page table is located through the page table entry in the primary (or master) page table which is indexed by the primary (or master) page number.

sector—A disk sector is the unit of information that a disk can read and write. It is also called a disk block. A disk sector is normally from 512 bytes to 16 K bytes.

security policy—The security policy in a computer system is a set of security rules that the protection mechanisms are used to enforce.

seek—A seek is the physical movement of the read/write heads in a disk system to the cylinder where the next read or write will take place. Most disk drives will automatically seek to the correct cylinder before a read or write operation although they also have a specific seek operation.

segment—A segment is an area in a virtual address space that contains data used for one purpose, that is, a code module, an array, a table, etc.

segment register—A segment register is a hardware register that contains the base address and length of a segment.

segmentation—Segmentation is a method of structuring virtual memory where each logical part of the program (a procedure, a table, an array, a storage pool, etc.) is placed in a separate segment. Segmentation leads to two-dimensional addressing where each byte is addressed by segment number and byte with the segment.

semaphore—A semaphore is a synchronization primitive with two operations: wait and signal (also called P and V). A semaphore is implemented with two data structures: a counter and a queue of blocked processes). The wait operation decrements the counter (if the counter is positive) or (if the counter is 0) blocks the process invoking the wait operation and puts it on the queue. The signal operation increments the counter (if the queue is empty) or (if the queue is not empty) removes a process from the queue and unblocks it.

separation of concepts—Separation of concepts is a design technique where a concept is divides into two concepts which can each be used separately. This can lead to greater flexibility and reusability.

separator character—A separator character is an ASCII character that is used to separate the parts of a compound (that is, multi-part) name. The separator character in UNIX is '/' (*/user/jeff*), in MS/DOS is '\' (*\user\jeff*), in MacOS is ':' (*:user:jeff*), etc.

serial port—A serial port is a connection which allows bit-serial (one bit at a time) communication between a device and a computer system.

serial port controller—A serial port controller is a device controller for connecting to serial devices like modems, printers, terminals, etc.

serially reusable resource—A serially reusable resource is a resource that can only be used by one process at a time but can be used by another process once the process currently using it is finished with it.

server—A server is a software process or hardware machine that provides services to other processes or machines over a network. A typical example is a file server which provides file services over a network.

server process—A server process is a process that is acts like a server, that is, that accepts requests for services and responds to them.

settling—A disk drive seeks by moving the heads in a single ballistic movement to the approximate place it expects to find the track it is seeking to. After this movement, it figures out which track it actually got to and make a few small adjustments to get to the correct track. These small adjustments are called settling.

shared-memory multiprocessors—A shared-memory multiprocessors is a computer system with several processes that all share some common memory. The processors may or may not have private memory of their own.

shell—A shell is a program that allows a user interactive access to the functions of an operating system. Another name for a shell is a command line processor.

short-term scheduler—A short-term scheduler decides which of the processes in memory will get to use the processor and for how long they will get to use it.

shortest job first scheduling—The shortest job first scheduling (SJF) scheduling algorithm is a non-preemptive scheduling algorithm that chooses the job that will execute the shortest amount of time.

signal—A signal is a notification that a specific event has occurred. A signal has a type but no information content beyond its type.

signaling—Signaling is a basic interprocess communication pattern where process A sends a signal to process B when process A reaches a specified point in its code. Process B will wait for that signal when it gets to a specific point in its code.

social engineering—Social engineering refers to a range of non-technical methods of gathering information that will assist in breaking into a computer system. These methods include: calling people on the phone and getting information from them (usually by lying to them), going through trash, getting a job as a janitor in a company, illegally breaking into an office, etc.

software interrupt—A software interrupt forces a process to execute an interrupt handling procedure when a specific event occurs. It is used to allow a process to respond quickly to events without having to poll for them. It mimics in software the effects of a hardware interrupt.

software page table lookup—Some newer computers do not have hardware to do page table lookups. Instead the hardware manages TLB lookups and interrupts to the operating system when a TLB lookup fails. The operating system then does the page table lookup to find the correct page table entry in software.

space division multiplexing—Space division multiplexing is a technique for sharing a resource by allocating parts of it to different processes. Memory is a good example of a resource that is allocated using space division multiplexing.

space resource—A space resource is a resource that can be divided up into pieces and can be used for space division multiplexing.

spatial locality—A process exhibits spatial locality if it is the case that if a memory cell is accessed then the memory cells around it are likely to be accessed very soon. Processes exhibit spatial locality in code because of sequential execution and loops and they exhibit spatial locality in data because variables in a procedure are using stored together and used together and because arrays are typically accessed sequentially.

spin lock—A spin lock is a busy-waiting lock where a processor checks a memory location over and over again to see if it contains a particular value.

spooling—Spooling is a technique for virtualizing a printer. It consists of writing printed lines to a disk file and later printing the disk file when the printer is not busy.

SSTF—SSTF stands for shortest seek time first. SSTF is a disk head scheduling algorithm where the request closest to the current position of the read/write heads (that is, the request the requires the shortest seek time) is chosen next.

standard input—The standard input of a process is an input file that is already opened and ready to read when the process is started. It defaults to the terminal the process was started from but it can be redirected from a file or another device.

standard output—The standard output of a process is an output file that is already opened and ready to write when the process is started. It defaults to the terminal the process was started from but it can be redirected to a file or another device.

starvation—Starvation is a resource management problem where a process does not get the resources it needs for a long time because the resources are being allocated to other processes.

state machine—A state machine is a mathematical model of a reactive system that accepts input data (or events), moves from state to state in response to these inputs, and sometimes produces outputs.

static data—Static data is data in a program that is local to a procedure but whose storage is allocated when the program begins and remains allocated (and retains it value) throughout the execution of the program.

static relocation—Static relocation is the technique of relocating a program to a new starting address before the program begins execution.

subject—A subject is an active entity in a protection system that will try to perform operations on objects.

superblock—A superblock is the UNIX name for a file system descriptor. It contains everything that UNIX needs to know about the file system.

swap area—A swap area is a disk partition (a logical disk) where the paging system stores pages that are not in memory. A swap area is not managed by the file system, it is managed directly by the paging system using the disk device drivers.

swapping—Swapping is a technique where processes are moved into and out of memory as memory is requested and becomes

free. Swapping is handled by a medium-term scheduler. Swapping is also used in paging systems where a process that is swapped out will release all its page frames for use by other processes.

symbol table—A symbol table is a part of an object module and a load module. The symbol table contains symbols defined in the module and their offset in the module. The symbol table also contains symbols used in the module (and defined in other modules) and the places in the module they are used.

symbolic link—A symbolic link is a file that refers to another file. A symbolic link is usually implemented as a short file that contains the name of the file it links to. Another name for a symbolic link is an alias (or a file alias).

synchronization—Synchronization is the activity whereby two processes coordinate their activities so that they can work together on a task.

synchronous—A synchronous system call is one where the action of the system call is completed before the system call returns. For example, if the system call requests that data be read from a file the data are read and placed in the user's buffer before the system call returns.

system call—A system call is a request by a process for the operating system to perform an operation for the process. This is usually an operation on an operating system object that the process cannot access directly. System calls are usually signaled by a system call instruction.

system call interface—The system call interface of an operating system is the set of system calls that the operating system implements. The system call interface defines the functionality of an operating system, that is, the objects it implements and the operations that are possible of these objects.

system call interrupt handler—The system call interrupt handler is the part of an operating system that first handles system calls. All system calls go first to the system call interrupt handler which determines which system call it is and directs the request to the appropriate part of the operating system.

system mode—System mode is a processor mode where all hardware instructions (including the privileged ones) are allowed.

system process—A system process is a process that runs in user mode but performs operating that are part of the operating system's functionality. System processes are part of the operating system but they do not run in system mode.

system stack—The system stack is the stack used by the operating system when it is running.

T

tape drive—A tape drive is an I/O device that can read or write data on a magnetic tape. Almost all of these now use cartridge tapes.

task—Task is the name used in the Mach operating system for process.

temporal locality—A process exhibits temporal locality if it is the case that if a memory cell is accessed then is is likely to be accessed again very soon. Processes exhibit temporal locality in code because of loops and they exhibit temporal locality in data because variables tend to be accessed several times in a row.

terminal capability database—A terminal capability database is a database of the instruction sets of a large number of terminals. The information about each terminal indicates how to do things like: clear the screen, write characters, move the cursor, make text bold, etc.

terminal emulator—A terminal emulator is a program that imitates the interface of a terminal. That is, it will accept the same commands the terminal accepts but write in a window rather than the terminal screen as a real terminal would do.

theory of program behavior—A theory of program behavior is the set of assumptions about how typical programs reference memory. Each paging algorithm tries to predict future page accesses from information about page references in the recent past. It makes this prediction using a theory of program behavior.

thrashing—If a paging system tries to load too many processes into memory then no process will have enough memory to run and so the page fault rate will get very high. As a result the system will be spending almost all of its time handling page fault interrupts. In this case the system is said to be thrashing.

thread—A thread is a software object that can be dispatched and executes in an address space. Several threads can exist in the same address space.

thread-safe—A program is thread-safe if it can be executed by two threads at the same time and it executes correctly for both threads. The thing that prevent a program from being thread-safe is the use of global or static data. Another name for thread-safe is reentrant.

three level paging—A three level paging system has three levels of page tables. The virtual address is divided into four parts: primary page number, secondary page number, tertiary page number and offset in the page. The primary page number is used to look up a page table entry in the primary (or master) page table. That page table entry points to the secondary page table and the secondary page number is used to find the page table entry of the tertiary page table. The tertiary page number is used to find the page table entry in that table. That page table entry will point to a page and the page offset is used to find the correct byte in that page.

throughput—Throughput is rate at which processes are serviced. Throughput is a measure of how efficiently a timesharing system is running.

time division multiplexing—Time division multiplexing is a technique for sharing a resource by allocating it to a processes for a short time and then allocating it to the next process. Time division multiplexing is good for resources that cannot be shared but can be preempted. The processor is a good example of a resource that is allocated using time division multiplexing.

time resource—A time resource is a resource that cannot be shared. Processor time is a good example.

time sharing—Time sharing is a technique for sharing the processor by giving each process use of the processor for short periods of time.

time slice—Time slice in another term for quantum.

timer interrupt handler—A timer interrupt handler is the interrupt handler that is called when the timer interrupts. Usually this means that a process has used up its quantum and must give up the processor to another process.

TLB—TLB stands for translation look-aside buffer.

transfer time—Transfer time is the time it takes to transfer a disk block (or blocks) to memory. A disk transfer incurs three delays: the seek time, the latency time, and the transfer time. Usually the transfer time is by far the shortest of these delays.

transformation—Transformation is the technique of creating a logical resource from a physical resource in such a way that the logical resource is an improved version of the physical resource. The logical resource will have simpler operations and may be more reliable than the physical resource.

translation look-aside buffer—A translation look-aside buffer is a set of hardware registers that act as a cache for the page table of the running process. When a virtual address is used, the virtual page is first looked up in the translation look-aside buffer. If it is found then the page table is not used and the page is accessed directly. If it is not found, then the page must be looked up in the page table. After it is looked up, the page table entry is stored in the translation look-aside buffer so it will be found the next time the page is looked up.

triple index block—A triple index block is a block that consists of the a series of disk block addresses of double index blocks.

Trojan horse problem—One way to penetrate security in a system is to get a person run run your program with their privileges. One way to do this is to create a useful program that people want to use but hide extra code inside it to do something else, like send a copy of all their files to you or to delete all their files. Such a program is called a Trojan horse program and the Trojan horse problem is how to prevent these programs from breaking your security system. The solution to the Trojan horse problem is to run all external programs in a protection domain that only allows them to do exactly what they are supposed to do.

true parallelism—True parallelism is the parallelism obtained from running processes on two or more physical processors. It is also called physical parallelism.

two dimensional address space—Segmentation produces a two dimensional address space. That is, all memory addresses have two parts, the segment number and the byte offset in the segment.

two handed clock—The two handed clock algorithm is a variation of the clock algorithm intended to free up page frame faster than the clock algorithm. The first hand visits all the page frames and turns off the referenced bit. The second hand follows the first hand by a certain distance (say 1000 page frames back). If the second hand encounters a page frame that is still not references (that is, it hasn't been referenced since the first hand passed it) then it immediately frees that page frame.

two level implementation—A system uses a two level implementation if the architecture is divided into two levels with the upper level being implemented using the functions defined in the lower level.

two level name space—A two level name space has a root directory which contains files and other directories but all the other directories can contain only files. Thus there can be only two levels of directories in any path name.

two level paging—A two level paging system has two levels of page tables. The virtual address is divided into three parts: primary page number, secondary page number and offset in the page. The primary page number is used to look up a page table entry in the primary (or master) page table. That page table entry points to the secondary page table and the secondary page number is used to find the page table entry of the page containing the byte we are accessing. That page table entry will point to a page and the page offset is used to find the correct byte in that page.

two phase locking—Two phase locking is a technique used in database access to avoid deadlock in record locking. In the first phase, a process only acquires locks and makes no changes to the database. If it fails to acquire a lock in the first phase, the process releases all it's locks and starts over. After it has acquired all the locks, the process enters the second stage. In the second stage, it does not acquire any locks but it can make the changes in the database. At the end of the second phase, the process releases all it's locks.

two queue scheduling—A two queue scheduling system is one where new processes go into the high priority queue for one quantum. If they do not finish in the quantum period then they go into the low priority queue. When the processor is free, the first process in the high priority queue is chosen (if the high priority queue it is not empty), otherwise the first process in the low priority queue is chosen.

U

undefined external symbol—An undefined external symbol is a symbol that is used in a module and is defined in another module.

uninitialized data section—The uninitialized data section is the part of an object module or load module that contains the data that is not given an initial value by the assembly language source code.

user—A user is a person who is using a computer system (by running processes on it).

user mode—When a processor is in user mode it cannot execute privileged instructions.

user threads—A user thread system is implemented by the process itself and the kernel does not know anything about it. This is faster than kernel threads but the whole process blocks if any user thread blocks.

V

vector graphics—Vector graphics is a hardware technique where the graphics are drawn directly on the phosphor by the electron beam. The alternative is raster graphics.

vertical retrace—The vertical retrace is the time period where the electron beam in a cathode ray tube is moving from the end of the last scan line to the beginning of the first scan line.

virtual computer—A virtual computer is a software abstraction implemented by an operating system. All processes run on virtual computers. A virtual computer has all the power of the physical computer but it is easier to use.

virtual memory—Virtual memory is a hardware technique where the system appears to have more memory that it actually does. This is done by time sharing the physical memory and storing parts of the memory one disk when they are not actively being used.

virtual memory object—A virtual memory object is an object in the Mach operating system that manages a section of the virtual address space. It uses a pager to transfer pages from the memory object into the physical memory.

virtual resource—A virtual resource is a software object that has the same capabilities as a physical resource does but is easier to use. It is implemented using a physical resource.

virtual swap space—Some operating systems allow some pages not to have assigned swap space. This can work because some pages will always be in memory and a page in memory does not require swap space until it needs to be replaced.

virtual terminal—A virtual terminal is a software emulation of a terminal.

virtual time—Virtual time is the time a process has been actually executing, that is, it does not include the time it spends waiting to be executed.

W

working directory—The working directory (also called the current directory) is the starting point of relative path names. Usually a user is working with the files in the working directory.

working set—The working set of a process (at a point in time) is the minimal set of pages it needs to run without excessive paging. In the working set algorithm it is the set of pages that have been accessed in the last N memory references (this range of past memory references is called the working set window).

working set page replacement—The working set page replacement algorithm is a page replacement algorithm that tries to keep the working set of each process in memory. It works by monitoring the working set of each process. If there is not enough room for the working set in memory then the process is swapped out until there is enough room.

worst fit—Worst fit is a memory allocation algorithm where a request for a block of memory is always filled with the free block that is as large as possible.

WSClock algorithm—The WSClock page replacement algorithm is a page replacement algorithm that tries to approximate the working set algorithm in the framework of a clock algorithm. It does this by approximating the time interval since each page has been referenced. If that interval is larger than the working set window then the page is replaced.

INDEX